AMERICAN BIOGRAPHIES

American Scientists

CHARLES W. CAREY, JR.

Facts On File

An imprint of Infobase Publishing

American Scientists

Facts On File, Inc.
An imprint of Infobase Publishing
132 West 31st Street
New York NY 10001

Library of Congress Cataloging-in-Publication Data

Carey, Charles W.
    American scientists / Charles W. Carey, Jr.
        p. cm.—(American biographies)
    Includes bibliographical references and indexes.
    ISBN 0-8160-5499-1 (acid-free paper)
    1. Scientists—United States—Biography. I. Title. II. Series.
    Q141.C214 2006
    509'.2'273—dc222005000683

Facts On File books are available at special discounts when purchased in bulk quantities for businesses, associations, institutions, or sales promotions. Please call our Special Sales Department in New York at (212) 967-8800 or (800) 322-8755.

You can find Facts On File on the World Wide Web at http://www.factsonfile.com

Text design by Joan M. Toro
Cover design by Cathy Rincon

Printed in the United States of America

VB Hermitage 10 9 8 7 6 5 4 3 2 1

This book is printed on acid-free paper.

CONTENTS

LIST OF ENTRIES

Simpson, George G.
Smalley, Richard E.
Smith, Hamilton O.
Snell, George D.
Sperry, Roger W.
Stakman, Elvin C.
Stanley, Wendell M.
Stein, William H.
Steinberger, Jack
Stern, Otto
Sumner, James B.
Sutherland, Earl W.
Tarter, Jill C.
Tatum, Edward L.
Taube, Henry
Taussig, Helen B.
Taylor, Joseph H.
Teller, Edward

Temin, Howard M.
Thomas, E. Donnall
Ting, Samuel C. C.
Torrey, John
Townes, Charles H.
Tsui, Daniel C.
Turner, Charles H.
Urey, Harold C.
Van Allen, James A.
Van de Graaff, Robert J.
Van Hise, Charles R.
Van Vleck, John H.
Varmus, Harold E.
Waksman, Selman A.
Wald, George
Watson, James D.
Weinberg, Steven
Welch, William H.

Weller, Thomas H.
Whipple, George H.
Wieman, Carl E.
Wieschaus, Eric F.
Wigner, Eugene P.
Wilczek, Frank
Wilson, Kenneth G.
Wilson, Robert W.
Wong-Staal, Flossie
Woodward, R. B.
Wright, Jane C.
Wright, Louis T.
Wright, Sewall
Wrinch, Dorothy Maud
Yalow, Rosalyn
Yang, Chen Ning
Zewail, Ahmed H

ACKNOWLEDGMENTS

I could never have written this book without the help of the vast number of sources from which it was drawn. Of them all, I relied most heavily on *American National Biography* (Oxford University Press, 1999); *Notable Twentieth-Century Scientists* (Gale Research, 1995 and 1998); Nobelprize.org, a marvelous Web site maintained by the Nobel Foundation, which awards the annual Nobel Prizes; and *Encyclopaedia Britannica,* from which I learned just about everything I know about biology, chemistry, and physics. Whatever merits this book has are owed to these sources; whatever faults it has are entirely my own.

I also want to acknowledge Elizabeth A. Blowers, who carefully read the manuscript and made a number of useful suggestions. And last but not least, my thanks to Nicole Bowen and Laura Shauger at Facts On File; if all editors were as professional and as easy to work with as they are, this would be a happy world indeed.

INTRODUCTION

Prior to 1901, the year the first Nobel Prize was awarded, the United States was a scientific backwater. Most of the cutting-edge research and theory was being done in Europe, especially Germany, where most of the world-class chemists, physicists, and medical researchers resided. As a result, most of the scientific output produced by 18th- and 19th-century Americans involved astronomy and botany, which at the time were focused on cataloging rather than explaining. As the nation developed economically and militarily into a world power following its victory in the Spanish-American War of 1898, American institutions of higher learning blossomed and with them the quality and quantity of American science. By 2004, Americans had won more than 200 Nobel Prizes in the sciences—physics, chemistry, and physiology or medicine—more than any other single nation.

ASTRONOMY AND ASTROPHYSICS

Astronomy and astrophysics offer the perfect example of how American science progressed. At first, astronomers were content to catalog and describe what they saw through their telescopes. As time progressed, however, they became more interested in explaining the origins of what they saw.

Around 1880, the Harvard Observatory's Edward Pickering undertook an ambitious project to identify and classify every visible star. Somewhat surprisingly, the "stars" of this project were women, not men. Gazing at the stars through a telescope for hours, and all night long at that, was an assignment too tedious to be given to male scientists, and so the door was opened for women to achieve success

in science. Over the next 50 years, WILLIAMINA FLEMING, ANTONIA MAURY, ANNIE J. CANNON, and HENRIETTA LEAVITT, among other women, photographed hundreds of thousands of stars and classified them according to systems that they had developed themselves.

The first U.S. astrophysicist, an astronomer who uses physics as a tool for understanding the heavenly bodies, was HENRY N. RUSSELL, who demonstrated that a star's brightness and color indicate its age. Russell and GEORGE ELLERY HALE pioneered the use of spectroscopic analysis, the study of materials by examining the waves of light they emit, as a tool for studying solar phenomena. Hale's techniques worked so well that other researchers used them to study the other visible stars. Hale also led the effort to construct four major telescopes, each one the largest in the world at the time of its completion.

It was through one of these telescopes that EDWIN HUBBLE, for whom the *Hubble Space Telescope* is named, made two important discoveries. In the 1920s Hubble, who had been a student of Hale's, proved the existence of galaxies other than the Milky Way, something that had been speculated about for centuries. Hubble further showed that the universe was expanding and had been for more than 10 billion years. This discovery suggested that the universe was still in the process of being created, a notion that seriously challenged the biblical version of creation.

Hubble's discovery led GEORGE GAMOW to develop the "big bang" theory in the 1940s. According to Gamow, about 15 billion years ago all of the matter in the universe was contained in a "ball," the size of which remains unknown. Then, at a critical moment, some entity—God, perhaps?—caused the ball to explode violently and disperse its matter throughout the vast void of empty space.

For many years, Gamow's theory was debated heatedly and even ridiculed, but it gained some valuable support in the 1960s from ARNO A. PENZIAS and ROBERT W. WILSON. Penzias and Wilson studied the stars by analyzing the radio waves they emit, and they discovered that a low level of electromagnetic radiation permeates the universe. Scientists have since concluded that this low-level radiation is the remnant of the intense flash of light that was generated by the big bang.

BOTANY

The first noteworthy American botanists, JOHN TORREY and ASA GRAY, strove to catalog as many species of North American flora as they could. Later, American botanists used their research to develop a better understanding of how plants grow and hence how to increase crop yields.

The two most important contributors to this effort were GEORGE WASHINGTON CARVER and ELVIN C. STAKMAN. Carver's research focused on finding ways to enhance the production of peanuts, soybeans, and cotton, thus improving the lives of impoverished southern farmers. Stakman used his botanical knowledge to develop disease-resistant strains of wheat, thus improving agriculture around the world and contributing to a significant reduction in world hunger.

GEOLOGY AND GEOPHYSICS

As with astronomers and botanists, the first American geologists were mostly interested in collecting and describing what they found. JOHN WESLEY POWELL conducted the first geological studies and developed the first topographical maps of the American West, while MATTHEW F. MAURY charted the currents and winds of the oceans.

Later, their work also contributed to a more profound understanding of natural processes. CHARLES R. VAN HISE cataloged the rock formations of the upper Midwest, but he also investigated the physical and chemical processes via which rock is formed and deformed. JAMES D. DANA developed a system for classifying minerals, but he also explained some of the physical processes that produce geological phenomena. The geologist LOUIS AGASSIZ and the paleontologists ALFRED S. ROMER and GEORGE G. SIMPSON put together impressive collections of fossils, but they also provided much evidence to back up Charles Darwin's theory of evolution. FRANK PRESS and CHARLES F. RICHTER acquired much knowledge about geophysics, the physical functions and aspects of the planet, but they also used that knowledge to prepare and protect westerners, especially Californians, from earthquakes.

MEDICINE AND PHYSIOLOGY

American contributions to medical science would fill an entire book. Perhaps the most important group of contributions can be classified as biomedical, with the most significant of these being the discovery of how genetics governs the body's biomedical functions.

The first American medical professional of note was BENJAMIN RUSH. His methods of bloodletting and administering purgatives have since been discredited, but during the 18th century he saved many a patient with these methods, which he taught to hundreds of students. Mercifully, a more enlightened method of medicine was practiced by the next generation of physicians. These practitioners emphasized medical research rather than the "heroic" approach, so called because it required a heroic effort on the part of the physician, not to mention the patient. This new generation was epitomized by WALTER REED, who used research to develop a cure for diphtheria and to discover how typhoid fever and yellow fever are transmitted.

By the dawn of the 20th century, Americans were founding what would become world-class institutions for medical education and research. During the 1890s WILLIAM H. WELCH established Johns Hopkins University in Baltimore, Maryland, as one of them. Hopkins was the first medical school in the United States to accept women, and its faculty included several prominent American female medical researchers, including FLORENCE SABIN, VIRGINIA APGAR, DOROTHY MAUD WRINCH, and HELEN B. TAUSSIG. In the 1910s SIMON FLEXNER established the Rockefeller Institute for Medical Research in New York City as a rival to Johns Hopkins, and in time this institution, later known as Rockefeller University, surpassed its rival. Rockefeller researchers were involved in virtually every conceivable aspect of medical research. One of its most important endeavors concerned the study of the biological features of the cell. Indeed, the field of cell biology was pioneered at Rockefeller by ALBERT CLAUDE, GEORGE E. PALADE, and GÜNTER BLOBEL.

Hopkins and Rockefeller inspired the creation of major medical centers across the United States, and by the late 20th century these centers were making important discoveries as well. At Washington University in St. Louis, Missouri, CARL and GERTY CORI identified the process by which the body breaks down and uses carbohydrates. MICHAEL S. BROWN and JOSEPH L. GOLDSTEIN of the University of Texas Southwestern Medical Center discovered the processes by which the cells metabolize cholesterol. At the University of Washington Medical School in Seattle, EDMOND H. FISCHER and EDWIN G. KREBS discovered the process by which enzymes activate and deactivate other enzymes.

Perhaps the most important contribution by American medical researchers was their work in genetics, work that ultimately resulted in the rise of biotechnology. The study of genetics was begun in earnest in America in the early 1900s by THOMAS HUNT MORGAN, the first native-born American to win the Nobel Prize in physiology or medicine, and HERMANN J. MULLER. Morgan and Muller demonstrated that genes are linked in a series on chromosomes and are responsible for identifiable, hereditary traits. While these two pioneers worked with fruit flies, later geneticists studied other organisms as well; for example, SEWALL WRIGHT worked with livestock, BARBARA MCCLINTOCK studied corn, and BERNARD O. DODGE worked with the bread mold *Neurospora*. Dodge's work laid the groundwork for GEORGE W. BEADLE and EDWARD L. TATUM, who matched up a number of *Neurospora*'s specific biochemical functions with the particular genes that control them. In time, other American researchers discovered relationships between genes and the processes they govern. For example, GEORGE D. SNELL and BARUJ BENACERRAF discovered

which genetic complex regulates the body's immune system, and H. ROBERT HORVITZ discovered which genes control programmed cell death.

A major advance in genetics came in the 1940s when ALFRED D. HERSHEY, MAX DELBRÜCK, and SALVADOR E. LURIA began studying the genetics of viruses, the simplest of all living things. In so doing, they established the field of molecular biology, the study of the biophysical principles by which living things grow and reproduce. In time, molecular biology contributed tremendously to a better understanding of genetics. JAMES D. WATSON was a molecular biologist who in the 1950s developed the double-helix model of DNA, the biomolecule that carries genetic coding. Over the next 50 years, molecular biology inspired geneticists to make a number of other important advances. The most impressive were the deciphering of genetic coding by ROBERT W. HOLLEY, H. GOBIND KHORANA, and MARSHALL W. NIRENBERG and the development of techniques for recombining DNA from different organisms, thus creating the field of biotechnology, by PAUL BERG, DANIEL NATHANS, HAMILTON O. SMITH, and RITA R. COLWELL.

Genetics and molecular biology helped virologists get a better understanding of how viruses cause cancer and other diseases. RENATO DULBECCO, DAVID BALTIMORE, and HOWARD M. TEMIN discovered how retroviruses, viruses that reverse the way genetic coding is transcribed, cause cancer, while HAROLD E. VARMUS and J. MICHAEL BISHOP showed that retroviruses have deposited potentially cancerous cells in virtually every living organism. More recently, FLOSSIE WONG-STAAL identified the retrovirus HIV as the cause of AIDS.

The pervasiveness of racism prior to 1960 kept most African Americans out of America's graduate science programs, but it also opened doors for blacks in the field of medicine. Hospitals and doctor's offices were just as segregated as any other aspect of American life, but segregation demanded the establishment of blacks-only hospitals where African-American physicians and nurses could practice. Consequently, the need for blacks-only medical schools arose, and these schools produced a number of skilled practitioners of the medical sciences. No African American has ever won a Nobel Prize in physiology or medicine; nevertheless, many blacks have made important contributions to the advancement of medical knowledge. W. MONTAGUE COBB demonstrated that the various races are virtually indistinguishable on the basis of anatomy. CHARLES R. DREW established the first large-scale blood bank program in the United States and developed many of the methods and procedures for handling and preserving blood in large quantities. WILLIAM A. HINTON developed tests for diagnosing syphilis and for detecting the presence of antibodies in spinal fluid. PERCY L. JULIAN developed techniques for producing a number of pharmaceutical drugs, including some of the first synthetic hormones. SAMUEL L. KOUNTZ, JR., developed many of the procedures and apparatus that are used in kidney transplant surgery. LOUIS T. WRIGHT and his daughter, JANE C. WRIGHT, were pioneers in the development of chemotherapy as a treatment for cancer.

CHEMISTRY

American chemists have made many contributions, but two in particular stand out. The first concerns the nature of chemical bonds, and the second involves the discovery of new elements and isotopes, forms of an element having the same number of protons but a different number of neutrons.

There were two great American chemists in the 19th century. The principal contribution of the first, J. WILLARD GIBBS, was the establishment of a new field, physical chemistry, which explores the relations between the physical properties of substances and their chemical composition and transformations. The second was THEODORE W. RICHARDS, who became the first American to win the Nobel Prize in chemistry. Richards and his students determined the exact atomic weights of 55 elements, or more than half the periodic table.

The early 20th century saw the rise of the next two important American chemists, GILBERT N. LEWIS and IRVING LANGMUIR. Their greatest contribution was the development around 1920 of the concept of the covalent bond. Although Lewis, who had studied under Richards, first advanced the idea, it was left to Langmuir to embellish and popularize it, and today it is accepted as a fundamental feature of most chemical bonds. Lewis carried forward Gibbs's pioneering work in physical chemistry

while Langmuir was an accomplished inventor who received patents for improvements to the light bulb and sophisticated rainmaking techniques. While developing the gas-filled light bulb in the 1910s, Langmuir discovered and named the physical phenomenon known as plasma, the mix of ions and electrons that results when a solid is vaporized by intense heat. Because plasma resembles neither a solid, liquid, nor gas, it is considered to be the fourth state of matter.

LINUS C. PAULING picked up where Lewis and Langmuir left off in terms of theorizing about the nature of the chemical bond. In the early 1930s Pauling demonstrated that atoms must be balanced in terms of their charges and aligned properly in terms of their angles before they can form a chemical bond. He also developed the theories of hybrid orbitals, resonance hybrids, and electronegativity as a means of providing a more sophisticated model for the chemical bonds that bind molecules. Later, he applied these theories to arrive at a more sophisticated understanding of how biochemical molecules interact, and in the 1950s he proposed a model for DNA that inspired JAMES D. WATSON and Francis Crick to develop their double-helix model.

Pauling's work with molecular bonds was carried forward by another important American chemist, ROBERT S. MULLIKEN. In the late 1930s Mulliken modified the Lewis-Langmuir model of covalent bonds to develop the molecular orbital theory. Whereas the covalent bond model has atoms bonding by sharing one electron each from their outer shell, the molecular orbital model has two atoms sharing a group of electrons that orbit both nuclei. This theory is virtually impossible to prove, but it explains the behavior of diatomic and small polyatomic molecules better than the covalent bond theory does.

The practical application of much of this theory about the nature of chemical bonding was left to R. B. WOODWARD, whose skills at synthesizing organic chemical compounds remain unsurpassed. Beginning in the 1940s, Woodward synthesized a number of biomedical compounds with important medicinal applications, such as quinine, penicillin, cortisone, and vitamin B_{12}. His skills resulted in large part from his ability to understand fully the nature of chemical bonds as developed by his predecessors. However, he also expanded on these theories by developing his own; in the 1960s he and ROALD HOFFMANN developed the Woodward-Hoffmann rules, which define certain chemical reactions in terms of the energy level and symmetry of shared electrons.

The first important American chemist in terms of the development of elements and isotopes was HAROLD C. UREY. A former student of Lewis's, in 1930 Urey coauthored the first American textbook of physical chemistry. He developed the concept of spin, or angular momentum, to explain the behavior of the electron during chemical analysis, and he correctly predicted the existence of two isotopes of hydrogen. His most important work involved the development of techniques for isolating isotopes and using them for everything from medical tracers in diagnostic medicine to building atomic bombs to determining the age of minerals. His most interesting work was his theory that Earth's earliest atmosphere consisted of methane, ammonia, and water vapor, and that life evolved via the reactions among these chemicals caused by ultraviolet radiation from the sun.

GLENN T. SEABORG is best remembered for collaborating with physicist EDWIN M. MCMILLAN in the discovery of the first transuranium, or human-made, elements. However, Seaborg made important contributions to chemical theory as well. Although his work does not involve chemical bonding per se, he did show how the human-made elements relate to the natural elements and placed the human-made elements in their proper place in the periodic table according to period, the number of rings of electrons, and group, the number of electrons in the outer ring.

PHYSICS

As with American chemists, American physicists have also played a major role in the development of science. Their theoretical contributions range from the nature of lightning to the nature of quantum electrodynamics. Their most important practical applications of theory include radar, the laser, the transistor, and the integrated circuit or computer chip.

America's first physicist was BENJAMIN FRANKLIN, one of the most accomplished Americans of all time.

At a time when the American colonies were still a scientific backwater, Franklin demonstrated that lightning is a huge discharge of electricity. He also developed the theory of conservation of charge and coined many of the terms used to describe electrical phenomena. The most important 19th-century American physicist was JOSEPH HENRY. His work with electromagnetism resulted in the discovery of induction, whereby an electric circuit can induce an electric current in another circuit to which it is not connected via means of an electromagnet, and self-induction, whereby an electromotive force can be induced in a circuit by varying the electrical current in that circuit. So important was Henry's contribution that the electrical unit of inductive resistance was named the "henry" in his honor.

The first American to win the Nobel Prize in physics was ALBERT A. MICHELSON. Michelson is best remembered for obtaining the first accurate measurement of the speed of light, but he won the Nobel in 1907 for developing methods and equipment for the measurement of length. The measurements he obtained include everything from the precise length of the meter to the diameters of distant stars.

American physicists played the leading role in the development of nuclear power during the mid-20th century. In the 1930s ENRICO FERMI and EMILIO SEGRÈ performed the first experiment involving nuclear fusion, the combining of atomic nuclei to produce energy. During World War II, Fermi oversaw the design and construction of the world's first atomic reactor under the football field at the University of Chicago, and he guided the production of the fissionable material used to make the two atomic bombs that were dropped on Japan. Meanwhile, the design and construction of the bombs themselves were overseen by JULIUS R. OPPENHEIMER in his capacity as head of the Manhattan Project's Los Alamos, New Mexico, facility.

The atomic bomb was important to Allied victory in World War II, but even more important was microwave radar, a major factor in the British victory over the German Luftwaffe during the Battle of Britain. Radar was designed by a joint British-American team, and the most prominent member of the U.S. group was I. I. RABI. Earlier, Rabi had used radio technology to develop the magnetic resonance method for observing nuclear phenomena, and this technology was the springboard for the development of radar. In the 1960s CHARLES H. TOWNES and ARTHUR L. SCHAWLOW used Rabi's work as a springboard from which to develop masers, devices that produce and amplify microwaves, and lasers, devices that produce a single-color beam of light so intense that it can vaporize heat-resistant materials.

American physicists played a leading role in the field of particle physics, the study of subatomic particles. In terms of experimental research, ERNEST O. LAWRENCE led the way in the 1930s by designing and building the first of several cyclotrons, or "atom smashers," for conducting research on particles at high energy levels. The most famous use of cyclotrons and other particle accelerators was by GLENN T. SEABORG and EDWIN M. MCMILLAN to discover transuranium elements, but other researchers used them as well to learn about the inner workings of the atomic nucleus and to discover new particles. One of the most fascinating discoveries came in the 1970s when MARTIN L. PERL discovered tau leptons. It is now believed that these massive particles existed in prodigious numbers in the days immediately following the big bang, but that they have since decayed radioactively into electrons.

The United States made major contributions to theoretical physics as well. In the 1930s HANS A. BETHE theorized that the stars generate energy via nuclear reactions, and he developed his theories so well that they continued to be valid for the next 70 years. Meanwhile, EUGENE P. WIGNER propagated many of the basic theorems of quantum mechanics, the study of subatomic particles and the physical laws they obey. Wigner's most important contribution to quantum mechanics is the supermultiplet theory. This theory emphasizes the symmetry of the forces acting on subatomic particles even when their electrical charges are different, which is usually the case within the nucleus. In the 1940s RICHARD P. FEYNMAN and JULIAN S. SCHWINGER

reworked the theories of quantum electrodynamics, the interactions of charged particles with each other and with the various forms of electromagnetic radiation such as light. These theories informed the work of ROBERT HOFSTADTER, whose experiments in the 1950s suggested that protons and neutrons are not indivisible particles but rather are constructed from even smaller particles. Hofstadter's work inspired MURRAY GELL-MANN, who in the 1960s developed a model that explains the behavior of particles within a nucleus in terms of the properties of quarks, the name Gell-Mann gave to Hofstadter's smaller particles.

American physicists were largely responsible for the development of solid-state physics, the study of how electrons flow through semiconductors, materials that are neither good nor bad conductors of electricity. The first major researcher to take an interest in solid-state physics was FELIX BLOCH. He explained electrical conductivity in terms of electron flow and developed several of the early theories to explain the behavior of semiconductors. Bloch's work led directly to the development of the transistor by JOHN BARDEEN, WALTER H. BRATTAIN, and WILLIAM B. SHOCKLEY. The transistor replaced the vacuum tube as the device of choice for generating and regulating the flow of electrons through a piece of electronic equipment, and it gave rise to the multimillion-dollar semiconductor industry. In turn, the transistor was replaced by the integrated circuit or computer chip, which was developed in the late 1950s by JACK S. KILBY and Robert Noyce.

The preceding discussion hardly does justice to the many contributions American men and women of science have made over the last three centuries. It has been slightly more than 100 years since the establishment of the Nobel Prize, the highest honor a chemist, physicist, or medical researcher can receive. During that century, American scientists, regardless of their discipline, have led the way in developing the theories and experiments that have propelled humankind's knowledge of science ever forward.

A

Agassiz, Louis
(Jean Louis Rodolpe Agassiz)
(1807–1873) *geologist*

Louis Agassiz was one of the foremost natural scientists of the mid-19th century. Swiss by birth, he transformed the way science was taught in the United States.

Agassiz was born on May 26, 1807, in Motier, Switzerland. His father, Rodolphe, was a Protestant minister, and his mother, Rose, was a homemaker. After completing his boyhood education, he attended several universities in Switzerland and Germany, receiving a Ph.D. from the University of Erlangen in 1829 and an M.D. from the University of Munich in 1830. He was more interested in pursuing a career as a natural scientist than as a medical doctor, however, and as a student he spent much time in Paris, France, where he became acquainted with several of the leading naturalists of his day. One of them, Johann Spix, possessed a remarkable collection of fish specimens from the Amazon River, which he left to Agassiz after his death. By 1829 Agassiz had finished cataloging the specimens, and that same year he published his work with the collection under the title *Selecta Genera et Species Piscium*. This work greatly impressed Alexander von Humboldt, one of Europe's foremost naturalists, who in 1832 helped Agassiz secure a position as professor of natural history at Switzerland's Collège de Neuchâtel. In 1833 he married Cécile Braun with whom he had three children. She died in 1848, and two years later he married Elizabeth Cary.

Agassiz's work with Amazon fishes led him to do similar work with the fishes of Europe, particularly the extinct species. Whenever he could break away from his duties at Neuchâtel, he traveled across Europe, inspecting public and private fossil collections. In the process he was able to identify more than 1,700 species of fishes that had once swum the rivers and lakes of Europe. He published his findings as he made them, and by 1843 he had published six volumes, known collectively as *Recherches sur le poissons fossiles*. He also studied the various fossils found alongside extinct fishes, and by 1843 he had published volumes on extinct mollusks and echinoderms, a phylum that includes starfishes and sea urchins. To ensure that his work received maximum exposure, he established his own printing operation with state-of-the-art photoduplicating capabilities.

At the time, the study of fossils was thought to be one of the activities of a geologist, and soon Agassiz's interest in fossils led to an interest in geology. While continuing his work with the fossils of water creatures, he took up the study of glaciers, large masses of perennial ice that form on land through the recrystallization of snow and that move forward under their own weight. Earlier naturalists had suggested that glaciers were once more prevalent in Europe than they were in the 19th century and that glaciers were responsible for carving out the valleys and depositing the tons of boulders that are prominent features in Switzerland. In 1836 he and several associates began to investigate these suggestions by studying the structure and movement of Switzerland's Aar Glacier, and four years later he published their findings in *Études sur les glaciers*. In it he argued that Switzerland had once been covered entirely by a sheet of ice, and that similar sheets had once covered every part of Europe where loose boulders could be found. He dubbed the period during which these ice sheets had proliferated the Ice Age, a term whose currency continues into the present. In 1847 he published *Système glaciare*, which further supported his theory by presenting evidence gathered from all over Europe.

A series of unfortunate incidents—his separation from his wife in 1845, followed by the closure of his publishing operation due to excessive debts—led Agassiz to visit the United States in 1846. His trip was made possible partly by a commission from the king of Prussia to produce a comparative study of the plants and animals of the United States and Europe, and partly by an invitation to deliver a series of lectures on natural science at the Lowell Institute in Boston, Massachusetts. The lectures proved to be so popular that in 1847 Harvard University offered him a position as professor of zoology and geology. In this capacity, he expanded his research interests to include all of the natural history of the United States, and he published comprehensive volumes on the fishes of Lake Superior, the embryology of turtles, and a classification of species most notable for its defense of creationism, the religious doctrine that holds that all life forms were created in six days, as opposed to evolution, the scientific theory that holds that the various life forms developed over billions of years.

Agassiz envisioned the development of a state-of-the-art museum of zoology at Harvard, and by 1859 his incessant lobbying of public and private funding sources had raised enough money to build the Museum of Comparative Zoology, also known as the Agassiz Museum. He stocked the museum with specimens of as many species as he could obtain, and by the time of his death it was the foremost center for the study of natural science in the United States. The museum emphasized Agassiz's most cherished belief about teaching natural science, that one must learn it from experiencing nature rather than reading about it in books. This belief was further communicated to students at a school he opened in 1873 on Penikese Island in

Massachusetts's Buzzards Bay. As the most prominent teacher of natural science of his day, he influenced the first generation of U.S. science teachers, who in turn influenced the science curriculum in public schools for years thereafter.

Agassiz worked to further the spread of scientific inquiry in other ways. He worked diligently for the creation of a national science foundation, and in 1863 his efforts were rewarded by the founding of the National Academy of Sciences. That same year he was appointed a regent of the Smithsonian Institution in Washington, D.C., and over the next 10 years he worked assiduously to raise funds for the Smithsonian's endeavors in natural history.

Toward the end of his career, Agassiz, once hailed as the "prince of naturalists," became embroiled in an extended brouhaha with the proponents of evolution. Agassiz never denied that species died out and were replaced by newer species, but he challenged the belief of Charles Darwin and his supporters that this happened via evolution. Instead, Agassiz believed firmly in creationism, not only as the origin of all living creatures but also as the origin of new species. He was convinced that species died out as the result of catastrophes, or "acts of God," such as the onset of the Ice Age, and that the new species that arose as a result of the catastrophe were created spontaneously by divine intervention. Many of his colleagues at that time believed the same thing, but as the evidence for evolution began to mount, they began to look for ways to combine religious faith with scientific fact. Agassiz never made such an attempt, refusing to his death to believe in or to teach evolution to his students. His dogmatic stance in this regard cost him the support of many of his former students, and he even became known in some circles as the "prince of charlatans."

Despite his refusal to accept Darwinism, Agassiz remained the most prominent American natural scientist of his day. He died in Cambridge, Massachusetts, on December 14, 1873.

Further Reading

Lurie, Edward. *Louis Agassiz: A Life in Science*. Chicago: University of Chicago Press, 1988.
———. *Nature and the American Mind: Louis Agassiz and the Culture of Science*. New York: Science History Publications, 1974.

The Museum of Comparative Zoology, Harvard University. "Louis Agassiz, 1807–1873." Available online. URL: http://www.mcz.harvard.edu/Departments/Fish/agassiz.htm. Downloaded on July 25, 2003.

Altman, Sidney
(1939–) *biochemist*

Sidney Altman codiscovered catalytic RNA, the first known biochemical substances other than enzymes that can catalyze, or initiate, a biochemical operation. For this discovery he was awarded a share of the 1989 Nobel Prize in chemistry.

Altman was born on May 7, 1939, in Montreal, Canada. His parents owned a grocery store. He came to the United States in 1956 to attend the Massachusetts Institute of Technology, receiving a B.S. in physics four years later. He then entered Columbia University's graduate physics program, but he transferred after two years to the University of Colorado Medical School where he changed his focus to biophysics and received a Ph.D. in molecular biology in 1967. After two years as a postdoctoral fellow at Harvard University and another two years as a researcher at the Medical Research Council Laboratory at England's Cambridge University, in 1971 he joined the faculty at Yale University as a professor of biology. In 1972 he married Ann Korner with whom he had two children, and he later became a naturalized U.S. citizen without relinquishing his Canadian citizenship.

At Cambridge, Altman worked under Francis Crick, who with JAMES D. WATSON had discovered the structure of deoxyribonucleic acid (DNA), the carrier of genetic information at the molecular level. Altman's research involved transfer ribonucleic acid (tRNA), the biomolecule that transfers genetic coding from the genes to the ribosomes where it initiates the production of proteins. Specifically, he was studying the way that *Escherichia coli* (*E. coli*), a bacterium commonly found in the intestines, synthesizes tRNA, and before he left Cambridge he discovered an intermediate form of *E. coli* tRNA. He continued to study this intermediate form at Yale, focusing his efforts on isolating and purifying the enzyme that catalyzes its production, which he called ribonuclease P (RNase P). To his

surprise, however, he discovered that RNase P cannot catalyze the production of mature tRNA in the absence of the intermediate form of tRNA. This suggested to Altman that the intermediate form constituted part of the active center of RNase P, and further research showed that the intermediate form of tRNA is capable of catalyzing its own production into the mature form of tRNA exactly as if it were an enzyme.

At the time, the early 1980s, such a suggestion was preposterous, as it was believed that all biochemical functions are catalyzed by enzymes and that only enzymes can catalyze biochemical functions. Consequently, Altman's findings were greeted with much skepticism. In 1982, however, those findings were corroborated by the work of THOMAS R. CECH, who had discovered what he called ribozymes, messenger RNA (mRNA) molecules that act like enzymes. Over the next several years, Altman was able to show that certain forms of tRNA and mRNA, known today as catalytic RNA, not only act like enzymes on themselves but also on other substances.

The discovery of catalytic RNA was important because it offered a possible answer to a question that has bothered medical researchers for decades: how to cure the common cold. Colds are caused by viruses, which are composed of RNA and not DNA. Armed with the knowledge that certain forms of RNA can act as catalysts, medical researchers began looking for ways to design vaccines made from catalytic RNA that are capable of chopping up a cold virus's RNA into little pieces. For the role he played in discovering catalytic RNA, Altman was awarded a half share of the 1989 Nobel Prize in chemistry; his corecipient was Cech.

Altman remained at Yale for the rest of his scientific career. He continued to study the function and structure of catalytic RNA in both *E. coli* and human cells, focusing on the possibility that catalytic RNA is capable of activating various genes in those cells. His other honors include election to the National Academy of Sciences and the American Academy of Arts and Sciences.

Further Reading
McMurray, Emily J., ed. *Notable Twentieth-Century Scientists*. Detroit: Gale Research, 1995, pp. 29–31.

Nobelprize.org. "The Nobel Prize in Chemistry 1989." Available online. URL: http://nobelprize.org/chemistry/laureates/1989. Downloaded on September 18, 2004.

Yale University. "Faculty—Sidney Altman." Available online. URL: http://xbeams.chem.yale.edu/GradBrach/html/altman.htm. Downloaded on March 23, 2005.

Alvarez, Luis W.
(Luis Walter Alvarez)
(1911–1988) *physicist*

Luis W. Alvarez won a Nobel Prize for using the hydrogen bubble chamber to discover the so-called resonance particles, subatomic particles with life spans of a fraction of a second. He also contributed in a number of ways to a better understanding of a wide range of topics from medical diagnostic applications to the extinction of the dinosaurs.

Alvarez was born on June 13, 1911, in San Francisco, California. His father, Walter, was a physician, and his mother, Harriet, was a teacher. At age 17 he entered the University of Chicago and received a B.S., an M.S., and a Ph.D. in physics in 1932, 1934, and 1936, respectively. While at Chicago, he demonstrated that most cosmic rays, particle beams that originate in outer space, have a positive charge. In 1936 he joined the faculty at the University of California at Berkeley and married Geraldine Smithwick with whom he had two children. They later divorced, and in 1958 he married Janet Landis with whom he had two children.

At Berkeley, Alvarez worked closely with ERNEST O. LAWRENCE on experiments related to particle accelerators, instruments that speed up subatomic particles so they can be used to initiate and study nuclear reactions. In 1938 he discovered that some radioactive elements decay because their nuclei capture some of their orbital electrons. When this happens, the electron becomes part of the nucleus, thus producing an element with a smaller atomic number. In 1939 he and FELIX BLOCH made the first measurement of the neutron's magnetic moment; magnetic moment is a function of magnetic strength, and in this case it equals the product of the neutron's pole strength and the distance between its poles. By beaming neutrons through a magnetic field with a variable strength and then observing the "spin," or change in orientation, of the neutrons as they passed through the field, Alvarez and Bloch were able to make a rough estimation of the magnetic moment. By the outbreak of World War II Alvarez had also discovered isotopes of hydrogen and helium and developed a method for producing particle beams of slow-moving neutrons. This latter development contributed to the development by other Berkeley researchers of the transuranium, or human-made, elements.

Alvarez spent the war years doing research on radar and the atomic bomb. He developed three important radar systems: the Ground Controlled Approach (GCA) system for landing airplanes in conditions of low visibility, the VIXEN airborne system for detecting submarines at sea, and the Eagle system for use in high-altitude bombing runs. He helped design the "trigger" used to detonate the atomic bombs dropped on Japan, and he flew as a scientific observer on the mission to bomb Hiroshima. After the war he returned to his work with particle accelerators, and in 1947 he built a 40-foot linear proton accelerator, a device for bombarding nuclei with high-energy protons. This device proved to be highly useful in the production of radioisotopes for medical diagnostic applications.

In 1953 Alvarez met DONALD A. GLASER, the inventor of the hydrogen bubble chamber. Glaser's invention consisted of a one-inch-diameter chamber filled with liquid hydrogen, and when subatomic particles passed through it they created a vapor trail that could be photographed. By bringing an external magnetic force field to bear on the chamber, any charged particles in the chamber could be deflected in such a way that their speed, charge, and mass could be determined. Alvarez modified Glaser's bubble chamber by making it bigger; by 1959 he had built a 72-inch-diameter chamber. He greatly improved the optical equipment used to photograph the vapor trails, and he computerized the procedure by which the photographs were analyzed, so that as many as a million photographs per year could be taken and studied. In 1960 he discovered resonance particles, subatomic particles created as a by-product of nuclear reactions. Some of these particles exist for as little as a tenthousandth of a millionth of a second, but in Alvarez's bubble chamber they left vapor trails that were several centimeters long. The bubble chamber as modified by Alvarez has since proved to be an indispensable tool for studying the debris of nuclear reactions, in the process giving scientists a much better understanding of what happens during such a reaction. For his work with the hydrogen bubble chamber, Alvarez was awarded the 1968 Nobel Prize in physics.

In 1967 Alvarez returned to his fascination with cosmic rays, and he developed a way to study them by using balloon-mounted superconducting magnets. He retired from Berkeley in 1978. Two years later he became involved in a controversy regarding the demise of the dinosaurs. His son, geologist Walter Alvarez, had discovered a worldwide layer of iridium-laced clay dating back to about 66 million years ago. Alvarez postulated that the iridium came from an asteroid or comet that had hit Earth so hard that it raised a huge cloud of dust that blocked out the sun, thus leading to the extinction of many species, including the dinosaurs.

Alvarez was awarded the National Medal of Science and elected to the National Academy of Sciences and the American Academy of Arts and Sciences. At the time of his death on September 1, 1988, in Berkeley, he held more than 40 patents for inventions related to radar, electronics, and optics.

Further Reading

Alvarez, Luis W. *Alvarez: Adventures of a Physicist.* New York: Basic Books, 1987.

Nobelprize.org. "The Nobel Prize in Physics 1968." Available online. URL: http://nobelprize.org/physics/laureates/1968. Downloaded on March 26, 2004.

Wasson, Tyler, ed. *Nobel Prize Winners.* New York: H. W. Wilson, 1987, pp. 12–14.

Anderson, Carl D.
(Carl David Anderson, Jr.)
(1905–1991) *physicist*

Carl D. Anderson was the first scientist to discover antimatter, subatomic particles that are analogous to common particles such as the electron but with opposite charges. His discovery of the positron earned for him a share of the 1936 Nobel Prize in

physics. He also discovered two other particles of antimatter, the muon and the strange particle.

Anderson was born on September 3, 1905, in New York City. His father, Carl, was a restaurant manager, and his mother, Emma, was a homemaker. At age six he moved with his family to Los Angeles, California, where he grew up. After finishing high school in 1923, he enrolled in the California Institute of Technology (Caltech) where he received a B.S. and Ph.D. in physics in 1927 and 1930, respectively. He remained at Caltech after graduation to work as a research assistant under ROBERT A. MILLIKAN, and in 1933 he was named a professor of physics. In 1946 he married Lorraine Bergman with whom he had two children.

As a graduate student, Anderson studied the ability of X-rays to eject electrons from the atoms the X-rays bombarded. The principal apparatus used during these experiments was a Wilson or cloud chamber. This device is essentially a closed vessel filled with supersaturated steam through which charged particles such as electrons leave a minute but visible trail that can be photographed. Millikan convinced Anderson to expand his research by conducting a related experiment involving cosmic rays, radiation that has its origins in outer space. Millikan made this suggestion for two reasons. First, he was involved in a dispute with ARTHUR H. COMPTON as to the nature of cosmic rays. Millikan believed that cosmic rays, like X-rays, consist of photons, or tiny packets of energy, while Compton believed that cosmic rays consist of charged particles. Millikan hoped that Anderson could settle the point. Second, in 1928 the French physicist Paul Dirac had postulated the existence of a so-called positive electron, a subatomic particle with the same mass as an electron but with a positive rather than a negative charge, and Millikan wished to discover this unknown particle, if possible.

Anderson modified his cloud chamber by wrapping a large electromagnet around the chamber. By magnetizing the flow of particles through the chamber, he would be able to distinguish those with negative charges from those with positive charges. He then directed a beam of cosmic rays through the chamber and photographed the results. In 1932, after studying thousands of photographs, he detected a positively charged particle with a mass about the same as an electron, which he named the positron; it was the first particle of antimatter to be discovered. In 1933 he discovered positrons in gamma rays, a form of radiation emitted by certain radioactive substances. Further investigation by other researchers showed that the positron is produced by the radioactive decay of a proton-rich nucleus. The positron is stable in a vacuum, but it quickly reacts with electrons, a reaction that causes it to disintegrate into gamma radiation. Today, it is used in positron emission tomography (PET), an imaging technique used in diagnosis and biomedical research. For discovering the positron, Anderson received a half share of the 1936 Nobel Prize in physics (his corecipient was the Austrian physicist Victor F. Hess).

Anderson continued to study cosmic rays after discovering the positron. His experiments took him to the tops of mountains such as Pikes Peak in Colorado and into high altitudes aboard airplanes, where cosmic rays are much stronger than at sea level. In 1935 he and Seth Neddermeyer, one of his students, discovered another unknown subatomic particle in cosmic rays. They named it the mesotron, thinking that it might be the particle with a mass between the electron and the proton that the Japanese physicist Yukawa Hideki had hypothesized. Later, this particle became known as the pi-meson, and today it is called a muon. A muon is similar to an electron in that it never interacts with nucleons (protons and neutrons), but it has more than 200 times the mass of an electron. Further investigation by other researchers showed that a muon decays via radioactivity into an electron and two neutrinos, particles that have no charge and virtually no mass. After World War II, Anderson discovered yet another new subatomic particle, this one so poorly understood that it is still called the "strange particle."

Anderson's other honors include election to the National Academy of Sciences and the American Academy of Arts and Sciences. In 1976 he retired from Caltech; he died on January 11, 1991, in San Marino, California.

Further Reading

Nobelprize.org. "The Nobel Prize in Physics 1936." Available online. URL: http://nobelprize.org/physics/laureates/1936. Downloaded on March 13, 2004.

Pickering, William H. "Carl David Anderson," National Academy of Sciences, *Biographical Memoirs* 73 (1998): pp. 24–39.

Wasson, Tyler, ed. *Nobel Prize Winners.* New York: H. W. Wilson, 1987, pp. 19–20.

Weiss, Richard J., ed. *The Discovery of Anti-Matter: The Autobiography of Carl David Anderson, the Youngest Man to Win the Nobel Prize.* River Edge, N.J.: World Scientific, 1999.

Anderson, Charles E.
(Charles Edward Anderson)
(1919–1994) *meteorologist*

Charles E. Anderson was a pioneer in the use of satellite data as a means of predicting the weather. His most important contribution to meteorology was the development of a computerized forecasting system that could predict tornadoes and hailstorms.

Anderson was born on August 13, 1919, in Clayton, Missouri; his parents were farmers. In 1929 he moved with his family to St. Louis, where he grew up. In 1941 he received a B.S. in chemistry from Lincoln (Mo.) University and joined the U.S. Army Air Corps, at the time part of the army. He was sent to the University of Chicago for further training, and in 1943 he received an M.S. in meteorology. Upon graduation he was assigned as a weather officer to the Tuskegee Airmen, a group of African-American fighter pilots who escorted bombing missions over Germany during World War II. In 1943 he married Marjorie Anderson with whom he had two children.

After the war Anderson was sent to the Polytechnic Institute of Brooklyn (N.Y.) where he received an M.S. in chemistry in 1948. He was then assigned to the Watson Laboratories in New Jersey as a research and development officer, but after a year he was transferred to Boston, Massachusetts, to help start up the Air Force's Geophysics Research Laboratory. As chief of the laboratory's cloud physics branch, he conducted research on the physics of cumulus cloud formation and behavior by studying the bands of ultraviolet light they emit under vacuum conditions at high altitudes. He also experimented with seeding clouds with chemicals as a way to make rain, and he invented a way to make the cloudlike trails of jet aircraft invisible. In 1960 he received a Ph.D. in meteorology from the Massachusetts Institute of Technology and resigned from the air force.

In 1961 Anderson became head of the atmospheric analysis group of the Douglass Aircraft Missiles and Space Systems Division in Los Angeles, California. In this capacity he was responsible for forecasting the structure of the atmosphere so that the optimum dates for launching rockets could be scheduled. Working with Joanne Simpson, he developed the first computer model of a moist cloud. In 1965 he was named director of the Environmental Science Service Administration's Office of Federal Coordination in Meteorology in Washington, D.C. In this capacity he coordinated U.S. involvement in World Weather Watch, the World Meteorological Organization's program for the near-instantaneous exchange of weather information across the entire globe.

In 1966 Anderson joined the faculty at the University of Wisconsin as assistant director of the Space Science and Engineering Center. Over the next 20 years he pioneered the use of satellite data and computer models to study severe storms, especially hailstorms and tornadoes. When a complex system of severe thunderstorms unleashed seven Force-5 tornadoes on Barneveld, Wisconsin, in 1984, he used computer analysis of the debris trail left by these tornadoes to identify the so-called Barneveld Tornado as a new type of tornadic storm, the spiral mesolow.

In 1987 Anderson left Wisconsin for North Carolina State University. There he developed a method for using remote sensing via satellite, a technique used by oceanographers to study the oceans, as a way to study severe storms and tornadoes. He developed a computer system for analyzing geosynchronous satellite imagery that could forecast tornadic storms by the way they spin, thus giving local residents up to an hour's warning before a tornado struck. He later modified this system so that it could also forecast hail-producing thunderstorms.

Anderson was elected to membership in the American Association for the Advancement of Science. He conducted weather-related research until his death on October 21, 1994, in Durham, North

Carolina. In 1999 the National Center for Atmospheric Research established the Charles Anderson Award in his honor.

Further Reading

Sammons, Vivian Ovelton. *Blacks in Science and Medicine.* New York: Hemisphere Publishing, 1990, p. 11.
Stamatel, Janet P. "Charles Edward Anderson," *Contemporary Black Biography* 37 (2003): pp. 4–7.

Anderson, Philip W.
(Philip Warren Anderson)
(1923–) *physicist*

Philip W. Anderson's work contributed to a better understanding of the magnetic and electronic structure of solids by showing how individual electrons interact in magnetic and electronic systems. For this contribution he was awarded a share of the 1977 Nobel Prize in Physics.

Anderson was born on December 13, 1923, in Indianapolis, Indiana. His father, Harry, was a biology professor at the University of Illinois in Urbana where he grew up, and his mother, Elsie, was a homemaker. After receiving a B.S. in physics from Harvard University in 1943, he joined the staff at the Naval Research Laboratory in Washington, D.C., where he designed antennas for use during World War II. After the war he returned to Harvard and received an M.A. and a Ph.D. in physics in 1947 and 1949, respectively. He then went to work for the Bell Telephone Laboratories (BTL) in Murray Hill, New Jersey, where he remained for the next 35 years. In 1947 he married Joyce Gothwaite with whom he had one child.

At BTL Anderson became an associate of JOHN BARDEEN and WILLIAM B. SHOCKLEY. Along with WALTER H. BRATTAIN, Bardeen and Shockley pioneered the study of solid-state physics and the use of semiconductors, elements that are neither good conductors of electricity nor good insulators, to control and amplify electric current in electronic applications. As a result of their influence, Anderson studied solid-state theory, later known as condensed matter theory, for the rest of his scientific career. While at BTL he also conducted research in other areas as well. One of his earliest achievements at BTL was to demonstrate how the magnetic properties of individual electrons, which act as if they were miniature bar magnets, contribute to the magnetic properties of substances in general. He also studied superconductivity, the ability of certain elements to lose all resistance to electron flow in extreme low-temperature conditions, in semiconductors.

In 1958 Anderson developed the theory known as Anderson localization to explain the flow of electrons in disordered solids, materials in which the distribution of ions, electrically charged atoms and molecules, is random and uneven. He demonstrated that an electron in a disordered solid, such as a sheet of glass, often becomes tied to a specific location from which it cannot roam about freely, and he also suggested how disordered solids might be designed to improve their conductivity. Among other things, this theory led to the use of amorphous silicon, which is much less expensive than pure silicon, in the manufacture of computer chips.

Between 1967 and 1975, Anderson split his time between BTL and Cambridge University, where he and British physicist Nevill Mott cochaired an experimental group studying the theory of condensed matter. Their collaboration focused on localization theory, and eventually they identified what became known as Mott-Anderson transitions, certain conditions whereby electron flow is disrupted, thus impeding conductivity. More importantly, they demonstrated that a properly controlled disordered solid can be just as valuable a conductor of electricity as a perfectly ordered solid.

In 1977 Anderson was awarded a one-third share of the Nobel Prize in physics. The prize was awarded not for any one discovery but rather in recognition of his overall contributions to the theories of magnetism and condensed matter. His corecipients were JOHN H. VAN VLECK, who had been his dissertation director at Harvard, and Mott.

Anderson left Cambridge in 1975 to become a professor of physics at Princeton University while continuing to work half-time at BTL. He retired from BTL in 1984 and from Princeton in 1997, but he continued to experiment with superconductivity for a number of years thereafter. In addition to his responsibilities at BTL and Princeton, he held important leadership positions at the Aspen (Colo.)

Center for Physics and the Santa Fe (N.Mex.) Institute, both of which are nonprofit organizations for promoting cooperative scientific research. His publications include *Notes on Theory of Magnetism* (1954), *Concepts in Solids* (1963), and *Basic Notions of Condensed Matter Physics* (1984). His honors include the National Medal of Science and election to the National Academy of Sciences and the American Academy of Arts and Sciences.

Further Reading

Anderson, Philip W. *A Career in Theoretical Physics.* Singapore: World Scientific, 1994.

Nobelprize.org. "The Nobel Prize in Physics 1977." Available online. URL: http://nobelprize.org/physics/laureates/1977. Downloaded on September 17, 2004.

Wasson, Tyler, ed. *Nobel Prize Winners.* New York: H. W. Wilson, 1987, pp. 20–22.

Anfinsen, Christian B.
(Christian Boehmer Anfinsen)
(1916–1995) *biochemist*

Christian B. Anfinsen demonstrated that an enzyme's three-dimensional form is critical to its ability to perform its function. For this discovery he was awarded a share of the 1972 Nobel Prize in chemistry.

Anfinsen was born on March 26, 1916, in Monessen, Pennsylvania. His father, Christian, was an engineer, and his mother, Sophie, was a homemaker. He received a B.A. in chemistry from Swarthmore (Pa.) College in 1937 and an M.S. in organic chemistry from the University of Pennsylvania in 1939. After a year as a visiting investigator at the Carlsberg Laboratory in Copenhagen, Denmark, he entered Harvard University and received a Ph.D. in biochemistry in 1943. He remained at Harvard for another seven years as a professor of biological chemistry. In 1950 he joined the staff at the National Heart Institute's laboratory of cellular physiology and metabolism, part of the National Institutes of Health (NIH) in Bethesda, Maryland. After a brief return to Harvard in 1962, the following year he was named director of the laboratory of chemical biology at NIH's National Institute of

Arthritis, Metabolism, and Digestive Diseases. In 1941 he married Florence Kenenger with whom he had three children; they divorced in 1978, and the following year he married Libby Ely.

Anfinsen's research focused on proteins, complex molecules that are the basis for all life processes in animals. He was particularly interested in enzymes, proteins that catalyze virtually every biochemical function. His early research involved the enzymes in the retina that regulate the chemical messengers associated with vision. Shortly after his first arrival at NIH, he became interested in the way that an enzyme's function is determined by its form. Like all proteins, enzymes are composed of peptides, or chains of amino acids. While any number of possible three-dimensional arrangements of the amino acids in a peptide and of peptides in a protein exists, only the "correct" arrangement results in an activated enzyme. Finding out how an enzyme "knows" which arrangement is the correct one fascinated Anfinsen, and he set out to do just that by studying ribonuclease, an enzyme that plays an important role in the synthesis of cellular protein.

Ribonuclease consists of 124 amino acids, and Anfinsen began his study by trying to synthesize a ribonuclease molecule by starting with the amino-terminal and adding to it one amino acid at a time. By 1954 he had worked for several years and had little progress to show for his efforts, so he completely reversed his approach. Instead of building up a ribonuclease molecule, he decided to tear it down by breaking its chemical bonds at key junctures. When he broke the bonds between sulfur atoms, the molecule refolded itself correctly, but when he broke the bonds in other places, it refolded itself into a three-dimensional form that was inactive. By 1962 he was able to show that when an inactive form of ribonuclease is placed in a chemical environment similar to the one in which it normally operates in the human body, it gradually refolds itself until it has assumed the active form. Further study showed that ribonuclease is able to refold itself correctly partly because of chemical coding contained within the linear sequence of the molecule's amino acids and partly because of the action of a previously unknown enzyme found in protoplasm.

Anfinsen's work dovetailed nicely with that of STANFORD MOORE and WILLIAM H. STEIN. By 1963 Moore and Stein had described the complete sequence of amino acids in ribonuclease, while Anfinsen had described the correct three-dimensional arrangement of those amino acids required to activate the enzyme. Their combined work marked the first time the composition and form of an enzyme was clearly demonstrated, and it contributed greatly to a better understanding of how enzymes work. For this achievement, Anfinsen was awarded a half share of the 1972 Nobel Prize in chemistry; his corecipients were Moore and Stein.

Following receipt of the Nobel Prize, Anfinsen turned his attention toward the isolation and description of other enzymes as well as the protein interferon, which plays a role in the suppression of viruses and tumor cells. By the time he retired from NIH in 1981, he had isolated and characterized interferon. Following a year at the Weizmann Institute of Science in Rehovot, Israel, in 1982 he became a professor of biology at Johns Hopkins University in Baltimore, Maryland. He concluded his career by studying bacteria that live in high-temperature environments in the hope of using them to deactivate and dispose of toxic materials.

Anfinsen's many honors include election to the National Academy of Sciences and to a term as president of the American Society of Biological Chemists. He edited *Advances in Protein Chemistry* for a number of years, and he wrote *The Molecular Basis of Evolution* (1959, 2nd ed. 1975), which describes the relationship between protein chemistry and genetics and how those fields can shed light on the process of evolution. He died on May 14, 1995, at his home in Pikesville, Maryland.

Further Reading

Nobelprize.org. "The Nobel Prize in Chemistry 1972." Available online. URL: http://nobelprize.org/chemistry/laureates/1972. Downloaded on August 1, 2004.

Profiles in Science, National Library of Medicine. "The Christian B. Anfinsen Papers." Available online. URL: http://profiles.nlm.nih.gov/KK. Downloaded on March 23, 2005.

Wasson, Tyler, ed. *Nobel Prize Winners*. New York: H. W. Wilson, 1987, pp. 24–26.

Apgar, Virginia
(1909–1974) *perinatologist and teratologist*

Virginia Apgar developed the Apgar Score as a means of identifying newborns in need of immediate medical attention. She also contributed to the development of perinatology, the treatment of newborns, and teratology, the treatment of birth defects, as separate medical specialties.

Apgar was born on June 7, 1909, in Westfield, New Jersey. Her father, Charles, was an insurance executive, and her mother, Helen, was a homemaker. After receiving an A.B. from Mount Holyoke (Mass.) College in 1929, she entered the Columbia University College of Physicians and Surgeons in New York City, receiving an M.D. in 1933. She spent the next two years studying surgery at Columbia-Presbyterian Medical Center, and then she went to the University of Wisconsin to become trained as an anesthesiologist. After a brief stint at New York's Bellevue Hospital, in 1936 she returned to the College of Physicians and Surgeons to teach anesthesiology. Two years later she was named clinical director of Presbyterian Hospital's anesthesiology department. In this capacity she assisted in a number of medical and surgical operations, including the delivery of more than 17,000 newborns.

In 1952 Apgar realized that a number of infants were born with conditions that required immediate medical attention, but instead they were bundled off to the nursery before a physician or nurse could examine them carefully. Because they had not been examined, many of these infants later developed serious complications or even died from conditions that were eminently treatable had they been attended to at once. This realization led her to devise a simple test that could be administered by delivery room personnel at the time of birth so that conditions requiring immediate attention could be attended to immediately. The simple test calls for examining a newborn in five areas: skin color, pulse, reflex irritability, muscle tone, and respiration. The test is administered one minute and five minutes after birth, and if the score of the second test is low, then the test is re-administered 10 minutes after birth as well. In each area, the newborn is rated from 0 to 2, with a 10 total being a perfect score. A score lower than seven alerts medical personnel to

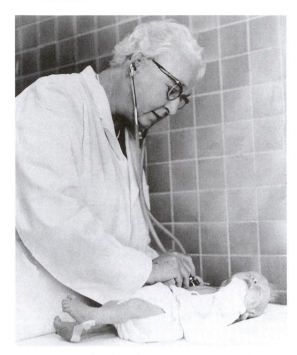

Virginia Apgar developed a means of assessing the health of newborns in a timely fashion so that infants who needed immediate medical treatment could receive it. *(Library of Congress, Prints and Photographs Division [LC-USZ62-131540])*

the need for careful monitoring, and a score lower than four calls for immediate action.

Published in 1953, the test became known as the Apgar Score, and it was put into practice in most delivering hospitals almost immediately. Ten years later, the *Journal of the American Medical Association* published an easy way to remember the five areas by relabeling them appearance, pulse, grimace, activity, and respiration, so that the first letters of the relabeled areas form the acronym Apgar. Apgar scoring continues to be used in virtually every delivery room in the world today, and it is credited with saving the lives of countless numbers of infants. Its adoption marks one of the first developments in perinatology as a medical specialty.

In 1959 Apgar received a master's degree in public health from Johns Hopkins University. That same year she became the director of birth defects for the National Foundation–March of Dimes, a nonprofit organization that seeks cures for polio and other children's diseases. In this capacity she lectured and raised money for further research, and in 1967 she was named director of basic research. Meanwhile, in 1965 she had left Columbia for Cornell University Medical College to teach pediatrics and teratology, thus becoming the first professor of teratology in the country. In 1973 she joined the faculty at Johns Hopkins University School of Hygiene and Public Health to teach medical genetics. That same year, she and Joan Beck coauthored *Is My Baby All Right? A Guide to Birth Defects,* which talks about congenital disorders in layman's terms and explains what the medical profession could and could not do about birth defects. She died, having never married, on August 7, 1974, in New York City. In 1994 the U.S. Postal Service issued a postage stamp in her honor.

Further Reading

Apel, Melanie Ann. *Virginia Apgar: Innovative Female Physician and Inventor of the Apgar Score.* New York: Rosen Publishing Group, 2004.

Calmes, Selma H. "Virginia Apgar: A Woman Physician's Career in a Developing Specialty," *Journal of the American Medical Women's Association* 39 (1984): pp. 184–188.

Yount, Lisa. *A to Z of Women in Science and Math.* New York: Facts On File, 1999, pp. 9–10.

Axel, Richard
(1946–) *physiologist*

Richard Axel helped demonstrate how odors are detected and identified by the nose as well as how sensory information related to odor is transmitted to the brain. For this contribution, he was awarded a share of the 2004 Nobel Prize in physiology or medicine.

Axel was born on July 2, 1946, in New York City. He received an A.B. from Columbia University in 1967 and an M.D. from Johns Hopkins University in 1970. He spent the next two years conducting research at Columbia's College of Physicians and Surgeons and its Institute of Cancer Research (ICR), and the two years after that as a research associate at the U.S. Public Health Service

research facility at the National Institutes of Health in Bethesda, Maryland. In 1974 he was appointed to ICR's faculty, and four years later he was named a professor of pathology and biochemistry, positions he has held ever since. In 1984 he took on the additional duty of investigator at the Howard Hughes Medical Institute at Columbia.

In 1980 Axel was joined by LINDA B. BUCK, who came to Columbia to conduct postdoctoral research in molecular biology, the specialty of Axel's laboratory. They soon decided to embark on a detailed investigation into how organisms detect and process sensory data related to smell. At the time, little was known about this process other than that odorant receptor cells, the cells that detect odor, are located far up in the nose, and that olfactory sensory data is transmitted to the olfactory bulb, where sensations of smell are decoded, via small canals in the nasal bone.

Axel and Buck spent the next 11 years expending on this small body of knowledge, focusing their early efforts on mice. They discovered that a mouse's olfactory system consists of approximately 1,000 different types of odorant receptors, and that the production of each type is regulated by a specific gene. The receptors are located on millions of olfactory receptor cells in the cell membranes in a small area in the mucosa, or lining, of the upper part of the mouse's nostril. Each type of receptor is designed to detect the molecules associated with a relatively small number of specific odors, and multiple copies of each receptor type are distributed randomly among the various receptor cells. Because a mouse's olfactory system is much more highly developed than a human's, a mouse can identify roughly 30,000 different scents, whereas humans, who have about 350 different types of odorant receptors, can identify about 10,000 different odors.

Axel and Buck also discovered how the sensory data collected by odorant receptors is transmitted to the brain from the nose. When odorant molecules bind to receptors, the receptors send an electric signal to structures known as glomeruli in the olfactory bulb. All of the receptors of the same type transmit their signals to the same glomerulus, which then transmits a signal to the brain indicating the type and intensity of the smell the receptors have detected. Axel and Buck began publishing their results in 1991, and 13 years later they were each awarded a half share of the 2004 Nobel Prize in physiology or medicine.

Axel and Buck ended their collaboration in 1991, when Buck departed for Harvard Medical School. Nevertheless, Axel continued to focus his research on the study of smell for a number of years thereafter. His other honors include election to the National Academy of Sciences and the American Academy of Arts and Sciences.

Further Reading

Altman, Lawrence K. "Unraveling Enigma of Smell Wins Nobel for 2 Americans," *New York Times,* October 5, 2004, p. A18.

Columbia University, Center for Neurobiology and Behavior. "Richard Axel." Available online. URL: http://cumc.columbia.edu/dept/neurobeh/Axel_center.html. Downloaded on March 25, 2005.

Nobelprize.org. "The Nobel Prize in Physiology or Medicine 2004." Available online. URL: http://nobelprize.org/medicine/laureates/2004. Downloaded on December 28, 2004.

Axelrod, Julius

(1912–2004) *neuropharmacologist*

Julius Axelrod discovered how the neurotransmitter noradrenaline is produced and neutralized by the nervous system. His discovery shed much light on how hallucinogenic drugs affect the nervous system as well as the nature of certain abnormal mental conditions. These discoveries won him a share of the 1970 Nobel Prize in physiology or medicine.

Axelrod was born on May 30, 1912, in New York City. His father, Isadore, was a basket maker, and his mother, Molly, was a homemaker. After studying briefly at New York University (NYU), he transferred to the City College of New York, receiving a B.S. in biology and chemistry in 1933. He worked for two years as a research assistant at NYU, after which he became a chemist at the Laboratory of Industrial Hygiene, a branch of the New York City Department of Public Health. Meanwhile, he returned to NYU as a student, receiving

an M.A. in chemistry in 1941. In 1938 he married Sally Taub with whom he had two children.

In 1946 Axelrod was assigned to study acetanilide, at the time a widely prescribed aspirin alternative. Certain patients taking the drug were developing methemoglobinemia, a condition that interferes with the ability of hemoglobin to carry oxygen to the cells. To solve the problem, he collaborated with Bernard Brodie of NYU's research division at Goldwater Memorial Hospital. Together Axelrod and Brodie discovered that the body converts acetanilide into acetaminophen, which explains the drug's analgesic properties; however, in some cases acetanilide is also converted into a compound that causes methemoglobinemia. This discovery led other researchers to develop techniques for synthesizing acetaminophen, which resulted in its widespread use as an alternative for both aspirin and acetanilide.

Axelrod's work came to the attention of the National Institutes of Health in Bethesda, Maryland, and in 1949 he was invited to join the staff of the National Heart Institute's section on chemical pharmacology. For the next six years Axelrod studied the effects on the heart of caffeine, amphetamine, mescaline, ephedrine, and the sympathomimetic amines, compounds that help prepare the body for strenuous activity. During this period he enrolled in the graduate program at George Washington University in Washington, D.C., receiving a Ph.D. in pharmacology in 1955. That same year he formed a pharmacology section for the National Institute of Mental Health (NIMH) and became its first chief.

At NIMH, Axelrod's research focused on neurotransmitters, chemical substances that transmit nervous impulses from one nerve ending to the next. Prior to the 1920s, it had been believed that nervous impulses were transmitted along a continuous, unbroken line of nerves physically connected to one another. This notion was proved false by English physiologist Henry Dale and German pharmacologist Otto Loewi, who won the 1936 Nobel Prize in physiology or medicine. Dale and Loewi demonstrated that nerve endings do not touch one another, and that nervous impulses are transmitted from one nerve to the next via neurotransmitters. Axelrod was particularly interested in the work of the Swedish biophysicist Ulf von Euler, who discovered the neurotransmitter noradrenaline, as well as how it is synthesized and stored. Axelrod built on von Euler's research by showing that noradrenaline is produced in excessive quantities by the nerves, but once it has transmitted a particular impulse it is neutralized immediately by the enzyme catechol-o-methyl transferase (COMT), which he discovered and named. Upon being neutralized, noradrenaline is then stored in the nerves until it is needed to transmit the next impulse.

Axelrod's discovery opened the door to a better understanding of how the entire nervous system works. Other researchers discovered that hallucinogenic drugs create dreamlike sensations by interfering with COMT's ability to neutralize noradrenaline in a timely fashion, thus causing nervous impulses to linger longer than normal. His work further suggested that abnormal mental conditions result in part from complicated physiology and brain chemistry, rather than psychological or environmental factors only. This discovery resulted in the development of pharmacological drugs designed to regulate the speed at which neurotransmitters operate. It was also shown that COMT counters the effects of certain hallucinogenic drugs, and that it is useful in research on hypertension and schizophrenia. For discovering COMT and for describing in detail its role in the transmission of neural impulses, Axelrod was awarded a one-third share of the 1970 Nobel Prize in physiology or medicine; one of his corecipients was von Euler, and the other was the British neuroscientist Bernard Katz.

Axelrod served as chief of NIMH's pharmacology section until his retirement in 1984. He continued to conduct research at NIMH, however, for a number of years as a guest researcher studying the biochemical regulation of cellular and molecular functions. In 1996 he was named a Scientist Emeritus of the National Institutes of Health. He died on December 29, 2004, in Rockville, Maryland.

Further Reading

Kanigel, Robert. *Apprentice to Genius: The Making of a Scientific Dynasty.* New York: Macmillan, 1986.

Nobelprize.org. "The Nobel Prize in Physiology or Medicine 1970." Available online. URL: http://nobelprize.org/medicine/laureates/1970. Downloaded on June 4, 2004.

Profiles in Science, National Library of Medicine. "The Julius Axelrod Papers." Available online. URL: http://profiles.nlm.nih.gov/HH. Downloaded on March 23, 2004.

Wasson, Tyler, ed. *Nobel Prize Winners.* New York: H. W. Wilson, 1987, pp. 42–44.

Bache, Alexander D.
(Alexander Dallas Bache)
(1806–1867) *science administrator*

Alexander Dallas Bache made no important scientific discoveries; nevertheless, he played an important role in the development of American science. He used his leadership and influence to professionalize the major scientific organizations of his day, and he cofounded and served as the first president of the National Academy of Sciences.

Bache was born on July 19, 1806, in Philadelphia, Pennsylvania. His father, Richard, was a postmaster, and his mother, Sophia, was a homemaker. At age 15 he entered the U.S. Military Academy, and in 1825 he graduated as a commissioned officer. He remained at West Point for a year to teach mathematics and natural philosophy (i.e., science) and then served for two years in Rhode Island with the Army Corps of Engineers. In 1828, the same year that he married Nancy Fowler with whom he had one child, he resigned from the army to teach natural philosophy and chemistry at the University of Pennsylvania in Philadelphia, a position he held until 1836. He spent the next six years serving as president of Girard College and superintendent of Central High School, both in Philadelphia.

Between 1828 and 1842, Bache developed a reputation as a scientific experimenter and administrator. His interest in geophysics led him to construct a laboratory wherein he took some of the first measurements of the Earth's magnetism ever taken in the United States. Meanwhile, he became involved in the affairs of the American Philosophical Society and the Franklin Institute, both of which were headquartered in Philadelphia. At the time, these two organizations were perhaps the two most important organizations to which an American scientist could belong.

Bache, a great-grandson of BENJAMIN FRANKLIN (for whom the Franklin Institute was named), used his considerable influence to rise to a leadership position in each, and then he worked to base membership on original scientific research. He also worked to get both institutions more involved in such research, and in 1830 he led the Franklin Institute's research project, which was funded by the federal government, into why steam boilers explode. This project was one of the first instances of Washington cooperating with a private scientific organization, and it set the stage for the establishment of the National Academy of Sciences as the primary scientific advisers to the federal government.

In 1843 Bache was named superintendent of the U.S. Coast Survey. Established in 1807, the Survey's mission was to develop maps and other navigational aids for mariners plying the U.S. Atlantic Coast. Bache used his position to expand that mission by making the Survey into one of the foremost scientific research institutions in the country. The Survey hired a number of scientists, both as employees and consultants, to study the stars and the weather, map large tracts of land and coastal waters, investigate terrestrial magnetism and the tides, and study the coastline's natural history, among other endeavors. Under his leadership, the Survey was the largest and most important organization for scientific research in the United States until the outbreak of the Civil War.

Having acquired a national reputation as a science administrator, Bache used his influence to professionalize the operations of national scientific organizations in much the same way he had in Philadelphia. Named to the board of regents of the Smithsonian Institution in 1846, he played an important role in getting it to support the advancement as well as the preservation of knowledge and to recruit the like-minded JOSEPH HENRY as its first secretary. In 1850 he was elected president of the American Association for the Advancement of Science, and in this position he worked to encourage and reward its members to perform original scientific research. In 1863 he helped organize the National Academy of Sciences and served as its first president. In this position, he guided the academy's efforts to help the federal government make use of new scientific and technological developments during the Civil War. Today, the academy remains one of the most important bodies for organizing, implementing, and assessing large-scale scientific research projects.

After the Civil War, Bache returned to his duties at the Coast Survey. He died on February 17, 1867, in Newport, Rhode Island.

Further Reading

Henry, Joseph. "Alexander Dallas Bache," National Academy of Sciences, *Biographical Memoirs* 1 (1877): pp. 205–212.

Odgers, Merle M. *Alexander Dallas Bache, Scientist and Educator, 1806–1867.* Philadelphia: University of Pennsylvania Press, 1947.

Slotten, Hugh R. *Patronage, Practice, and the Culture of American Science: Alexander Dallas Bache and the U.S. Coast Survey.* New York: Cambridge University Press, 1994.

Baltimore, David
(1938–   ) *virologist*

David Baltimore codiscovered retroviruses, cancer-causing viruses that replicate themselves by reversing the normal transmission of genetic coding. For this discovery, he was awarded a share of the 1975 Nobel Prize in physiology or Medicine.

Baltimore was born on March 7, 1938, in New York City to Richard and Gertrude Baltimore. After receiving a B.S. in chemistry from Swarthmore College in 1960, he entered the graduate program at the Massachusetts Institute of Technology (MIT) to study biophysics, but he left after one year to study animal virology at the Rockefeller Institute for Medical Research (today Rockefeller University), receiving a Ph.D. in 1964. Over the next four years he conducted postdoctoral research at MIT, the Albert Einstein College of Medicine in New York City, and the Salk Institute for Biological Studies in La Jolla,

David Baltimore helped discover that certain cancer-causing viruses replicate themselves by encoding from RNA to DNA. *(Courtesy of David Baltimore; photo by Bob Paz/Caltech)*

California; at the Salk Institute he worked with RENATO DULBECCO. In 1968, the same year he married Alice Huang with whom he has one child, he returned to MIT, this time to teach microbiology.

Baltimore's early research focused on poliovirus and other picornaviruses, the smallest of the viruses that infect mammals; picornaviruses are unusual in that their cores consist mostly of RNA rather than DNA. He was particularly interested in discovering how a picornavirus, or RNA virus, replicates itself. In 1962 Dulbecco showed that when certain DNA viruses invade a cell, the virus attaches its genome, a single set of chromosomes, to the DNA in the host cell's nucleus. In so doing, the virus permanently alters the cell by introducing what is, in essence, a new gene into its genetic makeup. The altered cell then produces daughter cells containing the viral genome that are not rejected by the host organism's immune system because they also contain the "correct" genetic coding. Dulbecco's finding, however, did not explain how an RNA animal virus was able to take over a host cell that contained DNA, because it was also understood that genetic coding could be transmitted only by messenger RNA from the DNA in a replicating cell to a daughter cell. In order for RNA animal viruses to behave as they evidently did, it was necessary for them to transmit genetic coding from RNA to DNA, which conventional wisdom held to be impossible.

By 1970 Baltimore was able to explain the secret of RNA animal virus replication. During the process of experimenting with Rauscher murine leukemia virus, he discovered a viral enzyme, later named reverse transcriptase, which replicates a single strand of RNA into a double strand of DNA. This discovery was duplicated independently that same year (1970) by HOWARD M. TEMIN, another former associate of Dulbecco's who had been working with an RNA animal virus that causes cancer in chickens, thus demonstrating conclusively that an RNA animal virus can integrate its genome into a host cell in the same way that a DNA virus does. Viruses that make use of reverse transcriptase to copy DNA from RNA are now known as retroviruses. For helping to dis-

cover them, Baltimore was awarded a one-third share of the 1975 Nobel Prize in physiology or medicine; his corecipients were Dulbecco and Temin.

In 1982 Baltimore became the founding director of MIT's Whitehead Institute for Biomedical Research. In this capacity he played an important role in galvanizing federal support for acquired immunodeficiency syndrome (AIDS) research, and he helped identify the virus that causes AIDS, the human immunodeficiency virus (HIV), as a retrovirus. He served as cochair of the National Academy of Sciences and Institute of Medicine's Committee on a National Strategy for AIDS and as chair of the National Institutes of Health AIDS Vaccine Research Committee.

Baltimore was elected to the National Academy of Sciences, the American Academy of Arts and Sciences, and the American Association for the Advancement of Science, and he was awarded the National Medal of Science. In 1990 he left MIT to return to Rockefeller University where he taught and served briefly as president. In 1994 he returned to MIT to teach molecular biology, and in 1997 he was named president of the California Institute of Technology.

Further Reading

Crotty, Shane. *Ahead of the Curve: David Baltimore's Life in Science.* Berkeley: University of California Press, 2001.

Nobelprize.org. "The Nobel Prize in Physiology or Medicine 1975." Available online. URL: http://nobelprize.org/medicine/laureates/1975. Downloaded on June 9, 2004.

Wasson, Tyler, ed. *Nobel Prize Winners.* New York: H. W. Wilson, 1987, pp. 50–51.

Banneker, Benjamin
(1731–1806) *astronomer*

Benjamin Banneker was typical of the self-trained scientists of the colonial period. Despite the lack of a formal education, he was able to teach himself astronomy and compute astronomical tables of the highest quality. He also used his astronomical skills to help survey the nation's capital.

Banneker was born on November 9, 1731, in Oella, Maryland. His parents, Robert and Mary, were farmers. His entire formal education consisted of several sessions in a one-room schoolhouse where he learned reading, writing, and arithmetic. Because he was a voracious reader, he was able to teach himself much about a number of subjects. He lived on the family farm his entire life; instead of marrying, he supported his parents until his mother's death in the late 1770s.

When he was in his early twenties, Banneker built a mechanical clock, a feat that bordered on the near-miraculous given his time and place. According to legend, he dismantled a pocket watch, examined its workings carefully, and then set out to build a chiming clock based on his observations. He carved most of the gears and other parts from hardwood, calculating himself the number of teeth each gear should have in order to keep precise time. The clock kept near-perfect time until after his death, and it gained for him a reputation as a man of learning throughout his community.

Except for a fortuitous event, Banneker might never have become a man of science. In 1771 George Ellicott, an entrepreneur from Philadelphia, Pennsylvania, moved into the neighborhood with the intention of making a fortune by raising and milling wheat. Ellicott happened also to have an interest in astronomy, and he brought his equipment and books to Oella, near present-day Ellicott City. Banneker expressed an intense interest in learning more about astronomy, and Ellicott taught him how to use a telescope. In 1789 Ellicott loaned Banneker a telescope and several astronomy books, and with this equipment Banneker was able to teach himself a great deal about astronomy. Within a short time he had learned enough to calculate an ephemeris, a table showing the calculated positions of a heavenly body on a number of future dates in a regular sequence. His success in this endeavor led him in 1790 to produce tables for a number of planets and stars for inclusion in an almanac for the year 1791.

In 1791 Banneker's ability as an astronomer came to the attention of Andrew Ellicott, the surveyor who had been put in charge of laying out Washington, D.C. Ellicott had asked his cousin George Ellicott, who was also a trained surveyor, to help him. George Ellicott, who was preoccupied with business in Maryland, suggested that Banneker take his place temporarily. For three months in early 1791, then, Banneker assisted Andrew Ellicott by supervising the surveying party's astronomy tent and the astronomical clock. At the time, surveyors used astronomical data to determine longitude and latitude, and the success of the party's efforts depended on Banneker's ability to provide accurate astronomical data.

Upon being relieved by George Ellicott, Banneker returned to his farm and began preparing astronomical tables for publication in an almanac of his own. At the time, almanacs were incredibly valuable publications as they contained the information farmers needed to know about when to plant and harvest crops, and much of this information was based on astronomical observations. Banneker's tables were published in Baltimore in 1792 under the title *Benjamin Banneker's Pennsylvania, Delaware, Maryland and Virginia Almanack and Ephemeris, for the Year of Our Lord 1792. . . .* It was so well received that he produced almanacs for the next five years as well. Although he stopped producing almanacs in 1797, he continued to calculate astronomical tables for his own amusement until 1804.

Banneker achieved international fame for his almanac after presenting a manuscript copy to Thomas Jefferson, who at the time was U.S. secretary of state. Jefferson, who shared Banneker's interest in astronomy, was so impressed with the latter's work that he distributed copies to his friends and contacts in Europe, where Banneker's calculations were compared favorably against those of more learned astronomers. Banneker died on October 19, 1806, at his home in Oella.

Further Reading

Bedini, Silvio A. *The Life of Benjamin Banneker: The First African-American Man of Science,* 2nd ed. Baltimore: Maryland Historical Society, 1999.

Cerami, Charles A. *Benjamin Banneker: Surveyor, Astronomer, Publisher, Patriot.* New York: J. Wiley, 2002.

Spangenburg, Ray, and Kit Moser. *African Americans in Science, Math, and Invention.* New York: Facts On File, 2003, pp. 8–10.

Bardeen, John
(1908–1991) *physicist*

John Bardeen is the only person to receive two Nobel Prizes in physics. The first came in 1956 for codiscovering the transistor effect in semiconductors, and the second came in 1972 for codeveloping the theory of superconductivity, also known as the BCS theory.

Bardeen was born on May 23, 1908, in Madison, Wisconsin. His father, Charles, was dean of the University of Wisconsin Medical School, and his mother, Althea, was a homemaker. At age 15 he graduated from high school and enrolled at Wisconsin, receiving a B.S. and an M.S. in electrical engineering in 1928 and 1929, respectively. In 1930 he went to work for the Gulf Research and Development Corporation in Pittsburgh, Pennsylvania, but left after three years to enter the graduate program at Princeton University, receiving a Ph.D. in physics in 1936. He spent the next two years doing postdoctoral research at Harvard University, followed by a three-year stint teaching physics at the University of Minnesota. During World War II he conducted war-related research at the U.S. Naval Ordnance Laboratory in Washington, D.C. In 1938 he married Jane Maxwell with whom he had three children.

In 1945 Bardeen became a colleague of WALTER H. BRATTAIN and WILLIAM B. SHOCKLEY at Bell Telephone Laboratories (BTL) in Murray Hill, New Jersey. Brattain and Shockley were developing an alternative to the vacuum tube, the primary means by which the flow of electrons was generated and controlled in an electronic apparatus. Although the vacuum tube worked well enough, it was too bulky, too energy-inefficient, and too short-lived for a growing number of critical applications. Specifically, Brattain and Shockley were experimenting with semiconductors, substances that conduct electricity better than nonconductors such as glass but not as well as good conductors such as copper. Shockley believed that the electrons in a semiconductor could be used to amplify an electrical signal flowing into the semiconductor, in much the same way that the electrons emitted by the electrodes in a vacuum tube amplify a signal passing through the tube. But when the trio's first attempt to do this failed, Bardeen suggested that the failure was caused by the way electrons are positioned close to the surface of a semiconductor.

After Brattain completed an extensive study of the surface properties of semiconductors that shed much light on their behavior relative to the flow of electrons, in 1947 he and Bardeen set out to build the first transistor. Within a year they had constructed what is now called a point-contact transistor. They passed an incoming electrical current through a wire to one side of a crystal of the semiconductor germanium, and a signal from an electrode to the other side of the crystal. As predicted, the signal from the electrode that emerged from the crystal was greatly amplified, even though the incoming current was much weaker than that required to generate the same level of amplification in a vacuum tube. Further experimentation by Bardeen, Brattain, and Shockley led to a full explanation of the so-called transistor effect, the ability of a semiconductor to amplify an electronic signal. By 1952 BTL researchers had developed a transistor for use in routing long-distance telephone calls, and before long virtually every electronic operation that had been performed by a vacuum tube was being performed by a transistor. For the part he played in discovering and harnessing the transistor effect, Bardeen was awarded a one-third share of the 1956 Nobel Prize in physics; he shared the prize with his collaborators, Brattain and Shockley.

Meanwhile, in 1951 Bardeen had left BTL to teach electrical engineering and physics at the University of Illinois in Urbana. Shortly thereafter he began experimenting with a phenomenon known as superconductivity, the ability of certain metals to lose all resistance to electron flow in extreme low-temperature conditions. Superconductivity was discovered in 1911 by Dutch physicist Heike Kamerlingh Onnes, but 40 years later its specific mechanics remained a mystery. In 1950 it was discovered that the isotopes of certain metals become superconductors at different temperatures and that the temperature at which they become superconductive is inversely proportional to the isotope's atomic mass. This latter discovery prompted Bardeen to speculate that superconductivity occurs because of an interaction between the electrons making up the metal and the electrons flowing through the metal. His supposition was based in part on the work of the German-American physicist Fritz London, who in 1935 had speculated that very low temperatures alter the physical properties of subatomic particles. Nevertheless, Bardeen's theory raised many eyebrows, because under normal conditions electrons repel rather than attract one another.

In 1955 Bardeen began collaborating in his research concerning superconductivity with LEON N. COOPER, who had just come to Illinois as a research associate. Within a year Cooper was able to prove Bardeen's theory about interacting electrons by demonstrating the existence of what is now called Cooper pairs. In a Cooper pair, one electron in the superconductor forms a bond with an electron flowing through the superconductor. As scores of Cooper pairs are created, the Cooper pairs interact with other pairs in such a way that the superconductor's resistance to electron flow is reduced to zero. Bardeen was further assisted by one of his graduate students, J. ROBERT SCHRIEFFER, who developed a mathematical model to explain the behavior of Cooper pairs. In 1957 Bardeen, Cooper, and Schrieffer published the first satisfactory theory of superconductivity, also known as the BCS theory after the initials of their last names. Almost 50 years after its publication, the BCS theory continues to inform all research involving superconductors.

Superconductivity promises to revolutionize the way electricity is transmitted and applied in a number of electronic applications. A better understanding of superconductivity was deemed so essential to scientific progress that the U.S. government had planned to fund the construction and operation of a multimillion-dollar research facility devoted to superconductivity until a budget crisis forced the project to be canceled. Meanwhile, in 1972 Bardeen was awarded a one-third share of the Nobel Prize in physics for his role in developing the BCS theory; his corecipients were his colleagues, Cooper and Schrieffer.

Bardeen was elected to the National Academy of Sciences. He served on the science advisory committees of presidents Dwight D. Eisenhower and John F. Kennedy and on the editorial boards of *The Physical Review* and *Reviews of Modern Physics.* He retired from Illinois in 1975, although he continued to study superconductivity for several years thereafter. He died on January 30, 1991, in Boston, Massachusetts.

Further Reading

Hoddeson, Lillian, and Vicki Daitch. *True Genius: The Life and Science of John Bardeen.* Washington, D.C.: Joseph Henry Press, 2002.

Nobelprize.org. "The Nobel Prize in Physics 1956." Available online. URL: http://nobelprize.org/physics/laureates/1956. Downloaded on February 22, 2004.

Nobelprize.org. "The Nobel Prize in Physics 1972." Available online. URL: http://nobelprize.org/physics/laureates/1972. Downloaded on February 22, 2004.

Wasson, Tyler, ed. *Nobel Prize Winners.* New York: H. W. Wilson, 1987, pp. 55–59.

Beadle, George W.
(George Wells Beadle)
(1903–1989) *geneticist*

George W. Beadle was one of the first practitioners of biochemical genetics, the study of the role genes play in controlling the biochemical functions of living organisms. His contributions to this field, and to genetics in general, were recognized in 1958 when he was awarded a share of the Nobel Prize in physiology or medicine.

Beadle was born on October 22, 1903, in Wahoo, Nebraska. His parents, Chauncey and Hattie, were farmers. In 1922 he entered the University of Nebraska College of Agriculture, receiving a B.S. and an M.S. in 1926 and 1927, respectively. He then enrolled in the graduate program at the University of Cornell and received a Ph.D. in genetics in 1931. In 1928 he married Marion Hill with whom he had one child. They divorced in 1953, and that same year he married Muriel Barnett.

While at Cornell, Beadle had participated in some of BARBARA McCLINTOCK's genetic experiments with maize, particularly *Zea mays,* popularly known as Indian corn, which has a different color pattern of kernels on each ear. In 1931 Beadle received a National Research Council fellowship to study genetics under THOMAS HUNT MORGAN at the California Institute of Technology (Caltech), where he shifted the focus of his research from maize to fruit flies. By 1935 Beadle's work had suggested that genes play some sort of role in biochemical functions, so that same year he went to the Institute of Biology and Physical Chemistry in Paris, France, to further explore this connection. He and the institute's Boris Ephrussi, who had spent the previous year at Caltech, repeatedly transplanted genetic material from one fruit fly larva into a larva of a different genetic heritage to see what effect this might have on determining eye color. At the end of a year, the results seemed to confirm Beadle's suspicion that genes affect biochemical functions, but they also showed that the biochemistry of genetics, even in such a simple organism as the fruit fly, is incredibly intricate, and that new methods needed to be developed before further progress in this area could be made.

In 1936 Beadle was named a professor of genetics at Harvard University, but he left after a year to accept a similar position at Stanford University. Over the next four years he and EDWARD L. TATUM tried to develop the methods that Beadle and Ephrussi's work had called for, but by 1941 they had concluded that the fruit fly was simply too complex an organism to work with. That same year they switched their focus to *Neurospora crassa*, a red bread mold, after realizing that they could manipulate the mold's environment in such a way that tracking genetic changes was relatively easy. They bombarded colonies of *Neurospora* with X-rays so as to cause certain genes to mutate, and then they varied the nutritional medium upon which the mutants grew so as to identify which biochemical functions had been affected by mutation. In this way they were able to match up a number of specific biochemical functions with the particular gene that controlled each function.

Beadle and Tatum's work led them to conclude that genes control the structure and function of enzymes, complex proteins that initiate biochemical reactions. Specifically, the results allowed them to hypothesize that each enzyme is controlled by one particular gene, the so-called one gene–one enzyme concept. Moreover, they showed that a mutation in a gene affects only the biochemical function initiated by the enzyme that the gene controls. Other researchers provided additional evidence to back up the one gene–one enzyme concept, which later proved to be invaluable to researchers studying cell metabolism, particularly how organisms produce amino acids, the building blocks of proteins. The one gene–one enzyme concept also led to new techniques for developing pharmaceutical drugs from living organisms. For their contributions to a better understanding of the biochemistry of genetics, Beadle and Tatum were each awarded a one-third share of the 1958 Nobel Prize in physiology or medicine.

Meanwhile, in 1946 Beadle had returned to Caltech to chair the biology division, a position that greatly restricted his ability to conduct research. In 1961 he was named president of the University of Chicago, a post he held for seven years. In 1968 he became director of the American Medical Association's Institute for Biomedical Research. In 1970 he retired to Pomona, California, although for several years thereafter he conducted genetic experiments concerning his first research interest, *Zea mays*. He was elected to the National Academy of Sciences and the American Academy of Arts and Sciences, and he served as president of the American Association for the Advancement of Science and the Genetics Society of America. He died on June 9, 1989, in Pomona.

Further Reading

Horowitz, Norman H. "George Wells Beadle," National Academy of Sciences, *Biographical Memoirs* 59 (1990): pp. 26–53.

Nobelprize.org. "The Nobel Prize in Physiology or Medicine 1958." Available online. URL: http://nobelprize.org/medicine/laureates/1958. Downloaded on April 20, 2004.

Wasson, Tyler, ed. *Nobel Prize Winners*. New York: H. W. Wilson, 1987, pp. 64–67.

Békésy, Georg von
(1899–1972) *physiologist*

Georg von Békésy discovered how the human ear transmits sound waves to the brain so that they can be recognized and translated by the brain. For this achievement, he was awarded a Nobel Prize.

Békésy was born on June 3, 1899, in Budapest, Austria-Hungary. His father, Alexander, was a diplomat, and his mother, Paula, was a homemaker. As a boy he traveled with his family to his father's posts in Germany, Switzerland, and the Ottoman Empire, but he returned to Budapest for his high school education. In 1916 he enrolled in the University of Berne, Switzerland, and received a B.S. in chemistry four years later. After a brief tour of duty in the Hungarian army, he entered the University of Budapest and received a Ph.D. in physics in 1923. He then went to work as a communications engineer for the Hungarian telephone system, and eventually became director of its research laboratory. From 1939 to 1946 he also taught experimental physics at Budapest.

In 1946 Békésy emigrated to Stockholm, Sweden, to conduct research at the Karolinska Institute and the Royal Institute of Technology, but he left a year later for a research position at Harvard University's Psycho-Acoustic Laboratory. While at Harvard, Békésy, who never married, became a U.S. citizen. Threatened with mandatory retirement in 1966, he left Harvard that same year for the University of Hawaii, where he finished out his career. In addition to teaching sensory sciences there, he conducted research for the telephone company in Hawaii.

Békésy first became interested in the mechanics of human hearing while working for the Hungarian telephone system. His primary research duties involved designing improvements to Hungary's long-distance service, but he eventually came to regard the ear as the most important feature of any telephone transmission system. Although the physiologists of the day understood how the ear was constructed, they did not know exactly how it worked. The most popular theory was the one advanced in 1863 by German physiologist Hermann von Helmholtz. According to Helmholtz, hearing occurs because sound vibrations excite the specialized nerve fibers in the auditory nerve in the inner ear. Helmholtz believed that each fiber vibrated in response to a particular frequency, and that the cumulative vibrating pattern of the fibers communicated to the brain the full range of what was being heard.

Békésy set out to determine the validity of Helmholtz's theory by building an oversized plastic model of the cochlea, a cavity in the inner ear that is divided in half by the basilar membrane, to which the specialized nerve fibers connect. He conducted experiments on the inner ears of guinea pigs by using microsurgical tools he designed and made himself. He also devised a method for preserving the ear tissues in cadavers by keeping them immersed in water, conducting his experiments on the human ear via means of an underwater microscope of his own design. During his short stay in Stockholm, he developed an audiometer that is patient-operated, thus permitting the researcher to obtain better feedback concerning what the patient hears. While at Harvard, he built a working mechanical model of the inner ear, complete with a nerve supply, which he constructed from skin from the arm. He published the results of the experiments he performed with these models and techniques in *Hearing: Its Psychology and Physiology* (1938) and *Experiments in Hearing* (1960).

By 1961 Békésy was able to describe in detail how humans hear. He discounted Helmholtz's theory by showing that hearing takes place as a result of the activity of the basilar membrane. This membrane vibrates according to the sound waves that reach it at its location in the inner ear. Tighter and thinner at its base than it is at the apex of the cochlea, the membrane vibrates in different places. The exact area of the membrane that is being caused to vibrate by a particular sound wave is transmitted along the auditory nerve to the brain, which translates that location into "sound." This discovery led to a host of developments, not the least of which were better ways to help the deaf regain their hearing. In recognition of his groundbreaking work, Békésy was awarded the 1961 Nobel Prize for physiology or medicine.

In addition to winning the Nobel Prize, Békésy was awarded a number of prizes and distinctions by European scientific organizations, including the academies of sciences of Berlin and Budapest. He was also awarded medals of honor by the American Otological Society and the Acoustical Society of America. He died on June 13, 1972, in Honolulu.

Further Reading

Nobelprize.org. "The Nobel Prize in Physiology or Medicine 1961." Available online. URL: http://nobelprize.org/medicine/laureates/1961. Downloaded on January 13, 2004.

Ratliff, Floyd. "Georg von Békésy," National Academy of Sciences, *Biographical Memoirs* 48 (1976): pp. 25–49.

Wasson, Tyler, ed. *Nobel Prize Winners*. New York: H. W. Wilson, 1987, pp. 76–78.

Benacerraf, Baruj
(1920–) *immunogeneticist*

Baruj Benacerraf discovered Ir genes, the genes that control the responses of the body's immune system. This discovery contributed to the creation of a new scientific field, immunogenetics, the study of the connection between immunology and genetics, while also winning for him a share of the 1980 Nobel Prize in physiology or medicine.

Benacerraf was born on October 29, 1920, in Caracas, Venezuela. His father, Abraham, was a textile merchant and importer, and his mother, Henriette, was a homemaker. At age five he moved with his family to Paris, France, where he grew up. In 1939 he returned with his family to Venezuela, where his father's businesses had continued to thrive, leaving the following year to attend Columbia University in New York City. After receiving a B.S. in 1942, he entered the Medical College of Virginia (today part of Virginia Commonwealth University). In 1943 he was drafted into the U.S. Army Medical Corps (although he remained in school), married Annette Dreyfus with whom he had one child, and became a naturalized U.S. citizen. After

Baruj Benacerraf showed that certain genes control the human immune system. *(Courtesy of Baruj Benacerraf)*

receiving an M.D. in 1945, he interned for a year at Queens General Hospital in New York City before being shipped by the army to Europe, where he served for two years.

In 1948 Benacerraf returned to New York City, this time as a research fellow at Columbia's Neurological Institute, but he left after a year for a research position at the Broussais Hospital in Paris. Over the next seven years, he divided his time between his scientific career and managing his father's businesses, relinquishing most of the latter duties in 1956 when he was named a professor of pathology at the New York University (NYU) School of Medicine. He remained at NYU until 1968, when he was named chief of the National Institute of Allergy and Infectious Diseases' immunology laboratory in Bethesda, Maryland, leaving two years later to become chair of the pathology department at Harvard University. In 1980 he retired from teaching to serve as president and chief executive officer of the Dana-Farber Cancer Institute in Boston, Massachusetts, a position he held until his retirement in 1996.

Benacerraf's early research focused on immunology, the process by which the body's immune system rejects the introduction of foreign biological matter. At the Neurological Institute he investigated hypersensitivity, the body's allergic reaction to the production of too many antibodies in response to the introduction of a toxic antigen. At the Broussais Hospital he studied the reticuloendothelial system, cells that attack intrusive substances such as bacteria, viruses, dead or abnormal cells, and foreign substances by completely surrounding and removing them. Upon settling at NYU, he began studying the relationship between immunology and genetics. This shift in focus was prompted by an observation he made while studying the antibody system in guinea pigs. After noting that certain guinea pigs responded, or produced antibodies, to the introduction of a particular antigen while other guinea pigs did not respond, he concluded that genetics played a role in the functioning of their immune systems. Further experiments demonstrated the existence of an immune response, or Ir, gene that controls the body's immune system. By 1970 he had located several Ir genes in a previously unmapped region of the major histocompatibility complex (MHC); discovered by GEORGE D. SNELL in the 1960s, the MHC is a linked group of genes that regulates the body's immune response.

Benacerraf showed that some Ir genes coordinate the activities of the different cell types that make up the immune system in order to bring about a certain response, while other Ir genes suppress responses of the immune system that threaten to get out of control. He concluded his research career in the 1970s by demonstrating the role played by Ir genes in the regulation of specific acquired immunity (immunity to a certain disease, such as measles, after having had the disease once) as well as the body's susceptibility to autoimmune diseases, whereby the body's immune system mistakenly attacks its own tissue. Because his discoveries contributed immensely to a better understanding of how the immune system works, Benacerraf was awarded a one-third share of the 1980 Nobel Prize in physiology or medicine; one of his corecipients was Snell while the other was the French immunologist Jean Dausset.

Benacerraf coauthored several books, including *Immunological Tolerance: Mechanisms and Potential Therapeutic Applications* (1974), *Immunogenetics and Immunodeficiency* (1975), and *The Role of Products of the Histocompatibility Gene Complex in Immune Response* (1976). His many honors include election to the National Academy of Sciences and the American Academy of Arts and Sciences, and he served as president of the American Association of Immunologists, the American Society for Experimental Biology and Medicine, and the International Union of Immunological Societies.

Further Reading

Benacerraf, Baruj. *From Caracas to Stockholm: A Life in Medical Science.* Amherst, N.Y.: Prometheus Books, 1998.

Nobelprize.org. "The Nobel Prize in Physiology or Medicine 1980." Available online. URL: http://nobelprize.org/medicine/laureates/1980. Downloaded on June 17, 2004.

Wasson, Tyler, ed. *Nobel Prize Winners.* New York: H. W. Wilson, 1987, pp. 81–83.

Berg, Paul
(1926–   ) *biochemist*

Paul Berg developed the techniques for recombining DNA from two different species, thus contributing to the development of genetic engineering and biotechnology. For this contribution he was awarded a share of the 1980 Nobel Prize in chemistry.

Berg was born on June 30, 1926, in Brooklyn, New York. His father, Harry, owned a garment factory, and his mother, Sarah, was a homemaker. After graduating from high school in 1943, he joined the U.S. Navy and served on a submarine chaser during World War II. He also spent some time during the war as a student at Pennsylvania State University, and in 1946 he returned to Penn State, receiving a B.S. in biochemistry two years later. Meanwhile, in 1947 he had married Mildred Levy with whom he had one child. In 1952 he received a Ph.D. in biochemistry from Western Reserve University (today Case Western Reserve University) in Cleveland, Ohio, and went off to Copenhagen, Denmark, for a year of postdoctoral research. Upon returning to the United States, he became a research assistant to ARTHUR KORNBERG at the Washington University School of Medicine in St. Louis, Missouri. Berg assisted Kornberg in his Nobel Prize–winning research, the synthesis of a molecule of DNA of *Escherichia coli* (*E. coli*), a bacterium commonly found in the human digestive tract. This experience led Berg to refocus his own research from the role played by enzymes in the production of amino acids to the study of how genetics regulates biochemical functions.

In 1959 Kornberg was named head of the department of biochemistry at the Stanford University School of Medicine in Palo Alto, California,

By demonstrating how to recombine DNA from two different species, Paul Berg cofounded the field of biotechnology. *(Courtesy of Paul Berg)*

and that same year he recruited Berg to join him as a professor in that department. At Stanford, Berg began studying how SV40, a virus that causes cancer in certain species of primates, spreads itself by recombining its DNA with the DNA of the host cells it infects so that the SV40 genome, or a complete set of chromosomes, becomes one of the host cell's genes. This study led him to become increasingly interested in the possibility of recombinant DNA technology, better known as genetic splicing. By 1969 he had become convinced that DNA from two different species could be combined in such a way as to shed light on the performance of the genes of both species. To this end he set out to combine DNA from SV40 with DNA from *E. coli*. By using a variety of different enzymes, in 1972 he was able to extract the three genes responsible for metabolizing the enzyme galactose in *E. coli* from *E. coli* DNA and splice them into the SV40 DNA genome. The result was the first synthetic molecule of recombinant DNA.

Gene splicing eventually became an important tool for analyzing the function and structure of mammalian genes because it allows a specific gene to be removed from its normal environment and studied in isolation from the other genes that normally modify its behavior. It also led directly to the rise of biotechnology, the genetic engineering of certain organisms to perform a specific task that they are otherwise incapable of performing. Recombinant DNA technology was first used to engineer a type of bacteria that produces large amounts of human insulin, but in time this technology became widespread in the production of antibiotics and other hormones as well. For his contribution to these developments, Berg was awarded a half share of the 1980 Nobel Prize in chemistry.

As the "inventor" of recombinant DNA technology, Berg was also the first to recognize the potential for disaster that gene splicing could cause. At one point he himself had planned to reverse his original experiment by injecting SV40 DNA into *E. coli* DNA, but he stopped short when he realized that the result might be the creation of a strain of killer *E. coli* capable of inducing tumors in humans. This realization led him to organize the first international conference, held in California in 1975, for establishing safety guidelines for the worldwide use of recombinant DNA technology. This conference also led to the passage of federal regulations governing genetic engineering in the United States, and the creation by the National Academy of Sciences of a committee on recombinant DNA molecules, which Berg chaired.

Berg finished out his scientific career at Stanford. In addition to taking over for Kornberg as department chair, he also served as director of the Beckman Center for Molecular and Genetic Medicine. He retired from his teaching and administrative duties in 2000, but he continued to conduct research, the focus of which was to target alterations in chromosomal genes of embryonic stem cells with a goal of creating mutant animals. His many honors include the National Medal of Science, election to the National Academy of Sciences and the American Academy of Arts and Sciences, and election to a term as president of the American Society of Biological Chemists. His publications include *Exploring Genetic Mechanisms* (1997), *Dealing with Genes: The Language of Heredity* (1992), and *Genes and Genomes: A Changing Perspective* (1991).

Further Reading

Hargittai, Istvan, and Magdolna Hargittai. *Candid Science II: Conversations with Famous Biomedical Scientists.* London: Imperial College Press, 2002, pp. 154–182.

Nobelprize.org. "The Nobel Prize in Chemistry 1980." Available online. URL: http://nobelprize.org/chemistry/laureates/1980. Downloaded on August 9, 2004.

Wasson, Tyler, ed. *Nobel Prize Winners.* New York: H. W. Wilson, 1987, pp. 85–87.

Bethe, Hans A.
(Hans Albrecht Bethe)
(1906–2005) *physicist*

Hans A. Bethe won a Nobel Prize for explaining how stars generate energy via nuclear reactions. He also contributed significantly to the development of theoretical physics in the United States, and his theories provided a better understanding of the forces governing the structures of atomic nuclei.

Hans Bethe showed that nuclear reactions are the processes by which the stars generate energy. *(Courtesy of Hans A. Bethe)*

Bethe was born on July 2, 1906, in Strasbourg, Alsace-Lorraine, at the time a part of Germany. His father, Albrecht, was a physiologist, and his mother, Anna, was a homemaker. At age six he moved with his family to Kiel, and three years after that to Frankfurt, where he grew up. He attended the University of Frankfurt for two years before transferring to the University of Munich, where he received a Ph.D. in theoretical physics in 1928. He spent the next seven years teaching physics and conducting research at various universities in Germany, England, and Italy. In 1935 he came to the United States to teach physics at Cornell University in Ithaca, New York, where he spent the rest of his academic career. In 1939 he married Rose Ewald with whom he had two children, and in 1941 he became a naturalized U.S. citizen.

Bethe was one of the first practitioners in the United States of theoretical physics or quantum theory, which eventually evolved into quantum mechanics, the study of subatomic particles. When he arrived at Cornell, the neutron had just been discovered, so quantum theory was still in its infancy. Moreover, since quantum theory had begun in Europe and the leading centers for its study were in Germany, he found that most American physicists were not up to speed on the latest developments. Consequently, he and several collaborators spent a year compiling what was known about quantum theory, and in 1936 they published it in a highly influential series of articles in *Reviews of Modern Physics*. These articles came to be known as the "Bethe bible."

Bethe was particularly interested in the theory of nuclear reactions. After attending a 1938 conference on theoretical physics in Washington, D.C., which was devoted to the role of quantum mechanics in astrophysics, Bethe began applying nuclear theory to the question of what produces energy in stars. It was generally agreed that some sort of nuclear reaction must be responsible because of the incredible amount of energy released by stars over the eons of their existence, but no one could explain the mechanics by which these reactions took place. In a brilliant paper that was published in 1939, Bethe theorized that there are actually two, and only two, types of nuclear reactions at work in the stars. The first takes place in smaller stars like the Sun, and it produces energy via a proton-proton reaction. In a series of four steps, four hydrogen atoms are converted via nuclear fusion into one helium atom and two protons; these two protons form the nuclei of two new hydrogen atoms, thus permitting the reaction to continue. The second takes place in massive stars, and it produces energy via the carbon-nitrogen cycle. In a series of six steps, one carbon atom and three hydrogen atoms are fused into one nitrogen atom, which then fuses with a hydrogen atom to create one helium atom and one carbon atom; in essence, the carbon atom acts like a catalyst, thus continuing the reaction.

Amazingly, given the lack of experimental data and the crude nature of technology at the time, Bethe's theory about energy generation in stars continued to be the standard theory for the next 30 years. As technology improved and observational evidence accumulated during this period, it only served to confirm what Bethe had already theorized. For contributing to a better understanding of how nuclear reactions fuel the stars and, ultimately, all life on Earth, Bethe was awarded the 1967 Nobel Prize in physics.

Bethe left Cornell during World War II to work on various weapons projects. In 1941 he joined a government project at the Massachusetts Institute of Technology that was developing radar; while there, he designed the Bethe coupler, a device for measuring an increase in electromagnetic waves. In 1942 he joined the Manhattan Project, the U.S. effort to build an atomic bomb, and was named director of the theoretical physics division at the Los Alamos, New Mexico, facility. In this capacity he devised, with the assistance of RICHARD P. FEYNMAN, the Bethe-Feynman formula for calculating the efficiency of a nuclear weapon. In 1946, however, he left the project because he wanted nothing more to do with the making of nuclear weapons, and from then on he worked actively for nuclear disarmament.

Upon returning to Cornell in 1946, Bethe returned to his studies of atomic and nuclear processes. This work is summarized in three books: *Elementary Nuclear Theory* (1947, 1956), a discussion of the experimental evidence concerning the forces acting inside the atomic nucleus; *Quantum Mechanics of One- and Two-Electron Atoms* (1957, 1977), which explains the properties of atomic nuclei in terms of the forces acting between protons and neutrons; and *Intermediate Quantum Mechanics* (1964, 1968, 1986), a theoretical description of atomic structure. He also did some of the early work on solid-state theory, which explains how electrons flow through a semiconductor, and he developed calculations for determining electron densities in crystals, the order-disorder states in alloys, the operational conditions of nuclear reactors, the ionization processes in shock waves, and the detection of underground nuclear explosions from seismographic records. He concluded his active career by returning to astrophysics in 1970 and following the discovery of neutron stars; these stars have used up their hydrogen and carbon, and so their nuclear reactions involve much higher elements, including iron and uranium.

Bethe retired from Cornell in 1975, but he maintained an office there for more than 25 years where he continued to work and write. During this period he wrote *The Road from Los Alamos* (1991), in which he reflects on the hydrogen bomb, weapons research, arms control, and nuclear power. His many honors include the Presidential Medal of Merit, the National Medal of Science, and election to the National Academy of Sciences. He died on March 6, 2005, at his home in Ithaca.

Further Reading

Bernstein, Jeremy. *Hans Bethe, Prophet of Energy.* New York: Basic Books, 1980.

Marshak, Robert E., ed. *Perspectives in Modern Physics: Essays in Honor of Hans A. Bethe on the Occasion of His 60th Birthday, July, 1966.* New York: Interscience Publishers, 1966.

Nobelprize.org. "The Nobel Prize in Physics 1967." Available online. URL: http://nobelprize.org/physics/laureates/1967. Downloaded on August 21, 2004.

Schweber, Silvan S. *In the Shadow of the Bomb: Bethe, Oppenheimer, and the Moral Responsibility of the Scientist.* Princeton, N.J.: Princeton University Press, 2000.

Wasson, Tyler, ed. *Nobel Prize Winners.* New York: H. W. Wilson, 1987, pp. 93–96.

Bishop, J. Michael
(John Michael Bishop)
(1936–   ) *molecular biologist*

J. Michael Bishop codiscovered that potentially cancerous cells lie dormant in virtually every living organism, waiting only for the right trigger to set them to work producing tumors. For this contribution he was awarded a share of the 1989 Nobel Prize in physiology or medicine.

Bishop was born on February 22, 1936, in York, Pennsylvania. His father, John, was a minister, and his mother, Carrie, was a homemaker. After receiving an A.B. in chemistry from Gettysburg College in 1957, he entered Harvard Medical School, receiving an M.D. in 1962. He spent the next six years completing his internship and residency at Boston's Massachusetts General Hospital and con-

ducting postdoctoral research at the National Institutes of Health in Bethesda, Maryland, and the Heinrich-Pette Institute in Hamburg, Germany. In 1968 he became a professor of microbiology at the University of California at San Francisco (UCSF). In 1959 he married Kathryn Putnam with whom he had two children.

Bishop's early research focused on animal viruses, particularly the virus that causes polio in humans. He eventually became interested in retroviruses, cancer-causing viruses that replicate themselves by using RNA to synthesize DNA, a reversal of the normal transmission of genetic coding. In 1970 HOWARD M. TEMIN and DAVID BALTIMORE discovered reverse transcriptase, the enzyme by which

J. Michael Bishop demonstrated that cancer is often caused by cells that have lain dormant within an organism for years. *(Courtesy of J. Michael Bishop)*

RNA encodes DNA. That same year, Bishop and HAROLD E. VARMUS, a UCSF colleague, began studying reverse transcriptase, and in short order they were able to describe the biochemical mechanism via which reverse transcriptase works. This success led Bishop and Varmus to undertake a study of viral RNA and viral DNA in both normal and infected cells, and from there to study viruses as a cause of cancer.

Bishop and Varmus focused on Rous sarcoma virus (RSV), a virus that causes cancer in chickens; it was the first virus known to cause cancer in mammals. PEYTON ROUS, its discoverer, had also demonstrated that cancer progresses slowly and by stages, not all of a sudden, and that cancer cells often lie dormant until some agent, like a virus or a chemical, awakens them. Other researchers had suggested that the spread of RSV was sparked by *src,* an RSV gene that the virus implants into the host cell's DNA at the time of infection. Bishop and Varmus, assisted by their junior colleagues Dominique Stehelin and Deborah Spector, discovered that *src* does indeed initiate the spread of RSV. However, they further discovered that *src* is actually a normal growth-controlling gene of the host cell that has been hijacked into the viral genome, or set of chromosomes, via recombination, the process whereby a virus and its host cell exchange genetic material. The *src* gene then lies dormant until some agent causes it to mutate into a cancer gene.

During the late 1970s and early 1980s, Bishop and Varmus looked for *src*-like genes in other species and discovered them in just about every species they examined. Moreover, they discovered that these genes, which they named proto-oncogenes, do not just lie dormant, but that they also perform their assigned role in regulating cellular functions, just as they did before they were hijacked into the viral genome. Proto-oncogenes trigger the production of cancer cells only after they are mutated by a particular agent, usually another retrovirus or a chemical carcinogen, but until then they function as normal, healthy genes of the organism to which they originally belonged.

Bishop and Varmus's discoveries were important steps forward in cancer research, as they indicated that potentially cancerous cells lie dormant in virtually every organism, including humans. Their work also explains why most human cancers occur late in life, as the necessary components to turn proto-oncogenes into cancer-producing genes take many years to come together. For their contributions to cancer research, Bishop and Varmus were each awarded a half share of the 1989 Nobel Prize in physiology or medicine.

Bishop remained at UCSF for the rest of his career. In 1981 he took on the additional duties of director of the University of California Medical Center's G. W. Hooper Research Foundation, and in 1998 he was named UCSF's chancellor as well. He also served as associate editor for two scientific journals, *Virology* and *Molecular Biology of the Cell.* His many honors include election to the National Academy of Sciences, the American Academy of Arts and Sciences, and the American Academy for the Advancement of Science.

Further Reading

Bishop, J. Michael. *How to Win the Nobel Prize: An Unexpected Life in Science.* Cambridge, Mass.: Harvard University Press, 2003.

McMurray, Emily J. *Notable Twentieth-Century Scientists.* Detroit: Gale Research, 1995, pp. 177–178.

Nobelprize.org. "The Nobel Prize in Physiology or Medicine 1989." Available online. URL: http://nobelprize. org/medicine/laureates/1989. Downloaded on July 9, 2004.

Blalock, Alfred
(1899–1964) *physiologist*

Alfred Blalock was one of the foremost surgeons of his day. He and his colleagues developed three important surgical procedures, the most important being an operation for curing "blue baby" syndrome.

Blalock was born on April 5, 1899, in Culloden, Georgia. His father, George, was a merchant, and his mother, Martha, was a homemaker. At age 11 he moved with his family to Jonesboro, where he grew up. In 1915 he entered the University of Georgia and received an A.B. three years later. He then enrolled in the Johns Hopkins Medical School in Baltimore, Maryland, and received an M.D. in

1922. After spending three years at the Johns Hopkins Hospital in various capacities, in 1925 he became a resident in surgery at the Vanderbilt University School of Medicine in Nashville, Tennessee, a position he held for 16 years. In 1930 he married Mary O'Bryan with whom he had three children. In 1941 he returned to Johns Hopkins as chairman of the department of surgery and chief surgeon of the school's hospital, positions he held until just before his death.

At Vanderbilt, Blalock became interested in shock, the failure of the circulatory system to supply sufficient blood to the peripheral tissues to meet basic metabolic requirements. Shock often occurs during surgery as a result of hemorrhaging, but at the time no one knew why. Blalock was the first to demonstrate that surgical shock usually results from the massive loss of blood, which in turn lowers blood pressure to the point that the circulatory system cannot do its job. He correctly reasoned that the proper treatment for shock was to begin replacing the lost blood with either plasma or whole blood as soon as shock set in. By the start of World War II, it had become a common practice to have plenty of blood on hand during surgery in case the patient went into shock, thus saving the patient's life in many cases.

Blalock is best remembered for his work with arterial anastomosis, the surgical connection of two different arteries. In the early 1930s he transplanted an adrenal gland, in the process performing the first successful surgical joining of blood vessels. This procedure led him to seek a surgical cure for coarctation, a condition in which the aorta, the body's main artery, gets blocked and constricts the flow of blood to the lower body. After conducting many experiments on dogs, in the early 1940s he figured out how to bypass the blockage by connecting the subclavian artery, which in humans carries blood from the heart to the arms, to the aorta below the blockage. In the course of these experiments, his surgical partners, Vivien Thomas and William Longmire, invented a device known as Blalock's clamp for clamping an artery during surgery. Working in conjunction with a colleague, G. Patrick Clagett, he helped develop the surgical procedure known as the Blalock-Clagett operation,

which relieves a congenital anomaly of the aorta. He and another colleague, C. Rollins Hanlon, devised the Blalock-Hanlon operation, whereby a hole is created in the wall of the atrium as a means of alleviating certain circulatory conditions.

Shortly after returning to Johns Hopkins, Blalock was approached by HELEN B. TAUSSIG about an idea of hers for surgically correcting "blue baby" syndrome. She had determined that the condition, wherein not enough oxygen reaches the tissues because not enough blood reaches the lungs, thus causing the baby's skin to turn slightly blue, is caused by a leaking septum, the wall that separates the chambers of the heart, and a too-narrow pulmonary artery, which connects the heart to the lungs. She convinced Blalock, who by now was one of the nation's foremost experts on anastomosis, that both problems could be corrected surgically, and they began to devise a procedure for doing just that.

In 1943 Blalock, Thomas, and Longmire successfully joined a dog's subclavian artery to its pulmonary artery, the type of procedure that Blalock and Taussig had determined was most likely to cure blue baby syndrome. The following year he performed a similar operation on a six-year-old "blue baby" via surgery, thus curing the condition completely. Taussig and Blalock published a joint account of the procedure in 1945, and in time the procedure became known as the Blalock-Taussig operation.

In addition to curing blue baby syndrome, the Blalock-Taussig operation demonstrated to surgeons that very sick children could be operated on successfully. It also led surgeons to perform more complicated operations on adults, culminating eventually with open-heart surgery. In terms of personal recognition, Blalock's role in developing the Blalock-Taussig operation, in addition to his other important contributions to medical science, led him to be elected to the National Academy of Sciences.

For the last 20 years of his life, Blalock concentrated on his duties as a teacher and surgeon at Johns Hopkins and consulted for visiting surgeons from around the country. He also played an important role in building up the Children's Medical and

Surgical Center in Baltimore. He retired from Johns Hopkins in 1964 and died that same year on September 15 in Baltimore.

Further Reading

Harvey, A. McGehee. "Alfred Blalock," National Academy of Sciences, *Biographical Memoirs* 53 (1982): pp. 49–82.

Ravitch, Mark M., ed. *The Papers of Alfred Blalock*. Baltimore, Md.: Johns Hopkins University Press, 1966.

Who Named It? "Alfred Blalock." Available online. URL: http://www.whonamedit.com/doctor.cfm/2036.html. Downloaded on August 29, 2003.

Blobel, Günter
(1936–) *cell biologist*

Günter Blobel discovered signal sequencing, whereby newly made proteins are provided with built-in signals that direct them to their correct destination within cells. This discovery won him the 1999 Nobel Prize in physiology or medicine.

Blobel was born on May 26, 1936, in Waltersdorf, Silesia, Germany, today a part of Poland. His father was a veterinarian and his mother was a homemaker. In 1945 he moved with his family to Freiburg, where he grew up. After finishing high school in 1954, he studied medicine at the universities of Frankfurt, Kiel, Munich, and Tübingen, receiving an M.D. from Tübingen in 1960. Two years later, having completed his internship and residency, he came to the United States and entered the University of Wisconsin, receiving a Ph.D. in oncology in 1967. That same year he became a postdoctoral fellow at the Laboratory of Cell Biology at the Rockefeller Institute for Medical Research (today Rockefeller University) in New York City, eventually becoming a Rockefeller professor and the laboratory's director. In 1986 he took on the additional duties of investigator at the Howard Hughes Medical Institute. At some point he married Laura Maioglio and became a naturalized U.S. citizen.

At Rockefeller, Blobel followed in the footsteps of two other Rockefeller researchers, ALBERT CLAUDE and GEORGE E. PALADE. Claude helped found the field of cell biology by using the electron microscope to discover the endoplasmic reticulum, a network of small, bladder-like cavities that makes up roughly half of the cell membrane. Palade, who had been Claude's assistant, was head of the Laboratory of Cell Biology when Blobel arrived, and he became Blobel's mentor. Palade, assisted by Blobel, showed that the mitochondria are the locations where the cell converts fat and sugar into adenosine triphosphate (ATP), the source of energy for all cellular functions, and that the ribosomes are the locations where protein synthesis takes place.

After Palade left Rockefeller in 1973, Blobel picked up where his mentor had left off. His primary interest was to discover how a protein that has just been synthesized manages to find its way through the endoplasmic reticulum to its proper organelle, a membrane-bound compartment within which the cell performs one of its many varied functions. In 1975 he postulated that each newly made protein is tagged with a chemical code, which he called a signal sequence, which directs the protein to and through the endoplasmic reticulum to its proper organelle, in much the same way that the address on an e-mail message routes the message through the Internet to its intended destination. He then developed an elaborate test-tube system that employed components obtained from the cells of mice, rabbits, and dogs, and over the next 20 years he compiled enough evidence to demonstrate that his signal hypothesis was indeed correct.

Blobel showed that each signal sequence consists of approximately 15 amino acid residues. Signal sequences open and close the protein-conducting channels in the endoplasmic reticulum so as to allow the protein to travel through the cell, and they open and close membranes so as to allow the protein to enter the proper organelle. Although a different system from the endoplasmic reticulum carries proteins to the nucleus, signal sequencing still controls their routing. Some signal sequences are permanent while others are temporary in that they detach themselves from the protein once it reaches a specific intermediary destination. He eventually demonstrated that signal sequences control the movement of proteins in all cells, plant and animal, and that signal sequencing has evidently been in place since the evolution of the very first cell.

Blobel's work provided biologists with important information regarding the operations of the cell. It also provided medical researchers with a better understanding of the mechanisms involved in conditions and diseases that are caused by the improper location of certain proteins. It also contributed to the rise of biotechnology in that it helped researchers learn how to custom-design cells that could produce a wide range of protein-based pharmaceuticals such as insulin and growth hormone. For his contribution, he was awarded the 1999 Nobel Prize in physiology or medicine.

Further Reading

Hargittai, Istvan, and Magdolna Hargittai. *Candid Science II: Conversations with Famous Biomedical Scientists.* London: Imperial College Press, 2002, pp. 252–266.

Nobelprize.org. "The Nobel Prize in Physiology or Medicine 1999." Available online. URL: http://nobelprize.org/medicine/laureates/1999. Downloaded on July 14, 2004.

Bloch, Felix
(1905–1983) *physicist*

Felix Bloch was a theoretical physicist whose work had tremendous practical applications. He codeveloped nuclear magnetic resonance (NMR), which won him a share of the 1952 Nobel Prize in physics and led eventually to the development of the CAT scan. By explaining electrical conductivity in terms of electron flow, he helped to lay the theoretical groundwork for the development of solid-state electronics. This latter contribution earned for him the unofficial title of "father of solid-state physics."

Bloch was born on October 23, 1905, in Zurich, Switzerland. His father, Gustav, was a wholesale grain dealer, and his mother, Agnes, was a homemaker. At age 19 he enrolled in the Federal Institute of Technology (FIT) in Zurich to study engineering, but while in school he decided that he was more interested in physics. In 1927 he entered the University of Leipzig (UL) in Germany, and the

following year he received a Ph.D. in theoretical physics, a branch of physics that studies quantum mechanics, the nature and behavior of subatomic particles (at the time, quantum mechanics was so new that it was called quantum theory). His doctoral dissertation explained electrical conductivity in terms of the wave behavior of electrons, and his explanation became known as the Bloch theorem. This theorem was the first in a series of theoretical developments whose practical result was solid-state electronics. Previously, electron flow in a piece of electronic equipment had been regulated by means of vacuum tubes. These devices are bulky and they generate too much heat to remain in service very long. Solid-state electronics, on the other hand, regulates electrons by means of transistors, which are much smaller and longer-lasting. In the late 20th century, solid-state electronics evolved into integrated circuitry, whereby transistors and other electronic apparatus are miniaturized and combined on a single chip.

Between 1927 and 1933 Bloch continued his work in solid-state theory at FIT and UL as well as several other universities in the Netherlands and Denmark. During this period he developed four important theorems. The first was the Bloch-Grüneisen relationship. This theorem used data gathered by the German physicist Eduard Grüneisen to suggest that a metal's temperature affects its ability to conduct electrons. The second was the Bloch T 3/2 law. This theorem suggested that the temperature of a ferromagnetic material, such as iron, affects its ability to hold a magnetic charge. The third was a description of the Bloch wall, the area in a magnetized ferromagnetic material, such as a bar magnet, where the "positive" and "negative" sections meet. The fourth was the Bethe-Bloch expression. This theorem used data gathered by the German-American physicist HANS A. BETHE to calculate the ability of a nucleus to absorb a charged subatomic particle, such as a proton or electron, attempting to pass through the nucleus.

In 1932 Bloch was given a permanent faculty position at UL. He gave it up the following year, however, when Adolf Hitler and the Nazis took control of the German government. Bloch, who was Jewish, took heed of the Nazis' anti-Semitic propaganda and left Germany as soon as he could. He spent a year at universities in France and Italy before accepting a faculty position at Stanford University in 1934. In 1939 he became a U.S. citizen, and in 1940 he married Lore C. Misch with whom he had four children.

Shortly after arriving at Stanford, Bloch began studying the magnetic properties of neutrons. This phenomenon fascinated him because neutrons have no electrical charge, and therefore logic told him they should not be susceptible to magnetism. In 1936 he theorized that the behavior of a neutron in a magnetic field could be predicted by measuring its magnetic moment, a function of its magnetic strength. Three years later, he and LUIS W. ALVAREZ successfully measured the magnetic moment of neutrons beamed through a magnetic field with a variable strength. By observing the "spin" of the neutrons as they passed through the field, Bloch and Alvarez were able to make a rough estimation of the magnetic moments.

During World War II, Bloch conducted counter-radar research at Harvard University's Radio Research Laboratory. During the course of his research, he realized that microwave technology offered a more precise way to measure a neutron's magnetic moment. After the war, his experiments with microwave technology led him to develop the nuclear induction method, better known today as nuclear magnetic resonance (NMR). This method involves passing a beam of neutrons through a magnetic field whose strength is varied by using microwave radio frequencies. He discovered that at a certain precise frequency neutrons reverse their spin, thus permitting their magnetic moments to be calculated precisely. Meanwhile, EDWARD M. PURCELL was pursuing an identical line of investigation, and he came up with the same results as did Bloch at about the same time. In 1952 Bloch and Purcell were jointly awarded the Nobel Prize in physics for their research involving NMR.

Although Bloch played no further role in its development, NMR proved to have enormously important practical applications. By using NMR, the precise identity of the atoms in a given sub-stance can be determined without altering those atoms in any way. In the 1970s ALLAN M. CORMACK and Gregory Hounsfield used NMR as the basis from which to develop computer-assisted tomography scanning equipment, better known today as the CAT scan. Put into commercial operation in the mid-1980s, the CAT scan makes it possible to observe the inner workings of the human body, thus giving it an essential role in modern diagnostic medicine.

Bloch devoted the last 20 years of his career to studying superconductivity, the phenomenon of electrical conductivity at temperatures approaching absolute zero, and statistical mechanics, the application of probability theory to quantum mechanics. He also served for a year (1954–55) as the first director of the European Nuclear Research Center in Geneva, Switzerland, which was devoted to finding peacetime applications for nuclear energy. In 1948 he was elected to the National Academy of Sciences, and in 1965 he was elected to a one-year term as president of the American Physical Society. In 1971 he retired from Stanford and returned to Zurich, Switzerland, where he died on September 10, 1983.

Further Reading

Chodorow, Marvin, et al., eds. *Felix Bloch and Twentieth-Century Physics.* Houston: William Marsh Rice University, 1980.

Hofstadter, Robert. "Felix Bloch," National Academy of Sciences, *Biographical Memoirs* 64 (1989): pp. 35–70.

Nobelprize.org. "The Nobel Prize in Physics 1952." Available online. URL: http://nobelprize.org/physics/laureates/1952. Downloaded on June 24, 2003.

Wasson, Tyler, ed. *Nobel Prize Winners.* New York: H. W. Wilson, 1987, pp. 102–104.

Bloch, Konrad
(Konrad Emil Bloch)
(1912–2000) *biochemist*

Konrad Bloch's work contributed to a better understanding of the nature of cholesterol and the way it is metabolized in the body. For this contribution, he was awarded a share of the 1964 Nobel Prize in physiology or medicine.

Bloch was born on January 21, 1912, in Neisse, Germany (today Nysa, Poland), to Fritz and Hedwig Bloch. After receiving a B.S. in chemical engineering from the Munich Technical Institute in 1934, he worked for two years at the Swiss Research Institute in Davos, Switzerland, before emigrating to the United States in 1936. He received a Ph.D. in biochemistry from Columbia University's College of Physicians and Surgeons in 1938 and then joined the Columbia faculty. In 1946 he left Columbia for the University of Chicago, and in 1954 he was named a professor of biochemistry at Harvard University. In 1941 he married Lore Teutsch with whom he had two children, and in 1944 he became a naturalized U.S. citizen.

Bloch's research focused on discovering the mechanism and regulation of the cholesterol metabolism. In 1942, when Bloch began investigating the biosynthesis of cholesterol, little was known about this complex molecule other than that it is a waxy substance that is present in the blood plasma and in all animal tissue; it was also thought to contribute to arteriosclerosis (hardening of the arteries) by building up on arterial walls. At that same time, however, new biochemical techniques involving the use of radioactive isotopes had just been developed, thus making it possible to trace the "life cycle" of a particular biochemical compound. Using radiocarbon, a radioactive isotope of carbon, Bloch was able to trace the movement of specific carbon atoms as they made their way through the cholesterol metabolism.

Over the course of the next 20 years, Bloch discovered that cholesterol is formed from acetic acid via a process that involves 36 different steps. The major intermediate compounds that are formed during cholesterol metabolism are, in order, acetate, acetyl coenzyme A, mevalonic acid, isoprene, squalene, and lanosterol. In the process, Bloch and his collaborators showed that cholesterol is a major building block in all of the body's cells. They discovered that it is a primary component of the cell membrane, and it is the intermediate compound for the biosynthesis of bile acids and one of the female sex hormones. They showed that cholesterol circulates in the bloodstream, and that it is synthesized by the liver and several other organs.

This synthesis is regulated according to a compensatory system that takes into consideration the amount of cholesterol ingested by the body in the form of food.

Bloch's work with cholesterol had several important results. Other researchers showed that cholesterol is an intermediate compound for the production of vitamin D and all of the steroid hormones, not just the one female sex hormone. These researchers also discovered that several diseases attributed to the presence of cholesterol actually result from malfunctions during its metabolism. For his discoveries regarding cholesterol, Bloch was awarded a half share of the 1964 Nobel Prize in physiology or medicine; his corecipient was the German biochemist Feodor Lynen, who had duplicated much of Bloch's work independently.

In the late 1960s, Bloch shifted his research away from cholesterol toward a study of the enzymatic formation of unsaturated fatty acids as well as of the various aspects of the process of long-term evolution involving biochemical functions. His many honors include election to the National Academy of Sciences and the American Academy of Arts and Sciences, and to a term as president of the American Society of Biological Chemists. He retired from Harvard in 1982 to his home in Burlington, Massachusetts, where he died on October 15, 2000.

Further Reading

Nobelprize.org. "The Nobel Prize in Physiology or Medicine 1964." Available online. URL: http://nobelprize. org/medicine/laureates/1964. Downloaded on June 3, 2004.

Wasson, Tyler, ed. *Nobel Prize Winners*. New York: H. W. Wilson, 1987, pp. 104–106.

Blodgett, Katharine B.
(Katharine Burr Blodgett)
(1898–1979) *physicist*

Monomolecular films, the scientific name for oily substances that are only one molecule thick, were discovered by IRVING LANGMUIR, but they were not

Irving Langmuir discovered monomolecular films, but Katharine Blodgett (above) showed how they work and what they are good for. *(Library of Congress, Prints and Photographs Division [LC-USZ62-118118])*

1918, and a Ph.D. in physics from England's Cambridge University in 1926.

During her senior year at Bryn Mawr, Blodgett visited the GE facilities in Schenectady to find out more about her father from the people he had worked with. While there she met Langmuir; they were mutually impressed, and Langmuir encouraged her to go to graduate school and study chemistry. Upon her graduation from Chicago, he hired her to work in his laboratory, thus making her GE's first woman researcher. He later used his influence to help get her admitted to Cambridge, thus making her one of its first women graduate students. For the next 15 years, except for the two years she attended Cambridge, she concentrated her research for GE on the flow of electrons, negatively charged subatomic particles, in lightbulbs and vacuum tubes.

In 1932 Langmuir won the Nobel Prize in chemistry for discovering monomolecular films. Because of their extreme thinness—less than one-millionth of an inch—monomolecular films often behave as if they are two-dimensional. Langmuir thought they might have some unusual applications, but he could never find any himself. In 1933 he encouraged Blodgett to focus her efforts on the further study of the behavior and application of monomolecular films.

Blodgett first experimented with monomolecular films made from stearic acid, an oily substance found in ordinary soap. Within a year she had discovered how to get a stearic acid film to adhere uniformly to a metal plate, as well as how to stack up hundreds of individual layers of film on a particular surface. In the process, she noticed that the stack of film layers changed colors as the number of layers increased and that the color reflected by a given number of layers was always the same. This discovery led her to develop a color gauge that could measure the thickness of extremely thin transparent or semitransparent substances with great precision simply by comparing the color of the substance with the colors of the layers in the gauge. Her gauge made it possible to accurately measure, for the first time, the thickness of such things as blood corpuscles and white blood cells.

properly understood until Katharine Blodgett began researching them. As a result of her extensive, groundbreaking work with monomolecular films, they eventually became known as Langmuir-Blodgett films.

Blodgett was born on January 10, 1898, in Schenectady, New York. Her father, George, was a patent attorney for the General Electric (GE) Company, and her mother, Katharine, was a child care worker. Blodgett's father was murdered before Katharine was born, and shortly after her birth she moved with her mother and brother to New York City. Her father left the family a considerable estate, thus making it possible for her to obtain a private education and to travel for extended periods throughout Europe. She received an A.B. in physics from Bryn Mawr College in 1917, an M.S. in chemistry from the University of Chicago in

Blodgett's invention of the color gauge led her to look for other practical uses for monomolecular films. In 1938 she discovered that applying exactly 44 layers of monomolecular film to a pane of ordinary window glass makes the glass "invisible." In fact, what happens is that the light reflected by the glass is counter-reflected by the film layers in such a way that the two reflections cancel out each other. By coating glass in this way, it can be made nonreflective. At the time, the only monomolecular films available to Blodgett were derived from stearic acid; not much stronger than the walls of a soap bubble, they quickly wore off and so were of limited value. Blodgett patented her process for making nonreflective glass, but then she abandoned further work in this area for other avenues of investigation involving monomolecular films. Later researchers, however, developed stronger films that were used to reduce or eliminate glare in window glass, photographic lenses, picture frames, automobile windshields, and thousands of other applications.

Blodgett postponed her work with monomolecular films during World War II to conduct war-related research. After the war she developed ways to make certain materials resistant to electricity by coating them with monomolecular films with low conductivity.

For her work with monomolecular films, Blodgett received the American Chemical Society's Francis Garvan Medal in 1951. That same year the mayor of Schenectady declared June 13 "Katherine Blodgett Day." She also received the Photographic Society of America's Progress Medal in 1972. In 1963 Blodgett, who never married, retired to her home in Schenectady, where she died on October 12, 1979.

Further Reading

Carey, Charles W., Jr. "Blodgett, Katherine Burr," *American Inventors, Entrepreneurs, and Business Visionaries.* New York: Facts On File, 2002, pp. 28–30.

Macdonald, Anne L. *Feminine Ingenuity: Women and Invention in America.* New York: Ballantine Books, 1994.

Yount, Lisa. "Blodgett, Katherine Burr," *A to Z of Women in Science and Math.* New York: Facts On File, 1999, pp. 22–23.

Bloembergen, Nicolaas
(1920–) *physicist*

Nicolaas Bloembergen developed important methods and techniques for using lasers as a tool for studying the interaction of subatomic particles in atoms and molecules. For this contribution, he was awarded a share of the 1981 Nobel Prize in physics.

Bloembergen was born on March 11, 1920, in Dordrecht, the Netherlands. His father, Auke, was a chemical engineer, and his mother, Sophia, was a homemaker. As a boy he moved with his family to Bilthoven where he grew up, although he attended school in nearby Utrecht. In 1938 he entered the University of Utrecht, and by 1943 he had earned the equivalent of a B.S. and an M.S. in physics. He spent the next two years trying to survive the Nazi occupation of Holland, finally leaving in 1945 to come to the United States. That same year he enrolled in the graduate physics program at Harvard University, where he became an assistant to EDWARD M. PURCELL. Over the next three years, Bloembergen, Purcell, and Robert V. Pound developed nuclear resonance absorption, a form of nuclear magnetic resonance (NMR). This method involves bombarding protons with microwave radio frequencies as a means of determining an atom's magnetic moment, a function of its magnetic strength. Since the atoms of each element possess unique magnetic moments, NMR permits researchers to determine the atomic composition of the element or compound under study. By 1948 Bloembergen, Purcell, and Pound had developed the ability to use NMR to determine the magnetic moments of liquids, gases, and certain solids.

In 1948 Bloembergen returned to the Netherlands and entered the University of Leiden, which awarded him a Ph.D. that same year for the work he had done on NMR at Harvard. In 1949 he returned to Harvard as a junior fellow, and for the next two years he conducted research concerning microwave spectroscopy, the study of the structure of atoms and molecules by examining the microwave radiation they emit. In 1951, the year after he married Deli Brink with whom he had three children, he was named a professor of physics at Harvard. In 1958 he became a naturalized U.S. citizen.

Between 1951 and 1956, Bloembergen headed a research group that used NMR to study the interactions between subatomic particles in alloys, ionic crystals, and ferromagnetic materials. Meanwhile, in 1953 CHARLES H. TOWNES had developed the maser, a spectroscopic device that produces and amplifies electronic radiation in the microwave region of the light spectrum. The maser provided researchers with a tool for seeing into an atom in a way that no other spectroscopic devices could do, so in 1956 Bloembergen proposed the development of a three-level solid-state maser capable of producing and amplifying microwaves of even greater intensity. This proposal was made obsolete, however, in 1958 when Townes and ARTHUR L. SCHAWLOW devised a methodology for building the laser, which produces and amplifies intense light from visible light.

Nicolaas Bloembergen developed techniques for using lasers as strobe lights for studying chemical reactions. *(Courtesy of Nicolaas Bloembergen; photo by Bachrach)*

At first, Bloembergen opposed the development of lasers on the grounds that they were too difficult and expensive for a modest academic laboratory to build. Nevertheless, by 1961 he was working with lasers, and he even developed a field that came to be known as nonlinear optics. Laser light can sometimes be so intense that it causes the matter upon which it is shone to resonate in ways that the theories of the day could not explain. In response, Bloembergen and his collaborators came up with a general theory to explain this phenomenon. They also developed new spectroscopic techniques for using lasers, including mixing two or more laser beams to produce laser light of a different wavelength. These techniques made it possible to generate bursts of laser light for periods of time as short as a few millionths of a billionth of a second, thus making it possible to watch in slow motion extremely rapid occurrences such as the stretching and breaking of chemical bonds. He published much of his work in this area in *Nonlinear Optics* (1965, 1996). In recognition of the importance of his contribution to spectroscopy in general, Bloembergen was awarded a quarter share of the 1981 Nobel Prize in physics; one of his corecipients was Schawlow (one-quarter share) and the Swedish physicist Kai M. Siegbahn (one-half share).

Bloembergen retired from Harvard in 1990. Much of his retirement was spent, however, as a visiting professor at the California Institute of Technology and at universities in Italy and Germany. He also served a term as president of the American Physical Society. His many honors include the National Medal of Science and election to the National Academy of Sciences and the American Academy of Arts and Sciences.

Further Reading

Levenson, Marc D., et al., eds. *Resonances: A Volume in Honor of the 70th Birthday of Nicolaas Bloembergen.* Teaneck, N.J.: World Scientific, 1990.

Nobelprize.org. "The Nobel Prize in Physics 1981." Available online. URL: http://nobelprize.org/physics/laureates/1981. Downloaded on August 29, 2004.

Wasson, Tyler, ed. *Nobel Prize Winners.* New York: H. W. Wilson, 1987, pp. 106–108.

Blumberg, Baruch S.
(Baruch Samuel Blumberg)
(1925–) *physician*

Baruch S. Blumberg discovered that the form of jaundice known as hepatitis B is caused by a virus, and he helped develop a screening test and a vaccine for hepatitis B. In addition to preventing hepatitis B, the vaccine was the first to prevent a human cancer, as hepatitis B often leads to primary liver cancer. These contributions won him a share of the 1976 Nobel Prize in physiology or medicine.

Blumberg was born on July 28, 1925, in New York City. His father, Meyer, was a lawyer, and his mother, Ida, was a homemaker. After finishing high school in 1943, he joined the U.S. Navy and saw action during World War II. While in the service, he also attended Union (N.Y.) College and received a B.S. in physics in 1946. He then entered Columbia University to study mathematics, but after a year he transferred to Columbia's College of Physicians and Surgeons, receiving an M.D. in 1951. After completing his internship and residency at New York's Bellevue Hospital and Columbia Presbyterian Medical Center, he entered Oxford University in England and received a Ph.D. in biochemistry in 1957. He then went to work for the National Institutes of Health (NIH) Section on Geographic Medicine and Genetics in Bethesda, Maryland. He left in 1964 to become the associate director of clinical research at the Institute for Cancer Research of the Fox Chase Cancer Center (FCCC) in Philadelphia, Pennsylvania. He remained at FCCC for the rest of his career, eventually being named distinguished scientist and senior adviser to the center's president. After 1977 he also taught medicine at the University of Pennsylvania, and from 1989 to 1994 he served as master of Oxford's Balliol College. In 1954 he married Jean Liebesman with whom he had four children.

As a medical student, Blumberg spent several months in a remote village in the Dutch colony of Surinam (today the nation of Suriname). He was struck by the different levels of susceptibility to disease of the many ethnic groups who comprised the village's population; for example, the parasitic disease known as elephantiasis plagued certain groups while not affecting other groups at all. This experience led him to study at Oxford inherited variation in susceptibility to disease. As with many researchers, he suspected that inherited variation had something to do with the blood, specifically the antibodies and other blood proteins that vary from person to person because of genetics. During his tenure at NIH he traveled to a number of countries, including Nigeria, the Philippines, India, Japan, Canada, Finland, and Australia, where he took and analyzed blood samples from members of as many different ethnic groups as possible.

In 1963 Blumberg discovered in the blood serum of an Australian aborigine a blood protein that became known as the Australia antigen. Further research showed that the Australia antigen, which is common in Asia and Africa, is rare in North America except in patients with leukemia and Down syndrome. Blumberg first considered that the Australia antigen might be an early indicator of one or both of these diseases, but in 1966 he concluded that it was more likely an indicator of hepatitis B, a form of jaundice that is transmitted via the transmission of blood to a recipient from an infected donor. The following year he showed that the Australia antigen is actually the protein shell that protects the virus that causes hepatitis B, at which point it was renamed hepatitis B virus antigen.

Blumberg's discovery made it possible to identify hepatitis B in potential blood donors, thus greatly reducing its transmission. He helped develop a simple test that screens out infected donors, thus making the supply of donated blood safer. This test was made a mandatory part of donor screening by the American Association of Blood Banks in 1971, after which the occurrence of hepatitis B in blood recipients declined significantly. He also helped develop a hepatitis B vaccine that became commercially available in 1982; this vaccine cut down on the incidence of hepatitis B in health-care workers. The vaccine also promised to cut down on the incidence of primary liver cancer, one of the world's three most deadly cancers. Primary liver cancer is particularly prevalent among males in Africa and Asia, and it is often preceded by chronic infection with hepatitis B. Under Blumberg's direction, FCCC developed a model liver-cancer prevention program, an important feature of which was worldwide vaccination of infants against hepatitis B, which promises to reduce the incidence of primary liver cancer in future generations by 80 percent.

Because of the wide-ranging applications that followed in the wake of the discovery of the Australia antigen, Blumberg was awarded a half share of the 1976 Nobel Prize in physiology or medicine; his corecipient was the American virologist D. CARLETON GAJDUSEK. His other honors include election to the National Academy of Sciences and the Inventors Hall of Fame.

Further Reading

Blumberg, Baruch S. *Hepatitis B: The Hunt for a Killer Virus*. Princeton, N.J.: Princeton University Press, 2002.

Nobelprize.org. "The Nobel Prize in Physiology or Medicine 1976." Available online. URL: http://nobelprize.org/medicine/laureates/1976. Downloaded on June 21, 2004.

Wasson, Tyler, ed. *Nobel Prize Winners*. New York: H. W. Wilson, 1987, pp. 108–110.

Adenosine triphosphate is the source of energy for all cellular functions, and Paul Boyer discovered how it is produced. *(Courtesy of Paul D. Boyer)*

Boyer, Paul D.
(Paul Delos Boyer)
(1918–) *biochemist*

Paul D. Boyer demonstrated that adenosine triphosphate (ATP), the source of energy for all cellular functions, is produced in a unique manner. This achievement won him a share of the 1997 Nobel Prize in chemistry.

Boyer was born on July 31, 1918, in Provo, Utah. His father, Dell, was a physician, and his mother, Grace, was a homemaker. In 1939, the same year he married Lyda Whicker with whom he had three children, he received a B.S. in chemistry from Brigham Young University. He then entered the graduate program at the University of Wisconsin, receiving an M.S. and a Ph.D. in biochemistry in 1941 and 1943, respectively. After two years as a research associate at Stanford University, he joined the faculty at the University of Minnesota. In 1963

he went to the University of California at Los Angeles (UCLA) to teach chemistry and biochemistry and to become the founding director of the Molecular Biology Institute.

Boyer's primary research concerned enzymes, the proteins that initiate virtually every biochemical function. He was particularly interested in discovering the enzyme that catalyzes oxidative phosphorylation, the process by which the energy in foods is converted into ATP. As part of this effort, in the early 1940s he demonstrated that potassium ions activate pyruvate kinase, an enzyme that plays a key role in the formation of one of the intermediate products in ATP metabolism.

During the 1960s, British chemist Peter D. Mitchell and other researchers discovered that the key enzyme in the production of ATP is ATP synthase and that ATP synthase is activated by hydrogen ions. However, they were unable to demonstrate exactly how ATP synthase works or what role the hydrogen ions play in ATP metabolism. Boyer took up the challenge of solving this riddle, and by the late 1970s he had developed an interesting hypothesis. Boyer concluded that ATP synthase produces ATP in a unique manner in that the enzyme functions somewhat like a mechanical mixer, and that the hydrogen ions provide the "biological electricity" that drives the mixer. In essence, ATP synthase is composed of several subunits; one resembles a bent mixing rod while the others form what is best described as a mixing bowl. An influx of hydrogen ions causes the rod to rotate in the bowl, which contorts the shapes of the subunits forming the bowl, in the process "mixing" adenosine diphosphate and phosphate building blocks into an ATP molecule. Once the ATP molecule has been formed, the rod continues to rotate, thus causing the bowl to revert to its original shape, which releases the ATP molecule just constructed and readies the bowl for the production of another molecule. This process, known as the binding change mechanism, was rejected by other biochemists because it involved what seemed like a mechanical operation, not a biochemical one. Not until 1994, when British biochemist John Walker produced X-ray images of ATP synthase crystals that verified Boyer's hypothesis, was the binding change mechanism accepted.

Boyer's discovery solved the long-standing puzzle surrounding a key aspect of oxidative phosphorylation. Just three years after Walker's verification of that discovery, Boyer was awarded a quarter share of the 1997 Nobel Prize in chemistry; one of his corecipients was Walker.

In addition to his other duties, Boyer served as director of the University of California Program for Research and Training in Biotechnology from 1985 to 1989. He edited or coedited *The Enzymes, Biochemical and Biophysical Research Communications,* and *Annual Review of Biochemistry.* His many honors include election to the National Academy of Sciences and the American Academy of Arts and Sciences and to a term as president of the American Society of Biological Chemists. He retired from UCLA in 1989 but he continued to conduct research there as a professor emeritus.

Further Reading

Krapp, Kristine M., ed. *Notable Twentieth-Century Scientists Supplement.* Detroit: Gale Research, 1998, pp. 53–55.

Nobelprize.org. "The Nobel Prize in Chemistry 1997." Available online. URL: http://nobelprize.org/chemistry/laureates/1997. Downloaded on August 8, 2004.

UCLA Department of Chemistry and Biology. "Paul D. Boyer." Available online. URL: http://www.chem.ucla.edu/dept/alumni/boyer/html. Downloaded on March 25, 2005.

Brattain, Walter H.
(Walter Houser Brattain)
(1902–1987) *physicist*

Walter H. Brattain played an integral role in the development of solid-state electronics, the use of transistors rather than vacuum tubes to control and amplify electronic signals. His work revolutionized the electronics industry by making it possible to construct radios and televisions that were smaller, more reliable, and more energy-efficient. It also made it possible to reduce tremendously the size and energy requirements of mainframe computers, thus making their construction and use more practical. Lastly, it set the stage for the development of the integrated circuit, or computer chip, and microchip technology. In recognition of his vital participation in the discovery that would make these later developments possible, Brattain was awarded a share of the 1956 Nobel Prize in physics.

Brattain was born on February 10, 1902, in Amoy, China. His father, Ross, was a schoolteacher, and his mother, Ottilie, was a homemaker. As a young boy he moved with his family to Tonasket, Washington, where he grew up. He received a B.S. in physics from Whitman (Wash.) College in 1924, an M.A. in physics from the University of Oregon in 1926, and a Ph.D. in physics from the University of Minnesota in 1929. Upon completing his education, he went to work for Bell Telephone Laboratories (BTL) in Murray Hill, New Jersey. In 1935 he married Keren Gilmore with whom he had one child. She died in 1957, and a year later he married Emma Jane Miller.

Brattain's research at BTL focused on learning more about the surface properties of solids, and then using that knowledge to improve the technology of communications. Much of this work was related to improving an electronic device known as the vacuum tube, so named because its three electrodes were enclosed in an evacuated glass housing. BTL's parent company, American Telephone & Telegraph (AT&T), had been using vacuum tubes since the mid-1910s to amplify long-distance telephone signals. Although the vacuum tube worked well enough as an amplifier, it was too bulky and too short-lived, mostly because it generated so much heat that its electrodes burned out rather quickly. One of the potential improvements Brattain dabbled with was the increased use of semiconductors, substances that conduct a flow of electrons better than insulators, such as glass, but not as well as good conductors, such as copper. Semiconductors were already being used in radio receivers as rectifiers, devices that change alternating current to direct current, but Brattain suspected that they might be useful in other ways as well.

In 1936 Brattain was joined at BTL by WILLIAM B. SHOCKLEY, whose thinking regarding semiconductors was further advanced than Brattain's. Shockley was mostly interested in developing an alternative to the vacuum tube, not simply improving it, and he believed that semiconductors were the key to such a development. Their superiors at BTL, however, preferred to channel resources into the development of other things, such as radar. Ironically, it was the vacuum tube's inability to handle satisfactorily the high-frequency microwave signals that radar employs that led BTL managers to give Brattain and Shockley permission to develop an alternative. By the time the United States entered World War II in 1942, they were studying in earnest the physical properties of semiconductors. Brattain focused on learning how semiconductors such as silicon and germanium conduct and rectify electrical current. His work was interrupted in 1942 by the war, during which he worked on ways to detect submarines via magnetism.

In 1945 Brattain and Shockley resumed their prewar experiments with semiconductors, but this time with the added assistance of JOHN BARDEEN. Shockley suggested that the electrons in a semiconductor could be used to amplify an electrical signal flowing into the semiconductor, in much the same way that the electrons emitted by the electrodes in a vacuum tube amplify a signal passing through the tube. When an attempt to do this failed, however, Brattain undertook an extensive study of the surface properties of semiconductors that shed much light on their behavior relative to the flow of electrons. Among other things, the study revealed that a semiconductor's ability to conduct electrons is greatly influenced by the percentage of impurities it contains. Upon concluding this study, in 1947 Brattain and Bardeen set out to build the first transistor, and by the following year they had constructed what is now called a point-contact transistor. They passed an incoming electrical current through a wire to one side of a germanium crystal containing a small amount of impurities, and a signal from an electrode to the other side of the crystal. As they had hoped, the signal from the electrode that emerged from the crystal was greatly amplified, even though the incoming current was much weaker than that required to create the same level of amplification in a vacuum tube.

Brattain continued to study the so-called transistor effect, the ability of a semiconductor to amplify a signal, and eventually he was able to demonstrate that a semiconductor's behavior is determined by the type and concentration of its impurities, the nature of the contact between the crystal and the wires carrying the signal and the amplifying current, and the loose bond a semiconductor's electrons have on its nuclei. In time, he and other BTL researchers were able to build transistors that were much smaller than vacuum tubes and that required very little current to produce a great deal of amplification. Because transistors generated very little heat, they lasted much longer than vacuum tubes, an added bonus. By 1952 BTL researchers had developed a transistor for use in routing long-distance telephone calls, but before long virtually every electronic operation performed by a vacuum tube was being performed by a transistor. For the part he played in discovering and harnessing the transistor effect, Brattain was awarded a one-third share of the 1956 Nobel Prize in physics; he shared the prize with his collaborators, Shockley and Bardeen.

Brattain continued to experiment with solid-state electronics until his retirement from BTL in 1967. That same year he returned to Whitman College to teach physics and experiment with the surface properties of living cells. He was elected to the National Academy of Sciences, the American Academy of Arts and Sciences, and the American Association for the Advancement of Science. He died on October 13, 1987, in Seattle, Washington.

Further Reading

Bardeen, John. "Walter Houser Brattain," National Academy of Sciences, *Biographical Memoirs* 63 (1994): pp. 68–87.

Nobelprize.org. "The Nobel Prize in Physics 1956." Available online. URL: http://nobelprize.org/physics/laureates/1956. Downloaded on February 19, 2004.

Wasson, Tyler, ed. *Nobel Prize Winners.* New York: H. W. Wilson, 1987, pp. 143–146.

von Braun, Wernher
(Wernher Magnus Maxmillian von Braun)
(1912–1977) *rocket scientist*

Wernher von Braun is generally considered to be the founder of the U.S. space program. Along with ROBERT H. GODDARD, he was the leading figure in the development of the modern rocket.

Von Braun was born on March 23, 1912, in Wirsitz, Germany, today part of Poland. His father, Magnus, was a baron, banker, and businessman, and his mother, Emmy, was a baroness. In 1920 he moved with his family to Berlin, where he grew up. Upon receiving a B.S. in mechanical engineering from Berlin's Charlottenburg Institute of Technology in 1932, he entered the University of Berlin and received a Ph.D. two years later.

Von Braun became interested in rocket science at age 13 when he read *The Rocket into Interplanetary Space,* a book by German rocket pioneer Hermann Oberth. While an undergraduate, von Braun joined the German Society for Space Travel and helped Oberth build liquid-fuel rocket motors; he also came to the attention of the Reichswehr, the German military, which had been experimenting with solid-fuel rockets for military purposes. In 1932 he was given a research grant by the Reichs-

Wernher von Braun holds a television camera that was used by Apollo 15's lunar roving vehicle. *(Courtesy of National Aeronautics and Space Administration)*

wehr and went to work at the Kummersdorf Army Proving Grounds near Berlin; his doctoral dissertation carried a security classification, as it involved the theory and development behind rocket engines designed to deliver military payloads. By 1934 he had developed the A-3, a rocket capable of reaching an altitude of 1 1/2 miles.

By 1934 the German rocket program had outgrown Kummersdorf, so the Reichswehr built a state-of-the-art rocket development center at Peenemünde on the Baltic Sea. Over the next 10 years, von Braun served as Peenemünde's technical director. In this position he supervised the development and testing of liquid-fueled rocket aircraft and jet-assisted takeoffs for the Luftwaffe, the German air force. He also developed a supersonic anti-aircraft missile known as the Wasserfall and the A-4, the first long-range ballistic missile. The A-4 was rechristened the V-2, for Vengeance Weapon, and was used by the Germans against British military and civilian targets during World War II.

In early 1945 von Braun and his staff surrendered to the U.S. Army. He and about 120 staffers were offered civilian contracts by the Army Ordnance Department and sent to Fort Bliss, Texas.

Here they assisted army efforts to develop and test missiles adapted from captured V-2s at a test site in White Sands, New Mexico. By the end of the war, this project had fired rockets to altitudes of more than 200 miles. Von Braun's German group remained at White Sands until 1952, when it was transferred to the Guided Missile Development Division in Huntsville, Alabama. Von Braun was named the division's technical director and later its chief, and he oversaw the development of the Redstone, Jupiter-C, Juno, and Pershing intercontinental ballistic missiles (ICBMs). In 1958 the first U.S. satellite, Explorer I, was launched into space on a modified Jupiter-C. Meanwhile, in 1947 von Braun had married Maria Louise Quistorp with whom he had three children, and in 1955 he had become a naturalized U.S. citizen.

In 1960 von Braun's division was made a part of the National Aeronautics and Space Administration (NASA), and he was named director of the George C. Marshall Space Flight Center in Huntsville. Between 1961 and 1970, von Braun's team developed the Saturn class of rocket boosters. These enormously powerful rockets launched the Mercury, Gemini, and Apollo missions, the latter including the first manned mission to the Moon, without a single mishap or delay related to rocket failure.

In 1972 von Braun transferred to NASA headquarters in Washington, D.C., where he served as the deputy associate administrator for planning. Two years later he resigned from NASA to become vice president of engineering and development for Fairchild Industries in Germantown, Maryland, and chairman of the board of the National Space Institute, a lobbyist effort to mobilize public support for increased federal spending on space missions. He died on June 16, 1977, at his home in Alexandria, Virginia.

Further Reading

Bergaust, Erik. *Wernher von Braun: The Authoritative and Definitive Biographical Profile of the Father of Modern Space Flight*. Washington, D.C.: National Space Institute, 1976.

Piszkiewicz, Dennis. *Wernher von Braun: The Man Who Sold the Moon*. Westport, Conn.: Praeger, 1998.

Spangenburg, Ray, and Diane K. Moser. *Wernher von Braun: Space Visionary and Rocket Engineer*. New York: Facts On File, 1995.

Stuhlinger, Ernst, and Frederick I. Ordway. *Wernher von Braun, Crusader for Space: A Biographical Memoir*. Malabar, Fla.: Krieger Pub., 1994.

Bridgman, P. W.
(Percy Williams Bridgman)
(1882–1961) *physicist*

P. W. Bridgman was the founder of high-pressure physics, the study of what happens to matter when it is subjected to extremely high pressures. His efforts in this field won him the 1946 Nobel Prize for physics.

Bridgman was born on April 21, 1882, in Cambridge, Massachusetts. His father, Raymond, was an author and journalist, and his mother, Mary Ann, was a homemaker. He spent his entire career at Harvard University; after receiving an A.B., M.A., and Ph.D. in physics in 1904, 1905, and 1908, respectively, he joined the faculty and became a full professor in 1919. In 1912 he married Olive Ware with whom he had two children.

Bridgman's research was devoted entirely to high-pressure physics. He was inspired in part by the experiments of the French physicist Emile-Hilaire Amagat. Because of the physical limitations of his equipment, Amagat could not proceed much beyond 3,000 atmospheres, or about 44,000 pounds per square inch (psi), one atmosphere being equal to 14.7 psi. Consequently, the primary obstacle Bridgman had to overcome was to design and build equipment that would allow him to experiment with increasingly higher pressures. To this end he learned the skills of a machinist and set up his own small machine shop, where he built many a piece of high-pressure apparatus. The most important apparatuses were a self-tightening, high-pressure seal that eliminated leakage around tube fittings and pistons and a set of high-pressure gauges that far exceeded anything available commercially. Thus equipped, he was able to take advantage of modern advances in metallurgy, such as the development of Carboloy, a high-strength alloy of tungsten carbide cemented in cobalt, to build the necessary pressure chambers, pistons, and other devices. Bridgman's equipment was so effective at achieving its desired results that, even today, his apparatuses remain the standards by which other high-pressure equipment is built. By 1941 he was able to experiment with pressures exceeding 400,000 atmospheres, or more than 5.8 million psi, the approximate pressure at the center of the Earth.

Bridgman's experiments focused on the effects of high pressure on the thermodynamic behavior of matter. Perhaps his most important discovery is that matter subjected to extreme pressure alters its behavior, and in many cases it experiences gross changes in its physical properties. For example, at 400,000 atmospheres, atoms lose their crystalline structure and become shapeless, and at lower pressures many elements experience a change in the pattern of their electrons. He discovered two forms of phosphorus, five forms of water-ice, and a thermoelectric effect known as internal Peltier heat, an anomaly in the production of heat in a conductor when a current flows through it, all of which exist only under high pressure. He contributed to the development of the Bridgman-Stockbarger method of "growing" crystals in a laboratory setting by subjecting the chemicals that make up a particular crystal to high temperature and pressure. Otherwise, his work contributed to a better understanding of the compressibility, thermoelectric conductivity, tensile strength, and viscosity of more than 100 different compounds. Much of his work in these and other areas is summarized in *The Physics of High Pressure* (1931), *The Thermodynamics of Electrical Phenomena in Metals* (1934), and *The Nature of Thermodynamics* (1941).

Bridgman's work had implications for a number of other disciplines. His methods and discoveries have informed physical chemists studying the nature of matter, geologists studying mineral reactions and the deformation of rocks, and astrophysicists studying the interiors of heavenly bodies. The Bridgman-Stockbarger method was later adapted to produce the world's first synthetic diamonds. In recognition of his contributions to high-pressure physics, in 1946 he was awarded the Nobel Prize for physics.

Throughout his career, Bridgman was interested in the philosophy of science. His most important contribution in this regard was his championing of the idea of operationism. Bridgman believed that the only meaningful scientific discussions that could take place were those that addressed concepts that could be measured, and measuring involved performing a certain set of operations. So, for Bridgman, if it could not be measured, it should not be discussed. In this way he hoped to rid science of much of what he considered to be metaphysics, philosophical discussions about concepts and entities that may or may not exist. He published his thoughts along these lines in *The Logic of Modern Physics* (1927) and *The Intelligent Individual and Society* (1938).

In addition to winning a Nobel Prize, Bridgman received many other honors. He presided over the American Physical Society; he was elected to the National Academy of Sciences, the American Association for the Advancement of Science, the American Academy of Arts and Sciences, and the Royal Society of London; and he received a number of medals, including the Franklin Institute's Cresson Medal. Having been diagnosed with an incurable form of bone cancer, he took his own life on August 20, 1961, at his summer home in Randolph, New Hampshire.

Further Reading

Kemble, Edwin C., and Francis Birch. "Percy Williams Bridgman," National Academy of Sciences, *Biographical Memoirs* 41 (1970): pp. 23–67.

Nobelprize.org. "The Nobel Prize in Physics 1946." Available online. URL: http://nobelprize.org/physics/laureates/1946. Downloaded on January 6, 2004.

Wasson, Tyler, ed. *Nobel Prize Winners.* New York: H. W. Wilson, 1987, pp. 150–151.

Brown, Herbert C.
(Herbert Charles Brown, Herbert Brovarnik)
(1912–2004) *chemist*

Unlike most chemists, Herbert C. Brown made important contributions in both organic and inorganic chemistry. Working with the boranes, chemical compounds made from boron and hydrogen, he developed sodium borohydride, which proved to be very useful to inorganic chemists. He also developed an entirely new class of compounds known as the organoboranes, which proved to be very useful to organic chemists. For these accomplishments, he was awarded a share of the 1979 Nobel Prize in chemistry.

Brown was born Herbert Brovarnik on May 22, 1912, in London, England. His father, Charles, was a cabinetmaker, and his mother, Pearl, was a homemaker. At age two his family immigrated to the United States and changed their last name to Brown; they settled near relatives in Chicago, Illinois, where his father opened a hardware store. Despite being an excellent student, young Herbert Brown was forced to drop out of high school to run the store when his father died in 1926, but he managed to finish his secondary education in 1930. He spent the next five years working at various jobs

Herbert Brown developed an entirely new class of chemical compounds known as the organoboranes. *(Courtesy of Herbert C. Brown)*

and studying at various junior colleges in Chicago before transferring to the University of Chicago, where he received a B.S. and a Ph.D. in chemistry in 1936 and 1938, respectively. In 1937 he married Sarah Baylen with whom he had one child.

While working on his doctorate, Brown became fascinated with boranes. Boranes do not exist in nature, and they were unknown until the German chemist Alfred Stock invented them in 1912. Boranes are unique in that they feature a three-center, electron-deficient bond whereby one electron pair is shared by three atoms—two boron and one hydrogen—rather than just two. Because of this unique arrangement, boranes, also known as borohydrides, make excellent reagents, substances that initiate reactions that synthesize two elements or simple compounds into one compound. Boranes are extremely reactive with oxygen, water, and alcohols, and they facilitate synthetic reactions that would otherwise be impossible. At the time, however, even the simplest of the boranes, diborane, was relatively rare and expensive to make.

During World War II, much of the work done by the Manhattan Project, the U.S. effort to construct an atomic bomb, was done at the University of Chicago, and Brown was asked to make some uranium borohydride as a means of producing pure uranium for the bomb. In order to produce enough uranium borohydride to satisfy the project's demands, he was forced to devise a faster and cheaper method of producing diborane, which is used in the preparation of uranium borohydride. By the war's end, he had discovered how to do this by reacting either lithium hydride or sodium hydride with boron trihalide, compounds which are relatively easy to obtain. In the process, he also developed, quite by accident, a previously unknown reagent, sodium borohydride, which eventually became one of the most used reagents in inorganic chemistry.

In 1943 Brown joined the faculty at Wayne State (Mich.) University as a professor of inorganic chemistry. During his four years at Wayne State, his research focused mostly on steric strains, deviations in the angles at which atoms bond with one another. By 1947 he had shown that steric strains play a major role in determining a compound's reactivity. That same year he was named a professor of chemistry at Purdue University, where he resumed and refocused his research with boranes. His earlier work had involved inorganic chemistry, but now he began venturing into the realm of organic chemistry by combining compounds that contain double-bonded carbon atoms with diborane. This innovative process, known as hydroboration, led Brown to develop a previously unknown class of organic compounds known as organoboranes. As with sodium borohydride, the organoboranes make excellent reagents, and they were eventually developed into some of the most useful reagents in synthetic organic chemistry; they are particularly valuable in the production of alkanes, alcohols, ketones, and related compounds.

Brown's work with boranes had important implications, both theoretical and practical, for organic and inorganic chemistry. While his research shed much light on the nature of chemical reactions involving reagents in general, it also provided the chemical industry with some of its most important tools for initiating synthetic chemical reactions. For his contributions, Brown was awarded a half share of the 1979 Nobel Prize in chemistry.

Meanwhile, in 1978 Brown had retired from his teaching duties at Purdue, although he continued to conduct research as a professor emeritus for a number of years. His many honors include the National Medal of Science and election to the National Academy of Sciences and the American Academy of Arts and Sciences. His many publications include *Hydroboration* (1962), *Boranes in Organic Chemistry* (1972), *Organic Syntheses via Boranes* (1975), *Borane Reagents* (1988), and *Organoboranes for Syntheses* (2001). He died on December 19, 2004, in West Lafayette, Indiana.

Further Reading

Brewster, James H., and Herbert C. Brown. *Aspects of Mechanism and Organometallic Chemistry: A Volume in Honor of Professor Herbert C. Brown.* New York: Plenum Press, 1978.

Davenport, Derek A., et al., eds. *Herbert C. Brown, a Life in Chemistry.* West Lafayette, Ind.: Department of Chemistry, Purdue University, 1980.

Nobelprize.org. "The Nobel Prize in Chemistry 1979." Available online. URL: http://nobelprize.org/ chemistry/laureates/1979. Downloaded on August 11, 2004.

Wasson, Tyler, ed. *Nobel Prize Winners.* New York: H. W. Wilson, 1987, pp. 154–156.

Brown, Michael S.
(Michael Stuart Brown)
(1941–   ) *molecular geneticist*

Michael S. Brown codiscovered the LDL and SREBP pathways, the processes by which the cells metabolize cholesterol. As a result, the medical community was alerted to the danger of high cholesterol levels in the bloodstream, one of the leading causes of heart attacks. This achievement won him a share of the 1985 Nobel Prize in physiology or medicine.

Brown was born on April 13, 1941, in New York City. His father, Harvey, was a textile salesman, and his mother, Evelyn, was a homemaker. At age 11 he moved with his family to Elkins Park, Pennsylvania, where he grew up. After receiving a B.S. in chemistry from the University of Pennsylvania in 1962, he entered the university's medical school, receiving an M.D. in 1966. He spent the next five years completing his internship and residency at Boston's Massachusetts General Hospital and working as a clinical associate at the National Institutes of Health in Bethesda, Maryland. During this period he became close friends with JOSEPH L. GOLDSTEIN, who would eventually become his lifelong collaborator. In 1971 he became affiliated with the University of Texas Southwestern Medical Center as a professor of internal medicine in its medical school and as a researcher in its division of gastroenterology. In 1964 he married Alice Lapin with whom he had two children.

In 1972 Brown was rejoined with Goldstein when the latter became affiliated with Southwestern. That same year they undertook a joint study of familial hypercholesterolemia; a genetic condition, its symptoms feature high levels of cholesterol in the blood. Cholesterol plays an important role in the formation of cellular membranes, the digestive acids, and steroid hormones. The body can produce its own cholesterol as well as ingest it from

Michael Brown (above) and Joseph Goldstein discovered how cells process cholesterol. *(Courtesy of Michael S. Brown; photo by David Gresham)*

food; consequently, most of the cholesterol in the body is found in the cells. Sometimes, however, enough cholesterol accumulates in the bloodstream that it inflames the walls of blood vessels, eventually leading to swollen or clogged arteries and heart attacks; patients with familial hypercholesterolemia usually die from heart attacks before the age of 30.

Brown and Goldstein studied cultures of connective tissue from healthy people in an effort to find out how the body metabolizes cholesterol. They discovered that healthy cells have molecules, called receptors, in their membranes that bind to low-density lipoproteins (LDLs), the primary carriers of cholesterol in the bloodstream. These receptors then carry the LDLs into the cell interior, where they are broken down into cholesterol and other chemicals, a process known as the LDL pathway. But when they studied the cells of patients with familial hypercholesterolemia, they

discovered that these cells have no LDL receptors because the gene that initiates the production of LDL receptors is defective. As a result, cholesterol accumulates in their bloodstreams until they die. The discovery of the LDL pathway alerted medical researchers that cholesterol-related diseases and conditions such as familial hypercholesterolemia might be treated via pharmaceuticals that could stimulate the production of LDL receptors. For this discovery, Brown and Goldstein were each awarded a half share of the 1985 Nobel Prize in physiology or medicine.

In the process of discovering the LDL pathway, Brown and Goldstein also discovered that the breakdown of LDLs causes the cell to cut down its production of LDL receptors. In an effort to find out why, they discovered a molecule they named the sterol regulatory element binding protein (SREBP). In cells that lack cholesterol, SREBP stimulates the gene that initiates the production of LDL receptors, but in cells that contain plenty of cholesterol, SREBP production is blocked and the production of LDL receptors is inhibited. The discovery of the SREBP pathway explained why so many people living in industrialized countries have such high levels of LDLs circulating in their bloodstreams, even though the gene that causes the production of LDL receptors is normal. Brown and Goldstein showed that these people consume large amounts of fat, which contains large amounts of cholesterol. As LDL receptors provide the cell with enough cholesterol to perform its tasks, the SREBP pathway shuts down the production of new LDL receptors, thus leaving dangerously high levels of cholesterol in the bloodstream. This discovery alerted the medical profession to the danger of high-fat, high-cholesterol diets, which led in turn to the development of a class of pharmaceutical drugs known as statins that can reduce the level of LDLs in the bloodstream.

Brown spent the rest of his career at Southwestern Medical Center, where he continued to collaborate with Goldstein on studies related to cholesterol in what became officially known in 1974 as the Brown-Goldstein Laboratory. His many honors include the National Medal of Science and election to the National Academy of Sciences and the American Academy of Arts and Sciences.

Further Reading

Nobelprize.org. "The Nobel Prize in Physiology or Medicine 1985." Available online. URL: http://nobelprize. org/medicine/laureates/1985. Downloaded on July 10, 2004.

UT Southwestern Medical Center. "Brown-Goldstein Laboratory." Available online. URL: http://www8. utsouthwestern.edu/utsw/cda/dept14857/files/ 114532.html. Downloaded on March 25, 2005.

Wasson, Tyler, ed. *Nobel Prize Winners*. New York: H. W. Wilson, 1987, pp. 156–157.

Buck, Linda B.
(1947–) *physiologist*

Linda B. Buck codiscovered the details concerning how the physiological systems associated with the sense of smell operate. For this contribution, she was awarded a share of the 2004 Nobel Prize in physiology or medicine.

Buck was born on January 29, 1947, in Seattle, Washington. After receiving B.S. degrees in psychology and microbiology from the University of Washington in 1975, she entered the University of Texas Southwestern Medical Center and received a Ph.D. in immunology in 1980. She spent the next four years doing postdoctoral research at Columbia University in New York City, and in 1984 she became an associate at Columbia's Howard Hughes Medical Institute.

At Columbia, Buck became affiliated with RICHARD AXEL, whose research covered a broad range of topics related to molecular biology. Buck developed an intense interest in how the nervous system deals with the tremendous amount of input it receives, and eventually decided to focus on how the sense of smell operates. At the time, it was known that most species rely heavily on their sense of smell for survival, and that many species have a more highly developed sense of smell than humans do. As for humans, it was known that odorant receptor cells, the ones that detect sensations of smell and then

cause them to be transmitted to the brain, are located far up in the nose, and that they transmit sensory data via small canals in the nasal bone directly to the olfactory bulb, where sensations of smell are decoded. Otherwise, little was known about the physiology of smell. Buck and Axel set out to change that via an exhaustive study that spanned 11 years, the results of which were first published in 1991.

Buck and Axel focused their early efforts on mice. They discovered that a mouse's olfactory system consists of approximately 1,000 different types of odorant receptors whose production is controlled by an equal number of genes. The receptors are located on the cell membranes of millions of olfactory receptor cells in a small area in the mucosa, or lining, of the upper part of the mouse's nostril, and each type of receptor is designed to detect the molecules associated with a relatively small number of specific odors. Multiple copies of each receptor type are distributed randomly among the various receptor cells. Because of this arrangement, a mouse can identify roughly 30,000 different scents. Buck and Axel eventually expanded their study to include humans, who have about 350 different types of odorant receptors and can identify about 10,000 different odors.

In addition to identifying the genes and cells associated with smell, Buck and Axel also demonstrated how olfactory sensations are communicated from the nose to the brain. When odorant molecules bind to receptors, the receptors send an electric signal to structures known as glomeruli in the olfactory bulb. All of the receptors of the same type transmit their signals to the same glomerulus, which then transmits a signal to the brain indicating the type and intensity of smell the olfactory system has detected. For demonstrating how the sense of smell works, Buck and Axel were each awarded a half share of the 2004 Nobel Prize in physiology or medicine.

Buck left Columbia in 1991 to teach neurobiology at the Harvard Medical School in Boston, Massachusetts. In 2002 she became a member of the division of basic sciences at the Fred Hutchinson Cancer Research Center in Seattle. While her research at the Hutchinson Center continued to focus on the physiology of smell, she also devoted considerable effort to understanding the mechanisms underlying aging and life span. Her other honors include election to the National Academy of Sciences.

Further Reading

Altman, Lawrence K. "Unraveling Enigma of Smell Wins Nobel for 2 Americans." *New York Times*, October 5, 2004, p. A18.

Nobelprize.org. "The Nobel Prize in Physiology or Medicine 2004." Available online. URL: http://nobelprize.org/medicine/laureates/2004. Downloaded on December 28, 2004.

Vitetta, Ellen S. *Linda B. Buck: The Making of a Nobel Laureate*. Dallas: University of Texas Southwestern Medical Center at Dallas, 2005.

Calvin, Melvin
(1911–1997) *chemist*

Melvin Calvin demonstrated the pathways via which plants absorb and process carbon dioxide during photosynthesis. For this achievement, he was awarded the 1961 Nobel Prize in chemistry.

Calvin was born on April 8, 1911, in St. Paul, Minnesota. His father, Elias, was a cigar maker, and his mother, Rose, was a homemaker. In the early 1920s he moved with his family to Detroit, Michigan, where his parents opened a small grocery store. After receiving a B.S. in chemistry from the Michigan College of Mining and Technology in 1931, he entered the University of Minnesota and received a Ph.D. in chemistry in 1935. He spent the next two years doing postdoctoral research at the University of Manchester in England, and in 1937 he was recruited by GILBERT N. LEWIS to join the faculty at the University of California at Berkeley. In 1942 he married Genevieve Jemtegaard with whom he had three children.

While at Manchester, Calvin became interested in the chemical composition of chlorophyll, the green coloring matter of leaves and plants, and the chemistry of photosynthesis, the process by which plants use sunlight to convert carbon dioxide, water, and inorganic salts into sugars and other organic compounds. Nevertheless, his early research at Berkeley focused on the molecular structure and behavior of coordination compounds, organic compounds that feature a metal atom at the center of an arrangement of nonmetallic atoms

or molecules. Oftentimes, coordination compounds have brilliant and intense hues, and in 1939 he and Lewis wrote an important paper about the color of organic substances. He also coauthored a textbook, *The Theory of Organic Chemistry* (1941).

After World War II, Calvin returned to his interest in photosynthesis. This move was prompted by the development during the war of techniques for producing significant amounts of a radioactive isotope of carbon known as carbon-14, or radiocarbon. Radioactive isotopes had been used as tracers in medical applications for a number of years, and it occurred to ERNEST O. LAWRENCE, at the time head of Berkeley's Radiation Laboratory, that the time had come to use radioactive isotopes as tracers for learning more about biochemical processes. In 1945 Lawrence recruited Calvin for the Laboratory's bio-organic chemistry group and convinced him to begin using radiocarbon as a tracer for learning how plants absorb carbon during photosynthesis.

Over the next nine years, Calvin studied photosynthesis in the green alga *Chlorella pyrerloidosa.* A colony of *Chlorella* were fed radioactive carbon dioxide and then allowed to grow to a certain point. The movement of radiocarbon through the algae's systems was then analyzed, and the process began again. Each time the algae were allowed to grow a little bit more than before, and in this way Calvin could follow precisely the pathway of carbon through the entire cycle of photosynthesis. In the process, he exploded two misconceptions regarding photosynthesis. First, he demonstrated that sunlight, which provides the energy needed during photosynthesis, acts only after it is absorbed into the chlorophyll, and not by interacting directly with carbon dioxide. Second, he showed that the first step in photosynthesis is not the immediate reduction of carbon dioxide but rather the fixation of carbon dioxide to a substance known as the carbon dioxide acceptor. This substance, a sugar derivative known as ribulose, then reacts with carbon dioxide to form phosphoglyceric acid, from which the plant manufactures the various carbohydrates that it needs. He published his work regarding radiocarbon and photosynthesis in 21 papers between 1948 and 1954, and in three books: *Isotopic Carbon* (1949), *The Path of Carbon in Photosynthesis* (1957), and *The Photosynthesis of Carbon Compounds* (1962).

Calvin showed that photosynthesis is much more complicated than anyone had supposed; the entire process involves the production of 10 intermediary compounds that are catalyzed by 11 different enzymes. Further research by other investigators showed that Calvin's findings for algae held true for higher forms of plant life as well, thus indicating that photosynthesis takes place in only one way. In addition to explaining in chemical terms the complete process of photosynthesis, which is also known as the Calvin cycle, Calvin opened the door to other studies of biochemical processes via the use of radioactive isotopes. For these contributions, he was awarded the 1961 Nobel Prize in chemistry.

In 1960 the Berkeley bio-organic chemistry group branched off to become the Laboratory of Chemical Biodynamics, and Calvin was named its director, a position he held until his retirement. He was elected to the National Academy of Sciences and the American Academy of Arts and Sciences, and he was awarded the National Medal of Science. He retired from Berkeley in 1980, but he continued to conduct research for a number of years thereafter. He died on January 8, 1997, in Berkeley.

Further Reading

Calvin, Melvin. *Following the Trail of Light: A Scientific Odyssey.* Washington: American Chemical Society, 1992.
Nobelprize.org. "The Nobel Prize in Chemistry 1961." Available online. URL: http://nobelprize.org/chemistry/laureates/1961. Downloaded on May 3, 2004.

Seaborg, Glenn T., and Andrew A. Benson. "Melvin Calvin," National Academy of Sciences, *Biographical Memoirs* 75 (1998): pp. 96–115.
Wasson, Tyler, ed. *Nobel Prize Winners.* New York: H. W. Wilson, 1987, pp. 176–177.

Cannon, Annie J.
(Annie Jump Cannon)
(1863–1941) *astronomer*

Annie Cannon was one of a group of women who made significant contributions to astronomy during the late 19th and early 20th centuries. She spent more than 40 years charting the heavens, and as a result she is known as the Census Taker of the Stars.

Cannon was born on December 11, 1863, in Dover, Delaware. Her father, Wilson, was a merchant, and her mother, Mary Elizabeth, was a homemaker. As a girl she demonstrated an interest in astronomy, which her father encouraged by helping her turn their attic into an observatory of sorts. After completing her secondary education, in 1880 she enrolled in Wellesley College in Massachusetts and received a B.S. in physics and astronomy four years later. While at Wellesley, she developed an ear infection that steadily worsened until she was almost totally deaf. Partly for this reason, and partly because scientific careers for women were exceptionally rare, she returned to Delaware after graduation and pursued an active social life for the next 10 years. Following the death of her mother in 1893, she returned to Wellesley to work as an assistant to Sarah Whiting, her former astronomy professor. In 1895 she enrolled in Radcliffe College as a special student and began taking graduate courses in astronomy at Harvard University, with which Radcliffe was associated.

At the time, the staff at the Harvard Observatory was attempting to identify and classify every star in the universe. Staff astronomers would photograph certain areas of the night sky through a telescope and a spectroscope, an optical device that measured the wavelengths, or spectra, of the various stars. The spectrograms, as the photographs were called, were then analyzed to see if they contained any previously unknown stars, as each star possesses its own unique spectrum. The project was made possible by a grant from the estate of Henry Draper, an amateur astronomer who in 1872 had taken the first photograph of a stellar spectrum, and it opened the door to a scientific career for many women. The project's director, Edward Pickering, believed that women were better suited to do the meticulous, oftentimes boring, work that examining spectrograms and classifying stars entailed, and he had hired a number of women to work on the project. Pickering was particularly impressed with Cannon's work as a graduate student, and in 1896 he offered her a position as an assistant to WILLIAMINA FLEMING, the observatory's curator of astronomical photographs.

Cannon immediately set about examining spectrograms with a magnifying glass. Before long she was able to tell, from a star's spectrum, its composition, heat, size, direction, and speed. She also began to tinker with the classification system that had been devised by Fleming and eventually

Annie J. Cannon developed a system for classifying newly discovered stars. *(Library of Congress, Prints and Photographs Division [LC-USZ62-115881])*

tweaked it into a system that classified stars by their surface temperatures. By 1910 this system had been adopted by astronomers around the world, and it remains in use today.

Cannon's ability to read spectrograms made her a legend in her own time. It was said that she could analyze as many as three spectra per minute, and over the course of her career she examined the spectra of approximately 350,000 stars. Many of these stars were classified by her at Harvard's Boyden Station in Arequipa, Peru, where she helped classify the stars of the southern hemisphere. She discovered five novae, stars that suddenly become thousands of times brighter and then fade to their original intensity, and approximately 300 variable stars, which vary markedly in brightness from time to time.

Cannon took over Fleming's position in 1911, and in 1918 she began overseeing the publication of the project's work. Known as the *Henry Draper Catalogue*, the first nine volumes, which appeared between 1918 and 1924, contained the spectra of more than 225,000 stars distributed over the entire sky. Two extension volumes, one published by Cannon in 1925 and the second published by her coworkers in 1949 after her death, contained another 133,000 stars. The *Catalogue* has been called one of the greatest collections of astronomical data of all time, and it continues to be used by astronomers and astrophysicists today.

In 1938 Cannon was appointed William Cranch Bond Astronomer, thus becoming one of the first women to be appointed to a named chair at Harvard. Other honors included the Draper Medal of the National Academy of Sciences in 1931. Two years later she used the monetary award that accompanied the medal to establish the Annie J. Cannon Prize of the American Astronomical Society, awarded every three years to a woman who has made an outstanding contribution to astronomy. In 1940 she retired to her home in Cambridge, Massachusetts, where she died, having never married, on April 13, 1941.

Further Reading

Bailey, Martha J. *American Women in Science: A Biographical Dictionary.* Santa Barbara, Calif.: ABC-CLIO, 1994, pp. 53–54.

Yount, Lisa. *A to Z of Women in Science and Math.* New York: Facts On File, 1999, pp. 29–31.

Carson, Rachel
(Rachel Louise Carson)
(1907–1964) *biologist*

If any one person can be credited with starting the environmental protection movement in the United States, that person would be Rachel Carson. A trained zoologist and a gifted writer, she brought to the attention of the American public the incredible dangers they faced from the indiscriminate use of pesticides. She also played a major role in convincing Americans that they needed to become "friends of the earth."

Carson was born on May 27, 1907, in Springdale, Pennsylvania. Her father, Robert, was a salesman, and her mother, Maria, was a teacher. As a child, Carson was encouraged by her mother to read and write about nature, especially the animals that she encountered on the farms and in the woods surrounding their home. At age 10 she published her first nature story in a children's magazine, and by the time she graduated from high school she had won several literary prizes. In 1925 she enrolled in the Pennsylvania College for Women (now Chatham College). Originally an English major, she changed her course of study after taking a biology course; she received an A.B. in zoology in 1929 and an A.M. in zoology from Johns Hopkins University in 1932. She spent several of her summers as a student working at the Woods Hole Marine Biological Laboratory in Woods Hole, Massachusetts. As a result of her work at Woods Hole, she became fascinated with the sea and the creatures that live in it.

From 1932 to 1936 Carson taught zoology at the University of Maryland. She also wrote scripts for a radio series about marine life as well as a number of natural history features for the Sunday supplement of a Baltimore newspaper. In 1936 she left teaching to work as a science writer and editor for the U.S. Commerce Department's Bureau of Fisheries, later part of the U.S. Fish and Wildlife Service. By 1937 her father and her older sister had died, leaving Carson the sole support of her mother and two orphaned nieces, whom she adopted and raised at her home in Silver Spring, Maryland.

In 1949 Carson was named Fish and Wildlife's editor-in-chief, thus putting her in charge of the service's publications. In that capacity she oversaw the development of a 12-pamphlet series called "Conservation in Action" and wrote four of the pamphlets herself. The series demonstrated both her command of basic biological principles and her growing sensitivity to ecological matters. Privately, she also wrote *The Sea Around Us* (1951), a book that presents scientific information about the fragility of the marine ecology while also expressing in lyrical terms the wonders of the sea, all in terms that the general public could understand and appreciate. The book topped the *New York Times* best seller list for 86 weeks, an unprecedented accomplishment for a book about nature, and won for her the John Burroughs Medal, the National Book Award, and the title "woman of the year in literature" from the Associated Press. It also led to the reissue of *Under the Sea-Wind,* her first book about the environment in which sea creatures live that first appeared in 1941. This book became a best seller, too. By 1952 she had earned enough in royalties that she was able to retire from Fish and Wildlife, build a summer cottage on the Sheepscot River in Maine, and concentrate on writing more books and articles about nature. In 1957 she published what became a third best seller, *The Edge of the Sea,* described by one reviewer as her "last volume in the sea's biography."

That same year Carson embarked on the project for which she would be best remembered. A friend, Olga Huckins, owned a bird sanctuary near Duxbury, Massachusetts, that had been sprayed by the state government as part of its mosquito control program. The spray contained the deadly pesticide dichlorodiphenyltrichloroethane—known popularly as DDT, in some circles it was half-jokingly referred to as "Drop Dead Twice." The spray greatly reduced the sanctuary's mosquito population, but it also killed a number of Huckins's birds, and she complained to Carson. While with Fish and Wildlife, Carson had become somewhat concerned with the growing use of pesticides, but now she began a full-scale investigation of DDT and other pesticides. Over the next four years Carson compiled scientific data regarding pesticides, and the more she learned the more appalled she became at the incredible amount of harm the unregulated application of pesticides in general, and DDT in particular, was capable of doing to nature as well as to people.

In 1962 Carson published her most important book, *Silent Spring;* the book takes its title from the opening scene, in which a spring is silent because all the birds and wildlife that should be drinking from it are dead. In it she condemned pest control practices that did not take into consideration their consequences for the ecology. For the first time, the book brought to the attention of the American people the fact that they lived in, and not outside of, nature, and it called on Americans to begin living in harmony with nature rather than trying to conquer it. Not surprisingly, *Silent Spring* was condemned by the pesticide and agribusiness industries for being overly emotional and not scientific enough. The scientific community, however, was more receptive to Carson's book, and in 1963 a special panel of President John F. Kennedy's Science Advisory Committee concurred with most of her conclusions.

Silent Spring, Carson's fourth best seller, created a tremendous stir in American society because it opened the eyes of Americans to the fact that nature is easily damaged without being easily repaired. It was a major contributor to the environmental protection movement that got under way shortly after the book's publication. Other results of the book were a federal government ban on the use of DDT and the creation of the U.S. Environmental Protection Agency. Meanwhile, Carson had developed breast cancer, and she died, having never married, on April 14, 1964, in Silver Spring. In 1980 President Jimmy Carter awarded her posthumously the Presidential Medal of Freedom.

Further Reading

Bailey, Martha J. *American Women in Science: A Biographical Dictionary.* Santa Barbara, Calif.: ABC-CLIO, 1994, pp. 56–57.

Brooks, Paul. *The House of Life: Rachel Carson at Work.* Boston: Houghton Mifflin, 1972.

McCay, Mary A. *Rachel Carson.* New York: Twayne, 1993.

Yount, Lisa. *A to Z of Women in Science and Math.* New York: Facts On File, 1999, pp. 33–35.

Carver, George Washington
(ca. 1860–1943) *botanist*

One of the best known American scientists is George Washington Carver. He invented hundreds of uses for peanuts, including the lunchtime staple, peanut butter. What few people realize, however, is that Carver's work with peanuts was part of a much larger effort to use scientific research to improve the lives of impoverished southern farmers.

Carver was born into slavery with the single name George sometime around 1860 on a farm in Diamond, Missouri. His mother, Mary, was a slave owned by Moses and Susan Carver, and his father, whose name is unknown, was probably a slave on a nearby farm who had died before George's birth. During the Civil War George and his mother were kidnapped by raiders from Arkansas. He was later ransomed back to the Carvers, who then raised him and his brother to young adulthood. Freed by the Civil War in 1865, George eventually took the last name Carver in honor of the kind treatment he had received from his former masters and foster parents.

In 1877 Carver left Diamond for Neosho, Missouri, so that he could attend a public school for blacks. Two years later he moved to Kansas, and over the next five years he attended school in several Kansas towns while supporting himself as a laundry worker and cook. During this period he met another African American named George Carver, so he took the middle name Washington to differentiate himself. In 1884 he graduated from the Minneapolis, Kansas, public high school and was accepted into Highland College. When the administration discovered that Carver was black, they denied him admission. Heartbroken, he spent the next six years drifting across Kansas, working variously as a wheat farmer and laundryman.

In 1890 Carver decided to reapply to college; this time he was permitted to attend Simpson College in Indianola, Iowa. Two years later he transferred to Iowa State College, and in 1894 he received a B.S. in horticulture and botany. He spent the next two years at Iowa State teaching freshman horticulture and managing the school's greenhouse while working on his M.S. in horticulture and botany, which he received in 1896.

George Washington Carver showed southern farmers how to farm scientifically. *(Library of Congress, Prints and Photographs Division [LC-J601-302])*

Upon completing his graduate studies, Carver accepted the position of head of the agriculture department at Tuskegee Institute in Tuskegee, Alabama, the black college founded and administered by Booker T. Washington. Shortly after his arrival, Carver began devoting his research efforts to helping southern farmers farm scientifically and therefore improve their lifestyles. Their biggest problem was that they had become overly dependent on growing cotton. Not only did cotton leach valuable nutrients from the soil, but its production also prevented farmers from growing much of their own food. Instead, they hoped to raise a bumper crop of cotton and use part of the proceeds to buy the additional food they needed. Unfortunately, this rarely happened, partly because poor farmers could not afford enough fertilizer to produce a bumper crop and partly because the boll weevil, an insect that infests cotton plants, destroyed millions of pounds of cotton annually.

Carver took several approaches to solve this thorny problem. First, he encouraged farmers to raise food crops that were easy to grow and full of nutrition. In 1897 he began experimenting with sweet potatoes, and soon he discovered how to raise a considerable amount on a small plot of marginal soil. Next, he developed more than 100 ways to prepare sweet potatoes, as well as ways to convert them into staples such as flour, sugar, and bread. He showed farmers how to increase their production of pork by shifting their hogs away from a diet of expensive cornmeal to a diet of acorns, which grew plentifully in the southern woods. Having developed these methods, he taught them to his students at Tuskegee, printed pamphlets for distribution to farmers, and outfitted a wagon into a demonstration school that he dispatched across the South.

Carver also worked to solve the southern farmer's dilemma by discovering new ways to reinvigorate the soil. In 1902 he began experimenting with black-eyed peas, a nitrogen-rich legume. He soon discovered that rotating a field between cotton one year and black-eyed peas the next kept the field completely restocked with all the nutrients needed to raise a considerable amount of cotton without having to buy expensive fertilizer. He also developed more than 40 recipes for converting black-eyed peas into delicious mealtime treats such as pancakes, pudding, and croquettes.

Carver's claim to fame came from his work with peanuts, which he began experimenting with in 1903. Before he became interested in peanuts, southern farmers had mostly fed them to their livestock. Carver realized that peanuts, a close relative to black-eyed peas, could also reintroduce much-needed nutrients into the soil, and he convinced farmers to grow them along with black-eyed peas. Once farmers began producing bumper crops of peanuts, which grow even better across the South than black-eyed peas, he began developing mealtime recipes for peanuts. He quickly discovered that peanuts are full of vegetable oil, which is easily extracted and which can be made into a variety of products. By 1916 he had developed from peanut oil more than 100 different products, including cheese, facial creams, printer's ink, medicine, shampoo, soap, vinegar, and wood stain.

The most popular food product Carver developed from peanuts is peanut butter. After much investigatory work, he discovered that roasted peanuts could be ground into a smooth, creamy butter that contains more protein than butter made from corn oil and that lasts longer than dairy butter. By the 1920s people across the United States had discovered that peanut butter spread on a slice of bread was a delicious, nutritious, and inexpensive snack.

Carver's third approach to helping southern farmers was to do something about the boll weevil. He had enjoyed much success breeding hybrid plants ever since his days at Iowa State, and in 1915 he managed to breed a hybrid cotton plant that was less susceptible to boll weevils. Known as Carver's Hybrid, this cotton plant matures quicker than other cotton plants, and its cotton bolls can often be harvested before the boll weevil has time to infest them.

Carver spent his entire professional career at Tuskegee Institute. He died, having never married, on January 5, 1943, in Tuskegee. He left his small savings to the institute to fund a research facility for agricultural chemistry.

Further Reading

Carey, Charles W., Jr. "Carver, George Washington," *American Inventors, Entrepreneurs, and Business Visionaries.* New York: Facts On File, 2002, pp. 61–63.

Gates, Henry L., and Cornel West. *The African-American Century: How Black Americans Have Shaped Our Country.* New York: Free Press, 2000.

McMurry, Linda O. *George Washington Carver: Scientist and Symbol.* Norwalk, Conn.: Easton Press, 1994.

Spangenburg, Ray, and Kit Moser. "Carver, George Washington," *African Americans in Science, Math, and Invention.* New York: Facts On File, 2003, pp. 38–40.

Tiner, John H. *100 Scientists Who Shaped World History.* San Mateo, Calif.: Bluewood Books, 2000.

Cech, Thomas R.
(Thomas Robert Cech)
(1947–   ) *chemist*

Thomas R. Cech discovered ribozymes, better known as catalytic RNA, the first known biochemical substances other than enzymes that can catalyze, or initiate, a biochemical operation. For this discovery he was awarded a share of the 1989 Nobel Prize in chemistry.

Cech was born on December 8, 1947, in Chicago, Illinois. His father, Robert, was a physician, and his mother, Annette, was a homemaker. As a boy he moved with his family to Iowa City, Iowa, where he grew up. In 1970 he received a B.S. in chemistry from Grinnell (Ia.) College and married Carol Martinson with whom he had two children. After receiving a Ph.D. in biochemistry from the University of California at Berkeley in 1975, he spent three years conducting postdoctoral research at the Massachusetts Institute of Technology. In 1978 he joined the faculty at the University of Colorado in Boulder as a professor of chemistry, where he remained for the rest of his career.

As a graduate student, Cech became interested in the structure of chromosomes, which contain hereditary information in the form of genes. This interest led him to investigate the process by which genetic coding is transferred from DNA to messenger

Thomas Cech discovered ribozymes, biochemical compounds that possess some of the properties of RNA and some of the properties of enzymes. *(Courtesy of Colorado University—Boulder Office of Public Relations; photo by Ken Abbott)*

RNA (mRNA), which then carries that coding to the cell's ribosomes where it initiates the production of proteins. Working with the single-cell protozoa known as *Tetrahymena thermophila*, he began searching for the specific enzyme that transfers genetic coding from DNA to mRNA. What he discovered was that no such enzyme exists; instead, mRNA seems to acquire genetic coding from DNA all by itself.

In 1977 the American biologist PHILLIP A. SHARP had discovered that, in higher order organisms, mRNA does not duplicate DNA exactly; rather, large sections of a DNA string are left out of the finished string of mRNA. Sharp identified two types of DNA sequences: exons, which carry genetic coding, and introns, which carry only "nonsense," or material that is not known to code for anything. Sharp believed that when genetic coding is transferred from DNA to mRNA, the introns are snipped out of the mRNA string by enzymes. Cech's research, however, suggested that the introns snip themselves out without aid of enzymes, and in 1982 he labeled these introns "ribozymes," since they combine features of ribonucleic acid and enzymes. Cech's findings were confirmed two years later by the American biochemist SIDNEY ALTMAN, who showed that ribozymes not only act as enzymes on themselves but also on other substances.

Prior to Cech's discovery of catalytic RNA, as ribozymes are more commonly known, it was generally believed that only proteins in the form of enzymes were capable of catalyzing a biochemical operation. Cech's work showed otherwise, and in so doing it led the way for a search for other enzyme-like nonproteins. His work also suggested a new approach for curing viral infections, as catalytic RNA might be used to snip out the exons that carry the coding for infections or genetic disorders. Lastly, his discovery suggested that catalytic RNA, because it is a much simpler molecule than a protein and because it initiates the production of proteins as well as itself, most likely was the original biomolecule in the history of evolution. For the role he played in discovering catalytic RNA, Cech was awarded a half share of the 1989 Nobel Prize in chemistry; his corecipient was Altman.

Cech continued to study catalytic RNA after winning the Nobel Prize, but he also branched out into another line of inquiry, the structure and replication of telomeres, the ends of chromosomes. Other researchers had shown that a cell must maintain the length of its telomeres in order to avoid death, and that failure to do so might also induce the cell to become cancerous. Cech began investigating telomerase, the enzyme that lengthens telomeres, as a possible agent in the prevention or treatment of cancer.

In addition to his duties at Colorado, Cech also conducted research as an investigator for the Howard Hughes Medical Institute. His many honors include election to the National Academy of Sciences and the American Academy of Arts and Sciences.

Further Reading

McMurray, Emily J., ed. *Notable Twentieth-Century Scientists.* Detroit: Gale Research, 1995, pp. 328–330.

Nobelprize.org. "The Nobel Prize in Chemistry 1989." Available online. URL: http://nobelprize.org/ chemistry/laureates/1989. Downloaded on August 11, 2004.

University of Colorado at Boulder. "Thomas H. [sic] Cech." Available online. URL: http://www.colorado. edu/chem/DEC/people/cecht.html. Downloaded on March 25, 2005.

Chamberlain, Owen
(1920–) *physicist*

Owen Chamberlain codiscovered the antiproton, a proton with a net negative charge. For this achievement he was awarded a share of the 1959 Nobel Prize in physics.

Chamberlain was born on July 10, 1920, in San Francisco, California. His father, Edward, was a radiologist, and his mother, Genevieve, was a homemaker. In 1941 he received a B.A. in physics from Dartmouth College and entered the University of California at Berkeley. He left school the following year to work on the Manhattan Project, the U.S. effort to build an atomic bomb during World War II. In 1943 he married Beatrice Copper with whom he had four children. After the war he entered the University of Chicago, receiving a Ph.D. in physics in 1949, the year after he returned to Berkeley as a professor of physics.

Chamberlain's early research involved the chemistry of plutonium, the first of the transuranium elements, which had been discovered at Berkeley the year he entered its graduate program. His work for the Manhattan Project involved investigating the spontaneous fission of plutonium, work which he performed at the project's facility in Los Alamos, New Mexico, under the direction of EMILIO SEGRÈ and which contributed to the design and construction of Fat Man, the 21-kiloton plutonium bomb that was dropped on Nagasaki, Japan.

Upon returning to Berkeley, Chamberlain rejoined Segrè, but now the focus of their collaboration shifted to the search for antimatter, subatomic particles that are analogous to common particles such as the electron but with opposite charges. In 1928 French physicist Paul Dirac had postulated the existence of a so-called positive electron, a subatomic particle with the same mass as an electron but with a positive rather than a negative charge. Four years later, the American physicist CARL D. ANDERSON demonstrated the correctness of Dirac's theory by discovering a particle whose mass was about the same as an electron but whose net charge was positive rather than negative; he named this particle the positron. Anderson's discovery raised the question as to whether or not the positron was the only form of antimatter, and in 1948 Segrè and Chamberlain set out to answer this question.

Since the neutron has no net charge, it was believed that an antineutron could not exist, so Segrè and Chamberlain set out to find an antiproton, a particle with the mass of a proton but with a negative rather than a positive charge. They used Berkeley's 184-inch synchrocyclotron—a sophisticated device that generates an electromagnetic field to accelerate subatomic particles to extremely high velocities and then propels them into other particles in an effort to create an atomic reaction—to propel protons into one another in the hope of creating an antiproton. As sophisticated as this device was, however, it was incapable of propelling protons at a high enough rate of speed to create antiprotons. In 1955 Berkeley put into operation a super-powerful synchrocyclotron known as the bevatron. That same year Segrè and Chamberlain, assisted by Clyde Wiegand and Thomas Ypsilantis, conducted a number of proton-proton bombardment experiments,

and the results clearly showed that antiprotons, protons with a net negative charge, do indeed exist, although they are short-lived. Meanwhile, other subatomic particles such as muons, pions, and K-mesons had been discovered, and researchers eventually discovered that they had antiparticles as well. In 1956 Segrè and Chamberlain discovered the antineutron, which has the same charge as a neutron but a different magnetic moment, a function of its magnetic strength. For their discovery of antiprotons, Segrè and Chamberlain each received a half share of the 1959 Nobel Prize in physics.

Chamberlain spent the rest of his career studying antiparticles. This work included investigating the interactions of antiprotons with hydrogen, the production of antineutrons from antiprotons, and the scattering of pi-mesons. He retired from teaching at Berkeley in 1989, although he continued to conduct experiments there for a number of years thereafter. His many honors include election to the National Academy of Sciences.

Further Reading

Nobelprize.org. "The Nobel Prize in Physics 1959." Available online. URL: http://nobelprize.org/physics/laureates/1959. Downloaded on August 26, 2004.

Science Matters @ Berkeley. "1955: Emilio Segrè, Owen Chamberlain, and the Matter of Antimatter." Available online. URL: http://sciencematters.berkeley.edu/archives/volume1/issue1/legacy.php. Downloaded on March 25, 2005.

Wasson, Tyler, ed. *Nobel Prize Winners.* New York: H. W. Wilson, 1987, pp. 197–199.

Chandrasekhar, Subrahmanyan (Chandra)
(1910–1995) *astrophysicist*

Subrahmanyan Chandrasekhar, or "Chandra" as he is known to the scientific community, won a Nobel Prize for formulating the currently accepted theory on the evolution of extremely massive stars into black holes. He contributed in major ways to so many other aspects of astrophysics, the study of the physics of heavenly bodies, that he is generally regarded as the most distinguished astrophysicist of the late 20th century.

Subrahmanyan Chandrasekhar developed a theory to explain the origins of black holes. *(Library of Congress, Prints and Photographs Division [LC-USW3-007566-C])*

Chandra was born on October 19, 1910, in Lahore, British India. His father, Chandrasekhara, was a railroad official, and his mother, Sitalakshmi, was a homemaker. In 1918 he moved with his family to Madras where he grew up. After receiving a B.Sc. in physics from Presidency College of the University of Madras in 1930, he attended the University of Cambridge in England and received a Ph.D. in physics in 1933. He spent the next four years as a fellow and lecturer at Cambridge's Trinity College, and then in 1937 he accepted a position at the University of Chicago, where he remained for the rest of his career. In 1936 he married Lalitha Doraiswarmy, with whom he had no children, and in 1953 he became a naturalized U.S. citizen.

Chandra began working on his theory of the evolution of massive stars while sailing from India to England to attend graduate school. At the time, it was believed that once all of a star's fuel is combusted, the star loses internal pressure and col-

lapses as a result of its own gravity into an Earth-sized star known as a white dwarf. Chandra recalculated the statistical mechanics of stellar structure in terms of Albert Einstein's special theory of relativity. In so doing, he concluded that a star with a mass greater than 1.44 times that of the Sun was incapable of degenerating into a white dwarf. Instead, the self-gravity of a collapsing massive star causes it to compress very tightly into a neutron star, a very dense star composed mostly of neutrons with an outer shell harder than steel. Part of the process of degenerating into a neutron star is the explosion of the star's gaseous outer layers, known as a supernova. In the case of an extremely massive star, degeneration results in a black hole, an incredibly dense dead star whose gravitational pull is so strong that not even light can escape it.

In 1935 Chandra presented his theory, today known as the Chandrasekhar mass limit, to the scientific community. It attracted so much ridicule from Cambridge's Arthur S. Eddington, at the time the world's foremost astrophysicist, that it was given little credence. Undaunted, Chandra continued to develop his theory, and he published a full explanation of stellar mass limit in *An Introduction to the Study of Stellar Structure* (1939). Over time, the scientific community would come to accept the Chandrasekhar mass limit as being the best explanation for the evolution of mature stars and the development of black holes. For explaining how massive stars end their existence, he was awarded a share of the 1983 Nobel Prize in physics.

Meanwhile, Chandra turned his attention to a number of other problems concerning astrophysics. In the late 1930s he began investigating how and why the motion of a star is affected by the gravitational pull of other "nearby" stars. In the process he developed the currently accepted theory for the evolution of star clusters, which he published in *The Principles of Stellar Dynamics* (1943). In the mid-1940s he focused on understanding how the energy transferred by radiation flows in a star's interior and its luminous visible surface. This line of inquiry led to the development of theories of stellar and planetary atmospheres and a theory of the illumination and polarization of the sunlit sky, which he published in *Radiative Transfer* (1950). In the early 1950s he turned his attention to the study of plasma, in physics a "soupy" mixture of disengaged subatomic particles that occurs under conditions of extreme high heat. Plasma is considered to be a fourth form of matter, and it is found extensively in stellar interiors and atmospheres and in interstellar gases. Chandra undertook an extensive study of the dynamical stability of plasma under the presence of magnetic fields and rotations such as occur in stars, and he published his findings in *Hydrodynamic and Hydromagnetic Stability* (1961). In the 1960s he collaborated with Norman R. Lebovitz on the study of the dynamics of rotating, self-gravitating spheroids of homogeneous incompressible fluids, the results of which appeared in *Ellipsoidal Figures of Equilibrium* (1968). This latter endeavor led him to study gravity from the perspective of Einstein's general theory of relativity. One result of this study was the discovery of the Chandrasekhar-Friedman-Schultz instability, a source of gravitational radiation from black holes, which he published in *The Mathematical Theory of Black Holes* (1983).

Chandra was elected to the National Academy of Sciences, and he was awarded the National Medal of Science. From 1952 to 1971 he served as editor of the *Astrophysical Journal*, in the process turning it into the most influential international publication dedicated to astrophysics. He retired from Chicago in 1985, after which he wrote two works of popular science, *Truth and Beauty: Aesthetics and Motivations in Science* (1987) and *Newton's Principia for the Common Reader* (1995). He died on August 21, 1995, in Chicago.

Further Reading

Nobelprize.org. "The Nobel Prize in Physics 1983." Available online. URL: http://nobelprize.org/physics/laureates/1983. Downloaded on March 21, 2004.

Parker, Eugene N. "Subrahmanyan Chandrasekhar," National Academy of Sciences, *Biographical Memoirs* 72 (1997): pp. 28–49.

Wald, Robert M., ed. *Black Holes and Relativistic Stars.* Chicago: University of Chicago Press, 1998.

Wali, Kameshwar C. *Chandra: A Biography of S. Chandrasekhar.* Chicago: University of Chicago Press, 1991.

Wasson, Tyler, ed. *Nobel Prize Winners.* New York: H. W. Wilson, 1987, pp. 199–201.

Chu, Steven
(1948–) *physicist*

Steven Chu developed the atom trap, a device for greatly reducing the velocity of atoms. For this achievement, he was awarded a share of the 1997 Nobel Prize in physics.

Chu was born on February 28, 1948, in St. Louis, Missouri. His father, Ju Chin, was a professor of chemical engineering, and his mother, Ching Chen, was an economist. At age four he moved with his family to New York City where he grew up. As an undergraduate he attended the University of Rochester, receiving an A.B. in mathematics and a B.S. in physics in 1970. He then entered the graduate physics program at the University of California at Berkeley, receiving a Ph.D. in 1976.

As a graduate student, Chu became interested in lasers, devices that produce and amplify electromagnetic radiation by using visible light. While studying the inner workings of atomic nuclei with a laser that he designed and constructed himself, he produced some of the first evidence to support the electroweak theory of STEVEN WEINBERG, Abdus Salam, and SHELDON L. GLASHOW. This theory postulates that electricity, magnetism, and the weak nuclear force (the force that governs the processes of radioactive disintegration in the nucleus) are all manifestations of one basic force.

After two years of postdoctoral research at Berkeley, in 1978 Chu joined the technical staff of the Bell Telephone Laboratories (BTL) in Murray Hill, New Jersey. Eventually he was named head of BTL's quantum electronics research department in Holmdel, New Jersey. At BTL he and Allen Mills used a laser as a strobe light to study the inner workings of an atom of positronium, which consists of one electron and one positron, an electron with a positive charge. Earlier attempts to study the positronium had failed because its life span is very short, approximately 140×10^{-9} seconds; nevertheless, Chu and Mills managed to obtain accurate measurements of the quantum electronic forces at work within the positronium.

In 1985 Chu became interested in using lasers to trap atoms, an idea that had been advanced several years earlier by his BTL colleague, Art Ashkin. Chu realized that the key to doing this was first to cool down the atoms to a temperature approaching absolute zero. He seemed certain that this could also be done with lasers, as had been suggested earlier by American physicist ARTHUR L. SCHAWLOW. Chu also drew on the work of Albert Einstein, who theorized that when an atom absorbs a photon, or a packet of light energy, it receives an impulse from that photon. If the photon's velocity is exactly opposite the atom's velocity, then the effect of the absorption is to slow down the atom, thus making it cooler. By adjusting the frequency of a laser beam so that the photons in the beam have the same frequency as the target atom, the atom can be slowed almost to a complete stop if it absorbs enough photons from the beam. Chu set out to put into practice the theories of Ashkin, Schawlow, and Einstein, and several months later he had designed and built the first atom trap, a device that slows down atoms from about 2,500 mph to about 1 mph.

In 1987 Chu left BTL to teach physics and applied physics at Stanford University, where he remained for the rest of his career. At Stanford he headed a research group that modified the atom trap to create so-called optical tweezers, which are used to trap microscopic particles in water. Optical tweezers can also be used to manipulate an individual DNA molecule by attaching micron-sized polystyrene spheres, or "handles," to the ends of the molecule. His group also used atom traps to develop an atomic fountain that measures time more accurately than the atomic clocks maintained by standard laboratories. They also developed a novel atom interferometer, a device that provides the most accurate measurements of everything from very small displacements to extremely long distances. For all these contributions, Chu was awarded a one-third share of the 1997 Nobel Prize in physics; His corecipients were the American physicist WILLIAM D. PHILLIPS and the French physicist Claude Cohen-Tannoudji. His other honors include election to the National Academy of Sciences and the American Academy of Arts and Sciences.

Further Reading

Broad, William J. "6 Men Share Nobels in Chemistry and Physics," *New York Times*, October 16, 1997, p. A16.
Nobelprize.org. "The Nobel Prize in Physics 1997." Available online. URL: http://nobelprize.org/physics/laureates/1997. Downloaded on September 1, 2004.

Claude, Albert
(1899–1983) *biologist*

Albert Claude was one of the founders of cell biology, the study of the individual components of living cells. His role in this endeavor won for him a share of a Nobel Prize.

Claude was born on August 24, 1899, in Longlier, Belgium. His father, Florentin, owned a bakery, and his mother, Glaudice, was a homemaker. As a boy he moved with his family to Athus, and at age 12 he went to work in a local steel mill. At age 15 he became a spy for the British during World War I, and he received several decorations for bravery. In 1922 he was admitted to the University of Liège Medical School, despite never having completed high school, and in 1928 he received an M.D.

While in medical school, Claude became interested in sarcomas, malignant tumors that originate in the connective tissue and generally attack the bones. A year of postdoctoral research in Berlin left him with a desire to conduct further research on the Rous sarcoma, which the American pathologist PEYTON ROUS had theorized was caused in chickens by a virus. Hoping to work with Rous at the Rockefeller Institute of Medical Research (today Rockefeller University), Claude applied there for a research position and was hired. He went to work at Rockefeller in 1929, but instead of joining Rous's research team, he was assigned to another team investigating the connection between viruses and cancer. Claude remained at Rockefeller for 20 years, in the process becoming a professor. Meanwhile, in 1938 he married Joy Gilder with whom he had one child, and in 1941 he became a U.S. citizen.

Once at Rockefeller, Claude began experimenting with tumor cells as part of his search for the agent that causes Rous sarcoma. He developed a process of cell fractionation whereby he used a centrifuge to break down cells into their constituent parts. In this manner he was able to identify a certain part of a tumor cell as being the most likely starting point from which a tumor could spread. Further investigation of individual cell components was made easier after 1942, when Claude obtained the use of an electron microscope.

Shortly thereafter, he was able to demonstrate the presence of the Rous sarcoma virus in the cell fragments he had isolated, thus proving that viruses can cause cancer.

In the course of his research with Rous sarcoma, Claude inadvertently pioneered the new field of cell biology. His fractionation process coupled with the use of the electron microscope were groundbreaking techniques that led to many discoveries concerning the components of living cells. Claude himself discovered the endoplasmic reticulum, a network of small, bladder-like cavities that makes up roughly half of the cell membrane. He also clarified the role played by the mitochondria—threadlike bodies in the cytoplasm—in the process whereby cells use oxygen to produce energy. For the role he played as one of the founders of cell biology, Claude was awarded a one-third share of the 1974 Nobel Prize for physiology or medicine. One of the people he shared the prize with was GEORGE E. PALADE, a former assistant of Claude's who perfected the use of the electron microscope in biological research, and the other was the Belgian biochemist Christian de Duve.

In 1949 Claude returned to Belgium to serve as director of the Jules Bordet Institute for Cancer Research at the Free University in Brussels while continuing to be affiliated with Rockefeller. By a special arrangement between the countries, he was permitted to be a citizen of both Belgium and the United States. In 1972 he resigned from both institutions to serve as director of the Catholic University of Louvain's Laboratory of Cellular Biology and Oncology, a position he held for the rest of his career. He died on May 22, 1983, in Brussels.

Further Reading

The Nobel Prize Internet Archive. "Albert Claude." Available online. URL: http://almaz.com/nobel/medicine/1974a.html. Downloaded on March 25, 2005.

Nobelprize.org. "The Nobel Prize in Physiology or Medicine 1974." Available online. URL: http://nobelprize.org/medicine/laureates/1974. Downloaded on January 15, 2004.

Wasson, Tyler, ed. *Nobel Prize Winners.* New York: H. W. Wilson, 1987, pp. 206–208.

Cobb, W. Montague
(William Montague Cobb)
(1904–1990) *physical anthropologist*

W. Montague Cobb demonstrated that racial differences between European Americans and African Americans, at least in terms of their bone structure, are virtually nil. He also put together one of the nation's largest collections of skeletons for purposes of anatomical research.

Cobb was born on October 12, 1904, in Washington, D.C. His father, William, was a printer, and his mother, Alexzine, was a homemaker. After receiving a B.A. in science from Amherst (Mass.) College in 1925, he spent a summer at the Woods Hole Marine Biology Laboratory on Cape Cod. There he met the American biologist ERNEST E. JUST, who convinced him to go to medical school at Howard University in Washington where Just taught. In 1929 Cobb received an M.D. from Howard and went off to Western Reserve University (today Case Western Reserve University) in Cleveland, Ohio, receiving a Ph.D. in physical anthropology in 1932. That same year he joined the Howard faculty as a professor of anatomy, a position he held for more than 40 years. At some point he married Hilda Smith with whom he had two children.

At Western Reserve, Cobb studied under T. Wingate Todd, who had put together the largest privately owned collection of skeletons in the country. The collection proved to be an invaluable tool for studying human anatomy and, upon settling at Howard, Cobb set out to amass his own skeleton collection. Over the years he prepared from cadavers more than 700 skeletons of both genders and from a considerable number of racial and ethnic backgrounds, and he was able to fully document the features of 300 more. In time the Cobb Collection, as it became known, was the third largest skeleton collection in the United States, and it served as an important training tool for Howard's medical students.

Cobb also used his collection as a research tool for studying the growth and development of human bones, especially those that form part of the skull. He demonstrated that the cranium develops quickly and remains stable after birth, but that the facial bones develop slowly and can be modified by environmental conditions such as diet. He also demonstrated that the closure of the cranial suture, the line of junction between two of the cranial bones, does not give any clues as to a skeleton's age, as had been previously believed. His most important contribution, however, was an exhaustive study he undertook in the 1930s comparing the bones of European Americans and African Americans. At the time it was believed that the Caucasian and Negroid races were dissimilar in a number of features, including bone structure, and that this latter difference permitted African Americans to perform better as athletes. Cobb's study proved conclusively that this is not the case, but rather that any differences in bone structures between the two races are virtually indistinguishable. He published his findings in this regard in "Race and Runners," *Journal of Health and Physical Education* (1936).

Cobb served as president of the National Medical Association (NMA), the African-American counterpart to the all-white American Medical Association, and for 28 years he edited the NMA's journal. In 1957 he founded the Imhotep National Conference on Hospital Integration as a way to secure better health care for African Americans (Imhotep was the Egyptian demigod of medicine). He also served a term as president of the American Association of Physical Anthropologists and as vice president of the American Association for the Advancement of Science. He retired from Howard in 1973, although he continued to do research and publish for another 14 years. He died on November 20, 1990, in Washington, D.C.

Further Reading

Hayden, Robert. *Eleven African-American Doctors*, rev. ed. New York: Twenty-First Century Books, 1992, pp. 72–87.

Spangenburg, Ray, and Kit Moser. *African Americans in Science, Math, and Invention*. New York: Facts On File, 2003, pp. 44–46.

Cohen, Stanley

(1922–) *biochemist*

Stanley Cohen was one of the first discoverers of growth factor, biochemical agents that stimulate the growth of cells. In recognition of his scientific contributions, he was awarded a Nobel Prize in 1986.

Cohen was born on November 17, 1922, in Brooklyn, New York. His father, Louis, was a tailor, and his mother, Fannie, was a homemaker. After finishing high school, he entered Brooklyn College and received a B.A. in biology and chemistry in 1943. As an undergraduate, he became interested in cell biology in general and embryonic development in particular, and he pursued this interest while obtaining an M.A. in zoology from Oberlin College in 1945 and a Ph.D. in biochemistry from the University of Michigan in 1948. He then joined the University of Colorado's pediatrics department where he spent the next four years conducting metabolic studies of premature infants. In 1951 he married Olivia Larson with whom he had three children; they later divorced, and in 1981 he married Jan Jordan.

In 1952 Cohen went to the Washington University of St. Louis to conduct postdoctoral research in radioisotope methodology. The following year he was invited to join the research team of Viktor Hamburger, a neuroembryologist at Washington University. Cohen's specific assignment was to help RITA LEVI-MONTALCINI isolate a nerve growth promoting agent she had identified several years earlier. Within three years they discovered that such an agent, now called nerve growth factor (NGF), was produced in abundant quantities by tumors in mice, and Cohen was able to collect and purify a considerable quantity of it. Over the next three years he discovered that snake venom and the salivary glands in male mice also contain large amounts of NGF. By 1959 he and Montalcini had identified the chemical composition of NGF and defined its molecular structure.

The discovery of NGF was the first time that a biochemical agent controlling the growth of cells had been identified and isolated. As a result, other researchers began looking for growth factors that stimulated the growth of other types of cells. By 1986 they had discovered somatomedin, which regulates the growth-promoting effect of growth hormone; platelet derived growth factor (PDGF), which stimulates the growth of cells making up connective tissues and blood vessels; and interleukin-2, which stimulates the growth of white blood cells in the immune system.

Cohen and Levi-Montalcini might have continued working together as a team, as they complemented and got along with each other well. Unfortunately, this was not to be; when Levi-Montalcini was promoted to a professorship in 1959, the same could not be done for Cohen. That same year he reluctantly broke off their partnership to accept a professorship at Vanderbilt University. He continued to experiment with NGF, however, and eventually made another important discovery concerning growth factor.

After injecting newborn mice with NGF extracted from the salivary glands of mice, Cohen discovered that their eyes opened and their teeth erupted several days earlier than normal. This result led him to conclude that the NGF extract contained some other kind of growth factor as well. He named this growth promoting agent epidermal growth factor (EGF) because it stimulated the growth of epithelial cells in skin. As he had done previously with NGF, he was able eventually to isolate and purify a quantity of EGF, as well as to identify its constituent amino acids and molecular structure. Further experimentation with EGF determined that it also stimulated a host of other activities, including the transport of glucose and amino acid to the cells, the activation of the synthesis of protein and DNA, and the replication of cells. EGF was also found to stimulate the growth of cells in the liver, thyroid, ovaries, pituitary glands, and the vascular system, as well as fibroblasts, which contribute to the formation of connective tissue fibers. In addition, he discovered that EGF promotes the healing of wounds to the epithelial cells in the skin and cornea.

By shedding light on the way healthy cells grow, Cohen contributed indirectly to the increase of knowledge concerning the behavior of cancer cells. Armed with his discoveries, other researchers have been able to search for clues as to why cancerous cells behave the way they do. One result of this line of inquiry was the discovery of oncogenes, which play a role in the transformation of cells.

For his work with growth factor in general and EGF in particular, Cohen received a number of awards. The biggest was the 1986 Nobel Prize in physiology or medicine, which he shared with Levi-Montalcini. Other major awards include election to the National Academy of Sciences in 1980 and the National Medal of Science in 1986. In 2000 Cohen retired from Vanderbilt to his home in Nashville, Tennessee.

Stanley Cohen discovered several of the biochemical compounds that cause cells to grow. *(Courtesy of Stanley Cohen)*

Further Reading

The Nobel Prize Internet Archive. "Stanley Cohen." Available online. URL: http://almaz.com/nobel/medicine/1986a.html. Downloaded on March 25, 2005.

Nobelprize.org. "The Nobel Prize in Physiology or Medicine 1986." Available online. URL: http://nobelprize.org/medicine/laureates/1986. Downloaded on August 31, 2003.

Wasson, Tyler, ed. *Nobel Prize Winners.* New York: H. W. Wilson, 1987, pp. 210–212.

Colwell, Rita R.
(Rita Rossi, Rita Rossi Colwell)
(1934–) *microbiologist*

Rita R. Colwell is a leading authority in marine bacteriology. Her research helped control the outbreak of cholera epidemics, and it also stimulated biotechnology researchers to pay more attention to marine bacteria.

Colwell was born Rita Rossi on November 23, 1934, in Beverly, Massachusetts. Her father, Louis, owned a construction company, and her mother, Louise, was a homemaker. She received a B.S. in bacteriology and an M.S. in genetics from Purdue University in 1956 and 1958, respectively, and a Ph.D. in oceanography from the University of Washington in 1961. After two years as a National Research Council fellow, in 1963 she joined the faculty at Georgetown University, leaving in 1972 to become a professor of microbiology at the University of Maryland. In 1956 she married Jack Colwell with whom she had two children.

Colwell's research focused on marine bacteriology. Her doctoral dissertation studied marine bacteria commensals, bacteria that live in or on marine animals without affecting them in any way, a project that led to the scientific classification of marine bacteria. At Georgetown she discovered that cholera bacteria are native to the Chesapeake Bay and similar estuaries, and that they maintain themselves in a dormant state by existing as commensals in and on marine crustaceans known as copepods. She theorized that increases in sea temperatures lead to outbreaks of cholera, as warmer waters foster the growth of the phytoplankton on which copepods feed, and thus to an increase in the number of cholera bacteria in the water. Further research showed that cholera outbreaks in Bangladesh are indeed related to climatic conditions that foster the growth of phytoplankton, and she related a cholera outbreak in Peru in 1991 to the onset of El Niño, an oceanic phenomenon occurring every several years or so off the tropical west coast of South America that features unusually warm ocean currents. Perhaps most importantly, she helped develop a simple method for eliminating cholera from drinking water by straining it through sari cloth, a material that is readily

Rita Colwell pioneered the use of marine bacteria in biotechnology. *(Courtesy of National Science Foundation; photo by Sam Kittner)*

available in even the poorest communities in Bangladesh. Her work concerning the connection between cholera and climate has spurred scientists to explore further the role played by climate in the spread of infectious diseases.

In 1983 Colwell began urging biotechnologists to pay more attention to marine bacteria and viruses. Her own research explored the possibility of cleaning up oil spills by developing petroleum-eating strains of certain marine bacteria. In 1985 she helped create the University of Maryland Biotechnology Institute and founded its Center of Marine Biotechnology in Baltimore; she later served as the institute's president.

In 1998 Colwell was named director of the National Science Foundation (NSF) in Arlington, Virginia, the U.S. government agency responsible for funding basic scientific and engineering research. In this capacity, she worked to develop programs for information sharing in a field that she calls "biocomplexity," multidisciplinary research designed to find other cross-disciplinary connections such as the cholera-climate one. In 2003 she left NSF to become chair of Canon US Life Sciences.

Colwell's published work includes *Estuarine Microbial Ecology* (1973), *Biotechnology of Marine Polysaccharides* (1985), and *Biomolecular Data: A Resource in Transition* (1989). Her many honors include election to the National Academy of Sciences and terms as president of the American Association for the Advancement of Science, the American Society for Microbiology, and the International Union for Microbiological Societies.

Further Reading

"Colwell, Rita R." *Current Biography Yearbook 1999.* New York: H. W. Wilson, 1999, pp. 148–152.

National Science Foundation, Office of Legislative and Public Affairs. "Dr. Rita R. Colwell's Biography." Available online. URL: http://www.nsf.gov/od/lpa/forum/colwell/rrcbio.htm. Downloaded on May 21, 2004.

Compton, Arthur H.
(Arthur Holly Compton)
(1892–1962) *physicist*

Arthur H. Compton is best remembered for discovering the Compton effect, a physical phenomenon that explains the relationship between X-rays and electrons. His discovery forced physicists to change the way they think about the relationship between energy and matter, and won him a share of the 1927 Nobel Prize in physics.

Compton was born on September 10, 1892, in Wooster, Ohio. His father, Elias, was a minister and college professor, and his mother, Otelia, was a homemaker. After receiving a B.S. from the College of Wooster in 1913, he entered Princeton University and received a Ph.D. in physics in 1916. That same year he married Betty McCloskey with whom he had two children. After teaching for a year at the University of Minnesota, in 1917 he went to work for the Westinghouse Lamp Company in Pittsburgh, Pennsylvania, as a research engineer.

Two years later he was off to Cambridge University in England to study experimental physics on a grant from the National Research Council. In 1920 he returned to the United States to become head of the department of physics at Washington University in St. Louis, Missouri.

Compton's primary research interest involved the interaction between electrons and X-rays, a form of electromagnetic radiation that is capable of penetrating solids. His doctoral dissertation examined the scattering of X-rays reflected from crystals as a means of determining the distribution of electrons in the crystals. He continued this line of investigation at Minnesota, where he reflected X-rays from a magnetite crystal that was exposed intermittently to an external magnetic field. He concluded from this experiment that electrons, and not atoms as a whole, carry the magnetic charge within an atom. Experiments conducted while he was with Westinghouse led him to conclude that the scattering of X-rays by a reflecting substance can best be explained by the presence of huge ring-shaped electrons in that substance. During his two years at Cambridge, he discovered that gamma rays, another form of penetrating radiation, behave much the same as X-rays when they are reflected from a substance. Meanwhile, he remained puzzled by the fact that X-rays are absorbed by reflecting substances to a lesser degree than the theories of classical mechanics predicted.

Upon arriving at Washington University, Compton began to experiment with X-rays in earnest by using a special type of spectrometer to make exact measurements of their wavelengths. By 1922 he had discovered that X-rays scattered by carbon experience an increase in their wavelengths and that this increase was directly proportional to the angle at which they were scattered. This discovery forced Compton to conclude that the nature of X-rays was completely different from what he had supposed it to be. He now theorized that X-rays, as well as other forms of radiation such as gamma rays, consisted of tiny packets of electromagnetic energy. These packets, which he named photons, have energy and momentum the same as subatomic particles such as electrons, but they also possess the characteristics of light, such as frequency and wavelength. He showed that the amount of energy in a photon is directly proportional to its frequency and inversely proportional to its wavelength. Most importantly, he demonstrated that when a photon collides with an electron, it transfers some of its energy and momentum to the electron. The result is the creation of a photon with less energy and momentum, which then scatters at an angle determined by the amount of energy it lost in the collision. He published his findings in 1923, and the process of energy and momentum loss he described became known as the Compton effect. A more thorough explanation of the Compton effect appeared in his book *X-Rays and Electrons* (1926).

The discovery of the Compton effect was a major step in the development of modern physics. Because it proved that energy and matter share some of the same characteristics, the Compton effect forced physicists to reconsider the relationship between energy and matter. Thus it contributed to the development of quantum mechanics, by which it is understood that the laws of classical physics do not always apply to subatomic particles. In recognition of his groundbreaking development, in 1927 Compton was awarded a share of the Nobel Prize in physics.

Compton left Washington University in 1923 to join the faculty of the University of Chicago. He continued to study the interaction between X-rays and electrons until 1931, when he became interested in cosmic rays, radiation of extremely high penetrating power that originates in outer space. That same year he organized a world survey of cosmic rays, in which expeditions equipped with identical cosmic-ray detectors were dispatched to the four corners of the globe. By 1934 these expeditions had gathered enough evidence to demonstrate that cosmic rays, unlike X-rays and gamma rays, consist of charged particles, not photons.

During World War II, Compton directed the Manhattan Project's Metallurgical Laboratory in Chicago; in 1942 the world's first extensive nuclear chain reaction took place there, thus making possible the construction of the atomic bomb. After the war, he returned to Washington University as chancellor, but he resigned this position in 1953 to teach natural philosophy. He died on March 15, 1962, in Berkeley, California.

Further Reading

Nobelprize.org. "The Nobel Prize in Physics 1927." Available online. URL: http://nobelprize.org/physics/laureates/1927. Downloaded on January 7, 2004.

Stuewer, Roger H. *The Compton Effect: Turning Point in Physics.* New York: Science History Publications, 1975.

Wasson, Tyler, ed. *Nobel Prize Winners.* New York: H. W. Wilson, 1987, pp. 212–215.

Cooper, Leon N.
(Leon Neil Cooper)
(1930–) *physicist*

Leon N. Cooper shared a Nobel Prize for his contributions to the BCS theory, which explains superconductivity. He also contributed to the BCM theory, which explains the physical mechanisms involved with human learning.

Cooper was born on February 28, 1930, in New York City. He studied physics at Columbia University, receiving an A.B. in 1951, an A.M. in 1953, and a Ph.D. in 1954. After an additional year at Columbia as a National Science Foundation fellow and a member of the Institute for Advanced Study, he became a research associate at the University of Illinois in Urbana. In 1969 he married Kay Allard with whom he had two children.

At Illinois, Cooper collaborated with JOHN BARDEEN in the study of superconductivity, the ability of certain metals to lose all resistance to electron flow in extreme low-temperature conditions. Bardeen had been studying superconductivity for several years, and by 1955 he had concluded that it occurs because of some sort of interaction that takes place between the electrons in the metal atoms and the electrons flowing through the metal, or superconductor. This conclusion met with much skepticism, however, because it was generally believed that electrons repel each other, so such an interaction as Bardeen proposed seemed impossible. By 1956 Cooper, Bardeen, and J. ROBERT SCHRIEFFER, one of Bardeen's graduate students, had proved that Bardeen's conclusion was essentially correct.

Cooper's contribution to the trio's success involved the discovery of what is now called Cooper pairs. In a Cooper pair, one electron in the superconductor forms a bond with an electron flowing through the superconductor. As scores of Cooper pairs are created, the Cooper pairs interact with other pairs in such a way that the superconductor's resistance to electron flow is reduced to zero. Schrieffer developed a mathematical model to explain the behavior of Cooper pairs, and in 1957 the three published the BCS theory, the first satisfactory theory of superconductivity. Almost 50 years later, the BCS theory continues to inform all research involving superconductors. Superconductivity promises to revolutionize the way electricity is transmitted and applied in a number of electronic applications, and for helping to explain how superconductivity works, Cooper, Bardeen, and Schrieffer were each awarded a one-third share of the 1972 Nobel Prize in physics.

In 1958 Cooper became a professor of physics at Ohio State University, but he left the following year for a similar position at Brown University in Providence, Rhode Island. During the 1960s he became increasingly interested in applying physics to problems of neuroscience, and in 1973 he was named the founding director of Brown's Center for Neural Science. Under his direction, the center focused on developing an understanding of memory and other brain functions, and in forming a scientific explanation for how the human mind operates. In 1982 Cooper and two Brown colleagues, Elie Bienenstock and Paul Munro, developed the BCM theory of visual cortical plasticity. This theory explains learning in terms of physical modifications to the synaptic junctions, or connections, between neurons, the nerve cells through which sensory impulses travel to the brain.

Cooper remained at Brown for the rest of his career. In addition to his duties there, however, he also cofounded and cochaired Nestor, Inc., a consulting firm that applies neural network systems to such things as pattern recognition and risk assessment for commercial and military clients. His publications include *Physics: Structure and Meaning* (1992), *How We Learn, How We Remember: Toward an Understanding of Brain and Neural Systems* (1995), and *Theory of Cortical Plasticity* (2004). His honors include election to the National Academy of Sciences and the American Academy of Arts and Sciences.

Further Reading

Brown University. "Leon N. Cooper." Available online. URL: http://biomed.brown.edu/Faculty/C/Cooper. html. Downloaded on March 25, 2005.

Nobelprize.org. "The Nobel Prize in Physics 1972." Available online. URL: http://nobelprize.org/physics/ laureates/1972. Downloaded on September 21, 2004.

Wasson, Tyler, ed. *Nobel Prize Winners.* New York: H. W. Wilson, 1987, pp. 215–216.

Corey, Elias J.
(Elias James Corey, William James Corey)
(1928–) *chemist*

Elias J. Corey developed retrosynthesis, a method for designing synthetic chemical reactions that made such reactions much more effective and successful. For this contribution, he was awarded the 1990 Nobel Prize in chemistry.

Corey was born William James Corey on July 12, 1928, in Methuen, Massachusetts. His father, Elias, was a businessman, and his mother, Fatina, was a homemaker. When he was 18 months old his father died, and his mother renamed him Elias in his father's memory. At age 16 he finished high school and entered the Massachusetts Institute of Technology, receiving a B.A. in chemistry in 1947 and a Ph.D. in organic chemistry in 1951. He then joined the faculty at the University of Illinois at Urbana-Champaign where he remained for eight years.

Corey's research ranged from physical chemistry to biochemistry. His earliest work explored the relationship between molecular orbital theory, the behavior of a molecule's electrons, and stereochemistry, the study of the three-dimensional arrangement of a molecule's elemental parts and functional groups. This work led him to experiment with various methods for synthesizing biochemical compounds, which at the time was still something of an art. Most biochemists of the day set out to synthesize a compound by relying primarily on intuition rather than detailed planning, and when they achieved success they were often unable to explain exactly why the experiment had worked. Frustrated by what seemed to him to be a less-than-scientific method, Corey began thinking about how to impose order on the chaos that was biochemical synthesis, so that he could establish fundamental guidelines and principles that could be learned and used by any reasonably competent chemist.

In 1957, while on sabbatical leave at Harvard University, Corey began developing the techniques of what became known as retrosynthesis. Rather than mixing chemicals together to see what happens next, he began with a diagram of the biomolecule he intended to synthesize. Then, working backward, he sketched out the simpler molecules from which the finished product could best be made, continuing in this manner until he had traced his way back to a collection of elements or compounds that were inexpensive and readily available. Thus, he had developed a method for planning a synthetic reaction that promised to revolutionize research in organic synthesis. He showed his first sketches, a plan for synthesizing longifolene, an essential oil derived from juniper trees, to

Elias Corey developed a very useful method for designing synthetic chemical reactions. *(Courtesy of Elias J. Corey)*

Harvard's R. B. WOODWARD, a world-renowned master of organic synthesis because of his innate ability to design an experiment. Woodward encouraged Corey to continue developing his innovative approach to organic synthesis, and in 1959 Woodward offered Corey a position on the Harvard faculty, which Corey accepted.

Once settled at Harvard, Corey used retrosynthesis to synthesize longifolene, and by 1961, the year he married Claire Higham with whom he had three children, he had succeeded. His next step was to synthesize the prostaglandins, a group of hormone-like biomolecules that regulate smooth-muscle contraction, blood pressure, and blood clotting, among other things. Because of their potency, prostaglandins occur at extremely low levels of concentration, and so they are very difficult to obtain by natural means. Prostaglandins are fatty acid derivatives that contain a 5-carbon ring, so their synthesis posed a bit of a challenge. Nevertheless, using retrosynthesis, by 1968 Corey had synthesized five different prostaglandins from some basic carbon compounds. Thereafter he used retrosynthesis to synthesize other biomolecules such as enzymes and non-prostaglandin fatty acid derivatives as well as several organometallic compounds, molecules that contain atoms of carbon bonded to those of metals. Altogether, he developed or improved existing methods for synthesizing approximately 100 compounds, many of them rare substances available only in trace quantities from natural sources. Perhaps most important, he developed and computerized step-by-step rules and "logic trees" so that graduate students could be taught to design sophisticated synthetic reactions in just three months. He published much of his work concerning retrosynthesis in *The Logic of Chemical Synthesis* (1989).

By systematizing methods for designing and carrying out synthesis reactions that the master chemists such as Woodward understood intuitively, Corey made a major contribution to the "art" of organic synthesis. This contribution was recognized in 1990 when he was awarded the Nobel Prize in chemistry for his methods as much as for what he had discovered with them.

Corey remained at Harvard for the rest of his career. He continued to experiment with organic and bio-organic chemistry, and one of his later projects involved the design and development of molecular robots, sophisticated enzyme-like catalysts for synthetic organic reactions. His many honors include election to the National Academy of Sciences and the American Academy of Arts and Sciences.

Further Reading

Harvard University. "Elias J. Corey." Available online. URL: http://www.chem.harvard.edu/faculty/corey. html. Downloaded on March 25, 2005.

McMurray, Emily J., ed. *Notable Twentieth-Century Scientists*. Detroit: Gale Research, 1995, pp. 399–400.

Nobelprize.org. "The Nobel Prize in Chemistry 1990." Available online. URL: http://nobelprize.org/chemistry/laureates/1990. Downloaded on August 14, 2004.

Cori, Carl F.
(Carl Ferdinand Cori)
(1896–1984) *biochemist*

Carl F. Cori and his wife GERTY T. CORI devoted themselves to identifying the carbohydrate cycle, the process by which the body breaks down and uses carbohydrates. For describing in detail how this cycle, known today as the Cori cycle, operates, he was awarded a share of the 1947 Nobel Prize in physiology or medicine.

Cori was born on December 5, 1896, in Prague, then a part of Austria-Hungary. His father, Carl, was a physician, and his mother, Martha, was a homemaker. As a boy he moved with his family to Trieste after his father was appointed director of the Marine Biological Station there. In 1914 the family returned to Prague, where he entered the Carl Ferdinand Medical School of Prague's German University. He was drafted into the Austrian army that same year and spent most of World War I in its medical corps. In 1918 he resumed his medical studies, and two years later he received an M.D. and married Gerty T. Radnitz with whom he had one child. After graduation he spent a year doing postdoctoral research at the University of Vienna, followed by a year as an assistant in pharmacology at the University of Graz.

As a result of Austria-Hungary's defeat in World War I, funding for medical research within its former borders became extremely scarce. By 1922 Cori realized that in order to conduct any sort of meaningful research, he would have to leave the country. That same year he was offered a position doing cancer research for the New York State Institute for the Study of Malignant Diseases (today the Roswell Park Memorial Institute) in Buffalo. That same year he and his wife emigrated to the United States. In 1928 he became a naturalized citizen. Three years later he became head of the pharmacology department at the Washington University School of Medicine in St. Louis, Missouri. In 1942 he was named professor of biochemistry.

Throughout his career, Cori collaborated with his wife Gerty, who served officially as his research assistant. The two developed a close working relationship and complemented each other extremely well. Generally speaking, Carl developed the couple's working hypotheses and theories, while Gerty designed experiments to either prove or disprove the theories and then oversaw the conduct of the experiments.

The Coris were primarily interested in discovering how carbohydrates are metabolized, or broken down and used, by the body. In Buffalo they had been assigned to find out how cancerous tumors metabolize carbohydrates, and their research made them curious as to how the process works in healthy cells. In their spare time, they began investigating how the body metabolizes glucose, a simple sugar that circulates freely in the bloodstream and is the source of energy for cell function. By 1929 they had discovered that glucose is stored in muscles as glycogen; when muscles are engaged in activity, the glycogen is broken down into glucose. They also found out that glucose is converted into glycogen in the liver, where it is also stored.

In 1936 the Coris discovered that glycogen passes through two intermediate stages on its way to becoming glucose. In the first stage, glycogen is converted into a substance called glucose-1-phosphate, better known today as the Cori ester. In the second stage, the Cori ester is metabolized into glucose-6-phosphate, also known as the Robison ester. The final stage involves the metabolization of the Robison ester into glucose. Moreover, they discovered that the cycle works in reverse when glucose is being converted into glycogen. Experiments designed to describe more fully the mechanism by which these stages took place showed that the second stage, the conversion of the Cori ester into the Robison ester, is catalyzed by an enzyme called phosphoglucomutase. In 1944 they discovered that the catalyst for the first stage, the conversion of glycogen into the Cori ester, was an enzyme known as phosphorylase.

At this point the Coris were able to describe the entire carbohydrate cycle. They had also discovered that the cycle is aided by the presence of the hormone epinephrine in the bloodstream, but when insulin, another hormone, is present instead, the cycle is retarded because glucose is removed from the bloodstream. Their complete description of the carbohydrate cycle, known today as the Cori cycle, was an important contribution to a fuller understanding of how enzymes and hormones regulate the body's biochemical processes, and in 1947 the Coris were awarded the Nobel Prize in physiology or medicine. They shared the prize with the Argentine physiologist Bernardo Houssay, whose research dovetailed with much of their own. Carl Cori received a number of other honors as well, including election to the National Academy of Sciences.

Carl and Gerty Cori continued to collaborate until her death in 1957. Three years later Cori married Anne Fitz-Gerald Jones. He continued to experiment with enzymes as a catalyst of biochemical processes until 1966, when he retired from the university and moved to Cambridge, Massachusetts. For a number of years thereafter, he conducted research in genetics at Massachusetts General Hospital. He died on October 20, 1984, in Cambridge.

Further Reading

Cohn, Mildred. "Carl Ferdinand Cori," National Academy of Sciences, *Biographical Memoirs* 61 (1992): pp. 79–109.

Nobelprize.org. "The Nobel Prize in Physiology or Medicine 1947." Available online. URL: http://nobelprize.org/medicine/laureates/1947. Downloaded on August 17, 2003.

Wasson, Tyler, ed. *Nobel Prize Winners*. New York: H. W. Wilson, 1987, pp. 216–218.

Cori, Gerty T.
(Gerty Theresa Radnitz, Gerty Theresa Radnitz Cori)
(1896–1957) *biochemist*

Gerty T. Cori and her husband, CARL F. CORI, led a research team that discovered the complete cycle by which carbohydrates are broken down, used, and stored in the body. For this discovery, she was awarded a share of the 1947 Nobel Prize in physiology or medicine.

Cori was born Gerty Theresa Radnitz on August 15, 1896, in Prague, then a part of Austria-Hungary. Her father, Otto, was a businessman, and her mother, Martha, was a homemaker. After finishing her secondary education, in 1914 she entered the Carl Ferdinand Medical School of the German University of Prague. In 1920 she received an M.D. and married Carl F. Cori with whom she had one child. After graduation she joined the staff of the Karolinen Children's Hospital in Vienna, Austria, where she conducted research on rare medical conditions affecting children.

Austria-Hungary was destroyed by World War I, and the effort to rebuild the nations that resulted from its breakup left little money for medical research. In 1922 Cori's husband, whose specialty was metabolic research, accepted an offer to join the New York State Institute for the Study of Malignant Diseases (today the Roswell Park Memorial Institute) in Buffalo. That same year she emigrated with her husband to the United States. Upon reaching Buffalo, she was able to prevail upon the director of the institute to give her a position as her husband's research assistant, despite a state rule prohibiting a married couple from working together. In 1928 she became a naturalized citizen. Three years later she and her husband became affiliated with the Washington University School of Medicine in St. Louis, Missouri, he as head of the pharmacology department and she as his research assistant. In 1944 she was elevated to associate professor, and three years later she was named a professor of biochemistry.

Despite the discrepancy in their official titles, positions, and pay for most of their careers, Gerty Cori was the equal of her husband as a researcher. Each possessed skills that complemented those of the other. While Carl's specialty was developing theories and hypotheses, Gerty's specialty was designing and conducting the experiments that either proved or disproved Carl's ideas.

The focus of the Coris' joint research was the way animals metabolize, or break down and use, carbohydrates. They began following this line of inquiry in Buffalo when they were assigned to experiment with the way cancerous tumors use carbohydrates. This led them to wonder how the body metabolizes glucose, a simple sugar that circulates freely in the bloodstream and is the source of energy for cell function. By 1929 they had discovered that the liver transforms glucose into glycogen, the form in which carbohydrate energy is stored in muscle, and that when the muscles go to perform a given task, they break down the glycogen into glucose. In time this process, and all the intermediate stages that compose it, would become known as the Cori cycle.

Further experimentation led the Coris to discover in 1936 what became known as the Cori ester. In essence, this ester, also known as glucose-1-phosphate, was the first stage through which glycogen passes on its way to becoming glucose as well as the last stage through which glucose passes on its way to becoming glycogen. At the same time, they discovered the second stage of the cycle, the metabolization of the Cori ester into glucose-6-phosphate, also known as the Robison ester, and that this second stage is catalyzed by the enzyme phosphoglucomutase. In 1944 they discovered that the conversion of glycogen into the Cori ester was catalyzed by an enzyme known as phosphorylase.

At this point the Coris were able to describe the entire Cori cycle with confidence. Glycogen is converted into the Cori ester, which is converted into the Robison ester, which is converted into glucose, which provides energy for the muscles; once the muscles have done their work, any leftover glucose is reconverted into glycogen in the liver, where it is also stored. They had also discovered that insulin facilitates the conversion of glucose into glycogen, and that epinephrine retards the conversion. Their complete description of the Cori cycle

was so important that in 1947, just three years after they published their complete findings, the Coris were awarded the Nobel Prize in physiology or medicine. They shared the prize with the Argentine physiologist Bernardo Houssay, who had conducted similar research at a similar time. She received a number of other honors as well, including election to the National Academy of Sciences.

During the last 10 years of her life, Cori returned to one of her first research interests, rare medical conditions affecting children. She discovered that several rare inherited diseases are caused by the absence of an enzyme that is vital to the Cori cycle. Without this enzyme, the body cannot break down glycogen, and it is stored in the liver and other organs, thus causing death.

In 1947 Cori was diagnosed with anemia. It was later discovered to be caused by an incurable disease of the bone marrow. Despite her condition, she continued to conduct research until her death on October 26, 1957, in St. Louis.

Further Reading

Bailey, Martha J. *American Women in Science: A Biographical Dictionary.* Santa Barbara, Calif.: ABC-CLIO, 1994, pp. 70–71.

Nobelprize.org. "The Nobel Prize in Physiology or Medicine 1947." Available online. URL: http://nobelprize.org/medicine/laureates/1947. Downloaded on August 17, 2003.

Wasson, Tyler, ed. *Nobel Prize Winners.* New York: H. W. Wilson, 1987, pp. 218–220.

Yount, Lisa. *A to Z of Women in Science and Math.* New York: Facts On File, 1999, pp. 40–42.

Cormack, Allan M.
(Allan MacLeod Cormack)
(1924–1998) *physicist*

Allan M. Cormack was one of the codevelopers of CAT scanning, whereby an X-ray beam scans a cross section of the body to develop a three-dimensional picture of that cross section. For his role in this development, he was awarded a share of the 1979 Nobel Prize in physiology or medicine. Incidentally, he is one of a few winners of the physiology/medicine Nobel Prize who have not held an M.D.

Cormack was born on February 23, 1924, in Johannesburg, South Africa. His father, George, was an engineer, and his mother, Amelia, was a teacher. As a boy he moved frequently with his family, eventually settling in Cape Town around 1936. He entered the University of Cape Town with the intention of studying engineering but changed his major to physics after two years, receiving a B.S. in 1944 and an M.S. in crystallography in 1945. He spent the next five years as a research student in England at Cambridge University's Cavendish Laboratory, returning to the University of Cape Town to teach physics in 1950. Six years later he emigrated to the United States; a year as a research fellow at Harvard University was followed by an offer to teach physics at Tufts University in Medford, Massachusetts, where he remained for the rest of his career. In 1950 he married Barbara Seavey with whom he had three children, and in 1966 he became a naturalized U.S. citizen.

Cormack's primary research interest was particle physics, particularly the scattering patterns of nucleons, and he came to the United States to have access to a cyclotron, something which did not exist in South Africa at the time. Nevertheless, while in South Africa he had spent some time as the resident medical physicist in the radiology department at Cape Town's Groote Schuur Hospital. This experience interested him in the problems associated with using radiation as a medical technique, particularly in terms of calculating radiation dosages for cancer therapy. Cormack realized immediately that any computation of such dosages should take into consideration the density of the tissue through which the radiation must pass, but the existing formulas did not take this important factor into account. This discovery led him to consider the other disadvantages of X-ray imaging, namely, that X-rays cannot distinguish between differences in the density of the various soft tissues, and that they reduce a three-dimensional object into a two-dimensional picture.

Cormack knew that tomography, X-ray photography of a selected plane in an object, was being used effectively in astronomy and oceanography, and he began to experiment with ways to apply tomography to medicine. By 1964 he had developed the mathematical and physical calculations

for computerized axial tomography (CAT) by using a simple desktop calculator. He then hooked up the calculator to an X-ray machine, which he used to develop accurate, three-dimensional cross sections of a variety of irregularly shaped objects from pennies to pork chops. He published his work in two articles in the *Journal of Applied Physics* in 1963 and 1964, but the articles received little attention, mostly because the computers of the day were incapable of completing in a timely fashion the vast number of calculations that a CAT scan requires. Not until 1972, when British engineer Godfrey Hounsfield developed a full-blown computerized system capable of implementing CAT scanning, did Cormack's work receive the proper attention it deserved.

Today CAT scans are used to examine all of the organ systems of the body. CAT scanning is particularly important, however, as a tool for diagnosing neurological disorders, as it permits physicians to forgo time-consuming and painful testing while making their diagnoses with greater certainty and precision. Because of the revolutionary effects CAT scanning promised to have on the medical profession, Cormack was awarded a half share of the 1979 Nobel Prize in physiology or medicine; his corecipient was Hounsfield.

Cormack taught physics at Tufts until his retirement in 1995. His other honors include the National Medal of Science and election to the National Academy of Sciences. He died on May 7, 1998, in Winchester, Massachusetts.

Further Reading

Nobelprize.org. "The Nobel Prize in Physiology or Medicine 1979." Available online. URL: http://nobelprize. org/medicine/laureates/1979. Downloaded on June 27, 2004.

Wasson, Tyler, ed. *Nobel Prize Winners.* New York: H. W. Wilson, 1987, pp. 220–222.

Cornell, Eric A.
(Eric Allin Cornell)
(1961–) *physicist*

Eric A. Cornell was one of the first developers of Bose-Einstein condensates, an unusual state of

Eric Cornell (above) and Carl Wieman demonstrated the existence of Bose-Einstein condensates, a state of matter wherein atoms behave like light waves rather than particles. *(Courtesy of Eric A. Cornell)*

matter in which atoms behave less like particles of matter and more like waves of light. For this development, he was awarded a share of the 2001 Nobel Prize in physics.

Cornell was born in 1961 in Palo Alto, California. His father, Allin, was a professor of civil engineering, and his mother, Elizabeth, was a high school teacher. Between his junior and senior years in high school, he moved with his family to San Francisco. As an undergraduate at Stanford University, where he received a B.S. in physics in 1985, he became interested in low-temperature physics, the study of what happens to matter at temperatures just above absolute zero. He continued with this interest at the Massachusetts Institute of Technology, where he received an M.S. and a Ph.D. in physics in 1985 and 1990, respectively.

In 1990 Cornell obtained a postdoctoral position with CARL E. WIEMAN at the Joint Institute for Laboratory Astrophysics (today known officially as JILA), a joint institute of the University of Colorado at Boulder and the National Institute of Standards and Technology. Wieman's primary research involved parity violation, or how the weak interaction of radioactive decay disrupts the symmetry of the wave function of subatomic particles, but he was also interested in laser cooling and trapping. Together, Cornell and Wieman embarked on an ambitious program to use laser cooling and trapping to develop Bose-Einstein condensates (BEC), a state of matter that exists only at temperatures near absolute zero and in which atoms merge into a single wavelike entity. The existence of BEC had been postulated in the 1920s by the world-renowned physicists ALBERT EINSTEIN and Satyendra Nath Bose. All attempts to develop them, however, had failed because no means existed to chill molecules to a sufficiently low temperature.

Cornell and Wieman spent the next five years solving the various problems connected with attaining temperatures of within one-millionth of a degree above absolute zero, the temperature at which BEC were supposed to develop. They solved the first problem, that of supercooling their sample of rubidium atoms in a dilute gas, by adapting a technique known as evaporative cooling. This technique was originally developed by MIT's Harold Hess, and it involves removing the fastest moving, or the "hottest," atoms from the sample while retaining the coldest ones. They solved the second problem, keeping the coldest atoms in the sample, by subjecting the sample to the effects of a rotating magnetic field. Finally, in 1995, they succeeded in supercooling about 2,000 atoms of rubidium gas, after which the atoms began behaving as if they were one gigantic atom. Further experiments by other researchers showed that BEC actually behaves more like a collection of photons, the packets of light energy that compose a beam of light, a finding that suggests that at extremely low temperatures matter and energy become interchangeable.

The development of BEC shed new light on the ability of matter to behave as if it were light. This development also promised to have many practical applications, especially for so-called quantum computers, futuristic computers that would operate with unimaginable speed. For developing BEC, Cornell and Wieman were each awarded a one-third share of the 2001 Nobel Prize in physics; their corecipient was the German physicist Wolfgang Ketterle. In 1995 Cornell married Celeste Landry with whom he had two children.

Further Reading

Glanz, James. "3 Researchers Based in U.S. Win Nobel Prize in Physics," *New York Times,* October 10, 2001, p. A14.

Nobelprize.org. "The Nobel Prize in Physics 2001." Available online. URL: http://nobelprize.org/physics/laureates/2001. Downloaded on September 4, 2004.

Cournand, André F.
(André Frédéric Cournand)
(1895–1988) *physician*

André F. Cournand pioneered the use of the catheter as a means of studying the human heart. For his work in this regard, he was awarded a shared Nobel Prize in physiology or medicine.

Cournand was born on September 24, 1895, in Paris, France. His father, Jules, was a dentist, and his mother, Marguérite, was a homemaker. He attended the Sorbonne, where he received a B.A. in 1913 and a diploma in physics, chemistry, and biology in 1914. After a year at the University of Paris Medical School, he joined the French army and served as a battalion surgeon during World War I, during which he was gassed, wounded, and awarded the Croix de Guerre. He returned to medical school after the war and received an M.D. in 1930. He then moved to the United States and became a resident at New York City's Bellevue Hospital. Four years later he joined the faculty of Columbia University's College of Physicians and Surgeons while continuing his duties at Bellevue. He remained at Bellevue and Columbia for the rest of his career, performing most of his experiments at the hospital's cardiopulmonary laboratory. In 1924 he married Sybille Blumer with whom he had four children. She died in 1959, and four years later he married Ruth Fabian; she died in 1973, and two years later he married Beatrice Berle. He became a U.S. citizen in 1941.

At first, Cournand's work at Bellevue involved studying tuberculosis, at the time a dreaded lung disease. In 1931 he and DICKINSON W. RICHARDS began collaborating on a study of the lungs, but they quickly discovered that they first needed to know much more about the heart and the circulatory system. In 1936, as part of their refocused efforts, Cournand went to Paris to learn more about catheterizing the heart. This technique had been invented in 1929 by German physician Werner Forssmann, who had inserted a catheter, a small tube, into his own heart via a vein at his right elbow. Forssmann had hoped that catheterization might offer a means of injecting drugs directly into the circulatory system for a faster, more direct effect, but Cournand believed that Forssmann's technique could be adapted for use as an effective way to learn more about the heart and the lungs. Upon returning to Bellevue, Cournand and Richards began inserting catheters into the hearts of laboratory animals without discovering any harmful side effects of the technique. Eventually, they learned how to insert a catheter all the way through the heart and into the lungs, in the process learning much about the operation of both organs.

In the early 1940s Cournand and Richards began experimenting with heart catheterization on humans. Eventually they were able to use the catheter to measure blood pressure and volume in the human heart, something that could be done only indirectly before. They also discovered how various organs are affected adversely when the volume of circulating blood is reduced due to certain malfunctions of the heart stemming from congenital heart disease, and how to reverse these effects by increasing volume via surgery and other therapeutic methods. In time, their work led to the use of heart catheterization as a means of diagnosing and treating virtually every kind of heart disease and condition. In 1956 Cournand, Richards, and Forssmann were awarded equal shares of the Nobel Prize in physiology or medicine.

Cournand's other honors include election to the National Academy of Sciences and being awarded the gold medals of the national medical academies of Belgium and France. He retired from Columbia and Bellevue in 1964 but continued to collaborate with Richards until 1973, when Richards died. Cournand died on February 19, 1988, in Great Barrington, Massachusetts.

Further Reading

Cournand, André F., with Michael Meyer. *From Roots— to Late Budding: The Intellectual Adventures of a Medical Scientist.* New York: Gardner Press, 1986.

Nobelprize.org. "The Nobel Prize in Physiology or Medicine 1956." Available online. URL: http://nobelprize. org/medicine/laureates/1956. Downloaded on January 10, 2004.

Wasson, Tyler, ed. *Nobel Prize Winners.* New York: H. W. Wilson, 1987, pp. 226–228.

Cowings, Patricia S.
(Patricia Suzanne Cowings)
(1948–) *psychophysiologist*

Patricia S. Cowings developed the Autogenic Feedback Training Exercise (AFTE) as a means of helping astronauts cope with space sickness. AFTE was later modified into effective methods for helping airplane pilots cope with motion sickness and for helping cancer patients cope with chemotherapy treatment.

Cowings was born on December 15, 1948, in New York City. Her father, Albert, owned a grocery store, and her mother, Sadie, was a teacher. After receiving a B.A. in psychology from the State University of New York at Stony Brook in 1970, she entered the graduate program at the University of California at Davis, receiving an M.A. and a Ph.D. in psychology in 1973. She spent the next two years at the National Aeronautics and Space Administration's (NASA) Ames Research Center at Moffett Field in California as a National Research Council research associate, and the two years after that as a research specialist for the San Jose State University Foundation. In 1977 she returned to the Ames Research Center as a research psychologist in the psychophysiological research laboratory. This unit specializes in the way the mind affects the body's physiological functions, and eventually she became its director. In 1980 she married William Toscano, a fellow NASA researcher, with whom she has one child.

Cowings was the first U.S. woman to undergo astronaut training, and she served as a backup payload specialist for one of the first science-oriented space shuttle missions. Ultimately she decided to stay on the ground and assist NASA missions as a researcher. Her primary involvement in this regard has been her efforts to overcome a condition known as zero-gravity sickness syndrome, or space sickness. This condition is similar to motion sickness, and as astronauts spend longer periods of time in outer space during a NASA mission, they become more susceptible to space sickness.

Cowings was put in charge of developing a program for combating space sickness that did not include the use of drugs, which impair an astronaut's performance. The result was the Autogenic Feedback Training Exercise (AFTE). This program consists of 12 30-minute sessions in which astronauts are taught biofeedback techniques so that they can monitor their physiological responses in the event of an attack of space sickness. Among other things, AFTE teaches astronauts how to control their heartbeat and blood pressure, overcome feelings of nausea and fainting, and relax certain muscles that are particularly susceptible to space sickness. About 65 percent of the graduates of the AFTE program are able to suppress completely the onset of space sickness, while an additional 20 percent are able to deal with space sickness sufficiently well so that it does not affect their job performance. After more than 10 years of development, AFTE's first test came in 1992 during the eight-day Spacelab-J mission, during which it proved to be a success. Her work regarding AFTE appeared in several articles she coauthored with her husband and as an essay in *Motion and Space Sickness* (1990).

Cowings's latest research involves developing exercises that permit astronauts to maintain muscle strength and tone while operating for extended periods in the zero-gravity conditions of outer space and the microgravity conditions of a space station. In addition to her duties at Ames, she teaches psychiatry at the University of California at Los Angeles. Her many awards include membership in the American Association for the Advancement of Science.

Patricia Cowings (right) strapped Leah Schafer, an Ames laboratory assistant, into a vertical acceleration device, one of the devices Cowings uses to train astronauts how to use biofeedback to overcome motion sickness. *(Courtesy of National Aeronautics and Space Administration)*

Further Reading

McMurray, Emily J., ed. *Notable Twentieth Century Scientists*. Detroit: Gale Research, 1995, pp. 417–418.

NASA Quest. "Patricia S. Cowings, Ph.D." Available online. URL: http://quest.arc.nasa.gov/people/bios/women/pc.html. Downloaded on March 25, 2005.

Spangenburg, Ray, and Kit Moser. *African Americans in Science, Math, and Invention*. New York: Facts On File, 2003, pp. 48–49.

Cram, Donald J.
(Donald James Cram)
(1919–2001) *chemist*

Donald J. Cram won a Nobel Prize for cofounding the field of host-guest chemistry. He also developed Cram's rule for predicting the outcomes of certain chemical reactions, and he founded the field of carceplex chemistry.

Cram was born on April 22, 1919, in Chester, Vermont. His father, William, was a cavalry officer and a lawyer, and his mother, Joanna, was a homemaker. At age two he moved with his family to Brattleboro where he grew up. He left home when he was 16, and he spent the next several years in Florida, Massachusetts, and New York, supporting himself by doing odd jobs while completing his secondary education. In 1937 he won a scholarship to Rollins (Fla.) College where he received a B.S. in chemistry in 1941. After receiving an M.S. from the University of Nebraska in 1942, he went to work as a research chemist for Merck & Company. He left after three years to attend Harvard University, where he received a Ph.D. in organic chemistry in 1947. He then joined the faculty at the University of California at Los Angeles (UCLA) where he spent the rest of his career. In 1940 he married Jean Turner; the marriage ended in 1968, and the following year he married Jane Maxwell. Both marriages were childless.

Once at UCLA, Cram focused his research efforts on stereochemistry, the principles by which atoms and molecules position themselves in a given compound and how these positions affect the compound's properties. He discovered and named the phenonium ion, which maintains the asymmetrical arrangement of two or more carbon atoms when a compound containing those atoms is dissolved in a

solvent. He undertook an exhaustive study of carbanions, negatively charged molecules containing a carbon atom that play an important intermediate role in the production of a wide range of compounds, which he published in *Fundamentals of Carbanion Chemistry* (1965). He developed Cram's rule, which describes how electrons are contributed during addition reactions involving carbonyls, molecules containing a carbon atom, and an oxygen atom connected by a double bond. He also coauthored, with George S. Hammond of the California Institute of Technology, the influential college chemistry textbook, *Organic Chemistry* (1960).

In 1968 CHARLES J. PEDERSEN announced the discovery of a highly unusual compound that he named a crown ether. Its distinguishing feature is a loose, two-dimensional flexible ring of carbon and oxygen atoms that does not break apart during a chemical reaction. Instead, a crown ether reacts with other atoms by "trapping" them inside the ring. Crown ethers have a strong affinity for metal atoms, and by varying the number of carbon and oxygen atoms in the ring, it is possible to develop a crown ether that will react with atoms of a particular metal and no other. Cram was immediately intrigued by this important new development in stereochemistry, and he devoted the next 20 years to the study of crown ethers. During this period, he developed three-dimensional crown ethers whose shape allows them to react selectively with nonmetallic compounds. This development made it possible to design synthetic compounds that behave like an enzyme, a biochemical compound that initiates a specific biochemical reaction by producing a specific biochemical substance. It also raised the possibility that medical researchers could one day produce synthetic enzymes that work better than the natural ones. The development of three-dimensional crown ethers marked the founding of a new branch of chemistry known as host-guest chemistry, whereby two compounds react without losing their essential form. For his work with crown ethers, Cram was awarded a one-third share of the 1987 Nobel Prize in chemistry; one of his corecipients was Pedersen and the other was the French chemist Jean-Marie Lehn.

In the late 1980s, Cram advanced host-guest chemistry by developing what he called carceplex chemistry. In host-guest chemistry, crown ethers capture an atom or molecule but leave certain of its surfaces exposed to the possibility of further reactions. In carceplex chemistry, a crown-ether derivative known as a carcerand completely encases the captured atom or molecule in a complex known as a carceplex. Cram then developed a hemicarcerand, a carcerand that has a small gap in one of its walls. By regulating the temperature of the hemicarcerand, it is possible to regulate the reactivity of the atom or molecule captured inside. Encasing highly unstable or reactive compounds such as benzyne and cyclobutadiene in a hemicarcerand made it possible to study these compounds for the very first time.

Cram was awarded the National Medal of Science and was elected to the National Academy of Sciences. In 1998 he was ranked among the 75 most important chemists of the past 75 years by *Chemical & Engineering News*. He retired from UCLA in 1991 to Palm Desert, California, where he died on June 17, 2001.

Further Reading

Cram, Donald J. *From Design to Discovery.* Washington, D.C.: American Chemical Society, 1990.

McMurray, Emily J., ed. *Notable Twentieth Century Scientists.* Detroit: Gale Research, 1995, pp. 421–423.

Nobelprize.org. "The Nobel Prize in Chemistry 1987." Available online. URL: http://nobelprize.org/chemistry/laureates/1987. Downloaded on May 11, 2004.

Cronin, James W.
(James Watson Cronin)
(1931–) *physicist*

James W. Cronin codiscovered that the radioactive decay of certain subatomic particles sometimes violates the fundamental principles of symmetry, principles that physicists had thought applied to all of the known physical forces. For this discovery, he was awarded a share of the 1980 Nobel Prize in physics.

Cronin was born on September 29, 1931, in Chicago, Illinois. His parents, James and Dorothy, were students at the University of Chicago. At age eight he moved with his family to Dallas, Texas, where his father had received a position as a professor of Latin and Greek at Southern Methodist University (SMU). After receiving a B.S. in mathematics and physics from SMU in 1951, James W. Cronin entered the University of Chicago and received an M.S. and a Ph.D. in physics in 1953 and 1955, respectively. He then became an assistant physicist at the Brookhaven National Laboratory on New York's Long Island. In 1954 he married Annette Martin with whom he had three children.

One of Cronin's colleagues at Brookhaven was CHEN NING YANG. In 1953 Yang and TSUNG-DAO LEE had discovered that the tau meson and the theta meson, which were considered to be two distinct subatomic particles because of the way they decay radioactively, were actually the same particle, known today as the K meson. This discovery led Yang and Lee to propose in 1956 the concept of parity violation. At that time, physicists assumed that every physical reaction occurs symmetrically, without regard to up, down, left, right, clockwise, or counterclockwise, thus conserving parity. Yang and Lee, however, showed that there was no experimental evidence to prove that parity is conserved during the weak interactions, one of which is a type of radioactive decay known as beta decay. When parity violation was demonstrated in 1957 to be a fact for the beta decay of K mesons, physicists were stunned. Almost immediately, many of them, including Cronin, set out to determine whether or not parity violation applies to particles other than K mesons and whether or not the other laws of conservation are also violated by the weak interactions.

Cronin's first project in this regard involved parity violation during the beta decay of hyperons, particles that are larger than nucleons (protons and neutrons) and that always decay radioactively into a nucleon. This project led him to collaborate with VAL L. FITCH, a Brookhaven colleague who also taught at nearby Princeton University, and in 1958 Fitch helped Cronin obtain a teaching position at Princeton. Their collaboration began as a study as to why a charged K meson sometimes disintegrates into three pi mesons but at other times into only two pi mesons. In the process, they discovered that the beta decay of a neutral K meson violates the law of charge conjugation conservation. According to this law, the products of neutral K meson decay should be evenly divided between matter and anti-matter. An antimatter particle is one that possesses the same mass as an elementary particle of matter but has the opposite charge; for example, an electron is a particle of matter while a positron, which has the same mass as an electron but carries a positive charge, is a particle of antimatter. Cronin and Fitch discovered that approximately one neutral K meson in 500 does not yield an even distribution of matter and antimatter, a minor but clear violation of charge conjugation conservation.

Coupled with the findings of Yang and Lee, Cronin and Fitch's findings offered clear proof of CP violation, that is, that two of the laws of conservation, charge conjugation (C) and parity (P), do not necessarily hold for the weak interactions. These findings had tremendous implications for astrophysicists, who had been wondering for years why the universe consists mostly of matter rather than an even distribution of matter and antimatter. Ever since Cronin and Fitch published their findings in 1964, astrophysicists have been considering the possibility that CP violation explains why the known universe consists almost entirely of matter rather than antimatter, and why that matter is distributed so unevenly throughout the universe. In 1980 the value of Cronin and Fitch's work was recognized when they each received a half share of the Nobel Prize in physics.

In 1971 Cronin returned to the University of Chicago, this time as a professor of physics, and he remained there until his retirement in 1996. In addition to continuing his study of CP violation concerning K mesons, he also investigated leptons, particles such as the electron that exist outside the nucleus. His honors include the National Medal of Science and election to the National Academy of Sciences and the American Academy of Arts and Sciences.

Further Reading

Nobelprize.org. "The Nobel Prize in Physics 1980." Available online. URL: http://nobelprize.org/physics/laureates/1980. Downloaded on September 24, 2004.

The University of Chicago Department of Physics. "James W. Cronin." Available online. URL: http://physics.uchicago.edu/x_astro.html#Cronin. Downloaded on March 25, 2005.

Wasson, Tyler, ed. *Nobel Prize Winners.* New York: H. W. Wilson, 1987, pp. 232–234.

Curl, Robert F.
(Robert Floyd Curl, Jr.)
(1933–) *chemist*

Robert F. Curl codiscovered the fullerenes, spherical arrangements of carbon atoms that possess amazing properties of strength, flexibility, and electrical conductivity. For this discovery he was awarded a share of the 1996 Nobel Prize in chemistry.

Curl was born on August 23, 1933, in Alice, Texas. His father, Robert, was a minister, and his mother, Lessie, was a homemaker. As a boy he moved with his family to a number of southern Texas towns before finally settling in San Antonio. After receiving a B.A. in chemistry from Rice Institute (today Rice University) in 1954, he entered the University of California at Berkeley and received a Ph.D. in physical chemistry in 1957. After a year of postdoctoral research at Harvard University, in 1958 he returned to Rice to teach chemistry. In 1955 he married Jonel Whipple with whom he had two children.

Curl's primary research interest was molecular spectroscopy, the study of molecules by examining the spectrum of light they emit. His graduate research focused on the infrared spectrum of disiloxane, a relatively simple molecule composed of two atoms of silicon and one of oxygen, while his postdoctoral research employed microwave spectroscopy to study the energy barriers within a molecule that inhibit the internal rotation of a group of atoms. His early work at Rice focused on using microwave spectroscopy to study stable free radicals, molecules that contain at least one electron that is not part of a covalent pair, and it eventually grew to encompass the use of tunable infrared lasers.

In 1976 Curl was joined at Rice by RICHARD E. SMALLEY, a molecular spectroscopist who had helped develop supersonic beam laser spectroscopy. Over the next decade, Curl and Smalley collaborated on the design and construction of increasingly sophisticated supersonic beam machines. By 1982 they had built the laser-vaporization supersonic cluster beam machine. This device froze its target molecules by means of a supersonic free jet so as to greatly reduce their rotation and vibration, thus making them easier to study. Then it vaporized them with a laser so that their structures could be studied via a spectroscope. Named AP2, this supersonic beam machine was capable of studying particles no larger than a nanometer, or one-millionth of a millimeter.

In 1985 Curl and Smalley froze and vaporized carbon in the AP2. Upon examining the results, they discovered that the carbon gas had condensed into molecules of C_{60}, which is composed of 60 atoms of carbon linked together in the shape of a soccer ball. They named their discovery buckminsterfullerene in honor of R. Buckminster Fuller, an American architect who had invented the geodesic dome, which a buckminsterfullerene closely resembles. Today, a buckminsterfullerene is more commonly known as a buckyball. Further experimentation revealed the existence of other fullerenes, or spherical arrangements of carbon atoms, such as C_{70} and C_{240}. Curl and Smalley also discovered that by adding a few atoms of nickel or cobalt, buckyballs can be elongated into buckytubes, tubes no longer than one nanometer that possess the strength and flexibility of polymers as well as the ability to conduct electricity.

The discovery of fullerenes revolutionized the world of organic chemistry, the study of carbon and its compounds, because it demonstrated that carbon can exist in previously unknown forms. This discovery also promised to lead to new technologies such as electrical wiring or structural materials made from buckytubes. For the role he played in the discovery of buckyballs, Curl was awarded a one-third share of the 1996 Nobel Prize in chemistry; one of his corecipients was Smalley, and the other was the British chemist Harold W. Kioto.

Around 1990, Curl ended his collaboration with Smalley and returned to his earlier work concerning free radicals. He also became part of the Laser Science Group, a Rice research group that uses laser spectroscopy in applications involving trace gas detection, environmental monitoring, chemical analysis, industrial process control, and medical diagnostics. His many honors include election to the National Academy of Sciences and the American Academy of Arts and Sciences.

Further Reading

Browne, Malcolm W. "Discoveries of Superfluid Helium, and 'Buckyballs,' Earn Nobels for 6 Scientists," *New York Times,* October 10, 1996, p. D21.

Nobelprize.org. "The Nobel Prize in Chemistry 1996." Available online. URL: http://nobelprize.org/ chemistry/laureates/1996. Downloaded on August 17, 2004.

D

Dana, James D.
(James Dwight Dana)
(1813–1895) *geologist*

James D. Dana was one of the foremost American geologists of the 19th century. His manuals concerning the classification of minerals and the physical processes that produce geological phenomena remained classics long after his death.

Dana was born on February 12, 1813, in Utica, New York. His father, James, owned a hardware store, and his mother, Harriet, was a homemaker. After finishing high school in 1830, he entered Yale University and received a B.A. in 1833. He spent the next three years teaching mathematics to midshipmen in the U.S. Navy. In 1834, while on a voyage to the Mediterranean Sea, he observed an eruption of Mount Vesuvius in Italy, and his report was published in the *American Journal of Science*. In 1836 he returned to Yale to assist Benjamin Silliman, under whom he had studied chemistry and mineralogy. Eight years later he married Silliman's daughter, Henrietta, with whom he had six children.

Once back at Yale, Dana set about developing an ambitious new system for classifying minerals. Using his and Silliman's mineral collections, he incorporated features of chemistry, physics, and mathematics to completely revise the way minerals are classified. In 1837 he published the results of his work as *A System of Mineralogy*. This groundbreaking work of almost 600 pages was revised three times by Dana before his death. In the third edition he placed greater emphasis on the chemical makeup of minerals as the basis for their classification, the method that remains in use today. The fourth edition of *A System of Mineralogy* continues to be used today as a primary reference tool.

In 1838 Dana was invited to serve as geologist and mineralogist aboard the USS *Peacock*, the flagship of a U.S. Navy oceanographic expedition that was to explore the South Pacific Ocean over the next four years. The expedition's main purpose was to chart previously unknown islands that had the potential to serve as bases for American merchant ships trading with the Far East. During the four years he was with the expedition, Dana collected so many zoological and mineral specimens that it took him until 1854 to classify them all. During much of this period he was an employee of the federal government, and he spent a great deal of time in Washington, D.C. His work with the *Peacock* specimens was published in *Report on Zoophytes* (1846), in which he identified more than 200 new species of invertebrate plant-like sea animals; *Report on the Geology of the Pacific* (1849), which dealt in large part with coral reefs and islands; and *Report on Crustacea* (1852–54), in which he identified 500 new species of hard-shelled sea creatures. All three works featured numerous illustrations hand-drawn by Dana.

In addition to his work with the *Peacock* specimens, Dana continued to teach at Yale and, after 1846, to serve as associate editor of the *American Journal of Science*, the foremost scientific journal of its day. In 1848 he published *A Manual of Mineralogy*, a textbook intended for college students, and in 1851 he took over as editor of the *Journal*. Four years later he was appointed to take Silliman's place as professor of natural history at Yale, and so he added another set of responsibilities to his already hectic schedule. The workload was too much, and in 1859 he suffered a nervous breakdown from which he never fully recovered. He stopped teaching in 1870, but he continued to publish and edit the *Journal*, even though he could work for only three hours a day without becoming exhausted. In 1876 he helped found Yale's Peabody Museum of Natural History, and he was largely responsible for building its mineral and geological collections.

Despite his medical condition, Dana played an important role as a guiding light for his fellow geologists. Through his editorials and reviews for the *Journal*, he presented his own insightful ideas on such matters as the origin and structure of continents and ocean basins, the physical processes that govern the building of mountains, and volcanic activity. One of his most influential works was *Manual of Geology* (1862); updated three times before his death, this handbook was so important that virtually every geologist in the United States owned a copy. Other important geological works include *A Textbook of Geology* (1864) and *Corals and Coral Islands* (1872). This latter work presented Dana's extensive knowledge about coral reefs, and it was the culmination of a study he had begun on the *Peacock*. In this work, he concurred with Charles Darwin, an eminent naturalist, that coral atolls are the remains of volcanoes that were active a great many years ago, and that their presence demonstrates that the Pacific Ocean floor was much shallower then than it is today. Whereas Darwin had merely presented his theories, Dana provided much of the evidence that proved Darwin correct.

By 1890 Dana's health had deteriorated to the point that he was forced to relinquish all of his official responsibilities at Yale and the *Journal*. He continued to work at his home in New Haven, Connecticut, where he died on April 14, 1895.

Further Reading

About Geology. "James Dwight Dana (1813–1895)." Available online. URL: http://www.geology.about.com/library/bl/blj-d-dana_bio.htm. Downloaded on July 27, 2003.

Stanton, William. "Dana, James Dwight," *Dictionary of Scientific Biography*. New York: Scribner, 1971, pp. 549–554.

Viola, H. J., and C. Margolis, eds. *Magnificent Voyagers: The U.S. Exploring Expedition, 1838–1842*. Washington, D.C.: Smithsonian Institution Press, 1985.

Davis, Raymond, Jr.
(1914–) *physicist*

Raymond Davis developed techniques for detecting solar neutrinos, thereby proving that the source of the Sun's energy is nuclear fusion. For this contribution, he was awarded a share of the 2002 Nobel Prize in physics.

Davis was born on October 14, 1914, in Washington, D.C. His father, Raymond, Sr., was a photographer, and his mother, Ida, was a homemaker. After receiving a B.S. in chemistry from the University of Maryland in 1938, he worked for a year for the Dow Chemical Company in Midland, Michigan, before returning to Maryland to earn an M.S. in chemistry. He then entered Yale University where he received a Ph.D. in physical chemistry in 1942. He spent the next three years in the U.S. Army, testing chemical weapons at the Dugway Proving Ground in Utah. After three years as a research chemist for the Monsanto Chemical Company in Miamisburg, Ohio, in 1948 he joined the staff at the Brookhaven National Laboratory on New York's Long Island. That same year he married Anna Torrey with whom he had five children.

Upon settling at Brookhaven, Davis became interested in neutrinos, subatomic particles with no electrical charge and little or no mass. Neutrinos had been postulated in 1931 by the Austrian physicist Wolfgang Pauli, but 17 years later they were still to be discovered, so Davis began looking for a way to prove their existence. The problem with detecting them, however, is that they rarely interact with other particles because they have no charge and virtually no mass, and so they are almost impossible to capture. His first experiment was to expose a 1,000-gallon tank of carbon tetrachloride to radioactive material from Brookhaven's graphite research reactor on the theory that an atom of chlorine and a neutrino would combine to form an atom of a radioactive isotope of argon. Unfortunately, the tank was far too small to capture even one neutrino, and so Davis's experiment failed. He continued to search for neutrinos using other methods until 1956, when FREDERICK REINES succeeded in demonstrating their existence.

Not long after Reines detected neutrinos, Davis began looking for a way to detect solar neutrinos. He was motivated to do so as a means of proving that the source of the Sun's energy, and for all stars, is proton-proton fusion, a process that generates countless trillions of neutrinos every second. Reasoning that an underground detection device would eliminate most of the background disturbances from cosmic rays that interfere with the chlorine-argon detection method, he placed a tank of perchloroethylene about 2,300 feet underground in a limestone mine near Akron, Ohio. Once again, the experiment yielded no neutrinos. Undaunted, in the early 1960s he shifted his experiment to the

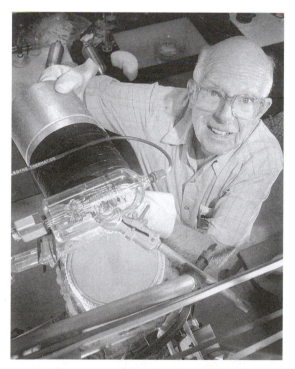

Raymond Davis proved that the Sun produces energy via nuclear fusion. *(Courtesy of Brookhaven National Laboratory)*

Homestake gold mine in Lead, North Dakota, putting a 100,000-gallon tank of perchloroethylene almost one mile below the Earth's surface. He also developed a sophisticated method for culling the argon atoms produced by the chlorine-neutrino interaction, and over the course of almost 30 years he was able to capture approximately 2,000 atoms of argon, thus proving the existence of solar neutrinos.

One further problem remained for Davis to solve, however, and that was the fact that his experiment yielded only about one-third the number of argon atoms that had been predicted. Further experimentation by other researchers demonstrated the existence of three kinds of neutrinos (electron, muon, and tau), that only about one-third of the solar neutrinos that reach the Earth's surface are electron neutrinos, and that the chlorine-argon detection method only detects electron neutrinos. Once all these facts were known, the value of Davis's contribution became clear, and he was awarded a quarter share of the 2002 Nobel Prize in physics. His corecipients were the Japanese physicist Masatoshi Koshiba (one-quarter share) and the American physicist RICCARDO GIACCONI (one-half share).

In 1984 Davis retired from Brookhaven and became a research professor at the University of Pennsylvania, where he continued his experiments with neutrinos. His honors include the National Medal of Science and election to the National Academy of Sciences.

Further Reading

Nobelprize.org. "The Nobel Prize in Physics 2002." Available online. URL: http://nobelprize.org/physics/laureates/2002. Downloaded on September 6, 2004.

Overbye, Dennis. "3 Nobels for Solving Longstanding Mysteries of the Cosmos." *New York Times,* October 9, 2002, p. A21.

Davisson, Clinton J.
(Clinton Joseph Davisson)
(1881–1958) *physicist*

Clinton J. Davisson demonstrated that, just like beams of light, beams of electrons can be diffracted, or made to bend around obstacles in their path.

This demonstration revolutionized the way physicists think about matter and won for Davisson a share of a Nobel Prize.

Davisson was born on October 22, 1881, in Bloomington, Illinois. His father, Joseph, was a painter and wallpaper hanger, and his mother, Mary, was a teacher. Because of his family's economic situation, he worked nights at the local telephone company and did not graduate from high school until age 20. He then entered the University of Chicago, where he came under the influence of future Nobel laureate ROBERT A. MILLIKAN. Davisson worked and studied part-time for seven years, receiving a B.S. in physics in 1908. Three years later he received a Ph.D. in physics from Princeton University, married Charlotte Richardson with whom he had four children, and joined the faculty at the Carnegie Institute of Technology in Pittsburgh, Pennsylvania. In 1917 he left teaching to accept an industrial research position in New York City with the engineering department of the Western Electric Company, the manufacturing branch of the American Telephone & Telegraph (AT&T) Company; in 1925 his department became part of Bell Telephone Laboratories (BTL), one of the foremost industrial research facilities of its day. In 1946 he retired from BTL to teach physics at the University of Virginia, where he spent the remainder of his career.

In 1919 Davisson began the line of research that would lead to the discovery of electron diffraction. AT&T was interested in amplifying and relaying long-distance telephone signals via electronic means, and Davisson was assigned to develop a coated filament for use in a vacuum tube, the first device used to control the flow of electrons in an electronic apparatus. He began by experimenting with nickel, a metal that makes an excellent protective coating for other metals. Within a year he had noticed that bombarding nickel with a stream of electrons sometimes causes the electrons to scatter instead of being amplified. Further investigation showed that subjecting nickel to intense heat, as happens in a vacuum tube, causes it to form into larger crystals than normal; furthermore, electrons beamed against heat-treated nickel scattered in a different pattern than they did when beamed against untreated nickel.

Not surprisingly, this result suggested to Davisson and Lester Germer, his research assistant, that the diffraction of the electrons was caused by the nickel crystal and not because of the structure of the electrons themselves.

In 1926 Davisson, while at a meeting at Oxford University, shared his findings with a group of British scientists, several of whom suggested that the scattering patterns he had observed might be explained by the theory of wave mechanics that French physicist Louis de Broglie had advanced in 1924. According to de Broglie's hypothesis, beams of subatomic particles behave like beams of light in that they possess some qualities of matter and some qualities of energy waves. He also hypothesized that the wavelength of a subatomic particle is directly proportional to its linear momentum. Upon returning to the United States, Davisson and Germer designed an experiment whereby slow-moving electrons would be beamed against a cubic nickel crystal, to prove or disprove de Broglie's theory. By 1927 they were able to diffract beams of electrons exactly as if they were beams of light, thus demonstrating conclusively that de Broglie's theory applied to beams of electrons. They further showed that the relationship between an electron's wavelength and its linear momentum was very close to what de Broglie had guessed it would be.

By proving the existence of electron diffraction, Davisson forced physicists to acknowledge that matter and energy are related in that they share certain properties. Inspired by Davisson's discovery, later researchers proved that de Broglie's formula concerning the wavelength of a subatomic particle also applies to atoms, molecules, neutrons, protons, and many other particles. In 1937 the importance of Davisson's contribution was recognized when he was awarded one-half of the Nobel Prize for physics. The other half was awarded to British physicist George P. Thomson, who had also arrived at Davisson's conclusion but by using a very different method.

Davisson continued to experiment with electrons for the rest of his career. He played a significant role in the invention of the electron microscope as well as the electron beam tube for use in televisions. His other honors include election to the National Academy of Sciences and medals from the Franklin

Institute and the Royal Society of London. He died on February 1, 1958, in Charlottesville, Virginia.

Further Reading

Kelly, Mervin J. "Clinton Joseph Davisson," National Academy of Sciences, *Biographical Memoirs* 36 (1962): pp. 51–84.

Nobelprize.org. "The Nobel Prize in Physics 1937." Available online. URL: http://nobelprize.org/physics/laureates/1937. Downloaded on January 5, 2004.

Wasson, Tyler, ed. *Nobel Prize Winners.* New York: H. W. Wilson, 1987, pp. 247–249.

De Bakey, Michael E.
(Michael Ellis De Bakey)
(1908–   ) *surgeon*

Michael E. De Bakey was a pioneer in surgery involving the circulatory system. He performed a number of the first successful surgical procedures involving replacement of the heart and arteries.

De Bakey was born on September 7, 1908, in Lake Charles, Louisiana. His father, Shaker, was a pharmacist, and his mother, Raheega, was a homemaker. In 1926 he entered Tulane University, earning enough credits after only two years to attend medical school. He spent the next two years working concurrently on his undergraduate degree and his M.D., receiving the latter in 1932. After a two-year internship at New Orleans's Charity Hospital, he spent a year doing research in Europe before returning to Tulane to receive an M.S. and join the faculty. His stay at Tulane was interrupted when the United States entered World War II, during which he served with the Surgeon General's Office; it came to an end in 1948 when he was named chair of the department of surgery at Baylor University School of Medicine in Waco, Texas. He remained at Baylor for the rest of his career, later serving as the medical school's president and chancellor. In 1936 he married Diane Cooper with whom he had four children. She died in 1972, and in 1974 he married Katrin Fehlhaber with whom he had one child.

While in medical school, De Bakey modified the roller pump so that it could be used during blood transfusions without damaging the blood.

This device was later incorporated into John H. Gibbons's heart-lung machine, which was used during open-heart surgery. During the 1950s De Bakey turned his attention to arterial disease, especially arteriosclerosis, or hardening of the arteries, a medical condition that was poorly understood. He developed a system for classifying arterial disease by location, characteristic, and pattern, thus making it easier to diagnose and treat. This research led him to develop procedures for correcting aneurysms, permanent enlargements of arteries, via surgery. At first he replaced damaged arteries with ones that had been grafted and frozen, but by 1953 he was using artificial arteries made from Dacron and Dacron-velour that he had sewn together himself. Over the next five years he performed the first successful surgical treatments of aneurysms in five different sections of the aorta—the major artery that routes blood from the heart to all parts of the body except the lungs—and the carotid artery, which carries blood from the aorta to the head, neck, and face. By 1963 he had also developed the standard procedure of therapy in arterial disease.

In the 1960s De Bakey began specializing in conditions of the heart. In 1964 he performed the first successful bypass surgery by using a vein from the patient's leg to reroute blood from the aorta to the coronary artery, which carries blood from the aorta back to the heart. He also began building artificial and partially artificial hearts, and in 1966 he successfully implanted an artificial heart into a human. Although the patient died four days later, the operation was hailed as a success, and it opened the door for future improvements in heart replacement surgery. Two years later he performed one of the first successful heart transplants—the first had been performed in 1967 by the South African surgeon Christiaan Barnard—but again the patient died after a short while. De Bakey abandoned this procedure until the 1980s, when better antirejection drugs and other technological advances made heart transplants more feasible. To further heart research, De Bakey helped found the Cardiovascular Research and Training Center at the Texas Medical Center in Houston and the De Bakey Heart Center at Baylor.

In the 1980s De Bakey returned to his earlier research with arteriosclerosis, this time to search for its cause. He and several colleagues discovered that the bloodstreams of patients with arteriosclerosis contain high levels of antibodies to cytomegalovirus (CMV), and they concluded that arteriosclerosis might result from a CMV infection early in life. They also demonstrated that although high cholesterol, smoking, a high fat diet, and high blood pressure might make a patient susceptible to arteriosclerosis, they do not cause it directly.

De Bakey made other important contributions to medicine. During World War II he helped establish the U.S. Army's mobile army surgical hospital (MASH) units, and he helped organize what became the Veterans' Administration's system of medical centers. He also helped establish the National Library of Medicine in Washington, D.C., as the world's foremost repository of medical archives. His many honors include the U.S. Medal of Honor and the National Medal of Science. Perhaps his greatest honor was the establishment by the surgeons he had trained—more than one thousand—of the Michael E. De Bakey International Surgical Society. He served as editor of the *Yearbook of Surgery* from 1958 to 1970, and his publications include *The Living Heart* (1977) and *The Living Heart Diet* (1984). A particularly gifted surgeon, he was still performing open-heart surgery at the age of 90.

Further Reading

McMurray, Emily J., ed. "Michael Ellis DeBakey," *Notable Twentieth Century Scientists*. Detroit: Gale Research, 1995, pp. 466–468.

Texas Medical Center News. "A Lifetime of Imagination and Dedication." Available online. URL: http://www.tmc.edu/tmcnews/10_15_98/page_02.html. Downloaded on May 27, 2004.

Dehmelt, Hans G.
(Hans Georg Dehmelt)
(1922–) *physicist*

Hans G. Dehmelt developed a method for trapping electrons so that their magnetic properties could be studied and measured with great accuracy. For this contribution he was awarded a share of the 1989 Nobel Prize in physics.

Dehmelt was born on September 9, 1922, in Görlitz, Germany. His father, Georg, was a real estate agent, and his mother, Asta, was a homemaker. After finishing high school in Berlin where he grew up, he joined the German army and served on the Russian and western fronts during World War II. In 1946 he was released from an American prisoner of war camp and entered the University of Göttingen, receiving a Ph.D. in physics in 1950. He spent the next two years conducting postdoctoral research at Göttingen, and in 1952 he was invited to conduct postdoctoral research at Duke University in Durham, North Carolina. In 1955 he was named a professor of physics at the University of Washington in Seattle. At some point he married Irmgard Lassow with whom he had one child; she later died, and in 1989 he married Diana Dundore. In 1962 he became a naturalized U.S. citizen.

Dehmelt's early research focused on atomic spectroscopy, the study of the inner workings of atomic nuclei by observing the electromagnetic radiation they emit. As a graduate student he used the magnetic resonance method, whereby a stream of gaseous molecules is passed through a series of magnetic fields whose strengths are manipulated by means of radio waves, to discover nuclear quadrupole resonance, the vibrational properties exhibited by an atom as it deviates from being spherical. This work led him to study the magnetic properties of electrons, which are miniature bar magnets in that they have a positive pole on one end and a negative pole on the other. By 1956 he had devised a method for aligning electrons according to their magnetic orientation by colliding them into target atoms in an electron impact tube. This method greatly improved the resolution of the electron's electromagnetic spectra and allowed Dehmelt to measure many of its magnetic properties with great precision.

Several properties remained unmeasured, however, and so Dehmelt began looking for alternative spectroscopic methods. He concluded that the first step was to slow down the electron, which moves incredibly fast, so that it could be viewed for a longer period of time. His first effort involved introducing a beam of electrons into a gaseous cloud of ions, or atoms with a net positive or negative charge, thus trapping the electrons momentarily. His next effort involved using a modified Penning ion gauge, which was invented by the Dutch physicist F. M. Penning; this device, which Dehmelt named the Penning trap, traps electrons between a strong magnetic field and a weak electric field and confines them to a very small area, thus maintaining electrons in a state where they could be easily observed for up to 10 seconds. Over the years Dehmelt devised methods for cooling electrons, thus further slowing them down, and removing them from the storage area until, by 1973, he was able to trap and observe a single electron for more than 10 months. By 1976 he had measured the frequencies of the electron's axial, cyclotron, and magnetron oscillations, all of which had been impossible to measure previously. Two years later he was able to obtain a highly accurate measurement of the electron's gyromagnetic ratio, or g-factor, a function of all of its magnetic properties, and in 1985 he obtained the most accurate measurement to date of the electron's radius. Meanwhile, Dehmelt and his associates also used the Penning trap to observe positrons, subatomic particles with the same mass as an electron but a positive charge, and ions.

The values obtained by Dehmelt greatly informed researchers working in the field of quantum electrodynamics, the branch of theoretical physics concerned with the interactions of charged particles with each other and with electromagnetic radiation. While his values supported much of the theoretical work that had been advanced previously, in one case they forced the rethinking of a particular theory. On the practical side, Dehmelt's trap proved very useful as a means of trapping atoms for use in the atomic clock, which measures time by counting the oscillations made by atoms. For his contributions to these developments, Dehmelt was awarded a quarter share of the 1989 Nobel Prize in physics. His corecipients were the German physicist Wolfgang Paul (one-quarter share) and the American physicist NORMAN F. RAMSEY (one-half share).

Dehmelt remained at the University of Washington for the rest of his career. His other honors include the National Medal of Science and election to the National Academy of Sciences and the American Academy of Arts and Sciences.

Further Reading

Broad, William J. "5 Win the Nobel Prizes in Chemistry and Physics," *New York Times*, October 13, 1989, Section I, p. 10.

Nobelprize.org. "The Nobel Prize in Physics 1989." Available online. URL: http://nobelprize.org/physics/laureates/1989. Downloaded on September 10, 2004.

Delbrück, Max
(1906–1981) *molecular biologist*

Max Delbrück was one of the earliest practitioners of molecular biology, the study of the biophysical principles by which living things grow and reproduce. For his discoveries concerning the behavior and replication of viruses, he was awarded a share of the 1969 Nobel Prize in physiology or medicine.

Delbrück was born on September 4, 1906, in Berlin, Germany. His father, Hans, was a history professor, and his mother, Lina, was a journalist. In 1924 he entered the University of Tubingen but transferred shortly thereafter to the University of Göttingen, where he received a Ph.D. in physics in 1930. He spent the next two years studying theoretical physics at the universities of Bristol, Zurich, and Copenhagen. At Copenhagen he studied with Niels Bohr who, among other things, had postulated the principle of complementarity. Bohr believed that one cannot understand the workings of a subatomic system without understanding both the wave behavior and the particle behavior of the system's components, two very different types of behavior. Complementarity also suggested that the physical principles governing all behavior, including that of living things, are different on a microscopic scale than they are on a larger scale. Delbrück was fascinated with this idea, and for the next 20 years he focused the bulk of his research on issues related to biophysics.

In 1932 Delbrück became a research assistant at the Kaiser Wilhelm Institute for Chemistry in Berlin, where his official duties involved studying the problems of nuclear fission. In his spare time, however, he studied fruit flies at the Institute for Biology, and eventually he developed a way to explain genetic stability and mutations in fruit flies in terms of quantum mechanics, the behavior of subatomic particles. In 1937 he was granted a three-year Rockefeller Fellowship in biology, so he left Germany for the United States, joining the faculty at the California Institute of Technology (Caltech). At Caltech he began studying bacteriophages, or phages, viruses that infect bacteria. Phages are the simplest form of life, consisting of a core of nucleic acid enclosed in a protein shell, and he believed that a proper understanding of how phages replicate and mutate would allow him to understand these same genetic functions in all life-forms. In 1939 he developed a simple process for growing phages whereby several hundred thousand could be grown in about an hour, thus yielding plenty of material upon which to conduct genetic experimentation.

In 1940 Delbrück was named a professor of physics at Vanderbilt University, but with the understanding that he could focus on biophysics. Over the next five years he helped establish the Carnegie Institution of Washington's department of genetics at Cold Spring Harbor, New York, where he spent his summers, as an annual meeting place for phage researchers in the United States. He also formed an informal partnership with SALVADOR E. LURIA and ALFRED D. HERSHEY, the three working independently but collaboratively on the problems of phage replication, mutation, and recombination. In 1946 Delbrück and Hershey discovered that two phages, by infecting the same bacterium at the same time, can recombine their genetic material, or mutate, into a new type of phage, an ability that was thought to be restricted to life-forms that reproduce sexually. This discovery suggested that genetic mutations in higher-order organisms were caused, at least in part, by viral infections of the organisms' cells, thus suggesting that genetic behavior was a biophysical function. Consequently, the discovery played an important role in establishing the "phage school" as perhaps the best way to investigate the underlying principles of molecular biology. It also served as a springboard for the research of JAMES D. WATSON, a member of the phage school, who with Francis Crick would discover the double-helix structure of deoxyribonucleic acid (DNA) in 1953.

Watson and Crick's discovery showed that biochemistry, and not biophysics in the form of molecular biology, held the keys to unlocking the secrets of genetic replication. As a result, the importance of the phage school was reduced significantly, and even Delbrück himself began to shift his research to other areas. Nevertheless, his study of phages had shed much light on the nature of viral behavior and genetic behavior. It also gave other researchers the tools they needed to develop vaccines against such viral diseases as measles, rubella, and mumps. For his contributions in these areas, Delbrück was awarded a one-third share of the 1969 Nobel Prize in physiology or medicine. His corecipients were Luria and Hershey.

In 1947 Delbrück returned to Caltech as a professor of biology. He continued to concentrate on phages until the mid-1950s, when he turned his attention to the molecular nature of sensory perception. He focused his research on the sense organs of the primitive fungus *Phycomyces*, this being one of the simplest life-forms having sensory perception. Although he pursued this line of research for the rest of his career, he made no discoveries to rival those he had made while studying phages.

Delbrück was elected to the National Academy of Sciences and the American Academy of Arts and Sciences. In 1941 he married Mary Manny with whom he had four children, and in 1945 he became a naturalized U.S. citizen. He continued to teach and conduct research at Caltech until his death on March 10, 1981, in Pasadena.

Further Reading

Fischer, Ernst P., and Carol Lipson. *Thinking about Science: Max Delbruck and the Origins of Molecular Biology*. New York: Norton, 1988.

Nobelprize.org. "The Nobel Prize in Physiology or Medicine 1969." Available online. URL: http://nobelprize. org/medicine/laureates/1969. Downloaded on April 16, 2004.

Wasson, Tyler, ed. *Nobel Prize Winners*. New York: H. W. Wilson, 1987, pp. 255–257.

Dodge, Bernard O.
(Bernard Ogilvie Dodge)
(1872–1960) *botanist*

Bernard O. Dodge was one of the foremost plant pathologists of his day. His work concerning the genetics of the bread mold *Neurospora* laid the groundwork for other researchers to win a Nobel Prize.

Dodge was born on April 18, 1872, in Mauston, Wisconsin. His parents, Eldridge and Mary Ann, were farmers. He graduated from high school at the age of 20, mostly because his duties on the family farm precluded him from going to school full-time. After graduation he taught school for eight years, and then in 1900 he entered the Milwaukee Normal School, receiving a teaching certificate the next year. He resumed teaching, and in 1906 he married Jennie Perry with whom he had no children.

In 1908 Dodge enrolled in the University of Wisconsin and received a B.A. in philosophy the following year. While at Wisconsin, he took a botany class under Robert A. Harper, who instilled in Dodge a great desire to learn more about plant life. Meanwhile, Harper was so impressed with Dodge that he encouraged Dodge to go to graduate school. In 1909, when Harper left Wisconsin for Columbia University, Dodge joined him as his research assistant.

After receiving a Ph.D. in botany and physics in 1912, Dodge remained at Columbia as a botany instructor and researcher. His primary research interest was fungi, one of several groups of plants whose distinguishing feature is a simple vegetative body that lacks leaves, roots, or stems. Fungi include such plants as mushrooms and molds, but they also include microscopic plants that cause disease in other plants, and it was in this latter group, known as plant pathogens, that Dodge took the most interest. At Columbia he studied the fungi that produce heart-rot in apple trees, as well as *Gymnosporangium*, the rust that causes a variety of diseases in cedar and apple trees. By 1920 Dodge was able to describe the life cycle, the form and structure, and the cell function of *Gymnosporangium*. He had also discovered heterothallism, an unusual method of reproduction, in *Ascobolus*, a parasitic sac fungus that preys on fruit trees.

Dodge's groundbreaking work with plant pathogens led to his recruitment in 1920 by the U.S. Department of Agriculture (USDA) as a plant pathologist with the Bureau of Plant Industry in Washington, D.C. In this position, he was responsible for investigating the diseases that affect fruit trees. His continued work with *Ascobolus* led directly to important findings in the development of plant disease control. In 1928 he returned to New York City as senior plant pathologist for the New York Botanical Garden (NYBG), and for the next 19 years he worked to control diseases in ornamental plants, particularly in irises, marigolds, and roses. In 1943 he and Harold W. Rickett coauthored *Diseases and Pests of Ornamental Plants*, which soon became a standard textbook on the subject of plant pathology.

Dodge's primary interest, however, concerned the red bread-mold fungi *Neurospora*. He and a USDA colleague, Cornelius L. Shear, had named *Neurospora* when they were assigned to study it in 1926. Because *Neurospora* was not a problem for ornamental plants, Dodge was not encouraged to continue his experiments with it after he became affiliated with NYBG. Nevertheless, he continued to study it in his spare time and at his own expense, and by the end of his career he had published more than 40 papers on *Neurospora*. Dodge discovered three species—*N. erythraea, N. sitophila,* and *N. tetrasperma*—and characterized the life cycles of all three. He also discovered that the first two species possess only one set of chromosomes, and that they inherited physical characteristics in the same way that animals and more sophisticated plants did. Perhaps most importantly, he developed methods by which *Neurospora* could be manipulated genetically, thus making it a valuable tool in the study of biogenetics, particularly the role of genes in biochemical processes. Dodge's work laid the groundwork for further experiments by GEORGE W. BEADLE and EDWARD L. TATUM, who won the 1958 Nobel Prize for physiology or medicine for their experiments concerning the genetic control of biochemical reactions in *Neurospora*.

Dodge retired from NYBG in 1947, but he continued to work part-time for another 10 years. Among his many professional positions, he served as editor of the *Bulletin of the Torrey Botanical Club*, president of the Mycological Society of America, and vice president of the 7th International Botanical Congress in Stockholm, Sweden. He was elected to membership in the National Academy of Sciences and the American Association for the

Advancement of Science. He died in New York City on August 9, 1960.

Further Reading

The New York Botanical Garden. "Bernard Ogilvie Dodge Records: Biographical Note." Available online. URL: http://www.nybg.org/bsci/libr/Dodge5. htm. Downloaded on November 28, 2003.

Robbins, William J. "Bernard Ogilvie Dodge," National Academy of Sciences, *Biographical Memoirs* 36 (1962): pp. 84–124.

Doisy, Edward A.
(Edward Adelbert Doisy)
(1893–1986) *biochemist*

Edward A. Doisy is best remembered for his role in discovering and arriving at a better understanding of vitamin K. For this contribution, he was awarded a share of the 1943 Nobel Prize in physiology or medicine.

Doisy was born on November 13, 1893, in Hume, Illinois. His father, Edward, was a traveling salesman, and his mother, Ada, was a homemaker. At age 16 he enrolled in the University of Illinois where he received a B.A. and an M.A. in chemistry in 1914 and 1916, respectively. After a year of graduate work at Harvard University, he spent two years in the U.S. Army Sanitary Corps. Discharged following the end of World War I, in 1919 he began teaching biochemistry at the Washington University School of Medicine in St. Louis, Missouri. Meanwhile, he continued to work on his Ph.D. in biochemistry, which he received from Harvard in 1920. In 1923 he was named head of the department of biochemistry at St. Louis University School of Medicine, where he remained for the rest of his career. In 1918 he married Alice Ackert with whom he had four children; she died in 1964, and the following year he married Margaret McCormick.

Doisy's first research interest involved female sex hormones, also known as estrogens. During the 1920s he and Edgar Allen, his research assistant, began extracting estrogens from the ovaries of mice, rats, and other animals. By 1936 they had isolated all three estrogens—estrone, estradiol, and estratiol—and developed methods for obtaining them in their pure forms. Doisy patented these processes and assigned them to St. Louis University. Over the years they proved to be worth millions of dollars, as more and more medical applications for estrone, estradiol, and estratiol were found. He published his work concerning estrogens in *Sex Hormones* (1936) and *Sex and Internal Secretions* (1939), the latter cowritten with Edgar Allen and Charles H. Danforth.

In the late 1930s, Doisy became interested in the work of Danish chemist Henrik Dam. Dam had discovered that baby chickens living on an artificial, fat-free diet were prone to hemorrhaging in different parts of their bodies, and the only way to stop the hemorrhaging was to put the chicks on a diet of hempseed. Dam concluded that hempseed contained a yet-undiscovered vitamin that played a role in blood clotting, and he eventually identified what he called vitamin K as the active ingredient that prevents hemorrhaging. Dam, however, was not able to isolate vitamin K in its pure form.

Taking up where Dam left off, Doisy and a graduate assistant, Ralph McKee, began working with vitamin K, which by now had been discovered in the seeds of several plants and in animal liver, which was found to produce it. They quickly discovered that Dam's vitamin K is actually two vitamins, K_1 and K_2. By 1939 they had produced both vitamins in their pure form, identified their chemical structures, and developed a process for producing them synthetically. Once again, Doisy patented these methods and assigned them to St. Louis University. At first, vitamins K_1 and K_2 were used to prevent hemorrhaging in newborn infants, a fairly common occurrence, but later they were put to use as well in preventing hemorrhaging associated with childbirth and with certain diseases of the liver, gall bladder, and intestines. For their roles in discovering and identifying vitamins K_1 and K_2, Doisy and Dam were awarded equal shares of the 1943 Nobel Prize in physiology or medicine.

Doisy served as president of the American Society of Biological Chemists, the Endocrine Society, and the Society for Experimental Biology and Medicine. In 1955 St. Louis University renamed its biochemistry department in his honor. He retired from St. Louis in 1965, but he continued to experiment with the estrogens and vitamins K_1 and K_2 in his old laboratory. He died on October 23, 1986, in St. Louis.

Further Reading

Edward A. Doisy Department of Biochemistry and Molecular Biology. "History." Available online. URL: http://biochemweb.slo.edu/history.html. Downloaded on March 25, 2005.

Nobelprize.org. "The Nobel Prize in Physiology or Medicine 1943." Available online. URL: http://nobelprize.org/medicine/laureates/1943. Downloaded on January 9, 2004.

Wasson, Tyler, ed. *Nobel Prize Winners.* New York: H. W. Wilson, 1987, pp. 265–266.

Drew, Charles R.
(Charles Richard Drew)
(1904–1950) *blood plasma scientist*

Charles R. Drew established the first large-scale blood bank program in the United States. He developed many of the methods and procedures for handling and preserving blood in large quantities that eventually made possible the establishment of a national blood collection program under the auspices of the American Red Cross.

Drew was born on June 3, 1904, in Washington, D.C. His father, Richard, was a carpet layer, and his mother, Nora, was a teacher. After completing high school, he attended Amherst (Mass.) College and received a B.A. in 1926. He spent the next two years teaching biology and chemistry at Morgan College (today Morgan State University) in Baltimore, Maryland. In 1928 he enrolled in McGill University Medical School in Montreal, Canada, and five years later he received an M.D. and a C.M. (master of surgery). Following a two-year internship and residency at Montreal General Hospital, in 1935 he returned to Washington to teach pathology at Howard University Medical School. Three years later he went to Columbia University Medical School in New York City to pursue a doctor of science in medicine degree. At Columbia, he became interested in blood banking, a concept that had just been introduced into the United States in 1937. Working in conjunction with John Scudder, a clinical surgeon at Columbia

University, in 1938 Drew established one of the first blood banks in the country at Presbyterian Hospital in New York. He also wrote his doctoral dissertation on the preservation of banked blood, and received his degree in 1940. That same year he returned to Howard to teach surgery and he married Minnie Robbins with whom he had four children.

Meanwhile, World War II had broken out in Europe, and the British government had contacted Drew about establishing a blood bank in England to supply blood to its wounded soldiers. In 1940 he joined the Blood for Britain Project, based in New York City, as its medical director; in this capacity he organized the preparation of liquid plasma from whole blood and its shipment from the United States to Great Britain. The quantities involved were much larger than had ever been handled previously by any blood bank, but Drew developed methods and procedures for collecting, preserving, and shipping large amounts of liquid plasma swiftly and effectively. In early 1941 he was named medical director of the American Red Cross (ARC) Blood Bank, which was established in the event that the United States should enter the war. His success in this effort led the ARC to undertake a national blood collection program in mid-1941. By that time, however, Drew had returned to Howard, this time as head of the surgery department. Nevertheless, he remained interested in the ARC's national program, and he protested its decision in late 1941 to refuse to accept blood from African-American donors on the grounds that there was no scientific evidence to prove that African-American blood and Caucasian blood were incompatible.

Drew spent the rest of his career at Howard, and in 1946 he took on the additional duties of medical director at Freedmen's Hospital. He died on April 1, 1950, in an automobile accident near Burlington, North Carolina. He received a number of posthumous awards, including the issuance of a U.S. postage stamp in his honor in 1981.

Further Reading

Love, Spencie. *One Blood: The Death and Resurrection of Charles R. Drew.* Chapel Hill: University of North Carolina Press, 1996.

Spangenburg, Ray, and Kit Moser. *African Americans in Science, Math, and Invention.* New York: Facts On File, 2003, pp. 63–64.

Wynes, Charles E. *Charles Richard Drew: The Man and the Myth.* Urbana: University of Illinois Press, 1988.

Dubos, René
(René Jules Dubos)
(1901–1982) *microbiologist*

René Dubos played an important role in the development of the first antibiotic drugs. He also contributed to a better understanding of the relation between science and society, which helped to inspire the environmental movement.

Dubos was born on February 20, 1901, in Saint-Brice-sous-Forêt, France. His father, Georges, was a butcher, and his mother, Adeline, was a homemaker. As a boy he moved with his parents to Henonville and then, in 1914, to Paris. After finishing high school, he enrolled in the Institut National Agronomique, graduating in 1921. He spent the next three years in Rome, Italy, as associate editor of the *Journal of International Agricultural Intelligence,* a publication of the League of Nations. In 1924 he emigrated to the United States, where he chanced to meet SELMAN A. WAKSMAN, who offered Dubos a research position at the New Jersey Agricultural Experiment Station. Dubos also enrolled in Rutgers University and received a Ph.D. in bacteriology in 1927. That same year he joined the staff of the Rockefeller Institute for Medical Research (today Rockefeller University) in New York City; except for a two-year stint during World War II as professor of tropical medicine at Harvard University Medical School, he remained at Rockefeller for the rest of his career. In 1934 he married Marie-Louise Bonnet; she died in 1942, and four years later he married Jean Porter.

Under Waksman, Dubos did his first experiments with soil microbiology, the study of microscopic organisms that live in soil. His doctoral dissertation involved using soil bacteria as agents to decompose cellulose; this project taught him that for every substance that occurs in nature, there is a microorganism capable of decomposing it. His first project at the Rockefeller Institute involved adapting his research with cellulose to finding a treatment for pneumonia. Previous attempts involved finding a way to break through the polysaccharide capsule that protects the pneumococcus, the bacteria that causes pneumonia, but they had all failed. Dubos devised a way to break down the capsule by identifying and cultivating soil bacteria that could decompose polysaccharides, since they decompose naturally in soil. By 1930 he had isolated the polysaccharide-decomposing enzyme that these bacteria produce, and he was able to produce enough of this enzyme to treat successfully laboratory animals with pneumonia. Before he could complete the testing necessary to use the enzyme medically, his approach was rendered unnecessary by the development of sulfa drugs, which can treat pneumonia as well as a host of other medical conditions.

Undaunted, Dubos turned his attention to finding a cure for tuberculosis, a deadly disease that killed his first wife and almost killed his second. By 1939 he had isolated another antibacterial substance, this one produced by the soil bacteria *Bacillus brevis,* which he named tyrothricin. At first, tyrothricin seemed capable of killing a wide range of infection-causing bacteria, especially those that were immune to penicillin. Upon further examination, however, he discovered that tyrothricin, when administered internally, is more deadly to test animals that it is to pathogens, which are killed by tyrothricin only under laboratory conditions. However, Dubos was able to extract another antibacterial substance from tyrothricin, which he called gramicidin. Gramicidin was also too toxic to be administered internally, but it was much more useful than tyrothricin as a means of inhibiting the growth of certain external bacterial infections.

Dubos's efforts to find a cure for tuberculosis failed. However, his discovery of tyrothricin and gramicidin contributed immeasurably to Waksman's discovery in 1943 of streptomycin, an antibiotic derived from soil bacteria that is highly effective in the treatment of tuberculosis, pneumonia, spiral meningitis, and typhoid fever. Dubos's microbiological investigations, which he summed up in *The Bacterial Cell in Its Relation to Problems of Virulence, Immunity and Chemotherapy* (1945), *Bac-*

terial and Mycotic Infections in Man (1948), and Bio-chemical Determinants of Microbial Diseases (1954), served to inform biomedical researchers and spur them to further discoveries.

In the latter half of his career, Dubos devoted much of his time and attention to writing about science for the general educated public. In these writings, which were as philosophical as they were scientific, he tried to connect science and society by making clearer the impact the one had on the other. In The White Plague: Tuberculosis, Man and Society (1952), he argued that science could not eradicate tuberculosis unless society addressed the poverty-stricken conditions in which tuberculosis, which he called a "social disease," thrived. In Mirage of Health: Utopias, Progress, and Biological Change (1959), he addressed the inability of science and technology to solve what were essentially social problems. In So Human an Animal: How We Are Shaped by Surroundings and Events (1968), he argued that global environmental problems are caused by local circumstances and choices, and therefore they can best be solved by local actions; this argument gave rise to the popular environmental slogan, "think globally, act locally." Unlike many pessimistic observers of the global environment, Dubos was optimistic about society's chances of "saving the planet" because he believed that the evolution of society made it possible for humans to reconsider their basic assumptions and change their actions in such a way that would create an ecologically responsible society.

Dubos was named professor emeritus at Rockefeller in 1971, but he continued to work until his death. His honors included editorship of the Journal of Experimental Medicine, election to the National Academy of Sciences, and a Pulitzer Prize for General Non-Fiction for So Human an Animal. In 1980 the René Dubos Center for Human Environment, a nonprofit education and research organization dedicated to resolving environmental problems, was named in his honor. He died on February 20, 1982, in New York City.

Further Reading
Hirsch, James G., and Carol L. Moberg. "René Jules Dubos," National Academy of Sciences, Biographical Memoirs 58 (1989): pp. 132–161.

Pace University Library. "René Jules Dubos (1902[sic]–1982)." Available online. URL: http://www.pace.edu/library/collection/Dubos.html. Downloaded on December 27, 2003.

Dulbecco, Renato
(1914–) virologist

Renato Dulbecco made important discoveries concerning how certain viruses cause healthy cells to become cancerous. For this contribution, he was awarded a share of the 1975 Nobel Prize in physiology or medicine.

Dulbecco was born on February 22, 1914, in Catanzaro, Italy. His father, Leonardo, was a civil engineer, and his mother, Maria, was a homemaker. As a boy he moved with his family to several Italian communities before settling in Imperia, where he grew up. At age 16 he entered the University of Turin Medical School and received an M.D. in 1936; one of his fellow medical students was SALVADOR E. LURIA. Dulbecco spent most of the next six years as a doctor in the Italian army, serving during World War II on the French and Russian fronts. Following the collapse of Benito Mussolini's government in 1942, he spent the next three years resisting the German forces that occupied Italy. He then returned to the University of Turin to teach anatomy, leaving in 1947 to join Luria at the University of Indiana in Bloomington. Married at an early age, in 1963 he divorced his first wife and married Maureen Muir with whom he had one child.

Dulbecco's research at Indiana involved bacteriophages, or phages, viruses that infect bacteria. His primary contribution to phage research was to demonstrate that white light can revive phages that have been inactivated by ultraviolet light. In the early 1950s, he turned his attention to viruses that plague animals. The first problem to overcome in this regard was to develop a method for determining how many units of a given virus were present in a culture of animal tissue. He solved this problem by adapting the plaque assay method, which had been developed by phage researchers. Dulbecco first used this method to study the biological properties of poliovirus, the results of which contributed

Renato Dulbecco showed how certain viruses can cause cancer in humans. *(Courtesy of the Salk Institute)*

in a major way to the development of ALBERT B. SABIN's live polio vaccine in 1954.

In 1949 Dulbecco left Indiana for the California Institute of Technology (Caltech) where he joined the viral research group of MAX DELBRÜCK. At Caltech Dulbecco began investigating the possibility that viruses can cause cancer. He was led to this line of inquiry by one of his graduate students, HOWARD M. TEMIN, who had been studying the Rous sarcoma virus, which had been discovered by PEYTON ROUS to cause cancer in chickens. In 1958 Dulbecco began studying polyoma virus, which causes cancer in mice. Over the next four years, he discovered much about how polyoma virus operates. Dulbecco showed that when polyoma virus invades a cell, it introduces its DNA into the cell's nucleus where it joins itself to the cell's DNA, in a sense becoming a new gene that permanently alters the cell. As the altered cell produces new cells, the DNA of the new cells includes the virus's DNA as well. Thus, the altered cell is transformed into a "factory" that manufactures cancerous cells that are not rejected by the mouse's immune system because they share the same genetic coding as the mouse's healthy cells. The process is continued as the cancerous cells reproduce themselves until the mouse dies.

Dulbecco's work provided further proof that viruses can cause cancer in animals, and thus potentially in humans, too. It also showed that the difference between a healthy cell and a cancerous cell is a matter of genetics. These contributions made possible a better understanding of the nature and mechanics of cancer, and they also gave other researchers additional tools with which to determine which human cancers, if any, are caused by viruses. As a result, in 1975 Dulbecco was awarded a one-third share of the Nobel Prize in physiology or medicine; one of his corecipients was Temin and the other was DAVID BALTIMORE.

In 1963 Dulbecco was named a resident fellow at the Salk Institute for Biological Studies in La Jolla, California, where he continued to study animal viruses. He left in 1972 for the Imperial Cancer Research Fund Laboratories in London, England, where he investigated the cause of human breast cancer. In 1977 he returned to the Salk Institute where he remained until his retirement in 1993, serving as the institute's president after 1988. From 1977 to 1981 he also taught at the University of California at San Diego Medical School. In 1986 he proposed the creation of the Human Genome Project, the international effort to study and map all human genes, and in 1990 he was named head coordinator of the Italian Human Genome Program as part of that project; since then he has divided his time between La Jolla and the Italian program's laboratories in Milan, Italy. His many honors include election to the National Academy of Sciences and the American Academy of Arts and Sciences.

Further Reading

Nobelprize.org. "The Nobel Prize in Physiology or Medicine 1975." Available online. URL: http://nobelprize. org/medicine/laureates/1975. Downloaded on June 7, 2004.

Salk Institute for Biological Studies. "Renato Dulbecco." Available online. URL: http://www.salk.edu/faculty/

faculty/details.php?id=16. Downloaded on March 25, 2005.

Wasson, Tyler, ed. *Nobel Prize Winners*. New York: H. W. Wilson, 1987, pp. 269–271.

Du Vigneaud, Vincent
(1901–1978) *biochemist*

Vincent Du Vigneaud was a leading expert on biochemical compounds composed in part of sulfur. His work in this regard led him to synthesize the hormones oxytocin and vasopressin, for which he won a Nobel Prize in chemistry.

Du Vigneaud was born on May 18, 1901, in Chicago, Illinois. His father, Alfred, was a machine designer and inventor, and his mother, Mary Theresa, was a homemaker. He studied organic chemistry at the University of Illinois at Urbana, receiving a B.S. and an M.S. in 1923 and 1924, respectively. After a year as an assistant biochemist at the Philadelphia (Pa.) General Hospital, he entered the University of Rochester and received a Ph.D. in biochemistry in 1927. He spent the next three years doing postdoctoral research as a National Research Council fellow at the Johns Hopkins University Medical School, the Kaiser Wilhelm Institute in Dresden, Germany, and the University of Edinburgh in Scotland. In 1930 he returned to Illinois to teach physiological chemistry, leaving two years later to become head of the biochemistry department at the George Washington University (GW) School of Medicine in Washington, D.C. He left GW in 1938 to accept a similar position at the Cornell University Medical College, where he remained for the rest of his career. In 1924 he married Zella Zon Ford with whom he had two children.

While a graduate student, Du Vigneaud became interested in the chemical composition of insulin, the hormone that regulates the metabolism of glucose and other carbohydrates as well as the level of sugar in the blood. He was particularly intrigued by the sulfur bonds that link together insulin's peptides (chains of amino acids) because he suspected that insulin was a derivative of the amino acid cystine, which has a high sulfur content. By 1937 he had proven his suspicion to be true, but he also showed that insulin is nothing more than amino acids, chief among them cystine, and a by-product of ammonia; that insulin gets all of its sulfur from cystine; and that insulin is regulated by its sulfur bonds with cystine and glutathione, a peptide consisting of the amino acids cysteine, glycine, and glutamic acid.

In the late 1930s, Du Vigneaud became interested in other sulfur-bearing biochemical compounds. In 1936 he synthesized glutathione, and by 1942 he had isolated and determined the chemical structure of biotin, or vitamin H. He then turned his attention to oxytocin, a hormone produced by the pituitary gland that stimulates the contraction of the uterus and the secretion of milk in pregnant women. He was able to determine quickly its chemical composition as oxytocin because it consists of only eight amino acids, whereas other hormones consist of hundreds. He then set out to synthesize oxytocin, but this task took him another 10 years because of the intricate way in which those eight amino acids are linked together in the oxytocin molecule. In 1952 Du Vigneaud's synthetic oxytocin was tested on pregnant women at the Cornell Medical Center, and it proved to be just as effective as natural oxytocin. Shortly thereafter he synthesized vasopressin, another hormone produced by the pituitary gland that increases blood pressure and decreases the flow of urine from the kidneys.

Du Vigneaud's work quickly resulted in a virtually unlimited supply of oxytocin and vasopressin for hospitals everywhere. It also demonstrated much about the nature of the sulfur-bearing polypeptide hormones, as he was the first ever to synthesize one. For this achievement, he was awarded the 1955 Nobel Prize in chemistry.

In the latter half of his career, Du Vigneaud focused on the metabolism of amino acids, but he also played a major role in the international effort to synthesize penicillin. Much of his work is summarized in *A Trail of Research in Sulfur Chemistry and Metabolism, and Related Fields* (1952). His many honors include election to the National Academy of Sciences. He retired from Cornell in 1975, and he died on December 11, 1978, in White Plains, New York.

Further Reading

Hofmann, Klaus. "Vincent Du Vigneaud," National Academy of Sciences, *Biographical Memoirs* 56 (1987), pp. 542–595.

Nobelprize.org. "The Nobel Prize in Chemistry 1955." Available online. URL: http://nobelprize.org/ chemistry/ laureates/1955. Downloaded on August 1, 2004.

Wasson, Tyler, ed. *Nobel Prize Winners*. New York: H. W. Wilson, 1987, pp. 275–277.

Edelman, Gerald M.
(Gerald Maurice Edelman)
(1929–) *biochemist*

Gerald M. Edelman codiscovered the chemical structure of antibodies and showed how antibodies fight against infections. For this contribution, he was awarded a share of the 1972 Nobel Prize in physiology or medicine.

Edelman was born on July 1, 1929, in New York City. His father, Edward, was a physician, and his mother, Anna, was a homemaker. He received a B.S. in chemistry from Ursinus (Pa.) College in 1950 and an M.D. from the University of Pennsylvania Medical School in 1954. After a year's internship at Boston's Massachusetts General Hospital, in 1955 he joined the U.S. Army Medical Corps and spent the next two years at an American hospital in Paris, France. He then entered the graduate program at New York City's Rockefeller Institute for Medical Research (today Rockefeller University), and in 1960 he received a Ph.D. and became a Rockefeller administrator and researcher. In 1950 he married Maxine Morrison with whom he had three children.

Edelman's early research involved antibodies, proteins that circulate in the blood and lymph in order to protect against foreign particles and microbes, collectively known as antigens. When he began this line of investigation in 1959, some physiologists argued that the production of each type of antibody was controlled by a specific gene, while others argued that there were not enough genes for

that to be the case since there are more than 50,000 different antibodies. Edelman hoped that a detailed description of the chemical structure of an antibody might answer that question. The biggest problem he faced was that an antibody molecule can contain hundreds of amino acids, the basic building blocks of proteins; however, it was also known that certain antibody molecules are composed of strings of amino acids, and so he set out to divide the molecule into its constituent strings.

In 1961 Edelman succeeded in splitting a molecule of the antibody known as IgG into two strings by dissolving the sulfide bonds that bind together its various amino acid strings. Further research over the next eight years by Edelman and the British biochemist Rodney Porter, who worked independently of Edelman, showed that the IgG molecule is composed of four strings, two identical "light" strings and two identical "heavy" strings. The strings are arranged in the shape of the letter "Y," with each light string forming one half of a branch and each heavy string forming one half of a branch and one half of the stem. By 1969 Edelman and Porter were able to describe precisely the chemical composition of both the light and the heavy strings, and to show that a single IgG molecule contains approximately 1,300 amino acids. They also showed that an antibody attacks an antigen by trapping the antigen between its branches and then binding to the antigen in such a way that alters the chemical structure of both antigen and antibody. This latter discovery led Edelman to theorize in 1967 that the production of antibodies in general is

Gerald Edelman discovered the chemical processes via which antibodies fight against infection. *(Courtesy of Gerald M. Edelman)*

controlled to a certain extent by genes, which explains why antibodies share so many common characteristics, but that, once produced, antibodies alter their chemical structures after coming in contact with certain antigens, which explains how humans become immune to certain diseases such as measles and mumps. Further research by other researchers eventually confirmed this theory as essentially correct.

Edelman and Porter's work shed much light on the workings of antibodies in particular and the immune system in general. As a result, medical researchers were better able to identify deficiencies in the immune system and devise treatments for immunological diseases and conditions. For their contribution to this development, Edelman and Porter were each awarded a half share of the 1972 Nobel Prize in physiology or medicine.

Edelman continued to study immunology until the late 1970s, when he shifted the focus of his research to neuroscience, the study of brain activity. He was intrigued by the similarities between the brain and the immune system, namely, that both had to be flexible enough to deal with a tremendous amount of incoming variables, data in the brain's case and antigens in the immune system's case. He explained the brain's flexibility in terms of what he called "neural Darwinism," the neural system's ability to develop a number of alternate pathways via which information flows rather than relying on a fixed pathway by which each particular piece of information must travel. In essence, Edelman envisioned the workings of the neural system in much the same way that the North American landline telephone system works, by routing calls along whichever route seems most effective and efficient at any given moment, so that no two calls from one specific phone to another specific phone ever travel by the exact same route. His work and theories concerning neuroscience are contained in several books, including *Neural Darwinism* (1987), *Bright Air, Brilliant Fire: On the Matter of the Mind* (1994), and *Consciousness: How Matter Becomes Imagination* (2001).

Edelman remained at Rockefeller University until the end of his career. In conjunction with his work in neuroscience, he also served as a director of the Neurosciences Institute in San Diego, California, and the Scripps Research Institute in La Jolla, California. His many honors include election to the National Academy of Sciences and the American Academy of Arts and Sciences.

Further Reading

Hargittai, Istvan, and Magdolna Hargittai. *Candid Science II: Conversations with Famous Biomedical Scientists.* London: Imperial College Press, 2002, pp. 196–220.

Nobelprize.org. "The Nobel Prize in Physiology or Medicine 1972." Available online. URL: http://nobelprize.org/medicine/laureates/1972. Downloaded on July 5, 2004.

Wasson, Tyler, ed. *Nobel Prize Winners.* New York: H. W. Wilson, 1987, pp. 282–284.

Einstein, Albert
(1879–1955) *physicist*

Albert Einstein is generally considered to be the leading theoretical physicist of the 20th century and one of the greatest scientists of all time. His work concerning Brownian motion and the photoelectric effect won him the 1921 Nobel Prize in physics. He is best remembered, however, for developing the special and general theories of relativity and for his work concerning the conversion of matter into energy and vice versa, which he expressed so famously in the formula $E=mc^2$.

Einstein was born on March 14, 1879, in Ulm, Germany. His father, Hermann, owned a small electrical plant and engineering works, and his mother, Pauline, was a homemaker. While an infant, he moved with his family to Munich and then, at age 12, to Milan, Italy. After completing his secondary education in Switzerland in 1896, he entered the Federal Polytechnic School in Zurich, receiving a diploma in physics and mathematics in 1901 and a Ph.D. in physics in 1905. During his time at Polytechnic, he also became a Swiss citizen (1901), went to work for the Swiss patent office (1901), and married Mileva Marić (1903) with whom he had two children. They divorced in 1919, and that same year he married Elsa Löwenthal.

Einstein's reputation as a theoretical physicist was established in 1905, when he published four groundbreaking papers in *Annalen der Physik*, an important German-language journal devoted to physics. The first paper, whose title in English is "On the Motion—Required by the Molecular Kinetic Theory of Heat—of Small Particles Suspended in a Stationary Liquid," offered the first theoretical explanation of Brownian motion. Named after the Scottish botanist Robert Brown, who in 1827 undertook its study, Brownian motion is the random movement of microscopic solid particles (atoms or

Albert Einstein (seated, second from left) is considered by many to be the greatest theoretical physicist who ever lived. In this photograph, taken at a 1931 dinner in his honor at the California Institute of Technology, he is flanked by fellow Nobel laureates Robert A. Millikan (seated, first from left) and Albert A. Michelson. *(©Bettmann/Corbis)*

molecules) suspended in a fluid (a liquid or gas). Einstein theorized that Brownian motion occurs because a particle is bumped continuously by adjacent particles, and that the rate of Brownian motion is affected by the size of the particle and the viscosity and temperature of the fluid in which it is suspended. He also developed a formula for computing the probability that Brownian motion will cause a given particle to move a given distance in a given direction during a given time interval. This work was verified experimentally over the next six years by the French physicist Jean-Baptiste Perrin.

The second paper, "On a Heuristic Viewpoint Concerning the Production and Transformation of Light," offered an explanation for the photoelectric effect, the emission of electrons by certain solids when they are struck by a beam of light. Einstein concluded that light waves are composed of individual and identical packets of energy that behave like particles; he named these packets quanta, but today they are known as photons. He theorized that the photoelectric effect is caused by the collision of two sets of particles, one set being the bombarded solid and the other being the bombarding quanta. He also developed a formula for calculating the kinetic energy of an electron emitted via the photoelectric effect. By 1916 this work had been verified experimentally by ROBERT A. MILLIKAN.

"On the Motion" and its subsequent proof by Perrin helped convince physicists that atoms and molecules exist as actual physical entities, a matter of intense debate at the time the paper was published. "On a Heuristic Viewpoint" and its subsequent proof by Millikan breathed new life into quantum theory, an early 20th-century attempt to explain the behavior of subatomic particles, and contributed to its development into quantum mechanics. For these two important contributions, Einstein was awarded the 1921 Nobel Prize in physics.

Ironically, the contributions Einstein made in his other two 1905 papers are at least as important as the ones that won him the Nobel Prize. "On the Electrodynamics of Moving Bodies" developed the special theory of relativity, the idea that the measurement of space and time depends on the relative motion of the observer making the measurements. Building upon the earlier work of the Irish physicist

George F. FitzGerald and the Dutch physicist Hendrik A. Lorentz, Einstein showed that, as an object's speed approaches the speed of light, its mass increases while the passage of time decreases. The special theory of relativity was exceptionally valuable to physicists developing particle accelerators, instruments that propel subatomic particles to speeds approaching the speed of light, as these particles behave in accordance with relativistic principles instead of "classical" ones.

"Does the Inertia of a Body Depend Upon Its Energy Content?" carried the special theory of relativity one step further by showing that mass and energy, rather than being conserved in every case, can be converted from one to the other. He presented in this paper the formula $E = mc^2$, where E is energy, m is mass, and c is the speed of light (approximately 186,000 miles per hour). Thus, one unit of mass can be converted into 186,000 × 186,000, or more than 34 billion, units of energy, and vice versa. This formula was exceptionally valuable to physicists experimenting with nuclear fission, the process by which nuclear reactors and bombs produce energy, and nuclear fusion, the process by which the stars produce energy.

The response generated by Einstein's 1905 work led directly to his appointment to increasingly important positions on the teaching faculties of universities in Berne, Zurich, and Prague. In 1914 he was named director of the Kaiser Wilhelm Physical Institute in Berlin, a position he held for 19 years. During his early days in Berlin he continued to think about relativity, and in 1916 he published "The Foundation of the General Theory of Relativity." He concluded that gravity is a curved field in the space-time continuum that results from the presence of mass. His conclusion was given credence three years later when it was demonstrated that starlight traveling close to the Sun is deflected by its gravitational pull in almost exactly the same manner that Einstein's equations regarding general relativity had predicted.

During the 1920s, Einstein focused on developing a unified field theory. Believing that electromagnetism and gravity are manifestations of a single universal force, he sought to develop the same sort of mathematical relationship between electromagnetism and gravity that he had established for energy and matter. In 1929 he published his preliminary findings concerning a unified field theory, but they were politely but firmly rejected by the scientific community. Undaunted, Einstein continued to pursue this project for the rest of his life, but without coming any closer to success.

The rise of Nazism in Germany in 1933 forced Einstein to renounce his German citizenship, which he had resumed in 1914, and accept a position at Princeton University's Institute for Advanced Study in Princeton, New Jersey. He became an American citizen in 1940, and he retired from Princeton in 1945. His book-length publications include *Relativity* (1920, 1950), *The Evolution of Physics* (1938), and *Out of My Later Years* (1950). He died on April 18, 1955, in Princeton.

Further Reading

Fox, Karen C. *Einstein A to Z*. Hoboken, N.J.: J. Wiley, 2004.

Kaku, Michio. *Einstein's Cosmos: How Albert Einstein's Vision Transformed Our Understanding of Space and Time*. New York: W. W. Norton, 2004.

Mih, Walter C. *The Fascinating Life and Theory of Albert Einstein*. Huntington, N.Y.: Kroshka Books, 2000.

Nobelprize.org. "The Nobel Prize in Physics 1921." Available online. URL: http://nobelprize.org/physics/laureates/1921. Downloaded on December 27, 2004.

Severance, John B. *Einstein: Visionary Scientist*. New York: Clarion Books, 1999.

Elion, Gertrude B.
(Gertrude Belle Elion)
(1918–1999) *pharmacologist*

In 1988 Gertrude Elion was awarded a share of the Nobel Prize for physiology or medicine. The award was unusual for two reasons: It was one of the few given to pharmaceutical drug researchers, and it was one of the few given to a woman.

Elion was born on January 23, 1918, in New York City. Her father, Robert, was a dentist, and her mother, Bertha, was a homemaker. As a girl, she was drawn to a career in science by two major influences. The first was her fascination with Marie Curie, who won two Nobel Prizes for her work with radium. The other was the profound effect made

upon her by the painful death of her grandfather, who died from stomach cancer when she was 15. After finishing high school, she enrolled in Hunter College and received a B.A. in chemistry in 1937.

Elion had a hard time finding a research position after graduation. For one thing, it was during the Great Depression, and jobs were scarce. For another, she was an attractive redhead, and at least one prospective employer refused to hire her because he feared she would distract the male researchers. She finally found a job as an assistant to Alexander Galat, a research chemist for a small pharmaceutical company, and then only because she offered to work for six months for free. In 1939 she enrolled in New York University and received an M.S. in chemistry two years later. During this period her fiancé died, and she never met anyone else whom she considered marrying.

Between 1941 and 1944 Elion worked as a quality control chemist for the Quaker Maid Company and as a research assistant for the pharmaceutical division of Johnson & Johnson. She found both positions to be quite boring, as the most difficult thing she was asked to do was measure the tensile strength of sutures. Desiring instead to help find a cure for cancer, in 1944 she went to work for GEORGE H. HITCHINGS, a research chemist with Burroughs Wellcome in Tuckahoe, New York, as his chief research assistant. Hitchings took a unique approach to developing new pharmaceutical drugs. Rather than invent a drug and then test it to see what it would do, he studied the biochemical differences between healthy cells and cells infected with the disease he was trying to cure. Once he understood the differences, he set out to design a drug that would affect the diseased cells while leaving the healthy ones alone. He also took a unique approach to managing Elion; rather than treating her as an attractive flunky, he considered her to be a valued colleague, and he generally allowed her to follow her own lead on research projects.

One of Elion's first assignments from Hitchings was to find a cure for leukemia, a type of blood cancer that ultimately leads to death, especially in children. Following Hitchings's guidelines, she first discovered how leukemia cells produce deoxyribonucleic acid, or DNA, which is essential to cell growth. Next, she set out to develop a drug that would interfere with the way leukemia cells produce DNA but that would not interfere with the DNA production of healthy cells. By 1948 she had developed such a drug, 2,6-diaminopurine. Unfortunately, the drug's side effects included such intense nausea and vomiting that it could not be prescribed.

Elion kept experimenting, and by 1951 she had developed 6-mercaptopurine, better known as 6-MP. This drug caused remission in child leukemia patients for up to one year without any deleterious side effects. More effective drugs for the treatment of leukemia have since been developed, but 6-MP continues to be prescribed to leukemia patients in remission. Meanwhile, 6-MP proved to have other applications. In 1957 Elion developed a derivative of 6-MP, azathioprine, which proved useful in suppressing the body's immune system during transplant operations. Five years later, JOSEPH E. MURRAY used azathioprine during the first successful kidney transplant in which the donor was not related to the recipient. In 1963 Elion discovered that allopurinol, a drug she developed to break down 6-MP, is useful as a treatment for gout and for certain parasitic infections such as leishmaniasis and Chagas' disease.

In 1967 Elion ended her 23-year stint as Hitchings's assistant to become head of Burroughs Wellcome's department of experimental therapy. Three years later she accompanied the department when it relocated to the Research Triangle Park near Chapel Hill, North Carolina. Her chief research activity in this capacity involved the development of acyclovir. The genesis of this research came in 1968, when she read a medical journal article that suggested that 2,6-diaminopurine could be enhanced so that it could keep DNA viruses from growing. Intrigued, she developed 2,6-diaminopurine arabinoside, which proved to be mildly effective against herpes viruses. She then directed a major research effort to design a much stronger drug, and in 1974 one of her researchers, Howard Schaeffer, developed acyclovir. One hundred times more potent than 2,6-diaminopurine arabinoside, acyclovir was the first drug to treat herpes viruses successfully.

In 1983 Elion retired from Burroughs Wellcome, but she continued to work as a consultant.

In this capacity she helped develop azidothymidine (AZT), the first drug approved by the Food and Drug Administration for the treatment of HIV/AIDS.

In 1988 Elion and Hitchings were awarded a share of the Nobel Prize for physiology or medicine; the third recipient was Sir James Black, who had developed drugs for treating heart disease and ulcers. The trio received the award not because of the particular drugs they had developed but because the innovative approach they had taken to develop them brought about major changes in the way pharmaceutical companies conduct research. In 1991 Elion became the first woman to be elected to the Inventors' Hall of Fame. That same year she also was awarded the National Medal of Science. She died on February 21, 1999, in Chapel Hill.

Further Reading

Carey, Charles W., Jr. "Elion, Gertrude Belle," *American Inventors, Entrepreneurs, and Business Visionaries.* New York: Facts On File, 2002, pp. 111–113.

Nobelprize.org. "The Nobel Prize in Physiology or Medicine 1988." Available online. URL: http://nobelprize.org/medicine/laureates/1988. Downloaded on June 24, 2003.

Wasserman, Elga. *The Door in the Dream: Conversations with Eminent Women in Science.* Washington, D.C.: Joseph Henry Press, 2000.

Yount, Lisa. "Elion, Gertrude Belle," *A to Z of Women in Science and Math.* New York: Facts On File, 1999, pp. 57–60.

Emeagwali, Philip
(Chukwurah Emeagwali)
(1954–   ) *computer scientist*

Philip Emeagwali is considered to be one of the founders of the Internet. He developed a program that allowed more than 65,000 computers in various locations to work together to solve the same problem, thus revolutionizing the way supercomputers are constructed and programmed.

Emeagwali was born Chukwurah Emeagwali on August 23, 1954, in Akure, Nigeria; his baptismal name is Philip. His father, James, was a nursing assistant, and his mother, Agatha, was a homemaker. In

1967 Biafra, the region in which the Emeagwalis were then living, seceded from Nigeria, and he dropped out of school and went to live with his family in a refugee camp. Two years later, at age 14, he was conscripted into the Biafran army and served as a cook until the war ended in 1970. He completed his first year of high school at Christ the King College in Onitsha before dropping out because of financial problems. Nevertheless, he was able to teach himself enough to pass a high school equivalency test administered by the University of London in 1973. He then obtained a scholarship to Oregon State University, where he received a B.S. in mathematics in 1977. After graduation he relocated to the Washington, D.C., area where he worked for the Maryland State Highway Administration and the National Weather Service while attending Howard University, George Washington University (M.S., environmental engineering, 1981; M.S., ocean, coastal, and marine engineering, 1986), and the University of Maryland (M.S., mathematics, 1986). In 1986 he moved to Wyoming to work as a civil engineer for the U.S. Bureau of Reclamation, but he left shortly thereafter to attend the University of Michigan, where he received a Ph.D. in applied mathematics in 1993. While working on his doctorate, he also conducted research at the Army High Performance Computing Research Center at the University of Minnesota. In 1981 he married Dale Brown with whom he had one child, and in 1983 he obtained a permanent U.S. residency visa.

Emeagwali's interest in computers began at Oregon State, where he wrote his first program and began hosting on ARPANET, a predecessor of the Internet. This interest led him to take up the problem of parallel processing, linking together a number of computers so that they could all work on the same problem at the same time. In 1974 he began thinking of how to hook up 64,000 computers around the Earth as a way to forecast the weather, an idea inspired by a science fiction story. He eventually put together a 1,000-page dissertation on how to do this, which later served as his doctoral dissertation in 1993. Before that, however, he received the opportunity to put his plan into action.

The Los Alamos National Laboratory had tried but failed to program an experimental computer system containing 65,536 central processing units.

Philip Emeagwali developed a way for tens of thousands of computers to work together, thus paving the way for the development of the Internet. *(Courtesy of Philip Emeagwali)*

In 1987 the agency invited bids from the general public on ways to solve the problem; Emeagwali had basically solved it already, so his proposal won the bid. Over the next two years he programmed the Los Alamos system from a remote location at the University of Michigan using the National Science Foundation Network, another predecessor of the Internet. When he finished in 1989, the system was able to compute more than three billion calculations per minute, or three times faster than the largest supercomputer then in existence.

Meanwhile, Emeagwali was also working on another very difficult computational problem, the development of a reservoir simulator for the petroleum industry. Oil corporations use reservoir simulators to determine the best strategies for pumping water into an oil field so that the maximum amount of oil and gas can be extracted. By developing a multi-computer program that took into account inertial forces within the oil field, in 1989 he developed the most successful reservoir simulator to date.

Emeagwali's successes proved that a number of small processors linked together properly were more powerful than a supercomputer, something which most experts had thought was impossible. This achievement led to the redesign of supercomputers so that they make use of thousands of smaller processors, in much the same way that Emeagwali's program did. It also won for him the Institute of Electrical and Electronic Engineers' Computer Society's 1989 Gordon Bell Prize, considered by many to be computer science's most prestigious award. His other honors include the National Technical Association's Computer Scientist of the Year Award and the World Bank/International Monetary Fund's Distinguished Scientist Award.

In 1993 Emeagwali returned to the Washington area to establish his own consulting firm, eventually settling in Baltimore, Maryland. By 2001 he had focused his research on developing what he called the World Wide Brain, a global superbrain that would link together millions of computers around the globe, thus taking the World Wide Web to a higher level.

Further Reading

Emeagwali.com. "Emeagwali." Available online. URL: http://emeagwali.com/booking/biography/for-high-school-students.shtml. Downloaded on May 12, 2004.

Sanchez, Brenna. "Philip Emeagwali," *Contemporary Black Biography* 30 (2002): pp. 61–63.

Spangenburg, Ray, and Kit Moser. "Emeagwali, Philip," *African Americans in Science, Math, and Invention.* New York: Facts On File, 2003, pp. 71–73.

Enders, John F.
(John Franklin Enders)
(1897–1985) *virologist*

John F. Enders played a major role in developing a method for growing the polio virus under laboratory conditions. This development made possible the development of a polio vaccine, and it won for Enders a share of the 1954 Nobel Prize in physiology or medicine.

Enders was born on February 10, 1897, in West Hartford, Connecticut. His father, John, was a banker, and his mother, Harriet, was a homemaker. After receiving a private school education, he entered Yale University in 1915. Two years later he joined the U.S. Naval Reserve and served during World War I as a flight instructor. He returned to Yale after being discharged in 1919, and he received a B.A. the following year. After selling real estate in Hartford for a year, he entered Harvard University with the intention of becoming an English teacher, receiving an M.A. in English in 1922. While working on a Ph.D., he became interested in bacteriology, so in 1927 he switched his program of studies from English to bacteriology and immunology, in which he received a Ph.D. in 1930. He then joined the faculty at Harvard, where he remained for the rest of his career. In 1927 he married Sarah Bennett with whom he had two children; she died in 1943, and eight years later he married Carol Keane.

Prior to 1939, Enders's research efforts focused on the relationship between the virulence, or strength, of *Pneumococcus,* the bacterium that causes pneumonia, and the resistance of the host organisms it seeks to infect. In 1939 he began studying other mammalian viruses, particularly influenza, measles, and mumps. He and his assistants, THOMAS H. WELLER among them, came up with new techniques for cultivating the mumps virus in laboratory cultures, which allowed them to develop blood and skin tests for the early detection of the mumps virus. They also demonstrated that even a mild strain of the virus immunizes its human host.

In 1946 Enders established a laboratory for investigating infectious diseases at the Boston Children's Hospital. Working in collaboration with Weller and FREDERICK C. ROBBINS, he began studying poliomyelitis, also known as polio and infantile paralysis, a crippling disease that plagued children. Prior to 1946, poliomyelitis was difficult to study because researchers could grow the polio virus only in the nerve tissue of live monkeys. Not only did this constraint limit the amount of the virus available to study, but also it prevented researchers from learning how polio develops in human tissue.

By 1949 Enders, Weller, and Robbins had adapted the culture-growing techniques Enders and Weller had devised while studying the mumps virus so that they were able to produce sufficient quantities of the polio virus to facilitate wide-scale experimentation. Basically, they placed cultures of kidney tissue from monkeys and human embryos in test tubes, into which were also introduced a bit of polio virus.

The result of Enders, Weller, and Robbins's achievement was the ability of medical researchers to observe the growth of the polio virus in living human cells under laboratory conditions. This development set the stage for JONAS E. SALK to develop a polio vaccine in 1954 as well as the development of ALBERT B. SABIN's oral polio vaccine in 1960. For their work regarding the in vitro growth of the polio virus, Enders, Weller, and Robbins were awarded equal shares of the 1954 Nobel Prize in physiology or medicine.

Enders continued to work with Weller and Robbins until 1952, when Robbins left Children's Hospital. In the late 1950s Enders and Weller produced a measles vaccine that went into widespread distribution in 1963. In 1977 Enders retired; he died on September 8, 1985, in Waterford, Connecticut.

Further Reading

Weller, Thomas H., and Frederick C. Robbins. "John Franklin Enders," National Academy of Sciences, *Biographical Memoirs* 60 (1991): pp. 47–65.

Nobelprize.org. "The Nobel Prize in Physiology or Medicine 1954." Available online. URL: http://nobelprize.org/medicine/laureates/1954. Downloaded on January 12, 2004.

Wasson, Tyler, ed. *Nobel Prize Winners*. New York: H. W. Wilson, 1987, pp. 300–302.

Erlanger, Joseph
(1874–1965) *physiologist*

Joseph Erlanger won a share of the 1944 Nobel Prize for medicine or physiology for his groundbreaking research concerning nerve fibers. His research work also contributed to a better understanding of the cardiovascular system, particularly how it sends and receives nervous impulses.

Erlanger was born on January 5, 1874, in San Francisco, California. His father, Herman, was a merchant, and his mother, Sarah, was a homemaker. After receiving a B.S. in chemistry from the University of California at Berkeley in 1895, he entered Johns Hopkins Medical School in Baltimore, Maryland. Upon receiving an M.D. in 1899, he interned for a year at Johns Hopkins Hospital and then he became an assistant in the school's physiology department. In 1906, the same year he married Aimée Hirtsel with whom he had three children, he founded the department of physiology at the University of Wisconsin's new medical school. Four years later he became chair of the department of physiology at Washington University in St. Louis, Missouri, where he remained for the rest of his career.

Prior to 1921, Erlanger's research focused primarily on the cardiovascular system. While a medical student, he designed improvements to the sphygmomanometer, a device for measuring blood pressure in the fingers. While an intern, he determined that orthostatic albuminuria, a condition whereby the kidneys secrete albumen into the urine, is caused by the pressure of the pulse on the kidney. While at Wisconsin, he determined that Stokes-Adams syndrome, a condition that causes fainting and slows down the heartbeat, is caused when the electrical impulse from the atrium telling the ventricle to contract is blocked. He also determined that the bundle of His, a small mass of muscular fibers at the base of the wall between the atria, is the connection by which impulses from the atria to the ventricles are routed.

In 1921 Erlanger refocused his research from the cardiovascular system to the nervous system. That same year he began conducting experiments with HERBERT S. GASSER, a former student of his at Wisconsin. Gasser had just been appointed chair of Washington University's department of pharmacology, but he was interested in measuring the electrical impulses that travel along nerve cells. Within a year Erlanger and Gasser developed a cathode-ray oscilloscope that was sensitive enough to measure accurately the minute currents of these impulses. Over the next 10 years they experimented with the workings of the various fibers within a single nerve cell as well as the speed at which nervous impulses travel.

By 1931, when Gasser left Washington University for Cornell Medical College, he and Erlanger had made several important discoveries concerning nerve fibers and the way they work. Their most important discovery was that there are three different types of nerve fibers in nerve cells. Called A-, B-, and C-fibers, the difference is found in their thicknesses, or diameters, with A-fibers being the thickest and C-fibers the thinnest. All three types of fibers conduct impulses at different rates, and these rates increase in direct proportion to the thickness of the fiber. For example, A-fibers, which are about 20 times thicker than C-fibers, transmit impulses up to 50 times faster than C-fibers and up to 10 times faster than B-fibers. The perception of pain is largely transmitted by C-fibers, while the impulses related to muscle sense and touch are transmitted by A-fibers. All three types of fibers are distributed throughout the nerve cells that transmit impulses up and down the spinal cord. Lastly, each fiber requires an electrical stimulus of a different intensity in order for it to transmit an impulse. For example, an A-fiber, which connects to the muscles, requires a more intense stimulus than a C-fiber, which transmits sensory feelings.

Erlanger and Gasser's work concerning the speed of transmission in nerve fibers confirmed the hypotheses of Swedish physiologist Gustav Göthlin and French physiologist Louis Lapicque, which was based on the speed of transmission in electrical cables. In recognition of their discoveries, Erlanger and Gasser were each awarded one-half of the 1944 Nobel Prize for medicine or physiology. The award was given partly for their discoveries concerning nerve fibers, and partly for the methods by which those discoveries were made. The prize committee was particularly impressed with the development of an oscilloscope capable of measuring minute currents, as this incredibly sensitive instrument opened the door to further research regarding the nerve fibers of the brain.

Erlanger retired from Washington University in 1946, but he continued to do research there for a number of years. He died on December 5, 1965, in St. Louis.

Further Reading

Davis, Hallowell. "Joseph Erlanger," National Academy of Sciences, *Biographical Memoirs* 41 (1970): pp. 111–139.

Nobelprize.org. "The Nobel Prize in Physiology or Medicine 1944." Available online. URL: http://nobelprize.org/medicine/laureates/1944. Downloaded on December 30, 2003.

Wasson, Tyler, ed. *Nobel Prize Winners.* New York: H. W. Wilson, 1987, pp. 302–304.

Faber, Sandra M.
(Sandra Moore, Sandra Moore Faber)
(1944–) *astronomer*

Sandra Faber helped develop several important theories that explain the formation and movement of galaxies. She also played an important role in improving the technology by which astronomers study outer space.

Faber was born Sandra Moore on December 28, 1944, in Boston, Massachusetts. Her father, Donald, was a civil engineer, and her mother, Elizabeth, was a homemaker. As a girl she moved with her family to Cleveland, Ohio, where she grew up. After receiving a B.S. in physics from Swarthmore College in 1966, she enrolled in Harvard University, receiving a Ph.D. in astronomy in 1972. She then became a professor of astronomy at the University of California at Santa Cruz and a member of the staff at the University's Lick Observatory. In 1967 she married Andrew Faber with whom she had two children.

Faber's research focuses on the origins and structure of galaxies. In 1975 she and Robert Jackson, one of her graduate students, discovered that a relationship exists between the size and brightness of elliptical galaxies and the orbital speeds of the stars they contain. This relationship, known as the Faber-Jackson relation, helped explain how elliptical galaxies evolve; it also helps determine distances between galaxies. By 1979 she had turned her attention to the problem of dark matter, invisible material that may constitute as much as 90 per-

cent of the matter in the universe. Dark matter cannot be seen because it neither emits nor absorbs light, and yet it exerts a gravitational pull so strong that it affects the movement of entire galaxies. Faber and several colleagues developed a theory that explains dark matter in terms of quantum physics, hypothesizing that dark matter is made up of relatively cold and relatively massive subatomic particles that interact weakly. Later, they theorized that galaxies evolve from "quantum seeds," massive chunks of dark matter that were distributed rather haphazardly throughout space by the big bang, GEORGE GAMOW's theory for the origins of the universe. In time, some of these chunks were somehow organized into visible matter that eventually became stars and planets, while most of them continued to exist as dark matter. The quantum seed theory was the first comprehensive attempt to explain the origins of the galaxies, and it is generally accepted by most astrophysicists as the best explanation to date for galaxy formation. It also offers the best explanation for the universe's "lumpiness," the uneven manner in which galaxies are distributed throughout space.

In the 1980s Faber took up the study of large-scale streaming, the phenomenon by which galaxies move through space at different rates of speed. By 1990 she and six of her colleagues, known collectively as the Seven Samurai, had discovered that one reason for this effect may be something known as the Great Attractor. One hundred and fifty million light years from Earth, the Great Attractor is 300 million light-years from end to end, and its mass exerts a gravitational pull equal to that of tens of thousands of galaxies. Meanwhile, the Great Attractor is itself being drawn toward an even larger mass somewhere else.

In addition to contributing to the advance of astrophysical theory, Faber has played an important role in advancing its technology as well. She was a member of the team that designed the *Hubble Space Telescope*, and she helped diagnose and then solve a problem with the Hubble's mirror after the telescope had been deployed in space. She also cochaired the steering committee that oversaw the development and construction of the twin 400-inch telescopes at the Keck Observatory in Hawaii, the largest telescopes in the world. Her many awards include election to the National Academy of Sciences and the American Academy of Arts and Sciences.

Further Reading

Lightman, Alan, and Roberta Brawer. *Origins: The Lives and Worlds of Modern Cosmologists.* Cambridge, Mass.: Harvard University Press, 1990, pp. 324–340.

Yount, Lisa. "Faber, Sandra Moore," *A to Z of Women in Science and Math.* New York: Facts On File, 1999, pp. 63–64.

Fenn, John B.
(John Bennett Fenn)
(1917–) *chemist*

John B. Fenn developed electrospray mass spectrometry (ESMS), a process that greatly speeds up the measurement of the molecular weights of protein molecules. For this contribution, he was awarded a quarter share of the 2002 Nobel Prize in chemistry.

Fenn was born on June 15, 1917, in New York City, but he spent his early childhood in nearby Hackensack, New Jersey. His father, Herbert, managed a manufacturing company and his mother, Jeanette, was a homemaker. At age 11 he moved with his family to Berea, Kentucky, where he grew up. After receiving an A.B. in chemistry from Berea College in 1937, he entered the graduate program at Yale University, receiving a Ph.D. in physical chemistry in 1940. He spent the next 12 years as a

research chemist for various chemical manufacturers, the last being Experiment, Inc. in Richmond, Virginia. In 1939 he married Margaret Wilson with whom he had three children.

In 1952 Fenn went to Princeton University to work on Project SQUID, a research and development project involving jet propulsion that was funded by the Office of Naval Research. While working on this project, he began adapting jet propulsion for use with the molecular beam as a tool for studying the chemical reactions that occur during combustion. Invented in 1911 by French physicist Louis Dunoyer, the molecular beam was used primarily by physicists to study the behavior of atoms and molecules in a free or noncolliding state. The technique involved injecting atoms or molecules in a gaseous state into a large vacuum through a tiny orifice so that they entered the vacuum in a thin beam. Fenn's idea was to use free jet expansion as the molecular beam's source so as to bring about reactive collisions between a beam of vaporized reactant molecules and other gaseous molecules. He was able to devote more time to this project after leaving Project SQUID in 1962, having become a professor of mechanical engineering at Princeton three years earlier.

In 1967 Fenn returned to Yale as a professor of applied science and chemistry. He continued his experiments with jet-propelled molecular beams until the mid-1980s, when he adapted jet propulsion for yet another purpose, mass spectrometry. Mass spectrometry measures the masses or molecular weights of individual atoms and molecules by giving them an electrical charge and then measuring how the trajectories of the resulting ions respond in vacuum to various combinations of electric and magnetic fields. This process is quite useful to physicists and chemists because it helps them identify precisely the atoms or molecules they are measuring. However, biochemists were unable to use mass spectrometry because protein molecules were too large to be vaporized by the methods of the day. Fenn changed this situation by developing electrospray mass spectrometry (ESMS). ESMS uses the principles of electrospray ionization (ESI) to mix proteins with water, vaporize the mixture, give it an electrical charge, and then spray it through an electrical field so that the water evaporates and only single droplets of protein are left. At this point the proteins can be weighed according to the standard methods of mass spectrometry.

ESMS permits biochemists to determine the exact chemical composition of a complex protein molecule in a matter of seconds. ESMS has proven to be of particular value in developing pharmaceuticals because it allows researchers to observe how a particular drug is broken down when it interacts with certain proteins. It also promises to be of great value as a tool for diagnosing cancer, because tumor cells have different concentrations of proteins than do healthy cells. For his contribution, Fenn was awarded a quarter share of the 2002 Nobel Prize in chemistry. His corecipients were the Japanese chemist Koichi Tanara (one-quarter share) and the Swiss chemist Kurt Wüthrich (one-half share).

Fenn retired from Yale in 1987, although he continued to conduct research concerning ESMS at Yale for the next six years; his first paper concerning ESMS was not published until 1989. In 1993 he returned to Richmond, Virginia, where he joined the faculty of Virginia Commonwealth University as a research professor of analytical chemistry.

Further Reading

Chang, Kenneth. "3 Whose Work Speeded Drugs Win Nobel," *New York Times*, October 10, 2002, p. A33.

Nobelprize.org. "The Nobel Prize in Chemistry 2002." Available online. URL: http://nobelprize.org/chemistry/laureates/2002. Downloaded on July 29, 2004.

VCU Department of Chemistry. "John B. Fenn." Available online. URL: http://www.has.vcu.edu/che/people/bio/fenn.html. Downloaded on March 25, 2005.

Fermi, Enrico
(1901–1954) *physicist*

Enrico Fermi performed the first experiment involving nuclear fusion, which led directly to the first experiment involving nuclear fission. For demonstrating the ability of slow-moving neutrons to start nuclear reactions, he was awarded the 1938 Nobel Prize in physics.

Fermi was born on September 29, 1901, in Rome, Italy. His father, Alberto, was a railroad inspector, and his mother, Ida, was a schoolteacher. At age 17 he entered the University of Pisa's undergraduate and graduate schools, receiving both an undergraduate degree and a Ph.D. in physics in 1922. He spent the next three years studying quantum mechanics at the universities of Göttingen and Leiden and teaching mathematics at the University of Rome, and in 1925 he took a position teaching mathematical physics at the University of Florence. Two years later he returned to Rome as a professor of theoretical physics, and over the next 11 years he helped the physics department develop into a world-class program. In 1928 he married Laura Capon with whom he had two children.

The first part of Fermi's career was devoted to theoretical physics, which attempts to explain physical behavior via mathematics rather than experiments. While in college he published papers addressing the properties of sound, the interactions of electric, magnetic, and mechanical phenomena, and ALBERT EINSTEIN's theory of general relativity, while his graduate thesis addressed the orbits of comets in terms of probability theory. In 1926 he published an influential paper on the statistical behavior of a perfect, hypothetical gas. That same year he became interested in Wolfgang Pauli's exclusion principle; in 1925 Pauli had stated that electrons cannot be paired at a given energy level within an atom unless their spins, a function of their magnetic properties, are opposite to each other. By 1927 Fermi had worked out the statistical laws governing the distribution of electrons in accordance with the Pauli exclusion principle. Later, it was discovered that neutrons and certain other subatomic particles also obey the Pauli exclusion principle; today these particles are known as fermions, while Fermi's statistical laws are known as the Fermi-Dirac statistics, after Fermi and the French physicist Paul Dirac, who discovered them at the same time as Fermi.

Fermi's work with the Pauli exclusion principle led him to develop, in 1928, a statistical model of the atom. He calculated the statistical averages of the individual wave functions of an atom's electrons to determine the approximate distribution of electrons around the nucleus at any given moment.

Enrico Fermi, a pioneer in the fields of nuclear fusion and nuclear fission, designed and oversaw the operation of the world's first nuclear reactor. *(©Corbis)*

This model became known as the Thomas-Fermi model, after Fermi and the British physicist Llewellyn Thomas, who, unknown to Fermi, had proposed a similar model the year before. In 1929 Fermi turned his attention to Dirac's theories concerning quantum electrodynamics, the interactions of charged particles with each other and with forms of electromagnetic radiation such as light, and by 1932 he had simplified Dirac's theories considerably. Over the next two years he reworked Pauli's theory of beta decay, which Pauli had proposed to explain certain types of radioactive disintegration. Pauli's theory had been advanced prior to the discovery of the neutron in 1932, so Fermi described beta decay as the radioactive disintegration of a neutron into a proton, an electron, and a neutrino—a subatomic particle with no charge and virtually no mass.

Despite these achievements, in 1934 Fermi gave up theoretical physics for experimental physics. He made this decision after hearing that French physicists Frédéric and Irène Joliot-Curie had created artificial radioactivity by bombarding various elements with alpha particles (an alpha particle consists of two neutrons and two protons). These developments gave Fermi the idea to create artificial radioactivity by using only neutrons instead of alpha particles, on the reasoning that neutrons possess no net charge and so they would most likely be able to penetrate the various layers of the atom with greater ease. He also reasoned that the neutrons would have to be slowed down to maximize their effect, which he did by passing them through a layer of water or paraffin. In the process he and EMILIO SEGRÈ, a University of Rome colleague, were able to create radioactive isotopes from every element except hydrogen, helium, and some of the ones that are already radioactive. When they bombarded uranium with slow-moving neutrons, however, they obtained something that did not seem to be a radioactive isotope of uranium. Although no one is entirely sure what it was, it is today believed that the result of their uranium bombardment experiment was actually the creation of the first transuranium element. In all likelihood, several of the uranium nuclei captured several of the slow-moving neutrons, thus being transformed into what is now known as neptunium.

Fermi's neutron bombardment experiment, known today as the Fermi-Segrè experiment, had two important repercussions. In 1938 three German physicists, Otto Hahn, Fritz Strassmann, and Lise Meitner, attempted to re-create the Fermi-Segrè experiment, but instead of obtaining a new element via nuclear fusion, they split several uranium nuclei into several parts via nuclear fission. Two years later the Fermi-Segrè experiment was re-created by EDWIN M. MCMILLAN and Philip H. Abelson; this time the neutrons were kept under better control, and the result was the first verified creation of neptunium, the first transuranium element, via nuclear fusion. Even before the McMillan-Abelson experiment, the importance of Fermi's use of neutrons to initiate nuclear reactions had been recognized, and in 1938 he was awarded the Nobel Prize in physics.

In 1938 Fermi left Italy for the United States, and in 1939 he was named professor of physics at Columbia University. That same year he learned that Hahn, Strassmann, and Meitner had obtained nuclear fission, and when he re-created their experiment he received the same results. Realizing the implications, especially considering that World War II had just broken out in Europe, he and several colleagues convinced President Franklin D. Roosevelt to begin a federally funded research project for exploring the development of nuclear fission into a military weapon. The result was the creation in 1942 of the Manhattan Project, the U.S. effort to build an atomic bomb. Fermi was put in charge of developing a controlled, self-sustaining nuclear chain reaction, and he assembled a team and established a laboratory at the University of Chicago. Here he constructed the world's first atomic pile, and in late 1942 the desired effect was achieved. He then devoted himself to solving the various problems associated with developing enough fissionable material for a bomb, thus playing a major role in the development of the bombs that were dropped on Hiroshima and Nagasaki in 1945. For his contribution to the success of the Manhattan Project, Fermi was made a naturalized U.S. citizen in 1944 and later awarded the Presidential Medal for Merit.

In 1946 Fermi was named Distinguished Service Professor for Nuclear Studies at the University of Chicago, a position he held until his death on November 28, 1954, in Chicago. His many honors include election to the National Academy of Sciences and receipt of the U.S. Atomic Energy Commission's first Fermi Award. The Fermi National Accelerator Laboratory in Batavia, Illinois, was named in his honor, as was fermium, transuranium element 100.

Further Reading

Latil, Pierre de. *Enrico Fermi: The Man and His Discoveries.* New York: P. S. Eriksson, 1964.

Nobelprize.org. "The Nobel Prize in Physics 1938." Available online. URL: http://nobelprize.org/physics/laureates/1938. Downloaded on May 5, 2004.

Segrè, Emilio. *Enrico Fermi: Physicist.* Chicago: University of Chicago Press, 1970.

Wasson, Tyler, ed. *Nobel Prize Winners.* New York: H. W. Wilson, 1987, pp. 314–316.

Feynman, Richard P.
(Richard Phillips Feynman)
(1918–1988) *physicist*

Richard P. Feynman was one of three physicists who resuscitated the outmoded theory of quantum electrodynamics (QED), the body of theory concerning the interactions of charged particles with each other and with forms of electromagnetic radiation such as light. For this achievement, he was awarded a share of the 1965 Nobel Prize in physics. His other achievements include contributing to the development of the theory of quarks, the basic building blocks of all matter.

Feynman was born on May 11, 1918, in New York City. His father, Melville, was a clothing salesman, and his mother, Lucille, was a homemaker. He received a B.S. in physics from the Massachusetts Institute of Technology in 1939 and a Ph.D. in physics from Princeton University in 1942. He spent World War II at the Manhattan Project's facility in Los Alamos, New Mexico, where he helped design the first atomic bombs. In 1945 he was named a professor of theoretical physics at Cornell University, but he left five years later to accept a similar post at the California Institute of Technology (Caltech), where he taught until his death. In 1941 he married

Arline Greenbaum; she died in 1945, and in 1952 he married Mary Louise Bell. They divorced in 1956, and in 1960 he married Gweneth Howarth with whom he had two children.

In his doctoral dissertation, Feynman applied a concept of classical physics, the principle of least action, to quantum mechanics, the study of subatomic particles, using it to predict which path a particle will take from one point to another. After World War II he began applying this principle to the problems encountered by quantum electrodynamics. QED is concerned primarily with the interaction between energy and matter. Specifically, it attempts to understand how certain subatomic particles, such as electrons and their positively charged counterparts, positrons, are formed from tiny packets of electromagnetic radiation known as photons, as well as how electrons and positrons can destroy each other and, in the process, be converted into photons. QED also studies the process by which photons transmit energy from one charged particle in a nucleus to another. QED originated in 1928 when French physicist Paul Dirac described the motion of electrons in terms of quantum theory and Albert Einstein's theory of special relativity. Two German physicists, Werner Heisenberg and Wolfgang Pauli, both of whom helped develop the theory of quantum mechanics, contributed to QED as well. In their hands, QED was used to develop equations for calculating certain magnetic properties of the electron and the positron, but they were unable to use it to develop equations for calculating such relatively simple things as the mass and charge of the positron and other particles found in the nucleus. As a result of this failure, by the late 1930s QED had become a discredited theory.

Feynman's approach to QED was to bypass considering the effects of the nucleus's electromagnetic field on particles and to consider instead the possible interactions between charged particles in a nucleus. In so doing, he developed the Feynman diagram, in essence a drawing of one particle interacting with another. He used Feynman diagrams to depict all the possible particle interactions, both individually and as groups. These diagrams were much more effective at explaining particle interactions than were the complicated mathematical equations that were also necessary to provide a complete understanding of QED. By 1948 he had essentially reconstructed the basic formulas and theories of QED, and his work in this regard is summarized in *Quantum Electrodynamics* (1961).

Meanwhile, Feynman's efforts were being duplicated independently by JULIAN S. SCHWINGER and Japanese physicist Shinichiro Tomonaga. Schwinger took a highly formal approach to the problem, and some of the mathematical equations he developed are very difficult to understand, even for physicists. Tomonaga, on the other hand, took a less abstract approach, as did Feynman, whose approach was the least abstract of all. Despite their different approaches, all three arrived at the same basic conclusions and solutions, thus transforming QED from a theory of questionable value into one of the most powerful tools of quantum mechanics. For his contribution to reformulating QED, Feynman was awarded a one-third share of the 1965 Nobel Prize in physics, as were Schwinger and Tomonaga.

After 1950 Feynman turned his attention from QED to other areas. In the early 1950s he explained superfluidity, the ability of certain liquids at temperatures near absolute zero to flow without resistance, in terms of quantum mechanics. He later tried using this same approach to explain superconductivity, the ability of certain metals at temperatures near absolute zero to conduct electricity without resistance, but failed. In 1958 he and MURRAY GELL-MANN developed a theory to explain why neutrons sometimes decay by emitting electrons, positrons, or neutrinos; the latter particles have no charge and virtually no mass. In the 1960s he and Gell-Mann collaborated on the development of the quark theory, which postulates that quarks are elementary particles that serve as "building blocks" for all other subatomic particles, including neutrons and protons. Today it is generally understood that the quark theory is essentially correct.

Feynman was elected to the National Academy of Sciences and the American Association for the Advancement of Science. He died on February 15, 1988, in Los Angeles, California.

Further Reading

Feynman, Richard P., as told to Ralph Leighton and edited by Edward Hutchings. *Surely You're Joking, Mr. Feynman: Adventures of a Curious Character.* New York: W. W. Norton, 1985.

Feynman, Richard P., as told to Ralph Leighton. *What Do You Care What Other People Think: Further Adventures of a Curious Character.* New York: W. W. Norton, 1988.

Nobelprize.org. "The Nobel Prize in Physics 1965." Available online. URL: http://nobelprize.org/physics/laureates/1965. Downloaded on March 29, 2004.

Schweber, Silvan S. *QED and the Men Who Made It: Dyson, Feynman, Schwinger and Tomonaga.* Princeton, N.J.: Princeton University Press, 1994.

Wasson, Tyler, ed. *Nobel Prize Winners.* New York: H. W. Wilson, 1987, pp. 316–319.

Fischer, Edmond H.
(Edmond Henri Fischer)
(1920–) *biochemist*

Edmond H. Fischer codiscovered reversible protein phosphorylation, the process by which enzymes activate and deactivate other enzymes. For his role in this discovery, he was awarded a share of the 1992 Nobel Prize in physiology or medicine.

Fischer was born on April 6, 1920, in Shanghai, China. His father, Otto, was an Austrian journalist, and his mother, Renée, was the daughter of a Swiss journalist. At age seven he was sent to school in Switzerland, where he eventually attended the University of Geneva, receiving a B.S. in chemistry and biology in 1943 and a Ph.D. in biochemistry in 1947. He remained at Geneva for the next six years, conducting postdoctoral research as a fellow of the Swiss National Foundation and the Rockefeller Foundation while also teaching biochemistry. In 1953 he became a research fellow at the California Institute of Technology, but he left that same year to teach biochemistry at the University of Washington Medical School in Seattle, where he remained for the rest of his career. At some point he married Nelly Gagnaux with whom he had two children; she died in 1961, and two years later he married Beverly Bullock. In 1958 he became a naturalized U.S. citizen.

Fischer's research focused on enzymes, proteins that regulate many of the activities of the cells. Upon settling at Washington, he and EDWIN G. KREBS took up the joint study of phosphorylase, an enzyme that plays an important role in the conversion of glucose (the source of energy for muscles) into glycogen (the form in which glucose is stored in the muscles). At the time, it was not known why phosphorylase exists in the bloodstream in both active and inactive forms. Previously, Fischer had studied phosphorylase at Geneva, while Krebs had studied it under CARL F. CORI and GERTY T. CORI. The Coris concluded that inactive phosphorylase requires the addition of a biochemical compound known as 5'-AMP (a form of adenosine monophosphate) to make it active, but their other research precluded them from pursuing this line of inquiry. Fischer's research, on the other hand, suggested that 5'-AMP has nothing to do with making inactive phosphorylase active. Consequently, Fischer and Krebs decided to find

Edmond Fischer (above) and Edwin Krebs showed how certain enzymes activate and deactivate other enzymes. *(Courtesy of Edmond Fischer)*

out what role, if any, 5'-AMP plays in the activation of phosphorylase.

Fischer and Krebs never did find the answer to this mystery, which was solved in the early 1960s by French biochemist Jacques Monod. Part of their failure stems from their discovery in 1959 of phosphorylase kinase, a discovery that redirected their research toward something much more important. Phosphorylase kinase activates phosphorylase by removing a phosphate group (phosphorus and oxygen) from adenine triphosphate (ATP), the biochemical compound that fuels the activities of the cells, and then attaching it to the phosphorylase molecule. Over the next nine years, they discovered another enzyme, phosphorylase phosphatase, which inactivates phosphorylase by removing the phosphate group. They also demonstrated that the production of phosphorylase kinase and phosphorylase phosphatase is affected by a variety of biochemical signals. Fear leads to the production of stress hormones, which in turn cause the production of phosphorylase kinase; however, a simple conscious decision to move about also results in the production of phosphorylase kinase. By the same token, the production of phosphorylase phosphatase can result from the recession of fear as well as by the conscious decision to stop moving.

The Fischer-Krebs partnership was interrupted in 1968 when Krebs left Washington for the University of California at Davis, but their work had a major impact on the world of biomedical research. Other researchers eventually discovered that virtually all enzymes are regulated by other enzymes acting in the same way that phosphorylase kinase and phosphorylase phosphatase act. A given enzyme's kinase activates it by adding a phosphate group, while its phosphatase deactivates the enzyme by removing the phosphate group. This process of enzyme activation and deactivation, known today as reversible protein phosphorylation, is now believed to be the cause of a number of diseases and medical conditions, especially such common ones as hypertension and tumors. Consequently, many researchers now seek cures for such conditions by looking for dysfunctions in the various phosphorylation cycles. Krebs and Fischer's discovery also led to a better understanding of cellular functions in general, almost all of which are initiated by enzymes. For being the first to discover an instance of reversible protein phosphorylation, Fischer and Krebs were each awarded a half share of the 1992 Nobel Prize in physiology or medicine.

Fischer resumed his partnership with Krebs in 1977, when the latter returned to the University of Washington. Fischer's many honors include election to the National Academy of Sciences and the American Academy of Arts and Sciences. In 1990 he was named a professor emeritus, and since then he has continued to study protein phosphorylation.

Further Reading

McMurray, Emily J., ed. *Notable Twentieth-Century Scientists*. Detroit: Gale Research, 1995, pp. 636–637.

Nobelprize.org. "The Nobel Prize in Physiology or Medicine 1992." Available online. URL: http://nobelprize. org/medicine/laureates/1992. Downloaded on June 11, 2004.

UW Seattle Office of Research. "Dr. Edmond Fischer." Available online. URL: http://www.washington.edu/ research/atuw/Fischer.html. Downloaded on March 25, 2005.

Fitch, Val L.
(Val Logsdon Fitch)
(1923–   ) *physicist*

Val L. Fitch codiscovered that neutral K mesons sometimes violate the fundamental principles of symmetry when they decay radioactively. For this discovery, he was awarded a share of the 1980 Nobel Prize in physics.

Fitch was born on March 10, 1923, near Merriman, Nebraska. His parents, Fred and Frances, were cattle ranchers. As a young boy he moved with his family to nearby Gordon where he grew up. After finishing high school, he joined the U.S. Army, and he spent World War II in Los Alamos, New Mexico, working on the Manhattan Project, which designed and built the atomic bombs that were dropped on Japan. After the war he studied electrical engineering at McGill University in Montreal, Canada, receiving a B.S. in 1948, and then he entered Columbia University, receiving a Ph.D. in physics in 1954. While at Columbia he collaborated with L. JAMES RAINWATER on an experiment

that showed that the radius of the nucleus of an atom of lead is much smaller than had been previously supposed. In 1949 he married Elise Cunningham with whom he had two children; she died in 1972, and in 1976 he married Daisy Harper.

In 1954 Fitch joined the faculty at Princeton University and the staff at the Brookhaven National Laboratory on New York's Long Island. Three years later, CHEN NING YANG, one of his colleagues at Brookhaven, and TSUNG-DAO LEE won a Nobel Prize for developing the theory of parity violation. At that time, physicists assumed that physical reactions take place symmetrically, without regard to up or down, left or right. This behavior is known as parity conservation, and it was assumed to be true for electromagnetism, the strong interactions (the forces that hold together protons and neutrons in an atomic nucleus), and the weak interactions (the forces that cause elementary particles to disintegrate via radioactive decay). Yang and Lee, however, showed that there was no experimental evidence to prove that parity is conserved during the radioactive decay of K mesons, particles whose behavior is so unique that physicists classify them as one of the "strange" particles. In 1957, when parity violation was proven for the beta decay of K mesons, physicists immediately set out to determine whether or not parity violation applies to particles other than K mesons and whether or not the other laws of conservation are also violated by the weak interactions.

In 1958 Fitch and JAMES W. CRONIN, another Brookhaven colleague, began investigating why K-meson decay violates parity in the first place. In the process, they discovered that the decay of a neutral K meson violates the law of charge conjugation conservation. According to this law, neutral K-meson decay should result in the production of equal amounts of matter and antimatter. An antimatter particle is one that possesses the same mass as an elementary particle of matter but has the opposite charge; for example, an electron is a particle of matter while a positron, which has the same mass as an electron but carries a positive charge, is a particle of antimatter. By 1964 Fitch and Cronin had discovered that for every 1,000 or so neutral K mesons that obey the law of charge conjugation conservation while undergoing decay, two violate it, proof enough that charge conjugation is not automatically conserved during a weak interaction.

Fitch and Cronin's findings combined with Yang and Lee's findings to demonstrate the existence of CP violation, that is, that two of the laws of conservation, charge conjugation (C) and parity (P), do not necessarily hold for the weak interactions. These findings had tremendous implications for astrophysicists, who had been wondering for years why the universe consists mostly of matter rather than an even distribution of matter and antimatter. Many astrophysicists believe that a better understanding of CP violation may be able to unlock this secret. For demonstrating the existence of CP violation, Fitch and Cronin were each awarded a half share of the 1980 Nobel Prize in physics.

Fitch remained at Princeton for the rest of his career, which was devoted to the study of the various properties of K mesons; he retired in 1994. His honors include the National Medal of Science and election to the National Academy of Sciences and the American Academy of Arts and Sciences.

Further Reading

Nobelprize.org. "The Nobel Prize in Physics 1980." Available online. URL: http://nobelprize.org/physics/laureates/1980. Downloaded on September 24, 2004.

Princeton University Department of Physics. "Val Fitch." Available online. URL: http://pupgg.princeton.edu/www/jhl/research/Fitch_Val.htmlx. Downloaded on March 25, 2005.

Wasson, Tyler, ed. Nobel Prize Winners. New York: H. W. Wilson, 1987, pp. 326–329.

Fleming, Williamina
(Williamina Paton Stevens Fleming)
(1857–1911) astronomer

Williamina Fleming was a pioneer in the spectrographic classification of stars. In addition to discovering hundreds of stars, she also helped develop a system for classifying them that bears her name.

Fleming was born Williamina Paton Stevens on May 15, 1857, in Dundee, Scotland. Her father, Robert, owned a carving and gilding business, and her mother, Mary, was a homemaker. An apt pupil, at age 14 she began teaching some of her peers while continuing her own education. At age 20 she married James Fleming with whom she had one child, but within two years they had emigrated to Boston, Massachusetts, and separated. After working for two years as a housekeeper for Edward Pickering, the director of the Harvard College Observatory, in 1881 she was hired by Pickering to do clerical and computational work for the observatory. Four years later, she was given the task of determining the photographic magnitude of some of the brighter stars.

In 1886 the Harvard Observatory received a major grant from the estate of Henry Draper, an amateur astronomer who in 1872 had taken the first photograph of a stellar spectrum. Pickering decided to use the grant to fund a project to classify every star in the universe. Staff astronomers began photographing specific areas of the night sky through a telescope and a spectroscope, an optical device that measures the wavelengths, or spectra, of the various stars. The spectrograms, as the photographs were called, were then analyzed by Fleming according to a system that she and Pickering developed. Known as the Pickering-Fleming system, it provided 13 different classifications for "normal" stars and a host of individual classifications for "peculiar" stars. The results of the project were published in 1890 as Draper Catalogue of Stellar Spectra, a volume that classified more than 10,000 of the brighter stars.

In 1891 the observatory established a branch operation in Arequipa, Peru, from where the stars of the southern sky could be photographed. Spectrograms from Peru were shipped back to Harvard where Fleming and her assistants could analyze them. It is estimated that over the course of her career, she personally analyzed more than 200,000 spectrograms. While so doing, she often came across stars that had been previously unknown. In 1887 she discovered Nova Persei, the first nova to be discovered via photography; in time she would discover nine more. She also discovered more than 300 variable stars, stars that vary markedly in brightness from time to time, as well as almost 100 meteor trails. In recognition of her outstanding contributions to the observatory's endeavors, in 1899 she was named curator of astronomical photographs.

Fleming also excelled as an author and teacher. In addition to her contributions to the Draper Catalogue, she published 28 articles under her own name and contributed to many more written by Pickering; most of these articles appeared in *Annals of Harvard College Observatory*, which she edited. She also trained a number of important American astronomers who worked under her, including ANTONIA MAURY, ANNIE J. CANNON, and HENRIETTA LEAVITT. Her honors include having a crater on the moon named after her. She died of pneumonia on May 21, 1911, in Boston.

Further Reading

Ogilvie, Marilyn Bailey. *Women in Science: Antiquity through the Nineteenth Century*. Cambridge, Mass.: MIT Press, 1986, pp. 85–86.

Ogilvie, Marilyn, and Joy Harvey, eds. *The Biographical Dictionary of Women in Science: Pioneering Lives from Ancient Times to the Mid-20th Century*. London: Routledge, 2000, pp. 453–454.

Flexner, Simon

(1863–1946) *pathologist*

Simon Flexner was the first director of the Rockefeller Institute for Medical Research. As its chief administrator for the first 30 years of its existence, he built up the institute into one of the foremost centers for medical research in the United States.

Flexner was born on March 25, 1863, in Louisville, Kentucky. His father, Morris, was a merchant, and his mother, Esther, was a seamstress. After serving a two-year apprenticeship with a local druggist, he entered the Louisville College of Pharmacy and graduated in 1882. He spent the next seven years working in his brother Jacob's drugstore while studying at the University of Louisville School of Medicine, receiving an M.D. in 1889. He then went to study pathology at Johns Hopkins University where he became the protégé of WILLIAM H. WELCH, and in 1891 he was named a fellow in pathology.

Johns Hopkins University placed heavy emphasis on research, and between 1891 and 1899 Flexner published more than 70 research papers, most of them related to bacteriology. In 1899 he chaired a Hopkins-sponsored commission to the Philippines to study tropical diseases. While there, he discovered the microbe that causes one of the most common forms of dysentery; today, the microbe is named *Shigella flexneri* in his honor. In 1899 he left Hopkins to become a professor of pathology at the University of Pennsylvania, and in 1903 he married Helen Thomas with whom he had two children.

In 1903 Flexner was named director of the laboratory at the newly established Rockefeller Institute for Medical Research (today Rockefeller University) in New York City. Under Flexner's leadership, the laboratory was modeled after the best research facilities in Europe, and by 1907 it was performing some remarkable work. For three years an epidemic of cerebrospinal meningitis had been plaguing New York City, but in 1907 Flexner and his research team developed an antiserum from the blood of monkeys in whom the bacteria that cause the disease had been allowed to grow. The antiserum was distributed for free, and it cut the number of deaths from the disease in half. That same year he and his staff began investigating poliomyelitis, commonly known as polio, by transferring it from humans to monkeys. In the course of their investigations, they determined that polio is caused by a viral infection; although they did not find a cure for polio at the time, their efforts contributed in a major way to the development of polio vaccines in the 1950s by JONAS E. SALK and ALBERT B. SABIN. Meanwhile, Flexner had provided facilities at the institute for the *Journal of Experimental Medicine* with the intention of using it as a forum for publishing the research he intended his staff to do, and from 1905 to 1946 he served as its editor.

In 1920 Flexner was named director of the Rockefeller Institute, a position he held until his retirement in 1935. Under his leadership, the institute became one of the most important centers for medical research in the world, but especially for research involving viral diseases. He also served on the board of directors of the Rockefeller Foundation, and he helped guide it on its course to becoming the world's most important dispenser of funding for medical treatment and research facilities. He served as president of the Association of American Physicians, the American Association for the Advancement of

Science, and the Congress of American Physicians, and he was elected to the National Academy of Sciences. He summed up his thoughts about administering a medical research facility in *The Evolution and Organization of the University Clinic* (1939). He died on May 2, 1946, in New York City.

Further Reading

American Philosophical Society. "Simon Flexner Papers." Available online. URL: http://www.amphilsoc.org/library/mole/f/flexner.htm. Downloaded on February 16, 2004.

Flexner, James T. *An American Saga: The Story of Helen Thomas and Simon Flexner.* Boston: Little, Brown, 1984.

Flory, Paul J.
(Paul John Flory)
(1910–1985) *polymer chemist*

Paul J. Flory was a pioneer in the field of polymer chemistry. His fundamental achievements helped establish polymer chemistry as a respected branch of organic chemistry and won for him the 1974 Nobel Prize in chemistry.

Flory was born on June 19, 1910, in Sterling, Illinois. His father, Ezra, was a minister, and his mother, Martha, was a schoolteacher. After receiving a B.S. in chemistry from Manchester (Ind.) College in 1931, he entered Ohio State University and received a Ph.D. in organic chemistry in 1934. He then went to work as a research chemist for E. I. du Pont de Nemours & Company (DuPont) in Wilmington, Delaware. In 1936 he married Emily Tabor with whom he had three children.

Upon arriving at DuPont, Flory was assigned to the research group headed by Wallace H. Carothers that developed neoprene, the first synthetic rubber, and nylon, the first synthetic polymer. At the time, the study of polymers, long chains of large molecules that occur in nature as well as in the laboratory, excited little interest among academic chemists. Nevertheless, the excitement generated by the accomplishments of the Carothers group led Flory to devote his professional career to polymer science.

Although he was part of the Carothers group for only four years, Flory made two major contribu-

tions to its success. First, he developed a mathematical formula for calculating the statistical distribution of polymer chain lengths. The formula was based on Flory's theory of equal reactivity, which held that the length of a polymer had nothing to do with its ability to grow longer. Instead, he hypothesized that the only consideration limiting the ability of a polymer to grow was the local conditions surrounding the molecule's active chemical group. Further research proved that Flory's theory was correct, and its application led to major breakthroughs in the production of very long polymers. Second, he developed a four-stage mechanism for controlling the length of polymers. This mechanism was based on Flory's theory of chain transfer, by which polymer growth could be stopped by transferring its growth to another molecule through the use of controlling agents or modifiers. Once again, further research proved this concept to be true, and for a number of years it was used extensively in the production of synthetic rubber.

In 1938 Flory left DuPont for the University of Cincinnati's Basic Science Research Laboratory. Here his work focused on the phenomenon of gelation, the process by which a polymer in a solution turns into a gel, thus bringing its growth to an end. As a means of preventing gelation, Flory developed a mathematical formula for predicting the gel point in any given polymeric process. In 1940, following the outbreak of World War II in Europe, he returned to industry, first with the Standard Oil Development Company in Linden, New Jersey, and then with the Goodyear Tire and Rubber Company in Akron, Ohio. At both companies his primary task was to develop methods that would increase dramatically the Allies' supply of synthetic rubber.

In 1948 Flory joined the faculty at Cornell University, where he taught polymer science for the next nine years. While at Cornell he produced his two most important contributions to polymer science. First, he demonstrated that at a particular temperature, which he called the theta temperature, dilute polymer solutions assume a certain "ideal behavior" condition that makes it possible to measure their physical properties. In time, "theta temperature" became known to polymer chemists as "Flory temperature." Second, he demonstrated that a constant ratio exists between a polymer's radius and its molecular weight; this value is known today as Flory's universal constant.

In 1957 Flory left Cornell to become executive director of research at the Mellon Institute in Pittsburgh, Pennsylvania. Four years later he was off again, this time to Stanford University where he remained for the rest of his career. While at Stanford, he began applying statistical mechanics, which combines statistics, classical physics, and quantum mechanics to explain the properties of chemical systems, to problems related to polymer chemistry, such as calculating the configurations of polymer chains from the physical properties of the simpler molecules of which they are composed. Over the course of his career, Flory developed a number of mathematical theories and experimental methods that have helped polymer chemists invent a number of plastics and synthetic fibers. For these contributions, he was awarded the 1974 Nobel Prize in chemistry.

Flory summed up most of his work in two influential textbooks, *Principles of Polymer Chemistry* (1953) and *Statistical Mechanics of Chain Molecules* (1969). He was awarded the National Medal of Science, and he was elected to the National Academy of Sciences. He died on September 8, 1985, at his home in Big Sur, California.

Further Reading

Johnson, William S., et al. "Paul John Flory," National Academy of Sciences, *Biographical Memoirs* 82 (2003): pp. 114–141.

Morris, Peter J. T. "Paul Flory," *Polymer Pioneers: A Popular History of the Science and Technology of Large Molecules.* Philadelphia: Center for History of Chemistry, 1986, pp. 70–73.

Nobelprize.org. "The Nobel Prize in Chemistry 1974." Available online. URL: http://nobelprize.org/chemistry/laureates/1974. Downloaded on May 1, 2004.

Wasson, Tyler, ed. *Nobel Prize Winners.* New York: H. W. Wilson, 1987, pp. 333–336.

Fossey, Dian

(1932–1985) *zoologist*

Dian Fossey specialized in the study of the mountain gorilla, one of the rarest primates on earth. Most of what is known about these gorillas today is a direct result of her work.

Fossey was born on January 16, 1932, in San Francisco, California. Her father, George, was an insurance agent, and her mother, Kitty, was a fashion model. Her parents divorced when she was three, and she was raised by her mother and stepfather, Richard Price. After completing two years at the University of California at Davis, she transferred to San Jose State College and received a B.A. in occupational therapy in 1954. She completed two additional years of clinical training, and in 1956 she was named head of the occupational therapy department at Kosair Crippled Children's Hospital in Louisville, Kentucky, a position she held for 10 years.

From childhood, Fossey had an intense interest in animals, and she had entered college with the intention of becoming a veterinarian. While in Louisville, she became fascinated with the idea of traveling to Africa to see the mountain gorillas of the Congo. In 1963 she spent two months in Africa, where she met the famous British anthropologists Louis and Mary Leakey. Her interest in gorillas and her resilient spirit impressed Louis Leakey, and he later invited her to study mountain gorillas, under the Leakeys' sponsorship, as part of his efforts to better understand the connections between humans and their ape-like ancestors, whose remains the Leakeys were excavating. By 1966 all the details of such a study had been worked out, and Fossey returned to Africa. She studied the work of George B. Schaller, one of the few zoologists who had studied gorillas in the field, and Jane Goodall, who was studying chimpanzees in Africa under Leakey's aegis. Fossey took up residence by herself in the Virunga Mountains of east central Africa. Within six months she was arrested and imprisoned by Congolese officials, escaped to Uganda, and resettled in Rwanda, where she established a permanent base camp, which later became known as the Karisoke Research Station.

Fossey quickly discovered that gorillas are anything but the fierce beasts Hollywood portrays them to be. Rather, she found them to be shy and retiring, and at first the only way she could observe them was through binoculars. For two years she watched several groups of gorillas from afar as they went about their daily activities, in the process learning more about the way gorillas eat, mate, communicate, and interact as families than was previously known. By 1968 she had gained their confidence by learning to imitate the loud belches and guttural noises they make while eating as well as how to walk, gorilla style. That same year, while she was observing a group of gorillas while hiding in the bushes, a male she had nicknamed Peanuts approached her and gently touched her. From that moment on, the rest of the gorillas in Peanuts' group seemed to welcome Fossey into their gatherings, and she was able to learn even more about the gorilla way of life by interacting with them.

By 1970 Fossey had much to tell the outside world about gorillas, but her lack of professional credentials denied her access to academic journals, where her information would be most appreciated. That same year she enrolled in Cambridge University and began working on a graduate degree in zoology under the direction of Robert Hinde, who had directed Goodall's dissertation. Upon receiving a Ph.D. in zoology in 1976, she returned to Africa to continue her observations. She realized almost immediately that the gorilla population was dwindling, and a census conducted by her indicated that it had been cut in half since 1960. The reasons were that central east Africa's growing human population was encroaching on the gorillas' natural habitat, plus poachers were killing adults in order to obtain the babies for sale to zoos.

In 1978 Fossey's favorite gorilla, a male she had nicknamed Digit, was found dead, probably killed by poachers. At this point Fossey shifted her emphasis from observation to conservation, and she undertook an active campaign to protect her beloved gorillas. In 1980 she returned to the United States to teach at Cornell University, to establish the Digit Fund, and to write the best seller *Gorillas in the Mist* (1983), all as a means of publicizing the gorillas' plight and raising money for their aid. In 1983 she returned to Africa to play a more aggressive role in protecting gorillas. Operating from the Karisoke Research Station, she captured and tortured poachers, kidnapped their children, and destroyed hunting equipment. Not surprisingly, such activities incited harsh reprisals, and on December 27, 1985, she was found hacked to death

by a machete. Her body was buried in the graveyard she had set up for her slain gorilla friends.

Further Reading

Hayes, Harold T. P. *The Dark Romance of Dian Fossey.* New York: Simon & Schuster, 1990.

Montgomery, Sy. *Walking with the Great Apes: Jane Goodall, Dian Fossey, Biruté Galdikas.* Boston: Houghton Mifflin, 1991.

Mowat, Farley. *Woman in the Mists: The Story of Dian Fossey and the Mountain Gorillas of Africa.* New York: Warner, 1987.

Yount, Lisa. *A to Z of Women in Science and Math.* New York: Facts On File, 1999, pp. 67–69.

Fowler, William A.
(William Alfred Fowler)
(1911–1995) *astrophysicist*

William A. Fowler was one of the first nuclear astrophysicists, physicists who study the nuclear reactions that take place in stars. For his contributions to this field, he was awarded a share of the 1983 Nobel Prize in physics.

Fowler was born on August 9, 1911, in Pittsburgh, Pennsylvania. His father, John, was an accountant, and his mother, Jennie, was a homemaker. At age two he moved with his family to Lima, Ohio, where he grew up. After receiving a B.S. in engineering physics from Ohio State University in 1933, he entered the graduate program at the California Institute of Technology (Caltech) in Pasadena, receiving a Ph.D. in physics in 1936. He spent the next three years as a Caltech research fellow, and in 1939 he accepted a position on the Caltech faculty. In 1940 he married Ardiane Omsted with whom he had two children. She died in 1988, and the following year he married Mary Dutcher.

In the late 1930s, Fowler worked under the direction of Charles C. Lauritsen, director of Caltech's Kellogg Radiation Laboratory. In 1939 Lauritsen and his associates became interested in gaining a better understanding of nuclear astrophysics. That same year HANS A. BETHE had advanced the so-called C-N cycle, the theory that stars generate the tremendous energy needed to keep them shining brightly for billions of years by converting carbon and nitrogen into helium. Lauritsen's team was investigating the C-N cycle when its work was interrupted by World War II. During the war, Fowler participated in the development of proximity fuses, radio-activated detonators for artillery and antiaircraft shells, and several of the key components of the first atomic bombs.

After the war, Fowler and three of his graduate students—Richard Crane, Lewis Delsasso, and Tommy Lauritsen—resumed the Caltech investigation of the C-N cycle, as well as an alternate Bethe theory, that stellar energy was generated via nuclear fusion, in this case the conversion of hydrogen into helium. Fowler's team demonstrated that the fusion of hydrogen into helium, and not the C-N cycle, was the way energy is generated in stars of up to 1.2 times the mass of the sun. In 1953 the team further demonstrated that the incredible heat produced by such fusion leads to the transmutation of helium into carbon and oxygen, which form the cores of many relatively young stars.

This last development was made with the assistance of Cambridge University's Fred Hoyle, and in 1954 Fowler went to Cambridge for a year to work more closely with Hoyle. Three years later Fowler, Hoyle, Geoffrey Burbidge, and Margaret Burbidge published "Synthesis of the Elements in Stars" in the October 1957 issue of *Reviews of Modern Physics*. This important paper outlines the steps via which stars evolve, a process known as nucleosynthesis. According to their theory, the nuclei of lighter elements such as hydrogen and helium are fused together into heavier elements such as carbon and oxygen, and as a star gets older and hotter it fuses the heavier elements into even heavier elements such as iron and uranium. By 1960 Fowler and Hoyle had determined the mechanisms for two types of supernova, the explosion of a dying massive star's gaseous outer layers right before it burns out and collapses into an incredibly dense core. That same year they developed the theory of nuclear cosmochronology, which provides an approximate timeline for the synthesis of the various elements in a stellar core. Much of this work appears in their joint effort, *Nucleosynthesis in Massive Stars and Supernovae* (1965), and in Fowler's *Nuclear Astrophysics* (1967). Several aspects of Fowler's ideas about nucleosynthesis and nuclear cosmochronol-

William Fowler won a Nobel Prize for his work concerning the nuclear reactions that take place in stars. *(Courtesy of the California Institute of Technology)*

ogy continue to be debated by astrophysicists, but his overall theory of stellar evolution remains the most convincing explanation for the life cycle of stars. For his contributions to nuclear astrophysics, Fowler was awarded a half share of the 1983 Nobel Prize in physics. His corecipient was SUBRAHMANYAN CHANDRASEKHAR.

Meanwhile, Fowler and Hoyle continued to collaborate off and on until 1988. Their later work involved the so-called radio galaxies, clusters of stars that give off extraordinarily large amounts of radio waves. They postulated that the sources of these radio waves are collapsed massive stars composed largely of radioactive materials, and that quasars, rare cosmic objects that are strong emitters of both light waves and radio waves, are simply larger versions of collapsed massive stars. On his own, Fowler studied pulsars, stars that emit regular pulses of radio waves, and neutrinos, subatomic particles having no electric charge and little or no mass that are released during nuclear reactions.

Fowler served a term as president of the American Physical Society. He was awarded the U.S. Medal for Merit and the National Medal of Science, and he was elected to the National Academy of Sciences. He retired from Caltech in 1982, and he died on March 14, 1995, in Pasadena.

Further Reading

Barnes, Charles A., Donald D. Clayton, and David N. Schramm, eds. *Essays in Nuclear Astrophysics: Presented to William A. Fowler, on the Occasion of His Seventieth Birthday.* New York: Cambridge University Press, 1982.

Nobelprize.org. "The Nobel Prize in Physics 1983." Available online. URL: http://nobelprize.org/physics/laureates/1983. Downloaded on March 26, 2004.

Wasson, Tyler, ed. *Nobel Prize Winners.* New York: H. W. Wilson, 1987, pp. 337–340.

Franklin, Benjamin

(1706–1790) *physicist*

Benjamin Franklin was one of the most remarkable Americans of all time. A successful publisher, inventor, and statesman, he was also one of the foremost scientists of his day. His famous experiments with lightning led Benjamin West, the American painter, to depict Franklin as the "god of electricity."

Franklin was born on January 6, 1706, in Boston, Massachusetts. His father, Josiah, was a soap maker and candle maker, and his mother, Abiah, was a homemaker. At age 12 he went to work for his brother James as an apprentice printer. Over the next five years he developed into a skilled typesetter and contributor of anonymous articles to James's newspaper, the *New-England Courant.* In 1723 Benjamin left James's employ and moved to Philadelphia, Pennsylvania. After working for a succession of printers in Philadelphia and London, England, in 1728 he and Hugh Meredith established their own printing business in Philadelphia. Franklin took over as sole proprietor in 1730, the same year he took Deborah Read as his common-law wife. They had two children and raised his illegitimate son by an unidentified woman.

Franklin was a skilled printer and a shrewd businessman. He acquired the printing contracts of the colonies of Pennsylvania, New Jersey, Delaware, and Maryland, and he published the *Pennsylvania Gazette,* the most influential newspaper published in colonial America. His most famous publication was *Poor Richard's Almanack,* a collection of educational and entertaining material that first appeared in 1732. By 1748 Franklin had made so much money as a printer and publisher that he was able to turn over the management of his business to his junior partner, David Hall, and devote himself to other endeavors, including the pursuit of scientific investigation.

As a scientist, Franklin is best known for his experiments with electricity. He and several colleagues began to experiment with electricity in late 1746, shortly after they received from Europe a collection of electrical apparatuses, including a Leyden jar. Invented in 1745 by Pieter van Musschenbroek, the Leyden jar was the first device capable of storing large amounts of electricity. In the process of conducting electrical experiments, Franklin developed the theory now known as the conservation of charge. According to this theory, the net sum of the charges within an isolated region is always constant. Franklin explained the theory by arguing in favor of the "one-fluid" theory. Developed by the English physician William Watson in the late 1740s this theory held that electricity was simply a single fluid. Franklin added to Watson's work by arguing that all matter contained greater or lesser amounts of electrical "fluid." Those with a greater than normal amount were "plus" or "positive," while those with a less than normal amount were "minus" or "negative." Franklin's explanation, which is essentially correct, informed the study of electricity for 100 years. Even though it was surpassed by more sophisticated theories, his use of the terms *plus, minus, positive,* and *negative* in conjunction with electricity continue to this day. Franklin reported the results of his and his colleagues' experiments to the Royal Society of London, the foremost body of scientific minds of the day, and in 1751 he published these reports as *Experiments and Observations on Electricity.*

By 1752 Franklin had concluded that an electrical discharge is caused when a body with a positive charge approaches one with a negative charge, with the discharge neutralizing the respective charges. This led him to the idea that lightning is nothing more than a huge discharge of electricity, and that the luminescence of lightning is caused by this discharge. To prove his theory, he connected a Leyden jar to a silk kite by means of a long piece of wet twine, from which was hung a metal key. Franklin then flew the kite, somewhat dangerously, during a violent thunderstorm. The kite-key-twine arrangement transferred electrical charge from the highly charged atmosphere to the Leyden jar, and he used this charge to perform various electrical experiments, thus proving his theory. Ever the practical inventor—Franklin invented the Franklin stove, bifocals, and the glass harmonica, among other things—he invented the lightning rod as a means of protecting tall structures from being blasted by lightning. The first lightning rod was attached to the steeple of Philadelphia's Christ Church in the mid-1750s.

The publication of Franklin's experiments with electricity made him famous among the learned minds of Europe. After 1757, when he became Pennsylvania's agent to Parliament, Franklin spent much time in London, and he was always welcome at the proceedings of the Royal Society. In 1765 Franklin met Joseph Priestley, who later discovered that oxygen is an element, at a Society function. Franklin lent Priestley his expertise and his books so that Priestley could write *The History and Present State of Electricity* (1767), a compendium of everything that was known about electricity to date.

Franklin also played a crucial role in the attainment of American independence from Great Britain. He is the only person to sign the Declaration of Independence, the Treaty of Paris ending the American Revolution, and the U.S. Constitution. The major achievements of his long and illustrious career are summed up in the famous epigram by Anne-Robert-Jacques Turgot, a French statesman: "He snatched the lightning from the skies and the sceptre from tyrants." Franklin died on April 17, 1790, in Philadelphia.

Further Reading

Brands, H. W. *The First American: The Life and Times of Benjamin Franklin.* New York: Doubleday, 2000.

Campbell, James. *Recovering Benjamin Franklin: An Exploration of a Life of Science and Service.* Chicago: Open Court, 1999.

Carey, Charles W., Jr. "Franklin, Benjamin," *American Inventors, Entrepreneurs, and Business Visionaries.* New York: Facts On File, 2002, pp. 132–134.

Crompton, Samuel W. *100 Americans Who Shaped American History.* San Mateo, Calif.: Bluewood Books, 1999.

Franklin, Benjamin, and L. Jesse Lemisch, ed. *The Autobiography and Other Writings.* New York: Signet Classics, 2001.

Friedman, Jerome I.
(Jerome Isaac Friedman)
(1930–) *physicist*

Jerome I. Friedman helped provide some of the earliest evidence for the existence of quarks, one of the basic building blocks of matter. For this contribution, he was awarded a share of the 1990 Nobel Prize in physics.

Friedman was born on March 28, 1930, in Chicago, Illinois. His father, Selig, owned a sewing machine repair business, and his mother, Lillian, was a homemaker. He studied physics at the University of Chicago, receiving a B.S. in 1950, an M.S. in 1953, and a Ph.D. in 1956. That same year he married Tania Letesky-Baranovsky with whom he had four children and moved to Palo Alto, California, where he was named a professor of physics at Stanford University and a staff member of Stanford's High Energy Laboratory.

At Stanford, Friedman became part of a research group that was studying the nature of the atomic nucleus. Headed by ROBERT HOFSTADTER, the group sought to determine whether nucleons, the protons and neutrons that comprise a nucleus, are elementary particles or whether they themselves consist of even more basic particles. Their experiments consisted of generating a beam of high-energy electrons in a linear accelerator, firing them into thin metal foil, and examining the scattering pattern that resulted when the electrons were deflected by the metal nuclei. The scattering patterns indicated that nucleons are indeed composed of smaller particles, and that some of these particles are pi mesons, or pions, particles with masses greater than an electron but smaller than a proton. The group was able to determine that pions orbit the cores of nucleons in "clouds," two positively charged clouds in the case of a proton and one positively charged and one negatively charged in the case of a neutron. However, these experiments were unable to shed further light on the nature of the nucleonic core itself, and they came to an end around 1957.

Two of Friedman's collaborators in the Hofstadter group experiments were HENRY W. KENDALL and Canadian physicist Richard E. Taylor. These three continued to collaborate until 1960, when Friedman left Stanford for the Massachusetts Institute of Technology (MIT). He resumed his collaboration with Kendall the following year, however,

Jerome Friedman helped demonstrate the existence of quarks, one of the basic building blocks of matter. *(Courtesy of Jerome I. Friedman; photo by Donna Coveney)*

when Kendall joined him at MIT. In 1967 Friedman and Kendall began working again with Taylor, who was now a group leader at the Stanford Linear Accelerator Center (SLAC). Since the conclusion of their work with Hofstadter, MURRAY GELL-MANN had theorized that the nucleonic cores Hofstadter had discovered are composed of elementary particles called quarks, but this theory had been received with much skepticism by the scientific community. To shed light on the possible existence of quarks, Friedman, Kendall, and Taylor decided to return to the experiments they had conducted with Hofstadter, but first they made two important changes. Hofstadter's experiments had generated high-energy electrons in a 300-foot linear accelerator, but Kendall, Friedman, and Taylor were able to use the new SLAC linear accelerator that was two miles long and thus capable of energizing electrons to much higher levels. Also, Hofstadter had focused on elastic collisions, whereby the bombarding electrons are deflected by the protons being bombarded, while the three collaborators focused on inelastic collisions, whereby the electrons penetrate the protons.

In 1968 Friedman, Kendall, and Taylor obtained scattering patterns that clearly indicated the existence of smaller particles inside the proton's core. By the mid-1970s, the trio was able to show that neutrons consist of smaller particles as well and to provide conclusive evidence for the existence of gluons, neutrally charged particles whose behavior holds together these smaller particles. This work provided the first experimental evidence to support Gell-Mann's quark theory, and in so doing it contributed to a more sophisticated understanding of the inner structure of matter. In recognition of their achievement, Friedman, Kendall, and Taylor were each awarded a one-third share of the 1990 Nobel Prize in physics.

Friedman remained at MIT for the rest of his career. In 1980 he was named director of MIT's laboratory of nuclear science. His honors include election to the National Academy of Sciences and the American Academy of Arts and Sciences.

Further Reading

McMurray, Emily J., ed. *Notable Twentieth-Century Scientists.* Detroit: Gale Research, 1995, pp. 698–699.

Nobelprize.org. "The Nobel Prize in Physics 1990." Available online. URL: http://nobelprize.org/physics/laureates/1990. Downloaded on October 7, 2004.

Physics@MIT. "Jerome I. Friedman." Available online. URL: http://web.mit.edu/physics/facultyandstaff/faculty/jerome_friedman.html. Downloaded on March 25, 2005.

Furchgott, Robert F.

(1916–) *biochemist*

Robert F. Furchgott discovered EDRF, the biochemical agent that facilitates the relaxation of the smooth muscles in blood vessels. For this discovery he was awarded a share of the 1998 Nobel Prize in physiology or medicine.

Furchgott was born on June 4, 1916, in Charleston, South Carolina. His father owned and managed a department store and his mother was a homemaker. At age 13 he moved with his family to Orangeburg where he grew up. After spending a year at the University of South Carolina, he transferred to the University of North Carolina at Chapel Hill, receiving a B.S. in chemistry in 1937. He then entered Northwestern University and received a Ph.D. in biochemistry in 1940. He spent the next nine years doing research at the Cornell University Medical School, and in 1949 he joined the faculty at the Washington University in St. Louis, Missouri, as a professor of pharmacology. In 1956 he was named chair of the pharmacology department at the State University of New York (SUNY) College of Medicine (today the SUNY Health Science Center) in Brooklyn.

Furchgott's early research covered a number of areas: the permeability of cell membranes, tissue metabolism, circulatory shock during hemorrhaging, and the effects of drugs on smooth muscles. This last subject led him to study the effects of enzymes, pharmaceuticals, and neurotransmitters, chemicals that transmit signals from one nerve cell to another, on the aorta, the body's major artery. He was particularly interested in learning more about how biochemical compounds react with the aorta's receptors, certain locations on cell membranes that regulate which biochemical compounds are allowed to enter the cell through the mem-

Robert Furchgott discovered the biochemical agent that makes the smooth muscles in blood vessels relax. *(Courtesy of Robert F. Furchgott)*

brane, and how pharmaceutical drugs can be used to modify that interaction. During one laboratory experiment in the mid-1950s, he was intrigued when acetylcholine, a drug that was known to be a powerful muscle relaxer, caused strips of aortic muscle tissue to contract rather than relax. Although he continued to investigate drug-receptor interactions for more than two decades, this unexpected result remained in the back of his mind the whole time.

In 1978 Furchgott made a discovery that explained the contradictory behavior of acetylcholine more than 20 years previously. The discovery arose out of the realization that, for decades, Furchgott had been preparing his strips of aortic muscle tissue in a way that removed the endothelium, the innermost layer of cells in a blood vessel. Once he began using strips that included endothelial cells, he discovered that the strips responded in a markedly different way to stimulation by various enzymes and drugs. For example, strips containing endothelial cells relax when stimulated with acetylcholine, whereas strips lacking endothelial cells contract. He concluded that the endothelium contains some agent, which he labeled endothelium-derived relaxing factor (EDRF), which works in conjunction with acetylcholine and other biochemical compounds to cause muscles to relax. In 1986 Furchgott identified EDRF as being nitric oxide, a short-lived gas that acts as a signaling mechanism between the endothelium and the muscles of the blood vessels. He also showed that EDRF actually plays an intermediary role in muscle relaxation in that it triggers the production of cyclic guanosine monophosphate (cyclic GMP), which in turn causes smooth muscles to relax. This finding was confirmed contemporaneously but independently by LOUIS J. IGNARRO and FERID MURAD.

The discovery and identification of EDRF explained why the administration of nitroglycerine, which metabolizes into nitric oxide, is such an excellent treatment for angina pectoris, a medical condition that is characterized by severe chest pain that results when certain arterial muscles cannot relax. It also gave medical researchers a better understanding of the way the muscles of the blood vessels work, and how defects in their performance might be overcome pharmaceutically. For his role in this discovery, Furchgott was awarded a one-third share of the 1998 Nobel Prize in physiology or medicine; his corecipients were Ignarro and Murad.

Furchgott retired from SUNY in 1989. However, he continued to do research there as a professor emeritus while also teaching pharmacology during the winter months at the University of Miami (Fla.) School of Medicine. His many honors include serving a term as president of the American Society for Pharmacology and Experimental Therapeutics. He has been married twice and has three children.

Further Reading

Hargittai, Istvan, and Magdolna Hargittai. *Candid Science II: Conversations with Famous Biomedical Scientists.* London: Imperial College Press, 2002, pp. 578–595.

Nobelprize.org. "The Nobel Prize in Physiology or Medicine 1998." Available online. URL: http://nobelprize.org/medicine/laureates/1998. Downloaded on July 14, 2004.

Gajdusek, D. Carleton
(Daniel Carleton Gajdusek)
(1923–) *virologist*

D. Carleton Gajdusek discovered the slow virus, a virus that takes years to complete its work of infecting and killing a victim. This discovery won for him a share of the 1976 Nobel Prize in physiology or medicine.

Gajdusek was born on September 9, 1923, in Yonkers, New York. His father, Karl, was a butcher, and his mother, Ottilia, was a homemaker. He began his scientific career at age 13 when he obtained a job synthesizing weed killer at the Boyce Thompson Institute for Plant Research in Yonkers. A gifted student, at age 19 he received a B.S. in biophysics from the University of Rochester and, three years later, an M.D. from Harvard Medical School. From 1945 to 1951 he studied clinical pediatrics and childhood diseases at Boston's Children's Hospital, Harvard, and Columbia University and virology and immunology at the California Institute of Technology. From 1951 to 1954 he studied viral and rickettsial diseases at the Walter Reed Army Medical Center in Washington, D.C., and the exotic epidemic diseases of western Asia at the Institut Pasteur in Tehran, Iran. From 1955 to 1958 he studied the exotic diseases of the indigenous peoples of Australia and New Guinea at the Hall Institute of Medical Research in Melbourne, Australia. In 1958 he became head of the virological and neurological research laboratories at the National Institutes of Health (NIH) in Bethesda,

Maryland, where he eventually established the Laboratory of Slow, Latent and Temperate Virus Infections as part of the National Institute of Neurological Diseases and Blindness.

Gajdusek's early research focused on viral childhood diseases, but in 1955 he became interested in a peculiar disease known only to affect the isolated Fore people of New Guinea. The disease, called kuru, is a chronic, degenerative, fatal viral disease that attacks the victim's central nervous system; its symptoms include unsteady gait, tremors, and involuntary purposeless movements. Once the symptoms appear, the victim dies within three to 20 months. At first it was suspected that kuru is a hereditary disease, especially since it affects only the Fore and no traces of infectious agents could be found in the victims' tissues or fluids. The major problem with this theory, however, is the fact that kuru affects mostly women and children, and very rarely adult men. The mystery was not solved until Gajdusek and his colleague, Clarence Gibbs, injected samples of the victims' brain tissue into live chimpanzees. The chimps developed the symptoms of kuru, but not until between 18 and 36 months after the injections. This result demonstrated to Gajdusek that kuru is caused by a virus that proceeds very slowly and perhaps is able to lie dormant in its victims for years before becoming active. Eventually, the cause of kuru was traced to a Fore funeral rite, which requires the women and children who are related to the deceased to handle and eat their dead relative's brains. Once the Fore began eliminating this form of ritual cannibalism from their funeral rites in 1959, the incidence of kuru declined markedly among children born after that year; nevertheless, many Fore women and a few adult men developed kuru for years thereafter, demonstrating the slow-working action of the kuru virus.

Gajdusek's discovery of the viral causes of kuru alerted medical researchers to the possibility that other slow-working viruses were at work in the world at large. Gajdusek and Gibbs also studied Creutzfeldt-Jakob disease, a rare condition that is marked by pre-senile dementia, and demonstrated that it is caused by a slow virus. The demonstration of the existence of slow viruses, which are not susceptible to the same immunological measures by which organisms overcome most normal-acting viruses, suggested that other neurological conditions such as multiple sclerosis, Parkinson's disease, and Alzheimer's disease might also be caused by slow viruses. For his work concerning slow viruses, Gajdusek was awarded a half share of the 1976 Nobel Prize in physiology or medicine; his corecipient was BARUCH S. BLUMBERG.

In addition to his work as a virologist, Gajdusek was also a rather accomplished anthropologist. He compiled extensive notes concerning his travels to exotic locales, and enough of these notes were published to comprise 18 volumes. Although he never married, Gajdusek adopted dozens of New Guinean boys and brought them to the United States where he educated them before sending them home to educate their fellow villagers. In 1997 he was convicted of sexually abusing one of those boys and sentenced to 18 months in prison. Since his release in 1998, he has been traveling the world and accepting the plethora of visiting professorships and fellowships that have been offered him by many of the world's leading viral research laboratories.

Further Reading

Eron, Carol. *The Virus That Ate Cannibals.* New York: Macmillan, 1981.

Hargittai, Istvan, and Magdolna Hargittai. *Candid Science II: Conversations with Famous Biomedical Scientists.* London: Imperial College Press, 2002, pp. 442–466.

Nobelprize.org. "The Nobel Prize in Physiology or Medicine 1976." Available online. URL: http://nobelprize. org/medicine/laureates/1976. Downloaded on June 21, 2004.

Wasson, Tyler, ed. *Nobel Prize Winners.* New York: H. W. Wilson, 1987, pp. 361–363.

Gamow, George
(Georgy Antonovich Gamov)
(1904–1968) *astrophysicist*

George Gamow is best remembered for developing the big-bang model of the origin of the universe. Ironically, he devoted most of his career to quantum mechanics, the study of subatomic particles.

Gamow was born Georgy Antonovich Gamov on March 4, 1904, in Odessa, Russia. His parents, Anton and Alexandra, were high school teachers. After spending a year at Novorossia University in Odessa, in 1923 he transferred to the University of Leningrad and received his undergraduate degree three years later. He then spent a year each at the University of Göttingen, the Copenhagen Institute of Theoretical Physics, and the University of Leningrad before receiving his Ph.D. from the latter in 1929. After one-year fellowships at Cambridge University and the Copenhagen Institute, in 1931 he returned to the University of Leningrad to teach theoretical physics. In 1933 he defected to the West, and the following year he was named a professor of physics at George Washington University (GW) in Washington, D.C. In 1956 he accepted a similar position at the University of Colorado at Boulder, where he spent the rest of his career. In 1931 he married Lyubov Vokhminzeva with whom he had one child; they divorced in 1956, and two years later he married Barbara Perkins. In 1940 he became a naturalized citizen of the United States.

At the time Gamow entered college, quantum mechanics was in its infancy, and he quickly became one of its early practitioners. During his first stay at the Copenhagen Institute, he explained varying rates of radioactive alpha decay in terms of the energy levels and average lifetimes of alpha particles (helium nuclei that consist of two protons and two neutrons), which are emitted during alpha decay. During his second stay at the institute, he began developing a model to explain how an atomic nucleus reacts to vibration. By 1935 he offered what became known as the "liquid drop" model, which proposes that a nucleus is like a drop of water in that nucleons (protons and neutrons) react flexibly and collectively to vibration by constantly changing the nucleus's shape. Although this theory was later supplanted by L. JAMES RAINWATER's unified theory in 1950, it served until then to offer a good model for the behavior of a nucleus. In 1936 Gamow and EDWARD TELLER developed a theory to explain radioactive beta decay, whereby beta particles (electrons) are emitted. Gamow's most important contribution to the development of quantum mechanics may be his sponsorship of the first annual Washington Conference on Theoretical Physics at GW in 1935. The conference soon became an international forum for discussing cutting-edge developments in the field, and the fifth conference, in 1939, helped initiate the study of nuclear fission in American research facilities.

During his second stay at Copenhagen, Gamow first applied quantum mechanics to astrophysics, the study of heavenly bodies, by helping to develop a model that explains the thermonuclear reactions taking place inside stars. This was his first venture into astrophysics, but not his last. In 1938 he devoted the fourth Washington Conference to the role of quantum mechanics in astrophysics, and shortly thereafter HANS A. BETHE developed a more sophisticated model for explaining stellar thermonuclear reactions. In 1942 Gamow and Teller developed a theory to explain the internal workings of red giant stars, the youngest stars in the universe, which are much cooler than older stars like the Sun.

Gamow's most important work concerning astrophysics involves the origin of the universe. In 1948 he and Ralph Alpher published a paper called "The Origin of Chemical Elements," which attempted to explain the distribution of the basic elements throughout the universe. Drawing on the work of EDWIN HUBBLE and others, who had proved that the universe is expanding, Gamow and Alpher reasoned that all the matter in the universe was once condensed into a relatively small area in which it was subjected to extremely high temperature and density. For some reason, this matter exploded so violently that even today, approximately 15 billion years later, it continues to spread outward from the source of the explosion. Meanwhile, the fragments of the "big bang" were reassembled via the process of successive neutron capture, whereby relatively slow-moving neutrons collided and combined into clusters. Eventually, these clusters attracted protons and electrons in proportion to the number of neutrons in the cluster, thus forming atoms. Meanwhile, they reasoned, a huge number of alpha and beta particles must have remained unattached to other matter, and the result, they predicted, would be a low level of radiation permeating the universe.

Initially, Gamow and Alpher's theory was met with much skepticism, especially on the part of critics who had not yet accepted the fact that the universe is still expanding. Their theory about the origin of atoms has been rejected, largely because it does not do a very good job of explaining the development of the heavier elements. In the 1960s ARNO A. PENZIAS and ROBERT W. WILSON proved the existence of universal radiation, and the big bang model now enjoys almost total acceptance in the scientific community.

In the 1950s Gamow became briefly but intensely interested in molecular biology. Upon hearing about the work being done by Francis Crick and JAMES WATSON, concerning the structure of deoxyribonucleic acid (DNA), he reasoned that the order of recurring triplets of nucleotides, the basic components of DNA, might contain some sort of genetic code. As originally expressed, his theory contained many flaws, but Crick later credited Gamow with putting him and Watson on the right track for making further discoveries about DNA.

In addition to being a brilliant theorist, Gamow also had the ability to write about cutting-edge science for the general educated public. Between 1939 and 1967 he wrote the *Mr. Tompkins* series, in which the mythical Mr. Tompkins explores the atom, learns where babies come from, and goes inside himself, among other things. His other popular writings include *The Birth and Death of the Sun* (1940), *One, Two, Three . . . Infinity* (1947), *The Creation of the Universe* (1952), *A Planet Called Earth* (1963), and *A Star Called the Sun* (1964). In 1956 the United Nations Educational, Scientific and Cultural Organization (UNESCO) awarded him the Kalinga Prize for his achievement as a popularizer of science. His other awards include election to the National Academy of Sciences. He died on August 20, 1968, in Boulder, Colorado.

Further Reading

Harper, E., W. C. Parke, and G. D. Anderson, eds. *The George Gamow Symposium: Sponsored by the George Washington University and the Carnegie Institution of Washington, 12 April 1997*. San Francisco, Calif.: Astronomical Society of the Pacific, 1997.

University of Colorado at Boulder. "The George Gamow Memorial Lecture Series." Available online. URL: http://www.colorado.edu/physics/Web/Gamow. Downloaded on June 24, 2005.

Gasser, Herbert S.
(Herbert Spencer Gasser)
(1888–1963) *neurophysiologist*

Herbert S. Gasser won a share of the 1944 Nobel Prize for medicine or physiology for his groundbreaking research concerning nerve fibers. Not only did Gasser's work serve to increase the body of knowledge available to neurophysiologists, scientists who study the function of the nervous system, but it also provided them with an electronic device, a supersensitive oscilloscope, that would revolutionize the way neurophysiologists conduct research.

Gasser was born on July 5, 1888, in Platteville, Wisconsin. His father, Herman, was a physician, and his mother, Jane, was a teacher. He attended the University of Wisconsin and received a B.A. in zoology and an A.M. in anatomy in 1910 and 1911, respectively. While at Wisconsin, he studied physiology under JOSEPH ERLANGER. After receiving an M.D. from Johns Hopkins Medical School in 1915, Gasser returned to Wisconsin to teach for a year. In 1916 he joined the faculty at Washington University in St. Louis, where Erlanger was now teaching, as an instructor of physiology.

Gasser and Erlanger became research collaborators shortly after Gasser arrived at Washington. At first, their experiments related to the circulatory system, Erlanger's specialty, and during World War I they studied the relationship between blood loss from battle wounds and shock. After the war,

Gasser's interests turned to the study of nerve cells, especially the way they transmitted and received information from each other. He and H. Sydney Newcomer used an electronic device known as a vacuum tube amplifier to construct an apparatus that could measure the minute electrical currents that constitute nervous impulses. Unfortunately, the device also introduced a considerable measure of distortion and was not as useful a tool as they had hoped. In 1921 Gasser and Erlanger, whose attention had turned to the nervous system, began looking for a way to eliminate the distortion, and within a year they had developed a cathode-ray oscilloscope capable of measuring nervous impulses clearly and precisely.

In 1922 Gasser and Erlanger began using their oscilloscope to study the workings of nerve fibers, the parts of a nerve cell that transmit nervous impulses. Over the next nine years they made several important discoveries concerning nerve fibers. Their most important discovery was that nerve fibers come in three different types: A-, B-, and C-fibers. The difference among them is their thicknesses, or diameters; A-fibers, the thickest, are about 20 times thicker than C-fibers, the thinnest. They also discovered that the different types of fibers conduct impulses at different rates, which increase in direct proportion to the thickness of the fiber. For example, A-fibers transmit impulses up to 50 times faster than C-fibers and up to 10 times faster than B-fibers. Also, the functions of the various fibers are different; for example, A-fibers transmit impulses related to muscle sense and touch while C-fibers transmit the impulses associated with pain. All three types of fibers are distributed throughout the nerve cells that transmit impulses up and down the spinal cord. Lastly, they found that each fiber type requires an electrical stimulus of a different intensity in order for it to transmit an impulse, with A-fibers requiring a more intense stimulus than C-fibers.

Earlier in the 20th century, Swedish physiologist Gustav Göthlin and French physiologist Louis Lapicque had hypothesized about the speed of transmission of nervous impulses. Lapicque's hypothesis was based on the speed of transmission in electrical cables, and it anticipated Gasser and Erlanger's findings, which confirmed it. In recognition of their discoveries, Gasser and Erlanger were awarded equal shares of the 1944 Nobel Prize for medicine or physiology. The award was given partly for their discoveries concerning nerve fibers, and partly for the methods by which those discoveries were made. The prize committee was particularly impressed with their oscilloscope, as this incredibly sensitive instrument made it possible to study the nervous system in a way that had been impossible before.

In 1931 Gasser left Washington University to teach physiology at Cornell Medical College, a move that ended his collaboration with Erlanger. Four years later he was named director of the Rockefeller Institute (today Rockefeller University) in New York City, one of the nation's most prestigious medical research facilities. Despite his administrative duties, he continued to experiment with neurophysiology, even after his retirement in 1953. He died, having never married, on May 11, 1963, in New York City.

Further Reading

Gasser, Herbert S. *Herbert Spencer Gasser, 1888–1963: Scholar, Administrator, Nobel Laureate: An Autobiographical Memoir of a Distinguished Career in Medical Science.* New York: Academic Press, 1964.

NASA Nemolab web. "Spotlight on Neuroscience: Herbert Spencer Gasser." Available online. URL: http://neurolab.jsc.nasa.gov/gasser.htm. Downloaded on March 25, 2005.

Nobelprize.org. "The Nobel Prize in Physiology or Medicine 1944." Available online. URL: http://nobelprize.org/medicine/laureates/1944. Downloaded on December 30, 2003.

Wasson, Tyler, ed. *Nobel Prize Winners.* New York: H. W. Wilson, 1987, pp. 368–370.

Geller, Margaret J.
(Margaret Joan Geller)
(1947–) *astrophysicist*

Margaret J. Geller discovered the Great Wall, an arc of galaxies that is the largest celestial structure ever seen. She is also one of the leaders of the effort to map the entire universe.

Geller was born on December 8, 1947, in Ithaca, New York. Her father, Seymour, was an X-ray crystallographer, and her mother, Sarah, was a homemaker. As a young girl she moved with her family to the Murray Hill, New Jersey, area where her father went to work for Bell Laboratories. In 1970 she received a B.A. in physics from the University of California at Berkeley and entered the graduate physics program at Princeton University, receiving an M.A. in 1972 and a Ph.D. in 1975. She spent the next 13 years at the Harvard-Smithsonian Center for Astrophysics in Cambridge, Massachusetts, interrupted by a 1 1/2-year stay in England at Cambridge University's Institute of Astronomy. In 1988 she was named a professor of astronomy at Harvard University.

Geller's early research involved the study of clusters, groups of a hundred galaxies or more that extend for millions of light-years; by comparison, the Milky Way, Earth's galaxy, is about 600,000 light-years from one end to the other. In 1981 she took up the challenge of mapping the universe, largely because of two developments that took place that same year. The first was the completion of a project to map the nearby universe; led by Marc Davis, one of Geller's Harvard-Smithsonian colleagues, the project had raised many questions about the nature of the universe. The second was the discovery by Robert Kirshner of an immense region, about 250 million light-years in diameter, which is completely void of galaxies. Kirshner's discovery astounded most astronomers, including Geller, because the conventional wisdom held that the "big bang," GEORGE GAMOW's theory of the origin of the universe, had distributed matter more or less evenly throughout space. Geller and John Huchra, a Harvard-Smithsonian astronomer, decided to resume Davis's project and to determine whether Kirshner's discovery was an anomaly or a universal pattern.

Three years later, Geller and Huchra had little to show for their effort, largely because they were trying to map a three-dimensional universe on a two-dimensional plane. In 1984 Geller decided that, rather than mapping the near universe in a 360° pattern, they should focus on mapping a pie-shaped strip extending as far out into the universe as they could see. By mid-1985 they and Valerié de Lapparent, one of Geller's graduate students, had plotted more than 1,000 galaxies, some of them hundreds of millions of light-years from Earth. This map revealed that almost all of them were arranged in a pattern that suggested thin walls surrounding vast empty regions like the one Kirshner had discovered. They then used the same technique to map other pie-shaped strips, mostly in the northern hemisphere of the Milky Way. This time they discovered the Great Wall, an arc of thousands of galaxies about 400 million light-years from Earth that is about 650 million light-years long, 250 million light-years wide, and "only" 20 million light-years thick. For the role she played in this discovery, Geller was elected to the National Academy of Sciences and the American Academy of Arts and Sciences.

Geller and Huchra continued to map galaxies, and by 1997 they had plotted more than 15,000. Together with collaborators from around the world and in both hemispheres, they have led the way in the development of a "universal map" that contains more than 100,000 galaxies. The overall pattern that has developed thus far is the one first described by Geller and Huchra in 1985. Meanwhile, the vast majority of the universe's hundreds of millions of galaxies remain uncharted.

Further Reading

Lightman, Alan, and Roberta Brawer. *Origins: The Lives and Worlds of Modern Cosmologists*. Cambridge, Mass.: Harvard University Press, 1990, pp. 359–377.

Yount, Lisa. "Geller, Margaret Joan," *A to Z of Women in Science and Math*. New York: Facts On File, 1999, pp. 76–78.

Gell-Mann, Murray
(1929–) *physicist*

Murray Gell-Mann won a Nobel Prize in physics for developing the theories of strangeness, SU(3) symmetry, and quarks. Each of these theories provided physicists with a more sophisticated way of understanding the world of subatomic particles.

Gell-Mann was born on September 15, 1929, in New York City. His father, Arthur, owned a language school, and his mother, Pauline, was a homemaker. At age 15 he graduated from high school and entered Yale University, receiving a B.S. in physics in 1948. Three years later he received a Ph.D. in physics from the Massachusetts Institute of Technology and joined the staff at the Institute for Advanced Study in Princeton, New Jersey. In 1952 he began teaching at the University of Chicago and conducting research at its Institute for Nuclear Studies.

As a theoretical physicist, Gell-Mann developed theories to explain how subatomic particles interact with one another, and in 1953 he developed the theory of strangeness. In the early 1950s, several of the newly discovered elementary particles that are known today as mesons and resonance particles exhibited behaviors that were forbidden by the prevailing theories of the day. These particles formed via the relatively fast-acting strong interactions, which bind together protons and neutrons in an atomic nucleus, but decayed via the relatively slow-acting weak interactions, which govern certain types of radioactive decay. Gell-Mann addressed this problem by proposing that these previously unknown particles possess a property he called strangeness. Particles that do not have strangeness radioactively decay via alpha decay, one of the strong interactions; for example, a neutron, which does not possess strangeness, decays via alpha decay into a proton. Particles with strangeness, however, decay via beta decay, a weak interaction.

Perhaps the most interesting aspect of Gell-Mann's theory of strangeness was that it proposed that strangeness is conserved by the strong interactions but not by the weak interactions. This notion flew in the face of a long-standing assumption that laws of conservation apply the same to all the forces of physics that involve particle interaction, such as electromagnetism and the strong and weak interactions. By theorizing that this is not necessarily so, Gell-Mann contributed indirectly to the success of CHEN NING YANG, TSUNG-DAO LEE, JAMES W. CRONIN, and VAL L. FITCH. In 1957 Yang and Lee showed that the weak interactions violate the law of parity conservation, while in 1964 Cronin and Fitch showed that the weak interactions violate the law of charge conjugation conservation.

In 1955 Gell-Mann left Chicago for the California Institute of Technology (Caltech). That same year he married Margaret Dow with whom he had two children; she died in 1981, and in 1992 he married Marcia Southwick. At Caltech he continued to think about particle interactions, and in 1962 he presented a model for understanding particles in terms of their fundamental properties. This model is known officially as SU(3) symmetry, for "special unitary group in three dimensions," but it is sometimes called the Eightfold Way, a takeoff on the Buddhist program for attaining enlightenment known as the Eightfold Path. The original version of SU(3) symmetry arranged all the known hadrons, or strongly interacting particles, into three symmetrical groups of eight and one group of 10 according to their spin, charge, and strangeness. At the time, the existence of the 10th member of the latter group, the omega-minus resonance particle, had yet to be demonstrated, but its discovery in 1964 offered further support for SU(3).

Meanwhile, Gell-Mann had been thinking about what causes strangeness, and in 1964 he developed the theory of quarks. At the time it was still believed that the elementary particles were indivisible, and yet SU(3) symmetry was able to arrange them according to three basic properties. Gell-Mann concluded from this that the elementary particles are not elementary at all but rather are constructed from something even more basic than themselves. He called this "something" a quark, after a fanciful term from *Finnegan's Wake* by Irish novelist James Joyce. Gell-Mann postulated the existence of three quarks, which he labeled up, down, and strange. He assigned the up quark a charge of +2/3 and the down and strange quarks charges of –1/3, while the strange quark was assigned a strangeness value of –1. He then theorized that a proton is made up of two up quarks and one down quark, thus giving it an overall charge of +1, while a neutron is composed of one up and two downs, for an overall charge of zero. Lastly, the various strange particles were thought to consist of either two or three quarks, at least one of which is a strange quark.

Given the nature of the equipment of the day and the incredible amount of activity that takes place in an atomic nucleus, physicists at first found it very difficult to verify the existence of quarks. In the 1970s, however, the development of sophisticated particle accelerators allowed

HENRY W. KENDALL, JEROME I. FRIEDMAN, and Richard E. Taylor to bombard protons with electrons whose high energy levels permitted them to penetrate the proton. The electron scattering pattern that resulted from these bombardments clearly verified the existence of quarks. Further experimentation showed that quarks are unable to escape from the particle they comprise, and so in all likelihood they are the most elementary particles of all. By the end of the 20th century, the existence of two more quarks, labeled charm and bottom (also known as beauty), had been discovered, and the existence of a sixth quark, top (also known as truth), was strongly suspected.

Gell-Mann's theories concerning strangeness, SU(3) symmetry, and quarks revolutionized the world of physics. These theories, which continued to

Murray Gell-Mann developed several important theories to explain the behavior of subatomic particles, including the theory of quarks, one of the basic building blocks of matter. *(Courtesy of Murray Gell-Mann; photo by Louis Fabian Bachrach)*

stand 40 years after he had advanced them, offer clear and compelling ways to understand why the elementary particles behave as they do and how they interact with one another. For his contributions, he was awarded the 1969 Nobel Prize in physics.

In 1993 Gell-Mann retired from Caltech and became a professor and distinguished fellow at the Santa Fe (N.M.) Institute. His work there involved what he called plectics, the study of simplicity and complexity as they apply to a broad range of subjects; for example, at one point he headed up a project studying the evolution of human languages. His publications include *Lectures on Weak Interactions of Strongly Interacting Particles* (1961), *The Eightfold Way* (1964), *Broken Scale Invariance and the Light Cone* (1971), *The Nature of Matter* (1981), and *Nonextensive Entropy: Interdisciplinary Applications* (2004). His honors include election to the National Academy of Sciences and the American Academy of Arts and Sciences.

Further Reading

Gell-Mann, Murray. *The Quark and the Jaguar: Adventures in the Simple and the Complex.* New York: W. H. Freeman, 1994.

Johnson, George. *Strange Beauty: Murray Gell-Mann and the Revolution in Twentieth-Century Physics.* New York: Alfred A. Knopf, 1999.

Nobelprize.org. "The Nobel Prize in Physics 1969." Available online. URL: http://nobelprize.org/physics/laureates/1969. Downloaded on September 28, 2004.

Schwarz, John H., ed. *Elementary Particles and the Universe: Essays in Honor of Murray Gell-Mann.* New York: Cambridge University Press, 1991.

Wasson, Tyler, ed. *Nobel Prize Winners.* New York: H. W. Wilson, 1987, pp. 370–372.

Giacconi, Riccardo

(1931–) *physicist*

Riccardo Giacconi pioneered the development of X-ray astronomy, a powerful technique for gathering information about celestial bodies in deep space. For this contribution, he was awarded a share of the 2002 Nobel Prize in physics.

Giacconi was born on October 6, 1931, in Genoa, Italy. His father, Antonio, was a business-man, and his mother, Elsa, was a high school teacher. As a young boy he moved with his family to Milan where he grew up. He eventually enrolled in the University of Milan, where he received a Ph.D. in 1954 and then taught physics for two years. In 1957 he married Mirella Manaira with whom he had two children.

While at Milan, Giacconi used a cloud chamber, a device that detects subatomic particles by tracking them through a cloud of water vapor, to study cosmic rays. Unlike most other rays, which consist of photons or tiny packets of light energy, cosmic rays consist of high-energy particles, mostly protons but also electrons, positrons, mesons, and neutrinos. Cosmic rays originate in deep space, and at the time they were considered to be an excellent source for the study of elementary particles. In 1956 he obtained a fellowship to continue his work on cosmic ray research at the University of Indiana at Bloomington, where he designed and built a newer and bigger cloud chamber, and at Princeton University, where he searched fruitlessly for a mysterious new particle that several Soviet scientists had claimed to discover.

In 1959 Giacconi was named a senior scientist by American Science & Engineering, Inc. (AS&E) in Cambridge, Massachusetts. For the next 14 years he coordinated the corporation's space science programs that were performed on behalf of the National Aeronautics and Space Administration (NASA). His efforts in this regard focused on X-ray astronomy, the study of X-rays that emanate from outer space. Unlike cosmic rays, X-rays dissipate in the Earth's upper atmosphere, so X-rays from outer space cannot be detected from the planet's surface. Consequently, in 1962 NASA launched *Aerobee*, a rocket carrying an X-ray telescope designed by Giacconi for determining whether or not the Moon reflected X-rays from the Sun. The answer was no, but, more importantly, the experiment demonstrated the existence of a large flow of X-rays from outside the solar system that seemed to be evenly distributed across the sky. This discovery amazed physicists, who previously had believed that X-rays emanate only from the Sun.

Giacconi designed improvements to the X-ray telescope and oversaw their deployment via rocket and high-altitude balloon. In short order he was able to demonstrate that X-rays emanate from double stars, whereby a star orbits a compact mass, either a neutron star or a black hole. He also oversaw the design, construction, and launch in 1970 of *Uhuru,* the first satellite dedicated to X-ray astronomy.

Giacconi left AS&E for Harvard University's Center for Astrophysics in 1973. He spent the next five years designing a successor to *Uhuru,* the *Einstein X-ray Observatory,* which was launched in 1978. *Einstein*'s telescope made detailed studies of a number of double stars as well as a host of normal stars. It also measured the X-ray radiation from the gas between galaxies in galaxy groups, thus permitting astrophysicists to make educated guesses about the nature of the so-called dark matter content of the universe, invisible matter that can be detected only by the gravitational pull it exerts on celestial bodies.

In 1981 Giacconi was named director of the Space Telescope Science Institute in Baltimore, Maryland, as well as a professor of astronomy at Johns Hopkins University. In addition to these duties, he participated in the development of the *Hubble Space Telescope,* named in honor of EDWIN P. HUBBLE, and oversaw the development of a successor to *Einstein,* the *Chandra X-ray Observatory,* named in honor of SUBRAHMANYAN CHANDRASEKHAR. Launched in 1999, *Chandra* sent back to Earth some amazingly detailed photographs of rapidly developing, high-energy events such as supernovas as well as the slow development of stars and constellations. After being correlated with data from conventional observatories, these photographs allowed astronomers to identify visually the sources of deep-space X-rays. Because X-ray astronomy gives astronomers and astrophysicists important new data with which to study the workings of the universe, Giacconi was awarded a half share of the 2002 Nobel Prize in physics.

In 1991 Giacconi returned to the University of Milan to teach physics and astronomy while also serving as director general of the European Southern Observatory near Munich, Germany. Eight years later he returned to the United States to be a research professor at Johns Hopkins and president of Associated Universities, Inc., in Washington, D.C. In the latter capacity, he over-

Riccardo Giacconi used X-rays to study celestial bodies in deep space. *(Courtesy of Riccardo Giacconi)*

saw the development of the Altacama Large Millimeter Array, a telescope complex being constructed in Chile's Altacama Desert. His honors include election to the National Academy of Sciences and the American Academy of Arts and Sciences. He became a naturalized U.S. citizen in 1967.

Further Reading

The Bruce Medalists. "Riccardo Giacconi." Available online. URL: http://phys-astro.sonoma.edu/brucemedalists/giacconi. Downloaded on March 25, 2005.

Gushy, Herbert, and Remo Ruffini. *Exploring the Universe: A Festschrift in Honor of Riccardo Giacconi.* River Edge, N.J.: World Scientific, 2000.

Nobelprize.org. "The Nobel Prize in Physics 2002." Available online. URL: http://nobelprize.org/physics/laureates/2002. Downloaded on September 6, 2004.

Overbye, Dennis. "3 Nobels for Solving Longstanding Mysteries of the Cosmos," *New York Times,* October 9, 2002, p. A21.

Giaever, Ivar
(1929–) *physicist*

Ivar Giaever showed that the tunneling effect applies to superconductivity as well as to semiconductivity. This demonstration won for him a share of the 1973 Nobel Prize in physics.

Giaever was born on April 5, 1929, in Bergen, Norway, but he grew up in Toten and Hamar. His father, John, was a pharmacist, and his mother, Gudrun, was a homemaker. After finishing high school, he worked for a year in a munitions factory before entering the Norwegian Institute of Technology. In 1952 he received a B.S. in mechanical engineering and married Inger Skramstad with whom he had four children. He spent the next two years as a corporal in the Norwegian army and as a patent examiner for the Norwegian government. In 1954 he left Norway for Canada and went to work for the General Electric (GE) Company's advanced engineering program in Peterborough, Ontario. Two years later he was reassigned to GE headquarters in Schenectady, New York, eventually being assigned to its research and development center. He also entered the graduate physics program at Rensselaer Polytechnic Institute (RPI) in nearby Troy, receiving a Ph.D. in 1964. That same year he became a naturalized U.S. citizen.

Giaever's early work at GE involved semiconductors, substances that conduct electricity better than nonconductors such as glass but not as well as good conductors such as copper. He was particularly interested in the work published in 1958 by Japanese physicist Leo Esaki concerning tunneling, a phenomenon whereby electrons make use of their wave properties to pass through what should be impenetrable force barriers. Esaki's work explained how tunneling works in semiconductors, but Giaever immediately saw that it also applied to superconductors, metals that lose all resistance to electron flow in extreme low-temperature conditions. In 1957 JOHN BARDEEN, LEON N. COOPER, and J. ROBERT SCHRIEFFER had published the BCS theory of superconductivity, which explains electron flow in terms of energy gaps that extremely low temperature creates in the superconductor's electron density. Giaever suspected that a device could be constructed that exploited the tunneling effect to make precise measurements of the energy gap in superconductors. In 1960 he placed a thin film of superconducting aluminum oxide between two thin films of aluminum so as to insulate them, and then he passed electrons from one aluminum film to the other through the aluminum oxide film via tunneling. He was then able to measure precisely the energy gap in the superconducting film by measuring the ratio of current to voltage that resulted during tunneling.

Once his experiment had been replicated in other laboratories, Giaever's tunneling method became the standard method of measuring activity in a superconductor. It also provided experimental evidence to support the BCS theory, thus helping Bardeen, Cooper, and Schrieffer win the 1972 Nobel Prize in physics. In so doing, Giaever helped himself win a quarter share of the 1973 Nobel Prize in physics; one of his corecipients was Esaki (one-quarter share) and the other was the British physicist Brian D. Josephson.

Meanwhile, Giaever had become interested in biophysics, specifically the behavior of protein molecules on metal films. After studying biophysics for a year at England's Cambridge University, in 1970 he returned to GE and devoted the next 18 years to inventing and perfecting Electric Cell-substrate Impedance Sensing (ECIS), an electrical method for studying in real time many of the activities of animal cells while they grow in tissue culture on small electrodes. In 1988 he left GE to become a professor of engineering and science at RPI. In 1991 he cofounded and became president of Applied BioPhysics, a private concern in Troy that manufactures and markets ECIS and other biotech equipment. His honors include election to the National Academy of Sciences and the American Academy of Arts and Sciences.

Further Reading
Nobelprize.org. "The Nobel Prize in Physics 1973." Available online. URL: http://nobelprize.org/physics/laureates/1973. Downloaded on September 29, 2004.

Physics Department, Rensselaer Polytechnic Institute. "Ivar Giaever." Available online. URL: http://www.rpi.edu/~giaevi. Downloaded on March 25, 2005.

Wasson, Tyler, ed. *Nobel Prize Winners.* New York: H. W. Wilson, 1987, pp. 372–374.

Giauque, William F.
(William Francis Giauque)
(1895–1982) *chemist*

William F. Giauque proved that the third law of thermodynamics is a basic law of nature, and he discovered the two isotopes of oxygen. For the former achievement, he was awarded a Nobel Prize in chemistry.

Giauque was born on May 12, 1895, in Niagara Falls, Ontario, Canada, to U.S. citizens. His father, William, was a railroad worker, and his mother, Isabella, was a homemaker. As a boy he moved with his family to Michigan, and then returned with them to Niagara Falls when he was 13. After finishing his high school education, he worked for two years at the Hooker Electrochemical Company, and then he enrolled in the University of California at Berkeley where he received a B.S. and a Ph.D. in chemistry in 1920 and 1922, respectively. He then joined the faculty at Berkeley where he remained for the rest of his career. In 1932 he married Muriel Ashley with whom he had two children.

Giauque's primary research interest involved the third law of thermodynamics. First proposed by German physicist Walther Nernst, this law was originally known as the Nernst heat theorem. Nernst reasoned that heat is caused by the movement of molecules, so the slower the molecules in a given system move, the less heat they will generate. Consequently, he theorized that the closer the temperature of a system gets to absolute zero (0 K, or Kelvin, which converts to −273.16° Centigrade and −459.69° Fahrenheit), the more difficult it becomes to extract energy from that system. Moreover, when that system reaches absolute zero, the point at which all molecular movement theoretically ceases, it is impossible to extract any energy from it at all. In 1906, when Nernst proposed his theorem, it was impossible to prove or disprove it, given the lack of equipment to generate temperatures low enough to conduct the necessary tests. Nevertheless, by 1920 the Nernst heat theorem had been accepted by the scientific community as the third law of thermodynamics, and Nernst won that year's Nobel Prize in chemistry for proposing it. Giauque made it his mission to prove or disprove that the Nernst heat theorem was indeed a basic law of nature.

In 1923 Giauque developed a method for supercooling glycerol to 70 K (room temperature is approximately 300 K). Further experiments indicated that the supercooled glycerol had a much higher level of entropy (a system's entropy level increases as its ability to release energy decreases) than did glycerol at normal temperature. By 1929 he was able to show that, when hydrogen molecules reach a temperature of 1 K, the spin of their protons becomes disordered in such a way that the molecules crystallize, thus leaving the molecules in a very high state of entropy.

Meanwhile, Giauque had conceived of a way to use magnetism to achieve temperatures lower than 1 K. Known as adiabatic demagnetization, this method involves changing a system's magnetic orientation so that the energy caused by its molecular spin can be siphoned off. Giauque conceived of this method in 1926, but it was not until seven years later that he was able to construct the equipment necessary to carry out the experiment. He subjected a crystal of the paramagnetic salt known as gadolinium sulfate to an 8,000-gauss magnet. The magnet realigned the dipoles of the molecules, and their heat was transferred to a surrounding bath of liquid helium. The result was a drop of the crystal's temperature to 0.53 K. Later that same year (1933), he subjected the crystal to more than 100,000 gauss and was able to reduce the temperature to 0.004 K. At these temperatures, he was able to prove, once and for all, that the Nernst heat theorem is indeed correct. He published his findings that same year, and in 1949 he was awarded the Nobel Prize in chemistry.

Giauque's experiments with extreme low temperatures led him to discover the isotopes of oxygen. Scientists had assumed that oxygen exists only in one form, with an atomic weight of 16, but in 1929 Giauque discovered that, in extremely rare cases, an oxygen atom can take on one or two additional neutrons, thus raising its atomic weight to 17 and 18, respectively. His discovery explained the discrepancy between the atomic weight value for oxygen used by chemists and the mass spectrometric scale value for oxygen used by physicists. As a result, the International Union of Pure and Applied Chemistry and the International Commission on Atomic Weights abandoned oxygen in favor of carbon as the standard by which all other elements are valued.

In addition to winning the Nobel Prize, Giauque was elected to the National Academy of Sciences and the American Academy of Arts and Sciences, and he was awarded the Franklin Institute's Elliot Cresson Medal. He retired from UC-Berkeley in 1962, but he continued to experiment there for a number of years thereafter. He died on March 28, 1982, in Berkeley.

Further Reading

Nobelprize.org. "The Nobel Prize in Chemistry 1949." Available online. URL: http://nobelprize.org/ chemistry/laureates/1949. Downloaded on January 9, 2004.

Pitzer, Kenneth S., and David A. Shirley. "William Francis Giauque." National Academy of Sciences, *Biographical Memoirs* 69 (1996), pp. 38–57.

Science Matters @ Berkeley. "1933: William F. Giauque and the Quest for Absolute Zero." Available online. URL: http://sciencematters.berkeley.edu/archives/ volume1/issue3/legacy.php. Downloaded on March 25, 2005.

Wasson, Tyler, ed. *Nobel Prize Winners*. New York: H. W. Wilson, 1987, pp. 374–375.

Gibbs, J. Willard
(Josiah Willard Gibbs)
(1839–1903) *physicist*

J. Willard Gibbs is generally regarded as the founder of physical chemistry, that branch of chemistry dealing with the relations between the physical properties of substances and their chemical composition and transformations. He also played a pioneering role in the mathematical field of vector analysis and the branch of physics known as statistical mechanics.

Gibbs was born on February 11, 1839, in New Haven, Connecticut. His father, Josiah, was a professor at Yale University, and his mother, Mary Ann, was a homemaker. At age 19 he received a bachelor's degree from Yale, which in 1863 also awarded him the first Ph.D. in engineering granted in the United States. For the next three years he tutored Yale students in Latin and natural philoso-phy; he also designed an improved railcar brake, for which he received a patent. In 1866 he went on a three-year working tour of Europe, spending a year each at the universities of Paris, Berlin, and Heidelberg; during this tour he attended the lectures of some of Europe's most prominent mathematicians and physicists. He returned to New Haven in 1869, and he devoted most of his time over the next two years to the study of engineering theory and invention. His most important contribution in this regard involved improvements to the governor, or speed regulator, of James Watt's steam engine. In 1871 Yale named him its first professor of mathematical physics, a position he held for the rest of his career. He remained a bachelor all his life.

In 1873 Gibbs published two groundbreaking papers in the *Transactions of the Connecticut Academy of Arts and Sciences*. Both papers dealt with chemical thermodynamics, the study of the relations between heat and energy in chemical reactions. "Graphical Methods in the Thermodynamics of Fluids" shows how to diagram what happens to fluids (gases and liquids) when they are subjected to changes in pressure or temperature. At the time, these changes were explained in terms of mathematical equations, a method that works well for gases but poorly for liquids. "A Method of Geometrical Representation of the Thermodynamic Properties of Substances by Means of Surfaces" shows how to develop three-dimensional diagrams for demonstrating the effects of energy (heat content), entropy (the amount of potential energy that cannot be converted into kinetic energy), and volume on a substance, be it a gas, liquid, or solid. The beauty of Gibbs's diagrams is that they show the range of states through which a given substance can pass, as well as those points of phase changes, that is when a substance changes from one state to another (i.e., from liquid to solid). Consequently, a Gibbs diagram can outline phase changes for a mixture of variable composition, not just a pure substance.

In 1876 Gibbs published the first part of his most influential paper, "On the Equilibrium of Heterogeneous Substances," in the *Transactions;* the paper's second part followed in 1878. This paper describes, in theory, how to predict which chemical reactions are possible and which are impossible, the amount of energy needed to drive a given chemical reaction, and the amount of heat released or absorbed by the reaction. In so doing, he propagated two critically important concepts, the phase rule and chemical potential. The phase rule defines precisely the likelihood of a system staying at equilibrium given changes to its pressure, temperature, or composition. This likelihood increases as the number of components increases or as the number of phases, or states in which the components exist, decreases, and vice versa. Chemical potential is Gibbs's term for the thermodynamic quantity necessary to change a given substance in a given system from one phase to another.

As impressive as Gibbs's work concerning chemical thermodynamics was, its significance was not entirely evident at first, partly because he published it in a rather obscure journal and partly because it was written in an obtuse style. Not until 1892, when German physicist Wilhelm Ostwald translated "On the Equilibrium . . ." into German and published it in the *Zeitschrift für physikalische Chemie* (*Journal of Physical Chemistry*), did the European scientific community become aware of Gibbs's groundbreaking work. The American community at least recognized that Gibbs's work was imbued with genius, although it was not quite sure what to make of it, and he was rewarded by being elected to the National Academy of Sciences, the American Association for the Advancement of Science, and the American Academy of Arts and Sciences. The latter group also presented him with its Rumford Medal, one of the most important awards for scientific achievement in the United States. In 1901 he was awarded the Royal Society of London's Copley Medal, one of the highest scientific honors of the day. Today, the phase rule is recognized as being essential for calculating chemical reactions, such as extraction, crystallization, distillation, precipitation, the use of freezing mixtures, and the identification of substances, for industrial applications.

After 1880 Gibbs focused his attention on physical problems, particularly the velocity and nature of light. He concluded that light was an electromagnetic phenomenon, and this led him to further study of the properties of electromagnetism. To this end he pioneered a new mathematical field, vector analysis, as a tool for better understanding electromagnetism; much of his work in this regard was published as *Vector Analysis* (1901). He also pioneered statistical mechanics, which today uses statistics, classical physics, and quantum mechanics to explain the properties of chemical systems. In 1902 he published the field's first important text, *Elementary Principles in Statistical Mechanics.*

Gibbs died on April 28, 1903, in New Haven. After his death, Yale honored his memory by creating the J. Willard Gibbs Professorship in Theoretical Chemistry.

Further Reading

Wheeler, Lynde Phelps. *Josiah Willard Gibbs, the History of a Great Mind.* New Haven, Conn.: Yale University Press, 1951.

Wikipedia, the Free Encyclopedia. "Josiah Willard Gibbs." Available online. URL: http://en.wikipedia.org/wiki/Willard_Gibbs. Downloaded on December 29, 2003.

Gilbert, Walter
(1932–) *molecular biologist*

Walter Gilbert's career made the transition from theoretical physics to molecular biology, the study of how genetics regulates biochemical functions. In the process, he developed a method for identifying the sequence of building blocks in a DNA molecule, an achievement that earned him a share of a Nobel Prize in chemistry.

Gilbert was born on March 21, 1932, in Boston, Massachusetts. His father, Richard, was an economist, and his mother, Emma, was a child psychologist. At age seven he moved with his family to Washington, D.C., where he grew up. He attended Harvard University and received a B.A. in chemistry and physics in 1953 and an M.A. in theoretical physics in 1954. He spent the next three years in England studying mathematical physics at Cambridge University, receiving a Ph.D. in mathematics in 1957. He then returned to Harvard for postdoctoral research and to assist JULIAN S. SCHWINGER, and in 1959 he joined the Harvard faculty as a professor of physics. In 1953 he married Celia Stone with whom he had two children.

In 1960 Gilbert began working with JAMES D. WATSON, at the time a Harvard colleague, on a study of messenger RNA (mRNA), the molecule that transfers genetic coding from the genes to the ribosomes, where it dictates the production of a certain protein. This project kindled his interest in molecular biology, and by the mid-1960s he had abandoned theoretical physics for experimental biology. His work with mRNA led to further study of how genetics regulates protein synthesis; specifically, he wondered why each gene does not continually call for the production of proteins. Earlier, French geneticists François Jacob and Jacques L. Monod had hypothesized the existence of some sort of repressor mechanism that signals certain genes to stop operating while others are allowed to continue. Gilbert began experimenting with *Escherichia coli* (*E. coli*), a bacterium commonly found in the human digestive tract that produces betagalactosidase, an enzyme that breaks down lactose. He soon

Walter Gilbert was one of a few scientists whose work involved biology, chemistry, and physics. *(Courtesy of Walter Gilbert)*

discovered that, in the absence of lactose, one of *E. coli*'s genes sends a chemical signal, known as a repressor, that "turns off" the gene that regulates the production of betagalactosidase. By 1970 he had isolated, characterized, and purified this repressor, thus demonstrating the validity of Jacob and Monod's hypothesis.

Gilbert then turned his attention to developing a method for determining the exact sequence of nucleotides, the building blocks from which DNA and RNA are constructed, in a DNA chain. First, he used radioisotopes to tag the various amino-acid bases, the most distinctive component of the building blocks from which nucleotides are constructed. Then, he used enzymes to break down a DNA chain into short strands, passed the strands through an electrically charged field, and exposed them to X-ray film. The film clearly captured the images produced by the various radioactive tags, thus making it possible to identify with relative ease the sequence of the amino-acid bases and, therefore, the nucleotides.

Rapid chemical DNA sequencing, as Gilbert's technique became known, enabled researchers to identify and then synthesize each of the nucleotides in a DNA molecule. This ability contributed in the late 1970s to the rise of biotechnology, the genetic engineering of certain organisms to perform a specific task that they are otherwise incapable of performing. For his contribution in this regard, Gilbert was awarded a quarter share of the 1980 Nobel Prize in chemistry.

Meanwhile, Gilbert's interests had shifted yet again. Having been named a professor of physics in 1959, of biophysics in 1964, of biochemistry in 1968, and of molecular biology in 1972, in 1978 he became involved in the commercial aspects of biotechnology. That same year he and a group of scientists and businessmen formed the biotech firm Biogen, with Gilbert as chair of the scientific board of advisers, and in 1981 he took a leave of absence from Harvard to become Biogen's chief executive officer. By 1984, however, he had become disillusioned with the firm's inability to live up to its potential, and that same year he resigned as CEO and returned to Harvard. Three years later he was named chair of the developmental biology department at Harvard, where he remained for the rest of his career. Nevertheless, he remained interested in biotechnology, and in 1987 he attempted to put together a private corporation that would develop, copyright, and sell information about DNA sequencing to other biotech firms. When the funding for this project fell through, he refocused his interests yet again, this time to the Human Genome Project. This project, headed by Gilbert's former collaborator, James D. Watson, attempts to map the 30,000-plus genes in the human chromosomes.

Further Reading

Hargittai, Istvan, and Magdolna Hargittai. *Candid Science II: Conversations with Famous Biomedical Scientists.* London: Imperial College Press, 2002, pp. 98–114.

Nobelprize.org. "The Nobel Prize in Chemistry 1980." Available online. URL: http://nobelprize.org/chemistry/laureates/1980. Downloaded on August 9, 2004.

Wasson, Tyler, ed. *Nobel Prize Winners.* New York: H. W. Wilson, 1987, pp. 378–380.

Gilman, Alfred G.
(Alfred Goodman Gilman, Jr.)
(1941–   ) *biochemist*

Alfred G. Gilman discovered G-proteins, which play an important role in helping a hormone initiate the activity of an enzyme within a cell. For this discovery, he was awarded a share of the 1994 Nobel Prize in physiology or medicine.

Gilman was born on July 1, 1941, in New Haven, Connecticut. His father, Alfred, was a professor of pharmacology, and his mother, Mabel, was a piano teacher. As a boy he moved with his family to White Plains, New York, where he grew up. He completed his high school education in Watertown, Connecticut, and then entered Yale University, receiving a B.A. in biology in 1962. After a brief stint at the Burroughs Wellcome research laboratory in Tuckahoe, New York, he enrolled in Case Western University in Cleveland, Ohio, receiving an M.D. and a Ph.D. in pharmacology in 1969. He spent the next two years as a research assistant to MARSHALL W. NIRENBERG at the National Institutes of Health in Bethesda, Maryland. In 1971 he

Alfred Gilman showed how hormones activate enzymes to perform certain biochemical functions. *(Courtesy of Alfred G. Gilman)*

became a professor of pharmacology at the University of Virginia, and in 1979 he was named chair of the department of pharmacology at the University of Texas Southwestern Medical Center in Dallas. In 1963 he married Kathryn Hedlund with whom he had three children.

Gilman's primary research interest involved cyclic adenosine monophosphate, or cyclic AMP. In the 1960s EARL W. SUTHERLAND had shown that cyclic AMP plays a major role in initiating the activity of enzymes within a cell. Sutherland's work demonstrated that, in order to prompt a particular enzyme into action, a hormone must attach itself to a specific location, or receptor, along the cell membrane so that its presence can be recognized by the cell. Once properly attached, the hormone triggers the production of cyclic AMP, the so-called second messenger, which then signals for the production of the enzyme associated with that particular receptor. In 1970 MARTIN RODBELL discovered that the process of cellular signal transduction requires a "third messenger" as well. Rodbell showed that a small intracellular molecule called guanosine triphosphate (GTP) carries the signal from the hormone through the cell membrane to the membrane's inner wall, where it signals for the production of cyclic AMP. However, Rodbell was not entirely sure how GTP made it through the cell membrane, so Gilman picked up this line of inquiry in the late 1970s.

Gilman discovered the existence of a previously unknown protein in the cell membrane that acts as a go-between between GTP and cyclic AMP. Gilman called this protein the G-protein, "G" standing for GTP, and showed that G-proteins serve as gates through which GTP, but nothing else, is allowed to pass through the membrane. It was later discovered that G-proteins also play a role in translating chemical signals from the sense organs into sensory perceptions in the brain.

The discovery of GTP and G-proteins provided medical researchers with a much better understanding as to how hormones govern cellular functions. Researchers also gained new insights into how certain diseases involving cellular malfunctions might be cured or treated by regulating the activities of G-proteins, and shortly after their discovery pharmaceutical companies began developing drugs that could do this. For their roles in this important medical development, Gilman and Rodbell were each awarded a half share of the 1994 Nobel Prize in physiology or medicine; Sutherland had been awarded the prize in 1971.

Gilman spent the rest of his career at Southwestern Medical Center, continuing his research into the workings of G-proteins. His many honors include election to the National Academy of Sciences.

Further Reading

Hargittai, Istvan, and Magdolna Hargittai. *Candid Science II: Conversations with Famous Biomedical Scientists.* London: Imperial College Press, 2002, pp. 238–252.

Krapp, Kristine M., ed. *Notable Twentieth-Century Scientists Supplement.* Detroit: Gale Research, 1998, pp. 178–180.

Nobelprize.org. "The Nobel Prize in Physiology or Medicine 1994." Available online. URL: http://nobelprize. org/medicine/laureates/1994. Downloaded on June 28, 2004.

Glaser, Donald A.
(Donald Arthur Glaser)
(1926–) *physicist*

Donald A. Glaser invented the hydrogen bubble chamber, a sophisticated device for observing extremely fast-moving subatomic particles. This invention won for him the 1960 Nobel Prize in physics.

Glaser was born on September 21, 1926, in Cleveland, Ohio. His father, William, was a businessman, and his mother, Lena, was a homemaker. In 1946 he received a B.S. in mathematics and physics from Cleveland's Case Institute of Technology (today Case Western Reserve University), and in 1950 he received a Ph.D. in mathematics and physics from the California Institute of Technology, although he had completed the requirements for the Ph.D. the year before. In 1949 he became a professor of physics at the University of Michigan.

Glaser's graduate research focused on the subatomic particles—protons, electrons, positrons, mesons, and neutrinos—that make up cosmic rays, which originate in the Sun and from unknown sources in deep space. One of the problems of studying such particles was that they were extremely difficult to detect with the relatively primitive equipment of the day. When he began his studies in the late 1940s, the most sophisticated piece of equipment for viewing subatomic particles was the cloud chamber. This device, which was invented by English physicist C. T. R. Wilson, consists of a gas chamber containing supersaturated water vapor. As a particle makes its way through the chamber it creates a vapor trail, much like a jet airplane creates a vapor trail in the sky. By using a strobe light, a researcher can photograph these vapor trails and observe particles as they undergo radioactive decay or fission. Glaser had used a cloud chamber to study the constituent particles of cosmic rays, but by the time he had arrived at Michigan his interest had shifted to "strange particles," so called because it takes them trillions of times longer to decay via radioactivity than it does for them to form. Because of their "strangeness," these particles are virtually impossible to observe in a cloud chamber.

To remedy this situation, Glaser conceived of building what is known today as the hydrogen bubble chamber. This device is similar to a Wilson cloud chamber except that it replaces the water vapor with superheated liquid hydrogen; instead of creating a vapor trail, particles create a bubble trail. The higher density of the liquid hydrogen, as compared to water vapor, makes it possible to observe particles, such as strange particles, that move at speeds approaching the speed of light. Moreover, the speed, charge, and mass of a particle detected in the bubble chamber can be determined simply by placing the chamber within a magnetic field whose strength can be adjusted. He finished building the first bubble chamber, which had a diameter of only one inch, in 1952, and he used it in conjunction with experiments concerning strange particles he conducted at the Brookhaven National Laboratory in New York. These experiments yielded important information about the lifetimes, modes of radioactive decay, and rotations of hyperons, which decay via radioactivity into protons and neutrons, and K mesons, which have about half the mass of a proton.

The hydrogen bubble chamber quickly became a piece of standard equipment for researchers studying particle physics. It came about around the time that high-energy particle accelerators were being developed, and it made it possible to examine the products of the extremely high-energy experiments these machines were capable of conducting. By 1960 other researchers, most notably LUIS W. ALVAREZ, had built bubble chambers as large as 72 inches in diameter and had incorporated computers to analyze the data they collected, which made it much easier to determine the various properties of subatomic particles. For inventing the hydrogen bubble chamber, Glaser was awarded the 1960 Nobel Prize in physics.

In 1959 Glaser left Michigan for the University of California at Berkeley. At Berkeley his research interest changed once again, this time from particle physics to biophysics. In 1964 he was named a pro-

fessor of molecular biology, and over the next 25 years his work gravitated toward neuroscience. By 2000 his research involved the development of computational models of the human visual system that explain its performance in terms of its physiology and anatomy.

In 1960 Glaser married Ruth Thompson. His honors include election to the National Academy of Sciences.

Further Reading

Achinstein, Peter, and Owen Hannaway, eds. *Observation, Experiment, and Hypothesis in Modern Physical Science.* Cambridge, Mass.: MIT Press, 1985, pp. 309–373.

Nobelprize.org. "The Nobel Prize in Physics 1960." Available online. URL: http://nobelprize.org/physics/laureates/1960. Downloaded on September 23, 2004.

Wasson, Tyler, ed. *Nobel Prize Winners.* New York: H. W. Wilson, 1987, pp. 382–384.

Glashow, Sheldon L.
(Sheldon Lee Glashow)
(1932–) *physicist*

Sheldon L. Glashow codeveloped the electroweak unification theory, which links together the seemingly unrelated physical forces of electromagnetism and the weak interactions. For this contribution, he was awarded a share of the 1979 Nobel Prize in physics.

Glashow was born on December 5, 1932, in New York City. His father, Lewis, was a plumber, and his mother, Bella, was a homemaker. Like STEVEN WEINBERG, he attended the Bronx High School of Science and received a B.S. in physics from Cornell University in 1954. He then entered the graduate physics program at Harvard University and received an M.A. and a Ph.D. in 1955 and 1959, respectively. Following postdoctoral work at the Institute for Theoretical Physics (today the Niels Bohr Institute) in Copenhagen, Denmark, the European Center for Nuclear Research (CERN) in Geneva, Switzerland, and the California Institute of Technology, in 1961 he joined the faculty at Stanford University. He left Stanford a year later for the University of California at Berkeley, and in 1966 he returned to Harvard as a professor of physics. In 1972 he married Joan Alexander with whom he had four children.

As a graduate student at Harvard, Glashow became interested in developing a theory that would unify electromagnetism and the weak interactions, the physical force that governs certain forms of radioactive decay. His doctoral dissertation explored the role played by the vector meson, a particle with a mass greater than an electron but smaller than a proton, in beta decay, a form of radioactive decay that is governed by the weak interactions. He and JULIAN S. SCHWINGER, his adviser at Harvard, collaborated on a preliminary effort to explain electromagnetism and the weak interactions as manifestations of one unified force, in much the same way that British physicist James Clerk Maxwell had demonstrated that electricity and magnetism are manifestations of electromagnetism.

Glashow continued to pursue a unified theory while in Europe, where he explored the algebraic structure of weak interactions. Using a combination of two mathematical symmetry groups known as $SU(2) \times (U)1$, in the early 1960s he developed a theory that combined electromagnetism and the weak interactions. The problem with the theory was that it hinged on the existence of four gauge bosons, messenger particles that actually carry the weak interactions in much the same way that electrons and photons, tiny packets of light energy, carry electromagnetism. Glashow's theory permitted the photon to be one of the gauge bosons, but the existence of the other three was problematic because they would have to have no mass, thus making them virtually impossible to detect.

By 1968, however, the problems with Glashow's theory had been worked out by Weinberg and Pakistani physicist Abdus Salam. Weinberg and Salam showed that the three missing gauge bosons did not have to be massless because the range of any given force tends to be inversely proportional to the mass of the particle transmitting it. Since the weak interactions operate over extremely short distances on the order of 10^{-16} centimeters, the gauge bosons that carry the weak interactions could be relatively large. Weinberg and Salam postulated the existence of three gauge bosons, labeled W^+, W^-, and Z^0, that carry the weak interactions as well as electrical charges of positive, negative, and neutral, respectively. Evidence to support this scheme was pro-

vided in 1973 by researchers at CERN, who in 1983 also demonstrated the existence of the W and Z particles.

The combined effort of Glashow, Weinberg, and Salam concerning unified theory is known today as the electroweak unification theory. Thirty-five years after its promulgation, it remains a valid attempt to unify the forces of electromagnetism and the weak interactions. The value of the theory was recognized in 1979 when Glashow, Weinberg, and Salam were each awarded a one-third share of the Nobel Prize in physics.

In 1982 Glashow moved to Texas where he was named a distinguished scientist at the University of Houston and a visiting professor at Texas A&M University; he retired in 2000. His publications include *The Charm of Physics* (1991). His honors include election to the National Academy of Sciences and the American Academy of Arts and Sciences.

Further Reading

Glashow, Sheldon, with Ben Bova. *Interactions: A Journey through the Mind of a Particle Physicist and the Matter of This World*. New York: Warner Books, 1988.

Nobelprize.org. "The Nobel Prize in Physics 1979." Available online. URL: http://nobelprize.org/physics/laureates/1979. Downloaded on October 2, 2004.

Wasson, Tyler, ed. *Nobel Prize Winners*. New York: H. W. Wilson, 1987, pp. 384–386.

Goddard, Robert H.
(Robert Hutchings Goddard)
(1882–1945) *rocket scientist*

Along with Russia's Konstantin E. Tsiolkovsky and Germany's Hermann Oberth, Robert H. Goddard is considered one of the founders of modern rocketry. His work served as the inspiration for the development of the U.S. space program under the auspices of the National Aeronautics and Space Administration (NASA).

Goddard was born on October 5, 1882, in Worcester, Massachusetts. His father, Nahum, owned a machine shop, and his mother, Fanny, was a homemaker. He attended public school in nearby Boston until age 16, when he was called on to stay home with his mother who had developed tuberculosis.

Robert Goddard, the "Father of American Rocketry," tinkers with an apparatus for studying solar energy. *(Courtesy of National Aeronautics and Space Administration and Mrs. Esther C. Goddard)*

Shortly thereafter he became fascinated with the possibility of traveling through space, and on October 19, 1899, he vowed to devote his life to making space travel a reality. He graduated from high school at age 21, and enrolled in the Worcester Polytechnic Institute, receiving a B.A. in 1908. He then entered Clark's graduate program and received an M.A. and a Ph.D. in physics in 1910 and 1911, respectively. After spending a year at Princeton University and more than a year recovering from tuberculosis, in 1914 he accepted a position teaching physics at Clark. In 1924 he married Esther Kisk with whom he had no children.

While a student, Goddard had conceived of using liquid oxygen and liquid hydrogen as propellants as well as multiple-stage rockets that could be discarded as they ran out of fuel. In 1907 he fired a powder-propelled rocket, his first ever, from the school campus; rather than get him expelled, it earned him the praise and interest of his professors because it showed his promise as a scientist. In 1914 he developed a double-base solid propellant consisting of 40 percent nitroglycerin and 60 percent nitrocellulose, and the following year he received a grant from the Smithsonian Institution to develop a rocket that could carry scientific instruments into the upper atmosphere. In a small rocket laboratory he built at Clark, he demonstrated that a rocket can propel itself through a vacuum, something that conventional wisdom held to be impossible. During World War I he experimented with rocket-propelled weaponry, and one of his ideas was later turned into the antitank bazooka that proved to be very effective in World War II. In 1919 he published "A Method of Reaching Extreme Altitudes" in the Smithsonian's *Miscellaneous Collections*. The essay proved mathematically that solid propellants could generate enough energy and thrust to propel a rocket into the upper atmosphere.

On March 16, 1926, Goddard used a combination of liquid oxygen and gasoline to launch the world's first liquid propellant rocket from his aunt's farm in Auburn, Massachusetts. The 10-foot rocket reached an altitude of 41 feet and stayed aloft for 2.5 seconds. He was unable to achieve significant improvements to this performance over the next three years, however, and in 1929 he was temporarily forced to give up his experiments when a rocket crashed and burned, thus causing the local authorities to ban further launches. Fortunately, Goddard's work had come to the attention of noted aviator Charles A. Lindbergh, who arranged for Goddard to receive a sizable grant from the Guggenheim Fund for the Promotion of Aeronautics. The grant, plus a smaller one from the Smithsonian, made it possible for Goddard to move his operations to a remote desert location near Roswell, New Mexico.

Between 1930 and 1942, Goddard and his associates designed, built, and tested the motors, fuel pumps, and cooling systems needed to propel a rocket. They also developed guidance systems using gyroscopes and vanes that permitted in-flight corrections of deviations from the flight plan. Goddard himself was granted more than 200 patents for rocket-related inventions, and in 1960 the rights to most of them were sold to the federal government for $1 million. In 1935 he launched the first rocket to travel faster than the speed of sound. Nevertheless, he was never able to reach an altitude higher than 10,000 feet, a major disappointment to him and his backers.

In 1942 Goddard shut down his Roswell operation to conduct war-related research at the U.S. Naval Engineering Experiment Station in Annapolis, Maryland. His efforts focused on building a rocket-assisted take-off (RATO) device to help heavily loaded aircraft get airborne. World War II ended before he could perfect such a device, but his work led others to do so.

In 1945 Goddard was diagnosed with cancer of the throat. He died on August 10, 1945, in Baltimore, Maryland. In recognition of his outstanding contribution to rocket science, in 1959 the National Aeronautics and Space Administration named its Goddard Space Flight Center in Greenbelt, Maryland, in his honor.

Further Reading

Lehman, Milton. *This High Man: The Life of Robert H. Goddard.* New York: Farrar, Straus, 1963.

National Aeronautics and Space Administration. "NASA Facts: Robert H. Goddard." Available online. URL: http://www.gsfc.nasa.gov/gsfc/service/gallery/fact_sheets/general/goddard/goddard.htm. Downloaded on February 6, 2004.

Goldstein, Joseph L.
(Joseph Leonard Goldstein)
(1940–   ) *molecular geneticist*

Joseph L. Goldstein codiscovered the LDL and SREBP pathways, the processes by which cells metabolize cholesterol. This work alerted the medical community to the importance of reducing cholesterol levels in the bloodstream as a means of preventing heart attacks. It also won for him a share of the 1985 Nobel Prize in physiology or medicine.

Goldstein was born on April 18, 1940, in Sumter, South Carolina. His parents, Isadore and Fannie, owned a clothing store in nearby Kingstree. After receiving a B.S. in chemistry from Washington and Lee (Va.) University in 1962, he entered the University of Texas Southwestern Medical Center's medical school in Dallas, receiving an M.D. in 1966. He spent the next six years completing his internship and residency at Boston's Massachusetts General Hospital, working as a clinical associate at the National Institutes of Health in Bethesda, Maryland, and studying medical genetics at the University of Washington. During this period he became close friends with MICHAEL S. BROWN, who would eventually become his lifelong collaborator. In 1972 he returned to Southwestern to teach internal medicine and to direct the division of medical genetics. Here he was rejoined with Brown, who had gone to Southwestern the previous year.

Goldstein's first research interest was familial hypercholesterolemia, a hereditary condition that is marked by high levels of cholesterol in the blood. Cholesterol plays an important role in the formation of cellular membranes, the digestive acids, and steroid hormones. In addition to ingesting cholesterol, the body can produce cholesterol on its own, and most of the cholesterol in the body is found in the cells. When it accumulates in the bloodstream, however, it becomes deadly as it inflames the walls of blood vessels, eventually leading to swollen or clogged arteries and heart attacks; a patient with familial hypercholesterolemia usually dies from a heart attack before the age of 30. In 1972 Goldstein and Brown began studying the processes by which cholesterol accumulates in the bloodstream, and their joint effort eventually grew to become the Brown-Goldstein Laboratory.

In an effort to find out how the body metabolizes cholesterol, Goldstein and Brown studied cultures of connective tissue from healthy people. They discovered that healthy cells have molecules, called receptors, in their membranes that bind to low-density lipoproteins (LDLs), the primary carriers of cholesterol in the bloodstream. These receptors then carry the LDLs into the cell interior, where they are broken down into cholesterol and other biochemical products; this process is known as the LDL pathway. By contrast, the cells of patients with familial hypercholesterolemia have no LDL receptors because of defects in the gene that initiates the production of LDL receptors. Consequently, cholesterol accumulates in their bloodstreams until it causes death, usually at an early age. The discovery of the LDL pathway alerted medical researchers that cholesterol-related diseases and conditions such as familial hypercholesterolemia might be treated via pharmaceuticals that could stimulate the production of LDL receptors. For this discovery, Goldstein and Brown were each awarded a half share of the 1985 Nobel Prize in physiology or medicine.

In the process of discovering the LDL pathway, Goldstein and Brown also discovered that the breakdown of LDLs causes the cell to cut down its production of LDL receptors. Further study showed the existence of a molecule they named the sterol regulatory element binding protein (SREBP). In cholesterol starved cells, SREBP stimulates the gene that initiates the production of LDL receptors, but in cells that contain plenty of cholesterol, the production of SREBP is blocked, thus the production of LDL receptors is inhibited. The discovery of the so-called SREBP pathway was particularly important because it explains why two-thirds of the people living in industrialized society have dangerously high levels of LDLs circulating in their bloodstreams, even though the gene that causes the production of LDL receptors is normal. Further study showed that industrialized people eat lots of fat, which contains lots of cholesterol. As the cell accumulates enough cholesterol to satisfy its needs, the SREBP pathway shuts down the production of new LDL receptors, thus leaving enough cholesterol in the bloodstream to inflame arteries and cause heart attacks. This discovery alerted the medical profession to the danger of high-fat, high-cholesterol diets, which led in turn to the development of a class of pharmaceutical drugs known as statins that can reduce the level of LDLs in the bloodstream.

Goldstein spent the rest of his career at Southwestern Medical Center, where he continued to collaborate with Brown on studies related to cholesterol. His many honors include the National Medal of Science and election to the National Academy of Sciences and the American Academy of Arts and Sciences. He also served a term as president of the American Society for Clinical Investigation.

Further Reading

Nobelprize.org. "The Nobel Prize in Physiology or Medicine 1985." Available online. URL: http://nobelprize.org/medicine/laureates/1985. Downloaded on July 10, 2004.

UT Southwestern Medical Center. "Brown-Goldstein Laboratory." Available online. URL: http://www8.utsouthwestern.edu/utsw/cda/dept14857/files/114532.html. Downloaded on March 25, 2005.

Wasson, Tyler, ed. *Nobel Prize Winners*. New York: H. W. Wilson, 1987, pp. 390–392.

Gourdine, Meredith C.
(Meredith Charles Gourdine)
(1929–1998) *physicist*

Meredith C. Gourdine was one of the first physicists to understand the principles of electrogasdynamics (EGD), the study of the forces produced by electrically charged particles suspended in a gas that is flowing through an electric field. Later in his career he became interested in magnetohydrodynamics (MHD), which is similar to EGD except that it substitutes a magnetic field for the electric field and its forces can be produced by a liquid as well as a gas. By the time of his death, he had contributed to a greater understanding of both EGD and MHD, and he had received more than 70 patents for applications and devices related to EGD and MHD.

Gourdine was born on September 26, 1929, in Newark, New Jersey. His father was a painting contractor, and his mother was a teletype operator. At age six he moved with his family to New York City where he grew up. In 1953 he received a B.S. in engineering physics from Cornell University and married June Cave with whom he had three children. They later divorced, and he married Carolina Bailing with whom he had one child.

After serving for two years as an officer in the U.S. Navy, in 1955 Gourdine entered the graduate program at the California Institute of Technology (Caltech), and in 1960 he received a Ph.D. in engineering physics. During his last three years at Caltech, he worked as a technical staffer for the Ramo-Woolridge Corporation and as a senior research scientist in the Jet Propulsion Laboratory (JPL), which Caltech administered for the National Aeronautics and Space Administration (NASA). As a graduate student he became interested in electrogasdynamics. EGD had been discovered in the 18th century, but its basic principles remained a mystery in the late 1950s. During his time at JPL, Gourdine worked out the solutions to many of the problems related to EGD so that EGD could be used to generate high-voltage electricity.

Caltech and NASA showed little interest in the practical applications of EGD, so in 1960 Gourdine left JPL to become the laboratory director at Plasmodyne Corporation, where he branched out into magnetohydrodynamics. MHD was almost as poorly understood as EGD, although by 1960 other researchers had developed an MHD generator capable of producing 10 kilowatts of electric power. Gourdine began experimenting with ways to use plasma, in physics the electrically charged particles produced when atoms in an extremely hot gas become ionized, as a source for generating power via MHD. Again, his superiors showed little interest in the practical applications of his work, and again Gourdine moved on, in 1962 to serve as chief scientist for the Curtiss-Wright Corporation's Aero Division and then in 1964 to Livingston, New Jersey, where he founded his own company, Gourdine Systems.

Once on his own, Gourdine began inventing ways to use EGD to solve everyday problems. Over the next 10 years he invented procedures to remove smoke from burning buildings, fog from airport runways, pollution from the air, and salt from seawater. He also made use of his knowledge of the underlying principles of EGD to design improvements to circuit breakers, acoustic imaging, air monitors, and spray-paint systems. In 1973 he moved to Houston, Texas, where he founded Energy Innovations, and for the next 25 years he designed direct energy-conversion devices using EGD and MHD, including generators that converted natural gas and low-grade coal into electricity.

In 1964 Gourdine was appointed by President Lyndon B. Johnson to serve on the President's Panel on Energy. He was later elected to the National Academy of Engineering for his contributions in the field of EGD. He died on November 20, 1998, in Houston.

Further Reading

Lemelson-MIT Program, Inventer of the Week. "Meredith C. Gourdine." Available online. URL: http://web.mit.edu/invent/iow/gourdine.html. Downloaded on March 25, 2005.

McMurray, Emily J., ed. *Notable Twentieth Century Scientists*. Detroit: Gale Research, 1995, pp. 805–807.

Spangenburg, Ray, and Kit Moser. *African Americans in Science, Math, and Invention*. New York: Facts On File, 2003, pp. 94–96.

Gray, Asa

(1810–1888) *botanist*

Asa Gray was one of the foremost botanists of the 19th century. His work did much to further the knowledge and understanding of North American flora. He also contributed significantly to the acceptance of Charles Darwin's theory of evolution in the United States.

Gray was born on November 18, 1810, in Sasquoit, New York. His parents, Moses and Roxana, were farmers. While attending high school in nearby Fairfield, he became fascinated with the incredible diversity of plant life. In 1829 he entered Fairfield Medical School and received an M.D. two years later. While practicing medicine over the next three years in western New York, he devoted his spare time to collecting plant specimens and teaching himself more about botany.

In 1834 Gray moved to New York City to assist JOHN TORREY, a professor of chemistry at New York's College of Physicians and Surgeons and one of the nation's foremost botanists. Over the next eight years, Gray collaborated with Torrey on several botanical projects. The most important one was the researching and writing of the first two volumes of *Flora of North America*, which came out in 1838 and 1843, respectively. Meanwhile, Gray wrote a textbook called *Elements of Botany* (1836) and did much of the preparatory work for the U.S. Exploring Expedition, better known as the Wilkes Expedition, which charted and explored the flora and fauna of a number of islands in the Pacific and Indian oceans. In 1838 he went to Europe for a year to observe North American flora on display in various herbariums.

In 1842 Gray was named professor of natural history at Harvard University. During his 46-year career at Harvard, he made many contributions to the advancement of botany in the United States. For one thing, he built up a collection of botanical specimens from all over North America without leaving Cambridge, Massachusetts. He accomplished this feat by corresponding regularly with hundreds of amateur collectors, who sent him specimens in exchange for help with classifying their specimens, specimens from other regions, collecting supplies, or money. He taught his correspondents how and what to collect, and then how to label and preserve what they collected, thus ensuring that he received from them the largest possible number of different plant types. In 1865 he donated his collection, which by now included thousands of plants and books, to Harvard on the condition that the university would house the collection suitably. This donation formed the basis for the formation of Harvard's department of botany.

In the process of obtaining his collection, Gray did much to teach botany to people all across the country. By teaching his correspondents about the whys and wherefores of botany, he also contributed immeasurably to a heightening of their botanical skills and the enjoyment they derived from botanical collecting. Moreover, the size and breadth of his collection enabled him to determine with considerable authority the range of a large number of plant species. He shared much of this knowledge with the general public by publishing *Manual of the Botany of* the *Northern United States;* this one-volume work first appeared in 1848, but it was updated by Gray five more times during his lifetime. *Gray's Manual,* as it was commonly known, was the most popular single-volume work on botany for a number of years, and many primary and secondary school teachers used it to teach botany to their students. In 1878 he published *Synoptical Flora of North America,* which updated and expanded the two volumes he and Torrey had produced.

Another of Gray's important contributions was the work he did toward getting the theory of evolution accepted in the United States. Gray corresponded regularly with Charles Darwin, whose *Origin of Species* (1859) introduced the general public to evolution, and he even helped Darwin by providing him with plant specimens from North America. One of Gray's most influential works, published in *Memoirs of the American Academy of Arts and Sciences* just a few months before *Origin of Species* came out, compared the flora of the eastern United States to that of Japan, and argued that the surprisingly large number of similarities among them result from them being descendants of a common stock that separated from each other during the Ice Age. Coming from Gray, this argument was easier to accept than if it had come from a relative unknown, and in turn it made it easier for many Americans to accept Darwin's theory, as it jibed in many ways with Gray's work. After *Origin of Species* appeared, Gray wrote a number of pieces in prestigious scientific journals in support of Darwin's general theory of evolution, even though Gray continued to believe that all species trace their roots back to a single act of divine creation, after which they evolved depending on local conditions.

In 1848 Gray married Jane Loring with whom he had no children. He died on January 30, 1888, in Cambridge.

Further Reading

Dupree, A. Hunter. *Asa Gray, American Botanist, Friend of Darwin.* Baltimore, Md.: Johns Hopkins University Press, 1988.

Keeney, Elizabeth B. *The Botanizers: Amateur Scientists in Nineteenth-Century America.* Chapel Hill: University of North Carolina Press, 1992.

Greengard, Paul
(1925–) *neurobiologist*

Paul Greengard made several key discoveries regarding the way neural signals are transmitted by nerves in the brain. For this achievement, he was awarded a share of the 2000 Nobel Prize in physiology or medicine.

Greengard was born on December 11, 1925, in New York City. His father, Benjamin, was a cosmetics wholesaler and his mother, Pearl, was a homemaker. In 1943 he graduated from high school and joined the U.S. Navy, spending World War II at the Massachusetts Institute of Technology where he helped build a radar system that could intercept kamikaze planes. After the war he attended Hamilton (N.Y.) College, receiving a B.S. in mathematics and physics in 1948. He then entered the graduate biophysics program at the University of Pennsylvania, but he transferred shortly thereafter to Johns Hopkins University in Baltimore, Maryland, receiving a Ph.D. in 1953. He spent the next five years in England as a postdoctoral fellow in biochemistry at the universities of London and Cambridge and the National Institute for Medical Research, returning to the United States in 1958 to do postdoctoral research at the National Institutes of Health in Bethesda, Maryland. A year later he was named director of the biochemistry department at Geigy Research Laboratories in Ardsley, New York, a position he held for eight years. In 1968 he joined the faculty at the Yale University School of Medicine as a professor of pharmacology and psychiatry, and in 1983 he became head of the Laboratory of Molecular and Cellular Neuroscience at the Rockefeller University in New York City.

As a researcher, Greengard was primarily interested in signal transduction in the nervous system, that is, the way nerve cells transmit sensory signals or impulses from one cell to another. Nerve cells are not connected directly to each other; instead, when a nerve wants to transmit a signal to the next nerve, it produces a tiny amount of a biochemical compound known as a neurotransmitter, which then bridges the gap (roughly one-millionth of a centimeter) between the two nerves, thus forming a temporary connection or synapse. While the chemical nature of synapses was clearly understood in the 1960s, the precise mechanisms by which they worked were not, so Greengard determined to find out what happens when neurotransmitters stimulate a nerve cell.

Greengard began his work by focusing on the slow neurotransmitters—so called because they can take as much as one full second to complete a synapse—that operate in the basal ganglia, dense masses of nerve cells located at the base of the brain. Slow neurotransmitters control our movements and also those processes in the brain that elicit emotions or react to addictive drugs such as cocaine, amphetamine, and heroin. He discovered that vesicles in the sending nerve cell release a neurotransmitter, which then activates receptors on the surface of the receiving cell. The receptors then activate enzymes in the cell wall, which starts the production of biochemical compounds known as second messengers. Second messengers travel into the cell and activate a class of enzymes known as protein kinases, which activate other proteins, which change the electrical activity of the cell so that the signal can be transmitted across the cell. In the process of studying slow neurotransmitters, Greengard and his colleagues discovered DARPP-32, a protein that regulates the activation and deactivation of virtually every known physiological aspect of signal transduction.

Greengard's work offered medical researchers new avenues by which to approach treatments for many neurological and psychiatric disorders, including schizophrenia, Parkinson's disease, Huntington's disease, depression, anxiety, attention-deficit/hyperactivity disorder, and drug abuse. Abnormalities in the activity of neurotransmitter signaling in the basal ganglia are now suspected to play a major role in causing these diseases and conditions, but it is hoped that pharmaceutical treatments aimed at modifying the activity of DARPP-32 may someday provide cures for all these diseases and conditions. For his contributions to a better understanding of signal transduction, Greengard was awarded a one-third share of the 2000 Nobel Prize in physiology or medicine. His corecipients were the Swedish physiologist Arvid Carlsson and the American neurobiologist ERIC R. KANDEL.

Greengard remained at Rockefeller University for the remainder of his career. His later research

focused on determining the components of signal transduction that are responsible for the regulation of the breakdown of a molecule known as Alzheimer Amyloid Precursor Protein (APP), with the aim of developing new targets for the treatment of Alzheimer's disease. He married Ursula von Rydingsvard with whom he had three children.

Further Reading

Nobelprize.org. "The Nobel Prize in Physiology or Medicine 2000." Available online. URL: http://nobelprize.org/medicine/laureates/2000. Downloaded on July 6, 2004.

Rowland, Lewis P. *NINDS at 50: An Incomplete History Celebrating the Fiftieth Anniversary of the National Institute of Neurological Disorders and Stroke.* New York: Demos Medical Pub., 2003.

Gross, David J.
(David Jonathan Gross)
(1941–) *physicist*

David J. Gross codeveloped a theory that explains why quarks, the basic building blocks of nucleons (protons and neutrons), cannot be separated from one another even though they sometimes behave as if they are separated. For this contribution, he was awarded a share of the 2004 Nobel Prize in physics.

Gross was born on February 19, 1941, in Washington, D.C. He received a B.S. and an M.S. in physics from the Hebrew University in Jerusalem, Israel, in 1962, and a Ph.D. in physics from the University of California at Berkeley in 1966. He spent the next three years as a junior research fellow at Harvard University, and in 1969 he was named a professor of physics at Princeton University.

In 1971 Gross was joined at Princeton by FRANK WILCZEK, at the time a graduate physics student. Gross and Wilczek were intrigued by a perplexing problem, the nature of the force that binds together quarks. The existence of quarks had been postulated in 1964 by MURRAY GELL-MANN and verified by numerous experiments in the late 1960s. However, the results of these experiments suggested that the strong nuclear force, the force that binds together quarks, gets stronger as the distance between quarks increases and weaker as the distance between them decreases. Thus, it is impossible to remove a quark from a nucleon, and a single quark has never been found outside a nucleon; yet, quarks seem to float freely within nucleons as if they are not bound together at all. This property, known as asymptotic freedom, is unknown in the other known forces of nature, for example, electromagnetism, gravity, and the weak nuclear force, which governs certain forms of radioactive decay. Each of these three forces gets weaker as the distance over which it must operate increases, and so theoretical physicists were unable to account for the contradictory behavior of the strong nuclear force in this regard.

After only two years of collaborating, however, Gross and Wilczek found the solution to the problem. They developed an ingenious mathematical formula for describing the asymptotic freedom of quarks. They were able to demonstrate that the beta function, which is always positive in formulas involving the other three forces, can be negative for the strong nuclear force, thus making it possible for physicists to understand mathematically the behavior of quarks. Gross and Wilczek published their formula in 1973 in an issue of the prestigious physics journal, *Physical Review Letters*. Ironically, that same issue also contained a paper by H. DAVID POLITZER, who had duplicated Gross and Wilczek's work independently. The formula was verified experimentally shortly thereafter, and it helped lay the groundwork for the development of quantum chromodynamics, the body of theory that explains in detail how quarks interact within a nucleon. For developing a mathematical explanation for asymptotic freedom, Gross, Wilczek, and Politzer were each awarded a one-third share of the 2004 Nobel Prize in physics.

Gross left Princeton in 1997 to become director of the Kavli Institute for Theoretical Physics at the University of California at Santa Barbara. His other honors include election to the National Academy of Sciences and the American Academy of Arts and Sciences.

Further Reading

Nobelprize.org. "The Nobel Prize in Physics 2004." Available online. URL: http://nobelprize.org/physics/laureates/2004. Downloaded on December 30, 2004.

Overbye, Dennis. "Three Americans Win Nobel for Particle Physics Work," *New York Times*, October 6, 2004, p. A18.

Guillemin, Roger
(Roger Charles Louis Guillemin)
(1924–   ) *neuroendocrinologist*

Guillemin cofounded the field of neuroendocrinology, the study of the interaction between the central nervous system and the endocrine system. For this achievement he was awarded a share of the 1977 Nobel Prize in physiology or medicine.

Guillemin was born on January 11, 1924, in Dijon, France. His father, Raymond, was a machine toolmaker, and his mother, Blanche, was a homemaker. After completing his undergraduate work at the University of Dijon in 1942, he received an M.D. from the University of Lyon Medical School in 1949 and a Ph.D. in physiology from the Institute of Experimental Medicine and Surgery at the University of Montreal in Canada in 1953. That same year he accepted a professorship in physiology at the Baylor University College of Medicine in Houston, Texas. From 1960 to 1963 he was also affiliated with the Collège de France in Paris. He left Baylor in 1970 to establish a neuroendocrinology laboratory at the Salk Institute for Biological Studies in La Jolla, California. In 1951 he married Lucienne Billard with whom he had six children, and in 1963 he became a naturalized U.S. citizen.

Guillemin became interested in endocrinology, the study of hormones and the glands that secrete them, while in medical school. At the time it was known that the various endocrine glands such as the thyroid and the adrenal glands were triggered to secrete hormones by the secretions of the pituitary gland, but no one knew what triggered the pituitary. In the 1930s English anatomist Geoffrey W. Harris had suggested that the pituitary was controlled by a secretion of the hypothalamus, an integral part of the brain that is located at the base of the brain just above the pituitary. Once he was settled at Baylor, Guillemin set out to obtain conclusive evidence to either prove or disprove Harris's hypothesis, and in 1957 he began collaborating with ANDREW V. SCHALLY, who also taught physiology at Baylor. Two years earlier, Schally had discovered the presence of corticotrophin-releasing hormone (CRH) in the tissues of the hypothalamus and the pituitary, a strong indication that CRH was the hypothalamic hormone that Harris had predicted.

Guillemin and Schally set out to prove conclusively that CRH is indeed secreted by the hypothalamus as a means of stimulating the pituitary to produce adrenocorticotropic hormone (ACTH), the hormone that stimulates the adrenal cortex to secrete steroids such as hydrocortisone. Unfortunately, their work proceeded very slowly, mostly because CRH is difficult to isolate as it is produced in extremely small amounts. In fact, they never found enough CRH to prove that they had found any at all, and they parted ways in 1960 when Guillemin began splitting his time between Texas and France. Nevertheless, both men continued to pursue their research independently in the quest to discover the hypothalamic hormone. That quest was aided tremendously in 1959, when ROSALYN YALOW announced the development of a technique known as radioimmunoassay (RIA), which had been specifically designed to measure the amount of hormones in blood and other bodily fluids.

Using RIA to study the contents of several tons of sheep hypothalamuses, in 1966 Schally isolated thyrotropin-releasing hormone (TRH), a hypothalamic hormone that induces the pituitary to stimulate the thyroid. Two years later, Guillemin determined the chemical structure of TRH, which led to his 1971 discovery of a second hypothalamic hormone, known both as luteinizing hormone-releasing hormone (LHRH) and gonadotropin-releasing hormone (GnRH); LHRH/GnRH induces the pituitary to secrete two hormones that stimulate the production of male and female sex hormones by the reproductive glands. That same year he isolated a third hypothalamic hormone, somatostatin, which inhibits the release of growth hormone by the pituitary.

Guillemin and Schally's work cofounded the field of neuroendocrinology by showing that the brain—specifically the hypothalamus—is directly responsible for regulating the secretions of the endocrine glands. Today it is known that the hypothalamus translates electrical neural impulses, particularly those related to emotion and stress, into hormones that control the endocrine system via the pituitary gland. They also presented medical researchers with a wider range of knowledge about the workings of the endocrine system and related diseases, and their work has had a profound effect on the study of hormone-related diseases and disorders, including thyroid diseases, problems of infertility, diabetes, and several types of tumors. For these contributions, Guillemin and Schally were each awarded a quarter share of the 1977 Nobel Prize in physiology or medicine; the winner of the other half share was Yalow.

Following his discovery of somatostatin, Guillemin stopped searching for other hypothalamic hormones. Instead, he focused his research on neurotransmitters, biochemical substances that transmit neural impulses from one nerve ending to another. In the process he discovered a new class of hormonal substances called endorphins. These opiate proteins occur naturally in the brain and play a role in regulating pain. It has been suggested that acupuncture "works" mostly because it stimulates the production of endorphins.

In 1989 Guillemin retired from the Salk Institute and the active pursuit of science. His other honors include the National Medal of Science and election to the National Academy of Sciences and the American Academy of Arts and Sciences.

Further Reading

Nobelprize.org. "The Nobel Prize in Physiology or Medicine 1977." Available online. URL: http://nobelprize.org/medicine/laureates/1977. Downloaded on June 26, 2004.

Wade, Nicholas. *The Nobel Duel: Two Scientists' 21-Year Race to Win the World's Most Coveted Research Prize.* Garden City, N.Y.: Anchor Press/Doubleday, 1981.

Wasson, Tyler, ed. *Nobel Prize Winners.* New York: H. W. Wilson, 1987, pp. 399–401.

H

Hale, George Ellery
(1868–1938) *astrophysicist*

George Ellery Hale was one of the foremost U.S. astrophysicists. He contributed immensely to the understanding of solar phenomena, particularly sunspot magnetism. He was a major force in the founding of three major observatories and the development of four large telescopes, each of which was the largest in the world at the time.

Hale was born on June 29, 1868, in Chicago, Illinois. His father, William, was a salesman, and his mother, Mary, was a homemaker. As a schoolboy, he developed an interest in astronomy, and by the time he turned 14 he had built his own telescope. While in high school he photographed partial solar eclipses and sunspots by means of a refracting telescope he had mounted on the roof of his house. As a student at the Massachusetts Institute of Technology (MIT) he served as a volunteer assistant at the Harvard College Observatory. During summer breaks from MIT, with financial help from his father, he built and operated a spectroscopic laboratory in a vacant lot next to his family's home in Chicago. He used this laboratory to photograph solar phenomena, particularly prominences, which are clouds of gas that rise high above the Sun's surface. In 1889 he designed and built the world's first spectroheliograph, an instrument that photographs the Sun using monochromatic light, or the light of a single wavelength of color.

In 1890 Hale received a B.A. from MIT and married Evelina Conklin with whom he had two children. He returned to his homemade laboratory in Chicago, and in 1891 he used an improved version of the spectroheliograph to take the world's first daytime photographs of prominences. That same year he opened Kenwood Observatory; built on the same property as his laboratory, the observatory's dome boasted a telescope with 12-inch disks. The following year he mounted the spectroheliograph to the Kenwood telescope and discovered flocculi, gaseous clouds that develop and change rapidly over the Sun's surface. He published these and other findings in nine scholarly articles, thus becoming one of the world's foremost authorities on solar phenomena. In 1892 he founded and coedited *Astronomy and Astrophysics,* a scholarly journal intended to bring together astronomers, who observe the heavens, and physicists, who experiment with physical phenomena, in a way that would be mutually beneficial. That same year he was invited to join the faculty of the University of Chicago as an assistant professor of astrophysics.

Shortly after accepting the Chicago appointment, Hale set out to build a major observatory in the Midwest. He obtained most of the funding from Charles T. Yerkes, a wealthy Chicago entrepreneur, and in 1897 the Yerkes Observatory opened in Williams Bay, Wisconsin. In addition to a 40-inch telescope that Yerkes paid for, the observatory included the dome, telescope, and equipment from Kenwood. Hale served as the observatory's director until 1904.

By 1904 Hale had convinced the Carnegie Institution of Washington, D.C., to build a world-class observatory on Mount Wilson near Pasadena, California. As its director, Hale had the Mount Wilson Observatory operational that same year. In 1905 he cofounded the International Union for Cooperation in Solar Research. In that same year he and his associates made a very important discovery, that sunspots are actually cooler, not hotter, than the surrounding surface. This discovery combined the observational advantages offered by Mount Wilson with the findings of a physical laboratory that correlated the spectral line strengths of various elements with the temperatures of those strengths. This data allowed Hale and his associates to calculate the temperatures of the various lines of the sunspot spectra. Later, other astrophysicists would continue this line of investigation to correlate temperature, brightness, and distance, thus making it possible to determine how far from Earth the brighter stars are.

In 1907 Hale and his associates made an observation that eventually led to the discovery that the Sun possesses a magnetic field similar to Earth. By observing a bright, narrow wavelength of the solar spectrum, they discovered that hydrogen flocculi known as solar vortices tend to swirl around sunspots. Hale observed further that the pattern of the vortices looked very much like the arrangement of iron filings around a magnet. For the rest of his career, he worked closely with laboratory physicists who gathered data that helped explain his observations, which he published in six books and more than 550 scholarly articles. By 1913 he was able to conclude that sunspot polarity reverses itself in the two solar hemispheres at the beginning of every sunspot cycle, which lasts 11 1/2 years. When this conclusion was confirmed in 1922, it was a major contribution toward proving that a solar magnetic field does indeed exist. For his discovery of sunspot magnetism, Hale was awarded the 1932 Sir Godfrey Copley Medal of the Royal Society, which noted in the presentation that the discovery was "the most vital thing accomplished in solar astronomy in 300 years."

Hale did not allow his observations of solar phenomena to detract from his duties as administrator of Mount Wilson. In 1908 he oversaw the development and installation at the observatory of a 60-inch telescope. He also designed a tower in

which to house the telescope that greatly reduced the blurring effect of heat waves at ground level, thus making it possible to observe the brighter stars in the same detail as the Sun had heretofore been observed. A taller tower was erected in 1910 and a 100-inch telescope was installed in 1917, both of which helped to provide increasingly detailed observations of the Sun and stars.

Hale resigned as director of Mount Wilson Observatory after suffering a nervous breakdown in 1921. Unable to retire entirely, he devoted himself to building a smaller observatory, the Hale Solar Observatory, in Pasadena, California. In 1928 he began lobbying the various scientific research organizations to donate the funds to develop a 200-inch telescope. He died 10 years before it could be completed, but when it was installed at the Hale Observatory in 1948 it was named the Hale Telescope in his honor.

In addition to his contributions to astronomy and astrophysics, Hale did much to further the advance of scientific research in general in the United States. In 1906 he became a trustee of Throop Polytechnic Institute, and he helped devise a plan to convert that school into the California Institute of Technology, which became one of the nation's most highly regarded scientific research institutions. In 1916 he proposed that the National Academy of Sciences, of which he had been a member since 1902, should aid the U.S. military effort in World War I. This proposal led eventually to the establishment of the National Research Council (NRC). As the NRC's first chairman, Hale worked to develop stronger ties among scientists, government officials, and philanthropic organizations to ensure greater funding for and improved efficiency in major research projects involving the physical sciences. Over time, the NRC would play a major role in coordinating and funding scientific research in the United States.

Hale directed the Hale Observatory until 1935. He died on February 21, 1938, in Pasadena.

Further Reading

Adams, Walter S. "George Ellery Hale," National Academy of Sciences, *Biographical Memoirs* 21 (1941): pp. 181–241.

Kevles, Daniel J. *The Physicists: The History of a Scientific Community in Modern America.* New York: Knopf, 1978.

Osterbrock, Donald E. *Pauper and Prince: Ritchey, Hale & Big American Telescopes.* Tucson: University of Arizona Press, 1993.

Wright, Helen. *Explorer of the Universe: A Biography of George Ellery Hale.* New York: Dutton, 1966.

Wright, Helen, et al., eds. *The Legacy of George Ellery Hale; Evolution of Astronomy and Scientific Institutions, in Pictures and Documents.* Cambridge, Mass.: MIT Press, 1972.

Hall, Lloyd A.
(Lloyd Augustus Hall)
(1894–1971) *chemist*

Lloyd A. Hall's career was devoted to finding better ways to process and preserve food. He developed the Ethylene Oxide Vacugas treatment for sterilizing spices and other products, and he was one of the first to experiment with artificial flavors.

Hall was born on June 20, 1894, in Elgin, Illinois. His father, Augustus, was a minister, and his mother, Isabel, was a homemaker. He developed an interest in chemistry while in high school, and after graduating he enrolled in Northwestern University, receiving a B.S. in pharmaceutical chemistry in 1916. He then went to work as a research chemist in the laboratory of the Chicago Department of Health while taking graduate courses in chemistry at the University of Chicago. He left after a year to work for the U.S. Army Ordnance Department as an inspector of gunpowder and explosives during World War I. In 1919—the same year he married Myrrhene Newsome with whom he had two children—he became chief chemist at John Morrell & Company, a meatpacking company in Ottumwa, Iowa. In 1921 he returned to Chicago to work as the chief chemist of Boyer Chemical Laboratory, but he left a year later to start his own consulting firm, called Chemical Products Corporation. In 1925 he was named chief chemist and director of research for Griffith Laboratories, where he spent the rest of his scientific career.

Hall's primary research interest involved the preservation of processed food, particularly meat.

At the time, meat processors used table salt to cure meat, a process by which its shelf life is prolonged. They also used sodium nitrate and potassium nitrate to preserve the meat's flavor and color. The problem was that the nitrates often worked faster than the salt, thus causing the meat either to deteriorate before it was cured or to taste funny. In 1932 Hall developed a process that avoided both negative results. He mixed up a strong solution of sodium chloride, or salt water, which contained small amounts of sodium nitrate and sodium nitrite. He then evaporated the solution by passing it over heated metal rollers, thus imbedding the nitrate and nitrite within the salt crystals. When these modified salt crystals were applied to meat during the curing process, the nitrate and nitrite imbedded in the crystals could not go to work until after the salt had dissolved into the meat, thus curing the meat completely while also preserving its flavor and color. He later developed an additive from glycerine and alkali metal tartrate that prevented the crystals from caking; not only did this additive permit a more even distribution of the crystals during curing, but it also prevented the crystals from absorbing moisture while in storage. Hall's method for curing meat was so effective that it soon became the standard method for preserving processed meat products, and it remained the standard for decades.

Hall next turned his attention to the problem of preserving meat by means of adding spices. For centuries, people had believed that spices helped to preserve food as well as to enhance its flavor. Hall, however, discovered that spices contain so many molds, yeasts, and bacteria, that the spices actually do more harm to food than good. Having made this discovery, he set out to find a way to decontaminate spices. For years, everything he tried changed either the flavor or the color of the spices, thus rendering them useless. Finally, he began experimenting with pesticides and insecticides as a means of sterilizing spices. He discovered that ethylene oxide gas worked as well on the microbes he was trying to eradicate as it did on insects. He devised a method whereby the spices were placed in a vacuum, thus drying them out completely, then filling the vacuum with the gas, thus killing off the microbes entirely. Hall's method, known as the Ethylene Oxide Vacugas treatment or the Vacugas sterilization treatment, worked so well that it was eventually adopted for use by manufacturers of pharmaceuticals, hospital supplies, and cosmetics as well as food.

Hall's next major contribution involved his work with antioxidants. While investigating what causes fatty or oily foods to become rancid, he discovered that the process involves the oxidation of certain ingredients in fats and oils. He further discovered that unrefined vegetable oils contain tocopherols, chemical compounds that retard oxidation and, thus, the onset of rancidity. He identified a number of chemical compounds that contain a high percentage of antioxidants, such as lecithin, propyl gallate, ascorbyl palmitate, citric acid, propylene glycol, and sodium chloride, and then he developed methods for using these compounds to treat foods, particularly bakery products, that are highly susceptible to oxidation.

Hall's last major contribution to food science was to develop a host of artificial flavors. By removing the water from plant proteins, he was able to create a group of flavoring materials known as protein hydrolysates. As a result of this development, Griffith Laboratories devoted a state-of-the-art manufacturing facility to the production of protein hydrolysates, which they sold with little difficulty to the food industry.

Hall was a cofounder of the Institute of Food Technologists, the first professional organization for chemists involved in food processing and preservation. He also served as a commissioner of the Illinois State Food Commission, a director of the American Institute of Chemists and the Science Advisory Board on Food Research, a member of the American Food for Peace Council, and a consultant to the United Nations' Food and Agricultural Organization. In 1959 he retired from Griffith Laboratories and moved to Pasadena, California. He died on January 2, 1971, in Altadena, California.

Further Reading

Smith, Caroline B. D. "Lloyd A. Hall." *Contemporary Black Biography* 8 (1994): pp. 99–102.

Spangenburg, Ray, and Kit Moser. *African Americans in Science, Math, and Invention.* New York: Facts On File, 2003, pp. 102–103.

Hartline, H. Keffer
(Haldan Keffer Hartline)
(1903–1983) *biophysicist*

H. Keffer Hartline was a pioneer in the discovery of the physiological processes of vision. For his contributions in this area, he received a share of the 1967 Nobel Prize in physiology or medicine.

Hartline was born on December 22, 1903, in Easton, Pennsylvania. His father, Daniel, was a biology professor, and his mother, Harriet, was an English teacher. He received from his father an intense interest in how living things operate, and after finishing high school he spent a summer at the marine laboratory in Cold Spring Harbor on Long Island, New York. After receiving a B.S. in biology from Lafayette (Pa.) College in 1923, he entered the Johns Hopkins University School of Medicine and received an M.D. in 1927. He remained at Johns Hopkins for two years as a National Research Council fellow in medical sciences, and he spent the two years after that in Germany studying mathematics and physics at the universities of Munich and Leipzig. In 1931 he became a fellow in medical physics at the Eldridge Reeves Johnson Foundation in Philadelphia, and in 1949 he returned to Johns Hopkins as professor and chair of the newly created department of biophysics. Four years later he left Johns Hopkins for the Rockefeller Institute for Medical Research (today Rockefeller University) in New York City, where he stayed for the rest of his career. In 1936 he married Elizabeth Kraus with whom he had three children.

Hartline's research focused on understanding the mechanics of vision. As a medical student, he studied how images are transmitted electrically from the eye to the brain via electric current running along the optic nerve. Using a string galvanometer, a device for determining the strength of small electric currents, he measured and charted the electric potential of retinal activity in frogs, cats, and rabbits. In 1931 he began experimenting with single nerve fibers that he had dissected from the optic nerve of a horseshoe crab, whose visual system is very simple. By the following year he had determined that visual information is transmitted along the optic nerve by variations in the current's frequency or number of wave cycles, and not its amplitude or wavelength. He also determined that the number of cycles in the frequency-modulated (FM) signals vary in accordance with the amount of light to which the retina is exposed.

In the 1930s Hartline temporarily abandoned his work with horseshoe crabs to study the optic nerve fibers of the frog, whose visual system is more sophisticated than the crab's. In 1940 he showed that different optic nerve fibers are connected to different receptor cells in the retina, and these fibers react to light in different ways; for example, some react only when the light is turned on, some react only when the light is turned off, and some provide a steady stream of information regarding changes in the light. The feedback from all these fibers is fed simultaneously through the optic nerve to the brain, where it is decoded into "images" of light, shadow, and color.

After 1940 Hartline returned to his studies of the horseshoe crab, and by 1949 he had discovered what he called lateral inhibition. When an optic nerve fiber becomes excited by light, its reaction causes nearby fibers to not react, thus sharpening the contrast between the electric signal from the excited fiber and those from the lateral, or adjacent, fibers whose reactions have been inhibited. Eight years later, he and Floyd Ratliff, a Rockefeller associate, developed a mathematical model that could predict almost exactly the excitations and inhibitions of the various nerve fibers as a result of virtually any pattern of light to which the retina could be exposed. Meanwhile, in 1952 he had discovered that amplitude modulation (AM) is also used in vision systems. Specifically, the electric potentials in the retinal receptor cells generate AM signals, which are sent to the optic nerve fibers. The AM signals are then translated into FM signals for transmission along the optic nerve to the brain.

Hartline's discoveries contributed enormously to a better understanding of the physical aspects by which the retina and the optic nerve convert sensory data into electric signals that can be converted into images in the brain. His efforts in this regard were rewarded in 1967 when he received a one-third share of the Nobel Prize in physiology or medicine. One of his corecipients was GEORGE WALD, whose work contributed to a better understanding of the biochemical aspects of vision, and the other was the Swedish physiological Ragnar Granit.

Hartline was elected to membership in the National Academy of Sciences and the American Academy of Arts and Sciences. In 1974 he retired from Rockefeller to Hydes, Maryland, and he died on March 18, 1983, in nearby Fallston.

Further Reading

Nobelprize.org. "The Nobel Prize in Physiology or Medicine 1967." Available online. URL: http://nobelprize. org/medicine/laureates/1967. Downloaded on April 13, 2004.

Ratliff, Floyd. "Haldan Keffer Hartline," National Academy of Sciences, *Biographical Memoirs* 59 (1990): pp. 196–213.

Wasson, Tyler, ed. *Nobel Prize Winners.* New York: H. W. Wilson, 1987, pp. 415–417.

Hartwell, Leland H.
(Leland Harrison Hartwell)
(1939–) *geneticist*

Leland H. Hartwell discovered that certain genes control certain steps in the cell division cycle, the process by which all organisms grow and reproduce. For this achievement, he was awarded a share of the 2001 Nobel Prize in physiology or medicine.

Hartwell was born on October 30, 1939, in Los Angeles, California. After spending his first year of college at Glendale Junior College in Los Angeles, he transferred to the California Institute of Technology, receiving a B.S. in biology in 1961. He then entered the Massachusetts Institute of Technology, receiving a Ph.D. in genetics in 1964. After a year of postdoctoral research at the Salk Institute for Biological Studies in La Jolla, California, he joined the faculty at the University of California in Irvine. In 1968 he became a professor of genetics at the University of Washington (UW) in Seattle. At some point he married Theresa Naujack with whom he had three children.

Hartwell was primarily interested in how genes regulate the cell division cycle, the process by which one cell grows and splits into two cells. He chose *Saccharomyces cerevisiae*, better known as baker's yeast, as his subject, partly because it is a one-cell fungus and partly because no one else was studying it. He soon demonstrated that yeast is as good a subject for studying genetics as fruit flies, red mold, or mice, the traditional subjects previously used by geneticists. By 1970 he had demonstrated that cell division, like virtually all cellular functions, is controlled by genes, and by 1974 he had identified dozens of genes that play a major role in the processes of protein synthesis and cell growth that result directly in cell division. Perhaps the most important of these genes, which he labeled cell division cycle (CDC) genes, is *CDC28*, which he showed initiates each step in the cycle. He also proved the existence of checkpoint genes, CDC genes that ensure that the steps in the cycle occur in the proper order, that no errors are made during a step, and that the next step in the cycle is not begun until the current one has been completed properly. Eventually, he isolated and identified the specific function of more than 50 of the 7,000 or so genes in baker's yeast.

Hartwell's work led him to hypothesize that defects in checkpoint genes might lead to cancer because they permit mutations in cells, a common feature of all cancers. He further hypothesized that cell division cycles in all organisms from yeast to humans might be controlled by genes that are more or less similar. This hypothesis was proven correct in 1987 by British geneticist Paul Nurse, who showed that certain genes perform the same function in different species. For his contributions to a better understanding of cell division and its role in cancer, Hartwell was awarded a one-third share of the 2001 Nobel Prize in physiology or medicine; one of his corecipients was Nurse and the other was British physiologist R. Timothy Hunt.

Meanwhile, Hartwell had become more interested in helping other people perform scientific research rather than in doing such himself. In 1996 he became senior scientific adviser at Seattle's Fred Hutchinson Cancer Research Center, and he immediately set out to create an interdisciplinary program that would encompass the center's education, training, and research efforts in order to make it easier for geneticists, biochemists, virologists, and other cancer researchers to share ideas about their work. The following year he was named president and director of the center, positions he held in addi-

tion to his teaching and research duties at UW. His many other honors include election to the National Academy of Sciences.

Further Reading

"Hartwell, Leland H.," *Current Biography Yearbook* 60 (1999): pp. 251–254.
Nobelprize.org. "The Nobel Prize in Physiology or Medicine 2001." Available online. URL: http://nobelprize. org/medicine/laureates/2001. Downloaded on July 9, 2004.

Hauptman, Herbert A.
(Herbert Aaron Hauptman)
(1917–   ) *biophysicist*

Herbert A. Hauptman helped develop the so-called direct method, a technique for determining the three-dimensional structure of crystalline biomolecules by using X-ray crystallography. For this achievement he was awarded a share of the 1985 Nobel Prize in chemistry.

Hauptman was born on February 14, 1917, in New York City. His father, Israel, was a printer, and his mother, Leah, was a homemaker. He received a B.S. in mathematics from City College of New York (CCNY) in 1937 and an M.A. in mathematics from Columbia University in 1939. He worked as a statistician for the U.S. Census Bureau until the United States entered World War II, at which point he joined the U.S. Army Air Force, serving as an electronics instructor and weather officer. Upon returning to civilian life in 1947, he became a physicist and mathematician at the Naval Research Laboratory (NRL) in Washington, D.C.; he was eventually named head of the mathematics branch of the optical sciences division. While at NRL he entered the graduate program at the University of Maryland, receiving a Ph.D. in mathematics in 1955. In 1940 he married Edith Citrynell with whom he had two children.

One of Hauptman's colleagues at NRL was JEROME KARLE, with whom he had shared several classes at CCNY. Hauptman and Karle soon became collaborators in a project of interest to them both, the development of an improved method for using X-ray crystallography to determine the three-dimensional structures of very small crystals such as crystalline biomolecules. At the time, biomedical researchers were just beginning to use X-ray crystallography as a method of investigating biomolecules such as vitamins and proteins. (Later JAMES D. WATSON and his collaborators would rely heavily on X-ray crystallography while developing their model of DNA.) Nevertheless, the methods then available were not easily applied to biochemistry, and it took up to two years to determine the structure of even a relatively simple biomolecule.

X-ray crystallography involves beaming X-rays into a crystal and then analyzing the pattern of spots created by the scattered beams on X-ray film as the beams are diffracted by the crystal. The pattern indicates the location and arrangement of the various atoms, which can be identified by analyzing

Herbert Hauptman used X-rays to study the chemical structures of biochemical compounds. *(Courtesy of Herbert A. Hauptman)*

the light intensity of the spots. The problem was that such scattered beams are out of phase with each other, and therefore it was difficult to compare the light intensities of the spots. Consequently, it was necessary to make educated guesses as to what the phase differences actually were, a process that involved much trial and error. By combining Hauptman's skill as a mathematician and Karle's skill as a physical chemist, the two collaborators solved the phase problem by developing what became known as the direct method because it eliminates the need for guesswork. In essence, the direct method uses the methods of statistical probability, in particular the joint probability distributions of several structure factors, as the essential tool for phase determination. Hauptman and Karle presented their findings in several journal articles and monographs between 1950 and 1956, the most important being *Solution of the Phase Problem, 1: The Centrosymmetric Crystal* (1953).

The direct method received little notice when it was first advanced, perhaps because its use required a great many mathematical calculations. With the advent of the modern computer, these calculations became much easier to make. By the mid-1980s, researchers using the direct method were able to determine the structure of a crystalline biomolecule in about two days, a fraction of the time that had once been required. For making X-ray crystallography a tool that can be used by just about any biomedical researcher, Hauptman and Karle were each awarded a half share of the 1985 Nobel Prize in chemistry.

In 1970 Hauptman left NRL to teach biophysical sciences at the State University of New York at Buffalo and to become head of the mathematical biophysics laboratory at the Medical Foundation of Buffalo, today the Hauptman-Woodward Medical Research Institute. His research at the institute focused on developing new methods of biomolecular structure determination, methods that he summarized in *Crystal Structure Determination: The Role of the Cosine Seminvariants* (1972) and *Direct Methods in Crystallography* (1978). He was named the institute's executive vice president and research director in 1972 and its president in 1986, a position he held until his retirement in 2001. His many honors include election to the National Academy of

Sciences and the American Association for the Advancement of Science and terms as president of the Association of Independent Research Institutes and the Philosophical Society of Washington.

Further Reading

Hauptman-Woodward Institute. "Herbert A. Hauptman, Ph.D." Available online. URL: http://www. hwi.buffalo.edu/personnel/Scientist/Hauptman/ Hauptman. html. Downloaded on March 25, 2005.

Nobelprize.org. "The Nobel Prize in Chemistry 1985." Available online. URL: http://nobelprize.org/ chemistry/laureates/1985. Downloaded on August 12, 2004.

Wasson, Tyler, ed. *Nobel Prize Winners*. New York: H. W. Wilson, 1987, pp. 418–420.

Hazen, Elizabeth L.
(Elizabeth Lee Hazen)
(1885–1975) *microbiologist*

Elizabeth L. Hazen was one of the first microbiologists to conduct research with actinomycetes, bacteria that live in soil. In the process she developed nystatin, an antifungal antibiotic drug that makes it safer to administer penicillin to humans.

Hazen was born on August 24, 1885, in Rich, Mississippi. Her parents, William and Maggie, were cotton farmers. Her parents died when she was four and she and her sister were raised by an aunt and uncle who lived in nearby Lula. After finishing high school, she enrolled in the Mississippi Industrial Institute and College (today Mississippi University for Women) and received a B.S. in science in 1910. After teaching high school science in Jackson, Mississippi, for six years, in 1916 she moved to New York City to enter the graduate program at Columbia University. She received an M.S. in bacteriology in 1917, then worked briefly for a West Virginia hospital before returning to Columbia to receive a Ph.D. in microbiology in 1927. She taught for four years at Columbia's College of Physicians and Surgeons, and then in 1931 she joined the New York State Department of Health's division of laboratories and research as a microbiologist. In this position, she devoted her research efforts to studying the spread of infectious diseases.

In 1941 Hazen changed the scope of her research to searching for an antibiotic drug that could kill fungus without harming humans. The need for such a drug had developed the year before, when penicillin was developed into an injectable drug. Although it was an excellent antibiotic, one of penicillin's side effects was that it stimulated the growth of fungus in the mouth and stomach, and these growths often developed into fatal infections. Hazen hoped to solve this problem by developing an antifungal antibiotic that could be administered in conjunction with penicillin, thus making it safe for humans.

In 1944 SELMAN A. WAKSMAN discovered that certain actinomycetes naturally produce substances that contain antibiotics. Later that year, Gilbert Dalldorf, the director of Hazen's division, introduced her to another division employee, Rachel Fuller Brown. Dalldorf's idea was that Hazen, a microbiologist, and Brown, a biochemist, would work together to develop antifungal antibiotics from actinomycetes. The two women agreed to collaborate, and for the next four years Hazen spent most of her time in the field searching for promising soil samples. Brown remained in the laboratory where she analyzed the actinomycetes in the samples sent her by Hazen. Brown sent whatever antibiotics they produced to Hazen, who then determined whether or not the antibiotics would kill fungus.

In 1948 Hazen collected a soil sample from a friend's farm near Warrenton, Virginia, that contained *Streptomyces noursei,* an actinomycete that produces two different antibiotics. One is so toxic that it is not safe to administer to humans. The other, however, proved to be strong enough to kill fungal infections in the central nervous system, mouth, lungs, and vagina without having any deleterious side effects on humans. For two years Hazen and Brown worked to develop their discovery into a drug that was both effective and safe. In 1950 they announced to the world the discovery of the new drug, which they named nystatin in honor of the New York State Department of Health. They obtained a patent for nystatin and licensed it to the pharmaceutical firm of E. R. Squibb and Sons. Squibb then marketed the drug in pill form under the trade name Mycostatin. Hazen and Brown eventually earned more than $13 million in royalties from the sale of Mycostatin, almost all of which they donated to medical research. Their most favored recipients were the Research Corporation, a nonprofit organization that conducted medical research of a general nature, and the Brown-Hazen Fund, which they cofounded to promote basic research in biology and related sciences.

Hazen discovered other antibiotic-producing actinomycetes, but none as useful as nystatin. In 1953 she and Brown developed phalamycin and in 1959 they developed capacidin. Despite early optimism, both proved to be too toxic to be administered to humans. However, the development of nystatin proved to be so important that they received two honors for its discovery alone. In 1955 they received the Squibb Award in chemotherapy, and in 1975 they became the first women to receive the American Institute of Chemists' Chemical Pioneer Award.

Hazen retired from the health department in 1960. For the next 13 years she worked as a guest investigator at Columbia University's Mycology Laboratory. In 1973 she moved to Seattle, Washington, to live near her sister. She died, having never married, in Seattle on June 24, 1975.

Further Reading

Baldwin, Richard S. *The Fungus Fighters: Two Women Scientists and Their Discovery.* Ithaca, N.Y.: Cornell University Press, 1981.

Carey, Charles W., Jr. "Brown, Rachel Fuller and Elizabeth Lee Hazen," *American Inventors, Entrepreneurs, and Business Visionaries.* New York: Facts On File, 2002, pp. 38–40.

Yount, Lisa. "Hazen, Elizabeth Lee," *A to Z of Women in Science and Math.* New York: Facts On File, 1999, pp. 86–87.

Heeger, Alan J.
(Alan Jay Heeger)
(1936–   ) *chemist*

Alan J. Heeger codiscovered conducting and semiconducting organic polymers, also known as synthetic metals. For this discovery he was awarded a share of the 2000 Nobel Prize in chemistry.

Alan Heeger (above) and Alan G. MacDiarmid codiscovered synthetic metals, polymers that conduct electricity. *(Courtesy of Alan J. Heeger)*

Heeger was born on January 22, 1936, in Sioux City, Iowa, but he grew up in nearby Akron. His father, Peter, managed a general store and his mother, Alice, was a homemaker. At age nine his father died, and he moved with his mother and siblings to Omaha, Nebraska, where he grew up. After receiving a B.S. in physics and mathematics from the University of Nebraska in 1957, the same year he married Ruthann Chudacoff with whom he had two children, he entered the graduate program at the University of California at Berkeley and received a Ph.D. in physics in 1961. He remained at Berkeley for a year before joining the faculty at the University of Pennsylvania.

At first, Heeger's research involved solid-state physics, the study of the various physical properties of semiconductors, substances that conduct electricity better than nonconductors such as glass but not as well as good conductors such as copper. He was particularly interested in magnetic impurities in metals and in the collective behavior of vast assemblies of interacting subatomic particles. As a result, he was quite intrigued to learn in 1973 that American chemist Mortimer Labes had recently demonstrated that the golden, film-like crystal known as polysulfurnitride acts like a semiconductor even though it is an organic polymer. Heeger immediately contacted ALAN G. MACDIARMID, a chemistry professor at Penn who had an interest and some experience in sulfurnitride chemistry. Heeger and MacDiarmid began studying the conducting properties of polysulfurnitride, and eventually they demonstrated that the addition of bromine increased polysulfurnitride's conductivity by a factor of 10.

In 1975 Heeger and MacDiarmid were joined by Hideki Shirakawa, a chemist at the Tokyo Institute of Technology who came to U-Penn as a visiting scientist. Shirakawa had developed a beautifully lustrous, silver-colored, film-like form of the organic polymer polyacetylene; like polysulfurnitride, Shirakawa's polyacetylene also possessed semiconducting properties. MacDiarmid and Shirakawa attempted to increase polyacetylene's conductivity by purifying it, but instead of making it more conductive they made it less so. They concluded that small amounts of impurities actually increase the conductivity of organic polymers just as they do in semiconductors, and so they added bromine to an impure sample of polyacetylene. To their surprise, its conductivity increased millions of times. In 1977 Heeger explained this phenomenon by showing that the bromine reacts with the carbon in such a way that it removes one electron from each of the carbon atoms that form every other link in polyacetylene's polymeric chain. These missing electrons create "holes" through which other electrons can flow, thus making the polymer as conductive as a metal.

Other researchers soon followed the lead of Heeger, MacDiarmid, and Shirakawa, and in the 1980s they developed other conducting and semiconducting polymers. These novel materials combine the electrical and optical properties of semiconductors and metals with the processing advantages and mechanical properties of polymers, and by the 1990s they were being used in such diverse applications as rechargeable batteries, electromagnetic interference shielding, antistatic dissipation, stealth applications, corrosion inhibition, flexible "plastic" transistors and electrodes, and electroluminescent polymer displays, among other things. For discovering conducting polymers, Heeger, MacDiarmid, and Shirakawa were each awarded a one-third share of the 2000 Nobel Prize in chemistry.

Meanwhile, in 1982 Heeger left U-Penn for the University of California at Santa Barbara (UCSB) where he was named director of the Institute for Polymers and Organic Solids, a position he has held since. In 1999 he cofounded and became chief scientist of UNIAX, a for-profit corporation devoted to developing the science and technology of conducting and semiconducting polymers for commercial purposes.

Further Reading

Epstein, Arthur J., et al. *Special Issue Celebrating the Year 2000 Nobel Prize in Chemistry to Alan Heeger, Alan MacDiarmid and Hideki Shirakawa for the Discovery and Development of Conductive Polymers.* Amsterdam, Holland: Elsevier, 2001.

Nobelprize.org. "The Nobel Prize in Chemistry 2000." Available online. URL: http://nobelprize.org/chemistry/laureates/2000. Downloaded on July 31, 2004.

Hench, Philip S.
(Philip Showalter Hench)
(1896–1965) *physiologist*

Philip S. Hench played a major role in the development of adrenal hormones, such as cortisone and adrenocorticotropic hormone (ACTH), into pain relievers for medical conditions such as rheumatoid arthritis. For his part in this development he was awarded a share of the 1950 Nobel Prize for physiology or medicine.

Hench was born on February 28, 1896, in Pittsburgh, Pennsylvania. His father, Jacob, was a teacher, and his mother, Clara, was a homemaker. After finishing high school he enrolled in Lafayette College and received a B.A. in 1916. He spent the next four years at the University of Pittsburgh Medical School;

while a medical student he served in the U.S. Army's Medical Enlisted Reserve Corps during World War I. He received an M.D. in 1920, and then spent a year as an intern at Pittsburgh's St. Francis Hospital. In 1921 he became a fellow of the Mayo Foundation for Medical Education and Research in Rochester, Minnesota. Two years later he joined the world-renowned Mayo Clinic as a first assistant in medicine, and in 1926 he was named chief physician of the department of rheumatic diseases. In 1927 he married Mary Genevieve Kahler with whom he had four children.

Hench devoted his medical career to studying the causes of muscle and joint inflammation and to finding ways to treat and cure the medical conditions that cause inflammation. He was particularly interested in rheumatoid arthritis, at the time a painful yet untreatable condition that, in extreme cases, was capable of causing joint deformation. By 1934 he had observed that patients with arthritis who also had jaundice did not experience as much pain as those who did not have jaundice. Since jaundice is caused by too much bilirubin—the yellowish pigment in bile—in the blood, Hench theorized that something in bilirubin relieved arthritic pain. He tried to prove his theory by administering bilirubin to non-jaundiced arthritic patients, but they continued to suffer as before.

In 1938 Hench made a second important observation, that women often gained temporary relief from arthritis during pregnancy. The blood of pregnant women, as well as of jaundice patients, contains abnormally high amounts of steroids, organic compounds synthesized from cholesterol that play important roles in a number of physiological activities. This realization led Hench to theorize that steroids might be a useful treatment for arthritis. At this point he began working closely with EDWARD C. KENDALL, a biochemist with the Mayo Foundation who had recently identified and isolated the various chemical components of six steroids produced by the adrenal cortex.

Over the next 12 years Hench administered the various compounds that Kendall derived from steroids to arthritic patients. In 1941 the two decided that the most promising results could probably be obtained by administering what Kendall called "Compound E," which was later christened cortisone by Hench. Unfortunately, the technology of the day made it exceptionally difficult to produce cortisone in sufficient quantities. The experiment was further delayed by World War II, during which Hench served as a lieutenant colonel in the U.S. Army Medical Corps at bases in Colorado and Arkansas. By 1948 Hench and Kendall had finally developed enough cortisone to permit a rigorous experiment. That same year they began administering cortisone and ACTH, a hormone produced by the pituitary gland that stimulates the adrenal cortex, to Mayo Clinic patients whose arthritic conditions were so bad that they were bedridden. Neither cortisone nor ACTH was capable of curing arthritis, and they caused mildly deleterious side effects; however, their continued combined application did much to alleviate the painful symptoms of the worst arthritic conditions.

The development of adrenal hormones into pain relievers was a major medical breakthrough, as they permitted the treatment of previously untreatable conditions. Modern technology has since led to the development of synthetic steroids that can be produced cheaply and plentifully and that have no harmful side effects, to the point that naturally derived cortisone and ACTH are rarely used today. At the time this discovery was so important that Hench and Kendall were awarded shares of the 1950 Nobel Prize for physiology or medicine. They shared the award with Tadeus Reichstein, a Polish-Swiss biochemist who had duplicated independently Kendall's work with steroids.

Hench continued to study rheumatic diseases at the Mayo Clinic until his retirement in 1957. He was a founding member of the Ligue International contre le Rheumatisme and the American Rheumatism Association and served as chief editor of *American Rheumatism Reviews* for 16 years. He received a host of awards from various medical and pharmaceutical organizations. He died on March 30, 1965, while vacationing in St. Ann's Bay, Jamaica.

Further Reading

Nobelprize.org. "The Nobel Prize in Physiology or Medicine 1950." Available online. URL: http://nobelprize. org/medicine/laureates/1950. Downloaded on July 4, 2003.

University of Virginia Health Sciences Library. "Philip Showalter Hench." Available online. URL: http://etext.lib.virginia.edu/healthsci/reed/hench.html. Downloaded on March 25, 2005.

Wasson, Tyler, ed. *Nobel Prize Winners.* New York: H. W. Wilson, 1987, pp. 433–435.

Henry, Joseph
(1797–1878) *physicist*

Joseph Henry was the foremost American scientist of his day. His work with electromagnetism led eventually to the development of the telegraph and the electrical transformer. As the first secretary of the Smithsonian Institution and a founder of the National Academy of Sciences, he played an important role in creating two of the nation's most important scientific institutions. He is also one of the few American scientists to have a unit of scientific measurement named after him.

Henry was born on December 17, 1797, in Albany, New York. His father, William, was a teamster, and his mother, Ann, was a homemaker. At age seven he went to live with his uncle and grandmother in nearby Galway, but he returned to Albany in his early teens when he worked for several years as an apprentice watchmaker and silversmith. At age 16 he discovered a book of popular science that so inspired him that he decided to devote his life to learning as much as he could about the laws of nature. Over the next 13 years he worked as a tutor and surveyor while spending his free time studying science on his own. In 1826 he was hired to teach mathematics and natural philosophy at his alma mater, the Albany Academy. In 1830 he married Harriet Alexander with whom he had four children.

While teaching at Albany Academy, Henry began experimenting with electricity. In 1820 the physical phenomenon of electromagnetism had been discovered by Danish physicist Hans Christian Ørsted when he demonstrated that a wire carrying electrical current can act like a magnet. Shortly thereafter English physicist William Sturgeon created the first electromagnet by wrapping bare copper wire around an iron bar. In 1829 Henry improved upon Sturgeon's electromagnet by using insulated wire; by wrapping hundreds of turns of wire around an iron bar, Henry was able to make an electromagnet capable of supporting more than a ton of iron.

Henry's work with electromagnetism led him to discover in 1830 the principle of induction, whereby an electric circuit can induce an electric current in another circuit to which it is not connected via means of an electromagnet. He did not publish his findings, however, until after English physicist Michael Faraday had published his in 1831, thus he is not given credit for the discovery. Meanwhile, Henry also discovered the principle of self-induction, whereby an electromotive force can be induced in a circuit by varying the electrical current in that circuit. Based on these discoveries, in 1831 Henry built the world's first telegraph line and invented the world's first electric motor.

Henry's telegraph line was only one mile long, and the signal sent from one end to the other did nothing more than ring a bell. Nevertheless, the line's success led him to predict that the telegraph would someday be used to transmit a host of information electrically. This vision became a reality in 1844, when Samuel F. B. Morse (with some technical assistance from Henry) sent a coded message between Washington and Baltimore via telegraph. Henry's electric motor, however, was a reciprocating motor, which is not as effective or efficient as the rotary motor invented by William Ritchie in 1833; the rotary motor remains the standard electric motor in use today. In 1832 Henry published his findings concerning self-induction.

By 1832 Henry's reputation in the American scientific community had grown to the point that the College of New Jersey (today Princeton University) offered him the position of professor of natural philosophy, despite the fact that Henry had never attended college. While at Princeton, he continued to experiment with electromagnetism and discovered the scientific principles governing the operation of the transformer, a device that uses electromagnetic induction to change the voltage and current in a circuit without changing its frequency. He also began studying other physical phenomena, including ultraviolet light, auroras, molecular cohesion, geophysics, meteorology, and terrestrial magnetism. He developed a thermoelectric device that could measure empirically the difference in temperature between sunspots and the solar surface, in the process proving that sunspots are actually cooler than the surface that surrounds them.

In 1846 the Smithsonian Institution was established in Washington, D.C., and Henry was chosen to serve as its first secretary, in effect its general manager. The institution was made possible by a generous bequest from British scientist James Smithson, who failed to specify what he wanted the institution to do. As secretary, Henry gave the Smithsonian some much-needed guidance in its earliest days, helping to steer it onto the path of becoming an international research center as well as the nation's foremost museum of science, technology, and natural history.

One of Henry's first endeavors in the area of scientific research was to supervise in 1849 the development of a nationwide chain of volunteer meteorologists, whose duties included recording weather data for their locality. A direct result of this work was the birth, in 1870, of the U.S. Weather Bureau; three years later, the Smithsonian turned over all its meteorological records and activities to the bureau. Other research efforts directed or encouraged by Henry were in the fields of anthropology, archaeology, astronomy, botany, geophysics, and zoology. He also oversaw the development of the Smithsonian Institution Press, which published those scientific works that could not be published, for economic reasons, by commercial publishing houses or learned societies.

During the Civil War, Henry served as one of President Abraham Lincoln's chief advisers on military technology. In this capacity he helped organize the National Academy of Sciences in 1863 to serve as the government's official adviser in matters related to science and technology. From 1868 to 1878 he served as the academy's second president. Previously, he had served as president of the American associations for the advancement of science and education. He died at his home in Washington, D.C., on May 13, 1878. In 1893 the electrical unit of inductive resistance was named the "henry" in his honor.

Further Reading

Coulson, Thomas. *Joseph Henry: His Life and Work.* Princeton, N.J.: Princeton University Press, 1950.

Moyer, Albert E. *Joseph Henry: The Rise of an American Scientist.* Washington, D.C.: Smithsonian Institution Press, 1997.

Herschbach, Dudley R.
(Dudley Robert Herschbach)
(1932–   ) *physical chemist*

Dudley R. Herschbach developed the crossed molecular beam technique, which provides chemists with an in-depth understanding of what happens to an individual molecule during a chemical reaction. For this contribution, he was awarded a share of the 1986 Nobel Prize in chemistry.

Herschbach was born on June 18, 1932, in San Jose, California. His father, Robert, was a building contractor, and his mother, Dorothy, was a homemaker. He attended Stanford University, receiving a B.S. in mathematics in 1954 and an M.S. in chemistry in 1955. After receiving an A.M. in physics in 1956 and a Ph.D. in chemical physics from Harvard University in 1958, he became a professor of chemistry at the University of California at Berkeley. Five years later he returned to Harvard, and in 1964, the same year he married Georgene Botyos with whom he had two children, he was named chair of Harvard's chemical physics program.

As a graduate student Herschbach became interested in chemical kinetics, the energy changes in atoms that bind them together into molecules or split molecules apart so their atoms can form new molecules. Because these energy changes affect the rate at which chemical reactions take place, he eventually became interested in studying the basic fundamentals concerning chemical reactions involving molecules. He was specifically interested in finding out what happens to an individual molecule during a chemical reaction. In the 1950s chemists had little more than a dim understanding of reaction dynamics. Chemists could explain what happened in terms of the changes that occurred to the chemical compounds they mixed together during a reaction, but they had little idea of how those reactions changed the shape or structure of the individual molecules themselves.

Meanwhile, physicists were making great strides at understanding the behavior of subatomic particles, atoms, and molecules. One of the tools they were using was the molecular beam; invented in 1911 by French physicist Louis Dunoyer, this technique involves injecting molecules in a gaseous state into a large vacuum through a tiny orifice so that they enter the vacuum in a thin beam. This technique makes it possible to study the molecules in a free or noncolliding state. Later, this method was modified so that two beams were collided into each other, or scattered, so that the molecules and fragments produced by the collisions could be studied.

Herschbach became familiar with molecular beam scattering while working on his doctorate, and it occurred to him that it could be used as a tool for chemical research as well. While he was at Berkeley, a leading center for physical research, he became more familiar with molecular beam scattering, and in 1962 he modified the molecular beam apparatus so that the molecules produced by the collisions were collected on an electrically charged metal filament. By measuring the variation in the filament's current caused by the collected molecules, he could study what had happened to an individual molecule during the collision, which in essence is a chemical reaction.

Dudley Herschbach developed a method for finding out what happens to an individual molecule during a chemical reaction. *(Courtesy of Dudley Herschbach; photo by Jane Reed/Harvard)*

The nature of the filament limited his research to relatively simple molecules containing the extremely reactive alkali metals, such as potassium and sodium. However, in 1967 he was joined at Harvard by YUAN T. LEE, who greatly modified and improved Herschbach's rather crude apparatus. The most important change Lee made was to replace the filament with a mass spectrometer. A spectrometer can measure the spectral, or light, wavelength of any molecule, so Herschbach was able to expand his research to study virtually any type of molecule. The spectrometer also allowed him to study the dynamics of a chemical reaction in terms of the changes it induces in the structure of a molecule's electrons.

Herschbach's crossed molecular beam technique greatly expanded chemists' knowledge of the mechanics of their experiments. Not only does this knowledge permit them to understand the results of their work better, but it also allows them to design more sophisticated experiments. For this contribution, Herschbach was awarded a one-third share of the 1986 Nobel Prize in chemistry; one of his corecipients was Lee.

Herschbach retired from his teaching duties in 2002, although he continued to study chemical kinetics by means of the crossed molecular beam technique for several years thereafter. His many honors include the National Medal of Science, election to the National Academy of Sciences and the American Academy of Arts and Sciences, and a term as associate editor of the *Journal of Physical Chemistry.* His publications include *Chemical Kinetics* (1976) and *Dimensional Scaling in Chemical Physics* (1993).

Further Reading

Harvard Department of Chemistry & Chemical Biology. "Herschbach." Available online. URL: http://www.chem.harvard.edu/herschbach/index.php. Downloaded on March 25, 2005.

Nobelprize.org. "The Nobel Prize in Chemistry 1986." Available online. URL: http://nobelprize.org/chemistry/laureates/1986. Downloaded on August 15, 2004.

Wasson, Tyler, ed. *Nobel Prize Winners.* New York: H. W. Wilson, 1987, pp. 438–440.

Hershey, Alfred D.
(Alfred Day Hershey)
(1908–1997) *molecular biologist*

Alfred D. Hershey was a pioneer in the field of molecular biology, the study of the biophysical principles by which living things grow and reproduce. For his discoveries concerning the behavior of viruses, particularly the manner in which they replicate, he was awarded a share of the 1969 Nobel Prize in physiology or medicine.

Hershey was born on December 4, 1908, in Owosso, Michigan. His father, Robert, worked in an automotive factory, and his mother, Alma, was a homemaker. In 1930 he received a B.S. in bacteriology from Michigan State University and entered its graduate program, receiving a Ph.D. in chemistry four years later. He then took a position as a bacteriologist with the Washington University School of Medicine in St. Louis, Missouri. In 1945 he married Harriet Davidson with whom he had one child.

Hershey's research at Washington University focused on discovering how organisms became immune to bacterial infections. In the late 1930s he became interested in bacteriophages (or phages), viruses that cause infections in bacteria. The simplest form of life, a phage consists of a core of nucleic acid encased in a protein shell. His interest in phages was further stimulated by the work of MAX DELBRÜCK, who in 1939 had developed a simple method for reproducing phages quickly. In 1942 Hershey and Delbrück met, and shortly thereafter Hershey joined Delbrück and SALVADOR E. LURIA as the core members of the so-called phage school. The phage school was an informal group of scientists who were doing related work with phages, and they met annually at the Carnegie Institution of Washington's genetics laboratory at Cold Spring Harbor, New York, every summer to exchange results and ideas. In 1946 Delbrück and Hershey, working independently of each other, discovered that when two phages infect the same bacterium at the same time, they can recombine their genetic material, or mutate, into a new type of phage. This ability, which Hershey christened genetic recombination, was thought to be possessed only by life-forms that reproduce sexually. The discovery of

genetic recombination in viruses suggested that genetic mutations in higher-order organisms were caused, at least in part, by viral infections. Coupled with Luria's discovery in 1947 that bacteria develop immunity to phages by a mutation process that is set in motion by viral infection, the discovery led a number of geneticists to seek a better understanding of genetic behavior by studying bacteria and viruses rather than higher-order organisms, and via biophysics rather than biochemistry.

In 1950 Hershey joined the research staff at Cold Spring Harbor on a full-time basis. Two years later he made a discovery that shifted the focus of geneticists from biophysics to biochemistry. By this time a number of researchers had become convinced that a form of nucleic acid known as deoxyribonucleic acid (DNA) carried genetic coding, and not viral protein as was held by the phage school. To settle the matter, he and Martha Chase, a Cold Spring Harbor colleague, tagged with radioactive markers the protein and nucleic acid in a colony of phages whose cores contained DNA and allowed the phages to begin infecting a colony of bacteria. Shortly after the infection process had begun, they ran the mix of bacteria and phages through a kitchen blender, thus interrupting the infection process before it was completed. Hershey and Chase discovered that phage protein remains outside the bacterial cell while phage DNA is injected into the cell where it replicates new phages. This result demonstrated that DNA and not viral protein is responsible for transmitting genetic coding. This discovery contributed to the discovery a year later by JAMES D. WATSON and Francis Crick of the double-helix structure of DNA.

As a result of these discoveries, the importance of the phage school was reduced significantly. Nevertheless, the study of phages had shed much light on the nature of viral behavior and genetic behavior. It also gave other researchers the tools they needed to develop vaccines against such viral diseases as measles, rubella, and mumps. For his contributions in these areas, Hershey was awarded a one-third share of the 1969 Nobel Prize in physiology or medicine. His corecipients were Delbrück and Luria.

Meanwhile, in 1962 Hershey had been named director of Cold Spring Harbor's genetic research unit. He continued to experiment with phage DNA, which he found to be different from human DNA. While the two strands of DNA in humans wind around each other like a spiral staircase, in phages the DNA is either single-stranded or circular.

Hershey was elected to the National Academy of Sciences and the American Academy of Arts and Sciences. He retired in 1974, but he remained active in his laboratory for a number of years thereafter. He died on May 22, 1997, at his home in Syosset, New York.

Further Reading

Nobelprize.org. "The Nobel Prize in Physiology or Medicine 1969." Available online. URL: http://nobelprize.org/medicine/laureates/1969. Downloaded on April 18, 2004.

Stahl, Franklin W. "Alfred Day Hershey," National Academy of Sciences, *Biographical Memoirs* 80 (2001): pp. 142–159.

Wasson, Tyler, ed. *Nobel Prize Winners*. New York: H. W. Wilson, 1987, pp. 440–442.

Hill, Henry A.
(Henry Aaron Hill)
(1915–1979) *chemist*

Henry A. Hill was one of the pioneers in the development of synthetic products from polymers. He is best remembered for the development of polymers for use as commercial dyes and as flame-retardant coatings for fabric and other textile products.

Hill was born on May 30, 1915, in St. Joseph, Missouri. His father, William, was a waiter, and his mother, Kate, was a homemaker. After finishing high school in 1931, he attended Lewis Institute (today part of the Illinois Institute of Technology) in Chicago for a year before transferring to Johnson C. Smith College in Charlotte, North Carolina, where he received a B.S. in mathematics and chemistry in 1936. Over the next six years he studied chemistry in the graduate programs at the University of Chicago and the Massachusetts Institute of Technology, receiving a Ph.D. from the latter in 1942. That same year he went to work as a research chemist for the North Atlantic Research Corporation in Newtonville, Massachusetts, and in 1946 he joined Dewey & Almy Chemical Company in Cambridge. In 1943 he married Adelaide Cromwell with whom he had one child.

Both North Atlantic Research and Dewey & Almy manufactured synthetic products. At the time, the plastics industry was still in its infancy, so Hill's research focused on learning more about polymerization, the chemical process by which plastic compounds such as polyethylene and polypropylene are made. Most polymers are formed by combining small molecules consisting mostly of hydrogen and carbon into long chains that can then be molded, spun into fibers, or developed into additives or coatings. Most polymeric processes involve the transformation of the raw materials into polymers through a series of steps, and the products produced by each step are called chemical intermediates. As the steps progress, the chemical intermediates become more complex, and understanding how to get them to react to produce the next desired intermediate becomes increasingly difficult. Within a few years, Hill had become one of the early experts on the production of chemical intermediates.

In 1952 Hill cofounded National Polychemicals, which specialized in the manufacture of chemical intermediates. Nine years later he founded and became president of Riverside Research Laboratory, a research and development/consulting firm that specialized in the development of polymers for use in the manufacture of textiles. Originally established in Watertown, the firm was later relocated to Haverhill. At Riverside, Hill played an important role in developing some of the first polymers for use in synthetic commercial dyes. He focused on making such polymers from the azo compounds, organic compounds that feature a double bond between two nitrogen atoms, and by 1963 he had developed azodicarbonide and barium azocarbonate. He then turned his attention to a new area, the development of synthetic flame-retardant coatings for textiles, and by 1967 he had developed one of the first coatings of this kind from a urea-formaldehyde resin.

Hill served terms as president of the American Chemical Society, chair of the chemistry section of the American Association for the Advancement of Science, and member of the National Commission on Product Safety. He died on March 17, 1979, in Haverhill.

Further Reading

The Chemical Heritage Foundation. "Chemical Achievers: Henry Aaron Hill." Available online. URL: http://www.chemheritage.org/EducationalServices/chemach/pop/hah.html. Downloaded on March 25, 2005.

McMurray, Emily J., ed. *Notable Twentieth Century Scientists.* Detroit: Gale Research, 1995, pp. 929–930.

Spangenburg, Ray, and Kit Moser. *African Americans in Science, Math, and Invention.* New York: Facts On File, 2003, pp. 116–117.

Hinton, William A.
(Augustus Hinton William)
(1883–1959) *pathologist*

William A. Hinton developed the Hinton test for diagnosing syphilis. He also helped to develop the Davies-Hinton test for detecting the presence of antibodies in spinal fluid.

Hinton was born on December 15, 1883, in Chicago, Illinois. His father, Augustus, was a railroad porter, and his mother, Marie, was a homemaker. As an infant he moved with his parents to Kansas City, Kansas, where he grew up. At age 17 he enrolled in the University of Kansas but transferred after two years to Harvard University, where he received a B.S. in 1905. He spent the next four years teaching science at Walden University in Nashville, Tennessee, and Oklahoma Agricultural and Mechanical College in Langston, Oklahoma. In 1909 he married Ada Hawes with whom he had two children and returned to Harvard, this time as a medical student.

Upon receiving an M.D. in 1912, Hinton went to work as an assistant at Harvard's Wasserman Laboratory, which specialized in the study of communicable diseases, and in the department of pathology at Massachusetts General Hospital. His work in both positions involved the study of syphilis, a communicable disease that is transmitted via sexual intercourse; untreated, syphilis causes the deterioration of virtually every organ and tissue in the body, but especially the brain and nervous system. Within two years he had learned so much about syphilis that he was invited to publish a paper on the way the disease acts in the bloodstream and to teach Harvard medical students how to diagnose syphilis in the laboratory. In 1915, when the Wassermann Laboratory was detached from Harvard and placed under the auspices of the Massachusetts Department of Public Health, he was put in charge of the laboratory and named assistant director of the department's division of biologic laboratories. Three years later he was also appointed instructor of preventive medicine and hygiene at Harvard Medical School, where he later taught bacteriology and immunology as well.

In 1915 Hinton began looking for a better way to diagnose syphilis in a patient. August von Wassermann, for whom the Wassermann Laboratory had been named, had devised a blood serum test for detecting syphilis in 1906. The Wassermann test detects the presence of antibodies to the protozoans that cause syphilis, and it works well enough that it is still used today. However, the Wassermann test is so sensitive that it gives a number of false positives, meaning that it sometimes indicates that a person is infected when in fact that person is not. Given the fact that the treatment for syphilis was long, painful, and dangerous, and that much shame was attached to people who had contracted syphilis, the high percentage of false positives yielded by the Wassermann test was deemed unacceptable.

For 12 years, Hinton experimented with various ways to diagnose syphilis, hoping to find one that would eliminate the number of false positives while also being quick, accurate, and simple to use. In 1927 he developed the Hinton test; although its 98 percent accuracy rate is not quite as high as the Wassermann's, it very rarely results in a false positive, thus making it more useful as a diagnostic tool. The Hinton test came into widespread use quickly, and in 1934 the U.S. Public Health Service cited it as being the best available method for detecting syphilis. The Hinton test was used extensively by the U.S. Army during World War II, and it contributed significantly to the army's successful effort to reduce syphilis among its troops.

Despite the Hinton test's value and success, Hinton continued to look for a test that would improve on its accuracy without losing its other benefits. In 1931 he and a colleague, John A. N. Davies, developed the Davies-Hinton test. This test made use of spinal fluid rather than blood serum, and it was as accurate as the Wassermann test. Because of the difficulty and danger of drawing spinal fluid, however, the Davies-Hinton test never achieved widespread use as a diagnostic tool for syphilis; instead, the Hinton test remained the test of choice for most public health departments.

By 1934 Hinton was one of the world's leading experts on syphilis. That same year he began to write a textbook regarding the detection and cure of syphilis for physicians, public health workers, and medical students. Published in 1936 as *Syphilis and Its Treatment*, it became a standard reference work in the United States and Europe.

In 1949 Hinton was named a full professor at Harvard Medical College. He retired from Harvard the following year, and in 1953 he retired from the state health department. On August 8, 1959, he died at his home in Canton, Massachusetts.

Further Reading

The Faces of Science: African Americans in the Sciences. "William Augustus Hinton." Available online. URL: http://www.princeton.edu/~mcbrown/display/hinton.html. Downloaded on March 25, 2005.

Kessler, James H., et al. *Distinguished African American Scientists of the 20th Century.* Phoeniz, Ariz.: Oryx Press, 1996, pp. 36–51.

Spangenburg, Ray, and Kit Moser. *African Americans in Science, Math and Invention.* New York: Facts On File, 2003, pp. 118–119.

Hitchings, George H.
(George Herbert Hitchings, Jr.)
(1905–1998) *pharmacologist*

George H. Hitchings revolutionized the way pharmaceutical drugs are designed, and with it the way pharmaceutical companies conduct research. For this contribution, as well as for the several innovative drugs he helped develop, he was awarded a Nobel Prize.

Hitchings was born on April 18, 1905, in Hoquiam, Washington. His father, George Sr., was a marine architect and shipbuilder, and his mother, Lillian, was a homemaker. As a boy he moved with his family to various places on the Pacific Coast, eventually settling in Seattle where he attended high school. He studied chemistry at the University of Washington, receiving a B.S. and an M.S. in 1927 and 1928, respectively. He then entered the graduate program at Harvard University where he received a Ph.D. in biochemistry in 1933. That same year he married Beverly Reimer with whom he had two children; she died in 1985, and four years later he married Joyce Shaver.

For nine years after finishing his education, Hitchings held a series of temporary research appointments. In 1942 he was hired to form and supervise a biochemistry department for Wellcome Research Laboratories, part of the pharmaceutical firm Burroughs Wellcome, in Tuckahoe, New York. In this capacity, he focused on developing drugs that could be used to treat or prevent cancer. Given a wide degree of latitude by his superiors, he was able to take his own tack as to how he went about his duties. He soon realized that inventing a drug and then testing it to see what it would do, the conventional practice in the pharmaceutical industry at the time, was of little help if one were trying to solve a particular problem. Instead, he decided to study the biochemistry of healthy cells and cells infected with the disease he was trying to cure. Once he understood how the healthy cells differed from the diseased ones, he began designing a drug that would attack the latter without harming the former. This approach was a revolutionary one, and in time most pharmaceutical drugs would be designed this way.

In 1944 Hitchings began designing a drug that could treat leukemia, a fatal form of blood cancer. This effort was supervised by Hitchings but carried out mostly by GERTRUDE B. ELION, his trusted associate for more than 30 years. By 1948 Hitchings, Elion, and their assistants had developed 2,6-diaminopurine, a drug that interferes with the way leukemia cells produce deoxyribonucleic acid (DNA), thus preventing them from growing. This drug, however, proved to cause unacceptable side effects in humans, and so it could be used only to treat patients with acute leukemia. Undaunted by this setback, the team continued to experiment, and three years later they developed 6-mercaptopurine, better known as 6-MP. This drug had none of the deleterious side effects of 2,6-diaminopurine, and it prolonged the lives of children with leukemia for up to 12 months. In 1957 the Hitchings team discovered that a derivative of 6-MP, azathioprine, was effective at suppressing the body's immune system during organ transplants and as a treatment for severe cases of rheumatoid arthritis and other autoimmune disorders.

By using Hitchings's method for designing drugs, he and his associates eventually developed a host of useful pharmaceutical therapies. These include pyrimethamine for treating malaria; thioguanine for treating leukemia; allopurinol for treating gout, leishmaniasis, and Chagas' disease; trimethoprim for treating bacterial infections of the urinary and respiratory systems; acyclovir for treating herpes; and zidovudine for treating AIDS. Their innovative approach to developing drugs led many major pharmaceutical firms to change the way they conduct research, and in 1988 Hitchings and Elion were each awarded one-third of the Nobel Prize for physiology or medicine. They shared the award with the British pharmacologist Sir James Black, who had used a similar approach while developing drugs for treating heart disease and ulcers.

In 1967 Hitchings gave up his laboratory responsibilities to become vice president of research for Burroughs Wellcome. The following year he moved with the company to the Research Triangle Park near Chapel Hill, North Carolina. In 1976 he returned to active research as a scientist emeritus with Burroughs Wellcome. He died on February 27, 1998, in Chapel Hill.

Further Reading

The Chemical Heritage Foundation. "Pharmaceutical Achievers. George Hitchings." Available online. URL: http://www.chemheritage.org/EducationalServices/pharm/chemo/readings/hitch.htm. Downloaded on March 25, 2005.

Nobelprize.org. "The Nobel Prize in Physiology or Medicine 1988." Available online. URL: http://nobelprize.org/medicine/laureates/1988. Downloaded on January 16, 2003.

Hoagland, Dennis R.
(Dennis Robert Hoagland)
(1884–1949) *botanist*

In his day, Dennis R. Hoagland was the world's foremost authority on the relationship between plants and the soil in which they grow. His work explored the complex interaction between plants and soil and resulted in a heightened understanding of the importance of proper plant nutrition.

Hoagland was born on April 2, 1884, in Golden, Colorado. The occupations of his parents, Charles and Lillian, are unknown. At age eight he moved with his family to Denver where he grew up. After finishing high school, he enrolled in Stanford University and received an A.B. in chemistry in 1907. He worked for several years as an assistant chemist for the University of California's Laboratory of Animal Nutrition in Berkeley, and in 1910 he took a position with the local office of the U.S. Food and Drug Administration investigating alleged injurious effects of food preservatives on humans. Two years later he enrolled in the University of Wisconsin; after receiving an M.A. in agricultural chemistry in 1913, he returned to UC-Berkeley to teach. In 1922, two years after he married Jessie Smiley with whom he had three children, he was named head of Berkeley's division of plant nutrition, a position he held for the rest of his career.

Hoagland's lifelong research interest concerned the interaction between plants and soil, both of which involved complex chemistries. His earliest investigations dealt with kelps, which grow in large beds off the coast of California. He first began investigating kelps after the outbreak of World War I, which cut off the United States from Germany, at the time its principal supplier of potash fertilizers. Hoagland's studies were intended to find ways to increase the supply of potash via the commercial production of kelps, which when burned yield potash. While studying kelps, Hoagland noticed that they accumulate potassium and iodide in quantities out of all proportion to the ratio of these elements in seawater. This discovery led him to investigate how plants are able to absorb selectively the minerals and salts they require from the environment in which they grow, while keeping out whatever they do not need. He discovered that plants do not accumulate nutrients via osmosis, as had been believed, but they do so metabolically. Ions of different elements are absorbed through the roots, but then they react with one another within the plant in such a way as to increase their concentration. He demonstrated that a number of factors contribute to this process, including light, temperature, hydrogen ion concentration, and oxygen supply, among others. One result of his work, which he published in 1944 as *Lectures on the Inorganic Nutrition of Plants*, was an increased awareness in the agricultural community of the need for proper fertilization techniques.

Hoagland's work with kelps led him to investigate other aspects of plant biochemistry as well. Previously, it had been believed that plants growing in soil need a neutral or slightly basic environment. He demonstrated, however, that plants can thrive in acidic conditions as well. As a result, he began growing plants hydroponically, or in water cultures, as a way of investigating exactly what chemicals and conditions plants need to grow. In the process, he discovered the biochemical role played by "trace" chemical elements, those elements required by living cells in minute amounts. Late in his career, he and a Berkeley colleague, Daniel I. Arnon, developed a superior water-culture method for growing plants without soil by combining calcium, nitrogen, potassium, phosphorus, magnesium, sulfur, iron, and trace elements of manganese, chlorine, zinc, copper, sodium, and molybdenum in water. Known today as Hoagland's solution, this water culture provides a nutritious environment in which plants can grow. More than 50 years after Hoagland's death, Hoagland's solution remains one of the most popular media for growing plants via hydroponics.

In addition to his research work concerning basic principles of plant growth, Hoagland also spent much time solving basic problems faced by California's farmers. Typical of this work is a study he did of the nutritional deficiencies of fruit trees, wherein he showed that many trees suffered not from disease but from malnutrition. He followed up this study with a circular on artificial nutrients.

Hoagland served as president of the American Society of Plant Physiologists (ASPP), the Western Society of Soil Science, the Western Society of Nat-

uralists, the Botanical Society of America's Pacific Division, and the American Association for the Advancement of Science's Pacific Division. He was consulting editor for *Soil Science, American Journal of Botany, Plant Physiology,* and *Plant and Soil,* and he cofounded the *Annual Review of Biochemistry.* He was elected to membership in the National Academy of Sciences. In 1985 the ASPP, which in 1929 had given him its highest award, named one of its awards in his memory. He retired in 1949 after several years of poor health, and he died in Oakland, California, on September 5, 1949.

Further Reading

Kelley, Walter P. "Dennis Robert Hoagland," National Academy of Sciences, *Biographical Memoirs* 29 (1956): pp. 123–143.

Online Archive of California. "Dennis Robert Hoagland, Plant Nutrition: Berkeley." Available online. URL: http://dynaweb.oac.cdlib.org:8088/dynaweb/uchist/public/inmemoriam/inmemoriam1949/@Generic_BookTextView/344. Downloaded on November 28, 2003.

Hoffmann, Roald
(Roald Safran)
(1937–) *chemist*

Roald Hoffmann helped demonstrate that the symmetry of the electrons that are shared during a chemical reaction plays an important role in determining the outcomes of certain chemical reactions. For this contribution, he was awarded a share of the 1981 Nobel Prize in chemistry.

Hoffmann was born Roald Safran on July 18, 1937, in Zloczow, Poland. His father, Hillel Safran, was a civil engineer, and his mother, Clara, was a school teacher. After his father was killed during World War II, his mother married Paul Hoffmann, who adopted young Roald. In 1949 he and his family emigrated to the United States and settled in New York City. He received a B.S. in chemistry from Columbia University in 1958 and an M.A. and a Ph.D. in chemical physics from Harvard University in 1960 and 1962, respectively. In 1960 he married Eva Börjesson with whom he had two children.

Roald Hoffmann provided scientists with a better understanding of how electrons help determine the outcomes of certain chemical reactions. *(Courtesy of Roald Hoffmann; photo by Clemens Loew)*

As a graduate student, Hoffmann became interested in the electronic structures of organic molecules. He was particularly fascinated by the boranes, synthetic compounds consisting of boron and hydrogen that do not exist in nature and whose unique three-center bond gives them a unique three-dimensional shape that is very stable despite their electron deficiency. In the course of his studies he wrote a computer program that became known as the extended Hückel method because it expanded on a series of calculations developed by the German chemist Erich Hückel. Hoffmann's program calculated the electronic structure of organic molecules, including the so-called sigma electrons, a covalent pair of electrons that occupy an orbital between the two atoms they bond.

After receiving his Ph.D. in 1962, Hoffmann remained at Harvard to conduct postdoctoral research. By this time he had come to the attention of ROBERT B. WOODWARD, a Harvard chemistry pro-fessor whose specialty was designing synthetic reactions. In 1964, while attempting to synthesize vitamin B_{12}, Woodward obtained an unexpected result, and he and Hoffmann began a collaboration to understand what had happened. This collaboration continued after Hoffmann was named a professor of chemistry at Cornell University in 1965. In time they discovered that Woodward had stumbled across what is now known as an electrocyclic reaction, one in which the symmetry of the molecular orbitals, the electrons that form the covalent pairs binding together atoms in a molecule, must be conserved in order to complete the reaction. This discovery led Hoffmann and Woodward to develop the Woodward-Hoffmann rules, which define certain chemical reactions in terms not only of the energy level of the shared electrons but also in terms of their symmetry. The Woodward-Hoffmann rules are explained in great detail in their book, *The Conservation of Orbital Symmetry* (1970). On his own, Hoffmann analyzed the molecular orbitals of most types of reactive intermediates—the temporary products of a reaction from which the final product is produced—in organic chemistry and showed that the same reactions involving the same compounds can yield entirely different results if the symmetry of the molecular orbitals is not conserved.

Hoffmann's role in developing the Woodward-Hoffmann rules took the understanding of the mechanisms of chemical reactions to a higher, more sophisticated level. As a result, chemists are better able to design reactions that are more likely to yield the products they are attempting to produce. For this contribution, Hoffmann was awarded a half share of the 1981 Nobel Prize in chemistry; his corecipient was the Japanese chemist Kenichi Fukui.

Hoffmann continued to study the mechanisms of chemical reactions at Cornell until 1996, eventually applying his methods to the study of the structure and reactivity of inorganic compounds and organometallic compounds, ones which contain both carbon and metal atoms. In 1996 he was named a professor of humane letters at Cornell, after which he devoted himself to writing poetry about science and other subjects. His many honors include the National Medal of Science and election to the National Academy of Sciences and the American Academy of Arts and Sciences. His scientific publications include *Solids and Surfaces: A Chemist's View of Bonding in Extended Structures* (1988).

Further Reading

Hoffmann, Roald, with Vivian Torrence. *Chemistry Imagined: Reflections on Science*. Washington, D.C.: Smithsonian Institution Press, 1993.

Nobelprize.org. "The Nobel Prize in Chemistry 1981." Available online. URL: http://nobelprize.org/chemistry/laureates/1981. Downloaded on August 16, 2004.

Wasson, Tyler, ed. *Nobel Prize Winners*. New York: H. W. Wilson, 1987, pp. 472–474.

Hofstadter, Robert

(1915–1990) *physicist*

Robert Hofstadter's work shed much light on the nature of the atomic nucleus and of the protons and neutrons from which nuclei are composed. For his contributions in this regard, he was awarded a share of the 1961 Nobel Prize in physics.

Hofstadter was born on February 5, 1915, in New York City. His father, Louis, owned a cigar store, and his mother, Henrietta, was a homemaker. In 1935 he received a B.S. in physics from the College of the City of New York (CCNY) and entered the graduate program at Princeton University, receiving an M.A. and a Ph.D. in physics in 1938. He spent the next four years conducting research and teaching physics at Princeton, the University of Pennsylvania, and CCNY, and the four years after that doing research related to the U.S. war effort in World War II at the National Bureau of Standards in Washington, D.C., and Norden Laboratories in New York City. He returned to teaching physics at Princeton in 1946, and in 1950 he joined the faculty at Stanford University in Palo Alto, California. In 1942 he married Nancy Givan with whom he had three children.

Hofstadter's first research efforts focused on examining the spectra of electromagnetic radiation given off by various elements and compounds. As a graduate student, he used the infrared waveband to study the nature of certain chemical bonds in organic molecules. In 1948 he discovered that crystals made of thallium-activated sodium iodide are particularly well-suited for use in scintillation counters, devices for detecting and measuring radioactivity. Two years later he showed that these same crystals could be used to great advantage in a spectrometer, a device that analyzes a given target's electromagnetic radiation, as a way of measuring the energy levels of X-rays and gamma rays. Further work in this area led to the development of improved scintillation counters using crystals of cesium fluoride and thallium chloride.

By 1950 Hofstadter had become more interested in the nature of the nucleus in general and of the nucleons (protons and neutrons) that comprise it. At the time, it was believed that nucleons were point-like particles, meaning that they were more or less solid and indivisible. Earlier, however, it had been believed that the atom itself was a point-like particle, and Hofstadter began to wonder if perhaps nucleons were more complex than scientists believed. To find out, he devised a variation on the experiment used by English physicist Ernest Rutherford in the early 1900s to discover the nucleus. Rutherford had scattered alpha particles (one alpha particle consists of two protons and two neutrons) from thin gold foil and measured the number of alpha particles scattered as a function of the angle of scatter. The surprisingly large number of particles that were scattered through large angles could be explained only by collisions with a small but heavy object inside the atom, which Rutherford called the nucleus.

Instead of alpha particles, Hofstadter decided to use high-energy electrons because they are much smaller and lighter than alpha particles. He reasoned that electrons are so small they could penetrate a nucleus and then be deflected easily by the strong electromagnetic forces operating inside the nucleus. Using Stanford's newly constructed linear electron accelerator (a device that speeds up electrons and then focuses them like a beam of light on a target), he scattered fast-moving electrons from targets of thin gold foil. Using a magnetic spectrometer of his own design, he then measured the distribution of these electrons as a function of the angle of scatter, similar to what Rutherford had done earlier. Not surprisingly, the results were similar to what Rutherford had discovered. Instead of being a single point-like particle, Hofstadter's results showed that a nucleon is like an atom in that it consists of a number of smaller particles; it was these many smaller particles that caused the wide angle of deflection of the electrons in Hofstadter's experiment.

Further experimentation showed that a nucleon has a charged core that is surrounded by two orbits of smaller particles. Today it is known that this core consists of particles known as quarks, while the orbiting particles are very small particles known as pions. By 1957 Hofstadter had discovered that the outer orbit of pions in both neutrons and protons is positively charged, while the inner orbit is positive in protons but negative in neutrons. Consequently, the two positive rings give a proton a positive charge, while the positive and negative rings in a neutron cancel out each other and give the neutron no charge at all. Today it is believed that the so-called strong nuclear force, the force that binds one nucleon to another in a nucleus, is generated by the activity of the double ring of pions. He also showed that the nuclei of the heavier elements such as uranium have a uniform density under a thin surface "skin," and that the amount of space a nucleus takes up, as well as its skin thickness, is extremely small but measurable; for example, the diameter of a nucleus is about one ten-billionth of a centimeter. For presenting what the Nobel committee called a "reasonably consistent" picture of the structure of nucleons and nuclei, Hofstadter was awarded a half share of the 1961 Nobel Prize in physics. His corecipient was the German physicist Rudolf Mössbauer.

In the 1960s Hofstadter refocused his research efforts on an earlier interest, the development of high-energy detectors. In 1968 he helped design a scintillation counter known as the "Crystal Ball" that was most effective in measuring the energy levels of collisions caused by the use of particle beams such as those generated by the linear electron accelerator. In 1970 he began working on the Energetic Gamma Ray Experiment Telescope (EGRET), a gamma-ray spectrometer that the National Aeronautics and Space Administration planned to base in outer space for measuring the energy levels of gamma rays in space. He also adapted his high-energy detectors for use as imaging equipment in medical diagnostics.

Hofstadter was elected to the National Academy of Sciences and awarded the National Medal of Science. He retired from Stanford in 1985, and he died on November 17, 1990, in Palo Alto.

Further Reading

Friedman, Jerome I., and William A. Little. "Robert Hofstadter," National Academy of Sciences, *Biographical Memoirs* 79 (2001): pp. 158–181.

Nobelprize.org. "The Nobel Prize in Physics 1961." Available online. URL: http://nobelprize.org/physics/laureates/1961. Downloaded on March 28, 2004.

Wasson, Tyler, ed. *Nobel Prize Winners.* New York: H. W. Wilson, 1987, pp. 474–475.

Holley, Robert W.
(Robert William Holley)
(1922–1993) *biochemist*

Robert W. Holley discovered transfer RNA, the nucleic acid molecule that plays a major role in protein biosynthesis. This discovery won for him a share of the 1968 Nobel Prize in physiology or medicine.

Holley was born on January 28, 1922, in Urbana, Illinois. His parents, Charles and Viola, were schoolteachers. After living in Illinois, California, and Idaho, he returned to Urbana where he graduated from high school. He received a B.A. in chemistry from the University of Illinois in 1942, and then he entered Cornell University in Ithaca, New York, receiving a Ph.D. in organic chemistry in 1947. After a year of postdoctoral research at Washington State University, he returned to Cornell to teach chemistry at its agricultural experiment station in Geneva. In 1958 he took on the additional duties of a research chemist at the U.S. Department of Agriculture's Plant, Soil and Nutrition Laboratory in Ithaca. In 1945 he married Ann Dworkin with whom he had one child.

Holley's research focused on the biochemical processes in plant life. In 1956 he became interested in the role played by the nucleic acids—DNA and RNA—in protein synthesis. Three years earlier, JAMES D. WATSON and Francis Crick had developed a model for DNA, and it was believed that some sort of biochemical process was involved in transferring genetic coding from the DNA in a cell's nucleus to the ribosomes in its cytoplasm, where the process of protein synthesis takes place. Holley began investigating the possibility that RNA plays some role in this transfer. In 1960 he discovered the existence of transfer RNA (tRNA), RNA molecules that attach themselves to loose amino acids and then transfer them to a ribosome, which attaches them to other amino acids to form a protein. By 1965 he was able to show that tRNA takes its instructions from messenger RNA (mRNA), which MARHALL W. NIRENBERG had recently shown to carry genetic coding from DNA to the ribosomes.

Holley demonstrated that each molecule of tRNA attaches to only one of the 20 or so amino acids that comprise proteins. Working with yeast, he used enzymes to isolate the tRNA that attaches to the amino acid alanine. He then demonstrated that this type of tRNA circulates among a cell's ribosomes to see if alanine is called for by any of the mRNA that is attached to the ribosomes. Once it reads the coding for alanine, the alanine tRNA attaches itself to the first alanine molecule it encounters and then transfers that molecule to the ribosome where alanine has been called for. Further experimentation showed that specific tRNA molecules exist for each of the protein-building amino acids, and that all tRNA works in the same fashion.

Holley's work complemented that of Nirenberg and H. GOBIND KHORANA, who had deciphered the coding by which mRNA calls for a specific amino acid. Together, their research shed much light on how the genetic coding in a gene's DNA is translated into the production of a specific protein. In so doing, the three made it possible for other researchers to investigate the possibility that organisms could be engineered in such a way as to alter their basic genetic traits, a development that held out much promise to medical researchers studying hereditary diseases. Because of the far-ranging implications of their work, Holley, Nirenberg, and Khorana were each awarded a one-third share of the 1968 Nobel Prize in physiology or medicine.

In 1968 Holley was named a resident fellow in molecular biology at the Salk Institute for Biological Studies in La Jolla, California. At the Salk Institute, he focused his research on the role played by non-RNA molecules, particularly hormones and amino acids, in the regulation of cell growth and replication. He was especially interested in the role played by a group of hormones known as transforming growth factors in the growth and replication of cancerous cells.

Holley's many honors included election to the National Academy of Sciences and the American Academy of Arts and Sciences. He died on February 11, 1993, in Los Gatos, California.

Further Reading

The Nobel Prize Internet Archive. "Robert W. Holley." Available online. URL: http://almaz.com/nobel/medicine/1968a.html. Downloaded on March 25, 2005.

Nobelprize.org. "The Nobel Prize in Physiology or Medicine 1968." Available online. URL: http://nobelprize.org/medicine/laureates/1968. Downloaded on June 18, 2004.

Wasson, Tyler, ed. *Nobel Prize Winners*. New York: H. W. Wilson, 1987, pp. 475–477.

Hopper, Grace
(Grace Brewster Murray, Grace Brewster Murray Hopper)
(1906–1992) *computer scientist*

Grace Hopper played a major role in the development of computer software. In addition to helping develop the first electromechanical computers, she played a crucial role in the conception and development of the compiler, a machine that programmers use to develop computer code. She also oversaw the successful effort to develop the first computer programming language.

Hopper was born Grace Brewster Murray on December 9, 1906, in New York City. Her father, Walter, was an insurance broker, and her mother, Mary, was a homemaker. After finishing high school she enrolled in Vassar College and received a B.S. in mathematics and physics in 1928. She then enrolled in the graduate program at Yale University and received an M.A. in mathematics in 1930 and a Ph.D. in mathematics and mathematical physics in 1934. She taught math at Vassar until 1941, then spent a year as a postdoctoral student at New York University's Courant Institute and a year teaching at Barnard College. In 1930 she married Vincent Hopper with whom she had no children; they divorced in 1945.

In 1943 Hopper decided to contribute to the U.S. war effort during World War II by joining the U.S. Naval Reserve. She was commissioned a lieutenant junior grade and assigned to Harvard University where the Navy's Bureau of Ordnance was working with the Automatic Sequence Controlled Calculator, better known today as the Mark I. The navy had commissioned the development of the Mark I as a faster and more accurate means of developing firing tables, complicated charts that are used to govern the firing of naval artillery. Hopper's specific duty was to write a user's manual for

Grace Hopper was a pioneer in the development of computer hardware and software. *(Library of Congress, Prints and Photographs Division [LC-USZ62-111439])*

the Mark I, an electromechanical computer that operated via a series of electric relay switches controlled by sequenced instructions punched into paper tape. It took up more than 400 square feet and could perform only three additions per second, thus making it much bigger and slower than the modern personal computer. The Mark I was blazing fast and much more accurate compared to mechanical calculators or human "computers," as people who performed mathematical calculations by hand were then known.

In 1946 Hopper was promoted to lieutenant commander and put on inactive reserve status. She remained at Harvard, however, as a research fellow and part-time mathematics professor so she could work on the next generation of electromechanical computers, the Mark II and the Mark III. One day, while trying to figure out why the Mark II refused to respond properly, she and her colleagues discovered that a dead moth had become lodged in one of the switches. They solved the problem by removing the moth, thus coining the term "debugging."

In 1949 Hopper went to work for the Eckert-Mauchly Corporation, developers of the Electronic Numerical Integrator and Calculator (ENIAC), the world's first all-electronic computer. A year later she became a senior computer programmer with Remington Rand, which had acquired Eckert-Mauchly, and was assigned to work on the Universal Automatic Computer (UNIVAC) I, the first computer that could handle alphabetical data just as easily as numerical data.

As senior programmer, Hopper's most daunting task was to find a better way for programmers to communicate with the computer. At the time, computer instructions were written in binary code, which consists of nothing more than zeroes and ones. Even the simplest instructions usually required the writing of a long string of zeroes and ones, and if the programmer inadvertently transposed a zero and a one, the entire line of code would be invalidated. Not surprisingly, programmers generally worked in a state of frustration, and they were abnormally susceptible to substance abuse, insanity, and suicide.

Hopper's solution to this knotty problem was to design an interface between the programmer and the computer. Known today as a compiler, this interface translated a short string of numerical code, such as "123," into a long string of binary code, such as several thousand zeroes and ones. The first compiler was put together by a team of programmers working under Hopper's direction; unveiled in 1952, it was known as the A-2 compiler. Then the team set out to develop a compiler that could translate alphanumeric code into binary code, and in 1957 the team developed the B-0 compiler. That same year it also made public the first programming language; known as Flow-Matic, this language enabled programmers to use words rather than numbers to write computer code.

The development of Flow-Matic spurred other programmers to develop their own programming languages. By 1960 two languages, Formula Translation (FORTRAN) and Common Business-Oriented Language (COBOL) had been developed for use by scientists and business people, respectively, with little or no programming background. Hopper played no role in the development of either FORTRAN or COBOL, but in the early 1960s she did oversee the development of several compilers for COBOL, the most popular computer language between 1960 and 1980.

In 1966 Hopper retired from Sperry-Rand, which had acquired Remington Rand 11 years earlier. She also retired from the Naval Reserve; however, seven months later she was recalled to active service at the rank of commander and assigned to the Office of the Chief of Naval Operations in the Pentagon as director of programming languages. Her primary duty was to oversee the standardization of the navy's computer operations. For the next 20 years she did everything from writing special computer languages for navy applications to convincing high-ranking officers that computers were not a problem but rather the solution to many problems. Her services were deemed of such importance that every year the navy lobbied Congress to pass a special bill exempting her from the mandatory retirement age. Meanwhile, she rose up through the ranks, and when she was finally allowed to retire in 1986 at age 79, she had attained the rank of rear admiral and the nickname "Amazing Grace."

After leaving the navy, Hopper went to work for the Digital Equipment Corporation as a senior consultant. In this capacity she continued to travel the country, giving four or more talks each week about computers and what they could do. In 1990 she retired, once and for all, to her home in Arlington, Virginia, where she died on New Year's Day, 1992.

Further Reading

Billings, Charlene W. *Grace Hopper: Navy Admiral and Computer Pioneer*. Hillside, N.J.: Enslow Publishers, 1989.

Carey, Charles W., Jr. "Grace Hopper," *American Inventors, Entrepreneurs, and Business Visionaries*. New York: Facts On File, 2002, pp. 190–192.

Yount, Lisa. "Grace Brewster Murray Hopper," *A to Z of Women in Science and Math*. New York: Facts On File, 1999, pp. 92–94.

Horvitz, H. Robert
(Howard Robert Horvitz)
(1947–) *biogeneticist*

H. Robert Horvitz contributed to a better understanding of programmed cell death, a central feature of the growth and development of all complex, multicellular organisms. This contribution won for him a share of the 2002 Nobel Prize in physiology or medicine.

Horvitz was born on May 8, 1947, in Chicago, Illinois. His father, Oscar, was an accountant, and his mother, Mary, was a school teacher. After receiving a B.A. in mathematics and economics from the Massachusetts Institute of Technology (MIT) in 1968, he entered the graduate biology program at Harvard University and received an M.A. in 1972 and a Ph.D. in 1974.

Horvitz spent the next four years in England doing postdoctoral research under Sydney Brenner at Cambridge University's Laboratory of Molecular Biology. Brenner's research focused on a species of roundworm known as *Caenorhabditis elegans*. *C. elegans* contains a total of only 959 cells and it is transparent, thus making it relatively easy for biologists to study its inner workings, and in 1974 Brenner demonstrated that it is easy to induce *C. elegans* to mutate, thus making it an excellent subject for geneticists as well. When Horvitz joined them, Brenner and his assistant, John E. Sulston, were trying to develop the first complete "wiring diagram" of a nervous system by studying *C. elegans*. Sulston was also working on a study of cell lineage, the relationships between and among cells as the one cell divides into two, those two divide into four, and so on, until the one cell eventually becomes a highly complex, multicellular adult organism. Horvitz joined Sulston in this latter study by focusing on the development of muscle cells in both normal and mutated worms, and in 1977 he and Sulston described in detail most aspects of cell lineage in the larva.

Meanwhile, Sulston had discovered that certain nerve cells always die at the same point in the cell lineage. Further experimentation led him to conclude in 1976 that a gene, which he called *nuc-1*, is responsible for this phenomenon, which became known as programmed cell death or apoptosis. In 1978 Horvitz returned to MIT to teach biology and to set up a laboratory for the study of *C. elegans*. Over the next five years he and his assistants studied every aspect of the roundworm's growth and development, focusing on the genetic aspects of apoptosis. Of particular interest to them was the fact that, in the process of growing from one cell to 959, *C. elegans* generates 131 cells that are not present in the mature roundworm, most of them in the nervous system.

In 1983 Edward M. Hedgecock, one of Sulston's assistants, discovered *ced-1* and *ced-2*, genes that signal certain cells to engulf cells that have died during apoptosis. That same year Horvitz and his team discovered *ced-3*, another gene that plays an important role in apoptosis, and described the process by which apoptosis takes place: *ced-3* initiates the death of a certain cell by signaling *ced-1* and *ced-2* to trigger the cell's engulfment and by signaling *nuc-1* to trigger the degradation of the cell's genetic material. By 1993 the Horvitz team had also discovered a second "death" gene, *ced-4*, which stimulates *ced-3* to take action, as well as an "anti-death" gene, *ced-9*, which inhibits *ced-4* from stimulating *ced-3*, thus protecting certain cells from undergoing apoptosis. Moreover, they also discovered that apoptosis in *C. elegans* is regulated by enzymes under the control of *ced-3*, *ced-4*, and *ced-9*, and that these enzymes closely resemble certain enzymes found in humans known as caspases.

Horvitz's discoveries explained in detail the process of programmed cell death in *C. elegans*, and they suggested that apoptosis takes place in similar ways in all organisms, including humans. These discoveries also raised the possibility that some human diseases and conditions have something to do with abnormalities in the process of apoptosis. This possibility is particularly high in those diseases involving the death or degeneration of neural cells, such as Alzheimer's, Parkinson's, and Huntington's diseases, but it is also significant in conditions affecting the deterioration of nonneural cells, such as in heart attacks and strokes. For his contribution, Horvitz was awarded a one-third share of the 2002 Nobel Prize in physiology or medicine; his corecipients were Brenner and Sulston.

Horvitz remained at MIT for the rest of his career. In 1988 he took on the additional duties of an investigator in MIT's branch of the Howard Hughes Medical Institute. In 1991 he married Martha Paton with whom he had one child. His many honors include election to the National Academy of Sciences and a term as president of the Genetics Society of America.

Further Reading

Altman, Lawrence K. "3 Win Nobel for Work on Suicidal Cells," *New York Times*, October 8, 2002, p. A22.

Massachusetts Institute of Technology web. "The Horvitz Laboratory" Available online. URL: http://web.mit.edu/horvitz/www. Downloaded on March 25, 2005.

Nobelprize.org. "The Nobel Prize in Physiology or Medicine 2002." Available online. URL: http://nobelprize.org/medicine/laureates/2002. Downloaded on July 22, 2004.

Hubble, Edwin
(Edwin Powell Hubble)
(1889–1953) *astronomer*

Edwin Hubble, one of the foremost astronomers of his day, made two incredibly important discoveries. The first was the existence of galaxies other than the Milky Way, and the second led directly to the development by others of the big bang model of the creation of the universe. In 1990 the *Hubble Space Telescope* was named in his honor.

Hubble was born on November 20, 1889, in Marshfield, Missouri. His father, John, was an insurance agent, and his mother, Virginia, was a homemaker. At age nine he moved with his family to the suburbs of Chicago, Illinois, where he grew up. In 1906 he enrolled in the University of Chicago, where he studied astronomy under GEORGE ELLERY HALE and received a B.A. in mathematics in 1910. A Rhodes Scholar, he studied at Oxford University and received a B.A. in law in 1913. He then joined his family in Louisville, Kentucky, and passed that state's bar examination. Instead of practicing law, however, he taught physics and coached basketball in nearby New Albany, Indiana, until he returned to the University of Chicago, where he received a Ph.D. in astronomy in 1917. He served in the U.S. Army during World War I, and upon being discharged in 1919 he accepted a position at the Mount Wilson Observatory in Pasadena, California. The observatory, which was directed by Hale, had recently installed a 100-inch telescope, at the time the largest in the world. Hubble remained at Mount Wilson for the rest of his career. In 1924 he married Grace Leib with whom he had no children.

At the time Hubble began his career as an astronomer, it was generally believed that the Milky Way Galaxy and the universe were one and the same. It was known that the edge of the Milky Way was populated by nebulae, clouds of matter that contain mostly gases and dust. Several astronomers had postulated that at least one of these nebulae was in fact a different galaxy, a cluster of stars revolving around a central gravitational point that is isolated by huge distances from other galaxies. In 1919 Hubble set about to investigate this question by studying the Andromeda nebula, a milky cluster about two million light-years from Earth; it had first been discovered in 964 by Arab astronomer as-Sūfi, and then rediscovered in 1612 by German astronomer Simon Marius. In 1924 Hubble announced that Andromeda was indeed a galaxy, and five years later he published the data that proved it, thus completely revolutionizing the standard conception of the universe. In addition, he and a colleague, Allan Sandage, discovered the presence of a number of incredibly bright stars in the Andromeda galaxy;

Edwin P. Hubble demonstrated that the universe is still expanding, a discovery that led to the development of the big bang theory of the origins of the universe. (©Bettmann/Corbis)

such stars are now known to be common in the giant galaxies and bear the name Hubble-Sandage variables.

Over the course of his career, Hubble was able to prove the existence of more than 500 additional galaxies; today, it is believed that there are more than 100 billion galaxies. As he discovered more and more galaxies, he found it necessary to devise a method for classifying them. He worked out such a system based on shape, with three main classes—spiral, elliptical, and irregular—each having a number of subclasses. He also began a series of investigations regarding the number of stars each galaxy contained, their brightness patterns, their distances from Earth, and their dimensions. His work concerning the classification of galaxies was compiled and published after his death by Sandage as *The Hubble Atlas of Galaxies* (1961).

In the course of these investigations, Hubble discovered that the universe is expanding. Prior to Hubble, most astronomers believed that the universe was static, meaning that it was neither growing nor shrinking. This notion was challenged by ALBERT EINSTEIN's theory of relativity, which suggested that the universe is expanding, and by Hubble's discovery of galaxies independent of the Milky Way. Consequently, several astronomers developed the theory that the galaxies on the edge of the universe are moving away from the center of the universe. Other astronomers disagreed, saying that the external galaxies only appear to be moving away because of some optical illusion, and that in fact they are not moving away at all. In 1928 Hubble set out to test the various hypotheses, mostly by using spectroscopy, the study of the light spectrum given off by a celestial body.

Via an ingenious method of analyzing the spectroscopic data, especially shifts in the red spectral lines, and several bold deductions, the following year he was able to prove that not only do the external galaxies move at a faster rate but also their velocities increase in direct proportion to their distance from the center. He calculated that median velocity increases at a rate of 150 kilometers per million light-years, a value that became known as Hubble's constant. Further experimentation with more sophisticated equipment established Hubble's constant at between 15 and 30 kilometers per million light-years.

For the second time, a Hubble discovery revolutionized the way astronomers looked at the universe. By proving that the universe is expanding, and by suggesting what its rate of expansion is, Hubble made it possible for others to speculate about the origins of the universe. In the 1940s GEORGE GAMOW and his colleagues used Hubble's discoveries, which were summed up in *Red Shifts in the Spectra of Nebulae* (1934), as a springboard for the development of the big bang model. According to this model, the universe began in a state of extremely high temperature and density, and then for some reason exploded so violently and so powerfully that matter continues to be propelled outward from the source of the explosion. If one accepts the big bang model, as the vast majority of scientists do, then using Hubble's constant makes it possible to date this explosion at roughly 15 billion years ago, thus offering a rough date for "creation."

During his lifetime, Hubble was honored by being elected to the National Academy of Sciences. He was also awarded gold medals by the Royal Astronomical Society and the Astronomical Society of the Pacific. He died on September 28, 1953, in San Marino, California.

Further Reading

Christianson, Gale E. *Edwin Hubble, Mariner of the Nebulae.* New York: Farrar, Straus and Giroux, 1995.

Mayall, Nicholas U. "Edwin Powell Hubble," National Academy of Sciences, *Biographical Memoirs* 41 (1970): pp. 175–214.

Sharov, Aleksandr S. *Edwin Hubble, the Discoverer of the Big Bang Universe.* New York: Cambridge University Press, 1993.

Hubel, David H.
(David Hunter Hubel)
(1926–   ) *neurobiologist*

David H. Hubel helped map out the visual cortex, that part of the brain that receives and decodes visual information from the retina. As a result of his work, scientists gained a much better understanding of how the brain processes neural information, as well as how quickly the brain develops after birth. For these contributions, he was awarded a share of the 1981 Nobel Prize in physiology or medicine.

Hubel was born on February 27, 1926, in Windsor, Ontario, Canada. His parents were U.S. citizens; his father, Jesse, was a chemical engineer, and his mother, Elsie, was a homemaker. At age three he moved with his family to Montreal where he grew up. He attended Montreal's McGill University, receiving a B.S. in mathematics in 1947 and an M.D. in 1951. After three years at the Montreal Neurological Institute, in 1954 he became a clinical neurologist at Johns Hopkins University in Baltimore, Maryland. The following year he was drafted into the U.S. Army and assigned to the Walter Reed Army Institute of Research's neurophysiology division. In 1953 he married Shirley Izzard with whom he had three children.

At Walter Reed, Hubel became interested in the activity of nerve cells during sleep. He devised a microelectrode about the thickness of a hair that could be inserted painlessly into the visual cortex area of a cat's brain. Upon attaching the microelectrode to an amplifier and loudspeakers, he was able to hear the sound a nerve cell makes as it transmits an electric impulse. This experiment so fascinated him that he soon began studying the neurophysiology of vision, specifically to identify the "firing pattern" of nerve cells during the process of seeing, so as to properly understand the role played by the optic nerve fibers.

Released from the military in 1958, Hubel returned to Johns Hopkins as an assistant to Stephen Kuffler, a noted expert in the neurophysiology of vision. Hubel continued the work he had begun at Walter Reed, but this time in collaboration with Swedish neurobiologist Torsten N. Wiesel, a Hopkins colleague. In 1959 Kuffler's entire laboratory staff, including Hubel and Wiesel, moved to Boston, Massachusetts, where they became affiliated with Harvard Medical School, eventually forming the school's department of neurobiology.

Whereas Kuffler had investigated how an image as seen by the eye is processed by the cells of the retina, Hubel and Wiesel extended this knowledge further by investigating how that image is processed by the cells of the visual cortex, which is located in the occipital lobes of the cerebrum. To this end they studied a section of the visual cortex known as Area 17, where the cells are arranged in columns. By using the microelectrodes and recording equipment devised by Hubel, they were able to correlate specific cells in Area 17 with specific cells in the retina. Thus, they were able to show that when a specific retinal cell is stimulated, it transmits an electric impulse to specific cells in Area 17 that decode the signal. As the signal travels along a particular column in Area 17, the various cells decode it in terms of contrast, linear patterns, and movement, with each cell in the column being responsible for decoding one specific bit of visual information. Further experimentation by Hubel and Wiesel showed that the ability of the visual cortex to decode retinal images is developed shortly after birth, and it is dependent on the eye being subjected to visual images at that time. Thus, a cat whose eyes are sutured shut shortly after birth, even though they remain sutured for only a few days, will suffer from permanently impaired vision.

Hubel and Wiesel's work shed much light on the inner language of the brain, specifically how it decodes electrical and chemical signals from the rest of the body. They also demonstrated that sensory perception plays an important role in the early development of the brain's higher functions. As a result, physicians learned of the importance of immediate surgical corrections of eye disorders in newborns, especially conditions such as congenital cataracts and strabismus, a muscular imbalance that prevents one of the eyes from focusing. For these contributions, Hubel and Wiesel were each awarded a quarter share of the 1981 Nobel Prize in physiology or medicine; their corecipient was the American psychobiologist ROGER W. SPERRY.

Hubel and Wiesel continued to collaborate on studies of visual neurophysiology until the mid-1980s. Afterward Hubel continued his work with a number of junior collaborators at Harvard, where he remained for the rest of his career, focusing on how the activation of brain cells is related to an animal's environment and behavior. Using both anesthetized and awake, alert macaque and squirrel monkeys as subjects, he studied the parts of the visual cortex known as V-1 (the striate cortex) and V-2 in an effort to learn more about all aspects of form, color, movement, and stereoscopic depth.

Further Reading

Hubel, David H., and Torsten N. Wiesel. *Brain and Visual Perception: The Story of a 25-Year Collaboration.* New York: Oxford University Press, 2005.

Nobelprize.org. "The Nobel Prize in Physiology or Medicine 1981." Available online. URL: http://nobelprize. org/medicine/laureates/1981. Downloaded on July 3, 2004.

Wasson, Tyler, ed. *Nobel Prize Winners.* New York: H. W. Wilson, 1987, pp. 484–486.

Huggins, Charles B.
(Charles Brenton Huggins)
(1901–1997) *surgeon*

Charles B. Huggins was one of the first medical researchers to be awarded a Nobel Prize for cancer research. He demonstrated the relationship between the sex hormones and the growth of tumors affecting the male prostate gland and the female breast.

Huggins was born on September 22, 1901, in Halifax, Nova Scotia, Canada. His father, Charles, was a pharmacist, and his mother, Bessie, was a homemaker. After receiving a B.A. from Acadia University in Nova Scotia in 1920, he entered Harvard Medical School and received an M.A. and an M.D. in 1924. Upon completion of a two-year internship at the University of Michigan Hospital, in 1926 he joined the faculty at Michigan's medical school. He left the following year for a similar position at the University of Chicago Medical School; with the exception of a brief stay in the late 1940s at Johns Hopkins University, he remained at Chicago for the rest of his scientific career. From 1951 to 1969 he directed the university's Ben May Laboratory for Cancer Research. In 1927 he married Margaret Wellman with whom he had two children, and in 1933 he became a naturalized U.S. citizen.

Huggins's early research efforts involved urology, the study of the urinary tract and its related organs and glands. He was particularly interested in the chemicals and hormones secreted by the prostate gland, the male reproductive organ that produces ejaculatory fluid. This interest led him to study prostate cancer, a condition that results in the enlargement of the prostate gland and the painful obstruction of the urinary tract. Untreated, prostate cancer can spread to the liver and bones, thus resulting in death. Using dogs as his research subjects, he discovered that prostate cancer caused the secretion of high levels of testosterone. He further discovered that reducing these levels of testosterone by either removing the testicles or administering the female hormone estrogen greatly inhibits the growth of the cancer, even after it has spread from the prostate to neighboring tissue or even to other organs. He also developed a procedure for diagnosing prostate cancer that measures the amount of the acidic and alkalinic forms of the enzyme phosphatase in the bloodstream, both of which are found in high levels in prostate cancer victims.

Despite the negative effect of castration on the body's production of male sex hormones, Huggins discovered that in some cases the body compensates by secreting male sex hormones from the adrenal glands, the endocrine glands that normally produce hormones such as epinephrine and cortisone. As these male sex hormones encourage prostate cancer to grow, he developed a treatment that called for removing the adrenal glands and administering cortisone. By 1953 he had fine-tuned his procedures so that he could prevent the further spread of prostate cancer in about 50 percent of his patients. Thus, patients who would otherwise have died had their lives prolonged by many years.

In the mid-1950s, Huggins turned his attention to breast cancer. Breast cancer was one of the most prevalent forms of cancer, and the speed with which it spread made it difficult to combat. Huggins began studying breast cancer by inducing mammary tumors in female rats. He soon discovered that, like prostate cancer, the spread of breast cancer is advanced by sex hormones. He then developed a treatment that combined removal of the ovaries and the adrenal glands with cortisone replacement therapy. When applied to humans, this procedure improved the conditions of almost 40 percent of patients with breast cancer, including some in the advanced stages of the disease. Further research on patients with cancers that did not affect the reproductive organs demonstrated that hormone treatment had little effect on inhibiting the growth of tumors in these cases. For demonstrating the relationship between hormones and certain types of cancer, Huggins was awarded a half share of the 1966 Nobel Prize in physiology or medicine; his corecipient was the American pathologist PEYTON ROUS. He received a number of other honors as well, including election to the National Academy of Sciences.

Shortly before winning the Nobel Prize, Huggins became involved in a controversy over the supposedly deleterious effects of the birth control pill, which had been made available to the general public in 1960. Many people feared that "the pill" would cause cancer of the breasts and the reproductive organs because it contained large amounts of synthetic progesterone, a female sex hormone. Huggins studied the effects of the pill on thousands of women, and by 1966 he had determined that women who took it did not increase their risk of contracting cancer.

In 1972 Huggins retired from the University of Chicago to become chancellor of his alma mater, Acadia University. He retired from Acadia in 1979 and returned to Chicago, Illinois, where he died on January 12, 1997.

Further Reading

Haddow, Alexander, et al. *On Cancer and Hormones; Essays in Experimental Biology.* Chicago: University of Chicago Press, 1962.

Nobelprize.org. "The Nobel Prize in Physiology or Medicine 1966." Available online. URL: http://nobelprize.org/medicine/laureates/1966. Downloaded on May 26, 2004.

Wasson, Tyler, ed. *Nobel Prize Winners.* New York: H. W. Wilson, 1987, pp. 486–488.

Hulse, Russell A.
(Russell Alan Hulse)
(1950–) *astrophysicist*

Russell A. Hulse codiscovered the first binary pulsar and provided some of the earliest evidence to support ALBERT EINSTEIN's theory of general relativity. These contributions won for Hulse a share of the 1993 Nobel Prize in physics.

Hulse was born on November 28, 1950, in New York City, to Alan and Betty Hulse. As a boy he attended the Bronx High School of Science and constructed his own radio telescope, a device that studies celestial bodies via the radio waves they emit. After receiving a B.S. in physics from Cooper Union (N.Y.) in 1970, he entered the graduate astronomy program at the University of Massachusetts.

Hulse's adviser at Massachusetts was JOSEPH H. TAYLOR, whose research interest involved pulsars, rapidly rotating stars that emit extremely regular pulses of radio waves. The first pulsar had been discovered in 1967 by English astronomers Jocelyn Bell and Antony Hewish, so at the time of Hulse's arrival at Massachusetts there was still much to be learned about pulsars. Today it is known that pulsars are created when the core of a supernova, a violently exploding star, collapses inward and becomes highly compressed. This compression creates a gravitational field so strong that radio waves, which are generated by the pulsar's extremely rapid

rotation, can escape it only at the magnetic poles where the gravitational pull is the weakest. As the pulsar rotates about its axis, the radio waves are projected in intense, sweeping beams that resemble the beams of light from a lighthouse. Most pulsars do not emit visible light, and so they can be studied only via a radio telescope.

In 1973 Hulse and Taylor began searching for pulsars by using the giant radio telescope in Arecibo, Puerto Rico. During the course of their collaboration, they discovered 40 new pulsars, including the first binary pulsar, known today as PSR1913+16. A binary pulsar consists of two pulsars that orbit each other at a distance roughly equal to the distance between the Earth and the Moon, and because of their intertwined orbits their radio pulses are irregular. Further study of PSR1913+16 showed that it rotates approximately 10 times faster than the speed at which the Earth orbits the Sun. The discovery of PSR1913+16 presented physicists with the perfect opportunity to investigate Albert Einstein's general theory of relativity. In 1905 Einstein had theorized that celestial bodies moving at rapid rates of speed would generate waves of gravitational radiation, or ripples in the curvature of the space-time continuum, but almost 70 years later no one had been able to provide evidence to support this theory. Hulse and Taylor were not able to provide direct evidence for the existence of gravitational radiation either, but they did show that PSR1913+16's orbiting period gradually diminishes with time. Moreover, they demonstrated that this is happening as a result of the emission of gravitational waves that are produced when the two stars are closest to each other, which is in accordance with Einstein's prediction. This demonstration has been interpreted by physicists as indicating that gravitational radiation does exist. For discovering PSR1913+16 and for providing evidence to support Einstein's theory of general relativity, Hulse and Taylor were each awarded a half share of the 1993 Nobel Prize in physics.

After receiving a Ph.D. in physics in 1975, Hulse spent two years conducting postdoctoral research at the National Radio Astronomy Observatory in Charlottesville, Virginia. Two years later he changed his focus from astrophysics to plasma physics and moved to Princeton University's Plasma Physics Laboratory (PPPL), where the bulk of his research involved the various aspects of hydrogen fusion, the process by which the Sun generates energy. In 1992 he was named principal research scientist at PPPL.

Further Reading

McMurray, Emily J., ed. *Notable Twentieth-Century Scientists*. Detroit: Gale Research, 1995, pp. 977–979.

Nobelprize.org. "The Nobel Prize in Physics 1993." Available online. URL: http://nobelprize.org/physics/laureates/1993. Downloaded on October 12, 2004.

I

Ignarro, Louis J.
(Louis Joseph Ignarro)
(1941–   ) *biochemist*

Louis J. Ignarro helped discover the chemical mechanisms involved in the relaxation of smooth muscles. For this discovery, he was awarded a share of the 1998 Nobel Prize in physiology or medicine.

Ignarro was born on May 31, 1941, in Brooklyn, New York, but he grew up in nearby Long Beach. His father was a carpenter and his mother was a homemaker. After receiving a B.A. in pharmacy from Columbia University in 1962, he entered the University of Minnesota's graduate program in pharmacology and received a Ph.D. in 1966. He spent the next two years doing postdoctoral research at the National Institutes of Health in Bethesda, Maryland, and in 1968 he went to work as a research biochemist for Geigy Pharmaceuticals on the outskirts of New York City. Five years later he joined the faculty at Tulane University in New Orleans, Louisiana, as a professor of pharmacology, leaving in 1985 to accept a similar position at the University of California at Los Angeles (UCLA) School of Medicine, where he remained for the rest of his career. His first marriage, which produced one child, ended in divorce in the mid-1980s, and in 1997 he married Sharon Williams.

Ignarro's research focused on the role played by cyclic guanosine monophosphate (cyclic GMP) in various physiological functions. His first experiments with cyclic GMP involved white blood cells and the heart, but in 1977 he became interested in the role cyclic GMP plays in the operation of blood vessels. For many years, physicians had known that nitroglycerine was an effective treatment for angina pectoris, a medical condition that is characterized by severe chest pain that results when certain arterial muscles cannot relax, but they did not know why nitroglycerine works. In 1977 FERID MURAD showed that nitric oxide, a product of the breakdown of nitroglycerine, increases the level of cyclic GMP in certain tissues, and he speculated that cyclic GMP was the biochemical agent responsible for relaxing smooth muscles, like the ones found in arteries and other blood vessels. The following year ROBERT F. FURCHGOTT discovered endothelium-derived relaxing factor (EDRF), a biochemical agent that is produced by the endothelium, the innermost layer of cells in a blood vessel. Furchgott showed that EDRF facilitates the relaxation of smooth muscles, but he was unable to identify its chemical composition. These two seemingly unrelated developments led Ignarro to speculate that EDRF is in fact nitric oxide, and that EDRF relaxes smooth muscles by triggering the production of cyclic GMP.

By 1979 Ignarro had shown that when a contracted strip of the coronary artery is treated with nitric oxide gas it immediately relaxes, a finding that supported his hypothesis that the chemical composition of EDRF is nitric oxide. Further experimentation linked the presence of nitric oxide in tissue with a dramatic increase in the production of cyclic GMP, a finding that strongly suggested that cyclic GMP is ultimately responsible for muscle relaxation. Two years later he demonstrated the complicated chain of reactions that nitroglycerine must go through to be broken down into nitric oxide, as well as the chemical process by which nitric oxide leads to the production of cyclic GMP. By 1984 he had determined conclusively that EDRF is nitric oxide, and that the body produces nitric oxide on its own, although it took him two more years to make his findings public. These discoveries enabled him to explain in detail the entire biochemical process involved in the relaxation of smooth muscles, thus explaining the ability of nitroglycerine to treat angina pectoris. For his work with nitric oxide and cyclic GMP, Ignarro was awarded a one-third share of the 1998 Nobel Prize in physiology or medicine; his corecipients were Murad and Furchgott.

Meanwhile, Ignarro continued to experiment with nitric oxide and cyclic GMP, particularly the roles they play in relaxing smooth muscles that are not part of the cardiovascular system. He demonstrated that male erectile dysfunction is marked by high levels of cyclic GMP in the tissue of the penis. This discovery led other medical researchers to develop Viagra, in essence a cyclic GMP inhibitor, the first of many pharmaceuticals designed to treat male erectile dysfunction. Much of his work regarding nitric oxide and cyclic GMP is summarized in *Nitric Oxide: Biochemistry, Molecular Biology, and Therapeutic Implications* (1995), which he coauthored with Murad, and *Nitric Oxide: Biology and Pathobiology* (2002).

Further Reading

Altman, Lawrence K. "Three Americans Awarded Nobel for Discoveries of How a Gas Affects the Body," *New York Times*, October 13, 1998, p. A14.

Nobelprize.org. "The Nobel Prize in Physiology or Medicine 1998." Available online. URL: http://nobelprize.org/medicine/laureates/1998. Downloaded on July 14, 2004.

UCLA Department of Molecular and Medical Pharmacology. "Louis J. Ignarro." Available online. URL: http://research.arc2.ucla.edu/departments/pharm_faculty.cfm?facultykey-1401. Downloaded on March 25, 2005.

Imes, Elmer S.
(Elmer Samuel Imes)
(1883–1941) *physicist*

Elmer S. Imes contributed to a better understanding of the quantum nature of molecules. His work played an important role in the development of quantum mechanics, the study of subatomic particles.

Imes was born on October 12, 1883, in Memphis, Tennessee. His father, Benjamin, was a minister, and his mother, Elizabeth, was a homemaker. After receiving his early education at schools in Ohio and Alabama, he entered Fisk University in Nashville, Tennessee, and received a B.A. in science in 1903. He spent the next seven years teaching mathematics and physics at Albany (Ga.) Normal Institute. In 1910 he returned to Fisk to teach mathematics and science while working on his M.S., which he received five years later. He then enrolled in the University of Michigan graduate program and received a Ph.D. in physics in 1918.

Imes's primary research interest involved the study of molecular structure through the use of high-resolution infrared spectroscopy. During his student days, quantum mechanics was still a theory, and the idea that atoms and molecules possessed energy in discrete amounts known as quanta had yet to be proven conclusively. Imes and Harrison M. Randall, a Michigan physics professor, used infrared spectroscopy, the study of the bands of infrared light emitted by a certain substance, to study the quantum properties of diatomic molecules, molecules that consist of only two atoms. The relative simplicity of diatomic molecules made them ideal candidates for Imes and Randall's groundbreaking procedure. By studying the infrared spectra of hydrogen chloride, hydrogen bromide, and hydrogen fluoride, they made the first accurate measurement of the distance between atoms in a molecule. They also showed that chlorine exists in isotopic form, meaning that the atomic weight of chlorine atoms is not identical. Although the existence of isotopes, forms of an element in which the nucleus has a different number of neutrons but whose physical properties are virtually identical to the normal form, had been demonstrated previously, theirs was the first discovery of an isotope of a nonradioactive element.

Imes and Randall's most important demonstration, however, was the quantization of the rotational spectra of diatomic molecules, meaning that the energy levels associated with the spectral lines that are emitted as the molecules rotate are discrete values that are integral multiples of some basic finite value. In 1919 they published their findings in the *Astrophysical Journal* and in 1920 in *Physical Review,* and in short order their work was being quoted extensively by other physicists conducting research involving quantum theory. Other researchers had previously demonstrated the quantization of the vibrational spectrum, so Imes and Randall's work helped transform quantum theory into quantum mechanics in the mid-1920s.

After graduating from Michigan, Imes moved to New York City where he worked as a consulting engineer and as a research physicist for several companies. In this capacity, he developed two procedures for measuring the properties of magnetic materials and then invented two pieces of apparatus for making such measurements. In 1919 he married Nella Larsen with whom he had no children; they divorced in 1933.

In 1930 Imes returned to Nashville to become head of Fisk's physics department, a position he held for the next 11 years. He also resumed his study of infrared spectroscopy, as well as the use of X-rays to study the properties of various materials. He died on September 11, 1941, in New York City.

Further Reading

The Faces of Science: African Americans in the Sciences. "Elmer Samuel Imes." Available online. URL: http://www.princeton.edu/~mcbrown/display/imes.html. Downloaded on March 25, 2005.

McMurray, Emily J., ed. *Notable Twentieth Century Scientists.* Detroit: Gale Research, 1995, p. 993.

Spangenburg, Ray, and Kit Moser. *African Americans in Science, Math, and Invention.* New York: Facts On File, 2003, pp. 125–126.

J

Julian, Percy L.
(Percy Lavon Julian)
(1899–1975) *chemist*

Percy L. Julian's career straddled the fence between pure research, discovery for discovery's sake, and industrial chemistry, discovery for practical uses. His particular genius was his ability to use vegetative sources, especially soybean oil, as a base from which to develop a host of valuable medical and commercial products.

Julian was born on April 11, 1899, in Montgomery, Alabama. His father, James, was a railway mail clerk, and his mother, Elizabeth, was a teacher. He developed an interest in chemistry at an early age, despite the fact that his segregated schools did not offer any chemistry courses. After finishing high school in 1916, he enrolled in DePauw University in Indiana and received an A.B. in chemistry in 1920. He taught chemistry at Fisk University for two years, and then he received a fellowship to attend Harvard University, where he received an M.A. in organic chemistry in 1923. He spent the next six years teaching chemistry at West Virginia State College and Howard University. Unable to gain admission to a Ph.D. program in the United States because he was an African American, in 1929 he enrolled in the University of Vienna in Austria and received a Ph.D. in organic chemistry two years later. Upon returning to the United States, he taught at Howard for one year and then obtained a permanent position on the faculty at DePauw. In 1935 he married Anna Johnson with whom he had two children.

Julian devoted his research efforts at DePauw to synthesizing physostigmine, a drug made from Calabar beans that is used to treat glaucoma and

Percy L. Julian developed methods for synthesizing human hormones such as cortisone from soybean oil. He is pictured here holding the Decalogue Society of Lawyers Annual Merit Award, which the Chicago-based society presents to people of outstanding merit. (©Bettmann/Corbis)

myasthenia gravis. In 1935 he published his findings concerning d, 1-eserethole, the compound from which synthetic physostigmine is derived. Julian's findings contradicted those of noted Oxford chemist Sir Robert Robinson, who had published on the same subject a year earlier, but further investigation proved that Julian, not Robinson, was correct.

Julian's next research effort involved extracting stigmasterol from soybean oil. Stigmasterol is a compound from which human sex hormones, which are used to treat a number of medical conditions, can be synthesized. He postponed this project in 1936 when he left DePauw to work as an industrial chemist for the Glidden Company in Chicago, Illinois. Glidden, a major manufacturer of paint, had decided to diversify its product line, and its management believed that soybean oil, which is relatively inexpensive to extract, had a number of undiscovered industrial and medical applications. Named director of research of Glidden's soya products division, Julian's first task was to oversee construction of a major soybean oil production facility. Once the facility was up and running, he set about discovering uses for the oil it was producing. His first discovery was that the vegetable protein in soybean oil makes a durable but inexpensive coating for paper. He later discovered how to use compounds derived from soybean oil in the manufacture of paint, animal feed, candy, cosmetics, food additives, ink, and textiles. He also developed Aero Foam, more popularly known as "bean soup," which was particularly effective at putting out petroleum fires.

In 1940 Julian returned to the stigmasterol experiments he had postponed four years earlier. A large vat of soybean oil had been contaminated with water, and the result was an oily paste that seemed to be useless. However, it occurred to Julian that the paste might be a good source from which stigmasterol and similar compounds could be produced, and a few experiments proved that his hunch was correct. Before long, Glidden was one of the world's largest producers of the female hormone progesterone and the male hormone testosterone; the former is used to prevent miscarriages and treat certain menstrual complications, while the latter is used to treat certain types of breast cancer. In 1949 Julian developed a way to synthesize cortisone, used to treat rheumatoid arthritis, from soybean oil.

In the 1940s Julian began looking for an even better source of synthetic hormones than soybean oil. His research led him to Mexico, where he discovered that the root of a wild yam known as *Dioscorea* was an excellent source of progesterone. In 1954 he left Glidden to found Julian Laboratories, which focused on the production of progesterone. Two years later, it was discovered that progesterone could be made into an oral contraceptive that was both safe and effective. In 1960 the U.S. Food and Drug Administration approved the contraceptive, known as the birth control pill, for sale to the general public. As owner of the world's foremost producer of the main ingredient in birth control pills, Julian soon became a millionaire. In 1961 he sold his company to Smith, Kline and French but served as its president for three more years.

In 1964 Julian founded the Julian Research Institute and Julian Associates, both of which focused on discovering and producing synthetic pharmaceutical drugs. He died on April 19, 1975, in Waukegan, Illinois.

Further Reading

Carey, Charles W., Jr. "Julian, Percy Lavon," *American Inventors, Entrepreneurs, and Business Visionaries.* New York: Facts On File, 2002, pp. 214–215.

Robinson, Louise. *The Black Millionaire.* New York: Pyramid Books, 1972.

Spangenburg, Ray, and Kit Moser. "Julian, Percy Lavon," *African Americans in Science, Math, and Invention.* New York: Facts On File, 2003, pp. 137–139.

Witkop, Bernhard. "Percy Lavon Julian," National Academy of Sciences, *Biographical Memoirs* 52 (1980): pp. 223–266.

Just, Ernest E.
(Ernest Everett Just)
(1883–1941) *biologist*

Ernest E. Just was one of the foremost investigators into the biochemical processes associated with the fertilization and growth of animal eggs. His major contribution was his espousal of the fertilizin theory, which explained the biochemical process by which a sperm cell fertilizes an egg cell.

Just was born on August 14, 1883, in Charleston, South Carolina. His father, Charles, was a carpenter, and his mother, Mary, was a teacher. When Ernest was four his father died, and he moved with his mother to nearby James Island where he grew up. At age 13 he entered the Colored Normal, Industrial, Agricultural and Mechanical College (today South Carolina State College) where he studied to be a teacher. Upon completing the program in 1899, he spent three years at Kimball Union Academy, a college-preparatory school in Meriden, New Hampshire, before enrolling in Dartmouth College. In 1907 he received a B.S. in biology and accepted a position on the faculty at Howard University in Washington, D.C. In 1912 he married Ethel Highwarden with whom he had three children; they divorced in 1939, and that same year he married Hedwig Schnetzler.

While at Dartmouth, Just had studied under the eminent zoologist William Patten and had contributed some of his research concerning frogs to Patten's book, *The Evolution of the Vertebrates and Their Kin* (1912). In turn, Patten recommended Just to Frank Lillie, director of the Marine Biological Laboratory at Woods Hole, Massachusetts. In 1909 Just was offered a summer position at Woods Hole as a research assistant, and for the next 20 years he spent most of his summers doing research there. Meanwhile, Lillie, who also headed the department of zoology at the University of Chicago, gave Just credit for his research toward a Ph.D. in experimental embryology, which Just received in 1916.

Just's primary research interest was the fertilization and growth of animal eggs. His association with Woods Hole led him naturally to investigate the eggs of marine animals, and in 1911 he took up the study of the breeding habits and fertilization process in sandworms and sea urchins. The following year he published his first of more than 50 articles on this and related topics. Most of these articles appeared in *Biological Bulletin*, the official

journal of Woods Hole for which he later served as editor. Much of his work involved the so-called fertilizin theory, whereby it was believed that the catalyst for the fertilization of an egg cell by a sperm cell was a substance called fertilizin. Though first developed by Lillie, Just eventually became the theory's foremost proponent. Later research showed that fertilizin is a gelatinous substance produced by eggs that causes sperm to stick to eggs. Much of his work regarding the fertilization of marine eggs was published in his book, *Basic Methods for Experiments on Eggs of Marine Animals* (1939). Previously he, Lillie, and THOMAS HUNT MORGAN had coauthored *General Cytology* (1924), a textbook covering the formation, structure, and functions of cells.

Despite his skill as a teacher, Just longed to devote his career to pure research, something that was impossible given his heavy teaching load at Howard. Consequently, he sought grants and fellowships that would allow him to take extended leaves of absence from teaching. In 1920 he was named the Julius Rosenwald Fellow in biology to the National Research Council, a position he held for 11 years. In 1929 he secured a grant that made it possible for him to work for a semester at the Zoological Station in Naples, Italy, in essence a European version of Woods Hole. In 1930 he resigned from Howard and Woods Hole, and for the next 10 years he remained in Europe to conduct research. Although he never found a permanent home in Europe, he had little trouble securing short-term appointments as a visiting professor at such distinguished institutions as the Kaiser Wilhelm Institute in Berlin and the Sorbonne in Paris.

While in Europe, Just published *Biology of the Cell Surface* (1939). The book was partly a compendium of a number of theories and ideas that Just had experimented with throughout his career and partly an exposition of a relatively new idea of his, that a cell's ectoplasm or outer surface plays an important role in the cell's development. At first, this theory received little attention, but after his death it was taken more seriously.

In 1940, shortly after the outbreak of World War II, Just was captured in France by the Germans and sent to a prisoner of war camp. Later that year he was released; unable to stay in Europe because of the war, he returned to Howard to resume his teaching duties. He died of cancer on October 27, 1941, in Washington, D.C. In 1997 the U.S. Postal Service issued a commemorative stamp in his honor.

Further Reading

Manning, Kenneth R. *Black Apollo of Science: The Life of Ernest Everett Just.* New York: Oxford University Press, 1983.

Spangenburg, Ray, and Kit Moser. *African Americans in Science, Math, and Invention.* New York: Facts On File, 2003, pp. 139–142.

K

Kandel, Eric R.
(Eric Richard Kandel)
(1929–) *neurobiologist*

Eric R. Kandel discovered the physical aspects involved in learning and the development of short-term and long-term memory. For this contribution, he was awarded a share of the 2000 Nobel Prize in physiology or medicine.

Kandel was born on November 7, 1929, in Vienna, Austria. His parents, Herman and Charlotte, owned and operated a toy store. At age nine he immigrated with his family to New York City where he grew up. After receiving a B.A. in European history and literature from Harvard University in 1952, he entered the New York City School of Medicine, receiving an M.D. in 1956. A one-year internship at New York's Montefiore Hospital was followed by three years of postdoctoral research at the National Institute of Mental Health in Bethesda, Maryland, two years as a resident at Boston's Massachusetts Mental Health Center, and a one-year postdoctoral fellowship at the Institut Morey in Paris, France. In 1963 he became a professor of psychiatry at Harvard Medical School, leaving in 1965 for New York University where he founded a research group devoted to cellular neurobiology and behavior. In 1974 he joined the faculty of Columbia University's College of Physicians and Surgeons where he founded the Center of Neurobiology and Behavior, and in 1984 he took on the additional duties of a senior investigator at Columbia's Howard Hughes Medical Institute. In 1956 he married Denise Bystryn with whom he had two children, and at some point he became a naturalized U.S. citizen.

As a medical student, Kandel was primarily interested in psychiatry and psychoanalysis, the sciences most concerned with the processes of thinking. These interests led him to study the biological aspects of neurophysiology, and eventually to abandon psychiatry in favor of a scientific investigation of the cellular and molecular mechanisms of learning and memory. In the 1950s nothing was known about these mechanisms, but the scientific techniques by which they might be studied were in the process of being developed. By 1960 Kandel's work with the hippocampus, a part of the brain that plays an important role in the development of conscious memory, had convinced him that learning and memory do not reside in the nerve cells themselves, but rather in the temporary connections, or synapses, that link them. Nerve cells are not connected directly to each other; instead, when a nerve wants to transmit a sensory signal or impulse to the next nerve, it produces a tiny amount of a biochemical compound known as a neurotransmitter, which then bridges the gap (roughly one-millionth of a centimeter) between the two nerves, thus forming a synapse. This fact led Kandel to wonder if learning and memory are controlled by synapses, which in turn are modified by the impulses that pass across them.

To answer this question, Kandel took up the study of *Aplysia,* a giant marine snail whose nervous

Eric Kandel's career was devoted to understanding how humans develop short-term and long-term memory. *(Courtesy of Eric R. Kandel)*

system is easy to study because its nerve cells are relatively large and few in number (about 20,000 total, as compared to approximately 100 billion in humans). Initially, he focused on *Aplysia*'s ability to learn in connection with a simple reflex; whenever its gills are touched, it withdraws them as a means of protecting them. Kandel discovered that when the gills are touched repeatedly but gently, the snail withdraws them less and less, suggesting that the snail has learned that the gills are not really in any danger. Conversely, when the gills are touched repeatedly but forcefully, the withdrawal motion is more pronounced than usual, suggesting that the snail has now learned that the gills are in greater danger. He then showed that this modified response to touching was controlled by the synapses. Repeated gentle touching results in less and less

neurotransmitter being produced, thus weakening the signal across the synapse along the neural pathway from the gills to the muscles responsible for contracting them, while repeated forceful touching results in the production of more and more neurotransmitter, thus strengthening the signal. He also showed that the production of neurotransmitter is regulated by a biochemical compound known as cyclic AMP, which is concentrated in a ganglion, or a dense mass of nerve cells, in the snail's abdomen. In turn, the strength of cyclic AMP's concentration is increased by the production of neurotransmitter.

Kandel then turned his attention to determining the molecular basis for how *Aplysia* translates short-term memory into long-term memory, in the process collaborating with PAUL GREENGARD. Kandel and Greengard eventually discovered that this process requires the synthesis of two enzymes known as PKA and MAP kinase. The repeated production of neurotransmitter increases the concentration of cyclic AMP in the ganglion to the point that the ganglion directs the translocation of PKA and MAP kinase into the nerve cell's nucleus where they trigger a gene regulator known as CREB-1. In turn, CREB-1 initiates a series of genetic actions that result in the development of newer, stronger synapses between the nerve cells in question, thus sustaining a long-term change in the gill-withdrawal reflex.

By 1990 Kandel had completed his demonstration of how learning and memory operate in *Aplysia,* and that same year he returned to his earlier studies of the hippocampus. Using genetically modified mice, he demonstrated that the development of long-term memory in the mouse hippocampus is similar to its development in snails in that cyclic AMP, PKA, and CREB-1 all play important roles in strengthening the synapses associated with conscious memory. By presenting a better understanding of the physiological basis for learning and memory, Kandel's work made it possible for other researchers to explore ways to cure learning disorders and to treat medical conditions affecting the memory, such as Alzheimer's disease. As a result, he was awarded a one-third share of the 2000 Nobel Prize in physiology or medicine; one of his corecipients was Greengard, and the other was the Swedish physiologist Arvid Carlsson.

Kandel spent the rest of his career at Columbia. His other honors include the National Medal of Science and election to the National Academy of Sciences and the American Academy of Arts and Sciences.

Further Reading

Howard Hughes Medical Institute. "HHMI Investigator: Eric R. Kandel." Available online. URL: http://www.hhmi.org/research/investigators/kandel.html. Downloaded on March 25, 2005.

Krapp, Kristine M., ed. *Notable Twentieth-Century Scientists Supplement.* Detroit: Gale Research, 1998, pp. 239–240.

Nobelprize.org. "The Nobel Prize in Physiology or Medicine 2000." Available online. URL: http://nobelprize.org/medicine/laureates/2000. Downloaded on July 6, 2004.

Karle, Jerome
(1918–   ) *physical chemist*

Jerome Karle was one of two developers of the so-called direct method, by which the three-dimensional structure of crystalline biomolecules can be determined via X-ray crystallography. For this achievement he was awarded a share of the 1985 Nobel Prize in chemistry.

Karle was born on June 18, 1918, in Brooklyn, New York. His father, Louis, was a businessman, and his mother, Sadie, was a homemaker. He attended the City College of New York (CCNY) where he majored in chemistry and biology and received a B.S. in 1937. After receiving an M.A. in biology from Harvard University in 1938, he worked for a year as a laboratory assistant at the New York State Health Department in Albany; while there he developed a method for measuring the amount of fluorine in drinking water. In 1940 he entered the graduate program at the University of Michigan, receiving a Ph.D. in physical chemistry in 1944. He then went to work for the U.S. Naval Research Laboratory (NRL), spending two years at their facility at Michigan before transferring to the main facility in Washington, D.C., in 1946.

HERBERT A. HAUPTMAN, one of Karle's former classmates at CCNY, came to work at NRL in Washington just a year after Karle had arrived. Soon they were collaborating on a project of mutual interest, the development of an improved method for using X-ray crystallography to determine the three-dimensional structures of very small crystals such as crystalline biomolecules. Biomedical researchers had just begun to use X-ray crystallography as a tool for learning about the chemical structures of biomolecules such as vitamins and proteins, and it played an important role in the development of the DNA model by JAMES D. WATSON and his collaborators. Nevertheless, X-ray crystallography was not readily accessible to anyone other than experts, and determining the structure of a biomolecule took months if not years to accomplish.

X-ray crystallography involves beaming X-rays into a crystal and then analyzing the pattern of spots created by the scattered beams on a photographic plate as the beams are diffracted by the crystal. The pattern indicates the location and arrangement of the various atoms, which can be identified by analyzing the light intensity of the spots. The problem was that the scattered beams are out of phase with each other, and therefore it was difficult to compare the light intensities of the spots. Consequently, it was necessary to make educated guesses as to what the phase differences actually were, a process that involved a great deal of trial and error. By combining Karle's skill as a physical chemist and Hauptman's skill as a mathematician, the two collaborators solved the phase problem by developing what became known as the direct method because it eliminates the need for guesswork. In essence, the direct method uses the methods of statistical probability, in particular the joint probability distributions of several structure factors, as the essential tool for phase determination. Karle and Hauptman presented their findings in several journal articles and monographs between 1950 and 1956, the most important being *Solution of the Phase Problem, 1: The Centrosymmetric Crystal* (1953).

The direct method received little notice when it was first advanced, perhaps because the mathematical equations involved are a bit daunting for a nonmathematician, but the development of the modern computer made these calculations much easier to make. By the mid-1980s, researchers using the direct method were able to determine the structure of a crystalline biomolecule in about two days, a fraction of the time that had once been required. For making X-ray crystallography a tool that can be used by just about any biomedical researcher, Karle and Hauptman were each awarded a half share of the 1985 Nobel Prize in chemistry.

Meanwhile, Karle and Hauptman had ended their collaboration, and after 1956 Karle began working more closely with his wife, the former Isabella Lugoski, whom he had married in 1942 and with whom he had three children. Like Karle, Isabella Karle was a trained physical chemist who also worked at NRL. Before Hauptman's arrival, the Karles had been experimenting with gas-electron diffraction analysis. This line of inquiry sought to determine molecular structures by bending, or diffracting, waves of electrons through a crystal and then recording the patterns of diffraction left by the electrons in a cloud of vapor, and it provided much of the underpinning for Karle and Hauptman's

development of the direct method. In the 1960s the Karles developed the "symbolic addition procedure," a more sophisticated version of the direct method, and returned to their earlier work with gas-electron diffraction analysis.

In 1968 Karle was named chief scientist of NRL's Laboratory for the Structure of Matter, a position he held for more than 35 years. Under his direction, the laboratory developed new methods for determining the structures of a broad range of subjects including gaseous molecules, amorphous solids, and fibers in addition to crystals and crystalline biomolecules. From 1951 to 1970 he also taught mathematics and physics at the University of Maryland. His many honors include election to the National Academy of Sciences and terms as president of the American Crystallographic Association and the International Union of Crystallography.

Further Reading

The Nobel Prize Internet archive. "Jerome Karle." Available online. URL: http://almaz.com/nobel/chemistry/1985b.html. Downloaded on March 25, 2005.

Nobelprize.org. "The Nobel Prize in Chemistry 1985." Available online. URL: http://nobelprize.org/chemistry/laureates/1985. Downloaded on August 12, 2004.

Wasson, Tyler, ed. *Nobel Prize Winners*. New York: H. W. Wilson, 1987, pp. 530–531.

Kendall, Edward C.
(Edward Calvin Kendall)
(1886–1972) *biochemist*

Edward C. Kendall played a major role in the development of pain relievers, such as cortisone and adrenocorticotropic hormone (ACTH), for treating medical conditions such as rheumatoid arthritis. His role in their development was rewarded in 1950 when he received a share of the Nobel Prize in physiology or medicine.

Kendall was born on March 8, 1886, in South Norwalk, Connecticut. His father, George, was a dentist, and his mother, Eva, was a homemaker. He developed an interest in chemistry while in high school, and he pursued that interest at Columbia University, where he received a B.S., an M.S., and a Ph.D. in chemistry in 1908, 1909, and 1910, respectively. After spending a year as a research chemist in the laboratories of Parke, Davis, a major pharmaceutical company, he joined the staff at St. Luke's Hospital in New York City where he established a biochemical laboratory. In 1914 he obtained a research position at the Mayo Clinic in Rochester, Minnesota. He remained with the clinic for 37 years, and in 1945 he was named head of its biochemistry laboratory. In 1915 he married Rebecca Kennedy with whom he had four children.

Kendall's first research interest was to isolate the hormone produced by the thyroid. In 1915 he was able to extract from the thyroid a crystalline, iodine-based substance he named thyroxine. Thyroxine, the active constituent of the thyroid hormone, proved to be useful in treating hypothyroidism, a medical condition caused by deficient activity of the thyroid gland and that leads to goiter in adults and cretinism in children. His biochemical studies of thyroxine led him to study glutathione, a tripeptide found in blood and tissue that plays an important role in tissue oxidation and in the activation of some enzymes, and by 1929 he was able to establish glutathione's chemical structure.

Kendall then set out to find and extract the active ingredient of the hormone secreted by the adrenal cortex in the hopes of finding a treatment for Addison's disease, a condition caused by the deterioration of the adrenal glands. By 1934 he had discovered that the adrenal cortex was much more complicated than anyone had suspected, and that it yielded more than one hormone. Within a year of that discovery, however, he isolated six substances, which he named Compounds A through F, from adrenal hormones. Moreover, he concluded that all but Compounds C and D potentially could be used to make therapeutic drugs.

At this point Kendall began working closely with PHILIP S. HENCH, a physician with the Mayo Foundation. Over the next 12 years Hench administered the various compounds that Kendall had derived to patients suffering from a number of ailments, but particularly from rheumatoid arthritis. In 1941 the two decided that the most promising results could probably be obtained from Compound E, which was later christened cortisone by Hench.

Unfortunately, the technology of the day made it exceptionally difficult to produce cortisone in sufficient quantities, so Kendall set out to produce it synthetically. The synthesis of cortisone for use as a painkiller received particular attention from the federal government during World War II, during which Kendall continued his work in this regard while serving on the Office of Scientific Research and Development's Committee on Medical Research.

By 1948 Kendall had finally produced enough synthetic cortisone to permit a rigorous experiment. That same year he and Hench began administering cortisone and ACTH, a hormone produced by the pituitary gland that stimulates the adrenal cortex, to Mayo Clinic patients whose arthritic conditions were so bad that they were confined to their beds. Instead of curing arthritis, cortisone and ACTH actually caused mildly deleterious side effects; however, Kendall and Hench discovered that the combined application of both substances alleviated the painful symptoms of even the worst arthritic conditions.

Because cortisone and ACTH permitted previously untreatable conditions to be treated, their development into pain relievers was a major medical breakthrough. Today naturally derived cortisone and ACTH are rarely used, mostly because modern technology has developed synthetic steroids that can be produced cheaply and plentifully and that have no harmful side effects. These advances were set in motion by Kendall and Hench's work, which was so important at the time that they were awarded shares of the 1950 Nobel Prize for physiology or medicine. They shared the award with Tadeus Reichstein, a Polish-Swiss biochemist who had independently duplicated Kendall's work.

In 1951 Kendall left the Mayo Clinic to teach chemistry at Princeton University, where he continued to experiment with the hormones of the adrenal cortex. He died on May 4, 1972, in Princeton, New Jersey.

Further Reading

Ingle, Dwight. "Edward C. Kendall," National Academy of Sciences, Biographical Memoirs 47 (1975): pp. 249–290.

Nobelprize.org. "The Nobel Prize in Physiology or Medicine 1950." Available online. URL: http://nobelprize.

org/medicine/laureates/1950. Downloaded on July 4, 2003.

Wasson, Tyler, ed. *Nobel Prize Winners*. New York: H. W. Wilson, 1987, pp. 542–544.

Kendall, Henry W.
(Henry Way Kendall)
(1926–1999) *physicist*

Henry W. Kendall helped provide some of the earliest evidence for the existence of quarks, one of the basic building blocks of matter. For this contribution, he was awarded a share of the 1990 Nobel Prize in physics.

Kendall was born on December 9, 1926, in Boston, Massachusetts. His father, Henry, was a businessman, and his mother, Evelyn, was a homemaker. As a boy he moved with his family to nearby Sharon where he grew up. After finishing high school, he entered the U.S. Merchant Marine Academy and spent the last year of World War II aboard a troop transport in the North Atlantic Ocean. In 1946 he enrolled in Amherst (Mass.) College, receiving a B.A. in mathematics in 1950. Four years later he received a Ph.D. in nuclear and atomic physics from the Massachusetts Institute of Technology (MIT). After two years as a postdoctoral fellow at the Brookhaven National Laboratory on New York's Long Island, in 1956 he joined the faculty at Stanford University in Palo Alto, California, and the staff of its High Energy Laboratory.

At Stanford, Kendall joined a research group headed by ROBERT HOFSTADTER. Hofstadter had been studying the nature of the atomic nucleus, particularly the nucleons (protons and neutrons) from which it is constructed. Hofstadter believed that nucleons are not indivisible particles but rather are constructed of something even more basic. He had developed an experiment whereby high-energy electrons were fired into thin metal foil and the scattering pattern caused by the electrons "bouncing" off the metal nuclei was examined. The results clearly showed that nucleons are indeed composed of smaller particles, but all Hofstadter was able to determine was that a nucleon consists of a core surrounded by two orbits of pions, particles with masses greater than an electron but

smaller than a proton. With the assistance of Kendall, JEROME I. FRIEDMAN, and Canadian physicist Richard E. Taylor, in 1957 Hofstadter showed that a proton carries a positive charge because both of its pion orbits are positively charged, while a neutron carries a neutral charge because one of its pion orbits is positively charged while the other is negatively charged.

Kendall, Friedman, and Taylor continued to collaborate after the conclusion of their work with Hofstadter. Their partnership was briefly disrupted in 1960 when Friedman left Stanford for MIT, as did Kendall in 1961. At MIT, Kendall and Friedman resumed their collaboration, and in 1967 they began working again with Taylor, who was now a group leader at the Stanford Linear Accelerator Center (SLAC). Specifically, they were intrigued by the theoretical work of MURRAY GELL-MANN, who in 1964 had theorized that the nucleonic cores that Hofstadter had discovered are composed of elementary particles called quarks. Most physicists were skeptical about the existence of quarks, so Kendall, Friedman, and Taylor set out to either prove or disprove Gell-Mann's quark theory.

Whereas Hofstadter's experiments had generated high-energy electrons in a 300-foot linear accelerator, Kendall, Friedman, and Taylor were able to use the new SLAC linear accelerator that was two miles long and thus capable of energizing electrons to much higher levels. Another primary difference between the trio's experiment and Hofstadter's is that Hofstadter had focused on elastic collisions, whereby the bombarding electrons are deflected by the protons being bombarded, while the three collaborators focused on inelastic collisions, whereby the electrons penetrate the protons. Within a year the trio showed that, although protons cannot be blasted into smithereens, the scattering patterns resulting from deep inelastic collisions demonstrate clearly the existence of smaller particles inside the proton's core. By the mid-1970s, the trio showed that neutrons consist of smaller particles as well, and they provided conclusive evidence for the existence of gluons, neutrally charged particles whose behavior holds together these smaller particles, which by then were being equated with Gell-Mann's quarks.

Because their work further advanced our understanding of the inner structure of matter, Kendall, Friedman, and Taylor were each awarded a one-third share of the 1990 Nobel Prize in physics.

Kendall remained at MIT for the rest of his career, although he spent about half of his time conducting experiments at SLAC and the Fermi National Laboratory (Fermilab) near Chicago, Illinois. In 1969 he cofounded the Union of Concerned Scientists (UCS), a public interest group that presses for control of potentially harmful or dangerous technologies such as nuclear power, nuclear weapons, and the excessive use of fossil fuels, and he served as its chair from 1974 to 1999. His efforts in this regard led him to write four books: *Energy Strategies—Toward a Solar Future* (1980), *Beyond the Freeze* (1982), *Fallacy of Star Wars* (1985), and *Crisis Stability and Nuclear War* (1988). His honors included election to the National Academy of Sciences and the American Academy of Arts and Sciences. He died, having never married, on February 15, 1999, during a scuba diving expedition in Wakulla County, Florida.

Further Reading

McMurray, Emily J., ed. *Notable Twentieth-Century Scientists*. Detroit: Gale Research, 1995, pp. 1,082–1,083.

MIT News Office. "MIT Nobelist Henry Kendall Dies at 72 while Scuba Diving in Florida Lake." Available online. URL: http://web.mit.edu/newsoffice/1999/kendall.html. Downloaded on March 25, 2005.

Nobelprize.org. "The Nobel Prize in Physics 1990." Available online. URL: http://nobelprize.org/physics/laureates/1990. Downloaded on October 7, 2004.

Khorana, H. Gobind
(Har Gobind Khorana)
(1922–) *biochemist*

H. Gobind Khorana helped decipher the genetic coding that governs the production of proteins by the cells. This discovery won for him a share of the 1968 Nobel Prize in physiology or medicine.

Khorana was born on January 9, 1922, in Raipur, Punjab, at the time in India but today in Pakistan. His father, Ganpat, was a government clerk, and his mother, Krishna, was a homemaker. After receiving an M.S. in chemistry from the University of Punjab in 1945, he entered the University of Liverpool in England, receiving a Ph.D. in organic chemistry in 1948. He spent the next four years as a postdoctoral fellow at the Swiss Federal Institute of Technology and Cambridge University. In 1952, the same year he married Esther Silber with whom he had three children, he was named director of the British Columbia Research Council's Organic Chemistry Section at the University of British Columbia in Canada. In 1960 he became codirector of the Institute for Enzyme Research at the University of Wisconsin, where he also taught biochemistry. In 1966 he became a naturalized U.S. citizen.

Khorana's early research focused on enzymes, the proteins that initiate biochemical functions. His major accomplishment in this field came in 1959, when he developed an inexpensive method for synthesizing acetyl coenzyme A from yeast. This compound catalyzes certain enzymes that process proteins, fats, and carbohydrates in the human body, and his method made acetyl coenzyme A readily available to researchers studying human digestion.

Khorana then turned his attention to the nucleic acids, DNA and RNA, which govern the production of proteins by the cells. In 1961 MARSHALL W. NIRENBERG had demonstrated the existence of messenger RNA, the nucleic acid that transmits the genetic coding carried in DNA from the genes to the ribosomes, where the coding determines which proteins the ribosomes will produce. Nirenberg had also begun to decipher genetic coding by demonstrating the existence of codons, groups of three consecutive nucleotides in a strand of RNA; each codon calls for the inclusion of a specific amino acid in the protein that a given ribosome is producing. As RNA contains four different nucleotides—adenine, cytosine, guanine, and uracil—the possible number of codons is 64; conversely, although there are more than 100 amino acids, only about 20 are used to make proteins. Consequently, much trial and error went into determining which 20 of the 64 possible codons are actually codes for the inclusion of a specific amino acid.

In 1964 Khorana began contributing to Nirenberg's efforts by deciphering several unidentified codons. He did this by synthesizing a short strand of messenger RNA of the intestinal bacterium *Escherichia coli* (*E. coli*), which contained the same codon repeated over and over. He then introduced the RNA strand into a colony of *E. coli,* and if the colony began producing amino acid chains consisting entirely of only one amino acid, it was then known that the repeated codon called for that specific amino acid. By 1966 he and Nirenberg had determined the codons that correspond to each of the 20 amino acids, and Khorana had also determined which codons signal a ribosome to begin and end the construction of a given protein.

By deciphering the genetic coding contained in the nucleic acids, Khorana and Nirenberg contributed immensely to a better understanding of genetics in general. Their work allowed other researchers to identify the causes of certain inherited traits, especially hereditary diseases, while raising the possibility that higher-order organisms could someday be engineered genetically so as to remove unwanted hereditary traits or to include desirable ones. Because of the far-reaching implications of their research, Khorana and Nirenberg were each awarded a one-third share of the 1968 Nobel Prize in physiology or medicine.

Meanwhile, Khorana had returned to his earlier work with yeast, this time to develop a synthetic copy of its DNA. Whereas RNA codons consist of single nucleotides, DNA codons consist of paired nucleotides—adenine, cytosine, guanine, and thymine—with adenine always paired with thymine and cytosine always paired with guanine. By 1970 he had synthesized not just a strand of yeast DNA but an entire yeast gene, the first time such a thing had ever been done.

In 1970 Khorana left Wisconsin to become a professor of biology and chemistry at the Massachusetts Institute of Technology. Here his research focused on the molecular mechanisms of visual transduction, specifically the way that rhodopsin, a biochemical receptor in the retina, transmits signals concerning light and color perception to the brain. His many honors include election to the National Academy of Sciences and the American Academy of Arts and Sciences.

Further Reading
MIT Department of Biology. "H. Gobind Khorana." Available online. URL: http://web.mit.edu/biology/facultyareas/facresearch/khorana.shtml. Downloaded on March 25, 2005.

Nobelprize.org. "The Nobel Prize in Physiology or Medicine 1968." Available online. URL: http://nobelprize.org/medicine/laureates/1968. Downloaded on June 18, 2004.

Wasson, Tyler, ed. *Nobel Prize Winners.* New York: H. W. Wilson, 1987, pp. 546–548.

Kilby, Jack S.
(Jack St. Clair Kilby)
(1923–   ) *electrical engineer*

Jack S. Kilby won a Nobel Prize in physics for his part in inventing the integrated circuit, popularly known as the microchip. This device revolutionized the electronics industry and eventually became the basis of a trillion-dollar-per-year industry of its own. He also invented the pocket calculator and the thermal printer.

Kilby was born on November 8, 1923, in Great Bend, Kansas. His father, Hubert, was the president of a small electric power company, and his mother, Vina, was a homemaker. In 1941 he entered the University of Illinois but he left after a semester to serve in the U.S. Army during World War II. He returned to Illinois after the war and received a B.S. in electrical engineering in 1947. He then moved to Milwaukee, Wisconsin, to work for the Centralab Division of Globe Union, Inc., which manufactured electronic parts for radios, televisions, and hearing aids. His duties at Centralab involved redesigning electrical circuits for printed circuit boards to make them smaller and more efficient. Meanwhile, he entered the graduate program at the University of Wisconsin and received an M.S. in electrical engineering in 1950. In 1948 he married Barbara Annegers with whom he had two children.

By 1958 Kilby had decided to devote himself full-time to the miniaturization of electronic components. Since Centralab lacked the facilities to support him in this endeavor, he went to work that same year for Texas Instruments (TI) in Dallas,

Texas. TI was already working with the U.S. military on the micro-module concept, whereby electronic components would be standardized and provided with built-in connections so they could be snapped together without wiring or soldering. Kilby, however, was not impressed with the micro-module concept; instead, he advocated reducing the number of individual parts, such as transistors, diodes, resistors, and capacitors, needed to make a complete electronic circuit. To this end he designed a device that combined the various components on a single silicon chip about half the size of a paper clip that could then be soldered to a circuit board. This device, which Kilby invented in 1958, was the first integrated circuit.

Kilby's integrated circuit had one major flaw, and that was that the various components were connected to one another on the chip by thin gold wire, a cost-prohibitive method. Meanwhile, researchers at the Fairchild Semiconductor Company in California were also designing an integrated circuit, and in early 1959 Robert N. Noyce, Fairchild's general manager, figured out how to connect the chip's components via a thin layer of conductive aluminum, a cheaper and more efficient method than Kilby's gold wire. Both TI and Fairchild received U.S. patents for inventing the integrated circuit, and after a long and heated debate in the electronics industry and the U.S. Patent Office it was decided that Kilby had invented the integrated circuit but that Noyce had made it work.

The integrated circuit made possible the development of smaller, faster computers, thus revolutionizing the way people all over the world work and access information. For the part he played in inventing the integrated circuit, Kilby was awarded a half share of the 2000 Nobel Prize in physics. Had Noyce been alive at the time—he had died in 1990—he almost certainly would have shared the prize as well. Kilby's corecipients were the Russian physicist Zhores I. Alferov and the German physicist Herbert Kroemer.

Having invented the integrated circuit, Kilby devoted the next 10 years to applying it in various missile systems and computers. Perhaps the most notable device he applied it to was the handheld, or pocket, calculator. At the time it was believed that there would be little interest in such a device as virtually every engineer and engineering student was proficient in the use of the slide rule, but in 1971 TI went ahead with production anyway. The first pocket calculator, known as the Pocketronic, weighed more than two pounds and cost $250. Nevertheless, it proved to be highly popular with consumers, and for years it was the most popular application of the integrated circuit. Kilby also used the integrated circuit to design and build the thermal printer, which was used extensively in portable data terminals.

In 1970 Kilby took a leave of absence from TI; although he never worked full-time for the company again, he worked as a part-time consultant until 1984 and maintained a working relationship with the company long after that. After eight years as a self-employed consultant, in 1978 he joined the faculty at Texas A&M University as a professor of electrical engineering. He retired in 1984, although he continued to consult part-time and to serve on the boards of directors of various companies in the electronics industry. His honors include the National Medal of Science and the National Medal of Technology and election to the National Academy of Engineering.

Further Reading

McMurray, Emily J., ed. *Notable Twentieth-Century Scientists*. Detroit: Gale Research, 1995, pp. 1,094–1,096.

Nobelprize.org. "The Nobel Prize in Physics 2000." Available online. URL: http://nobelprize.org/physics/laureates/2000. Downloaded on October 15, 2004.

Reid, T. R. *The Chip: How Two Americans Invented the Microchip and Launched a Revolution*. New York: Random House, 2001.

Knowles, William S.
(William Standish Knowles)
(1917–) *chemist*

William S. Knowles developed asymmetrical hydrogenation, a catalytic technique used in the production of many pharmaceutical drugs. For this contribution he was awarded a share of the 2001 Nobel Prize in chemistry.

Knowles was born on June 1, 1917, in Taunton, Massachusetts. His father, George, was in the textile business, and his mother, Alice, was a homemaker. As a boy he moved with his family to New Bedford where he grew up. After receiving a B.S. in chemistry from Harvard University in 1939, he entered Columbia University and received a Ph.D. in steroid chemistry in 1942. He then went to work as an industrial chemist for Thomas and Hochwalt Laboratories in Dayton, Ohio. Two years later, after the company was bought by the Monsanto Corporation, he transferred to Monsanto's headquarters in St. Louis, Missouri. In 1945 he married Lesley Cherbonnier with whom he had four children.

For the first 20 years of his career at Monsanto, Knowles focused his efforts on making the company's production facilities, which manufactured industrial chemicals as well as pharmaceutical drugs, operate as efficiently as possible. In the mid-1960s, however, he embarked on a study of a more theoretical nature. At the time, chemists were just beginning to understand that a molecule's structure, or the three-dimensional arrangement of its atoms, affects its reactivity just as much as the physical properties of the atoms themselves do. Pharmaceutical chemists had known for years that many of the drugs they produce involve molecules that come in two versions, a "right-hand" and a "left-hand" version. Although the two versions are composed of the exact same atoms, their structures mirror each other as the right hand mirrors the left hand. No one thought much about this situation because the only known solution was to separate out the preferred version and discard the other. This procedure cost so much, however, that, had it been implemented, it would have made the price of pharmaceuticals prohibitively high.

Then, in the early 1960s, a great tragedy involving the drug thalidomide occurred. Between 1959 and 1962, almost 3,000 babies in Germany and Great Britain were born with flipper-like appendages instead of arms. It was eventually determined that the cause of the birth defects was thalidomide, which had been prescribed to pregnant women as a treatment for nausea. Further study showed that the "right-hand" version of the drug does indeed inhibit nausea, but that the "left-hand" version causes serious birth defects.

This sobering demonstration of the importance of molecular structure got the attention of most pharmaceutical chemists and drug company executives, and Knowles decided to look for a cost-effective way to solve the right-hand/left-hand problem. He set out to design a catalyst, a chemical compound that initiates a chemical reaction, which would produce "right-hand" molecules without also producing "left-hand" ones. Eventually he found a catalyst that inserts two hydrogen atoms between two carbon atoms in such a way that the new molecule twists outward, the direction of the twist determining whether a "right-hand" or a "left-hand" version of the new molecule is produced. Knowles discovered that he could modify the molecular structure of the catalyst so that it causes all of the molecules it catalyzes to twist in only one way, thus preventing the "left-hand" version of the molecule from even being produced. This process became known as asymmetrical hydrogenation.

In 1968 Knowles used asymmetrical hydrogenation to produce L-dopa, a pharmaceutical that is prescribed as a treatment for some of the symptoms of Parkinson's disease. While the "right-hand" version of L-dopa is therapeutic, the "left-hand" version, known as D-dopa, is toxic. Normal production of L-dopa, as with all pharmaceuticals produced from two-version molecules, yields roughly 50 percent of each version, but by using asymmetric hydrogenation Knowles was able to increase the yield of L-dopa to 97.5 percent of a given batch. That same year Monsanto began using asymmetrical hydrogenation to produce L-dopa commercially, and before long it was standard procedure for the manufacture of virtually every pharmaceutical drug that has a right-hand and a left-hand version.

Asymmetrical hydrogenation revolutionized the pharmaceutical industry by giving manufacturers a way to produce more effective drugs at a fraction of the cost. For his role in developing it, Knowles was awarded a quarter share of the 2001 Nobel Prize in chemistry. His corecipients were the Japanese chemist Ryoji Noyori (one-quarter share) and the American chemist K. BARRY SHARPLESS (one-half share).

Knowles worked at Monsanto until his retirement in 1986. He worked as a consultant for several years thereafter and eventually retired for good, first to his home in St. Louis and later to Kelly, Wyoming.

Further Reading

Chang, Kenneth. "3 Win Nobel for Better Chemical Reactions," *New York Times*, October 11, 2001, p. A20.

The Nobel Prize Internet Archive. "William S. Knowles." Available online. URL: http://almaz.com/nobel/chemistry/2001a.html. Downloaded on March 25, 2005.

Nobelprize.org. "The Nobel Prize in Chemistry 2001." Available online. URL: http://nobelprize.org/chemistry/laureates/2001. Downloaded on August 18, 2004.

Kohn, Walter
(1923–) *physicist*

Walter Kohn played a leading role in the development of the density functional theory, which explains mathematically how atoms are bound together to form molecules. For this contribution, he was awarded a half share of the 1998 Nobel Prize in chemistry.

Kohn was born on March 9, 1923, in Vienna, Austria. His father, Solomon, was an art publisher, and his mother, Gittel, was a homemaker. A refugee from the Nazi takeover of Austria, he emigrated at age 16 to England but left the following year for Canada, where he spent several years in various internment camps. In 1942 he enrolled in the University of Toronto, leaving after his junior year to serve in the Canadian army during World War II. He returned to Toronto after the war and received a B.A. in mathematics and physics and an M.A. in applied mathematics in 1945 and 1946, respectively. He then entered the graduate physics program at Harvard University and received a Ph.D. in 1948. He taught physics at Harvard for two years before joining the faculty at the Carnegie Institute of Technology (today Carnegie-Mellon University) in Pittsburgh, Pennsylvania, where he taught physics for 10 years. In 1960 he left Carnegie-Mellon for a similar position at the University of California at San Diego (UCSD). He was married twice and had three children, and in 1957 he became a naturalized U.S. citizen.

Kohn's early research involved quantum field theory, the study of the interaction of subatomic particles. While at Harvard, he assisted JULIAN S. SCHWINGER, a pioneer in quantum electrodynamics, and he developed what is today known as the Kohn variational principle for scattering. This elementary mathematical formulation is used to determine the distribution of the subatomic particles that comprise a target atom or molecule after the target has been bombarded by other subatomic particles. He also developed a variational approach for studying the wave functions of electrons in certain types of crystals.

By 1950 Kohn had become more interested in solid-state physics, the study of the various physical properties of semiconductors, substances that conduct electricity better than nonconductors such as glass but not as well as good conductors such as copper. From 1953 to 1966 he spent his summers at the Bell Telephone Laboratory in Murray Hill, New Jersey, where he collaborated with JOHN BARDEEN, WALTER H. BRATTAIN, and WILLIAM B. SHOCKLEY, the pioneers of solid-state physics and the inventors of

Walter Kohn explained how atoms bind together to form molecules. *(Courtesy of Walter Kohn)*

the transistor, a device that was fundamental to the early development of solid-state electronics. During this period he described the so-called Kohn anomaly, a particular type of interaction between the surface of constant energy that surrounds a semiconductor's electrons and the vibrational energy of an electron trying to flow through the semiconductor.

By 1963 transistors were being constructed from alloys of semiconductors and other elements, and Kohn became interested in the electronic structures of these new alloys. Previously, physicists and metallurgists had tried to understand electronic structures in terms of the wave function of electrons, but they had enjoyed little success because this approach depends on the positions of all the electrons in a wave and thus is too complex to be of much use except in the simplest of cases. Kohn realized that an electronic structure's energy level is directly proportional to its electron density, which is a function of only three positional coordinates. By 1965 he and his collaborators, Pierre Hohenberg and Lu J. Sham, had developed and published a set of relatively simple equations by which the energy level and electron density of an electronic structure can be calculated.

Kohn's work with electronic structures became known as the density functional theory (DFT), and it proved to have applications beyond solid-state electronics. DFT made it much easier, for example, for chemists to understand the bonds that hold together chemical compounds and for biochemists to understand what happens during chemical reactions involving enzymes. In fact, because of DFT's wide-ranging applications to chemistry and biochemistry, Kohn, a theoretical physicist, was awarded a half share of the 1998 Nobel Prize in chemistry.

Meanwhile, in 1979 Kohn left UCSD to become the founding director of the National Science Foundation's Institute of Theoretical Physics at the University of California at Santa Barbara (UCSB). He stepped down as director in 1984 and retired from teaching in 1991, but he remained at UCSB as a research professor and continued to conduct experiments concerning electronic structures and other problems related to theoretical

chemistry. His many honors include the National Medal of Science and election to the National Academy of Sciences and the American Academy of Arts and Sciences.

Further Reading

Kohn, Walter, Matthias Scheffler, and Peter Weinberger. *Walter Kohn: Personal Stories and Anecdotes Told by Friends and Collaborators.* New York: Springer, 2003.
Nobelprize.org. "The Nobel Prize in Chemistry 1998." Available online. URL: http://nobelprize.org/chemistry/laureates/1998. Downloaded on July 30, 2004.

Kornberg, Arthur
(1918–) *biochemist*

Arthur Kornberg was the first to synthesize deoxyribonucleic acid (DNA), the carrier of genetic information at the molecular level. For this achievement, and for discovering the mechanisms by which DNA is produced naturally, he was awarded a share of the 1959 Nobel Prize in physiology or medicine.

Kornberg was born on March 3, 1918, in New York City to Joseph and Lena Kornberg. After receiving a B.S. from the College of the City of New York in 1937, he entered the University of Rochester (N.Y.) School of Medicine, receiving an M.D. in 1941. He then interned for a year at Rochester's Strong Memorial Hospital, and in 1942 he was commissioned an officer in the U.S. Public Health Service and assigned to the National Institutes of Health (NIH) in Bethesda, Maryland. In 1943 he married Sylvy Levy with whom he had three children.

While in medical school, Kornberg became interested in enzymes, complex proteins that initiate biochemical reactions, and he continued to study them at NIH. He focused his research on better understanding the "one gene–one enzyme" principle discovered by GEORGE W. BEADLE and EDWARD L. TATUM in 1941, by which the production and activity of each particular enzyme is controlled by one particular gene. He also helped discover the biochemical functions by which cells produce the coenzymes flavin adenine dinucleotide and diphosphopyridine nucleotide.

In 1953 Kornberg left NIH to teach microbiology at Washington University in St. Louis, Missouri. That same year JAMES D. WATSON and Francis Crick developed a model for the structure of DNA, and Kornberg became interested in synthesizing the DNA molecule. The Watson-Crick model showed that the DNA molecule looks like two long intertwined ladders, the so-called double helix. Each rung consists of two compounds known as nucleotides, either adenine and thymine or cytosine and guanine, that are connected end-to-end at the middle of the rung. The rungs are connected by links made of a phosphate compound and a sugar known as deoxyribose, and they are arranged so that only the deoxyribose touches the rungs. The rungs can be arranged in infinite varieties of adenine-thymine pairs and cytosine-guanine pairs, and in most DNA molecules the ladders contain thousands of rungs.

Using the common intestinal bacteria *Escherichia coli* (*E. coli*), the subject of some of Tatum's research, Kornberg discovered that the enzyme DNA polymerase plays an important role in DNA replication. Watson and Crick had hypothesized that genetic coding is carried along the middle of the DNA ladder rungs. When the DNA molecule replicates itself, the ladders split in half along the middle of the rungs and then reconstruct themselves into complete ladders that are identical to the original ladders. Kornberg discovered that DNA polymerase interprets the coding from the ladder half to be replicated and then assembles the four nucleotides in the proper sequences in the new DNA ladder half. Using methods developed by SEVERO OCHOA, in 1957 Kornberg and his associates produced a giant molecule of artificial *E. coli* DNA; although it resembled "real" DNA exactly in terms of its chemical and physical composition, it could not be replicated. Nevertheless, this development corroborated the Watson-Crick hypothesis about DNA replication, and it led to a Nobel Prize for Watson and Crick. It also led to Kornberg being awarded a half share of the 1959 Nobel Prize in physiology or medicine; his corecipient was Ochoa.

In 1959 Kornberg was named head of the department of biochemistry at the Stanford University School of Medicine in Palo Alto, California,

where he continued to experiment with synthetic DNA. He soon discovered that the reason his *E. coli* DNA did not "work" was because the DNA polymerase he had used was not pure enough. Other enzymes had affected it in a way that caused it to rearrange the nucleotides incorrectly. Abandoning *E. coli* as a research subject, he and Mehran Goulian, a Stanford colleague, switched to Phi X174, a virus that infects *E. coli*. Phi X174 DNA is single stranded and circular rather than double stranded and helical like *E. coli*, and therefore it promised to be much easier to replicate. Using a much purer sample of DNA polymerase, in 1966 Kornberg and Goulian were able to synthesize a perfect ring of Phi X174 DNA, which consists of approximately 6,000 rungs. When this synthetic DNA was introduced into a colony of *E. coli*, it quickly infected the colony exactly as if it had been "real" Phi X174 DNA. This result opened the door to the possibility that future researchers will be able to alter viral DNA in such a way that makes deadly viruses harmless, and it is potentially more important than the one that won him the Nobel Prize. As a means to further such research, in 1980 he cofounded DNAX Research Institute of Molecular and Cellular Biology, a division of the pharmaceutical firm Schering-Plough, Inc., and he served on the scientific and advisory boards of several other biotech companies.

Kornberg remained at Stanford for the rest of his career. In the 1990s he switched the focus of his research from DNA to inorganic polyphosphate, a linear polymer that plays an important role in facilitating the behavioral functions of certain microorganisms. He was awarded the National Medal of Science, he was elected to the National Academy of Sciences and the American Academy of Arts and Sciences, and he served a term as president of the American Society of Biological Chemists. His books include *Enzymatic Synthesis of DNA* (1962), *DNA Synthesis* (1974), *DNA Replication* (2nd ed., 1992), and *The Golden Helix: Inside Biotech Ventures* (1995).

Further Reading

Hargittai, Istvan, and Magdolna Hargittai. *Candid Science II: Conversations with Famous Biomedical Scientists.* London: Imperial College Press, 2002, pp. 50–72.

Kornberg, Arthur. *For the Love of Enzymes: The Odyssey of a Biochemist*. Cambridge, Mass.: Harvard University Press, 1989.

Nobelprize.org. "The Nobel Prize in Physiology or Medicine 1959." Available online. URL: http://nobelprize.org/medicine/laureates/1959. Downloaded on May 9, 2004.

Wasson, Tyler, ed. *Nobel Prize Winners*. New York: H. W. Wilson, 1987, pp. 570–572.

Kountz, Samuel L., Jr.
(Samuel Lee Kountz, Jr.)
(1930–1981) *medical researcher*

Samuel L. Kountz was the foremost kidney transplant specialist of his day. He developed many of the procedures and apparatuses that are still used in kidney transplant surgery.

Kountz was born on October 20, 1930, in Lexa, Arkansas. His father, Samuel, was a minister, and his mother was a homemaker. After receiving a B.S. in 1952 from Arkansas Agricultural, Mechanical and Normal College (today the University of Arkansas at Pine Bluff), he entered the graduate chemistry program at the University of Arkansas. Two years later he transferred to the university's medical school, receiving an M.S. in chemistry in 1956 and an M.D. in 1958. That same year he married Grace Akin with whom he had three children. Following a one-year internship at San Francisco (Calif.) General Hospital, he entered the Stanford University School of Medicine to study surgery. In 1961, while still a resident, Kountz and Roy Cohn, one of his professors, performed the first successful kidney transplant between two people who were not twins.

Kountz was affiliated with Stanford until 1967, having been named a professor of surgery the previous year. During this period he began experimenting on dogs in an effort to find ways to prevent the body from rejecting a donor kidney, a problem that continued to plague kidney recipients despite his and Cohn's success. Kountz soon discovered that the steroid methylprednisolone could reverse the rejection process if large amounts of it were administered immediately following surgery, but if too much methylprednisolone were administered the dog would die. Further observation revealed that the process of kidney rejection begins at the junction between the blood vessels of the body and the kidney, so that the donated kidney eventually dies from lack of blood. To solve this problem, he developed a method for monitoring the flow of blood to the donated kidney; when the flow slowed, more methylprednisolone was administered, but when the flow resumed, the drug treatment was suspended until flow slowed again.

In 1967 Kountz was named chief of the kidney transplant service at the University of California at San Francisco (UCSF), and over the next five years he developed a first-rate kidney transplant research center at UCSF. That same year he began collaborating with Folker Belzer, a UCSF colleague, on ways to preserve a kidney after it had been removed from a donor's body. This work led eventually to the development of the Belzer kidney perfusion machine, which was capable of keeping alive a donated kidney for up to 50 hours outside a body. He led a team of researchers in developing tissue-typing tests as an aid in ensuring that a donor's kidney had the best possible chance of not being rejected by its recipient. Having come to realize that a patient's psychological outlook played an important role in whether or not kidney transplantation was successful, he established intense, personalized nursing care for kidney recipients and started a support group where prospective recipients could discuss their concerns with kidney transplant survivors and health-care professionals. In 1972 Kountz left UCSF for the State University of New York's Downstate Medical Center in Brooklyn; he was also named chief of surgery at Kings County Hospital. Over the next five years he built up Downstate's organ transplant unit into one of the best on the East Coast.

During his career, Kountz performed more than 1,000 kidney transplants. In addition to his other duties, he traveled the world to teach his methods to other medical researchers; on one of these trips he performed the first successful kidney transplant in the Middle East. In 1977 he developed brain damage from an undiagnosed disease he caught while visiting South Africa, and he was never able to perform surgery again. He died from this disease on December 23, 1981, in Great Neck, New York.

Further Reading

The Faces of Science: African Americans in the Sciences. "Dr. Samuel L. Kountz, Jr.: Kidney Specialist." Available online. URL: http://www.princeton.edu/~mcbrown/display/kountz.html. Downloaded on March 25, 2005.

McMurray, Emily J., ed. *Notable Twentieth Century Scientists*. Detroit: Gale Research, 1995, pp. 1,130–1,131.

Spangenburg, Ray, and Kit Moser. *African Americans in Science, Math, and Invention*. New York: Facts On File, 2003, pp. 150–152.

Krebs, Edwin G.
(Edwin Gerhard Krebs)
(1918–) *biochemist*

Edwin G. Krebs codiscovered reversible protein phosphorylation, the process by which enzymes activate and deactivate other enzymes. For his role in this discovery, he was awarded a share of the 1992 Nobel Prize in physiology or medicine.

Krebs was born on June 6, 1918, in Lansing, Iowa. His father, William, was a minister, and his mother, Louise, was a homemaker. As a boy he moved with his family to the Illinois towns of Newton, Greenville, and Urbana. He received a B.S. in chemistry from the University of Illinois in Urbana in 1940, and then he entered the Washington University School of Medicine in St. Louis, Missouri, receiving an M.D. in 1943. After completing his internship at Barnes Hospital in St. Louis, he joined the U.S. Navy and served as a medical officer during World War II. In 1946 he returned to Washington University as a postdoctoral fellow in the laboratory of CARL F. CORI and GERTY T. CORI, leaving four years later to teach pharmacology and biochemistry at the University of Washington Medical School in Seattle, where he remained for the rest of his career. In 1945 he married Virginia French with whom he had three children.

Krebs's research focused on phosphorylase, an enzyme that plays an important role in the Cori cycle. Discovered by the Coris, this cycle describes the pathway by which glucose, a simple sugar that circulates freely in the bloodstream and is the source of energy for cell function, is stored and released for use by the muscles. The Coris under-

Edwin Krebs (above) and Edmond Fischer showed how certain enzymes activate and deactivate other enzymes. *(Courtesy of Edwin G. Krebs)*

stood the role played by phosphorylase—it adds phosphorus to glucose so that it can be stored in the muscles—but they could not explain why phosphorylase appears in the bloodstream in both an active and an inactive form. They concluded that inactive phosphorylase requires the addition of a biochemical compound known as 5'-AMP (a form of adenosine monophosphate) to make it active, while active phosphorylase does not. Krebs studied phosphorylase at Washington University under the Coris and at the University of Washington on his own. In 1953 he formed a partnership with EDMOND H. FISCHER to find out what role 5'-AMP plays in the activation of phosphorylase.

Krebs and Fischer never did find the answer to this mystery—it was solved in the early 1960s by French biochemist Jacques Monod—mostly because in 1959, while they were looking for it, they discovered phosphorylase kinase. This enzyme activates phosphorylase by transferring to it a phosphate group (phosphorus and oxygen) from adenine triphosphate (ATP), the biochemical compound that fuels the activities of the cells. Over the next nine years, Krebs and Fischer discovered that the activation of phosphorylase is reversible; another enzyme, phosphorylase phosphatase, inactivates phosphorylase by removing the phosphate group. They also discovered that the production of phosphorylase kinase and phosphorylase phosphatase is affected by a variety of biochemical signals. Phosphorylase kinase, which results in the muscles being supplied with energy, can be activated by means of a stress hormone, as when one is preparing to fight or flee, as well as by a simple act of will, as when one decides to walk across the room. By the same token, the deactivation of stress hormones or the decision to sit down can cause the production of phosphorylase phosphatase. This process is today known as reversible protein phosphorylation, so named because enzymes are proteins.

Krebs and Fischer interrupted their partnership in 1968 when Krebs went to the University of California at Davis to establish a department of biochemistry, but their work influenced a number of other researchers. In time, these researchers discovered that virtually every enzyme is regulated by other enzymes acting in the same way that phosphorylase kinase and phosphorylase phosphatase act. The protein kinase that is specific to a given enzyme activates it by adding a phosphate group, while the specific protein phosphatase deactivates the enzyme by removing the phosphate group. Thus, a number of diseases and medical conditions, especially such common ones as hypertension and tumors, could be investigated based on the possibility that they are caused by a dysfunction in the phosphorylation process. Krebs and Fischer's discovery also led to a better understanding of cellular functions in general, almost all of which are initiated by enzymes. Consequently, their discovery opened the door to a new field of biomedical research, and they were each awarded a half share of the 1992 Nobel Prize in physiology or medicine.

Meanwhile, in 1977 Krebs returned to the University of Washington, this time as chair of the department of pharmacology, and resumed his collaboration with Fischer. Krebs's many honors include election to the National Academy of Sciences and the American Academy of Arts and Sciences. In 1988 the University of Washington named him a professor emeritus, and since then he has continued to study protein phosphorylation, particularly the role it plays in apoptosis, the programmed death of a cell.

Further Reading

McMurray, Emily J., ed. *Notable Twentieth-Century Scientists.* Detroit: Gale Research, 1995, pp. 1,132–1,133.

National Academy of Sciences. "Membership Listing: Krebs, Edwin G." Available online. URL: http://www4.nationalacademies.org/nas/naspub.nsf/0/DF5F42393949DB3D852569DF006EF86A?open document. Downloaded on March 25, 2005.

Nobelprize.org. "The Nobel Prize in Physiology or Medicine 1992." Available online. URL: http://nobelprize.org/medicine/laureates/1992. Downloaded on June 11, 2004.

Kuiper, Gerard P.
(Gerard Peter Kuiper, Gerrit Pieter Kuiper)
(1905–1973) *astronomer*

At a time when most astronomers were more interested in studying the distant stars, Gerard Kuiper remained focused on the solar system. He made a number of important discoveries concerning the moons of the system's planets, and he played an integral role in the success of the Apollo mission to put a man on the Moon in 1969.

Kuiper was born Gerrit Pieter Kuiper on December 7, 1905, in Harenkarspel, the Netherlands. His father, Gerrit, was a tailor, and his mother, Antje, was a homemaker. At age 19 he enrolled in the astronomy program at the University of Leiden and received a B.Sc. in 1927 and a Ph.D. in 1933. While at Leiden, he worked as an assistant in the university observatory and went to Sumatra as part of a Dutch solar eclipse expedition. In 1933 he accepted a position as a staff astronomer at the Lick Observatory in California, but he left two years later for a similar position at the Harvard College Observatory. In 1936 he became a professor of astronomy at the University of Chicago and a member of the staff of its Yerkes Observatory. That same year he married Sarah Fuller with whom he had two children, and in 1937 he became a naturalized citizen of the United States.

While at Chicago, Kuiper focused his research efforts on exploring the solar system, particularly the moons of the various planets. In 1944 he discovered that Titan, a moon of Saturn, has a methane atmosphere; prior to this discovery, it was believed that no moon in the solar system possessed an atmosphere of any kind. In 1948 he discovered Miranda, the fifth moon of Uranus, and Nereid, the second moon of Neptune. That same year he discovered carbon dioxide in the atmosphere of Mars, an indication that the planet might once have sustained plant life similar to that of Earth. In 1951 he proposed the existence of an area between the orbits of Uranus and Pluto that contained debris from the solar system's formation. He also suggested that this area serves as the origin for a number of the comets that pass through the solar system. Little was made of this suggestion until 1992, when other researchers confirmed its existence. Today this area is known as the Kuiper belt.

In 1960 Kuiper left Chicago for the University of Arizona in Tucson to become head of its new Lunar and Planetary Laboratory (LPL). In this capacity he enjoyed a long association with the National Aeronautics and Space Administration. Right about the time that Kuiper established LPL, NASA was working to put a man on the Moon, and the agency supported LPL with millions of dollars for buildings and telescopes. In return, Kuiper helped NASA solve sev-

Gerard Kuiper briefs the press before the Ranger VII lunar mission. *(Courtesy of National Aeronautics and Space Administration)*

eral problems related to the Moon mission. His most important contribution in this regard involved the Ranger lunar probe project. After the first five Rangers failed to complete their missions, Kuiper was invited to reorganize the project and redesign the probe. As a result, Rangers 7, 8, and 9 transmitted back to Earth more than 17,000 high-resolution photographs of the Moon, many from as close as 1,000 feet above the lunar surface. These photographs made it possible to select the best area for the Apollo lunar lander to touch down, thus contributing to humankind's first steps on the Moon.

In addition to his duties at LPL, Kuiper also helped survey new locations for observatories, including important facilities at Cerro Tololo in Chile and Mauna Kea in Hawaii. On Christmas Eve, 1973, while on a similar trip to Mexico, he suffered a heart attack and died in Mexico City.

Kuiper's many honors included election to the National Academy of Sciences, appointment to the Dutch Order of Orange-Nassau, and receipt of the Janssen Medal of the French Astronomical Society. After his death, craters on the Moon, Mars, and Mercury were named in his honor. In 1975 the Kuiper Airborne Observatory was named in his honor; this 36-inch telescope mounted in a C-141 airplane permits the observation of infrared radiation from planets, stars, and galaxies that is filtered out by Earth's lower atmosphere. In 1984 the Division for Planetary Sciences of the American Astronomical Society named one of its annual prizes in his honor.

Further Reading

Cruikshank, Dale P. "Gerard Peter Kuiper," National Academy of Sciences, *Biographical Memoirs* 62 (1993): pp. 258–295.

The Encyclopedia of Astrobiology, Astronomy, and Spaceflight. "Kuiper, Gerard Peter (1905–1973)." Available online. URL: http://www.daviddarling.info/encyclopedia/K/KuiperGP/html. Downloaded on December 19, 2003.

Kusch, Polykarp
(1911–1993) *physicist*

Polykarp Kusch won a share of the 1955 Nobel Prize in physics for discovering the anomalous mag-netic moment of the electron. This achievement had a profound effect on the development of quantum electrodynamics, the body of theory concerning the interactions of charged particles within a nucleus's electromagnetic field.

Kusch was born on January 26, 1911, in Blankenburg, Germany. His father, John, was a minister, and his mother, Henrietta, was a homemaker. The year after his birth his family moved to the United States and settled in Cleveland, Ohio, where he grew up, and in 1922 he became a naturalized U.S. citizen. After receiving a B.S. in physics from the Case School of Applied Science (today Case Western Reserve University) in Cleveland in 1931, he entered the graduate program at the University of Illinois and received an M.S. and a Ph.D. in physics in 1933 and 1936, respectively. He spent the next two years teaching physics at the University of Minnesota. In 1938 he accepted a faculty position at Columbia University in New York City. Three years earlier he had married Edith McRoberts with whom he had three children; she died in 1959, and the following year he married Betty Pezzoni with whom he had two children.

At Columbia, Kusch collaborated with I. I. RABI on the development of an experimental tool known as molecular beam magnetic resonance, also known as the magnetic resonance method. This procedure beams molecules through a series of magnetic fields whose strengths are increased or decreased via radio frequency. In 1940 Kusch, Rabi, and Sidney Millman coauthored a paper on the radio frequency of atoms. Their partnership was broken up, however, by World War II, during which Kusch experimented with microwave vacuum tubes as a means of generating the microwaves used by radar.

In 1946 Kusch turned his attention to the magnetic properties of electrons, which behave like miniature magnets. Specifically, he wanted to measure exactly a spinning electron's magnetic moment, the product of its pole strength and the distance between its poles. The prevailing theory of quantum electrodynamics held that the magnetic moment of a spinning electron was $1.00119 \times 9.273 \times 10^{-21}$ erg/gauss/particle (the second number is the value of the Bohr magneton, the unit of magnetic moment used in the study of subatomic particles).

However, certain measurements of electronic behavior suggested that the multiplier 1.00119 might be inaccurate.

By 1948 Kusch had developed a procedure for determining the exact value of the multiplier by generating magnetic resonance via microwave vacuum tubes. In the process, he determined that the correct value was 1.00116, not 1.00119, and the difference between the two values became known as the anomalous magnetic moment. Although the value of the anomalous magnetic moment—a mere three hundred-thousandths—seems too minuscule to be important, it was actually quite a significant discovery, because it called for the complete reworking of quantum electrodynamics theory in order to explain the difference. Over the years, other physicists, most notably RICHARD P. FEYNMAN and JULIAN S. SCHWINGER, did exactly that, in the process arriving at a more sophisticated and accurate understanding of quantum electrodynamics. For his contribution to this development, Kusch was awarded a half share of the 1955 Nobel Prize in physics, his corecipient was the American physicist WILLIS E. LAMB.

Kusch's other honors include election to the National Academy of Sciences. In 1972 he retired from Columbia and moved to Dallas, Texas, where he taught physics at the University of Texas. He retired from Texas in 1982, and he died on March 20, 1993, in Dallas.

Further Reading

The Nobel Prize Internet Archive. "Polykarp Kusch." Available online. URL: http://almaz.com/nobel/physics/1955b.html. Downloaded on March 25, 2005.

Nobelprize.org. "The Nobel Prize in Physics 1955." Available online. URL: http://nobelprize.org/physics/laureates/1955. Downloaded on March 22, 2004.

Wasson, Tyler, ed. *Nobel Prize Winners*. New York: H. W. Wilson, 1987, pp. 579–580.

L

Lamb, Willis E., Jr.
(Willis Eugene Lamb, Jr.)
(1913–   ) *physicist*

Willis E. Lamb discovered the Lamb shift, an important step in the development of quantum electrodynamics. This contribution won him a share of the 1955 Nobel Prize in physics.

Lamb was born on July 12, 1913, in Los Angeles, California. His father, Willis Sr., was a telephone engineer, and his mother, Marie, was a homemaker. He was educated at the University of California at Berkeley, receiving a B.S. in chemistry in 1934 and a Ph.D. in theoretical physics in 1938. That same year he became a professor of physics at Columbia University, and the following year he married Ursula Schaefer; she died in 1996, and that same year he married Bruria Kaufman.

As a graduate student, Lamb became interested in the electromagnetic properties of atoms and molecules. He continued to pursue this interest at Columbia, where he became a collaborator of I. I. RABI. In 1937 Rabi had developed the magnetic resonance method, by which the magnetic properties of molecules could be measured by beaming the molecules through a series of magnetic fields, the strengths of which were modified via radio waves, and Lamb worked with Rabi on several projects that utilized the magnetic resonance method. During World War II, Lamb and Rabi collaborated on projects related to the development of microwave technology for use in radar.

After the war, Lamb became involved in atomic spectroscopy, the study of the inner workings of atoms and molecules by examining the light spectra they emit. Using microwave technology to enhance the magnetic resonance method, he began studying the fine structure, the splitting of a spectral line into two or more components, each of which represents a slightly different wavelength of a single electron in an atom's outermost orbit. In 1928 English physicist Paul Dirac had developed a set of equations to describe the behavior of electrons, but no one had been able to verify the correctness of the equations via experimental data. In fact, much of the experimental data suggested that Dirac's equations were inaccurate in terms of describing the fine structure. In an effort to verify or disprove Dirac's theory as it applies to the fine structure, Lamb began studying the fine structure of hydrogen, which has only one electron, and in 1947 he was able to demonstrate conclusively the deficiencies in Dirac's theory. Lamb showed that the two fine structure lines for hydrogen that should coincide according to the Dirac theory are in reality shifted relative to each other by a certain amount, which he explained in terms of the interaction between the electron and the electromagnetic radiation it absorbs from subatomic particles in its nucleus. This amount eventually became known as the Lamb shift, and much of his subsequent research was devoted to measuring this shift with great accuracy.

The actual amount of the Lamb shift is exceedingly small. Nevertheless, its discovery resulted in a complete overhaul of quantum electrodynamics, the interactions of subatomic particles with each other and with the various forms of electromagnetic radiation such as light, much of which was performed by JULIAN S. SCHWINGER and RICHARD P. FEYNMAN. For his contribution, Lamb was awarded a half share of the 1955 Nobel Prize in physics.

In 1951 Lamb left Columbia, and over the next 23 years he was affiliated with Stanford University (1951–56), Oxford University in England (1956–62), and Yale University (1962–74). In 1974 he was named a professor of physics and optical sciences at the University of Arizona, and in 1983 he was named head of the Arizona Research Laboratory. Despite the frequent change of locale, his research continued to focus on the quantum mechanics of optical phenomena and the theory of its measurement. His publications include *Laser Physics* (1974) and *The Interpretation of Quantum Mechanics* (2001). His other honors include the National Medal of Science and election to the National Academy of Sciences.

Further Reading

Nobelprize.org. "The Nobel Prize in Physics 1955." Available online. URL: http://nobelprize.org/physics/laureates/1955. Downloaded on September 5, 2004.

Ter Haar, Dik, and Marlon O. Scully, eds. *Willis E. Lamb, Jr.: A Festschrift on the Occasion of His 65th Birthday.* New York: North Holland Pub. Co., 1978.

Wasson, Tyler, ed. *Nobel Prize Winners.* New York: H. W. Wilson, 1987, pp. 589–591.

Landsteiner, Karl

(1868–1943) *biochemist*

Karl Landsteiner was the foremost authority on human blood of his day. He discovered the four types of human blood, and he collaborated in the discovery of the Rh factor by which blood is classified as being either positive or negative. These discoveries revolutionized the way the medical community regards and handles blood, and won him a Nobel Prize.

Landsteiner was born on June 14, 1868, in Vienna, Austria. His father, Leopold, was a journalist and newspaper publisher, and his mother, Fanny, was a homemaker. After completing his preparatory schooling, he studied medicine at the University of Vienna and received an M.D. in 1891. Over the next five years he studied chemistry at several European universities and served as an assistant in the University of Vienna's medical and surgical clinics. In 1896 he became an assistant at the university's Institute of Hygiene, where he began the first of many experiments involving human blood. Studying the effects of immune blood serum on bacteria cultures led him to become interested in the new field of immunology, and in 1898 he transferred to the university's Institute of Pathological Anatomy.

Like many medical researchers of the day, Landsteiner was perplexed by the relatively low success rate of blood transfusions involving two humans. Sometimes a transfusion benefited the recipient greatly, but more often than not it caused the recipient of the blood more harm than good. This curious fact led Landsteiner to theorize that there is more than one type of human blood, and over the next several years he devoted his research efforts to either proving or disproving this theory.

In 1900 Landsteiner observed that every time a blood transfusion resulted in complications for the recipient, clumping occurred among some of the recipient's red corpuscles. He then focused his research on the study of red corpuscles, and in 1901 he discovered the existence of two types of agglutinogens, which stimulate the production of antibodies, which in turn attack organisms foreign to the body. He further discovered that some red corpuscles contain one type, which he labeled "A," some contain the other type, which he labeled "B," and some contain neither type. As a result of these discoveries, he concluded that there are three different types of human blood; "A" blood contains "A" agglutinogens, "B" blood contains "B" agglutinogens, and "C" blood contains no agglutinogens. In 1902 his research associates discovered that some red corpuscles contain both "A" and "B" agglutinogens. This discovery led him to reclassify the blood types into four groups; A, B, AB, and O (Landsteiner renamed "C" blood "0," for zero agglutinogens, but it later became known as "O").

It took doctors and hospitals about 10 years to fully grasp the implications of the existence of four types of human blood instead of just one, but by the outbreak of World War I in 1914, the medical community had realized the need and developed the technology to identify donor and recipient blood types before giving a blood transfusion. The discovery also made it possible to successfully perform operations that involve a tremendous loss of blood, such as those involving the heart, lungs, and circulatory system, as the patient could now be transfused with the proper type of blood. By 1930 the magnitude of Landsteiner's work was fully understood, and that same year he was awarded the Nobel Prize for physiology or medicine.

Meanwhile, Landsteiner had temporarily abandoned the study of blood to focus more on pathology, the study of the origin, nature, and course of diseases. Between 1902 and 1912 he discovered that exposure to cold causes paroxysmal hemoglobinuria (the presence of hemoglobin pigment in the urine), he improved the Wassermann test for detecting syphilis, and he concluded that poliomyelitis (polio) was caused by a viral infection. During this period he began teaching pathology at the University of Vienna and joined the pathology staff at Vienna's Royal-Imperial Wilhelmina Hospital.

Medical research in Vienna was brought to a virtual standstill following Austria's defeat in World War I, and in 1919 Landsteiner decided to pursue better opportunities elsewhere. He spent three years at the R.K. Hospital in The Hague, the Netherlands, and in 1922 he joined the staff of the Rockefeller Institute for Medical Research (later known as Rockefeller University) in New York City. Here he returned to his earlier fascination with the chemistry of human blood. After conducting a three-year comparative study of human, monkey, and ape blood, he concluded that the three bloods are too different for humans to have descended from any existing primate species, but that the three bloods are so similar that all three species are probably descended from a common primate ancestor.

Landsteiner had earlier become convinced that, despite the existence of the four blood types, each person's blood is unique. In 1925 he embarked on a search for other distinguishing factors in human blood, and two years later he and Philip Levine discovered three new agglutinogens, which they labeled "M," "N," and "P." Further investigation, however, determined that these agglutinogens usually occur only in abnormal blood. In 1940 Landsteiner, Levine, and Alexander S. Weiner discovered a blood antigen known as the Rh factor in red blood cells. Further investigation by the three Rockefeller colleagues determined that 85 percent of the population is Rh positive while the remaining 15 percent is negative, and that mixing positive and negative blood, even of the same blood type, can have the same result as mixing two blood types. As a pathologist as well as a biochemist, Landsteiner was able to use this discovery to develop a treatment for erythroblastosis, a condition involving the dissolution of red corpuscles in fetuses and newborns whose father is Rh positive and whose mother is Rh negative.

In addition to the Nobel Prize, Landsteiner received a number of awards during his lifetime, including election to the French Legion of Honor in 1911 and the National Academy of Sciences in 1932. He was married in 1916 to the former Helene Wlasto with whom he had one child, and in 1929 he became an American citizen. He died on June 26, 1943, in New York City.

Further Reading

Nobelprize.org. "The Nobel Prize in Physiology or Medicine 1930." Available online. URL: http://nobelprize. org/medicine/laureates/1930. Downloaded on July 5, 2003.

Speiser, Paul, and Ferdinand Smekal. *Karl Landsteiner, the Discoverer of the Blood-Groups and a Pioneer in the Field of Immunology.* Vienna, Austria: Hollinek, 1975.

Wasson, Tyler, ed. *Nobel Prize Winners.* New York: H. W. Wilson, 1987, pp. 593–595.

Langmuir, Irving
(1881–1957) *chemist*

Irving Langmuir was one of the leading researchers and inventors of his day. He received more than 60 patents during his career, and his achievements as an industrial researcher inspired many companies and government agencies to establish research laboratories of their own. In 1932 he was awarded the Nobel Prize in chemistry.

Langmuir was born on January 31, 1881, in Brooklyn, New York. His father, Charles, was an insurance executive, and his mother, Sadie, was a homemaker. After receiving a public school education, he enrolled in the Columbia University School of Mines and received a B.S. in metallurgical engineering in 1903. He spent the next three years at the University of Göttingen in Germany where he studied under Walther Nernst, one of the first scientists to study the relationship between physics and chemistry, and he received a Ph.D. in chemistry in 1906. That same year he joined the faculty of the Stevens Institute of Technology (today New Jersey Institute of Technology) as an instructor of chemistry. Three years later he left teaching to accept a research position with the General Electric (GE) Research Laboratory in Schenectady, New York, where he remained for the rest of his career. In 1912 he married Marion Mersereau with whom he had two children.

Langmuir's first research project for GE involved making improvements to the tungsten-filament lightbulb, which GE researchers had invented in 1907. While at Göttingen he had studied the effects of heat generated by a lamp on metals and gases in the immediate vicinity of the lamp, and he applied what he had learned during the course of this investigation to his work at GE. The result was Langmuir's invention of the gas-filled incandescent bulb. The first lightbulbs had been evacuated (all the air removed), so he filled the bulb with nitrogen as a means of extending the life of the tungsten filament. Later he began experimenting with the inert gases, and by 1913 he had settled on a mixture of nitrogen and argon. Combined with other improvements GE researchers made to the tungsten filament, the company's gas-filled incandescent bulb drove virtually all other incandescent bulbs from the marketplace.

Langmuir's work with the lightbulb led him to make a host of related inventions. Vacuum tubes, also known as electron tubes, were the first devices used to control the flow of electrons in electronic circuitry; they were later replaced by transistors and then by integrated chips. The tube itself is much like a lightbulb, in that a heated filament, or cathode, generates electrons that are collected by a plate, or anode, both of which are contained within a glass bulb. In 1907 Lee De Forest built the first three-element vacuum tube, and by 1912 Langmuir had developed an improved version. Called the pliotron, Langmuir's vacuum tube proved to be useful in amplifying signals for radio and telephone systems. In 1913 he invented two gauges for measuring vacuum, each more sensitive than anything previously available. By the following year he had developed a welding process that used atomic hydrogen, single atoms of hydrogen that result from the breaking down of hydrogen molecules by the intense heat of a filament or another red-hot body. The atomic hydrogen welding process generates temperatures greater than 6,000°F, thus making it possible to weld metals that cannot be welded by the oxyacetylene torch. In 1915 he invented the mercury condensation vacuum pump, a more effective way of evacuating a space.

In addition to being an inventor, Langmuir was also a brilliant theoretician. While inventing the gas-filled lightbulb, he discovered that, when a solid is vaporized by intense heat, the result is a mix of ions and electrons that resembles neither a solid, liquid, nor gas. He named this mix "plasma" because it reminded him of blood plasma, and he theorized that it constitutes a fourth state of matter. Scientists have since estimated that 99 percent of the universe's matter exists in the plasma state, including all of the matter making up the stars and the outer atmospheres of the planets. In 1921 he published his concentric theory of atomic structure, in which he postulated that chemical reactivity is a function of an atom trying to complete its outer shell by sharing electrons with other atoms. He played such a major role in popularizing GILBERT N. LEWIS's theory of the covalent bond (which Langmuir named), whereby two atoms share two electrons in their outer shells, that the theory became known as the Lewis-Langmuir theory.

Langmuir is best remembered for his theoretical work concerning surface chemistry, the study of what happens on the surface of a solid when it comes into contact with a gas or liquid; the most common phenomena related to surface chemistry is condensation. Langmuir's research concerning surface chemistry began when he started looking for ways to preserve the life of a lightbulb's tungsten filament. By the time he was done, surface chemistry had become a separate field of physical chemistry, the study of the physical properties of chemical elements and compounds. Along the way, he clarified the true nature of adsorption, the gathering of a gas, liquid, or dissolved substance on a surface in a condensed layer. Aided by a supersensitive microbalance of his own invention, he proved the existence of monolayers, surface films so thin (one ten-millionth of an inch thick) that they act as if they are two-dimensional. He also proposed a theory to explain chemisorption, the adsorption of reactants by the catalyst in a chemical reaction, in terms of the behavior of monolayers.

Langmuir's work with surface chemistry eventually led to his being awarded the 1932 Nobel Prize for chemistry. Later researchers would apply Langmuir's discoveries to everything from developing innovative manufacturing processes to gaining a better understanding of the biochemistry and biophysics of cell membranes. One such researcher was KATHARINE B. BLODGETT, a member of Langmuir's staff, whose work with monomolecular films stemmed from Langmuir's work with monolayers.

The Nobel Prize was only one of Langmuir's many honors. He presided over the American Chemical Society (ACS) and the American Association for the Advancement of Science. He won 22 medals, among them the ACS's Perkin Medal and the Royal Society of London's Rumford Medal, and Alaska's Mount Langmuir is named in his honor. He died on August 16, 1957, while vacationing in Woods Hole, Massachusetts.

Further Reading

Nobelprize.org. "The Nobel Prize in Chemistry 1932." Available online. URL: http://nobelprize.org/ chemistry/laureates/1932. Downloaded on January 2, 2004.

Suits, C. Guy, ed. *The Collected Works of Irving Langmuir, with Contributions in Memoriam, Including a Complete Bibliography of His Works.* Vol. 12, *Langmuir, the Man and the Scientist,* by Albert Rosenfeld. New York: Pergamon Press, 1962.

Wasson, Tyler, ed. *Nobel Prize Winners.* New York: H. W. Wilson, 1987, pp. 597–599.

Laughlin, Robert B.

(1950–   ) *physicist*

Robert B. Laughlin provided the theoretical explanation for the fractional quantum Hall effect, whereby electrons behave as if they possess a fraction of their electrical charge. This contribution awarded him a share of the 1998 Nobel Prize in physics.

Laughlin was born on November 1, 1950, in Visalia, California. His father was a lawyer and his mother was a schoolteacher. After receiving a B.A. in mathematics from the University of California at Berkeley in 1972, he spent two years in the U.S. Army before entering the graduate physics program at the Massachusetts Institute of Technology. Upon receiving a Ph.D. in theoretical physics in 1979, he went to work for the Bell Telephone Laboratories (BTL) in Murray Hill, New Jersey. Also in 1979 he married Anita Perry with whom he had two children.

While at BTL, Laughlin became interested in the work of German physicist Klaus von Klitzing concerning magnetism's effect on electron flow. Klitzing's work involved the Hall effect, which was named after its discoverer, American physicist Edwin H. Hall. In 1879 Hall had discovered that when an electric current flows through a solid material in the presence of a strong magnetic field, the electrons are drawn to one side of the material, thus creating a transverse electric field at right angles to the direction of the current. Furthermore, Hall showed that the voltage generated by the transverse field varies with changes in the magnetic field's strength in a smooth and continuous pattern. Klitzing's experiment involved chilling the electrons to temperatures approaching absolute zero and then greatly increasing the strength of the magnetic field through which they flowed. The result was that the Hall-effect voltage varied not in a continuous pattern but in discrete steps, as if in accordance with the laws of quantum mechanics. In his first important theoretical paper, Laughlin explained the quantum Hall effect in terms of localization, a state of motion in which an electron may be found anywhere within a particular region. Furthermore, he showed that the Hall conductance was accurately quantized because it was a measurement of the charge of the electron being localized.

In 1982 Laughlin left BTL for the Lawrence Livermore Laboratory in Berkeley, California. Although Livermore's work focused primarily on nuclear physics, in his spare time he continued to investigate the quantum Hall effect. Meanwhile, that same year two of his former BTL colleagues, DANIEL C. TSUI and Horst L. Störmer, had carried Klitzing's work to a new level. Using lower temperatures and stronger magnets than Klitzing had used, they showed that Klitzing's quantized steps were actually a collection of peaks and valleys that bore only a passing resemblance to discrete steps. More importantly, they showed that these peaks and valleys corresponded to fractional, not integral, values. They concluded that these fractional peaks and valleys result from the presence of electrons that have only a fractional negative charge. The problem with this conclusion was that every scientist knew that an electron carries an integral charge of 1 and that an electron cannot be fragmented into smaller, constituent particles, and therefore the conclusion could not possibly be correct.

Laughlin thought about the fractional quantum Hall effect for about a year, and in 1983 he advanced a theory to explain it. He postulated that low temperature and high magnetism combine to create a kind of quantum fluid, and that the magnetic field further acts upon the fluid in the same way that a storm acts upon the sea. The magnetic field, or "wind," creates excitations, or "eddies," in the quantum fluid, thus forcing the electrons to share their electrical charges with the eddies. In turn, the eddies take on some of the characteristics of particles in that they carry a small fraction of an electron's charge. Fifteen years later, this theory remained the best explanation for the fractional quantum Hall effect, and Laughlin was awarded a one-third share of the 1998 Nobel Prize in physics for advancing it; his corecipients were Tsui and Störmer.

In 1985 Laughlin joined the faculty at Stanford University. In addition to developing mathematical models based on the fractional quantum Hall effect, he also investigated high-temperature superconductivity, the ability of certain metals to lose all resistance to electron flow. His honors include election to the National Academy of Sciences and the American Academy of Arts and Sciences.

Further Reading

Browne, Malcolm W. "5 Quantum Theorists Share 2 Nobel Prizes in Sciences." *New York Times*, October 14, 1998, p. A16.

Nobelprize.org. "The Nobel Prize in Physics 1998." Available online. URL: http://nobelprize.org/physics/laureates/1998. Downloaded on October 13, 2004.

Stanford University Department of Physics. "Robert B. Laughlin." Available online. URL: http://www.stanford.edu/dept/physics/people/faculty/laughlin_robert.html. Downloaded on March 25, 2005.

Lawrence, Ernest O.
(Ernest Orlando Lawrence)
(1901–1958) *physicist*

Ernest O. Lawrence won a Nobel Prize for designing and developing the cyclotron, a device that revolutionized the study of nuclear physics. He also played an important role as a science administrator, and he helped to transform the nature of scientific research in the United States into a large-scale, multimillion-dollar enterprise.

Lawrence was born on August 8, 1901, in Canton, South Dakota. His parents, Carl and Gunda, were schoolteachers. He spent one year at St. Olaf College in Northfield, Minnesota, and then transferred to the University of South Dakota where he received a B.A. in chemistry in 1922. The following year he received an A.M. in physics from the University of Minnesota and enrolled in the University of Chicago to work on his doctorate, but he transferred after a year to Yale University, where he received a Ph.D. in physics in 1925. He taught physics for three years at Yale, and then in 1928 he was named a professor of physics at the University of California at Berkeley, where he spent the rest of his career. In 1932 he married Mary Blumer with whom he had six children.

While at Yale, Lawrence's research primarily involved the photoelectric effect, the emission of electrons by a surface, usually metallic, after the surface has been bombarded by light or some other form of electromagnetic radiation. His doctoral dissertation investigated the photoelectric effect in potassium vapor as a function of the frequency of light, and he later measured the time lag between bombardment and emission as being approximately three-billionths of a second. However, he was also interested in nuclear physics, and he made the most accurate measurements up to that time of the amount of energy required to strip away an electron from a mercury atom (approximately 10 volts) and of the ratio of an electron's charge to its mass.

Shortly after arriving at Berkeley, Lawrence became interested in developing a better way to initiate nuclear reactions by bombarding nuclei with subatomic particles. In 1919 English physicist Ernest Rutherford had transmuted nitrogen into oxygen by bombarding it with naturally occurring radioactive helium ions. Further work in this regard, however, was limited as such ions were extremely difficult to come by and such bombardment required a prohibitively large amount of voltage. In 1929 Lawrence learned of a Norwegian engineer, Rolf Wideröe, who had built a linear particle accelerator capable of accelerating potassium ions to 50,000 electron volts (eV). Lawrence had calculated that it would take at least several million eV to accelerate a beam of particles to the energy level required to initiate a nuclear reaction, and that a linear accelerator capable of generating this many eV would be incredibly long and therefore impractical to build. However, Wideröe's invention gave Lawrence the idea to build a circular particle accelerator, and he and M. Stanley Livingston, one of his students, set out to construct one.

The basic idea behind the circular particle accelerator, or cyclotron as it came to be known, was to propel charged particles in a circular path via means of magnetic resonance acceleration. An oscillating magnetic field was synchronized so that each time a particle passed a certain point, the field gave the particle a slight boost in speed. Once the required speed had been reached, a beam of particles was deflected into a vacuum chamber where the beam collided with its target. The first cyclotron, which was completed in 1930, was made of glass and red sealing wax and was only four inches in diameter. A metal cyclotron of the same dimensions was built shortly thereafter, and it was capable of generating a proton beam with a power of 80,000 eV while drawing only 2,000 volts. By 1932 a 37-inch cyclotron capable of generating a beam of 8 million eV had been built by Lawrence and his associates.

Lawrence's original intention in building the cyclotron was simply to bombard atomic nuclei as a way of learning more about nuclear structure. However, the 37-inch cyclotron also made it possible to develop large quantities of radioactive isotopes, which have a number of applications. By 1936 the cyclotron had opened up so many fruitful avenues for researchers that Berkeley constructed the Radiation Laboratory (today called the Lawrence Berkeley Laboratory) specifically for further experimentation with the cyclotron, and Lawrence was named its director.

The Rad Lab, as it was known, was the first modern laboratory devoted to nuclear physics. Under Lawrence's direction, it ushered in the era of "big science," large-scale research projects featuring large staffs and plenty of funding, as opposed to "little science," one researcher working alone or with a few students or assistants. Lawrence was as successful at obtaining grants of money from private corporations and foundations as he was at experimenting, and after World War II he put into operation a 184-inch synchrocyclotron designed by EDWIN M. MCMILLAN. He established a second "Rad Lab" in Livermore, California (today the Lawrence Livermore Laboratory) and oversaw the development of a "bevatron," a cyclotron capable of generating a particle beam of more than one billion eV. He made the various cyclotrons at both facilities available to a host of researchers from around the world, who carried out a number of different experiments. The most spectacular of these experiments involved the discovery of several transuranium, or man-made, elements by McMillan, GLENN T. SEABORG, and others. However, the most beneficial use of the cyclotron was the production of vast amounts of radioactive isotopes for use by medical researchers and practitioners around the world.

Lawrence played a critical administrative role in the two most important scientific research projects of World War II. He helped establish a major research facility at the Massachusetts Institute of Technology for the development of radar, and he masterminded the development of the uranium and plutonium isotopes used to manufacture the atomic bombs that were dropped on Hiroshima and Nagasaki. In 1958 he represented the United States at a conference of experts to study the possibility of detecting violations of a possible agreement on suspension of nuclear tests.

For his work in developing the cyclotron, Lawrence was awarded the 1939 Nobel Prize in physics. He also won a number of other awards and medals, including election to the National Academy of Sciences. In 1961 the transuranium element 103, discovered by a team of Berkeley researchers, was named lawrencium in his honor. He died from cancer on August 27, 1958, in Palo Alto, California.

Further Reading

Alvarez, Luis W. "Ernest Orlando Lawrence," National Academy of Sciences, *Biographical Memoirs* 41 (1970): pp. 251–294.

Childs, Herbert. *An American Genius: The Life of Ernest Orlando Lawrence.* New York: Dutton, 1968.

Heilbron, John L., and Robert W. Seidel. *Lawrence and His Laboratory: A History of the Lawrence Berkeley Laboratory.* Berkeley: University of California Press, 1989.

Nobelprize.org. "The Nobel Prize in Physics 1939." Available online. URL: http://nobelprize.org/physics/laureates/1939. Downloaded on March 10, 2004.

Wasson, Tyler, ed. *Nobel Prize Winners.* New York: H. W. Wilson, 1987, pp. 603–606.

Leavitt, Henrietta
(Henrietta Swan Leavitt)
(1868–1921) *astronomer*

Henrietta Leavitt was one of several important women astronomers who worked at the Harvard College Observatory in the late 19th and early 20th centuries. While there, she discovered the period-luminosity relation, which was later used by other astronomers to calculate the distances between Earth and the stars.

Leavitt was born on July 4, 1868, in Lancaster, Massachusetts. Her father, George, was a minister, and her mother, Henrietta, was a homemaker. As a girl she moved with her family to Cleveland, Ohio, where she grew up. In 1886 she enrolled in Oberlin College in Ohio, but transferred after two years to the Society for the Collegiate Instruction of Women (today Radcliffe College) in Massachusetts. After receiving an A.B. in 1892, she remained

at the school for a year to do graduate work in astronomy at the Harvard College Observatory in Cambridge, Massachusetts. From 1893 to 1902 she taught high school, traveled, and volunteered at the observatory when not suffering from poor health, which eventually led to a partial loss of hearing.

In 1902 Leavitt was hired to work full-time at the Harvard observatory. At the time, the observatory was in the middle of a project to identify and classify every star in the universe; astronomers photographed the heavens through a spectroscope, an optical device that measured the wavelengths, or spectra, of the various stars, mounted to a telescope. Any stars appearing on the spectrograms, as the photographs were called, were then classified according to their own unique spectra. For five years Leavitt analyzed spectrograms under the direction of WILLIAMINA FLEMING, curator of the observatory's astronomical photographs.

In 1907 Leavitt was named director of the observatory's photographic photometry department. In this capacity, she developed an improved system for calculating the brightness of stars. This system was made necessary by the fact that a star's brightness appears differently to the eye peering through a telescope, the old way of classifying stars, than it does on a photograph, the method employed at the observatory. By classifying the spectra of 46 stars of all degrees of brightness near the North Star, she devised what became known as the North Polar Sequence. In 1913 Leavitt's system was adopted by the International Committee on Photographic Magnitudes as its standard for determining stellar brightness.

In the course of devising the North Polar Sequence, Leavitt became interested in variable stars, stars that get brighter and dimmer on a regular schedule. She focused her research on variable stars to 25 stars in a group called the Cepheids in the Small Magellanic Cloud in the southern hemisphere. She studied these stars for five years by photographing each star at certain intervals and then comparing its brightnesses in the various spectrograms. In so doing, she discovered approximately 2,400 previously unidentified variable stars over the course of her career. A catalogue listing 1,777 of them appeared in the *Annals of the Astronomical Observatory of Harvard College* in 1908.

By 1912 Leavitt had determined that a variable star's period, the time it takes to make one complete cycle from brightest to dimmest, is directly proportional to its luminosity, or the brightness of a star in comparison to the Sun. Since all 25 Cepheids were about equally distant from Earth, she concluded in a 1912 article in the *Harvard College Observatory Circular* that their different periods were probably indicative of their true brightness, and not just their brightness as it appeared on film.

Leavitt was prevented from pursuing this conclusion to its logical conclusion by her duties at the observatory. However, other astronomers, notably Danish astronomer Ejnar Hertzsprung, quickly realized that Leavitt's period-luminosity relation could be used to determine a star's distance from Earth. Eventually, the period-luminosity relation became the standard tool by which to compute stellar distances, largely as the result of the work of Harlow Shapley, director of the Harvard Observatory. Shapley figured out how to determine the true brightness of a variable star by calculating its period, and by comparing its true brightness to its apparent brightness as seen from Earth, he was able to calculate its distance from Earth. In this way, he discovered that the Small Magellanic Cloud is not part of the Milky Way, as had been thought, but rather that it belonged to a different galaxy, a conclusion that was hotly debated by astronomers for years thereafter.

Leavitt, who never married, spent her entire scientific career at the Harvard Observatory. Cancer forced her to abandon her duties shortly before her death on December 12, 1921, in Cambridge.

Further Reading

Bailey, Martha J. *American Women in Science: A Biographical Dictionary.* Santa Barbara, Calif.: ABC-CLIO, 1994, p. 205.

Yount, Lisa. *A to Z of Women in Science and Math.* New York: Facts On File, 1999, pp. 118–120.

Lederberg, Joshua
(1925–) *geneticist*

Joshua Lederberg discovered that bacteria are capable of producing new strains by recombining their genetic material, something that was previously thought to be possible only for organisms that reproduce sexually. He also discovered that viruses play a role in genetic recombination in bacteria. For these discoveries, he was awarded a share of the 1958 Nobel Prize in physiology or medicine.

Lederberg was born on May 23, 1925, in Montclair, New Jersey. His father, Zvi, was a rabbi, and his mother, Esther, was a homemaker. As a boy he moved with his family to New York City where he grew up. After receiving a B.A. in zoology at Columbia University in 1944, he entered Columbia's College of Physicians and Surgeons with the idea of becoming a medical doctor. However, he soon discovered that he was more interested in research, and in 1946 he transferred to Yale University to study biochemical genetics under EDWARD L. TATUM. That same year he married Esther Zimmer with whom he had no children. They later divorced, and he married Marguerite Stein with whom he had two children.

By 1946 Tatum had already made several notable discoveries concerning biochemical genetics. By experimenting with mutated specimens of the red bread mold *Neurospora crassa*, he and GEORGE W. BEADLE had demonstrated that every biochemical reaction is regulated by a particular gene in that the gene controls the structure and function of the enzyme that initiates the reaction. Lederberg and Tatum adapted the techniques that Tatum and Beadle had used to study *Neurospora* so they could see if genes control the biochemical reactions in bacteria as well. After selecting the K-12 strain of the bacteria *Escherichia coli* (*E. coli*) as the focus of their study, they decided to see what would happen when a colony of K-12 *E. coli* was combined with a colony of a different strain of *E. coli*. The result was the production of a third strain of *E. coli* that was clearly the genetic offspring of the two combined colonies. Previously, it had been thought that bacteria reproduce via simple cell division, but this result demonstrated that bacteria can exchange genetic material, an ability that was thought to be restricted to life-forms that reproduce sexually.

In 1948 Lederberg received a Ph.D. in microbiology from Yale and joined the faculty at the University of Wisconsin. At Wisconsin he organized a department of medical genetics and continued his experiments with the genetic behavior of bacteria. In 1952 he and Norton D. Zinder, a Wisconsin graduate student, showed that genetic recombination in bacteria is sometimes facilitated by bacteriophages, or phages, viruses that infect bacteria, in a process they dubbed viral transduction. When a phage invades a bacterium, it uses the bacterium's material to create new phages. If one of these phages infects a bacterium of a different strain and that bacterium lives, in some cases it transforms into a new strain of bacteria by virtue of the genetic material transduced into it by the phage.

Lederberg's work with genetic recombination in bacteria opened the door to a better understanding of the basic process of cell function and cell growth, a development that promised to greatly facilitate cancer research. For this contribution, he was awarded a half share of the 1958 Nobel Prize in physiology or medicine; his cowinners were Tatum and Beadle. In addition, Lederberg was elected to the National Academy of Sciences and, later, awarded the National Medal of Science.

In 1959 Lederberg left Wisconsin for Stanford University Medical School, where he organized a department of genetics and directed the Kennedy Laboratory for Molecular Medicine. In 1978 he was named president of Rockefeller University in New York City, a position he held until his retirement in 1990. Since then he has continued to conduct laboratory research on bacterial and human genetics and to advise government and industry on global health policy, biological warfare, and the threat of bioterrorism.

Further Reading

Hargittai, Istvan, and Magdolna Hargittai. *Candid Science II: Conversations with Famous Biomedical Scientists.* London: Imperial College Press, 2002, pp. 32–50.

Nobelprize.org. "The Nobel Prize in Physiology or Medicine 1958." Available online. URL: http://nobelprize.org/medicine/laureates/1958. Downloaded on May 9, 2004.

Profiles in Science, National Library of Medicine. "The Joshua Lederberg Papers." Available online. URL: http://profiles.nlm.nih.gov/BB/Views/Exhibit/narrative/biographical.html. Downloaded on May 9, 2004.

Wasson, Tyler, ed. *Nobel Prize Winners.* New York: H. W. Wilson, 1987, pp. 611–613.

Lederman, Leon M.
(Leon Max Lederman)
(1922–   ) *physicist*

Leon M. Lederman codeveloped the neutrino beam method for studying the weak nuclear interactions, and then he used that method to discover the muon neutrino. For these contributions he was awarded a share of the 1988 Nobel Prize in physics.

Lederman was born on July 15, 1922, in New York City. His father, Morris, owned and operated a laundry, and his mother, Minna, was a homemaker. After receiving a B.S. in chemistry from the City College of New York in 1943, he spent three years in the U.S. Army Signal Corps. He then entered New York's Columbia University, and as a student in the graduate physics program he helped construct some of the equipment that comprised Nevis Laboratories, Columbia's facility for researching high-energy subatomic particles. After receiving a Ph.D. in 1951, he joined the Columbia faculty.

Lederman's early research involved mesons, subatomic particles with more mass than an electron but not as much as a proton. As a graduate student, he measured the lifetimes of the two different types of pi mesons, or pions, the elementary particles that are chiefly responsible for the strong interactions, the forces that bind together protons and neutrons in an atomic nucleus. In 1956 he was part of the team that discovered the neutral K meson; one of the so-called strange particles because of the way it decays via radioactivity, the neutral K meson was shown later by JAMES W. CRONIN and VAL L. FITCH to violate the fundamental principles of symmetry.

In 1959 Lederman shifted the focus of his research from mesons to neutrinos, subatomic particles with no electrical charge and virtually no mass. The existence of neutrinos had just been detected three years earlier by FREDERICK REINES and Clyde L. Cowan, Jr. Because of its charge and mass, a neutrino rarely interacts with matter, but when it does it induces the production of either an electron or a muon, a particle that carries the same electrical charge (negative) as an electron but that has about 200 times the mass. Physicists wondered if this meant that there are two different types of neutrinos, so Lederman and two of his Columbia colleagues, MELVIN SCHWARTZ and JACK STEINBERGER, decided to find out. They moved their operations from Nevis to the Brookhaven National Laboratory on Long Island because Brookhaven had a particle accelerator, a device that energizes subatomic particles to extremely high energy levels, that was much more powerful than the one at Nevis.

Lederman, Schwartz, and Steinberger devised an experiment whereby a beam of high-energy protons was generated in the accelerator and then fired into a block of the metal beryllium. Behind the beryllium was a 40-foot-thick barrier of steel plates, and behind the plates was a detector consisting of 90 one-inch aluminum sheets with a layer of neon gas separating each sheet. The beam struck the block with so much force that the beryllium atoms were blasted into smithereens, in the process generating a beam of approximately one hundred thousand billion neutrinos. All of the debris except the neutrinos was trapped by the steel plates, and as the neutrino beam passed through the plates into the detector, a grand total of 51 neutrinos was collected. By 1962 the three experimenters were able to verify the existence of two distinct types of neutrinos: electron neutrinos, which generate electrons, and muon neutrinos, which generate muons.

The "two-neutrino experiment," as it became known, was important for two reasons. First, it demonstrated the existence of the previously unknown muon neutrino. Second, it provided physicists with the neutrino beam, a powerful new tool for investigating nuclear forces. Previously, particle accelerators had generated beams of particles that operate according to the strong interactions, so it was difficult for them to investigate the weak interactions, certain processes of radioactive decay. Since neutrinos are affected only by the weak interactions but not by the strong interactions, the neutrino beam became the perfect tool for investigating the weak interactions, about which little was known. For devising and carrying out the two-neutrino experiment, Lederman, Schwartz, and Steinberger were each awarded a one-third share of the 1988 Nobel Prize in physics.

Leon Lederman developed a method for studying certain forms of radioactive decay. *(Courtesy of Leon M. Lederman; photo by Ellen Lederman)*

From 1961 to 1978, Lederman served as director of the Nevis Laboratories. In addition to his duties at Nevis, he also conducted research at the Fermi National Accelerator Laboratory (Fermilab) in Batavia, Illinois, and in 1977 he led the team that discovered the bottom or beauty quark, one of the basic building blocks of matter. He left Columbia in 1979 to become the director of Fermilab. In this position he oversaw the design and construction of the first superconducting synchrotron, at the time the most powerful particle accelerator in the world. He also led the effort to build an even more powerful particle accelerator, the Superconducting Super Collider; although this project received preliminary funding from the U.S. Congress, it was eventually scrapped because of the prohibitive cost to build it.

In 1989 Lederman retired from Fermilab and returned to teaching physics, first at the University of Chicago (1989–92) and then at the Illinois Institute of Technology (since 1992). He was married twice, in 1945 to Florence Gordon with whom he had three children and in 1981 to Ellen Carr. His publications include *The God Particle: If the Universe Is the Answer, What Is the Question?* (1989)

and *From Quarks to the Cosmos: Tools of Discovery* (1993). His honors include the National Medal of Science, election to the National Academy of Sciences, and a term as president of the American Association for the Advancement of Science.

Further Reading

Lederman Science Center at Fermilab. "Leon M. Lederman." Available online. URL: http://www-ed.fnal.gov/samplers/hsphys/people/lederman.html. Downloaded on March 25, 2005.

McMurray, Emily J., ed. *Notable Twentieth-Century Scientists.* Detroit: Gale Research, 1995, pp. 1,206–1,207.

Nobelprize.org. "The Nobel Prize in Physics 1988." Available online. URL: http://nobelprize.org/physics/laureates/1988. Downloaded on October 4, 2004.

Lee, David M.
(David Morris Lee)
(1931–   ) *physicist*

David M. Lee codiscovered superfluidity in an isotope of helium known as helium-3. For this discovery, he was awarded a share of the 1996 Nobel Prize in physics.

Lee was born on January 20, 1931, in Rye, New York. His father, Marvin, was an electrical engineer, and his mother, Annette, was a schoolteacher. After receiving a B.S. in physics from Harvard University in 1952, he spent two years in the U.S. Army and served in Korea during the Korean War. He became interested in low temperature physics, the study of what happens to the thermal, electrical, and magnetic properties of matter at temperatures approaching 0 K, or absolute zero, following a chance conversation with a fellow soldier who was a former graduate student of Paul Zilsel, a specialist in low temperature physics at the University of Connecticut. Based partly on that meeting, Lee decided to enroll in Connecticut's graduate physics program where he studied low temperature physics and received an M.S. in 1955. He continued in this vein at Yale University, where he received a Ph.D. in physics in 1959; that same year he was named the founding director of what became known as the Laboratory of Atomic and Solid State Physics (LASSP) at Cornell University in Ithaca, New York. Also in

1959, he married Dana Thorangkul with whom he had two children.

Lee's research at LASSP focused on superfluidity, the unusual properties exhibited by liquid helium when it is cooled to 2.18 K. These properties include frictionless flow, including the ability to overflow its containment vessel in defiance of the laws of viscosity, and very high heat conductivity. He was particularly intrigued by the different phenomena exhibited by the two isotopes of helium, the more common helium-4, which has four nucleons (two protons and two neutrons), and the exceedingly rare helium-3, which has three nucleons (two protons but only one neutron); whereas helium-4 demonstrated superfluidity, helium-3 had not. The standard explanation involved the difference between bosons and fermions. Bosons contain an even number of nucleons while fermions contain an uneven number of nucleons, and therefore their angular momentums, or spin, are different. Consequently, it was believed that helium-4 becomes a superfluid because it is a boson while helium-3 cannot become a superfluid because it is a fermion.

Lee was joined at LASSP in 1966 by ROBERT C. RICHARDSON and in 1967 by DOUGLAS D. OSHEROFF, and together they embarked on a project to study magnetism in solid helium-3. By 1972 they had managed to cool helium-3 to 0.002 K, at which point they discovered that it, too, becomes a superfluid. Moreover, helium-3 in the superfluid phase possesses certain magnetic properties that helium-4 in the superfluid phase does not. Not only did this discovery nullify the conventional wisdom regarding the conditions required for superfluidity, but also it permitted physicists to conduct some very interesting research concerning the differences in behavior between bosons and fermions, as now a boson (helium-4) and a fermion (helium-3) could be studied in a superfluid phase. For their discovery, Lee, Richardson, and Osheroff were each awarded a one-third share of the 1996 Nobel Prize in physics.

Lee stepped down as director of LASSP in 1990, although he continued to study low temperature physics at Cornell for the rest of his career. His many honors include election to the National Academy of Sciences and the American Academy of Arts and Sciences.

Further Reading

Browne, Malcolm W. "Discoveries of Superfluid Helium, and 'Buckyballs,' Earn Nobels for 6 Scientists," *New York Times,* October 10, 1996, p. D21.

Cornell University Laboratory of Atomic and Solid State Physics. "David M. Lee." Available online. URL: http://www.lassp.cornell.edu/lassp_data/dmlee.html. Downloaded on March 25, 2005.

Nobelprize.org. "The Nobel Prize in Physics 1996." Available online. URL: http://nobelprize.org/physics/laureates/1996. Downloaded on August 23, 2004.

Lee, Tsung-Dao
(1926–) *physicist*

Tsung-Dao Lee codeveloped the theory that the laws of parity conservation do not necessarily apply to the weak interactions, one of the four principal physical forces. For the role he played in promulgating this theory, known today as parity violation, he was awarded a share of the 1957 Nobel Prize in physics.

Lee was born on November 24, 1926, in Shanghai, China. His father, Tsing Kong, was a businessman, and his mother, Ming Chang, was a homemaker. As a boy he moved with his family to Kanchow in Kiangsi Province where he grew up. In 1943 he entered the National Chekiang University but transferred after a year to the National Southwest Associated University (NSAU), receiving a B.S. in physics in 1946. He then came to the United States and entered the graduate program at the University of Chicago. In 1950 he received a Ph.D. in theoretical physics and married Hui Chung Chin with whom he had two children. After a year as a research associate at the University of California at Berkeley, he joined the staff at the Institute of Advanced Study (IAS) in Princeton, New Jersey. In 1953 he was named a professor of physics at Columbia University in New York City. Except for a brief return to IAS that lasted from 1960 to 1963, he spent the rest of his career at Columbia.

One of Lee's fellow students at NSAU was CHEN NING YANG. Although they hardly knew each other then, they became collaborators at Chicago, where Yang was also a graduate student. They resumed their collaboration in 1951 when Lee joined Yang at IAS, and they continued it after Lee moved on to Columbia, meeting once a week to exchange ideas. They shared a common interest in the theory of the weak interactions, of which there are now known to be at least 20. They were particularly intrigued by the tau and theta mesons, which in 1953 they concluded were actually the same particle, known today as the K-meson. The reason the K-meson was thought to be two different particles is because of the behavior it exhibits during beta decay, one of the weak interactions; sometimes a K-meson yields three pi mesons, but at other times it yields only two. This situation suggested to Lee and Yang that K-mesons violate the laws of parity conservation. These laws state that every physical reaction occurs symmetrically, without regard to up, down, left, right, clockwise, or counterclockwise. For example, when an ice cube melts, the water does not flow mostly to the left but in all directions evenly. In 1953 physicists assumed that the weak interactions, like all the other physical forces, obey the laws of parity conservation as do all the other physical forces, namely, electromagnetism, gravity, and the strong interaction, the force that binds together protons and neutrons in the nucleus. Consequently, Lee and Yang deter-

Tsung-Dao Lee showed that the process of radioactive decay occasionally violates some of the basic laws of physics. *(© Caron [NPP] Philippe/Corbis SYGMA)*

mined to find out what experimental evidence, if any, supports the notion that parity conservation holds for the weak interactions.

Lee and Yang spent the next three years reviewing the literature regarding experiments concerning the weak interactions. In 1956 they concluded that there was no experimental evidence to support the assumption that the weak interactions obey the laws of parity conservation, even though every experiment they read about had been conducted on that assumption. Consequently, they concluded that parity violation might explain the behavior of K-mesons during beta decay, and they suggested a set of experiments that could be performed to determine whether or not this is the case. In early 1957 Chinese-American physicist Chien-shiung Wu conducted their experiments with a radioactive isotope of cobalt, cobalt-60. Wu showed that as cobalt-60 undergoes beta decay, the particles it emits have a remarkable preference for moving in the "up" direction, a clear violation of parity conservation.

The implications of parity violation, as demonstrated by Wu and as theorized by Lee and Yang, were monumental. Parity violation forced particle physicists to stop assuming that the laws of conservation that apply to electromagnetism and the strong interactions also apply without question to the weak interactions. Over the next several years, other researchers offered further support for parity violation during other weak interactions, and they also showed that the laws of conservation regarding charge conjugation and time are also violated during certain weak interactions. For proposing the experiments that forced this reevaluation, Lee and Yang were each awarded a half share of the 1957 Nobel Prize in physics.

In the latter part of his career, Lee contributed to a better understanding of some of the other major questions facing theoretical physics. He proposed a theory of high-temperature superconductivity, the ability of certain metals to lose all resistance to electron flow, in terms of angular momentum, which is a function of the way an atom rotates about its axis. He also proposed modifications to the theory of quantum chromodynamics, which explains the strong interactions in terms of the various properties of quarks, the basic building blocks of protons and neutrons. His

publications include *Elementary Particles and Weak Interactions* (1957), which he coauthored with Yang; *Particle Physics and Introduction to Field Theory* (1981, 1990); and *Symmetries, Asymmetries, and the World of Particles* (1988). His honors include election to the National Academy of Sciences and the American Academy of Arts and Sciences.

Further Reading

Nobelprize.org. "The Nobel Prize in Physics 1957." Available online. URL: http://nobelprize.org/physics/laureates/1957. Downloaded on September 24, 2004.

Novick, Robert, ed. *Thirty Years since Parity Nonconservation: A Symposium for T. D. Lee*. Boston: Birkhaüser, 1988.

Wasson, Tyler, ed. *Nobel Prize Winners*. New York: H. W. Wilson, 1987, pp. 615–617.

Lee, Yuan T.
(Yuan Tseh Lee)
(1936–) *chemist*

Yuan T. Lee made significant improvements to the apparatus that employed the crossed molecular beam technique, a technique that made it possible to understand what happens to a molecule during a chemical reaction. For this contribution he was awarded a share of the 1986 Nobel Prize in chemistry.

Lee was born on November 29, 1936, in Hsinchu, Taiwan. His father, Tsefan, was an artist, and his mother, Pei, was a schoolteacher. After receiving a B.S. in chemistry from the National Taiwan University in 1959 and an M.S. in chemistry from the National Tsinghua University in 1961, in 1962 he went to the United States to work on his doctorate at the University of California at Berkeley.

As a graduate student at Berkeley, Lee became interested in various methods for determining the structures of chemical compounds. He was particularly interested in the crossed molecular beam technique, which was developed in 1962 by DUDLEY R. HERSCHBACH, at the time a chemistry professor at Berkeley. This technique is an offshoot of the process of molecular scattering, whereby two beams of molecules in a gaseous state are injected into a large vacuum in such a way that they collide with each other. Molecular scattering had been invented by physicists to study the molecules, atoms, and subatomic particles that result from the collisions, but Herschbach adapted it so that he could study what happens to a molecule in a chemical reaction.

Lee received his Ph.D. from Berkeley in 1965, but he remained for another 18 months to conduct postdoctoral research. During this period he built and experimented with a crossed molecular beam scattering device of his own design. Meanwhile in 1963 Herschbach had moved from Berkeley to Harvard, and when Lee completed his postdoctoral research at Berkeley in 1967, Herschbach recruited him to become a postdoctoral fellow at Harvard. Over the next year Lee made major improvements to Herschbach's crossed molecular beam apparatus, which was a crude piece of equipment. The part that collected collided molecules, for example, was a thin filament of platinum wire, and the changes that the molecules underwent during the collisions, which in essence are chemical reactions, were measured by determining the variation they caused to the electrical current running through the filament. This arrangement, however, limited research to relatively simple molecules containing the extremely reactive alkali metals, such as potassium and sodium. Lee replaced the filament with a mass spectrometer, which measures the spectral, or light, wavelength of a molecule, so that the apparatus could measure changes in virtually any type of molecule. The spectrometer also allowed Lee and Herschbach to study the dynamics of a chemical reaction in terms of the changes it induces in the structure of a molecule's electrons.

In 1968 Lee joined the faculty at the University of Chicago, returning six years later to Berkeley where he was named a professor of chemistry. At both schools he built successively more sophisticated machines for using the crossed molecular beam technique and then used them to generate a tremendous amount of detailed information regarding what happens to an individual molecule during a chemical reaction. This information permitted chemists to understand the results of their experiments better as well as to design more sophisticated experiments. For this contribution, Lee was awarded a one-third share of the 1986 Nobel Prize in chemistry; one of his core-

cipients was Herschbach and the other was the Canadian chemist John C. Polanyi.

In 1963 Lee married Bernice Wu with whom he had three children, and in 1974 he became a naturalized U.S. citizen. That same year he was named a principal investigator at the Lawrence Berkeley Laboratory, one of the nation's preeminent institutions devoted to the study of matter, a position he held until 1997. His many honors include the National Medal of Science and election to the National Academy of Sciences and the American Academy of Arts and Sciences.

Further Reading

The Nobel Prize Internet Archive. "Yuan T. Lee." Available online. URL: http://almaz.com/nobel/chemistry/1986b.html. Downloaded on March 25, 2005.

Nobelprize.org. "The Nobel Prize in Chemistry 1986." Available online. URL: http://nobelprize.org/chemistry/laureates/1986. Downloaded on August 15, 2004.

Wasson, Tyler, ed. *Nobel Prize Winners*. New York: H. W. Wilson, 1987, pp. 617–619.

Levi-Montalcini, Rita
(1909–) *neuroembryologist*

Rita Levi-Montalcini was the first researcher to discover the existence of a biological factor that promotes cell growth. Together with STANLEY COHEN, she received the 1986 Nobel Prize for physiology or medicine.

Levi-Montalcini was born Rita Levi on April 22, 1909, in Turin, Italy. Her father, Adamo, owned a factory, and her mother, Adele, was a homemaker. She so admired her mother that later in life she added her maiden name, Montalcini, to her last name. She received a finishing school education in preparation for a good marriage, but at age 20 she decided that she would rather pursue a career as a physician. After a year of extensive tutoring, she passed the entrance examinations for the University of Turin Medical School. Two of her classmates at Turin were future Nobel laureates SALVADOR E. LURIA and RENATO DULBECCO. After receiving an M.D. in 1936, she remained at Turin for postdoctoral studies in neurology and psychiatry. During this period she became interested in the development of the nervous system in chick embryos.

In 1938 the fascist regime of Benito Mussolini declared that Jews could no longer teach or conduct research at state universities. Undaunted, Levi-Montalcini continued to conduct research on chick embryos in a makeshift laboratory she constructed in her bedroom. After World War II broke out, she fled with her family to a small house in the Piedmont, and then later to Florence; food was so scarce that the family often ate the embryos after she was finished experimenting with them.

Despite these primitive conditions, however, Levi-Montalcini was able to make some interesting discoveries. One set of experiments was intended to replicate the findings of German neuroembryologist Viktor Hamburger, who in 1934 had discovered that nerves growing into a limb in an embryo stop growing if the limb is amputated. Levi-Montalcini, however, discovered that the nerves continued growing to maturity after the amputation, even though they soon died because there was no limb for them to grow into. She suspected that some nerve growth–promoting agent in the embryo was responsible, and she reported her findings and her conclusion in a small European medical journal.

At some point Hamburger read Levi-Montalcini's article. Rather than being insulted by it, in 1947 he invited her to assist him for one school year at Washington University in St. Louis, Missouri, where he now taught. She accepted and then remained at Washington University for 30 years. Her work with embryonic nerve development was spurred when she discovered that certain mouse tumors, when grafted in place of an amputated limb, have a tremendously stimulating effect on nerve growth. She concluded that the nerve growth promoting agent whose existence she had earlier suspected must exist in large quantities in the tumor.

Levi-Montalcini's work received a further boost in 1953, when she began to work closely with Stanley Cohen, a biochemist. By 1956 they had been able to purify a nerve growth promoting agent from a mouse tumor that contained both protein and nucleic acids. They soon discovered that snake venom and the salivary glands in male mice also contain large amounts of what is now called nerve growth factor (NGF). By 1959 they had identified NGF as a molecule composed of two chains of 118 amino acids each.

Levi-Montalcini and Cohen's discovery was the first time a cell growth factor had been identified and isolated. This important contribution stimulated other researchers to look for other factors that stimulate the growth of other types of cells. Over the next 25 years, these researchers discovered that somatomedin regulates the growth-promoting effect of growth hormone, that platelet derived growth factor (PDGF) stimulates the growth of cells making up connective tissues and blood vessels, and that interleukin-2 stimulates the growth of white blood cells in the immune system. In each case, the work of these researchers was informed by the experiments of Levi-Montalcini and Cohen. In 1986 the importance of their work was validated when they were jointly awarded the Nobel Prize for physiology or medicine.

Levi-Montalcini became a U.S. citizen in 1956, the same year she was named a professor at Washington University. Nevertheless, she retained her Italian citizenship, and in 1962 she opened a research facility in Rome. For the next 15 years she divided her time between Rome and St. Louis. Upon her retirement from Washington University in 1977, she returned to Rome to focus solely on her duties as director of the Institute of Cell Biology of the Italian National Council of Research, a position she had held since 1969. Although she retired again in 1979, she continued to conduct research. In 1986 she discovered that NGF also stimulates the growth of brain cells, and that a link exists between NGF and the body's immune system. These last two discoveries hold out the hope that NGF might someday be used to treat conditions such as Alzheimer's disease and strokes.

Further Reading

Hargittai, Istvan, and Magdolna Hargittai. *Candid Science II: Conversations with Famous Biomedical Scientists*. London: Imperial College Press, 2002, pp. 364–376.

Levi-Montalcini, Rita. *In Praise of Imperfection: My Life and Work*. New York: Basic Books, 1988.

Nobelprize.org. "The Nobel Prize in Physiology or Medicine 1986." Available online. URL: http://nobelprize.org/medicine/laureates/1986. Downloaded on August 31, 2003.

Wasson, Tyler, ed. *Nobel Prize Winners.* New York: H. W. Wilson, 1987, pp. 625–627.

Lewis, Edward B.
(1918–2004) *geneticist*

Edward B. Lewis made important discoveries concerning the way genes govern an organism's development from embryo to adulthood. This discovery earned him a share of the 1995 Nobel Prize in physiology or medicine.

Lewis was born on May 20, 1918, in Wilkes-Barre, Pennsylvania, to Edward and Laura Lewis. He received a B.A. in biostatistics from the University of Minnesota in 1939, a Ph.D. in genetics from the California Institute of Technology (Caltech) in 1942, and an M.S. in meteorology from Caltech in 1943. He spent the next two years as a weatherman and oceanographer with the U.S. Army Air Force, and served in the Pacific theater during World War II. In 1946, the same year he married Pamela Harrah with whom he had three children, he returned to Caltech to teach biology. Except for one-year stints as a Rockefeller Foundation Fellow at Cambridge University in England (1947–48) and as a visiting professor at the University of Copenhagen's Institute of Genetics in Denmark (1975–76), he remained at Caltech for the rest of his career.

Lewis's interest in genetics began in high school when he and a friend paid one dollar for 100 fruit flies from a university biology department. At the time, fruit flies were the subject of choice for geneticists because they are inexpensive, small, and they breed quickly, a new generation being hatched every 10 days. Indeed, by the time he went off to college, he had already bred several mutant fruit flies and had begun to study the cause of genetic mutations.

Lewis focused his research on understanding how genes control the fruit fly's physiological development from larva to adult. He was particularly fascinated by how a fruit fly could develop a double set of wings, and he was eventually able to show that this development is accompanied by the development of two thoraxes, the body segment that contains the wings. By 1978 he had made a

Edward Lewis showed how genes guide and regulate the development of an organism from an embryo to adulthood. *(Courtesy of the California Institute of Technology)*

number of other important discoveries. He showed that the positioning, or mispositioning, of genes on a chromosome has an important effect on the development of a mutated fly. He demonstrated that the genes governing the development of the fruit fly's 14 body segments are arranged in order on the chromosome. He discovered that genes not only have their own individual roles to play, but also that they work together as part of what he called a gene complex to regulate the growth and development of large sections—segments, in the case of the fruit fly—of an organism. He also demonstrated the role played by each of the fruit fly's chromosomes that regulate the development and arrangement of each of the fruit fly's segments.

Other researchers later showed that genes and gene complexes operate in humans the same way they do in fruit flies, and that the genes that regulate the growth and development of humans and fruit flies from the embryo to maturity are arranged on the chromosome in the same order. In turn, this discovery shed much light on how vertebrates develop. For his contributions in this regard, Lewis was awarded a one-third share of the 1995 Nobel Prize in physiology or medicine. His corecipients were the German physiologist Christiane Nüsslein-Volhard and the American embryologist ERIC F. WIESCHAUS.

Lewis was elected to the National Academy of Sciences and the American Academy of Arts and Sciences, and he was awarded the National Medal of Science. In 1988 he retired from Caltech to his home in San Marino, California, although he continued to study and publish articles about the genetics of fruit flies. He died on July 21, 2004, in Pasadena, California.

Further Reading

Hargittai, Istvan, and Magdolna Hargittai. *Candid Science II: Conversations with Famous Biomedical Scientists.* London: Imperial College Press, 2002, pp. 350–364.

Krapp, Kristine M., ed. *Notable Twentieth-Century Scientists Supplement.* Detroit: Gale Research, 1998, pp. 283–284.

Nobelprize.org. "The Nobel Prize in Physiology or Medicine 1995." Available online. URL: http://nobelprize.org/medicine/laureates/1995. Downloaded on June 10, 2004.

Lewis, Gilbert N.
(Gilbert Newton Lewis)
(1875–1946) *chemist*

Gilbert N. Lewis never won a Nobel Prize, but he is generally considered to have been one of the most important American chemists of all time. His major contribution shed light on the nature of the covalent bond, a basic feature of chemical reactivity.

Lewis was born on October 23, 1875, in Weymouth, Massachusetts. His father, Francis, was a lawyer, and his mother, Mary, was a homemaker. At age nine he moved with his family to Lincoln, Nebraska, where he grew up. After attending the University of Nebraska for a year, he transferred to Harvard University where he studied under THEODORE W. RICHARDS and received a B.A., an

M.A., and a Ph.D. in chemistry in 1896, 1898, and 1899, respectively. Over the next six years, he taught chemistry at Harvard, studied at the universities of Leipzig and Göttingen in Germany, and supervised the bureau of weights and measures in the Philippines, at the time a U.S. possession. In 1905 he joined the faculty at the Massachusetts Institute of Technology (MIT), but he left after seven years to become dean of the college of chemistry at the University of California at Berkeley, where he remained for the rest of his career. Under his tutelage, Berkeley's chemistry program developed into one of the best in the country, and in time it would turn out more Nobel Prize winners than any other. In 1912 he married Mary Sheldon with whom he had three children.

Throughout his career, Lewis strove to make chemistry more of an exact science. At the dawn of the 20th century, most chemists tried to apply the laws of thermodynamics to chemical reactions involving solutions. These laws, however, are based on the behaviors of ideal gases and liquids, and so they are of little value in predicting the outcomes of actual experiments. In 1900 Lewis began looking for ways to make chemistry more exact in dealing with reactions involving real gases and solutions. While teaching at Harvard, he proposed the use of concepts such as fugacity (the tendency of a component in a liquid mixture to vaporize from the mixture) and free energy (the amount of work—energy—that a particular reaction is capable of doing—releasing). While teaching at MIT, he proposed the concept of activity, which states that a solution's ability to react equals its ideal reactivity minus the reactivity lost due to the interaction of its constituents. In so doing, Lewis established himself as one of the leading American practitioners of physical chemistry, the branch of science that studies chemistry via the application of the laws of physics. His ideas concerning physical chemistry were published in *Thermodynamics and the Free Energy of Chemical Substances* (1923).

Lewis's most important work involved the nature of electron sharing in a chemical reaction. The electron was discovered in 1895 by British physicist J. J. Thomson, and shortly after its discovery other physicists began postulating that it might have something to do with chemical reactions. The most common theory was that two atoms reacted by exchanging one or more electrons. In 1902 it occurred to Lewis that, rather than exchange electrons, atoms might instead share electrons in their valence, or outer, shell. By 1916 he had concluded that the electron-pair bond, whereby two atoms each share an electron in the valence shell, is a primary feature of chemical reactions, and he developed a theory that explained the wide range of situations involving equal as well as nonequal conditions of sharing.

At first, Lewis's theory was rejected by American chemists. After 1919, when IRVING LANGMUIR popularized it and renamed the electron-pair bond the covalent bond, it began to gain wider acceptance. By 1923 Lewis had expanded his thinking about electrons to use them to provide a better understanding of the difference between acids and bases. An acid, he stated, is any substance that can accept an electron pair, while a base is any substance that can donate an electron pair. He published his ideas concerning electron pairs and related concepts in *Valence and the Structure of Atoms and Molecules* (1923), a classic in modern bonding theory.

The latter part of Lewis's career was devoted to a number of different research interests. In the mid-1930s he experimented with the separation of isotopes, forms of a chemical element that have the same number of protons but a different number of neutrons. In the late 1930s he studied the ultraviolet absorption spectra, and in the 1940s he examined the spectra of fluorescence and phosphorescence. He died as the result of a laboratory accident on March 23, 1946, in Berkeley.

Further Reading

Hildebrand, Joel H. "Gilbert Newton Lewis," National Academy of Sciences, *Biographical Memoirs* 31 (1958): pp. 209–235.

Lachman, Arthur. *Borderland of the Unknown: The Life Story of Gilbert Newton Lewis, One of the World's Great Scientists.* New York: Pageant Press, 1955.

The Woodrow Wilson National Fellowship Foundation. "Gilbert Newton Lewis." Available online. URL: http://www.woodrow.org/teachers/chemistry/institutes/1992/Lewis.html. Downloaded on January 31, 2004.

Libby, Willard F.
(Willard Frank Libby)
(1908–1980) *chemist*

Willard F. Libby developed the radiocarbon dating technique for determining the age of organic compounds that are thousands of years old. For this achievement, he was awarded the 1960 Nobel Prize in chemistry.

Libby was born on December 17, 1908, in Grand Valley, Colorado. His parents, Ora and Eva, were farmers. At age five he moved with his family to Santa Rosa, California, where he grew up, although he attended school in nearby Sebastopol. In 1927 he entered the University of California at Berkeley, receiving a B.S. in chemistry in 1931 and a Ph.D. in chemistry in 1933. He then taught chemistry at Berkeley for the next eight years. In 1940 he married Leonor Hickey with whom he had two children; they divorced in 1966, and that same year he married Leona Marshall with whom he had two children.

Libby's research at Berkeley focused on radioactivity, the process by which certain elements decay; isotopes, uncommon forms of an element that possess the same number of protons as the most common form but a different number of neutrons; and the behavior of chemical elements in gaseous states. His work in these areas qualified him for a research fellowship at Princeton University, where he went in 1941. It also qualified him to work on the Manhattan Project, the U.S. effort during World War II to build the first atomic bombs, and in 1942 he moved to Columbia University to work on the project. For the next three years he helped design and perfect a gaseous-diffusion process by which the highly fissionable uranium isotope known as U-235 could be separated from the more abundant forms of uranium for use in an atomic bomb. In 1945 he was named professor of chemistry at the University of Chicago and a staff member of its Enrico Fermi Institute for Nuclear Studies.

After the war, Libby resumed the study of an earlier interest, the use of radioactive isotopes as a dating technique. In 1939 researchers at New York University discovered that cosmic rays, rays of particles that originate in outer space, cause a chain reaction in Earth's upper atmosphere that results in a small amount of nitrogen atoms decaying via radioactivity into a radioactive isotope of carbon known as carbon-14 or radiocarbon. It occurred to Libby that radiocarbon then bonded with oxygen in the atmosphere to form carbon dioxide, an essential ingredient in plant photosynthesis. Since virtually all living organisms nourish themselves, either directly or indirectly, on plants, it stood to reason that all living organisms maintain a low level of radioactivity throughout their lives. Upon dying, however, the degree of radioactivity in the organism would decrease in accordance with the half-life, or speed of decay, of the radiocarbon. At the time, radiocarbon was believed to have a half-life of about 5,600 years (modern measuring techniques have shown it to be 5,730 years). Libby concluded that the age of any organic compound between 500 and 70,000 years old could be determined accurately if the amount of radiocarbon in the organism

Willard Libby developed the radiocarbon dating technique, thus providing archaeologists with a useful tool for dating artifacts. *(Courtesy of the University of Chicago)*

could be measured accurately; today, the upper limit of the accuracy of radiocarbon dating is known to be between 40,000 and 50,000 years.

Libby published his theory in 1947 and expanded upon it in *Radiocarbon Dating* (1952; 2nd ed. 1955). His next step was to develop a measuring device capable of testing his theory. By adapting techniques developed by German physicist Walther Bothe in the 1930s, in 1953 Libby developed a radiation detector that could detect and measure extremely low levels of radioactivity. He tested his device on a number of ancient artifacts whose dates were known, as well as on sequoia trees, whose exact age could be determined from counting their rings. Having developed both the theory and the device, Libby made it possible for archaeologists, paleontologists, and other researchers who deal with ancient organic material to date that material more accurately than ever before. The importance of his contribution was noted in 1960 when he was awarded the Nobel Prize in chemistry. By that same year, more than 40 radiocarbon testing centers had been established around the world. Radiocarbon dating also inspired other researchers to use radioactive isotopes to develop dating techniques for inorganic material, such as potassium-argon dating, which is capable of dating rocks that are millions of years old.

Libby left Chicago in 1954 to serve on the general advisory committee of the U.S. Atomic Energy Commission. In 1959 he returned to academia by joining the faculty at the University of California at Los Angeles (UCLA). Three years later he was named director of UCLA's Institute of Geophysics and Planetary Physics, a position he held until his retirement in 1976. He died on September 8, 1980, in Los Angeles.

Further Reading

E Museum @ Minnesota State University, Mankato. "Willard Frank Libby." Available online. URL: http://www.mnsu.edu/emuseum/information/biography/klmno/libby_willard.html. Downloaded on March 25, 2005.

Nobelprize.org. "The Nobel Prize in Chemistry 1960." Available online. URL: http://nobelprize.org/chemistry/laureates/1960. Downloaded on April 30, 2004.

Wasson, Tyler, ed. *Nobel Prize Winners.* New York: H. W. Wilson, 1987, pp. 632–634.

Lipmann, Fritz A.
(Fritz Albert Lipmann)
(1899–1986) *biochemist*

Fritz A. Lipmann received a share of a Nobel Prize for discovering the first coenzyme, a relatively small organic molecule that activates an enzyme. His research contributed to a better understanding of how the human body converts carbohydrates into energy.

Lipmann was born on June 12, 1899, in Königsberg, Germany (today Kaliningrad, Russia). His father, Leopold, was a lawyer, and his mother, Gertrud, was a homemaker. In 1917 he entered the University of Königsberg, but he left after a year to serve in the German army during World War I. Discharged in 1919, he entered the University of Munich and graduated in 1922. He then enrolled in the University of Berlin where he received an M.D. in 1924 and a Ph.D. in chemistry in 1927. Over the next 14 years he conducted biochemical research at the universities of Berlin and Heidelberg, the Rockefeller Institute for Medical Research (today Rockefeller University) in New York City, the Biological Institute of the Carlsberg Foundation in Copenhagen, Denmark, and Cornell Medical School in Ithaca, New York. In 1941 he was named head of the biochemical research laboratory at Boston's Massachusetts General Hospital (MGH) and professor of biological chemistry at Harvard Medical School, positions he held for the next 16 years. In 1957 he joined the faculty at Rockefeller University in New York City, where he remained for the rest of his career. In 1931 he married Elfreda Hall with whom he had one child, and in 1944 he became an American citizen.

Prior to becoming affiliated with MGH, Lipmann's research involved the biochemical reactions occurring in muscle and tissue and the metabolism of fibroblasts, cells that contribute to the formation of connective tissue fibers. He also investigated the chemical composition of phosphoproteins, compounds that contain protein and phosphorus, and the role played in the metabolism of embryo cells by glycolysis, the decomposition of glucose and related carbohydrates. To a lesser extent, he also participated in cancer research.

In 1941 Lipmann began to focus on a series of biochemical reactions known collectively as the tricarboxylic acid cycle, commonly known as the Krebs cycle in honor of its discoverer, German-British biochemist Hans A. Krebs. The Krebs cycle is an important part of the process by which carbohydrates are converted into the compounds that provide almost two-thirds of the energy used by the human body. In 1937 Krebs was able to describe the tricarboxylic acid cycle to a considerable degree, but he was not able to explain every detail as to how it worked. Much of the confusion centered on several enzymes that became activated during the cycle in some mysterious way, so Lipmann set out to see if he could shed light on this mystery.

Lipmann's first conclusion was that the enzymes were activated by acetyl phosphate, a combination of acetic acid and phosphorus acid. Lipmann based this conclusion partly on the fact that much acetic acid is produced during the Krebs cycle. His colleagues, however, rejected this idea and even denied that the production of acetyl phosphate had anything to do with the Krebs cycle. Undaunted, Lipmann continued to experiment, and by 1947 he had isolated a compound he called Coenzyme A, also known as CoA. Lipmann showed that Coenzyme A reacts with an acetyl compound and then with oxaloacetic acid to produce citric acid, which activates seven enzymes whose activities are crucial to the operation of the Krebs cycle. By 1953 he was able to describe in detail the activities and molecular composition of Coenzyme A. Previously the existence of coenzymes was unknown, so Lipmann's discovery opened up an entirely new field for biochemists to investigate. Today it is known that Coenzyme A is involved in the conversion of amino acids, steroids, fatty acids, and hemoglobins into energy, and that a host of other coenzymes activate a number of critical biochemical reactions. In recognition of his discovery, Lipmann was awarded a half share of the 1953 Nobel Prize in physiology or medicine; the recipient of the other half was Krebs.

In 1940 Lipmann had proposed that a substance known as adenosine triphosphate (ATP) is the common form by which energy is exchanged in many cells, a proposal that is generally accepted today. Much of his research after 1953 investigated the activity of several phosphate and sulfate derivatives involved with the transfer of ATP. He also investigated the biochemical synthesis of protein and peptides, certain compounds containing two or more amino acids.

In addition to the Nobel Prize, Lipmann was awarded the National Medal of Science and elected to the National Academy of Sciences. He died on July 24, 1986, in Poughkeepsie, New York.

Further Reading

Lipmann, Fritz. *Wanderings of a Biochemist.* New York: Wiley-Interscience, 1971.

Nobelprize.org. "The Nobel Prize in Physiology or Medicine 1953." Available online. URL: http://nobelprize.org/medicine/laureates/1953. Downloaded on February 18, 2004.

Wasson, Tyler, ed. *Nobel Prize Winners.* New York: H. W. Wilson, 1987, pp. 634–636.

Lipscomb, William N.
(William Nunn Lipscomb, Jr.)
(1919–   ) *physical chemist*

William N. Lipscomb demonstrated that, in certain instances, covalent bonds can bind together three atoms instead of just two. He also showed that a chemical compound's three-dimensional shape is an important factor in its ability to react with other compounds. For these contributions, he was awarded the 1976 Nobel Prize in chemistry.

Lipscomb was born on December 9, 1919, in Cleveland, Ohio, to William and Edna Lipscomb. As a baby he moved with his family to Lexington, Kentucky, where he grew up. In 1941 he received a B.S. in chemistry from the University of Kentucky and entered the California Institute of Technology, where he conducted research for the U.S. Office of Scientific Research and Development. After receiving a Ph.D. in physical chemistry in 1946, he joined the faculty of the University of Minnesota. In 1944 he married Mary Adele Sargent with whom he had two children; they divorced in 1983, and that same year he married Jean Evans with whom he had one child.

William Lipscomb demonstrated that a chemical compound's reactivity is determined in part by the three-dimensional arrangement of its atoms. *(Courtesy of William N. Lipscomb)*

Lipscomb's early research involved boranes, also known as boron hydrides, chemical compounds made from boron and hydrogen. Boranes do not exist in nature, and they were unknown until German chemist Alfred Stock invented them in 1912. Boranes proved to be of great interest to physical chemists because of the unique nature of their chemical bond. Most chemical bonds are covalent, whereby two atoms share an electron pair. Boranes, however, are electron-deficient, meaning they do not seem to have enough electrons in their outer shells for all of their atoms to be bound in covalent bonds. Several chemists, including LINUS C. PAULING, Lipscomb's thesis adviser at Caltech, had advanced interesting theories about the structure of boranes. By 1949 the most likely explanation was that boranes feature a three-center bond whereby two boron atoms and one hydrogen atom are linked together. However, no one could demonstrate conclusively that this unique arrangement is indeed the case.

In the early 1950s Lipscomb took up the problem of borane structure, and in 1954 he was able to offer a more sophisticated explanation. He beamed X-rays into a crystalline borane compound and then recorded on a photographic plate the pattern in which the beams were scattered, thus marking the exact location of the atoms in the crystal. As a result, he was able to show that covalent bonds do indeed bind boranes together, as they do all known chemical compounds, but in the three-center bond the three atoms share only two covalent pairs, so that these pairs orbit three atoms instead of just two. He then began studying the nature of the three-dimensional structure of the boranes by using nuclear magnetic resonance (NMR), and eventually he showed that the unique three-center bond gives the boranes a unique three-dimensional shape that is very stable despite their electron deficiency. He published his work concerning the boranes in *Boron Hydrides* (1963) and *NMR Studies of Boron Hydrides and Related Compounds* (1969). Because his work shed much light on the nature of chemical bonds and structures, Lipscomb was awarded the 1976 Nobel Prize in chemistry.

Meanwhile, in 1959 Lipscomb had left Minnesota to become a professor of chemistry at Harvard University. Although he continued to experiment with boranes, at Harvard he also began to investigate how the three-dimensional structure of an enzyme affects its ability to initiate biochemical reactions. He was particularly interested in the mechanisms of allosteric control, whereby a small regulatory molecule either inhibits or activates a particular enzyme by altering its three-dimensional shape.

Lipscomb retired from his teaching duties at Harvard in 1990, although he continued to conduct research there for a number of years. His many honors include election to the National Academy of Sciences and the American Academy of Arts and Sciences and a term as president of the American Crystallographic Association.

Further Reading

Eaton, Gareth R., et al., eds. *Structures and Mechanism: From Ashes to Enzymes.* New York: Oxford University Press, 2002 [preface is an autobiography of Lipscomb].

Nobelprize.org. "The Nobel Prize in Chemistry 1976." Available online. URL: http://nobelprize.org/chemistry/laureates/1976. Downloaded on August 12, 2004.

Wasson, Tyler, ed. *Nobel Prize Winners.* New York: H. W. Wilson, 1987, pp. 638–640.

Luria, Salvador E.
(Salvador Edward Luria)
(1912–1991) *molecular biologist*

Salvador E. Luria was one of the first molecular biologists, scientists who study the biophysical principles by which living things grow and reproduce. His research contributed to a better understanding of how viruses replicate and mutate, for which he received a share of the 1969 Nobel Prize in physiology or medicine.

Luria was born on August 13, 1912, in Turin, Italy. His father, David, was an accountant and printer, and his mother, Ester, was a homemaker. At age 17 he entered the University of Turin Medical School and received an M.D. in 1935. He spent the next three years as a medical officer in the Italian army, after which he spent two years as a research fellow studying medical physics and radiology at the Institute of Radium in Paris, France. In 1940 he accepted a position as a research assistant in surgical bacteriology at the University of Columbia's College of Physicians and Surgeons in New York City, but he left after three years to teach bacteriology at the University of Indiana. In 1950 he was named a professor of microbiology at the University of Illinois, and in 1959 he took a similar position at the Massachusetts Institute of Technology (MIT), which he held until his death. From 1974 to 1985 he also served as director of MIT's Center for Cancer Research. In 1945 he married Zella Hurwitz with whom he had one child, and in 1947 he became a naturalized U.S. citizen.

Luria began experimenting with viruses while at the Institute of Radium, where he studied the effects of radiation on the ability of viruses and bacteria to replicate and mutate. In 1941 he met MAX DELBRÜCK, a researcher at the California Institute of

Technology, who for several years had been studying replication and mutation in bacteriophages, or phages, viruses that infect bacteria. One of the simplest forms of life, a phage consists of a core of nucleic acid enclosed in a protein shell, and Delbrück and Luria hoped that their research would shed light on the genetic functions of more sophisticated life-forms. Using a simple process for growing phages that Delbrück had devised, the two began working independently on similar experiments in the hope of stimulating each other's thinking without duplicating each other's efforts. In 1942 they were joined by ALFRED D. HERSHEY of the Washington University in St. Louis, Missouri, and together the three formed the core of the so-called phage school, an informal group of researchers conducting closely related experiments on phages.

Shortly after meeting Delbrück, Luria began investigating the ability of bacteria to develop resistance to phages. Researchers knew that a phage could not kill all the bacteria in a single colony, even if they all had been cloned from the same original bacterium. The question was whether immunity resulted because exposure to the phage had caused immunity in one or more of the bacteria, which then passed it on to the next generation, or whether the virus-resistant bacteria had already existed, via mutation, in the colony prior to the colony's exposure to the phage. To answer this question, Luria spent the next six years developing and perfecting the so-called fluctuation test, and in 1947 he demonstrated that bacteria develop immunity by mutating. This discovery led a number of geneticists to shift their work from higher-order organisms, such as fruit flies, to bacteria because of the ease and speed with which multiple generations can be produced, thus making it easier to check the effects of an experiment on the genetic behavior and characteristics of multiple generations.

Meanwhile Luria continued to focus on phages. By 1952 he had become convinced that phage protein is the carrier of genetic coding in all living things, and that genetic mutations are caused by viral infections that induce a cell's genes to mutate so as to develop immunity to the infection. He was soon forced to abandon this idea, however, when Hershey demonstrated that same year that a phage replicates by injecting its nucleic acid, and not its protein, into a bacterial cell. Coupled with the discovery by JAMES D. WATSON and Francis Crick of the double-helical structure of DNA the following year, this discovery demonstrated that biochemistry, and not biophysics in the form of molecular biology, offered the best approach to understanding the mechanics of genetic replication. As a result, the importance of the phage school was reduced significantly. Nevertheless, the phage school had provided a considerable amount of invaluable information regarding the behavior of viruses. It also gave other researchers the tools they needed to develop vaccines against such viral diseases as measles, rubella, and mumps. Luria's contribution in this regard was acknowledged in 1969 when he, Delbrück, and Hershey were each awarded a one-third share of the Nobel Prize in physiology or medicine. He was also elected to the National Academy of Sciences and the American Academy of Arts and Science.

The latter portion of Luria's career was devoted to investigating viral infections as a potential cause of cancer. He died on February 6, 1991, in Lexington, Massachusetts.

Further Reading

Luria, Salvador E. *A Slot Machine, a Broken Test Tube: An Autobiography.* New York: Harper & Row, 1984.

Nobelprize.org. "The Nobel Prize in Physiology or Medicine 1969." Available online. URL: http://nobelprize. org/medicine/laureates/1969. Downloaded on April 16, 2004.

Wasson, Tyler, ed. *Nobel Prize Winners.* New York: H. W. Wilson, 1987, pp. 648–649.

M

MacDiarmid, Alan G.
(Alan Graham MacDiarmid)
(1927–) *chemist*

Alan G. MacDiarmid codiscovered electrically conducting organic polymers, also known as synthetic metals. For this discovery he was awarded a share of the 2000 Nobel Prize in chemistry.

MacDiarmid was born on April 14, 1927, in Masterton, New Zealand. His father, Archibald, was an engineer and his mother, Ruby, was a homemaker. During the Great Depression he moved with his family to Lower Hutt, a suburb of Wellington, where he grew up. At age 16 he entered Victoria University in Wellington, receiving a B.Sc. and an M.Sc. in chemistry in 1948 and 1950, respectively. He then came to the United States to study at the University of Wisconsin, receiving an M.S. and a Ph.D. in inorganic chemistry in 1952 and 1953, respectively. Postdoctoral studies at Cambridge University in England earned him a second Ph.D. in 1955, the same year he joined the faculty in the department of chemistry at the University of Pennsylvania. In 1954 he married Marian Mathieu with whom he had four children.

MacDiarmid's early research focused on sulfurnitride chemistry, the study of the compounds that can be obtained by combining sulfur (S) and nitrogen (N). As an undergraduate he became fascinated with S_4N_4, a beautiful bright orange crystal, and he wrote his master's thesis on its highly colorful derivatives. He later turned his attention to inorganic chemistry, particularly the molecular silicon compounds. He rekindled his interest in sulfurnitride chemistry in 1973 when ALAN J. HEEGER, a physics professor at Penn, informed him that American chemist Mortimer Labes had recently demonstrated that $(SN)_x$, a golden, film-like crystal known as polysulfurnitride, is capable of conducting electricity even though it is an organic polymer. MacDiarmid and Heeger began studying the conducting properties of polysulfurnitride, and eventually they demonstrated that the addition of bromine increased polysulfurnitride's conductivity by a factor of 10.

In 1975 MacDiarmid went to a conference in Japan where he met Hideki Shirakawa, a chemist at the Tokyo Institute of Technology. Shirakawa had developed $(CH)_x$, a beautifully lustrous, silver-colored, film-like form of the organic polymer polyacetylene, but unlike $(SN)_x$ it was only semiconductive. MacDiarmid recruited Shirakawa to come to Penn as a visiting scientist, and once Shirakawa had arrived he and MacDiarmid attempted to increase $(CH)_x$'s conductivity by purifying it. Instead, they made it less conductive. Concluding that small amounts of impurities actually increase the conductivity of organic polymers as they do in semiconductors, they then added bromine to an impure sample of $(CH)_x$, and its conductivity increased millions of times. In 1977 Heeger explained this phenomenon by showing that bromine removes some of the electrons from the carbon atoms that form every other link in $(CH)_x$'s polymeric chain. These missing electrons create "holes" through which other electrons can flow, thus making the polymer as conductive as a metal.

The work of MacDiarmid, Heeger, and Shirakawa led other researchers to develop a host of other conductive and semiconductive polymers. Because conducting polymers combine the high conductivity of metals with the flexibility and low weight of plastics, by the 1990s they had found ready acceptance in such diverse applications as rechargeable batteries, electromagnetic interference shielding, antistatic dissipation, stealth applications, corrosion inhibition, flexible "plastic" transistors and electrodes, and electroluminescent polymer displays, to name but a few. For discovering conducting polymers, MacDiarmid, Heeger, and Shirakawa were each awarded a one-third share of the 2000 Nobel Prize in chemistry.

Shirakawa returned to Japan in 1977, but MacDiarmid continued to collaborate with Heeger until 1982, when Heeger left Penn for the University of California at Santa Barbara. At that point MacDiarmid, who remained at Penn for the rest of his career, found a new collaborator in Arthur J. Epstein, and the two continued to study electrically conducting polymers, particularly polyaniline, the most technologically important conducting polymer.

Further Reading

Epstein, Arthur J., et al. *Special Issue Celebrating the Year 2000 Nobel Prize in Chemistry to Alan Heeger, Alan MacDiarmid, and Hideki Shirakawa for the Discovery and Development of Conductive Polymers.* Amsterdam: Elsevier, 2001.

Nobelprize.org. "The Nobel Prize in Chemistry 2000." Available online. URL: http://nobelprize.org/chemistry/laureates/2000. Downloaded on July 31, 2004.

Marcus, Rudolph A.
(Rudolph Arthur Marcus)
(1923–) *physical chemist*

Rudolph A. Marcus made important contributions to the theory of electron transfer reactions in chemical systems. For these contributions, he was awarded the 1992 Nobel Prize in chemistry.

Marcus was born on July 21, 1923, in Montreal, Canada, to Myer and Esther Marcus. He studied chemistry at Montreal's McGill University, receiving a B.S. in 1943 and a Ph.D. in 1946, and then went off to Ottawa to conduct postdoctoral research for the National Research Council of Canada. In 1949, the same year he married Laura Hearne with whom he had three children, he became a postdoctoral fellow at the University of North Carolina.

Shortly after arriving in the United States, Marcus became interested in the theory associated with chemical reaction rates. Although it was possible at the time to determine the speed of a number of reactions, the speeds themselves often seemed to make no sense. For example, many of the reactions involving the transfer of a single electron between ions in an aqueous solution take hours, while other reactions involving the transfer of one electron take place almost instantaneously. Several theories had been advanced to explain this phenomenon, as well as to calculate in general the rates of chemical reactions, but none were entirely

Rudolph A. Marcus pioneered the study of genetics in the United States. *(Courtesy of the California Institute of Technology)*

satisfactory. Marcus combined the Rice-Ramsperger-Kassel theory, which treats the rate at which a single electron is transferred from one atom to another in a unimolecular gas reaction as a function of the molecule's energy, with transition-state theory, which takes into account only the molecule's statistical properties, to derive a relatively simple mathematical equation for computing reaction rates. Published in 1952, his work in this regard is known today as the Rice-Ramsperger-Kassel-Marcus (RRKM) theory.

In 1951 Marcus became a professor of physical chemistry at the Polytechnic Institute of Brooklyn, New York. He continued to study electron transfer reactions in solution, extending the focus of the RRKM theory to include redox reactions, oxidation and reduction reactions in which the reactants exchange electrons. He was particularly interested in the role played during redox reactions by the molecules of solvent surrounding the reactants. By 1965 he had concluded that, during a redox reaction, the molecular structures of the reactants and the solvent undergo minute changes. These changes temporarily increase the energy of the system, thus permitting the movement of an electron from one reactant to the other. More importantly, he also concluded that reaction rates are governed by the reaction's free energy change, or driving force. Using simple quantities such as ionic radii and ionic charges, he developed a mathematical equation for expressing the relationship between reaction speed and driving force. The parabola described by the equation shows that, once a reaction's driving force reaches a certain level, it actually serves to decrease the reaction rate rather than increase it.

This latter portion of Marcus's theory aroused much controversy and skepticism among physical chemists, partly because it defied logic and partly because there was no experimental evidence to confirm it. When such evidence became available in the mid-1980s, the value of Marcus's work became more apparent. Today it is applied to the study of a wide range of phenomena from photosynthesis to chemiluminescence, or cold light. In recognition of his contribution to a better understanding of how electrons are transferred during chemical reactions, he was awarded the 1992 Nobel Prize in chemistry.

Meanwhile, in 1964 Marcus, who had become a naturalized U.S. citizen six years earlier, was named a professor of physical chemistry at the University of Illinois at Champaign-Urbana. In 1978 he took a similar position at the California Institute of Technology, where he continued his investigations concerning electron transfers. His many honors include the National Medal of Science and election to the National Academy of Sciences and the American Academy of Arts and Sciences.

Further Reading

McMurray, Emily J., ed. *Notable Twentieth-Century Scientists.* Detroit: Gale Research, 1995, pp. 1,316–1,317.

Nobelprize.org. "The Nobel Prize in Chemistry 1992." Available online. URL: http://nobelprize.org/chemistry/laureates/1992. Downloaded on August 13, 2004.

Maury, Antonia
(Antonia Caetana De Paiva Pereira Maury)
(1866–1952) *astronomer*

Antonia Maury was one of a group of women who made significant contributions to astronomy in the late 19th century. Her most important contribution was to modify an existing system for classifying stars to make it more comprehensive.

Maury was born on March 21, 1866, in Cold Spring, New York. Her father, Mytton, was a clergyman and the editor of *Maury's Geographical Series*, and her mother, Virginia, was a homemaker. After completing most of her elementary and secondary education under the tutelage of her father, she enrolled in Vassar College and received a B.A. in astronomy, physics, and philosophy in 1887. While at Vassar she studied under MARIA MITCHELL, a noted astronomer.

In 1888 Maury went to work as an assistant at the Harvard College Observatory. The observatory was in the process of identifying and classifying every star in the heavens, a project that had been funded by the estate of Maury's uncle, Henry Draper. One of her first tasks was to determine the period of rotation of Mizar; discovered by the observatory's director, Edward Pickering, Mizar is a spectroscopic binary or double star, a pair of stars so close together that they appear to be one from the vantage point of Earth. In 1889 she discovered another double star, Beta Aurigae.

Despite her brilliant work, Maury soon incurred Pickering's displeasure. He and WILLIAMINA FLEMING had devised a stellar classification system that Maury thought was too simple. The project involved photographing stars through a telescope and a spectroscope, an optical device that measured the wavelengths, or spectra, of the various stars. The spectrograms, as the photographs were called, were then analyzed and the stars contained thereon were identified and classified according to their spectra. In addition to classifying stars according to their brightness, Maury preferred to subclassify stars as normal, hazy, or sharp according to the sharpness of their spectral lines, whereas Pickering and Fleming thought that Maury's subclassification was unnecessary and time-consuming. For almost eight years, Pickering chided Maury for what he thought was her slowness, when in fact she was simply paying meticulous attention to a number of details that Pickering did not care about. In time Maury's subclassifications would be adopted by astronomers around the world—in 1943 she was awarded the American Astronomical Society's ANNIE J. CANNON Prize in recognition of her system—but in 1896 her devotion to them resulted in her resignation from the observatory.

From 1896 to 1918 Maury pursued a multifaceted career in science. For most of the period, she taught physics and astronomy at a variety of high schools and, for a while, at Cornell University. She also lectured on the need to preserve historic sites and to conserve natural resources. From time to time she would visit Harvard Observatory to conduct research on double stars.

In 1918 Pickering retired from the observatory, and that same year Maury rejoined the observatory's staff. In addition to her stellar classification work, she devoted a considerable amount of time to researching double stars, especially Beta Lyrae, a double star in the northern constellation Lyra. Discovered by John Goodricke in 1784, Beta Lyrae's twin stars are so close together that they exchange material and share a common atmosphere, and they are steadily losing mass to an expanding ring of gases that surround them. In 1933 she published her findings regarding the spectral changes of Beta Lyrae in *Annals of the Harvard College Observatory*.

Maury retired from the observatory in 1935. She spent the next three years as curator of the Draper Park Observatory Museum in the former home of Henry Draper in Hastings-on-Hudson, New York. In 1938 she retired from the museum to her own home in Hastings-on-Hudson, although she visited the Harvard Observatory annually. She died on January 8, 1952, having never married, in Dobbs Ferry, New York.

Further Reading

Bailey, Martha J. *American Women in Science: A Biographical Dictionary.* Santa Barbara, Calif.: ABC-CLIO, 1994, pp. 240–241.

Yount, Lisa. *A to Z of Women in Science and Math.* New York: Facts On File, 1999, pp. 140–141.

Maury, Matthew F.
(Matthew Fontaine Maury)
(1806–1873) *oceanographer*

Matthew F. Maury is generally recognized as one of the founders of modern oceanography. His pioneering studies of the oceans' winds and currents established the scientific basis for more extensive scientific investigations in this regard. They also led to the establishment of generally accepted shipping lanes, thus contributing to Maury's sobriquet "Pathfinder of the Seas." His work regarding the depth of the Atlantic Ocean's floor provided guidelines by which all of the world's seabeds could later be mapped.

Maury was born on January 14, 1806, in Spotsylvania County, Virginia, near Fredericksburg. His parents, Richard and Diana, were farmers. At age five he moved with his family to a farm on the outskirts of Franklin, Tennessee, where he grew up. His older brother was an officer in the U.S. Navy, which inspired Maury to pursue a similar career. In 1825 he joined the navy as a midshipman and spent most of the next 14 years at sea. His most memorable voyage occurred between 1826 and 1830, when he sailed around the world aboard the USS *Vincennes*. He also served as ship's astronomer on a voyage of exploration to the Pacific Ocean and surveyed several harbors in the southeastern United States. In 1834 he married Ann Herndon with whom he had eight children.

In 1839 Maury was forced to retire from active duty after a stagecoach accident left him lame, but he continued to serve on shore. In 1842 he was appointed superintendent of the Depot of Charts and Instruments and superintendent of the Naval Observatory in Washington, D.C. When these two commands were united as the U.S. Naval Observatory and Hydrographic Office in 1854, he was named its first superintendent.

Maury's career as an oceanographer began in 1836 when he published *A New Theoretical and Practical Treatise on Navigation*. Intended to be used as a handbook on navigation for naval officers, the book demonstrated Maury's growing interest in gathering and disseminating scientific data concerning winds and ocean currents. He devoted himself full-time to this interest after taking over the Depot of Charts and Instruments. In this capacity, he requested that the captains of U.S. naval vessels on duty in the Atlantic Ocean keep detailed logbooks concerning winds and currents. By 1847 he had collected enough data from the logbooks to publish *Wind and Current Chart of the North Atlantic,* which included a detailed treatise on the Gulf Stream. This effort, the first scientific study of the sea, was followed up the following year by *Abstract Log for the Use of American Navigators,* which was reissued in 1850 under the title *Notice to Mariners*. In 1851 he published *Explanations and Sailing Directions to Accompany the Wind and Current Charts,* which outlined the best routes for sailing between the various ports on both sides of the Atlantic. This work proved to be so valuable that it was updated and reissued eight times; the 1855 edition suggested the establishment of eastbound and westbound lanes in the foggy, heavily traveled North Atlantic so as to avoid head-on collisions, a suggestion that was generally adopted within short order.

Maury next turned his attention to providing mariners with wind and current charts of the entire globe. At first he attempted to glean the necessary information from old ships' logs, but soon he developed a detailed form, which he distributed to naval and merchant marine captains, on which all the data he required could be easily and succinctly

recorded. As data poured in from all over the world, the Depot of Charts and Instruments produced wind and current charts for the South Atlantic Ocean as well as the Pacific and Indian Oceans. In 1853, while representing the United States at an international meeting of oceanographers in Brussels, Belgium, he convinced a number of his counterparts to begin collecting data from their nations' mariners so that comprehensive wind and current charts could be published for the entire globe. At this meeting he also played an instrumental role in the founding of the International Hydrographic Bureau, the first international organization devoted to the study of the world's oceans.

While studying global winds and currents, Maury had developed an interest in the geography of the ocean bed. In order to gain more information in this regard, he requested ships' captains to take regular soundings and record them on forms, which were forwarded to the depot. Although he never gathered enough data to produce a satisfactory map of the entire Atlantic floor, by 1855 he was able to confirm the feasibility of laying a transatlantic telegraph cable between the United States and Ireland, which had already been connected by underwater cable to Great Britain, and to suggest the route that the cable should take. That same year he published what he had learned about the world's seabeds in *The Physical Geography of the Sea,* which is widely regarded as the first modern text on oceanography.

In addition to contributing to a better scientific understanding of the world's oceans, Maury's work had a practical application. By identifying prevailing winds and currents, he made it possible for ships' captains to plan the optimum routes for their voyages, thus reducing significantly the amount of time required to travel from one place to another by sea. For example, during the California Gold Rush in the late 1840s and early 1850s, Maury's charts helped reduce the time of the trip from New York to San Francisco by almost one-third. In recognition of his contributions, he received a number of awards and commendations from mercantile groups and scientific organizations alike.

Maury's oceanographic endeavors ended in 1861 when he resigned from the U.S. Navy (by now he had advanced to the rank of commander) to join the Confederate navy. For the next four years he supervised the defense of the Confederacy's coasts, harbors, and rivers. After the Civil War ended, he went to Mexico and accepted the position of commissioner of immigration; in this capacity he attempted unsuccessfully to establish a colony in that country for former Confederates. In 1866 he left Mexico for England but returned to the United States two years later to accept an appointment as professor of meteorology at the Virginia Military Institute in Lexington. He died on February 1, 1873, in Lexington.

Further Reading

American Studies at the University of Virginia. "Matthew Fontaine Maury." Available online. URL: http://xroads.virginia.edu/~UG97/monument/maurybio.html. Downloaded on July 24, 2003.

Jahns, Patricia. *Matthew Fontaine Maury and Joseph Henry, Scientists of the Civil War.* New York: Hastings House, 1961.

Williams, Frances L. *Matthew Fontaine Maury: Scientist of the Sea.* New Brunswick, N.J.: Rutgers University Press, 1963.

Mayer, Maria Goeppert
(Maria Gertrude Goeppert)
(1906–1972) *physicist*

Maria Goeppert Mayer developed the shell model, one of the most useful theories about how protons and neutrons behave in the atom. For this achievement, she was awarded a share of the 1963 Nobel Prize in physics.

Mayer was born Maria Gertrude Goeppert on June 28, 1906, in Kattowitz, Germany. Her father, Frederich, was a pediatrician, and her mother, Maria, was a homemaker. At age four she moved with her family to Göttingen, Germany, where her father had become a professor at the University of Göttingen. She later enrolled in Göttingen to study mathematics but changed her major to theoretical physics after coming into contact with Max Born, one of the German physicists who were developing the new theory of quantum mechanics, the study of subatomic particles. In 1930 she received a Ph.D. in theoretical physics and married Joseph E. Mayer with whom she had two children. Her husband was

Maria Goeppert Mayer developed a model to explain how protons and neutrons behave in an atomic nucleus. *(Library of Congress, Prints and Photographs Division [LC-USZ62-118262])*

an American physical chemist whom she had met at the University of Göttingen, and shortly after their marriage they moved to Baltimore, Maryland, where he had been named a professor of chemistry at Johns Hopkins University. She became a naturalized U.S. citizen in 1933.

Mayer's husband's career took the couple to Columbia University in 1940, the University of Chicago in 1946, and the University of California at San Diego in 1960. Until 1960 the rules of nepotism prevented Mayer from getting a full-time position anywhere her husband taught, and so the only academic positions she could obtain were either part-time or volunteer ones. These rules had relaxed somewhat by 1960, and at San Diego she was named to a full-time position as a professor of physics. Despite these constraints, she found support for her own research from her husband and from her colleagues at the various schools. At Hopkins she and Karl Herzfeld worked together to apply quantum mechanics to the study of chemistry. In 1940 she and her husband coauthored *Statistical Mechanics.* At Columbia she collaborated with ENRICO FERMI in the study of the chemical properties of neptunium and plutonium, the first two man-made elements. During World War II she worked with HAROLD C. UREY and EDWARD TELLER on building the first nuclear weapons. At Chicago she became affiliated with the Atomic Energy Commission's Argonne National Laboratory, where she, Fermi, and Teller continued to collaborate on studies related to the development of nuclear energy.

In 1948 Mayer and Teller took up a study of the fundamental properties of the natural elements in the hope of shedding light on their origins. Mayer focused on cataloguing the known isotopes, variations of an element whose atoms have the same number of protons as atoms of the most common form but a different number of neutrons. In the course of this study, she discovered that the most stable isotopes are the ones that have either 2, 8, 20, 28, 50, 82, or 126 nucleons (neutrons and protons) in their nuclei. These numbers correspond roughly to the number of electrons in the most stable elements, the noble or inert gases: helium (2), neon (10), argon (18), krypton (36), xenon (54), and radon (86). Since it was understood that the inert gases do not interact with other elements because their outer electron shells are full, it occurred to Mayer that the numbers she was seeing for stable isotopes might represent similarly full shells in the nucleus. This theory contradicted the conventional wisdom about the nature of the nucleus, which held that the nuclear forces were so strong that nucleons could not possibly orbit in the nucleus the same way that electrons orbit around the nucleus. Instead, physicists accepted the so-called liquid drop model of GEORGE GAMOW, which proposes that a nucleus is like a drop of water in that nucleons react flexibly and collectively to vibration by constantly changing the nucleus's shape.

By 1949 Mayer, in collaboration with her husband and Fermi, had worked out a fully articulated theory, known as the shell model, concerning the nature of the nucleus. According to the shell model, nucleons revolve in shells just like electrons do, and the maximum number of nucleons that can exist in a particular shell are, from innermost shell to outermost shell, 2, 6, 12, 18, 22, 32, and 44, respectively. This model was given added support by German physicist J. Hans D. Jensen, whose own team of researchers had arrived independently at the same conclusion as Mayer. Further investigation by other researchers indicated that the shell

model works particularly well for atoms that are spherically shaped, hence its other name, the spherical-shell model. Eventually, JAMES L. RAINWATER would develop a unified theory that combined those of Gamow and Mayer into a more comprehensive model, but in the meantime the shell model served as a good model for the nucleus. In 1955 Mayer and Jensen coauthored *Elementary Theory of Nuclear Shell Structure,* and in 1963 they were each awarded a quarter share of the Nobel Prize in physics. Their corecipient was the American physicist EUGENE P. WIGNER.

Mayer's other honors include election to the National Academy of Sciences. After winning the Nobel Prize, she continued to teach and conduct research until her death on February 20, 1972, in San Diego.

Further Reading

Dash, Joan. *A Life of One's Own: Three Gifted Women and the Men They Married.* New York: Harper & Row, 1973.

Nobelprize.org. "The Nobel Prize in Physics 1963." Available online. URL: http://nobelprize.org/physics/laureates/1963. Downloaded on March 15, 2004.

Sachs, Robert G. "Maria Goeppert Mayer," National Academy of Sciences, *Biographical Memoirs* 50 (1979): pp. 311–328.

Wasson, Tyler, ed. *Nobel Prize Winners.* New York: H. W. Wilson, 1987, pp. 677–680.

McClintock, Barbara
(1902–1992) *geneticist*

As a geneticist, Barbara McClintock went against the grain of her day. While most other geneticists studied DNA, she studied plants, specifically corn. While the conventional wisdom taught that genetic coding could not be passed from one gene to another, she proved otherwise. Although her ideas were treated with a healthy skepticism during much of her career, they were also given due consideration and led eventually to her being awarded a Nobel Prize.

McClintock was born on June 16, 1902, in Hartford, Connecticut. Her father, Thomas, was a physician, and her mother, Sara, was a homemaker.

At age six she moved with her family to Brooklyn, New York, where she grew up. In 1919 she entered Cornell University's College of Agriculture. During her junior year she took a course in genetics, which at the time was a relatively new field. She did so well that her professor invited her to take a graduate course in genetics, which she did. Upon receiving her B.S. in biology in 1923, she remained at Cornell to do graduate work in the relatively new field of cytogenetics, the study of the genetic content of chromosomes.

As a graduate student, McClintock experimented with maize, particularly *Zea mays*, popularly known as Indian corn, which has a different color pattern of kernels on each ear. She developed a method for preparing Indian corn cells for microscopic examination that allowed her to view each of a cell's 10 chromosome pairs and to distinguish them from one another. In 1927 she received a Ph.D. in botany and was hired to teach botany at Cornell. That same year she began working to match up the 10 chromosomes in an Indian corn cell with the plant's various genetic traits. In 1931 she and her graduate assistant, Harriet Creighton, published a paper identifying the genetic role of each chromosome.

By 1931 McClintock had realized that she much preferred to conduct research than to teach, and for the next five years she conducted research as a fellow of the National Research Council and the Guggenheim Foundation. Following a five-year stint as a botany professor at the University of Missouri, during which she focused more on research than on teaching, in 1941 she became affiliated with the Carnegie Institution of Washington's genetics laboratory at Cold Spring Harbor in Huntington, New York, on Long Island.

At Missouri, McClintock had experimented with the effect of X-rays on the chromosomes of Indian corn. She discovered that X-rays damaged chromosomes by destroying or changing genes, the result of which was an increase in the number of mutations, or random changes, in kernels. She continued this line of investigation at Cold Spring Harbor, and by 1944 she had discovered that a certain mutation did not occur randomly but rather at a regular and predictable rate. This led her to believe that mutations are not random at all but rather are controlled by some mechanism, probably located in the genes, that is capable of "jumping" from one chromosome to another. For the next six years she studied this phenomenon, and in 1950 she publicly presented her findings confirming the existence of transposable genetic elements, or transposons, as she called them. In essence, she had discovered that genes can change their places on a chromosome and even move from one chromosome to another, in the process interacting with other genes and changing the way these other genes behave.

McClintock's findings were not readily accepted by the scientific community. The prevailing opinion at the time was that chromosomes were much more stable than her work suggested. Moreover, the recent discovery that deoxyribonucleic acid (DNA) carried most genetic information had captured the attention of most geneticists, who generally ignored McClintock's work. She remained undaunted by this reception, partly because several of her former colleagues at Cornell supported her work. Also, in 1944 she had been elected to the National Academy of Sciences, becoming only the third woman to be so honored, and to a term as president of the Genetics Society of America, both major validations of her standing in the scientific community.

Despite the lack of enthusiastic acceptance of her ideas, McClintock continued her experiments with Indian corn, and eventually came to a startling discovery. She noted that the mutation rate of Indian corn increased whenever the corn was placed under environmental stress, such as too much sun or not enough rain, the result being a mutant strain of Indian corn that was better suited to survive in the new environmental situation. She reasoned from this that some genes are "turned on" by environmental factors, which in turn enables them to "turn on" the genes next to them, either on the same chromosome or on a chromosome to which they jump. This led her to the conclusion that the evolution of a particular species is determined in part by the environment and to a certain degree by the response of the members of that species to their environment.

McClintock continued to present her findings to skeptical geneticists until the late 1950s, but most were unable to accept what they thought were weird theories that contradicted what everyone "knew" about genetics. Nevertheless, her work made an impression, as indicated by her being awarded the Botanical Society of America's Merit Award in 1957, the National Academy of Sciences' Kimber Genetics Award in 1967, and the National Medal of Science in 1970. Not until the 1970s, however, did other researchers begin to validate her concepts in experiments of their own with bacteria, insects, animals, and humans, and as they did so McClintock's professional stature soared even higher. In 1983 she was awarded the Nobel Prize in physiology or medicine for her discovery of "mobile genetic elements."

McClintock spent the last 40 years of her scientific career at Cold Spring Harbor. She "retired" in 1967, but she continued to work there for another 25 years as a distinguished member. From 1965 to 1992 she also taught at Cornell as the Andrew White Professor at Large. She died, having never married, on September 2, 1992, in Huntington.

Further Reading

Bailey, Martha J. *American Women in Science: A Biographical Dictionary.* Santa Barbara, Calif.: ABC-CLIO, 1994, pp. 221–222.

Keller, Evelyn Fox. *A Feeling for the Organism: The Life and Work of Barbara McClintock.* San Francisco: W. H. Freeman, 1983.

Nobelprize.org. "The Nobel Prize in Physiology or Medicine 1983." Available online. URL: http://nobelprize. org/medicine/laureates/1983. Downloaded on August 29, 2003.

Wasson, Tyler, ed. *Nobel Prize Winners.* New York: H. W. Wilson, 1987, pp. 680–683.

Yount, Lisa. *A to Z of Women in Science and Math.* New York: Facts On File, 1999, pp. 131–134.

McMillan, Edwin M.
(Edwin Mattison McMillan)
(1907–1991) *physicist*

Edwin M. McMillan is best known for his work with the "atom smasher," the popular name for the cyclotron. His experiments with the cyclotron resulted in the creation of the first man-made element and won for him a Nobel Prize.

McMillan was born on September 18, 1907, in Redondo Beach, California. His father, Edwin H., was a physician, and his mother, Anna Marie, was a homemaker. As an infant he moved with his family to Pasadena where he grew up. As a high school student he attended many of the free lectures put on by the nearby California Institute of Technology (Caltech). After finishing high school he attended Caltech and received a B.S. in physics in 1928 and an M.S. in physics in 1929. He spent the next three years studying the behavior of subatomic particles at Princeton University and received a Ph.D. in physics in 1932. That same year he received a two-year National Research Council fellowship to do research at the University of California at Berkeley. Upon completion of the fellowship, he became a research associate at the Berkeley Radiation Laboratory (now Lawrence Berkeley Laboratory) and began his first experiment with cyclotrons.

Invented by ERNEST O. LAWRENCE and M. Stanley Livingston, two Berkeley researchers, the cyclotron generates an electromagnetic field to accelerate subatomic particles to extremely high velocities and then propels them into atomic nuclei in an effort to create an atomic reaction. Between 1934 and 1940, McMillan used the Lawrence-Livingston cyclotron to transmute aluminum and nitrogen, to create radioactive oxygen, and to investigate gamma rays and artificial radioactivity.

During this period McMillan became interested in the work of two Italian physicists, ENRICO FERMI and EMILIO SEGRÈ. In 1934 Fermi and Segrè had bombarded uranium nuclei with slow-moving neutrons; one of the results of this experiment may have been the creation of the first transuranium element, although no one knows for sure. If so, it would have occurred because several of the neutrons would have been fused to several of the uranium nuclei, thus increasing by one the nuclei's atomic number and transforming them into what is now known as neptunium. In 1938 three German physicists—Otto Hahn, Fritz Strassmann, and Lise Meitner—attempted to re-create the Fermi-Segrè experiment, but instead of obtaining a new element via nuclear fusion, they split several uranium nuclei into several parts via nuclear fission.

In 1940 McMillan and Philip H. Abelson used the Lawrence-Livingston cyclotron to conduct their own version of the Fermi-Segrè experiment. The major difference in the McMillan-Abelson version was that the velocity of the bombarding neutrons was greatly reduced. In so doing, they succeeded in getting enough neutrons to fuse with enough uranium nuclei that a new element, with an atomic number of 93, was created. The new element, a silvery metal, was christened neptunium in honor of the planet Neptune.

Neptunium was the first transuranium, or man-made, element, but it was not the last. Inspired by McMillan and Abelson, physicists the world over vied with one another to create more artificial elements, and by 1984 they had succeeded in creating a total of 15 transuranium elements. Meanwhile, his role in getting this line of experimentation under way earned for McMillan a share of the 1951 Nobel Prize for chemistry. His corecipient was the American physicist GLENN T. SEABORG.

Between 1940 and 1945 McMillan postponed his experimentation involving cyclotrons to conduct war-related research. He spent two years on various projects involving the development of sonar and microwave radar, and in 1942 he joined the Manhattan Project, which resulted in the development and detonation of the first atomic bomb. In 1941 he married Elsie Blumer with whom he had three children.

After World War II ended, McMillan began work on a second-generation cyclotron known today as a synchrocyclotron. An interesting feature about subatomic particles is that their mass increases as they approach the speed of light, thus causing them to decelerate. This in turn threw them out of synch with the oscillating electric pulses generated by the Lawrence-Livingston machine, which caused the particles to get lost somewhere inside the cyclotron. To solve this problem, McMillan synchronized the oscillating pulses so that they slowed down as the mass of the particles increased, thus keeping the particles in synch with the electromagnetic field.

McMillan continued to experiment with cyclotrons at the Berkeley Radiation Laboratory until he retired in 1973. During the last 17 years of his affiliation with the laboratory, he served as its director. He also served on the advisory committees of a number of scientific and government commissions and agencies, and from 1968 to 1971 he chaired the National Academy of Sciences. He died on September 7, 1991, in El Cerrito, California.

Further Reading

McMurray, Emily, ed. "Edwin M. McMillan," *Notable Twentieth-Century Scientists*. Detroit: Gale, 1995, pp. 1,352–1,353.

Nobelprize.org. "The Nobel Prize in Chemistry 1951." Available online. URL: http://nobelprize.org/chemistry/laureates/1951. Downloaded on July 5, 2003.

Seaborg, Glenn T., with Eric Seaborg. *Adventures in the Atomic Age: From Watts to Washington*. New York: Farrar, Straus and Giroux, 2001.

Wasson, Tyler, ed. *Nobel Prize Winners*. New York: H. W. Wilson, 1987, pp. 683–684.

Merrifield, R. Bruce
(Robert Bruce Merrifield)
(1921–) *biochemist*

R. Bruce Merrifield developed solid phase peptide synthesis, an automated method for the mass production of peptides, or chains of amino acids. For this contribution he was awarded the 1984 Nobel Prize in chemistry.

Merrifield was born on July 15, 1921, in Fort Worth, Texas. His father, George, was a salesman, and his mother, Lorene, was a homemaker. At age two he moved with his family to California, eventually settling in Montebello where he grew up. In 1939 he entered Pasadena (Calif.) Junior College, transferring two years later to the University of California at Los Angeles (UCLA) where he received a B.A. in chemistry in 1943. After a year as a research chemist with the Philip R. Park Research Foundation, he returned to UCLA, receiving a Ph.D. in biochemistry in 1949. That same year he married Elizabeth Furlong with whom he had six children and joined the faculty at the Rockefeller Institute for Medical Research (today Rockefeller University).

Merrifield's research involved proteins, the complex molecules that regulate virtually every biochemical process. He was particularly interested in amino acids (the basic building blocks of proteins) and peptides (the chains of amino acids from which proteins are constructed). After 10 years of research he concluded that peptide research was too difficult to do unless a better method for synthesizing peptides could be found, as the existing method required weeks if not months to prepare a single peptide. One problem involved in peptide synthesis was that, as the peptide got longer, the number of its potential bonding points increased, each of which had to be deactivated chemically before another amino acid could be added to the chain. Another problem was that after each link was added, the peptide had to be separated from the chemicals that remained from the reaction that added the link, a process that took time and involved a certain amount of loss of the synthesized peptide.

In 1959 Merrifield devised a method that circumvented both problems. By anchoring the amino acid from one end of a peptide to an insoluble polymeric base, he found that all of the peptide's bonding points could easily be deactivated except the one on the end of the chain to which the next amino acid would be attached. This method also negated the need to separate the peptide from byproducts and unused reactants, and when the process was complete the peptide could be detached easily from the base simply by using the proper solvent. By 1962 Merrifield was synthesizing peptides that were longer and purer than had been possible via the old method, and he was doing so in much less time. In 1965 he further improved the process by constructing the first automated peptide synthesizer, in essence a computerized mixer. Four years later he succeeded in synthesizing the enzyme known as ribonuclease, which consists of 124 different amino acid links. This process requires more than 300 different chemical reactions performed in more than 11,000 steps, but Merrifield's machine and method cut the time required to complete the peptide to a fraction of what it had been before.

The automation of solid phase peptide synthesis revolutionized the study and production of biochemical compounds. It is widely used in the development of new pharmaceutical drugs as well as in the manufacture of a wide range of drugs and biomedical compounds including hormones, growth factors, antibiotics, toxins, neuropeptides, antigens, ion carriers, and enzymes. For his work concerning solid phase peptide synthesis, Merrifield was awarded the 1984 Nobel Prize in chemistry.

Merrifield retired from Rockefeller in 1992. Nevertheless, he remained as a professor emeritus and continued to conduct research on various aspects of the development and application of solid phase synthesis in protein chemistry. His many honors include election to the National Academy of Sciences.

Further Reading

The Nobel Prize Internet Archive. "Robert Bruce Merrifield." Available online. URL: http://almaz.com/nobel/chemistry/1984a.html. Downloaded on March 25, 2005.

Nobelprize.org. "The Nobel Prize in Chemistry 1984." Available online. URL: http://nobelprize.org/chemistry/laureates/1984. Downloaded on August 9, 2004.

Wasson, Tyler, ed. Nobel Prize Winners. New York: H. W. Wilson, 1987, pp. 691–693.

Michelson, Albert A.
(Albert Abraham Michelson)
(1852–1931) *physicist*

Albert A. Michelson is best remembered for being the first to accurately measure the speed of light. However, he won a Nobel Prize not for this achievement but for developing more precise methods for measuring distances of all kinds.

Michelson was born on December 19, 1852, in Strelno, Prussia. His father, Samuel, was a merchant, and his mother, Rozalia, was a homemaker. At age two he emigrated with his family to the United States; they eventually settled in San Francisco, California, where he grew up. After graduating from the U.S. Naval Academy in 1873, he spent the next two years at sea and then returned to the academy to teach physics and chemistry. In 1877 he married Margaret Heminway with whom he had three children. They divorced in 1897, and two years later he married Edna Stanton with whom he had three children.

While teaching at the academy, Michelson became fascinated with the idea of measuring the speed of light. Encouraged by his commanding officer and his father-in-law, who helped pay for the necessary apparatus, Michelson assembled an arrangement of mirrors and lenses, and in 1879 he arrived at the most accurate value for the speed of light achieved to that date. Despite this impressive achievement, he believed he could obtain an even more accurate reading if he could obtain more knowledge about optics. After a year at the Nautical Almanac Office, where he served under SIMON NEWCOMB, in 1880 he obtained a leave of absence from the navy and went to Europe. For the next three years he studied optics at the leading scientific institutions of Germany and France. While in Europe he began working on the instrument that would allow him to achieve his goals, the Michelson interferometer.

The principles behind the interferometer were first described in 1862 by French physicist A.-H.-L. Fizeau. The interferometer divides a beam of light into two or more beams and makes them travel unequal paths. When the beams are reunited, the difference in their intensities creates interference, which appears as a pattern of alternating light and dark bands. In the Michelson interferometer, a half-silvered mirror divides the light beam into two equal beams; one is transmitted to a fixed mirror and the other is reflected at a perpendicular angle to a movable mirror. Analyzing the changes in the band patterns created by adjusting the movable mirror permits the precise measurement of the beam's movement, and therefore its velocity. Upon returning to the United States in 1883, having resigned his naval commission two years earlier, Michelson used his interferometer to determine the speed of light at 186,329 miles per second.

In 1883 Michelson moved to Cleveland, Ohio, to teach physics at the Case School of Applied Sciences (today Case Western Reserve University). That same year he began collaborating with Edward W. Morley in an effort to prove the existence of "luminiferous ether," a mysterious medium in space that made the transmission of light waves possible. Michelson and Morley theorized that, if luminiferous ether existed, then light waves would travel at one speed in the direction of the Earth's movement but at a different speed perpendicular to the Earth's movement. Between 1883 and 1887,

Michelson and Morley conducted a number of experiments with increasingly sensitive Michelson interferometers, but all of the experiments showed that light waves travel at exactly the same speed regardless of their direction relative to the Earth's movement. The negative results of the so-called Michelson-Morley experiment cast grave doubt on the existence of luminiferous ether and caused the scientific community to rethink the whole matter of light waves and their transmission. The issue was finally solved in 1905 when ALBERT EINSTEIN proposed that the speed of light is a universal constant.

In 1889 Michelson left Case for a similar position at Clark University in Worcester, Massachusetts. While at Clark, he realized that the interferometer made it more accurate, and more universally accessible, to base standard lengths, such as the meter, on a particular wavelength of light. He began experimenting with various wavelengths, and in 1893 he concluded that the best measurement for the meter could be obtained from measuring the wavelengths of the red light emitted by heated cadmium. He campaigned energetically for the adoption of such a standard, but it was not until 1960 that his proposal won universal acceptance. Nevertheless, the incredible precision of measurement that the Michelson interferometer made possible impressed the scientific community so much that in 1907 he was awarded the Nobel Prize in physics.

It was also at Clark that Michelson began using the interferometer to measure planetary distances. In 1891 he used the 36-inch telescope at the Lick Observatory in California to obtain close estimates of the diameters of Jupiter's four largest moons. He continued to experiment in this vein after leaving Clark in 1892 for the University of Chicago, where he formed a physics department and then served as its first head. By 1919 he had perfected his techniques and equipment to the point that he was able to determine the diameters of seven nearby stars. The following year he used the 100-inch telescope at the Mount Wilson Observatory near Pasadena, California, to determine the diameter of the star Betelgeuse as being almost 240 million miles, or roughly 300 times the diameter of the Sun.

In 1923 Michelson returned to his original interest, measuring the speed of light. Using a much more sensitive interferometer than before, he calculated the speed of light at 186,295 miles per second. In 1933 an experiment he had begun before his death yielded a value of 186,280 mps; this value stood until the 1970s, when the current value of 186,282.4 mps was determined.

Michelson published three classic works, *Velocity of Light* (1902), *Light Waves and Their Uses* (1899–1903), and *Studies in Optics* (1927). He served as president of the National Academy of Sciences, the American Association for the Advancement of Science, and the American Physical Society. In addition to the Nobel Prize, he received a host of honors and awards including the Royal Society of London's Copley Medal and the Franklin Institute's Elliot Cresson and Franklin medals. In 1929 he retired from the University of Chicago to work full-time at the Mount Wilson Observatory. He died on May 9, 1931, in Pasadena.

Further Reading

Jaffe, Bernard. *Michelson and the Speed of Light.* Garden City, N.Y.: Anchor Books, 1960.

Livingston, Dorothy M. *The Master of Light: A Biography of Albert A. Michelson.* New York: Scribner, 1973.

Nobelprize.org. "The Nobel Prize in Physics 1907." Available online. URL: http://nobelprize.org/physics/laureates/1907. Downloaded on January 19, 2004.

Wasson, Tyler, ed. *Nobel Prize Winners.* New York: H. W. Wilson, 1987, pp. 698–700.

Millikan, Robert A.
(Robert Andrews Millikan)
(1868–1953) *physicist*

Robert A. Millikan won the 1923 Nobel Prize in physics for determining the electrical charge of a single electron and for validating ALBERT EINSTEIN's photoelectric equation, but he also made important contributions to American science as an educator, administrator, and popular writer.

Millikan was born on March 22, 1868, in Morrison, Illinois. His father, Silas, was a minister, and his mother, Mary Jane, was a teacher. As a boy he moved with his family to Maquoketa, Iowa, where he grew up. After receiving a B.A. and an M.A. in physics from Oberlin College in 1891 and 1893,

respectively, he entered Columbia University, receiving a Ph.D. in physics in 1895. He spent the next year doing postdoctoral research at the universities of Berlin and Göttingen before joining the faculty at the University of Chicago in 1896. In 1902 he married Greta Blanchard with whom he had three children.

Millikan's career at Chicago was focused primarily on teaching. To this end he wrote or cowrote a number of physics textbooks for use in colleges and high schools, including *A College Course in Physics* (1898), *Mechanics, Molecular Physics, and Heat* (1902), *A First Course in Physics* (1906), *A Laboratory Course in Physics for Secondary Schools* (1907), *Electricity, Sound, and Light* (1908), and *The Electron* (1917). Nevertheless, he remained intensely interested in research, particularly as it concerned the nascent field of quantum mechanics, the study of subatomic particles.

Millikan's most famous experiment is the so-called oil-drop experiment, by which he measured, in 1909, the electrical charge of an electron. He dropped a microscopic oil droplet through a small hole in the top of a closed box with a metal top and bottom and transparent sides. Using a microscope, he measured the gravitational force pulling the droplet slowly downward through the box. He then brought the droplet to a complete stop by adjusting the potential difference, or voltage, between the metal top and bottom so that the upward electrical force was exactly equal to the downward gravitational force. Dividing the value of the upward electrical charge by the number of electrons in the droplet yielded the value of the charge of a single electron, 1.602×10^{-19} coulomb. In 1910 he demonstrated that the electrical charge of a drop of any size is a whole-number multiple of this value.

Millikan next turned his attention to the photoelectric effect, the phenomenon that involves the emission of electrons from some solids when struck by light. Einstein had postulated that light is composed of individual quanta, today called photons, which possess the characteristics of both matter and energy. In 1905 he had predicted that the kinetic energy of an electron emitted in the photoelectric effect can be determined by the formula $hv - P$, where h equals Planck's constant (the ratio between the energy and the frequency in a photon of radiation), v equals the frequency of the light, and P equals the amount of work produced by the electron upon striking the solid. By 1916 Millikan had developed a way to measure v and P, and the values he obtained yielded a more precise value for h that was nevertheless consistent with the results of earlier experimenters. This result validated Einstein's photoelectric equation, and it was a major factor in Einstein being awarded the 1921 Nobel Prize in physics. For contributing to a better understanding of the photoelectric effect, and for determining the electrical charge of an electron, Millikan was awarded the 1923 Nobel Prize in physics.

In 1921 Millikan left Chicago to become chairman of the executive committee and director of the physics laboratory at the California Institute of Technology. By this time his research was focused on the hot-spark spectroscopy of the elements, or the exploration of the region of the light spectrum between the ultraviolet and X-radiation bands. In the process, he demonstrated that the ultraviolet spectrum extends downward far beyond the then known limit. He next became interested in cosmic radiation, although he came out on the losing side of an argument with ARTHUR H. COMPTON on the nature of cosmic rays. Millikan insisted that cosmic rays consist of photons, while Compton correctly identified their components as charged particles.

Later in his career, Millikan devoted some of his time to writing books and magazine articles about science for the general educated public. These works include *Science and Life* (1924), *Evolution in Science and Religion* (1927), *Science and the New Civilization* (1930), *Time, Matter, and Values* (1932), and *Electrons (+ and –), Protons, Photons, Neutrons, Mesotrons, and Cosmic Rays* (1947); the latter was a revised edition of *The Electron*. In these works he attempted to reconcile science and religion by showing that they complement each other in their contributions to human progress. In so doing, he became one of the most popular and influential science writers of his day.

Millikan served as president of the American Physical Society, and he was elected to membership in the National Academy of Sciences (NAS) and the American Association for the Advancement of Science. His many other awards include NAS's

Comstock Prize and the Edison Medal of the American Institute of Electrical Engineers. He retired from Caltech in 1946. He died on December 19, 1953, in San Marino, California.

Further Reading

Du Bridge, Lee A., and Paul Epstein. "Robert Andrews Millikan," National Academy of Sciences, *Biographical Memoirs* 33 (1959): pp. 241–282.

Kargon, Robert H. *The Rise of Robert Millikan: Portrait of a Life in American Science*. Ithaca, N.Y.: Cornell University Press, 1982.

Millikan, Robert A. *Autobiography*. New York: Prentice Hall, 1950.

Nobelprize.org. "The Nobel Prize in Physics 1923." Available online. URL: http://nobelprize.org/physics/laureates/1923. Downloaded on January 30, 2004.

Wasson, Tyler, ed. *Nobel Prize Winners*. New York: H. W. Wilson, 1987, pp. 700–703.

Minot, George R.
(George Richards Minot)
(1885–1950) *pathologist*

George R. Minot was one of three physicians who developed liver therapy as an effective treatment for the fatal medical condition known as pernicious anemia. For this discovery, he was awarded a share of the 1934 Nobel Prize in medicine.

Minot was born on December 2, 1885, in Boston, Massachusetts. His father, James, was a physician, and his mother, Elizabeth, was a homemaker. As a youngster he developed a keen interest in natural history, and by age 18 he had published two papers on butterflies and moths. After receiving a B.A. from Harvard University in 1908, he entered Harvard Medical School and received an M.D. four years later. He spent the next three years as an intern at Massachusetts General Hospital and as a laboratory assistant at Johns Hopkins Medical School. In 1915, the same year he married Marian Weld with whom he had three children, he was appointed to the medical staff at Massachusetts General. In 1923 he was named physician in chief at Harvard's Collis P. Huntington Memorial Hospital while also becoming an attending physician at Peter Bent Brigham Hospital (today Brigham and

Women's Hospital). In 1928 he became director of Boston City Hospital's Thorndike Memorial Laboratory, a position he held for the rest of his career. From 1915 to 1947 he also taught at Harvard Medical School.

Minot's primary research interest concerned diseases and medical conditions of the blood and the organs that form blood. As an intern at Massachusetts General, he had become interested in anemia, a deficiency of hemoglobin in the blood that leads to a reduction in the number of red blood cells and causes weakness and breathlessness. While at Johns Hopkins, he conducted experiments related to the behavior of red blood cells in patients with pernicious anemia, a fatal condition caused by the body's reduced ability to absorb vitamin B_{12}. One such experiment led to the discovery that patients with pernicious anemia experience temporary remissions during the course of their illness, and that an increase in the number of reticulocytes, or new red blood cells, takes place during these remissions. As a hospital physician, he studied the diets of pernicious anemia patients and found that they lacked vitamins, in much the same way as do the diets of patients with other dietary deficiency diseases.

In the early 1920s Minot became associated in private practice with WILLIAM P. MURPHY, a colleague at Brigham who shared his interest in pernicious anemia. Both were fascinated with the work of GEORGE H. WHIPPLE, who in 1920 began investigating the relationship between anemia and diet. Whipple had induced anemia in dogs by bleeding them, after which he fed them a variety of diets in order to see which boosted the animals' red blood count the fastest. In so doing, he discovered that a diet rich in raw liver provided the fastest relief from the symptoms of anemia. Intrigued by the possibilities, in 1925 Minot and Murphy began feeding raw liver to some of their anemic private patients. When the red blood counts increased, they began putting their hospital patients with pernicious anemia on liver-rich diets. In 1926 Minot and Murphy were able to report that the best treatment for pernicious anemia was a diet that was rich in liver. Later, they demonstrated that eating at least one-half pound of raw liver per day greatly stimulates the formation of reticulocytes, and that such a diet actually serves to eliminate the symptoms of pernicious anemia completely, often within two weeks.

Most patients, however, could hardly bear to consume that much raw liver on a daily basis, even if it did prolong their lives. At first, Minot and Murphy addressed this problem by pulverizing liver and mixing it with orange juice. Later, Minot and Harvard chemist Edwin J. Cohn collaborated in an effort to prepare liver extracts. By 1928 they had succeeded in developing liver extracts that could be taken orally in small doses but which were just as effective as eating raw liver. Lastly, Murphy and pharmacologist Guy W. Clark developed an extremely concentrated extract that could be administered by injection. These treatments, known as liver therapy, supplanted the standard treatments for pernicious anemia, the administration of arsenic and the removal of the spleen, both of which provided only temporary relief and had harmful side effects. Liver therapy remained the treatment of choice for patients with pernicious anemia until 1948, when William B. Castle isolated and extracted vitamin B_{12}. Meanwhile, in 1934 Minot, Murphy, and Whipple were awarded equal shares of the Nobel Prize in physiology or medicine for their roles in discovering and developing liver therapy.

Minot devoted the rest of his career to studying blood-related diseases and medical conditions, and he eventually became one of the world's foremost experts in this field. In 1947 he suffered a stroke and had to retire from teaching and practicing medicine. He died on February 25, 1950, in Brookline, Massachusetts.

Further Reading

Castle, William B. "George Richards Minot," National Academy of Sciences, *Biographical Memoirs* 45 (1974): pp. 337–383.

Nobelprize.org. "The Nobel Prize in Physiology or Medicine 1934." Available online. URL: http://nobelprize.org/medicine/laureates/1934. Downloaded on January 20, 2004.

Rackemann, Francis M. *The Inquisitive Physician: The Life and Times of George Richards Minot.* Cambridge, Mass.: Harvard University Press, 1956.

Wasson, Tyler, ed. *Nobel Prize Winners.* New York: H. W. Wilson, 1987, pp. 707–709.

Mitchell, Maria
(1818–1889) *astronomer*

Maria Mitchell was the first American woman to establish a career for herself as a scientist. She was the first woman professor of astronomy and the first woman to direct an observatory in the world.

Mitchell was born on August 1, 1818, in Nantucket, Massachusetts. Her father, William, was a banker, and her mother, Lydia, was a librarian. William Mitchell was also an amateur astronomer who made stellar observations for the U.S. Coast Survey (USCS) and synchronized the chronometers of Nantucket whalers with the correct solar time. As a girl and young woman, she assisted her father with these tasks, at first making astronomical observations from the roof of their home and then later from the roof of his bank building. After finishing her secondary schooling, she taught school until 1836, when she became the town librarian.

In 1847, while scanning the skies by herself, Mitchell discovered a previously unknown comet. Sightings of new comets were so rare that 16 years earlier the king of Denmark had offered to give a gold medal to the next person who discovered a comet by using a telescope. Mitchell's discovery not only entitled her to the prize but it opened the door to a scientific career as well. In 1848 she became the first woman to be elected to the American Academy of Arts and Sciences. In 1849 she was hired by the *American Ephemeris and Nautical Almanac*, an annual compilation of astronomical tables for mariners, to compute information about the movements of the planet Venus. That same year she was invited to join several USCS astronomers for the summer at Mount Independence, Maine, where she had access to state-of-the-art equipment. In 1850 she was elected to the American Association for the Advancement of Science, and she remained its only female member until her death. In 1857 she traveled to Europe where she was given ready access to the observatories at Greenwich, England; Cambridge University; and the Vatican. By 1860 she had become the best-known female scientist, and the only one able to make a living as a scientist, in the United States.

In 1861 Mitchell's mother died, and she and her father moved to Lynn, Massachusetts, where her sister lived. For the next four years she made astronomical observations from a small observatory she had built in Lynn. In 1865 she was named professor of astronomy at Vassar College, a newly established all-female college in Poughkeepsie, New York, and director of the college's observatory, positions she held for the next 23 years.

Mitchell was one of the first astronomers to photograph sunspots through a telescope, which led her to discover that sunspots are whirling vertical cavities rather than clouds, as was generally believed. However, she placed more emphasis on her teaching duties than on research. Over the course of her career at Vassar, she trained some of the country's most prominent woman scientists, including ANTONIA MAURY. She also became a staunch advocate for scientific education for women as well as for opening more scientific careers to women. In 1873 she cofounded the Association for the Advancement of Women, and later she served a one-year term as its president. Her advocacy and training helped a number of American women find work as astronomers beginning in the late 19th century.

Mitchell retired from Vassar in 1888 and returned to Lynn where she continued to observe the heavens from a small observatory her nephew built for her. She died, having never married, in Lynn on June 28, 1889.

Further Reading
Albers, Henry, ed. *Maria Mitchell: A Life in Journals and Letters*. Clinton Corners, N.Y.: College Avenue Press, 2001.
Bailey, Martha J. *American Women in Science: A Biographical Dictionary*. Santa Barbara, Calif.: ABC-CLIO, 1994, pp. 253–255.
Yount, Lisa. *A to Z of Women in Science and Math*. New York: Facts On File, 1999, pp. 151–153.

Molina, Mario J.
(Mario José Molina)
(1943–) *chemist*

Mario J. Molina codiscovered that chlorofluorocarbons (CFCs) delete the ozone layer of the upper atmosphere. For this discovery, he was awarded a one-third share of the 1995 Nobel Prize in chemistry.

Molina was born on March 19, 1943, in Mexico City, Mexico. His father, Roberto, was a lawyer, and his mother, Leonor, was a homemaker. At age 17 he enrolled in the chemical engineering program at the National University of Mexico (UNAM), receiving a B.S. in 1965. After studying physical chemistry at the University of Freiburg in Germany for two years, he returned to UNAM to set up a graduate program in chemical engineering. In 1968 he entered the University of California at Berkeley, receiving a Ph.D. in physical chemistry four years later. He remained at Berkeley to conduct postdoctoral research for a year, and in 1973, the same year he married Luisa Tan with whom he had one child, he joined the research group of F. SHERWOOD ROWLAND at the University of California at Irvine. In 1975 he was named a professor of chemistry at Irvine.

Rowland was a specialist in photochemistry, the chemical action of light, and the previous year he had become concerned about the presence of chlorofluorocarbons (CFCs) in the upper atmosphere. These man-made molecules are key ingredients in such products as aerosol-spray propellants, refrigerants, and solvents, and they were slowly building up in the upper atmosphere where it was thought they would remain inert, thus making them excellent chemical tracers. Rowland knew from his work with photochemistry, however, that CFCs would not remain inert forever because of the effects of solar radiation. When Molina joined him at Irvine in 1973, the two decided to undertake a study to find out what would happen to CFCs in the atmosphere.

Molina and Rowland started by looking for atmospheric mechanisms that destroy CFCs in the lower atmosphere. When they found none, they developed what is now known as the CFC–ozone depletion theory. According to this theory, CFCs drift into the upper atmosphere where they are decomposed by solar radiation. The chlorine atoms released as a result of this decomposition then catalyze a photochemical reaction that destroys ozone molecules, thus causing a significant depletion of the ozonosphere. This region in the upper atmosphere prevents temperatures on Earth from getting too hot; it also filters out certain forms of solar radiation that, if allowed to reach the Earth's surface,

would kill or injure most living things. They published their findings in 1974, but because of the perceived danger to life on Earth they presented their findings to public policymakers as well. Stirred to action by Molina and Rowland's findings, by 1980 the United States, Canada, and the Scandinavian nations banned the use of CFCs in aerosol-spray dispensers.

In 1982 Molina left Irvine to become a senior research scientist in the molecular physics and chemistry section of the California Institute of Technology's Jet Propulsion Laboratory. Focusing on the chemistry of the stratospheric clouds over the South Pole, he showed that the presence of ice crystals in these clouds promotes chlorine-activation reactions of the very type he and Rowland had called attention to in the CFC–ozone depletion theory. This discovery explained the discovery in 1985 by other researchers that ozone depletion was taking place in the ozone layer over Antarctica. Although this depletion was shown to occur naturally at regular intervals, it was also shown that CFCs exacerbate the depletion process. These two discoveries led more than two dozen nations in 1987 to impose strict reductions on the manufacture and use of CFCs over the next 12 years. For alerting the world to the dangers of CFCs, Molina was awarded a one-third share of the 1995 Nobel Prize in chemistry; one of his corecipients was Rowland.

In 1989 Molina joined the faculty at the Massachusetts Institute of Technology. His research since then has focused on air pollution in the lower atmosphere over urban areas, especially Mexico City, one of the world's largest megalopolises. Much of his work in this regard is summarized in *Air Quality in the Mexico Megacity: An Integrated Assessment* (2002), which he coedited. His many honors include election to the National Academy of Sciences.

Further Reading

Massachusetts Institute of Technology Chemistry. "Mario J. Molina." Available online. URL: http://web.mit.edu/chemistry/www/faculty/molina.html. Downloaded on March 25, 2005.

Nobelprize.org. "The Nobel Prize in Chemistry 1995." Available online. URL: http://nobelprize.org/chemistry/ laureates/1995. Downloaded on August 19, 2004.

Oleksy, Walter. *Hispanic-American Scientists*. New York: Facts On File, 1998.

Moore, Stanford
(1913–1982) *biochemist*

Stanford Moore played a major role in determining the molecular structure of ribonuclease and then relating its structure to its biochemical function. His work marked the first time an enzyme was so completely understood, and it won for him a share of a Nobel Prize.

Moore was born on September 4, 1913, in Chicago, Illinois. His father, John, was a law student, and his mother, Ruth, was a homemaker. In 1919 he moved with his family to Gainesville, Florida, where his father had accepted an appointment to the faculty of the University of Florida Law School. As the senior Moore's career progressed, the family later moved from Gainesville to Macon, Georgia, and, in 1924, to Nashville, Tennessee, where Moore grew up. In 1931 he entered Vanderbilt University and received a B.S. in chemistry four years later. He spent the next four years at the University of Wisconsin and received a Ph.D. in organic chemistry in 1939.

At Wisconsin, Moore had experimented with breaking down the double-ring chemical compound known as benzimidazole into its constituent molecules. His work came to the attention of Max Bergmann, a German chemist affiliated with the Rockefeller Institute of Medical Research (today Rockefeller University) in New York City. Bergmann was trying to determine the molecular construction of protein, and he convinced Moore to come to Rockefeller to assist him. For three years, Moore and WILLIAM H. STEIN, another Bergmann assistant, experimented with the proteins albumin and fibroin in an effort to identify their constituent amino acids, the building blocks from which proteins are made. Moore and Stein dissolved the proteins in various solutions of reagents and then separated the resulting fractions by filtering the solutions through a narrow column packed with potato starch. By 1942, when their work was interrupted by World War II, Moore and Stein had identified four of the two proteins' amino acids: serine, alanine, phenylalanine, and leucine.

Moore spent the war years conducting research for the Office of Scientific Research and Development and the U.S. Army Chemical Warfare Service. In 1945 he and Stein returned to Rockefeller and resumed their experiments with albumin and fibroin. Over the next several years they identified four more of the proteins' amino acids: isoleucine, methionine, tyrosine, and valine.

In 1953 Moore and Stein set out to identify the amino acids in ribonuclease, an enzyme that plays an important role in the synthesis of cellular protein. Ten years later they had completely identified the sequence of amino acids in ribonuclease, and they were able to describe how the amino acids that make up the enzyme's structure govern its function. This achievement marked the first time that the amino-acid sequence of an enzyme had been described, and it won for Moore and Stein a half share of the 1972 Nobel Prize for chemistry. The other half was awarded to CHRISTIAN B. ANFINSEN, whose findings concerning the relationship between ribonuclease's structure and function dovetailed with Moore and Stein's work.

One positive side effect of Moore and Stein's experiments with protein chemistry was that several noteworthy contributions were made to the field of chromatography, the separation of mixtures and solutions into their constituent parts via various filtering methods. During World War II, two English researchers, Archer Martin and Richard Synge, had developed a technique for filtering solids known as partition chromatography. Moore and Stein adapted this technique to the filtering of liquids. In 1949 they developed an automatic fraction collector, a device that used a photoelectric cell to count the drops being filtered out of a solution. This device was later adapted by other researchers and eventually gained widespread acceptance as a chromatographical tool. In 1951 they adapted the techniques of ion-exchange chromatography, whereby a positively or negatively charged filtering medium filters out the desired fraction by exchanging ions with it, so that they could be used with liquids. They also contributed to the advancement of column chromatography, the method they had originally used, by replacing potato starch with resonated polystyrene resins. Because the resins act in a more discriminating manner than the starch, they permit the collection of a greater amount of a particular fraction in a much shorter period of time.

Moore continued his investigations in protein and enzyme chemistry at Rockefeller until his death. In addition to the Nobel Prize, he won a number of awards, including election to the National Academy of Sciences in 1960. He served on a number of scientific boards and commissions and presided over the American Society of Biological Chemists and the Federation of the American Societies for Experimental Biology. Toward the end of his life, he contracted a disease that caused his nerves and muscles to degenerate, and this condition eventually drove him to suicide. He died, having never married, on August 23, 1982, in New York City.

Further Reading

Nobelprize.org. "The Nobel Prize in Chemistry 1972." Available online. URL: http://nobelprize.org/ chemistry/laureates/1972. Downloaded on July 5, 2003.

Smith, Emil L., and C. H. W. Hirs. "Stanford Moore," National Academy of Sciences, *Biographical Memoirs* 56 (1987): pp. 355–385.

Wasson, Tyler, ed. *Nobel Prize Winners*. New York: H. W. Wilson, 1987, pp. 729–731.

Morgan, Thomas Hunt
(1866–1945) *geneticist*

Thomas Hunt Morgan demonstrated that genes are linked in a series on chromosomes and are responsible for identifiable, hereditary traits. For this contribution to the field of genetics, in 1933 he was awarded a Nobel Prize.

Morgan was born on September 25, 1866, in Lexington, Kentucky. His father, Charlton, was a diplomat, and his mother, Ellen, was a homemaker. At age 16 he entered the State College of Kentucky (today the University of Kentucky) and received a B.S. in zoology in 1886. Four years later he received a Ph.D. in biology from Johns Hopkins University. After a year of research at Hopkins and the Naples Zoological Station in Italy, in 1891 he began teach-

ing biology at Bryn Mawr College. In 1904, the same year he married Lilian Sampson with whom he had four children, he became professor of experimental zoology at Columbia University. In 1928 he was named head of the biology department at the California Institute of Technology, a position he held for the rest of his career.

Early in his career, Morgan's primary interest involved morphology, a branch of biology that concerns the proper classification of species. His major contribution in this area was to demonstrate that sea spiders are more closely related to true spiders than they are to crabs and lobsters, whom they resemble. Morphology, however, was largely descriptive, as were most biological fields at the time, and he soon abandoned it in favor of other research venues that stressed experimentation. He began focusing on embryonic development and differentiation, and by 1897, when he published *The Development of the Frog's Egg,* he had become one of the country's leading embryologists. Upon moving to Columbia, he shifted his primary focus to cytology, the study of cells and their formation, structure, and function. This line of research brought

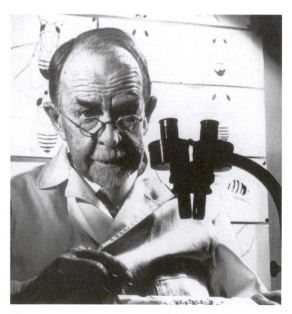

Thomas Hunt Morgan pioneered the study of genetics in the United States. *(Courtesy of the California Institute of Technology)*

him into contact with the work of Austrian botanist Gregor Mendel, who laid the mathematical foundations for the study of genetics. At first, Morgan was skeptical about Mendel's theories of heredity for the same reasons he was skeptical about Charles Darwin's theories about evolution. Morgan thought both were too simplistic because they did not properly account for the spontaneity of nature. In time, however, his own research with genetics led him to accept, and to contribute to a better understanding of, both theories.

By 1908 Morgan's research interests had shifted to genetics, and he began experimenting with *Drosophila melanogaster,* the common fruit fly. Fruit flies were the perfect species for genetic experimentation because they are inexpensive to breed, millions of them can be bred in a relatively small space, and changes in their hereditary characteristics over a large number of generations can be observed in a relatively short time. In 1909 Morgan discovered among his millions of red-eyed fruit flies a white-eyed mutant, and he began cross-breeding this mutant with red-eyed flies. In time, he discovered that all of the white-eyed flies were male, which led him to conclude that some genetic variations were linked to sex. He further concluded that these variations were controlled by the X-chromosomes of females. Later, he discovered that many sex-linked changes are inherited together, which led him to conclude that the X-chromosome carries a number of hereditary units. He called these units genes, a name he borrowed from Danish botanist Wilhelm Johannsen, and he hypothesized that they are arranged in linear fashion on the chromosome.

In 1911 Morgan and his assistants, one of whom was HERMAN J. MULLER, began mapping gene positions on the four fruit fly chromosomes. Published in 1913, this map verified Morgan's hypothesis concerning the linear arrangement of genes. They also showed conclusively that the closer two genes are to each other on the chromosome, the more likely they are to link with each other. Later, their work demonstrated that some genes modify the expression of other genes, that a gene's position on a chromosome can shift, that such a shift modifies a gene's expression, and that a gene's expression can be changed by changing the environmental conditions in which it develops. These findings were published in *Heredity and Sex* (1913), *The Mechanism of Mendelian Heredity* (1915), *A Critique of the Theory of Evolution* (1925), and *The Theory of the Gene* (1926).

Morgan and his colleagues provided the foundation for the modern study of genetics. The gene map concept was later used by a number of other genetic researchers, including BARBARA MCCLINTOCK, to study genetics in a wide range of plants and animals. Morgan's work proved conclusively that Mendel's theories about hereditary were essentially correct. It also gave strong scientific support to Darwinian evolution by explaining the mechanism via which organisms evolve and via which spontaneous mutations occur. Lastly, Morgan's work demonstrated that biology does not have to be a descriptive science, but that it can be just as experimental as physics or chemistry. This last contribution may be his most important one, because it inspired hundreds of biologists to embark on research projects of their own, in the process immeasurably advancing the body of biological knowledge. For these contributions, Morgan was awarded the 1933 Nobel Prize in physiology or medicine.

Although he is best known for his work with genetics, Morgan never lost his interest in experimental embryology. Prior to moving to California, he spent most of his summers at the Marine Biological Laboratory in Woods Hole, Massachusetts, where he experimented with sea creatures. Once at Caltech, he used Woods Hole as the model for the Marine Laboratory on Corona del Mar, which he established. While studying the phenomenon of regeneration, he demonstrated that the hermit crab is capable of regenerating a number of body parts other than limbs, thus refuting the theory that regeneration only involved the replacement of critical body parts. His work in this area was published in *Experimental Embryology* (1927) and *Embryology and Genetics* (1934).

Morgan served as president of the National Academy of Sciences, the American Association for the Advancement of Science, and the Sixth International Congress on Genetics. He continued to teach and conduct research until his death on December 4, 1945, in Pasadena, California.

Further Reading

Allen, Garland E. *Thomas Hunt Morgan: The Man and His Science*. Princeton, N.J.: Princeton University Press, 1978.

Nobelprize.org. "The Nobel Prize in Physiology or Medicine 1933." Available online. URL: http://nobelprize.org/medicine/laureates/1933. Downloaded on January 26, 2004.

Shine, Ian, and Sylvia Wrobel. *Thomas Hunt Morgan, Pioneer of Genetics*. Lexington: University Press of Kentucky, 1976.

Sturtevant, Alfred H. "Thomas Hunt Morgan," National Academy of Sciences, *Biographical Memoirs* 33 (1959): pp. 283–325.

Wasson, Tyler, ed. *Nobel Prize Winners*. New York: H. W. Wilson, 1987, pp. 731–733.

Muller, Hermann J.
(Hermann Joseph Muller, Jr.)
(1890–1967) *geneticist*

Hermann J. Muller won a Nobel Prize for developing the radiation techniques that greatly facilitated the study of genetics. He also generated much controversy by becoming involved in more than one debate over the causes and benefits of artificial genetic mutation.

Muller was born on December 21, 1890, in New York City. His father, Hermann, owned an art metal works, and his mother, Frances, was a homemaker. His early interest in science led him to cofound a science club at his high school and a biology club at Columbia University, where he received a B.A. in zoology in 1910, an M.A. in physiology in 1911, and a Ph.D. in genetics in 1916. In 1920, after two 2-year stints teaching genetics at the Rice Institute (today Rice University) in Houston, Texas, and zoology at Columbia, he was named a professor of zoology at the University of Texas in Austin. In 1923 he married Jessie Jacobs with whom he had one child. They divorced in 1934, and five years later he married Dorothea Kantorowicz, with whom he had one child.

While a graduate student, Muller became involved with THOMAS HUNT MORGAN's genetic experiments with fruit flies, and he was one of Morgan's coauthors on *The Mechanism of Mendelian Heredity* (1915). Muller was particularly interested

in speeding up the occurrence of mutations, by which so much is learned about genetic behavior. At the University of Texas he continued to experiment with fruit flies, but by using X-rays to alter genetic behavior. In 1927 he demonstrated that bombarding fruit flies with radiation resulted in a number of bizarre mutations, including flies with two heads and no legs. Five years later he showed that radiation could not only alter genetic behavior but also could alter the genes themselves. Overexposure to X-rays or gamma rays can result in the rupture of a chromosome, thus resulting in the loss of one or more of its genes. Another effect of radiation is that the ruptured ends of one chromosome might not reconnect with each other, but rather with the ruptured ends of other chromosomes, thus altering the behavior of the genes they contain. In all cases, the result is to greatly increase the percentage of mutations produced in a single generation, sometimes to the point that every member of a generation is a mutant, even if only slightly so.

Muller's work was important for two major reasons. First, he developed techniques that other researchers could use to speed up the mutation rate in whatever organism it was they were working with. The most beneficial results in this regard were achieved by plant researchers, who used radiation bombardment to develop mutant strains of crops that are capable of withstanding certain diseases or of thriving in a wider range of climatic conditions. Second, he raised the possibility that human beings can be genetically reengineered, thus making them hardier and healthier. This possibility is much more controversial than the first because it involves eugenics, the improvement of offspring by the careful selection of their parents. Unfortunately, this noble sentiment has resulted in several misguided attempts to improve the human race, the most notorious being experiments conducted by scientists in the concentration camps in Nazi Germany, and Muller's suggestion that human genes could be manipulated in a beneficial way elicited cries of outraged indignation. Nevertheless, Muller's work was of such incredible importance to all types of biological research that in 1946 he was awarded the Nobel Prize in physiology or medicine.

Meanwhile, Muller had become involved in a scientific debate that ultimately transcended science because it involved cold war politics. Muller was a socialist, and in 1933 he went to the Soviet Union where he hoped his ideas about genetics and eugenics would be better received. While there he ran afoul of Trofim D. Lysenko, the Soviet Union's leading biologist. Lysenko insisted that plants and animals were able to mutate simply by being placed in an appropriate environment; at one time Lysenko went so far as to claim that wheat plants cultivated under conditions conducive to growing rye would produce seeds of rye. As far-fetched as they were, Lysenko's ideas made a favorable impression on Soviet dictator Joseph Stalin. Stalin believed that Lysenkoism, as Lysenko's ideas became known, could greatly increase the yield of Soviet crops at a time when the Soviet Union was unable to feed its entire people. Because Lysenkoism offered Soviets the possibility of being independent from capitalist food suppliers, especially its archrival the United States, Stalin made it a tenet of faith for Soviet geneticists, even going so far as to imprison and kill those scientists who refused to accept it. Muller was foolish enough to denounce Lysenkoism while still at the Institute of Genetics in Moscow, and in 1937 he was forced to flee the country to avoid being executed by Stalin. Despite being officially denounced by the Soviet government, Muller continued to denounce Lysenkoism for the rest of his career.

Upon leaving the Soviet Union, Muller took a position at the University of Edinburgh in Scotland. In 1940 he returned to the United States; after spending World War II at Amherst College in Massachusetts, in 1945 he joined the faculty at the University of Indiana in Bloomington. The latter part of his career continued to be marked by controversy. He once proposed that the sperm of notable individuals should be frozen and used for purposes of selective breeding. He also raised concerns over the testing of nuclear weapons, warning that the high levels of radiation released during aboveground tests were capable of causing mutations in humans that might not show up for several generations. Such were the fears he raised that the U.S. Atomic Energy Commission once refused to let him present a paper regarding the effects of nuclear radiation on human genetics.

Muller served as president of the American Humanist Association, and he was elected to membership in the National Academy of Sciences and the American Academy of Arts and Sciences. In 1964 he retired from Indiana, only to spend the next two years teaching at the University of Wisconsin. He died on April 5, 1967, in Bloomington.

Further Reading

Carlson, Elof A. Genes, Radiation and Society: The Life and Work of H. J. Muller. Ithaca, N.Y.: Cornell University Press, 1981.

Muller, Hermann J. Out of the Night: A Biologist's View of the Future. New York: Vanguard Press, 1935.

Nobelprize.org. "The Nobel Prize in Physiology or Medicine 1946." Available online. URL: http://nobelprize.org/medicine/laureates/1946. Downloaded on February 11, 2004.

Wasson, Tyler, ed. Nobel Prize Winners. New York: H. W. Wilson, 1987, pp. 740–742.

Mulliken, Robert S.
(Robert Sanderson Mulliken)
(1896–1986) chemist

Robert S. Mulliken developed the molecular orbital theory, which explains the chemical bond that occurs between certain types of small molecules. For this achievement, he was awarded the 1966 Nobel Prize in chemistry.

Mulliken was born on June 7, 1896, in Newburyport, Massachusetts. His father, Samuel, was a chemist, and his mother, Katherine, was a homemaker. In high school he became interested in electrons, which were discovered the year before he was born, and at his graduation ceremony he presented a paper entitled "Electrons: What They Are and What They Do." After receiving a B.Sc. in chemistry from the Massachusetts Institute of Technology in 1917, he went to work as a chemical engineer for the U.S. Bureau of Mines in Washington, D.C. Two years later he took a research position with the New Jersey Zinc Company, but he left after a year to enter the graduate program of the University of Chicago, where he received a Ph.D. in chemistry in 1921. He spent the next five years as a National Research Council (NRC) fellow at Chicago and at Harvard University. In 1926 he was named a professor of physics at New York University, but he left after two years to accept a similar position at Chicago. In 1929 he married Mary Ellen von Noé with whom he had two children.

Mulliken's early career involved the separation and identification of isotopes, forms of an element that have the same number of protons but a different number of neutrons than the normal form. As an NRC fellow, he participated in a project to identify isotopes in molecules according to the light waves, or band spectra, that the molecules emitted. This project led him to return to the subject that had fascinated him as a schoolboy, the behavior of electrons. He discovered that certain analogies exist between the behavior of a diatomic (two atoms) molecule and the element having the same number of electrons as that molecule; for example, O_2 (diatomic oxygen) behaves in ways that are similar to one atom of sulfur because both have 16 electrons. This discovery led him to consider the structure of atoms and molecules in terms of the arrangement of their electrons.

In 1925 and 1927, Mulliken visited a number of European scientists; among them was Friedrich Hund, who specialized in spectroscopy (the study of spectral lines) and quantum mechanics (the behavior of subatomic particles). Over the next five years, Mulliken and Hund shared their ideas about the nature of chemical bonding. As a result of this exchange, in 1932 Mulliken proposed an entirely new way of looking at chemical bonding in diatomic molecules. GILBERT N. LEWIS and IRVING LANGMUIR had earlier proposed the concept of covalent bonding, whereby two atoms combine by sharing one electron each from their outer shell. Mulliken suggested that, in some cases, the two atoms in a diatomic molecule create what he called molecular orbitals, that is, a group of electrons that orbit both nuclei. Mulliken theorized that the two nuclei in a diatomic molecule combine to form one nucleus, and all of the electrons from the two atoms orbit this combined nucleus as if the molecule were actually only one atom. This theory became known as the molecular orbital theory and the Hund-Mulliken theory. In 1935 Mulliken expanded this theory to include small polyatomic molecules, molecules composed of three or more atoms. Although the molecular orbital theory has so far been impossible to prove, it explains the

Robert Mulliken explained how chemical bonds form between certain types of small molecules. *(Courtesy of the University of Chicago)*

behavior of diatomic and small polyatomic molecules better than the covalent bond theory does, and other researchers have given it credence by examining the band spectral lines of diatomic and small polyatomic molecules.

Mulliken continued to explore the implications of the molecular orbital theory for the rest of his career. By 1960 he had advanced several related concepts, including hyperconjugation (the stabilizing interaction that results from the interaction of molecular orbitals) and population analysis (which suggests that the strength of a chemical bond is determined by the overlap of molecular orbitals). In 1966 he was awarded the Nobel Prize in chemistry for his work concerning the molecular orbital theory.

In 1961 Mulliken retired from the University of Chicago, although he continued to serve as a professor emeritus until 1985. From 1964 to 1971 he taught chemical physics at Florida State University, after which he returned to his home in Chicago. He was elected to membership in the National Academy of Sciences and the American Academy of Arts and Sciences. He received a number of awards in addition to the Nobel Prize, including five medals from the American Chemical Society. He died on October 31, 1986, while visiting his daughter in Arlington, Virginia.

Further Reading

Mulliken, Robert S. *Life of a Scientist: An Autobiographical Account of the Development of Molecular Orbital Theory with an Introductory Memoir by Friedrich Hund.* Edited by Bernard J. Ransil. New York: Springer-Verlag, 1989.

Nobelprize.org. "The Nobel Prize in Chemistry 1966." Available online. URL: http://nobelprize.org/chemistry/laureates/1966. Downloaded on February 13, 2004.

Wasson, Tyler, ed. *Nobel Prize Winners.* New York: H. W. Wilson, 1987, pp. 744–746.

Mullis, Kary B.
(Kary Banks Mullis)
(1944–) *chemist*

Kary B. Mullis developed polymerase chain reaction (PCR), a method that permits the rapid reproduction and analysis of genetic material. This contribution won for him a share of the 1993 Nobel Prize in chemistry.

Mullis was born on December 28, 1944, in Lenoir, North Carolina, to Cecil and Bernice Mullis. As a boy he moved with his family to Columbia, South Carolina, where he grew up. He received a B.S. in chemistry from the Georgia Institute of Technology and a Ph.D. in biochemistry from the University of California at Berkeley in 1972. He spent the next seven years teaching biochemistry at Berkeley, conducting postdoctoral research in pediatric cardiology at the University of Kansas Medical School, and conducting postdoctoral research in pharmaceutical chemistry at the University of California at San Francisco. In 1979 he became a DNA chemist with the Cetus Corporation, a biotechnology firm in Emeryville, California, that manufactured oligonucleotides, the biochemical compounds used in genetic cloning.

In 1983 Mullis conceived of polymerase chain reaction (PCR) as a means of rapidly cloning snippets of DNA. At the time, genetic cloning was the basis for biotechnology, which recombines specific genes from different organisms to create new organisms capable of performing a specific biochemical function such as the production of human insulin. Genetic cloning was also how medical researchers investigating hereditary diseases and conditions obtained enough DNA samples to conduct their experiments. The process of cloning DNA, however, was a time-consuming affair that reproduced all of a strand of DNA, not just the specific genes wanted. To obtain these genes, researchers had to use special enzymes that snip out the sections of the DNA that contain the required genetic material. PCR, on the other hand, reproduces only the DNA snippet, and it does this so rapidly that a million copies of the snippet can be produced in a matter of hours.

PCR employs polymerases, naturally occurring enzymes whose job is to copy genetic material. PCR requires a template molecule (the snippet of DNA that is to be copied) and two primer molecules to get the copying process started. The primers are short, single-stranded chains of the four different nucleotides, or chemical building blocks, from which DNA is made. The primers must be duplicates of nucleotide sequences on either side of the template molecule, which means that the exact order of the primers' nucleotides must already be known. These flanking sequences can be constructed in the lab or purchased from commercial suppliers.

There are three basic steps in PCR. First the target genetic material must be denatured; that is, the strands of its helix must be unwound and separated by heating it to between 90 and 96°C. Then the primers must bind to their complementary bases on the now single-stranded DNA. Last a polymerase synthesizes the DNA by reading a template strand and matching it with complementary nucleotides very quickly. All three steps are performed in the Thermal Cycler, the machine Mullis designed to automate the PCR process. The result is two new helixes in place of the first, each composed of one of the original strands plus its newly assembled complementary strand.

PCR had a profound influence on basic research in biology. By making it easier to clone and sequence genes, PCR made it easier to study genetic and evolutionary relationships, even in ancient fossils containing only fragments of DNA. This aspect of PCR inspired the popular novel and movie, *Jurassic Park,* in which PCR is used to recreate dinosaurs. It has also become a useful tool in drug design, the diagnosis of viral and bacterial infections including HIV, and in forensic medicine, which uses PCR to analyze the DNA content of a drop of blood or a strand of hair. For developing PCR, Mullis was awarded a half share of the 1993 Nobel Prize in chemistry. His corecipient was the Canadian chemist Michael Smith.

In 1986 Mullis left Cetus to become director of molecular biology at Xytronyx, Inc., a research firm in San Diego, but he left a year later to form his own biochemical research consulting firm and to work as a Distinguished Researcher at Children's Hospital and Research Institute in Oakland. He was married three times, the last time to Nancy Cosgrove in 1998, and he has three children.

Further Reading

Hargittai, Istvan, and Magdolna Hargittai. *Candid Science II: Conversations with Famous Biomedical Scientists.* London: Imperial College Press, 2002, pp. 182–196.

Mullis, Kary B. *Dancing Naked in the Mind Field.* New York: Pantheon Books, 1998.

Nobelprize.org. "The Nobel Prize in Chemistry 1993." Available online. URL: http://nobelprize.org/chemistry/laureates/1993. Downloaded on August 16, 2004.

Murad, Ferid
(1936–) *biochemist*

Ferid Murad codiscovered the roles played by nitric oxide and cyclic GMP as agents for signaling the initiation of certain biochemical functions. For this discovery, he was awarded a share of the 1998 Nobel Prize in physiology or medicine.

Murad was born on September 14, 1936, in Whiting, Indiana. His parents, Jabir and Henrietta, owned and managed a restaurant. In 1958 he received a B.A. in chemistry from DePauw (Ind.) University and married Carol Ann Leopold with whom he had five children. He then entered West-

ern Reserve University in Cleveland, Ohio, receiving an M.D. and a Ph.D. in pharmacology in 1965. He spent the next five years completing his internship and residency at Boston's Massachusetts General Hospital and conducting postdoctoral research at the National Institutes of Health (NIH) in Bethesda, Maryland. In 1970 he accepted an invitation to form a clinical pharmacology division at the University of Virginia Medical School. In 1981 he left Virginia to become chief of medicine at the Veterans Administration (VA) Medical Center in Palo Alto, California, and a professor of internal medicine and pharmacology at Stanford University. In 1989 he left academia for the world of biotechnology, working first as vice president of pharmaceutical research and development of Abbott Laboratories and then as president and chief executive officer of the Molecular Geriatrics Corporation; both companies were located on the outskirts of Chicago, Illinois. In 1997 he was named chair of the

Ferid Murad showed that certain biochemical functions are initiated by nitric oxide. *(Courtesy of Ferid Murad)*

department of integrative biology, pharmacology, and physiology at the University of Texas Medical School at Houston.

Murad's research focused on "second messengers," biochemical agents that trigger a certain cellular function after being themselves triggered by another agent. As a medical student he assisted EARL W. SUTHERLAND, who discovered that cyclic adenosine monophosphate (cyclic AMP) acts as a second messenger in the production of a number of enzymes inside cells. Murad's research at NIH suggested that cyclic guanosine monophosphate (cyclic GMP) might also be an important second messenger, and his work after 1970 focused on cyclic GMP. He soon became interested in the relationship between cyclic GMP and nitroglycerine, which is used to treat angina pectoris, a medical condition that is characterized by severe chest pain that results when certain arterial muscles cannot relax. By 1977 he had shown that nitric oxide, a product of the breakdown of nitroglycerine, increases the level of cyclic GMP in certain tissues. This discovery led him to speculate that cyclic GMP was the second messenger responsible for relaxing certain smooth muscles, specifically the ones found in arteries and other blood vessels.

Murad's work with cyclic GMP informed the research of LOUIS J. IGNARRO. In 1979 Ignarro confirmed Murad's findings regarding the ability of nitric oxide to increase the level of cyclic GMP. Two years later Ignarro demonstrated the complicated chain of reactions through which nitroglycerine must go to be broken down into nitric oxide, as well as the chemical process by which nitric oxide leads to the production of cyclic GMP. Together, Murad and Ignarro's work informed the research of ROBERT F. FURCHGOTT, who confirmed Murad's hypothesis that cyclic GMP acts as the second messenger in the relaxation of smooth vascular muscles.

The work of Murad, Ignarro, and Furchgott explained why nitroglycerine causes arteries to relax, a phenomenon that physicians had known for years but had never understood. Their work also opened the door to further research with nitric oxide and cyclic GMP, and other researchers found a number of cellular functions that are triggered by these two signaling agents. For their contributions, Murad, Ignarro, and Furchgott each won a one-third share of the 1998 Nobel Prize in physiology or medicine.

Murad remained at the University of Texas-Houston for the rest of his career. Much of his work concerning second messengers is summarized in *Cyclic GMP: Synthesis, Metabolism and Function* (1994) and *Nitric Oxide: Biochemistry, Molecular Biology, and Therapeutic Implications* (1995), which he coauthored with Ignarro.

Further Reading

"Ferid Murad, MD, PhD, A Conversation with the Editor," *American Journal of Cardiology* 94, no. 1 (2004): pp. 75–91.

Nobelprize.org. "The Nobel Prize in Physiology or Medicine 1998." Available online. URL: http://nobelprize. org/medicine/laureates/1998. Downloaded on July 14, 2004.

Murphy, William P.
(William Parry Murphy)
(1892–1987) *pathologist*

William P. Murphy played a major role in the development of liver therapy as an effective treatment for pernicious anemia. As a result, he was awarded a share of the 1934 Nobel Prize in physiology or medicine.

Murphy was born on February 6, 1892, in Stoughton, Wisconsin. His father, Thomas, was a minister, and his mother, Rose, was a homemaker. As a youngster he moved with his family to Oregon, where his father held several pastorates. After receiving an A.B. from the University of Oregon in 1914, he taught high school mathematics and physics for two years before entering the University of Oregon Medical School. He transferred after a year to Harvard Medical School and received an M.D. in 1920. After interning at Rhode Island Hospital in Providence, in 1923 he joined the staff at Boston's Peter Bent Brigham Hospital (today Brigham and Women's Hospital). From 1924 to 1958 he also taught at Harvard Medical School. In 1919 he married Pearl Adams, with whom he had two children.

In the early 1920s Murphy entered into private practice with GEORGE R. MINOT, a colleague of his at

Brigham who shared his interest in blood disorders. The two were particularly interested in anemia, a deficiency of hemoglobin in the blood that leads to a reduction in the number of red blood cells and causes weakness and breathlessness. Consequently, they were intrigued with the research of GEORGE H. WHIPPLE, who in 1920 began investigating the relationship between anemia and diet. Whipple had induced anemia in dogs by bleeding them, after which he fed them a variety of diets in order to see which diet induced the fastest recovery of the dogs' red blood count. In the process he discovered that a diet rich in raw liver provided the fastest relief from the symptoms of anemia. Curious as to whether or not such a diet might have the same effect in anemic humans, in 1925 Murphy and Minot began feeding raw liver to some of their private patients. When the results indicated yes, they placed many of their hospital patients with pernicious anemia on liver-rich diets. In 1926 Murphy and Minot reported their findings, that a diet rich in liver offered an effective treatment for pernicious anemia. Later, they demonstrated that eating at least one-half pound of raw liver per day greatly stimulates the formation of new red blood cells, thus eliminating the symptoms of pernicious anemia completely, often within two weeks.

The only drawback to this treatment was that most patients could not stand the taste of raw liver. At first, Murphy and Minot overcame patient objections by finding a way to pulverize liver and mix it with orange juice so that patients could drink it. Later, Minot and Harvard chemist Edwin J. Cohn began preparing liver extracts. By 1928 they had succeeded in developing liver extracts that could be taken orally in small doses but which were just as effective as eating raw liver. Lastly, Murphy and Guy W. Clark, a pharmacologist with Lederle Laboratories, developed an extremely concentrated extract that could be administered by injection. These treatments, known collectively as liver therapy, took the place of the standard treatments for pernicious anemia, the administration of arsenic and the removal of the spleen, treatments that provided only temporary relief and had harmful side effects. Liver therapy remained the treatment of choice for patients with pernicious anemia until 1948, when William B. Castle isolated and extracted vitamin B_{12}. Meanwhile, in 1934 Murphy, Minot, and Whipple

were awarded equal shares of the Nobel Prize in physiology or medicine for their roles in discovering and developing liver therapy.

Murphy continued to experiment with blood disorders until his retirement in 1958. He died on October 9, 1987, in Brookline, Massachusetts.

Further Reading

The Nobel Prize Internet Archive. "William Parry Murphy." Available online. URL: http://almaz.com/nobel/medicine/1934c.html. Downloaded on March 25, 2005.

Nobelprize.org. "The Nobel Prize in Physiology or Medicine 1934." Available online. URL: http://nobelprize.org/medicine/laureates/1934. Downloaded on January 20, 2004.

Wasson, Tyler, ed. *Nobel Prize Winners*. New York: H. W. Wilson, 1987, pp. 746–777.

Murray, Joseph E.
(Joseph Edward Murray)
(1919–) *surgeon*

Joseph E. Murray was one of the foremost plastic surgeons in the United States, and he was particularly adept at reconstructing the heads and necks of cancer victims. His major claim to fame, however, involved organ transplants, and for his work in this regard he was awarded a share of the 1990 Nobel Prize in physiology or medicine.

Murray was born on April 1, 1919, in Milford, Massachusetts. His father, William, was a judge, and his mother, Mary, was a schoolteacher. After receiving an A.B. from the College of the Holy Cross (Mass.) in 1940, he entered Harvard Medical College and received an M.D. in 1943. He interned for a year at Boston's Peter Bent Brigham Hospital (today Brigham and Women's Hospital), and then he was commissioned a first lieutenant in the U.S. Army Medical Corps and assigned to Valley Forge (Pa.) General Hospital. Upon leaving the military in 1947, he returned to Brigham where he remained for the rest of his career. In 1945 he married Virginia Link with whom he had six children.

As a surgeon, Murray was primarily interested in plastic surgery. At Valley Forge Hospital he performed

Joseph Murray made important contributions to the theory and practice of plastic surgery and organ transplants. *(Courtesy of Joseph E. Murray, M.D.)*

reconstructive surgery on hundreds of military casualties, especially burn patients, and at Brigham he served as head of the plastic surgery division for more than 20 years, in the process becoming one of the most highly regarded plastic surgeons in the world. Nevertheless, he was also very much interested in the workings of the immunological system, which researchers such as British zoologist Peter Medawar had shown to be responsible for the process via which the body accepts skin grafts from itself but rejects skin grafts from other bodies. His interest in the mechanics of tissue rejection led him to become involved in the work of John Merrill and David Hume, Harvard researchers who had been using Brigham's facilities to experiment with kidney transplants involving dogs. By the early 1950s Merrill and Hume had succeeded in attaching kidneys from cadavers to the thighs of patients whose kidneys were damaged but in a state of recovery. Although this arrangement did not last long because the patient's immune system eventually rejected the connections linking the patient to the foreign kidney, it lasted long enough for the damaged kidney to recover and function on its own.

The qualified success of this procedure led the Merrill-Hume team to conclude that a kidney transplant involving two live humans could succeed if both the donor and the recipient were closely related to one another, because in this case the recipient's immune system was least likely to reject the donor kidney. Meanwhile, Murray had developed a surgical technique for connecting the blood vessels in the donor kidney to the blood vessels in the recipient's abdomen, and he had begun looking for a suitable donor-recipient pair on whom to operate. In 1954 he performed the world's first successful kidney transplant on humans, taking a kidney from Ronald Herrick and transplanting it to his identical twin brother, Richard Herrick.

Although Murray continued to perform transplant surgery on identical twins, he also began looking for a way to override the immunological process by which the body rejects foreign tissue so that he could perform transplants involving non-related humans. Extensive experimentation showed that X-ray treatments and bone marrow transplants would keep the body from rejecting transplanted tissue, but only for a few additional weeks. Meanwhile, in 1957, GERTRUDE B. ELION developed azathioprine, a pharmaceutical drug she derived from another drug used to treat leukemia. It was soon demonstrated that animals that had been administered azathioprine were much less likely to reject foreign protein, thus setting the stage for its use by Murray. In 1962, after extensive testing of azathioprine demonstrated its effectiveness in suppressing the human immune system, and thus minimizing rejection of a transplanted organ, Murray used the drug during the first successful kidney transplant in which the donor and the recipient were not related.

Murray's success inspired other surgeons and researchers to develop ways to transplant other organs between non-related humans. By 1990 transplants involving kidneys, livers, pancreases, and even hearts and lungs had become almost commonplace. That same year, in recognition of his contribution to medical science, Murray was awarded a half share of the Nobel Prize in physiology or medicine. His corecipient was the American physician E. DONNALL THOMAS.

Meanwhile, in 1970 Murray took on the additional duties of professor of surgery at Harvard while continuing to perform kidney transplants and plastic surgery at Brigham. In 1986 he retired as a surgeon, but he continued at Brigham as an administrator. In 1997 Harvard Medical School established the Joseph E. Murray Professorship in Plastic and Reconstructive Surgery in his honor.

Further Reading

Murray, Joseph E. *Surgery for the Soul: Reflections on a Curious Career.* Canton, Mass.: Science History Publications, 2001.

Nobelprize.org. "The Nobel Prize in Physiology or Medicine 1990." Available online. URL: http://nobelprize. org/medicine/laureates/1990. Downloaded on June 16, 2004.

N

Nathans, Daniel
(1928–1999) *molecular biologist*

Daniel Nathans was the first to use enzymes as a recombinant DNA technique, a basic tool in the field of biotechnology as well as many areas of medical research. For this contribution, he was awarded a share of the 1978 Nobel Prize in physiology or medicine.

Nathans was born on October 30, 1928, in Wilmington, Delaware. His father, Samuel, was a businessman, and his mother, Sarah, was a homemaker. He received a B.S. in chemistry from the University of Delaware in 1950 and an M.D. from Washington University in St. Louis, Missouri, in 1954. Over the next five years he completed his internship and residency at Columbia-Presbyterian Medical Center in New York City and worked as a clinical associate at the National Institutes of Health in Bethesda, Maryland. In 1959 he became a guest investigator at New York City's Rockefeller Institute for Medical Research (today Rockefeller University), leaving three years later to teach microbiology and genetics at Johns Hopkins University in Baltimore, Maryland. In 1956 he married Joanne Gomberg with whom he had three children.

Nathans's early research involved the synthesis of protein by bacteria, but he soon took up the study of viruses that infect bacteria, known as bacteriophages or phages. He was specifically interested in discovering how bacteria sometimes change the genetics of the phages that infect them. In 1968 he refocused his research once again, this time devoting his efforts to learning how animal viruses, in particular SV40, a virus that infects monkeys and other simians, cause cancerous tumors.

This latter project led Nathans to become interested in the work of Werner Arber, a Swiss microbiologist who discovered restriction/modification phenomena, and HAMILTON O. SMITH, one of Nathans's colleagues at Johns Hopkins. Arber was interested in how bacteria defend themselves against lysogeny, the process by which a phage inserts its genome, a complete set of genes, into a bacterium's core so that the phage's genome becomes a gene on the bacterium's chromosome. Thus, when an infected bacterium replicates, the replicated bacteria already contain phage virons. Rather than kill the infected bacteria immediately, these virons live in their cores in a parasitic manner and are released only when the bacteria are exposed to a specific phenomenon such as a chemical or ultraviolet light. Arber showed that bacteria produce two kinds of enzymes that fight against lysogeny. Modification enzymes coat bacterial DNA chains so that phages cannot splice their genomes into them, while restriction enzymes restrict the growth of phages by cutting up viral DNA into bits. The restriction enzymes discovered by Arber were able to recognize specific sequences in viral DNA, but they cut those sequences at random locations in the DNA chain.

Smith built on Arber's work by discovering the Type II restriction enzyme. Unlike Arber's, or Type I, restriction enzymes, Type IIs always cut a DNA chain at the same exact point in the sequence. In 1969 Smith, who knew about Nathans's work with SV40, notified Nathans about a Type II restriction enzyme Smith had developed from the bacterium *Hemophilus influenzae* (*H. influenzae*). Like Smith, Nathans realized that such an enzyme might help him dissect SV40 DNA chains into manageable parts so that the virus's genetics could be studied more easily. Using Smith's *H. influenzae* enzyme, in 1971 Nathans was able to cleave the SV40 DNA chain into 11 specific pieces. After further research, he was also able to write the complete chemical formula for SV40 DNA and identify the genes that control specific functions along the SV40 DNA chain. Perhaps most important, by 1972 he had developed mutant strains of SV40 from which certain portions of the DNA sequencing had been deleted.

Nathans's ability to develop mutant viral strains by using a Type II restriction enzyme was perhaps the first major event in the history of biotechnology, which was born in the early 1970s. Biotechnology involves the development of new organisms, such as strains of bacteria that biodegrade oil spills and toxic wastes or organisms that produce insulin for human consumption, by cutting and splicing, or recombining, DNA from two or more organisms, and Type II restriction enzymes make DNA recombination possible. Recombinant DNA techniques are also widely used by medical researchers looking to cure cancer or a variety of hereditary diseases because they allow DNA chains to be dissected into well-defined segments that subsequently can be used for structural investigations or in genetic experiments. For his contribution to these areas, Nathans was awarded a one-third share of the 1978 Nobel Prize in physiology or medicine; his corecipients were Smith and Arber.

After winning the Nobel Prize, Nathans refocused his research yet again, this time taking up the study of cellular responses to growth signals. To this end he isolated and characterized some of the first cellular genes whose expression was regulated by growth factor treatment. He remained at Johns Hopkins for the rest of his career, serving for one year as interim president of the university. His other honors include the National Medal of Science and election to the National Academy of Sciences and the Amer-ican Academy of Arts and Sciences. He died on November 16, 1999, at his home in Baltimore.

Further Reading

DiMaio, Daniel. "Daniel Nathans," National Academy of Sciences, *Biographical Memoirs* 79 (2001): pp. 262–279.

Hargittai, Istvan, and Magdolna Hargittai. *Candid Science II: Conversations with Famous Biomedical Scientists.* London: Imperial College Press, 2002, pp. 142–154.

Nobelprize.org. "The Nobel Prize in Physiology or Medicine 1978." Available online. URL: http://nobelprize.org/medicine/laureates/1978. Downloaded on July 4, 2004.

Wasson, Tyler, ed. *Nobel Prize Winners.* New York: H. W. Wilson, 1987, pp. 755–757.

Newcomb, Simon
(1835–1909) *astronomer*

Simon Newcomb developed one of the first methods for calculating the effect of interplanetary gravity on a planet's movement. His research and influence also resulted in the adoption of a standardized set of tables by the major seafaring nations of the world.

Newcomb was born on March 12, 1835, in Wallace, Nova Scotia, Canada. His father, John, was a schoolteacher, and his mother, Emily, was a homemaker. Newcomb possessed amazing ability when it came to mathematics, and by age seven he had mastered every mathematical function up to and including the extraction of cube roots. Despite his ability, he received little formal education as a child, although with his father's encouragement he became well-read. After spending most of his childhood working on neighbors' farms, at age 16 he was apprenticed to an herb doctor in Salisbury, New Brunswick. Two years later he ran away and went to live with his father, who by now had relocated to the outskirts of Washington, D.C.

Newcomb earned his living as a teacher and tutor in rural Maryland, but he spent much of his free time at the Smithsonian Institution in downtown Washington. He soon made the acquaintance of the institution's director, JOSEPH HENRY, who introduced Newcomb to several of his colleagues.

In 1856 one of them arranged a job for Newcomb at the Nautical Almanac Office in Cambridge, Massachusetts. In this position he helped compute ephemerides—tables that listed the computed positions of celestial bodies on specific dates—for use by mariners as navigation aids. He also enrolled in Harvard University's Lawrence Scientific School to study mathematical astronomy and received a B.S. in mathematics in 1858. He continued to work at the Almanac Office after graduation, taking time off to join a solar eclipse expedition to Saskatchewan and to conduct independent research concerning the origins of the asteroid belt between Mars and Jupiter. In 1861 he returned to Washington, D.C., as a commissioned naval officer and professor of mathematics at the U.S. Naval Observatory. In 1863, the year before he became a naturalized citizen, he married Mary Hassler with whom he had three children.

The Naval Observatory had better equipment than the Almanac Office, and in the early 1870s it acquired a 26-inch telescope, at the time the largest in the country. Newcomb was able to use this equipment to show that the accepted values for the celestial longitudes of the bright fixed stars were substantially incorrect, and his 14 years with the observatory were devoted mostly to recalculating these values. However, he also made time to conduct research concerning the movements of the Moon, Uranus, and Neptune; he was specifically interested in calculating the effects on the three of the gravitational pull of other planets so that their positions could be plotted more accurately. His work in this regard won him the 1874 Gold Medal of the Royal Astronomical Society of London.

In 1877 Newcomb was appointed superintendent of the Nautical Almanac Office, which by now had been put under the auspices of the navy and relocated to Washington. In this position, he implemented a basic research program designed to recalculate all the positional values for the planets and the bright fixed stars, as many of these values had been determined more than 100 years earlier using equipment that was not up to the standards of Newcomb's day. He began publishing his work in this regard in 1879 in the first volume of *Astronomical Papers Prepared for the Use of the American Ephemeris and Nautical Almanac,* and he continued to publish his updated tables in its pages through its next eight volumes. Much of this work was also published in *The Elements of the Four Inner Planets and the Fundamental Constants of Astronomy* (1895). He continued to work on this project after his retirement from the Almanac Office in 1897 via a generous grant from the Carnegie Institute. The tables Newcomb prepared concerning the positioning of the Sun, Mercury, Venus, Mars, Uranus, and Neptune were so accurate that they were used until well into the mid-20th century, long after much better equipment than Newcomb had to work with was put into use.

In 1895 Newcomb began working to update the nautical almanacs of other countries besides the United States. After consulting with his counterpart in the British Nautical Almanac Office, in 1896 he headed up a conference of the directors of the national almanacs of the United States, Great Britain, France, and Germany. The result of the conference was that all four nations adopted Newcomb's updated tables for use in their nautical almanacs. A similar conference, held in 1950, voted unanimously to continue using Newcomb's system of constants.

In addition to his work with nautical almanacs, Newcomb wrote and taught for the general public. From 1884 to 1893 he taught astronomy at Johns Hopkins University in Baltimore, Maryland. His popular works on astronomy include *Popular Astronomy* (1878), *The Stars* (1901), *Astronomy for Everybody: A Popular Exposition of the Wonders of the Heavens* (1902), and *A Compendium of Spherical Astronomy* (1906). He also wrote with great understanding about economics, his most important work in this regard being a textbook, *Principles of Popular Economy* (1885). He cofounded and served as president of the American Astronomical Society, he presided over the American Association for the Advancement of Science, and he was elected to membership in the National Academy of Sciences. He died on July 11, 1909, in Washington.

Further Reading

Carter, Bill, and Merri Sue Carter. *Latitude: How American Astronomers Solved the Mystery of Variation.* Annapolis, Md.: Naval Institute Press, 2002.

Moyer, Albert E. *A Scientist's Voice in American Culture: Simon Newcomb and the Rhetoric of Scientific Method.* Berkeley: University of California Press, 1992.

Nirenberg, Marshall W.
(Marshall Warren Nirenberg)
(1927–) *biochemist*

Marshall W. Nirenberg discovered how genetic coding is transmitted from DNA to the ribosomes, the centers of protein synthesis. This discovery won for him a share of the 1968 Nobel Prize in physiology or medicine.

Nirenberg was born on April 10, 1927, in New York City to Harry and Minerva Nirenberg. At age 12 he moved with his family to Orlando, Florida, where he grew up. He received a B.S. in zoology and chemistry and an M.S. in zoology from the University of Florida in 1948 and 1952, respectively, and then entered the University of Michigan, receiving a Ph.D. in biological chemistry in 1957. That same year he became a research fellow at the National Institutes of Health (NIH) in Bethesda, Maryland. He remained at NIH for the rest of his career, eventually becoming chief of the National Heart, Lung and Blood Institute's laboratory of biomedical genetics. In 1961 he married Perola Zaltzman.

Nirenberg's early research focused on the role played by the nucleic acids—DNA and RNA—in the biosynthesis of proteins, the complex molecules that carry out the biochemical functions of the cells. Four years before he arrived at NIH, JAMES D. WATSON and Francis Crick had developed a model of DNA, which carries the genetic coding for the production of a living organism's proteins. Although Watson and Crick also provided a model for how DNA replicates itself, they did not suggest how the genetic coding carried by DNA is translated into the production of proteins, a problem that Nirenberg set out to solve.

Proteins are made from amino acids. Although approximately 100 amino acids exist, only about 20 are used to make proteins. Conversely, the number of ways in which DNA's four main building blocks—adenine, cytosine, guanine, and thymine— can be arranged in pairs to form a single "step" in the DNA ladder is only four, since adenine always pairs with thymine and cytosine always pairs with guanine. Consequently, it was not clear how a single DNA step dictates the production of a specific amino acid, since there are far more amino acids than there are step arrangements. Nirenberg answered this question when he showed that it takes three DNA steps, also called a triplet or codon, to call for one specific amino acid.

Like many scientists, Nirenberg believed that RNA had something to do with the transfer of genetic coding from DNA to proteins. In 1960 he and German biochemist Heinrich J. Matthaei began studying the four main building blocks of RNA: adenine, cytosine, guanine, and uracil (one difference between RNA and DNA is that in RNA uracil is substituted for thymine). Working with a colony of *Escherichia coli* (*E. coli*), a bacterium found in the human colon, they synthesized a strand of *E. coli* RNA that contained codons consisting entirely of uracil and introduced the strand into the colony. When the *E. coli* began producing amino acid chains consisting entirely of phenylalanine, one of the 20 protein-building amino acids, they realized that the poly-U codon was the genetic code that called for the incorporation of phenylalanine. This experiment, which was concluded in 1961, demonstrated that messenger RNA is the medium via which genetic coding is transmitted from the DNA in a cell's nucleus to the ribosomes in its cytoplasm. In essence, each codon in a strand of messenger RNA tells a ribosome to include a specific amino acid in the protein it is synthesizing. Further experimentation over the next five years identified most of the codons that call for the production of other protein-making amino acids.

By figuring out how to decipher the genetic coding contained in the nucleic acids, Nirenberg opened the door for further experimentation in genetics. His work made it possible to better identify the causes of certain inherited traits, especially hereditary diseases. It also raised the possibility that genetic engineering involving higher-order organisms would someday become commonplace. Because of the far-reaching implications of his research, Nirenberg was awarded a one-third share of the 1968 Nobel Prize in physiology or medicine.

After winning the Nobel Prize, Nirenberg shifted the focus of his research from biochemistry to neurobiology. He was specifically interested in learning how the nervous system employs biochemical compounds to transmit mental information in much the same way that DNA employs biochemical compounds to transmit genetic information. He was elected to the National Academy of Sciences and the American Academy of Arts and Sciences. His other honors include the National Medal of Science and the National Medal of Honor.

Further Reading

Hargittai, Istvan, and Magdolna Hargittai. *Candid Science II: Conversations with Famous Biomedical Scientists.* London: Imperial College Press, 2002, pp. 130–142.

Nobelprize.org. "The Nobel Prize in Physiology or Medicine 1968." Available online. URL: http://nobelprize.org/medicine/laureates/1968. Downloaded on June 18, 2004.

Wasson, Tyler, ed. *Nobel Prize Winners.* New York: H. W. Wilson, 1987, pp. 767–769.

Northrop, John H.
(John Howard Northrop)
(1891–1987) *chemist*

John H. Northrop won a Nobel Prize for proving that enzymes are composed of protein. He also contributed to a better understanding of the composition of viruses.

Northrop was born on July 5, 1891, in Yonkers, New York. His parents, John and Alice, were biologists. After receiving a B.S. (1912), an M.A. (1913), and a Ph.D. (1915) in chemistry from Columbia University, he took a position as a research chemist at New York's Rockefeller Institute for Medical Research (today Rockefeller University). In 1917 he married Louise Walker with whom he had two children.

While at Columbia, Northrop became interested in enzymes because they catalyze, or start, every biochemical reaction and also because they were so poorly understood at the time. He rekindled his interest in enzymes during World War I; assigned to the U.S. Army Chemical Warfare Service, he developed a fermentation process using enzymes to speed up the production of acetone and ethyl alcohol for warfare purposes. He returned to Rockefeller after the war, and in 1926 he transferred to its general physiology laboratory in Princeton, New Jersey. That same year he began assembling a team to conduct further research with enzymes. The catalyst for this decision was the announcement in 1926 by JAMES B. SUMNER that he had isolated the enzyme urease, and that urease was a protein. Sumner's claims were rejected by a large group of German biochemists, including Nobel Prize winner Richard Wilstätter, who had been trying to isolate an enzyme for years without success. The Germans believed that enzymes are composed of some sort of unknown chemical compound and are encased in a protein "wrapper," and they were sure that what Sumner had "isolated" was nothing more than the wrapper.

Northrop and his team set out to verify the results of Sumner's experiments. They developed and perfected techniques for isolating enzymes via crystallization that were more sophisticated and precise than those used by either Sumner or Wilstätter. In 1929 Northrop was able to crystallize pepsin, one of the enzymes that catalyzes digestion. By 1935 he and his associates had crystallized the digestive enzymes trypsin and chymotrypsin, as well as chymotrypsinogen and pepsinogen, the chemical substances from which chymotrypsin and pepsin, respectively, are formed. Further experimentation brought the Sumner-Wilstätter debate to a close by demonstrating that enzymes are not encased in protein but are themselves proteins. Northrop's results, which he published in *Crystalline Enzymes* (1939), settled the debate over the nature of enzymes in Sumner's favor.

Meanwhile, in 1935 one of Northrop's Rockefeller colleagues, WENDELL M. STANLEY, had used Northrop's crystallization techniques to isolate a virus. Stanley's achievement led Northrop to shift the focus of his research from enzymes to viruses, and in 1938 he crystallized a bacteriophage, in this case a virus that attacks the bacteria that cause staphylococcal infections. Further research indicated that the virus is composed of protein and DNA, a result that contributed to a better understanding of the nature of viruses. The importance of

Northrop, Sumner, and Stanley's work was validated in 1946, when they were awarded the Nobel Prize in chemistry.

In 1947 the Rockefeller Institute closed its Princeton facility. Rather than return to New York City, Northrop accepted a position as professor of bacteriology at the University of California at Berkeley. Although the transfer greatly curtailed his staff and facilities, he continued to investigate viruses. In 1951 he theorized that a virus is nothing more than a DNA center with a protein shell, and that the protein helps the virus enter a healthy cell so that its DNA can transform the cell. This work helped later researchers understand that DNA is the material that replicates and produces genetic changes within cells.

Northrop edited the *Journal of General Physiology* for many years. His many honors include election to the National Academy of Sciences. In 1970 he retired from Berkeley to Wickenburg, Arizona, where he died on May 27, 1987.

Further Reading

Herriott, Roger. "John Howard Northrop," National Academy of Sciences, *Biographical Memoirs* 63 (1944): pp. 423–450.

Nobelprize.org. "The Nobel Prize in Chemistry 1946." Available online. URL: http://nobelprize.org/chemistry/laureates/1946. Downloaded on February 9, 2004.

Wasson, Tyler, ed. *Nobel Prize Winners.* New York: H. W. Wilson, 1987, pp. 772–773.

Ochoa, Severo
(1905–1993) *biochemist*

Severo Ochoa developed a method for duplicating ribonucleic acid (RNA) that was later used to duplicate deoxyribonucleic acid (DNA). His achievement was a major step forward in understanding how hereditary traits are passed from one cell to another, and it won for Ochoa a share of the 1959 Nobel Prize in physiology or medicine.

Ochoa was born on September 24, 1905, in Luarca, Spain. His father, Severo, was a lawyer, and his mother, Carmen, was a homemaker. At age seven he moved with his family to Málaga where he grew up. After receiving a B.A. from Málaga College in 1921, he remained for a year in that school's premedical program and then entered the University of Madrid Medical School, receiving an M.D. in 1929. He spent the next two years conducting postdoctoral research at the Kaiser-Wilhelm Institute for Medical Research in Berlin, Germany, and in 1931, the same year he married Carmen Cobian, he began teaching physiology and biochemistry at Madrid. The following year he was off to the National Institute for Medical Research in London, England, for two more years of research before returning to teach at Madrid, which named him head of the department of medicine in 1935.

Ochoa left Spain in 1936 following the outbreak of the Spanish Civil War. Over the next five years, he was associated for brief periods of time with the Kaiser-Wilhelm Institute, the Marine Biological Laboratory in Plymouth, England, and the department of biochemistry at England's Oxford University. In 1941 he joined CARL F. CORI and GERTY T. CORI at Washington University in St. Louis, Missouri, but he left after a year for the New York University (NYU) School of Medicine. He taught biochemistry and pharmacology at NYU until 1954, when he was named chair of the biochemistry department. In 1956 he became a naturalized U.S. citizen.

Prior to settling at NYU, Ochoa's research involved a wide variety of projects: the biochemistry and physiology of muscle, the function in the body of vitamin B_1 (thiamine), the way enzymes catabolize (break down) and metabolize (build up) carbohydrates, and the process by which yeast ferments, to name a few. Once at NYU, however, he was able to focus his research on one main line, the synthesis and transfer of energy in living organisms via enzymes, proteins that trigger the biochemical functions. In the early 1950s he isolated triphosphopyridine nucleotide (TPN), one of the chemical compounds that facilitate photosynthesis. He then began experimenting with adenosine triphosphate (ATP), the coenzyme that carries chemical energy produced by the catabolism of food to the cells. By 1954 he had demonstrated that the oxidation, or burning, of one molecule of glucose yields 36 molecules of ATP.

In 1954 Ochoa began exploring the role played by enzymes in the formation of DNA. Most enzymes break down chemical compounds into simpler ones, but Ochoa believed that the nucleotides from which DNA is built were strung together with the help of an enzyme. Although he never found a DNA enzyme, in 1955 he discovered an enzyme in an acetic acid bacterium that facilitates the production of RNA, the biochemical compound that transfers genetic coding from the DNA in a cell's nucleus to its cytoplasm, where protein is synthesized. The enzyme, named polynucleotide phosphorylase by Ochoa, strips away half of the phosphoric acid residues from ribonucleotides having twice the ratio of such residues as RNA, and then it links together the "stripped" nucleotides to form RNA molecules that are indistinguishable from the "real thing."

Ochoa's discovery opened the door for other researchers to begin duplicating other processes involving the transfer of hereditary traits from cell to cell. His method for synthesizing RNA was quickly duplicated by ARTHUR KORNBERG, who used an enzyme he had discovered in the bacterium *E. coli* to synthesize DNA. These two discoveries led other researchers to begin looking for cures for hereditary diseases by investigating ways in which "defective" traits can be eliminated by altering an organism's DNA or RNA. They also stimulated researchers looking for cures to viral diseases and cancer, as they held out the promise of permitting changes to be made to the DNA of harmful viruses or tumorous cells. For his discovery, Ochoa was awarded a half share of the 1959 Nobel Prize in physiology or medicine; his corecipient was Kornberg.

In 1974 Ochoa retired from NYU, only to become associated with the Roche Institute of Molecular Biology in New Jersey, where he continued to conduct research involving RNA and DNA. In 1985 he returned to Spain to teach biology at the University Autonoma in Madrid. He died on November 1, 1993, in Madrid.

Further Reading

Kornberg, Arthur, et al., eds. *Reflections on Biochemistry: In Honour of Severo Ochoa's 70th Birthday.* New York: Pergamon Press, 1976.

Nobelprize.org. "The Nobel Prize in Physiology or Medicine 1959." Available online. URL: http://nobelprize.org/medicine/laureates/1959. Downloaded on June 3, 2004.

Wasson, Tyler, ed. *Nobel Prize Winners.* New York: H. W. Wilson, 1987, pp. 773–775.

Olah, George A.
(George Andrew Olah)
(1927–) *chemist*

George A. Olah gave chemists a better understanding of the structure and behavior of carbocations, positively charged molecules centered on an atom of carbon. Carbocations, also known as carbonium ions, play an important role in the production of synthetic hydrocarbons such as thermoplastics and high-octane gasoline. For this contribution to organic chemistry, he was awarded the 1994 Nobel Prize in chemistry.

Olah was born on May 22, 1927, in Budapest, Hungary. His father, Julius, was a lawyer, and his mother, Magda, was a homemaker. In 1949 he received a B.S. and a Ph.D. in organic chemistry from the Technical University of Budapest and married Judith Lengyel with whom he had two children. He taught chemistry at the Technical University for five years and then became associate director of the Central Chemical Research Institute, where he established a small research group in organic chemistry. In 1956 he left Hungary for England, settling the following year in Canada where he took a job as a research chemist with Dow Chemical in Sarnia, Ontario. He was eventually promoted to company scientist and given the time and resources to conduct experiments of his own choosing.

One of Olah's duties at Dow was to oversee the production of ethylbenzene, a synthetic hydrocarbon (a compound containing only carbon and hydrogen atoms) used in the manufacture of styrene, from which clear plastic and synthetic rubber are made. Dow was producing ethylbenzene via a Friedel-Crafts reaction, which employs aluminum chloride as a catalyst to synthesize hydrocarbons. At the time it was strongly suspected that the intermediates, short-lived temporary products of a reaction from which the final product is formed, during a Friedel-Crafts reaction are carbocations. However, the actual existence of carbocations had yet to be proven because they normally exist for less than a billionth of a second, and the technology of the day was unable to detect such short-lived intermediates. Consequently, a lively debate had arisen among organic chemists as to the existence and nature of carbocations.

Upon being named company scientist, Olah set out to prove the existence of carbocations. By 1965 he had developed a method, using special solvents (which do not react with cations) and fluorine-based superacids (with strengths billions of times stronger than concentrated sulfuric acid), to increase both the life span and the concentration of carbocations so that they could be studied. That same year he returned to academia by joining the chemistry faculty at Case Western Reserve University in Cleveland, Ohio, where he focused his research efforts exclusively on carbocations.

In 1977, seven years after he became a naturalized U.S. citizen, Olah was named a professor of chemistry at the University of Southern California and founding director of its Loker Hydrocarbon Research Institute. He continued to experiment with carbocations, eventually demonstrating the existence of two groups of carbocations: trivalent, in which the carbon atom is surrounded by three hydrogen atoms; and pentacoordinated, in which the carbon atom is surrounded by five hydrogen atoms. Pentacoordinated carbocations feature a three-center bond, whereby the carbon atom and two of the hydrogen atoms are linked by a unique covalent bond in which they share two covalent pairs of electrons instead of the usual three. Previously, it had been believed that a carbon atom could not bind with more than four atoms, so Olah's demonstration of the existence of pentacoordinated carbocations forced chemists to rethink one of the basic premises of organic chemistry, which is the study of carbon and its compounds.

Olah also discovered that, in some cases, a superacid donates a proton to a pentacoordinated carbocation, thus allowing the carbocation to undergo further reactions. This discovery was of major importance to the petrochemical industry, which now uses proton-modified carbocations to produce gasoline and diesel fuels that are cleaner and have higher octane ratings, thus reducing the need for toxic additives. He also developed methods for using carbocations to convert methane into higher hydrocarbons from which ethylene and propylene can be produced.

Olah's work with carbocations contributed significantly to a better understanding of the structure of carbon compounds. This work proved to have important applications in the chemical, petrochemical, plastics, and rubber industries because it gave chemical engineers more detailed knowledge about one of the key steps in the reactions they use to develop their products. For the significance of his contributions to hydrocarbon chemistry, Olah was awarded the 1994 Nobel Prize in chemistry.

Olah's work with carbocations led him to investigate the so-called onium ions, positively charged molecules centered on an atom of oxygen or one of the halogens. One of his last research projects involved finding ways to produce hydrocarbons from carbon dioxide and water, a development that held great promise for addressing the problems of air pollution and dwindling petroleum reserves. His many honors include election to the National Academy of Sciences and the American Academy of Arts and Sciences. His publications include *Superacids* (1985), *Cage Hydrocarbons* (1990), *Chemistry of Energetic Materials* (1991), *Synthetic Fluorine Chemistry* (1992), *Hydrocarbon Chemistry* (1995), and *Onium Ions* (1998).

Further Reading

Nobelprize.org. "The Nobel Prize in Chemistry 1994." Available online. URL: http://nobelprize.org/chemistry/laureates/1994. Downloaded on August 13, 2004.

Olah, George A. A *Life of Magic Chemistry: Autobiographical Reflections of a Nobel Prize Winner.* New York: Wiley-Interscience, 2001.

Onsager, Lars
(1903–1976) *chemist*

Lars Onsager was one of the foremost practitioners of statistical mechanics, which uses statistics, classical physics, and quantum mechanics to explain theoretically the properties of chemical systems. He authored the Onsager reciprocal relation, today considered by many to be the fourth law of thermodynamics. For this achievement, he was awarded the 1968 Nobel Prize in chemistry.

Onsager was born on November 27, 1903, in Oslo, Norway. His father, Erling, was a lawyer, and his mother, Ingrid, was a homemaker. In 1925 he received a degree in chemical engineering from the

Norwegian Institute of Technology. While a student, he proposed a correction to the Debye-Hückel equation, a mathematical expression that explains certain properties of strong electrolytes, salts that are good conductors of electricity when dissolved in solutions. One of the authors of the equation, Dutch physical chemist Peter Debye, was so impressed with the correction that in 1926 he invited Onsager to become his research assistant at the Federal Institute of Technology in Zurich, Switzerland. After two years in Zurich, Onsager went to the United States to teach chemistry at Johns Hopkins University, but he left after a year to accept a similar position at Brown University. In 1933, the same year he married Margarethe Arledter with whom he had four children, he became a professor of theoretical chemistry at Yale University, a position he held for almost 40 years. In 1935 Yale awarded him a Ph.D. in chemistry on the basis of his published work, and in 1945 he became a naturalized U.S. citizen.

Onsager's entire scientific career was devoted to explaining the processes involved in complex chemical reactions in terms of statistical mechanics, which at the time was poorly understood. Most of his research involved explaining the behavior of solutions of strong electrolytes. His most important contribution in this regard is today known as the Onsager reciprocal relation, and it describes the reciprocal relations between fluxes and forces that take place in simultaneous irreversible processes. A common example of such processes would be the dissolving of a powdered sweetener in a hot beverage; while the heat of the beverage raises the temperature of the sweetener, the water in the beverage causes the sweetener to dissolve. Onsager was more interested in explaining what happens when a strong electrolyte is dissolved in a solution. Using statistical mechanics, he proved that the equations governing the one-way flow of ions could be written in such a way that certain simple connections would exist between these equations. These connections, the reciprocal relations, make it possible to describe theoretically what happens during simultaneous irreversible processes. For example, he used reciprocal relations to demonstrate that changes to a system's entropy, the amount of potential energy that cannot be converted into kinetic energy, taking place during simultaneous irreversible processes are symmetrical and held to a minimum.

The Onsager reciprocal relation was first proposed when Onsager submitted it to the Norwegian Institute of Technology as his Ph.D. dissertation. Its importance was not recognized at the time, however, and it was rejected, not only as a useful theory but also as an acceptable dissertation. In 1931 he published an article describing reciprocal relations in *Physical Review,* but again its importance was not immediately grasped. In the 1960s, however, it was shown to be of great use to researchers in physics, chemistry, biology, and technology, and in 1968, almost 40 years after being propagated, it earned for Onsager the Nobel Prize in chemistry.

Meanwhile, Onsager had made other contributions to chemistry by using statistical mechanics. In 1936 he published a correction to the mathematical formula for calculating the dielectric constant of molecules with permanent dipole moments. His work concerning the separation of isotopes later proved to be of value to researchers trying to construct the first atomic bomb from an isotope of uranium. Perhaps his greatest achievement was to demonstrate that statistical mechanics can explain theoretically the transition of matter from one phase (i.e., solid, liquid, gas) to another.

Onsager was awarded the National Medal of Science, and he was elected to the National Academies of Science and the American Academy of Arts and Sciences. In 1971 he retired from Yale, but the following year he took a position with the University of Miami's Center for Theoretical Studies. He died on October 5, 1976, in Coral Gables, Florida.

Further Reading

Mintz, Stephan L., ed. *Quantum Statistical Mechanics in the Natural Sciences: A Volume Dedicated to Lars Onsager on the Occasion of His Seventieth Birthday.* New York: Plenum Press, 1974.

Nobelprize.org. "The Nobel Prize in Chemistry 1968." Available online. URL: http://nobelprize.org/chemistry/laureates/1968. Downloaded on April 28, 2004.

Wasson, Tyler, ed. *Nobel Prize Winners.* New York: H. W. Wilson, 1987, pp. 783–785.

Oppenheimer, Julius R.
(Julius Robert Oppenheimer)
(1904–1967) *physicist*

J. Robert Oppenheimer was the driving force behind the design and construction of the first atomic bombs. He was also an able teacher and researcher, and he built up first-class programs in theoretical physics at two major universities.

Oppenheimer was born on April 22, 1904, in New York City. His father, Julius, was a textile importer, and his mother, Ella, was a painter. After receiving a B.A. in physics from Harvard University in 1925, he studied in Europe at Cambridge University and the University of Göttingen, receiving a Ph.D. in theoretical physics from the latter in 1927. He spent the next two years conducting research at the universities of Leiden and Zurich in Europe, Harvard, and the California Institute of Technology (Caltech). In 1929 he accepted offers to teach physics at both Caltech and the University of California at Berkeley, and for the next 13 years he taught during the fall semester at one school and during the spring at the other. In 1940 he married Katharine Harrison with whom he had two children.

Oppenheimer is best remembered for his administrative work, but he also made several contributions as a researcher. In 1927 he and Max Born, one of his professors at Göttingen, developed a quantum theory of molecules that described the motion of electrons around the combined nuclei as well as the motion of the nuclear skeleton. They also developed the Born-Oppenheimer approximation, a greatly simplified method for making calculations concerning electron structures. Over the next 13 years Oppenheimer calculated the photoelectric effect for hydrogen and for X-rays, the radiation in the form of X-rays produced in the collision of an electron with a nucleus with a positive charge, and the capture of electrons by ions of other atoms. He also developed theories to describe the extraction of electrons from metal surfaces by very strong electric fields and the multiplicity of electron showers in cosmic radiation. His most important contribution was to explain in quantitative terms the so-called Oppenheimer-Phillips process, whereby a deuteron (one proton and one neutron) entering a heavy nucleus is split into one proton and one neutron so that one is retained by the nucleus while the other is reemitted.

Despite these contributions, Oppenheimer's strength as a physicist was as a teacher and research director. At Berkeley he established the School for Theoretical Physics where many of the United States's leading physicists received at least part of their training. He focused his attention and the school's on quantum mechanics, the study of subatomic particles, which was still in its infancy in the early 1930s. As a research director he was exceptionally gifted in his ability to suggest cutting-edge problems to study, and then to guide the resulting investigations of more than a dozen students at the same time. Many of his students went on to become leading physicists in their own right. In recognition of his contributions as a researcher and teacher, in 1941 he was elected to the National Academy of Sciences.

In 1942 Oppenheimer was recruited to work on the Manhattan Project, the U.S. effort during World War II to construct an atomic bomb. While others directed the production of the necessary nuclear fuel, Oppenheimer was put in charge of building the actual bomb. He chose for his laboratory a site in the remote Pecos Valley of New Mexico, the former Los Alamos Ranch School, and he recruited about 50 or so of the best physicists in the country, including HANS A. BETHE and EDWARD TELLER. Unlike other divisions of the Manhattan Project, which limited information to researchers on a strict need-to-know basis, Oppenheimer encouraged his researchers to share information, thus stimulating an unusual number of ideas about how to solve the sticky problems facing the design team. Oppenheimer contributed little in terms of theory to the project, but the contributions he made as a research director and morale booster ensured the overall success of the Los Alamos Laboratory's efforts.

The Manhattan Project's leaders were uncertain as to which type of fissionable material would be developed sooner, so Oppenheimer's team had to design and test two entirely different bombs, one using uranium and one using plutonium. In the end, sufficient amounts of both materials were ready at about the same time, so Oppenheimer's team was able to build two bombs: a uranium bomb, nicknamed "Little Boy," was dropped on Hiroshima; and a plutonium bomb, "Fat Man," was dropped on Nagasaki. The two bombs brought the war against Japan to an immediate end, and in 1946 Oppenheimer was awarded the U.S. Medal of Merit.

In 1946 Oppenheimer was named to chair the general advisory committee of the U.S. Atomic Energy Commission (AEC). The committee included such luminaries as ENRICO FERMI, I. I. RABI, and GLENN T. SEABORG, and it was charged with advising the commission on scientific matters and general policy concerning the development of nuclear energy for both peacetime and military uses. In 1954 Oppenheimer was removed as committee chair for security reasons. In the 1930s he had flirted with the Communist Party, although he had never joined it, and he had contributed money to several left-wing organizations. More damning was his decision in 1949 to oppose the development by the United States of the hydrogen bomb, a decision that some officials took to be a sign that Oppenheimer was "soft on communism." He was partially exonerated from the taint that the removal had on his career and reputation in 1963, when President Lyndon B. Johnson arranged for Oppenheimer to receive the AEC's Enrico Fermi Award.

Meanwhile, in 1947 Oppenheimer was named director of the Institute for Advanced Study at Princeton University. In this capacity, he developed a world-class program in theoretical physics at Princeton while also enhancing its offerings in the social sciences and the humanities. He became interested in the relation between modern science and modern culture, and he wrote a number of books and articles about science for the general public, including *Science and Common Understanding* (1954), *The Open Mind* (1955), and *The Flying Trapeze: Three Crises for Physicists* (1961). He retired from Princeton in 1966, and he died on February 18, 1967, in Princeton, New Jersey.

Further Reading

Bacher, Robert F. *Robert Oppenheimer, 1904–1967.* Los Alamos, N.Mex.: Los Alamos Historical Society, 1999.

Bethe, Hans A. "J. Robert Oppenheimer," National Academy of Sciences, *Biographical Memoirs* 71 (1997): pp. 175–220.

Smith, Alice Kimble, and Charles Weiner, eds. *Robert Oppenheimer, Letters and Recollections.* Cambridge, Mass.: Harvard University Press, 1980.

Osheroff, Douglas D.
(Douglas Dean Osheroff)
(1945–) *physicist*

Douglas D. Osheroff codiscovered superfluidity in an isotope of helium known as helium-3. For this discovery, he was awarded a share of the 1996 Nobel Prize in physics.

Osheroff was born on August 1, 1945, in Aberdeen, Washington. His father, William, was a physician, and his mother, Bessie, was a homemaker. After finishing high school, he entered the California Institute of Technology, receiving a B.S. in physics in 1967. While at Caltech he became interested in low-temperature physics, the study of what happens to the thermal, electrical, and magnetic properties of matter at temperatures approaching 0 K, or absolute zero. Upon entering the graduate physics program at Cornell University in Ithaca, New York, he joined DAVID M. LEE and ROBERT C. RICHARDSON in collaboration on projects involving low-temperature physics at Cornell's Laboratory of Atomic and Solid State Physics (LASSP).

Lee and Richardson were particularly interested in superfluidity, the unusual properties exhibited by liquid helium when it is cooled to 2.18 K. These properties include frictionless flow, involving the ability to overflow its containment vessel in defiance of the laws of viscosity, and very high heat conductivity. Specifically, Lee and Richardson wanted to learn more about helium-3, an isotope of helium that did not become a superfluid at low temperatures. The standard explanation for this phenomenon involved the difference between bosons and fermions. Helium-4, the more common isotope of helium, is a boson because it contains an even number of nucleons (protons and neutrons), while helium-3 is a fermion because it contains an uneven number of nucleons. The difference between having an even or odd number of nucleons is significant

Douglas Osheroff's work helped explain how extremely low temperatures affect the physical properties of matter. *(Courtesy of Douglas D. Osheroff; photo by Linda Cicero)*

K, at which point they discovered that it, too, becomes a superfluid. Moreover, helium-3 in the superfluid phase possesses certain magnetic properties that helium-4 in the superfluid phase does not. Not only did this discovery nullify the conventional wisdom regarding the conditions required for superfluidity, but also it permitted physicists to conduct some very interesting research concerning the differences in behavior between bosons and fermions, as now a boson (helium-4) and a fermion (helium-3) could be studied in a superfluid phase. For their discovery, Osheroff, Lee, and Richardson were each awarded a one-third share of the 1996 Nobel Prize in physics.

In 1973 Osheroff received a Ph.D. in physics from Cornell. The previous year he had gone to work as a member of the technical staff of AT&T Bell Laboratories in Murray Hill, New Jersey, and in 1981 he was named head of the solid state and low temperature research department. During his time at Bell Labs he continued his work with low-temperature physics, measuring many of the important characteristics related to magnetism of the superfluid phases. In 1987 he was named a professor of physics at Stanford University, where he remained for the rest of his career. His many honors include election to the National Academy of Sciences and the American Academy of Arts and Sciences. In 1970 he married Phyllis Liu.

Further Reading

Browne, Malcolm W. "Discoveries of Superfluid Helium, and 'Buckyballs,' Earn Nobels for 6 Scientists," *New York Times*, October 10, 1996, p. D21.

Nobelprize.org. "The Nobel Prize in Physics 1996." Available online. URL: http://nobelprize.org/physics/laureates/1996. Downloaded on August 23, 2004.

Stanford University Department of Physics. "Douglas D. Osheroff." Available online. URL: http://www.stanford.edu/dept/physics/people/faculty/osheroff_douglas.html. Downloaded on March 25, 2005.

because it determines angular momentum, or spin; bosons and fermions behave differently from each other because they have different spins. Consequently, it was believed that helium-4 becomes a superfluid because it is a boson while helium-3 cannot become a superfluid because it is a fermion.

Shortly after Osheroff's arrival at Cornell, he, Lee, and Richardson began collaborating on a study of the magnetic properties of solid helium-3. By 1972 they had managed to cool helium-3 to 0.002

P

Palade, George E.
(George Emil Palade)
(1912–   ) *cell biologist*

George E. Palade was one of the founders of cell biology as a recognized field of research in the biological sciences. His discoveries shed much light on the structure and functions of the cell. For these contributions, he was awarded a share of the 1974 Nobel Prize in physiology or medicine.

Palade was born on November 19, 1912, in Jassy (Iaşi), Romania. His father, Emil, was a philosophy professor, and his mother, Constanta, taught elementary school. In 1930 he entered the University of Bucharest School of Medicine, receiving an M.D. in 1940. He remained at the university as an anatomy professor until 1946, when he emigrated to the United States. In 1941 he married Irina Malaxa with whom he had two children; she died in 1969, and in 1970 he married Marilyn Farquhar, a fellow cell biologist. In 1952 he became a naturalized U.S. citizen.

Shortly after arriving in the United States, Palade found a research position at New York University's biology laboratory. There he met ALBERT CLAUDE of the Rockefeller Institute for Medical Research (today Rockefeller University), who in late 1946 invited Palade to become his assistant. Although Claude's primary research interest was the potential role played by viruses as a cause of cancer, he also pioneered the new field of cell biology. He was one of the first researchers to make extensive use of the electron microscope, and as his assistant, Palade developed several of the techniques required for preparing cell tissue for examination under the electron microscope. Between 1946 and 1949, when Claude returned to his native Belgium, he and Palade collaborated on several studies, including the first stages of an investigation into the nature of the Golgi apparatus, an irregular network of small fibers and cavities that is involved in constructing the cell membrane, storing proteins and lipids, and transporting particles across the cell membrane.

Following Claude's departure, Palade pursued several of the lines of research that his mentor had initiated. He first focused on the structures in the cytoplasm, that area of the cell outside the nucleus, that Claude had labeled "secretory granules." Palade showed that these structures, today known as mitochondria, are the locations where the cell converts fat and sugar into adenosine triphosphate (ATP), the source of energy for all cellular functions. He also showed that ATP is transported throughout the cytoplasm via the Golgi apparatus.

Next Palade turned his attention to the so-called microsomes, small bodies in the cytoplasm that Claude had discovered. At the time it was believed that microsomes were fragments of mitochondria, but Palade showed that they were actually part of the endoplasmic reticulum, a series of double-layered membranes that he discovered. Claude has shown that microsomes were rich in ribonucleic acid (RNA), the complex molecule that transmits genetic coding during protein synthesis, but Palade showed that they were also rich in protein. Further study of the microsomes, renamed ribosomes by Palade, showed that they are the locations where protein synthesis takes place. He also showed that proteins are transported from the ribosomes via the endoplasmic reticulum to larger ribosomes, which assemble the proteins into amino acids and amino acid chains, and to the Golgi apparatus, where excess proteins are stored. Lastly, he discovered much about how the membranes of the various cellular structures interact during the transportation of the various biochemical materials. For all these discoveries, Palade was awarded a one-third share of the 1974 Nobel Prize in physiology or medicine; one of his corecipients was Claude.

In 1973 Palade left Rockefeller for the Yale University Medical School. While at Yale he taught cell biology and investigated how defects in the cellular production of protein cause certain medical conditions. In 1990 he was named dean of scientific affairs at the University of California at San Diego, where he also taught cellular and molecular medicine. His many honors include election to the National Academy of Sciences and serving as the founding editor of the *Journal of Cell Biology*.

Further Reading

Nobelprize.org. "The Nobel Prize in Physiology or Medicine 1974." Available online. URL: http://nobelprize.org/medicine/laureates/1974. Downloaded on June 6, 2004.

University of California San Diego Cellular & Molecular Medicine. "George E. Palade, M.D. "Available online. URL: http://cmm.ucsd.edu/palade. Downloaded on March 25, 2005.

Wasson, Tyler, ed. *Nobel Prize Winners*. New York: H. W. Wilson, 1987, pp. 789–791.

Pauling, Linus C.
(Linus Carl Pauling)
(1901–1994) *chemist*

Linus C. Pauling is considered by many to have been the greatest chemist of the 20th century. His research concerning the nature of chemical bonds in molecules, and his ability to show how those bonds affect the operation of complex molecules in living organisms, were rewarded with the 1954 Nobel Prize in chemistry.

Pauling was born on February 28, 1901, in Portland, Oregon. His father, Herman, was a druggist, and his mother, Lucy, was a homemaker. At age 16 he entered Oregon Agricultural College (today Oregon State University), receiving a B.S. in chemical engineering in 1922. He then enrolled in the graduate program at the California Institute of Technology (Caltech) and received a Ph.D. in chemistry in 1925. After spending the next two years studying theoretical physics in Europe at the universities of Munich, Zurich, and Copenhagen, in 1927 he returned to Caltech to teach theoretical chemistry. In 1923 he married Ava Miller with whom he had four children.

Linus Pauling won two Nobel Prizes, one in chemistry and the other in peace. *(Courtesy of the California Institute of Technology)*

In 1919, while still an undergraduate student, Pauling had read a paper by IRVING LANGMUIR concerning GILBERT N. LEWIS's views on the nature of the covalent bond, a basic feature of chemical reactivity. This paper led Pauling to devote the first part of his scientific career to arriving at a better understanding of the basic principles of chemical bonds. He pioneered the use of X-ray crystallography, the study of the way crystallized molecules cause X-rays to change course as they pass through the molecules, as a way to understand the inner structure of molecules. This technique allowed him to measure the distance between two atoms in a molecule as well as the angles at which atoms bond, and he took such measurements for hundreds of crystallized molecules. He was then able to demonstrate that atoms must be balanced in terms of their charges and aligned properly in terms of their angles before they can form a chemical bond.

Pauling developed three concepts that were very influential in the early days of structural chemistry, the study of how atoms are arranged in molecules. The first was the concept of hybrid orbitals. Like Langmuir and Lewis, Pauling believed that all chemical bonds are valence bonds, that is, bonds formed by sharing one or more electrons in an atom's valence, or outermost, orbit or shell. Pauling showed that molecular bonding can also involve the sharing of electrons in orbits other than just the valence orbit. The second was the concept of resonance hybrids. According to Pauling, a molecule's true structure does not fluctuate from one structure to another as electrons are being shared back and forth. Rather, the molecule maintains itself, or resonates, between two or more bond structures, thus lowering its energy level to a point that makes the molecule more stable than any of the individual bond structures. The third was the concept of electronegativity, which states that an atom in a molecule is better able to attract electrons than if it were a free atom. These concepts, among others, were published in *The Nature of the Chemical Bond, and the Structure of Molecules and Crystals* (1939), a widely used college chemistry textbook that went through three editions. Some of its ideas were later discarded; for example, some of Pauling's ideas about valence bonds have been replaced by the concept of molecular bonding as first developed in

the 1930s by ROBERT S. MULLIKEN. Nevertheless, many chemists regard *The Nature of the Chemical Bond* as the most influential treatise on structural chemistry to be published in the 20th century.

In 1934 Pauling began applying his knowledge of structural chemistry to problems related to biochemistry, the study of the chemical functions that take place in living organisms. He was particularly interested in proteins, the complex molecules that are necessary for all biochemical processes. One of his first discoveries was that the bonds formed by hydrogen atoms help maintain the integrity of a protein's structure. He then explained the behavior of antibodies, proteins that fight foreign substances in a living organism, in terms of the way their molecules react with both native and foreign substances. His most important work, however, involved hemoglobin, the protein coloring matter in red blood corpuscles that carries oxygen to the tissues. By 1950 he had shown that sickle-cell anemia, a medical condition that is hereditary among people of African descent, is caused by a genetic deformity in the hemoglobin molecule that hampers its ability to bond with oxygen. This deformity leads in turn to the deformed, sickle-like shape of the red corpuscle, hence the name of the condition. This demonstration was the first time that a hereditary disease was explained in terms of a molecule's structural chemistry. In 1962 he demonstrated that the study of the evolution of hemoglobin might hold some of the answers concerning the evolution of species. By analyzing the differences in the amino-acid makeup of hemoglobin between modern-day humans and horses and their ancestors from about 130 million years ago, he developed a "molecular clock" for predicting how often the amino acids in hemoglobin change. Based on this clock, he hypothesized that humans and gorillas diverged from one another about 10 million years ago, and that all living creatures diverged from a common ancestor about 600 million years ago.

Pauling also sought to understand the exact nature of the composition of proteins, and to this end he set out to build models of various protein molecules. He demonstrated that polypeptides, the molecules from which proteins are built, are constructed in the form of a single helix. In 1952 he proposed that deoxyribonucleic acid (DNA) molecules are shaped like triple helixes, a theory that was later proved to be wrong. Nevertheless, his work in this area guided the work of JAMES D. WATSON and Francis Crick, who in 1953 developed the double-helix model of DNA. For his achievements as both a structural chemist and a biochemist, in 1954 Pauling was awarded the Nobel Prize in chemistry.

In 1963 Pauling left Caltech to teach the biological and physical sciences at the Center for the Studies of Democratic Institutions in San Diego. Four years later he was named professor of chemistry at the University of California at San Diego, and in 1969 he accepted a similar position at Stanford University. In 1973 he became a fellow of the Linus Pauling Institute of Science and Medicine in Menlo Park, California, where he remained for the rest of his career. His honors and awards include the U.S. Medal for Merit, the National Medal of Science, and election to the National Academies of Science and the American Association for the Advancement of Science. He also won the 1962 Nobel Prize in peace for his antiwar activities, especially his efforts to secure an international ban on nuclear testing. He died on August 19, 1994, in Big Sur, California.

Further Reading

Goertzel, Ted, and Ben Goertzel. *Linus Pauling: A Life in Science and Politics.* New York: Basic Books, 1995.

Hager, Thomas. *Force of Nature: The Life of Linus Pauling.* New York: Simon and Schuster, 1995.

Mead, Clifford, and Thomas Hager, eds. *Linus Pauling: Scientist and Peacemaker.* Corvallis: Oregon State University Press, 2001.

Nobelprize.org. "The Nobel Prize in Chemistry 1954." Available online. URL: http://nobelprize.org/chemistry/laureates/1954. Downloaded on April 23, 2004.

Wasson, Tyler, ed. *Nobel Prize Winners.* New York: H. W. Wilson, 1987, pp. 798–802.

Pedersen, Charles J.
(Charles John Pedersen)
(1904–1989) *chemist*

Charles J. Pedersen discovered the crown ether, a synthetic chemical compound that is capable of performing as if it were an enzyme or some other bio-

logical molecule. For this discovery, he was awarded a share of the 1987 Nobel Prize in chemistry.

Pedersen was born on October 3, 1904, in Pusan, Korea. His father, Brede, was a Norwegian mining engineer, and his mother, Takino, was the daughter of a prominent Japanese businessman. At age eight he was sent to a convent school in Nagasaki, Japan, and two years later he entered St. Joseph College, a preparatory school in Yokohama. He came to the United States in 1922 to study chemical engineering at the University of Dayton in Ohio. After receiving a B.S., he entered the Massachusetts Institute of Technology, receiving an M.S. in organic chemistry in 1927. He then went to work as a research chemist for the E. I. du Pont de Nemours (DuPont) & Company's Jackson Laboratory in Deepwater, New Jersey.

Pedersen's early research at DuPont focused on improving petroleum products. One of his first accomplishments was to develop improvements to the process for making tetraethyl lead, at the time a gasoline additive. He then turned his attention to the degradative effect oxidation has on petroleum products, and by 1947 he had received patents for more than 30 antioxidants. The most important patents were for organic metal deactivators that prevent trace amounts of metal in gasoline, refined oil, and synthetic rubber from reacting with and breaking down their "host" product. Pedersen produced these deactivators by using coordination chemistry; this branch of chemistry deals with compounds that contain a metal atom at the center of a cluster of nonmetallic atoms or molecules.

In 1947, the same year he married Susan Aulf with whom he had two children, Pedersen was named a DuPont research associate. This position gave him the privilege of choosing his own research projects, rather than taking those that were assigned to him. Over the next 12 years he experimented with photochemistry, the chemical action of light, as a catalyst for producing the intermediate chemical compounds from which enamels, printing inks, automotive finishes, and dyes are manufactured. He also developed several compounds for catalyzing the chain reactions by which polymers are manufactured, and he designed several exotic polymers.

In 1959 Pedersen transferred to DuPont's elastomers division at the company's Experimental Station in Wilmington, Delaware, where he experimented briefly with hydrocarbon polymers. In 1960 he returned to the study of coordination chemistry, this time as it involves the metal vanadium, in hopes of developing a ligand that could enhance vanadium's catalytic properties. By 1968 he had developed a highly unusual compound that he named a crown ether. This two-dimensional compound contains a loose, flexible ring of carbon and oxygen atoms that remains unbroken during chemical reactions. Instead, an atom reacting with a crown ether forms one or more bonds inside the ring where it is "trapped." He also showed that crown ethers have a strong affinity for metals, particularly alkali metal ions, which previously had demonstrated a marked resistance to bonding. By varying the number of carbon and oxygen atoms in the ring, he found that he could custom design a crown ether that would react with atoms of a specific metal and no other.

Pedersen's discovery inspired other researchers, most notably DONALD J. CRAM and Jean-Marie Lehn, to synthesize other chemical compounds capable of behaving like enzymes in that they can "recognize" and react with a certain atom or molecule to the exception of all others. Cram and Lehn adapted Pedersen's work with two-dimensional crown ethers to develop three-dimensional compounds capable of reacting selectively with nonmetallic compounds, thus opening the door to the synthetic production of artificial enzymes that work as well as, if not better than, those that are produced biochemically. For his contribution to this development, Pedersen was awarded a one-third share of the 1987 Nobel Prize in chemistry; his corecipients were Cram and Lehn.

Pedersen retired from DuPont in 1969, but he continued to experiment with crown ethers for a number of years thereafter. He died on October 27, 1989, in Salem, New Jersey.

Further Reading

Nobelprize.org. "The Nobel Prize in Chemistry 1987." Available online. URL: http://nobelprize.org/chemistry/laureates/1987. Downloaded on April 30, 2004.

Schroeder, Herman. "The Productive Scientific Career of Charles J. Pedersen," *Pure and Applied Chemistry* 80 (April 1988): pp. 445–451.

Penzias, Arno A.
(Arno Allan Penzias)
(1933–) *astrophysicist*

Arno A. Penzias codiscovered that cosmic microwave background radiation permeates the universe. This discovery provided some of the first evidence to support the big bang theory of the creation of the universe and won for him a share of the 1978 Nobel Prize in physics.

Penzias was born on April 26, 1933, in Munich, Germany, to Karl and Justine Penzias. At age six he left Germany with his family, and after a brief stay in England, in 1940 they settled in New York City. In 1954 he received a B.S. in physics from the City College of New York and joined the U.S. Army Signal Corps. Upon completion of his two-year tour of duty, he entered the graduate physics program at Columbia University, receiving an M.A. in 1958 and a Ph.D. in 1962. At Columbia, he studied microwave physics under I. I. RABI and POLYKARP KUSCH, two of the developers of radar, and CHARLES H. TOWNES, the inventor of the maser, the microwave-amplifying device that inspired the invention of the laser. Under Townes's direction, Penzias built a maser and then used it in an experiment involving radio astronomy, which uses various wavebands of electromagnetic radiation to explore outer space.

In 1961 Penzias went to work for the Bell Telephone Laboratories (BTL) in Holmdel, New Jersey, as a member of the radio research laboratory's technical staff. In this position he participated in the development of the communications systems for Echo and Telstar, two of the first telecommunications satellites. At the same time, he began a series of radio astronomy experiments designed to detect and measure the distribution of various molecules and chemical compounds in deep space. In 1963 he was joined by ROBERT W. WILSON, and over the next 10 years they discovered significant amounts of carbon monoxide, hydrocyanic acid, and ethyl alcohol, as well as an isotope of hydrogen known as deuterium.

In 1964 Penzias and Wilson began using a new, highly sensitive horn reflector antenna. In the process of tuning it to seven centimeters, a bandwidth they hoped would minimize background noise from cosmic interference, they discovered quite by

Arno Penzias provided evidence to support the big bang theory of the creation of the universe. *(Courtesy of Bell Laboratories)*

accident the existence of a low-level noise signal at about three degrees above absolute zero that was faint yet persistent. They began searching for the origin of this signal, and eventually they were forced to conclude that there is no single source, but rather that the noise signal permeates the universe.

This discovery provided the first experimental evidence to confirm GEORGE GAMOW's big bang theory. Drawing on the work of EDWIN HUBBLE and others, who had proved that the universe is expanding, in 1948 Gamow hypothesized that the universe originated when a highly condensed ball of matter underwent a rapid and violent expansion about 15 billion years ago. Part of Gamow's theory held that a low level of radiation must permeate the universe, just as a flash of light permeates the air in the vicinity of a giant firecracker immediately after it explodes. At first this theory met with much skepticism, but once Penzias and Wilson proved the existence of Gamow's lingering "flash of light," the theory gained acceptance. Over the next 40 years it

became accepted by the scientific community as the best explanation for the origins of the universe. For the role they played in confirming the big bang theory, Penzias and Wilson were each awarded a quarter share of the 1978 Nobel Prize in physics.

Penzias remained at BTL for the rest of his career. He was promoted to head of the radio physics research department in 1972, director of the radio research laboratory in 1976, director of the communications sciences research division in 1979, and vice president of research in 1981. In this latter position he oversaw BTL's transformation in the wake of the breakup of the Bell/AT&T system. In light of the lost revenue from the departed local telephone companies, Penzias refocused BTL's research away from pure research in the classical academic disciplines and into those areas that held the most promise for the development of emerging technologies and commercially valuable devices and systems.

Penzias was married twice, in 1954 to Anne Penzias with whom he had three children and in 1996 to Sherry Levit. He retired from BTL in 1998. His publications include *Ideas and Information: Managing in a High-Tech World* (1989), and his honors include election to the National Academy of Sciences and the American Academy or Arts and Sciences.

Further Reading

Bernstein, Jeremy. *Three Degrees Above Zero: Bell Labs in the Information Age.* New York: Charles Scribner's Sons, 1984.

Nobelprize.org. "The Nobel Prize in Physics 1978." Available online. URL: http://nobelprize.org/physics/laureates/1978. Downloaded on September 29, 2004.

Wasson, Tyler, ed. *Nobel Prize Winners.* New York: H. W. Wilson, 1987, pp. 806–808.

Perl, Martin L.
(Martin Lewis Perl)
(1927–) *physicist*

Martin L. Perl discovered the tau lepton, a negatively charged subatomic particle whose origins date back to the earliest days of the universe. For this discovery he was awarded a share of the 1995 Nobel Prize in physics.

Perl was born on June 24, 1927, in New York City. His parents, Oscar and Fay, owned a printing and advertising company. At age 16 he finished high school and entered the Polytechnic Institute of Brooklyn (today Polytechnic University) to study chemical engineering. His studies were interrupted by World War II, during which he served in the merchant marine and the U.S. Army; he did not receive a B.S. until 1948. He spent the next two years working for the General Electric (GE) Company's electron tube production factory in Schenectady. While at GE he took a course in atomic physics at Schenectady's Union College, which led him to give up chemical engineering for physics. In 1950 he entered the graduate physics program at Columbia University, and five years later he received a Ph.D. and joined the faculty at the University of Michigan. In 1963 he left Michigan for Stanford University where he joined the staff at the Stanford Linear Accelerator Center (SLAC).

Perl's research at Michigan involved the detailed study of the behavior of subatomic particles via bubble chamber physics, whereby particles are observed as they track through a vapor cloud. At SLAC, however, his work focused on the search for new subatomic particles, particularly leptons, particles that exist outside the nucleus. This interest was sparked in part by new discoveries concerning the muon, a lepton that is more than 200 times heavier than an electron. The muon was discovered in 1935, but at first it was believed to be what is now called the meson, a particle that plays a major role in holding together protons and neutrons in the nucleus. By the 1960s, however, it was known that muons are leptons, and that they decompose via radioactive decay into electrons. This discovery led many physicists to wonder if the muon was an intermediate step between the electron and an even heavier precursor dating back to the big bang, the origins of the universe that occurred between 10 billion and 20 billion years ago. In the mid-1960s, Perl began looking for this theoretical particle by using a linear accelerator, a device that induces miniature nuclear reactions by propelling subatomic particles into other particles at high rates of speed and high energy levels.

In 1973 SLAC's BURTON RICHTER completed construction of a particle accelerator known as SPEAR, for Stanford Positron-Electron Accelerating Ring. SPEAR was a different type of apparatus in that it accelerated a beam of electrons and a beam of positrons, particles with the same mass as electrons but with a positive charge, in concentric rings and then directed them to collide head-on with each other. Perl used SPEAR to re-create miniature "big bangs" by propelling electrons into positrons at extremely high temperatures and energy levels such as supposedly existed in the moments before the big bang. Because electrons and positrons annihilate each other when they collide, SPEAR enabled him to produce some very interesting reactions. In 1974 one of these reactions resulted in the production of the tau lepton, a negatively charged particle with approximately 3,500 times the mass of an electron. Further experimentation showed that a tau lepton decays into a muon, an electron, and a host of neutrinos,

Martin Perl's work provided insights into the nature of matter in the early days of the universe. *(Courtesy of Martin L. Perl)*

particles that have no electrical charge and virtually no mass.

As the precursor to the muon, the tau lepton provides physicists with an important link between present-day particles and their ancestors from the days immediately following the big bang. It is now believed that electrons are actually the third generation in the evolution of leptons, particles that exist outside the nucleus, the first generation being the tau lepton and the second generation being the muon. The discovery of tau leptons gave researchers important new insights into what the universe was like in its earliest days, and what some far distant corners of the universe might be like today. For this contribution, Perl was awarded a half share of the 1995 Nobel Prize in physics. His corecipient was the American physicist FREDERICK REINES.

Perl remained at SLAC for the rest of his career; from 1991 to 1997 he chaired its high-energy physics faculty. His most recent research has involved the search for new leptons such as the hypothetical tau neutrino, a big bang precursor to the neutrino, the most common particle in the universe. His publications include *High Energy Hadron Physics* (1975) and *Reflections on Experimental Science* (1996). His honors include election to the National Academy of Sciences and the American Academy of Arts and Sciences.

Further Reading

Nobelprize.org. "The Nobel Prize in Physics 1995." Available online. URL: http://nobelprize.org/physics/laureates/1995. Downloaded on September 7, 2004.
SLAC HEP Faculty. "Martin L. Perl." Available online. URL: http://www.slac.stanford.edu/slac/faculty/hepfaculty/perl.html. Downloaded on March 25, 2005.
Wilford, John N. "2 Americans Win Nobel for Finding Tiny Particles," *New York Times*, October 12, 1995, p. B6.

Phillips, William D.
(William Daniel Phillips)
(1948–) *physicist*

William D. Phillips developed the magneto-optic trap, a device for greatly reducing the velocity of atoms. For this achievement, he was awarded a share of the 1997 Nobel Prize in physics.

Phillips was born on November 5, 1948, in Wilkes-Barre, Pennsylvania. His parents, William and Mary Catherine, were social workers who lived in nearby Kingston. At age eight he moved with his family to Butler, and then three years later to Camp Hill where he grew up. In 1970 he received a B.S. in physics from Juniata (Pa.) College, married Jane Van Wynen with whom he had two children, and entered the graduate physics program at the Massachusetts Institute of Technology (MIT). At MIT he became interested in spectroscopy, the study of the inner workings of atoms and molecules by examining the various kinds of electromagnetic radiation they emit. Using a maser, a device that produces and amplifies microwave radiation, he studied the magnetic moment, a function of magnetic strength, of the protons in a molecule of water. This project led him to use a laser, similar to the maser except that it substitutes visible light for microwaves, to study what happens when atoms collide with each other.

After receiving a Ph.D. in 1976, he stayed at MIT for another two years to conduct postdoctoral research, and in 1978 he accepted a position in the physics laboratory of the National Bureau of Standards, today the National Institute of Standards and Technology (NIST) in Gaithersburg, Maryland. His work at NIST involved using lasers as spectroscopic tools, but he also became interested in using them in other applications. He was particularly interested in the work of ARTHUR L. SCHAWLOW, who had suggested that lasers could be used to cool atoms in a vapor to within fractions of a degree above absolute zero. Normally atoms travel at speeds of up to 2,500 mph, but cooling them to extremely low temperatures would slow them down and make it easier to study them. After American physicist STEVEN CHU developed the first atom trap in 1985, Phillips shifted the focus of his own research to modifying this new device. Two years later he had designed and built the magneto-optic trap. This device slows down atoms by turning a cloud of target atoms into a field of "optical molasses" at the intersection of three pairs of mutually opposite laser beams, and then trapping the cloud in a magnetic field. Despite a number of

William Phillips developed a method for slowing down atoms, thus making them easier to study. *(Courtesy of William D. Phillips)*

improvements to the basic design by other researchers, the magneto-optic trap remained the most commonly used atom trap almost 20 years after its development.

The magneto-optic trap slows down atoms and pens them into a confined space so that they can be more easily studied by spectroscopists. It also played a major role in the development of improvements to such devices as optical tweezers, a laser-driven device for manipulating individual molecules of DNA, and the atomic clock. For his contributions to the development of atom traps, Phillips was awarded a one-third share of the 1997 Nobel Prize in physics; one of his corecipients was Chu and the other was the French physicist Claude Cohen-Tannoudji.

Phillips continued to experiment with atom traps and their various applications at NIST for the rest of his career. Much of this work laid the groundwork for ERIC A. CORNELL and CARL E. WIE-

MAN, who used atom traps to study Bose-Einstein condensates, a state of matter that exists only at temperatures near absolute zero and in which atoms merge into a single wavelike entity that is much like a beam of laser light. His other honors include election to the National Academy of Sciences and the American Academy of Arts and Sciences.

Further Reading

Broad, William J. "6 Men Share Nobels in Chemistry and Physics," *New York Times,* October 16, 1997, p. A16.

National Institute of Standards and Technology. "William D. Phillips." Available online. URL: http://physics.nist.goo/News/Nobel/phillips.html. Downloaded on March 25, 2005.

Nobelprize.org. "The Nobel Prize in Physics 1997." Available online. URL: http://nobelprize.org/physics/laureates/1997. Downloaded on September 1, 2004.

Politizer, H. David
(Hugh David Politizer)
(1949–) *physicist*

H. David Politizer codeveloped the mathematical formula that served as the foundation for the development of quantum chromodynamics, the study of the behavior of quarks, the building blocks of protons and neutrons. For this contribution, he was awarded a share of the 2004 Nobel Prize in physics.

Politizer was born on August 31, 1949, in New York City to Alan and Valerie Politizer. After receiving a B.S. in physics from the University of Michigan in 1969, he entered the graduate physics program at Harvard University. His graduate research focused on developing a better theoretical explanation for the strong nuclear force, the force that binds together quarks, the basic building blocks of nucleons (protons and neutrons). MURRAY GELL-MANN had postulated the existence of quarks in 1964, and by 1969 his theory had gained support from the results of a number of experiments. These experiments, however, also suggested something very peculiar about the strong nuclear force, that it gets stronger as the distance between quarks increases and weaker as the distance between them decreases. While physicists found it impossible to remove a quark from a nucleon, or even to find a single quark outside a nucleon, quarks seem to move about freely within nucleons as if they are not bound together at all. This property, known as asymptotic freedom, does not hold true for particles under the influence of the other known forces of nature. Electromagnetism, gravity, and the weak nuclear force, which governs certain forms of radioactive decay, get weaker as the distance between the particles or bodies they affect increases. Because of asymptotic freedom, theoretical physicists were unable to explain mathematically how the strong nuclear force governs the behavior of quarks, and so they were unable to develop a convincing body of theory concerning quarks.

In 1973 Politzer came up with a solution for this problem. He devised an ingenious mathematical formula for describing asymptotic freedom as it applies to quarks by demonstrating that the beta function, a factor that is always positive in formulas involving electromagnetism, gravity, and the weak nuclear force, can be negative for the strong nuclear force. Politzer's formula thus made it possible for physicists to arrive at a mathematical understanding of asymptotic freedom and therefore the behavior of quarks. He published his formula in a 1973 issue of the prestigious physics journal *Physical Review Letters*. That same issue also contained a paper by DAVID J. GROSS and FRANK WILCZEK, who had duplicated Politzer's work independently. The Politzer-Gross-Wilczek formula was verified experimentally in short order, and over the next few years it formed the basis for the development of quantum chromodynamics. For developing a mathematical explanation for asymptotic freedom, Politzer was awarded a one-third share of the 2004 Nobel Prize in physics; his corecipients were Gross and Wilczek.

Politzer received a Ph.D. from Harvard in 1974, but he remained for an additional three years as a junior research fellow. In 1977 he joined the faculty at the California Institute of Technology, where he remained for the rest of his career.

Further Reading

Nobelprize.org. "The Nobel Prize in Physics 2004." Available online. URL: http://nobelprize.org/physics/laureates/2004. Downloaded on December 30, 2004.

Overbye, Dennis. "Three Americans Win Nobel for Particle Physics Work," *New York Times*, October 6, 2004, p. A18.

Powell, John Wesley
(1834–1902) *geologist*

John Wesley Powell was the foremost explorer of the West in his day. His geological studies and topographical maps—the latter performed under his aegis as director of the U.S. Geological Survey—did much to increase the American public's awareness of the West. His policy recommendations, although they got him into political trouble during his career, eventually formed the basis for federal land use policies in the West.

Powell was born on May 24, 1834, in Mount Morris, New York. His father, Joseph, was a tailor, and his mother, Mary, was a homemaker. He moved westward several times with his family, who finally settled on a farm in Wheaton, Illinois. He attended nearby Wheaton College and Oberlin College in Ohio, but graduated from neither. As a young man he farmed and taught school, but his real interest was in natural history and archaeology. He put together impressive collections of specimens in both fields that he had obtained on trips up and down the Ohio and Mississippi Rivers, and in 1861 he was elected secretary of the Illinois Society of Natural History. That same year he enlisted in the Union army, and he stayed in it for the duration of the Civil War; during the Battle of Shiloh, he lost his right arm below the elbow. In 1862 he married Emma Dean with whom he had one child.

In 1865 Powell became a professor of natural science at Illinois Wesleyan College. The following year he accepted a similar position at Illinois Normal College (now Illinois State University at Normal) as well as that of curator of the school's museum of natural history. In 1867 he made the first of many trips to the western United States, this one to the Colorado Rockies. The following winter he returned to that area to explore the upper reaches of the Colorado River. In 1869 he led a boating expedition, backed by several Illinois colleges, the Smithsonian Institution, and the U.S. Army, down the previously uncharted Green and

Colorado Rivers. As far as is known, this expedition was the first party to float through the Grand Canyon and live to tell the tale.

In 1871 Powell organized a second expedition to retrace the path of the 1867 group so that he could better record the geological features—especially the deep trenches through which the Colorado and its branches run—that are unique to the Colorado River system. In 1875 he published *Exploration of the Colorado River of the West and Its Tributaries,* a record of the two trips that was republished in 1895 as *Canyons of Colorado.* In this work Powell advanced a number of terms and concepts that later became part of the specialized language of geology. One such concept, that of "antecedent rivers," theorized that the Colorado River and its branches had arrived at their present levels by cutting deeper throughout the eons into strata that were, at the same time, being elevated. This concept was Powell's most important contribution to geology, as it explains how rivers sometimes cut through mountains rather than detour around them.

Powell's heroic voyages brought him to the attention of the federal government as well as the general public. In 1871 he was appointed to head a geologic and geographic survey of federally owned lands in the West, a project that occupied him for the next eight years. Much of his work in this regard was published in 1878 as *Report on the Lands of the Arid Region of the United States.* In it he argued that the land use policies that had worked so well east of the Missouri River were simply untenable for the vast expanse between the Missouri and the Rocky Mountains, given the scant amount of rainfall in this area. Rather than dismiss this region as being the Great American Desert, as Zebulon Pike had done in the early 1800s, Powell recommended an enlightened program of western land and resource management whereby the federal government would develop and regulate the flow of water for farmers, ranchers, and communities. Powell's recommendations met with much flak from western developers, then and now, but in time his vision informed federal land development policy in the West, particularly after the dust bowl catastrophe of the 1920s. This policy came to include damming the Colorado River in several

places and constructing dozens of dams on other western rivers.

Powell's work contributed in large part to the establishment in 1879 of the U.S. Geological Survey (USGS) as part of the Department of the Interior. Two years later he took over as director of the USGS, and in this capacity he developed a plan for mapping and classifying all lands held in the public domain. In time this project was expanded to include the development of topographic maps for the entire United States.

Powell also contributed to a better understanding of Native American ethnology. During his two Colorado River expeditions, he studied the ways and languages of the various tribes he encountered. From 1872 to 1873 he served as a special commissioner of Indian affairs for Utah, Nevada, and northern Arizona, and in this capacity he continued his studies. Much of his work concerning Native Americans was published in 1877 as *Introduction to the Study of Indian Languages.* He and his colleagues developed a dictionary of North American Indian languages and discovered the identity of the Moundbuilders, ancient Indians who had constructed large burial mounds in the Ohio and Mississippi River basins. From 1879 to 1894, while also directing the USGS, he served as director of the U.S. Bureau of Ethnology, and in this capacity he oversaw the publication of numerous important works on Indian ethnography, linguistics, and archaeology.

Politics forced Powell to resign from the USGS in 1894, but he continued to direct the Bureau of Ethnology for another eight years. He died on September 23, 1902, at his summer home in Haven, Maine.

Further Reading

deBuys, William, ed. *Seeing Things Whole: The Essential John Wesley Powell.* Washington, D.C.: Island Press/Shearwater Books, 2001.

Dolnick, Edward. *Down the Great Unknown: John Wesley Powell's 1869 Journey of Discovery and Tragedy through the Grand Canyon.* New York: HarperCollins, 2001.

Worster, Donald. *A River Running West: A Life of John Wesley Powell.* New York: Oxford University Press, 2001.

Press, Frank

(1924–) *geophysicist*

Frank Press was a leading seismologist of his day. He developed modern techniques by which seismology could be used to answer many fundamental questions about the geophysical properties of the Earth.

Press was born on December 4, 1924, in Brooklyn, New York, to Solomon and Dora Press. After finishing high school in 1941, he entered the City College of New York and received a B.S. in physics three years later. He then enrolled at Columbia University to study geology, and he received an M.A. in 1946 and a Ph.D. in 1949. After graduation he was offered a full-time faculty position at Columbia, which he accepted. In 1944 he married Billie Kallick with whom he had three children.

Press's research interest was geophysics (the physics of the Earth), especially seismology (the study of earthquakes and their phenomena). At Columbia he collaborated with W. Maurice Ewing to develop a seismograph capable of recording seismic waves of more than one minute's duration, thus making it possible to record a broader range of seismic activity. In 1955 Press became a professor of geophysics at the California Institute of Technology. Two years later he assumed the duties of director of Caltech's Seismological Laboratory. In this capacity he investigated the theory of Beno Gutenberg, codeveloper of the Richter scale for measuring earthquakes, that a layer of molten rock lays beneath the Earth's crust. Press developed a sophisticated method for interpreting seismic waves in much the same way that a sonar expert uses sound waves to determine the distance to an object underwater. By 1959 he had accumulated enough evidence to be able to announce that Gutenberg was right, and that the molten layer begins about 90 miles below the Earth's surface.

Meanwhile, in 1957 Press and Ewing had taken up another joint effort, this time to determine the thickness of the North American continent. That same year tremors from an earthquake centered near Samoa in the South Pacific Ocean had been recorded by 42 seismological stations in the United States and Canada. By analyzing the data collected at these stations, in 1958 Press and Ewing were able to determine that North America's continental crust is between 19 and 32 miles thick. Moreover, they refuted the theory that the Earth's crust is thinner below a mountain range than it is below a plain. Press and Ewing demonstrated that the Earth's surface mirrors the crust beneath it; in other words, the crust below the Rocky Mountains is just as thick as the crust below the Great Plains.

In 1958 Press took part in an expedition to Wilkes Land in Antarctica to determine whether Antarctica was really a continent or just a continent-size iceberg. Once again, Press developed a method for analyzing seismic data that demonstrated that Antarctica's icy surface is connected by rock to the Earth's core. For his contribution to this expedition, Mt. Press in Antarctica was named in his honor.

The year 1959 was very productive for Press. First, he joined a team of seismologists to study a major earthquake that had taken place earlier that year in Chile. During their investigation, the team discovered that the Earth vibrates like a ringing bell for up to three weeks after a major earthquake. Next, the National Aeronautics and Space Administration (NASA) chose Caltech as one of two schools to develop a lunar seismograph, and Press took the lead role in developing the Caltech version. Last, he was chosen to represent the United States at a nuclear test-ban conference in Geneva, Switzerland. One of the key issues was whether or not to ban underground testing, and Press was the U.S. expert on whether or not seismological practices were sophisticated enough to tell the difference between an earthquake and an underground blast.

Press attended three more test-ban conferences over the next four years, and he played a major role in advising the key negotiators about the feasibility of various methods of monitoring nuclear tests. Partly as a result of his performance at these conferences, in 1961 he was chosen to serve as one of President John F. Kennedy's science advisers. He also served in this capacity for two of Kennedy's successors, Lyndon B. Johnson and Jimmy Carter. During the Johnson administration, Press served on a blue-ribbon commission to develop methods for predicting earthquakes.

In 1965 Press became a professor of geophysics and chairman of the Massachusetts Institute of Technology's (MIT) department of earth and planetary sciences. In 1981 he was appointed chairman of the National Research Council, a position he held for 12 years. One of the major duties of his position was to oversee the debate concerning which scientific research projects are most deserving of federal research grants. Another was to coordinate to a certain degree those projects that are found deserving of federal support.

In 1993 Press left MIT to become a senior fellow at the Carnegie Institution of Washington. Four years later he joined the Washington Advisory Group as a principal. In this capacity he provides strategic counsel and management consulting to the leaders of companies, universities, governments, and nonprofit organizations that are directly engaged in research, development, or higher education.

During his academic career, Press published more than 150 technical papers and books, but perhaps his most influential publication was a college textbook. *Understanding Earth,* which he coauthored with Ray Siever, is an introductory text that explains the basics of physical geology to students who are new to science as well as to geophysics. It also discusses how science and public policy interact and how geologic research continues to overturn much of what geophysicists think they know. The book first appeared in 1982, and in 2003 it appeared in a fourth edition; one student reviewer called it "straight-forward and casual," while science reviewers have praised it for the breadth of its coverage.

For his many achievements, Press was awarded the U.S. National Medal of Sciences. His other honors include election to the National Academy of Sciences and the American Association of Arts and Sciences.

Further Reading

Press, Frank, et al. *Understanding Earth,* 4th ed. New York: W. H. Freeman, 2003.

The Washington Advisory Group LLC. "Frank Press." Available online. URL: http://www.theadvisorygroup. com/principals_press_bio.html. Downloaded on August 4, 2003.

Prusiner, Stanley B.
(Stanley Ben Prusiner)
(1942–   ) *neurobiologist*

Stanley B. Prusiner discovered the prion, the first known infectious agent that does not possess genetic material or reproduce itself. For this discovery, he was awarded the 1997 Nobel Prize in physiology or medicine.

Prusiner was born on May 28, 1942, in Des Moines, Iowa. His father, Lawrence, was an architect, and his mother, Miriam, was a homemaker. At age 10 he moved with his family to Cincinnati, Ohio, where he grew up. After receiving an A.B. in chemistry from the University of Pennsylvania in 1964, he entered the university's medical school, receiving an M.D. in 1968. He spent the next four years completing an internship and residency in medicine at the University of California at San Francisco (UCSF) Medical School and conducting research at the National Institutes of Health in Bethesda, Maryland. In 1972 he returned to UCSF, this time as a resident in neurology, and two years later he was named a professor of neurology.

Prusiner's primary research interest was rare neurodegenerative diseases, especially the ones that develop slowly over a period of years. He was particularly inspired by D. CARLETON GAJDUSEK, who discovered that kuru, a neurodegenerative disease that is found only among certain cannibals in New Guinea, is caused by a slow-acting virus. In 1972 Prusiner began studying Creutzfeldt-Jakob disease, a rare condition that is marked by pre-senile dementia, as well as an animal disease known as scrapie, so called because it causes sheep to scrape the wool from their bodies. Like kuru, both diseases were thought to be caused by slow viruses, and Prusiner hoped to be able to define the molecular structures of these viruses and to explain why the immune system develops no response to infection by slow viruses.

Focusing at first on scrapie, Prusiner was puzzled to discover that scrapie-infected tissue samples showed no signs of nucleic acid. This puzzled him because viruses typically cause infection by injecting their nucleic acid, either DNA or RNA, into the target cells. Instead, he found traces of protein that seemed to be foreign to sheep protein. When he added enzymes that destroy the nucleic acid in genes to the tissue samples and then injected the samples into hamsters, he discovered that the hamsters still developed scrapie, thus indicating that scrapie is not caused by a virus.

By 1981 Prusiner had become convinced that the causative agent in scrapie is a rogue protein he labeled a prion, a protein in the brain that has spontaneously altered its normal three-dimensional conformation in such a way that makes it malignant. Having altered itself, a prion is able to alter the conformation of the proteins to which it is attached, thus forming malignant clusters that eventually kill off a part of the brain by turning it into a porous, spongy area. Depending on which part of the brain is affected, the resulting symptoms are dementia, loss of memory, loss of muscle control, or insomnia. Because prions are proteins that have been present in the organism since birth and therefore contain the proper genetic coding, the body's immune system does not recognize them as being a threat and so it leaves them alone. By 1992 he had shown that prion-related diseases, which he called spongiform encephalopathies, can also be inherited; when a certain gene is removed from mice via selective breeding, the mice are immune to spongiform encephalopathies. He also showed that spongiform encephalopathies can be passed from one species to another; for example, a human can become infected after eating the meat of a cow infected with bovine spongiform encephalopathy, better known as mad cow disease.

Prusiner's work shed much light on the nature of neurodegenerative diseases in general. It suggested that many of these diseases, including Alzheimer's and Parkinson's diseases, may be caused by prions. It further suggested that spongiform encephalopathies, because they result to a certain degree from genetic defects, may therefore be treatable by properly designed pharmaceutical drugs. For his contribution to medical science, Prusiner was awarded the 1997 Nobel Prize in physiology or medicine.

Prusiner remained at UCSF for the rest of his career, eventually becoming director of the Institute for Neurodegenerative Disease. He published his work in several books, including *Prion Biology and Diseases* (2003). He is married to the former Sandy Turk with whom he had two children.

Further Reading

Krapp, Kristine M., ed. *Notable Twentieth-Century Scientists Supplement.* Detroit: Gale Research, 1998, pp. 378–380.

Nobelprize.org. "The Nobel Prize in Physiology or Medicine 1997." Available online. URL: http://nobelprize.org/medicine/laureates/1997. Downloaded on July 14, 2004.

UCSF Neuroscience Participating Faculty. "Stanley Prusiner, M.D." Available online. URL: http://www.ucsf.edu/neurosc/faculty/neuro_prusiner.html. Downloaded on March 25, 2005.

Purcell, Edward M.
(Edward Mills Purcell)
(1912–1997) *physicist*

Edward M. Purcell codeveloped nuclear magnetic resonance (NMR), a discovery that led eventually to the development of the CAT scan. For this contribution, he was awarded a share of the 1952 Nobel Prize in physics.

Purcell was born on August 30, 1912, in Taylorsville, Illinois. His father, Edward, managed an independent telephone company, and his mother, Mary Elizabeth, was a homemaker. At age 14 he moved with his family to Mattoon, Illinois. He received a B.S. in electrical engineering from Purdue University in 1933, and then he studied physics at the Technische Hochschule in Karlsruhe, Germany, for a year before entering the graduate physics program at Harvard University. After receiving a Ph.D. in 1938, he taught at Harvard for two years before joining the staff of the Massachusetts Institute of Technology's Radiation Laboratory in 1940. In 1937 he married Beth Busser with whom he had two children.

Purcell's time at the Radiation Laboratory coincided with World War II, during which the laboratory's researchers cooperated with British researchers to develop microwave radar. His involvement in this project led him to realize that microwave technology also offered a more precise way to measure an atom's magnetic moment, a function of its magnetic strength. Since atoms of a given element and molecules of a given compound have their own unique magnetic moments, he hoped to devise a method for identifying atoms and molecules by using microwaves. By 1946 he and two Radiation Lab colleagues, Henry C. Torrey and Robert V. Pound, had developed nuclear resonance absorption, better known today as nuclear magnetic resonance (NMR). This method involves bombarding protons with microwave radio frequencies, which the protons absorb; at a certain precise frequency the protons alter their spin, thus permitting their magnetic moments to be calculated precisely. Over the next two years Purcell, Pound, and the American physicist NICOLAAS BLOEMBERGEN perfected their methods and equipment, and by 1948 they had developed the ability to use NMR to determine the magnetic moments of liquids, gases, and certain solids.

NMR proved to have enormously important practical applications. By using NMR, the precise identity of the atoms in a given substance can be determined without altering those atoms in any way. In the 1970s ALLAN M. CORMACK and Gregory Hounsfield used NMR as the basis from which to develop computer-assisted tomography scanning equipment, better known today as the CAT scan. Put into commercial operation in the mid-1980s, the CAT scan makes it possible to observe the inner workings of the human body, thus giving it an essential role in modern diagnostic medicine. Even before the development of the CAT scan, the value of Purcell's contribution had been recognized, as he was awarded a half share of the 1952 Nobel Prize in physics. He shared the award with FELIX BLOCH, who had developed a similar method of NMR at about the same time.

In 1946 Purcell returned to his teaching duties at Harvard. He continued to experiment with microwave technology, and in 1951 he made a discovery that was of great importance to astronomers. Seven years earlier Dutch astronomer Hendrik C. van de Hulst had postulated that electromagnetic radio waves were emitted by hydrogen atoms in deep space in the 21-centimeter, or 1,420-megahertz, wavelength. Working together with Harold I. Ewen, a Harvard graduate student, Purcell developed a method for detecting these radio waves, whose frequency is actually 1,421 megahertz. Since then, 21-centimeter radiation has provided astronomers with a valuable tool for studying the Milky Way galaxy because it allows them to penetrate the clouds of interstellar dust that cannot be seen through a telescope.

Prior to 1960, Purcell's career was devoted primarily to the study of nuclear magnetism. He was particularly interested in phenomena associated with the interactions between subatomic particles, related problems of molecular structure, measurement of atomic constants, and nuclear magnetic behavior at low temperatures. In the early 1960s, however, he became more interested in astrophysics, particularly the problem of understanding the mechanisms of the interactions of interstellar dust and light propagation throughout the Milky Way. He went on to develop the image of interstellar dust grains brought into states of high-speed rotation, which he called suprathermal rotation, by their interactions in space.

Purcell retired from Harvard in 1980, although he continued to conduct research and write for a number of years thereafter. His publications include *Electricity and Magnetism* (1985). His many honors include the National Medal of Science and election to the National Academy of Sciences and the American Academy of Arts and Sciences. He died on March 7, 1997, in Cambridge, Massachusetts.

Further Reading

Nobelprize.org. "The Nobel Prize in Physics 1952." Available online. URL: http://nobelprize.org/physics/laureates/1952. Downloaded on August 27, 2004.

Pound, Robert V. "Edward Mills Purcell," National Academy of Sciences, *Biographical Memoirs* 78 (2000): pp. 182–205.

Wasson, Tyler, ed. *Nobel Prize Winners.* New York: H. W. Wilson, 1987, pp. 841–843.

Quarterman, Lloyd A.
(Lloyd Albert Quarterman)
(1918–1982) *chemist*

Lloyd A. Quarterman was the most accomplished fluorine chemist of his day. His most notable success was the making of several chemical compounds from fluorine and the inert gas xenon, thus proving that inert gases are capable of reacting with other elements.

Quarterman was born on May 31, 1918, in Philadelphia, Pennsylvania. In 1943 he received a B.S. in chemistry from St. Augustine's College in Raleigh, North Carolina, and moved to Chicago to work on the Manhattan Project, the U.S. effort to build an atomic bomb during World War II. After the war, the project's Chicago facilities were converted into the Argonne National Laboratories and given the mission to conduct basic atomic research and to develop peaceful uses for nuclear energy. Quarterman remained at Argonne for the rest of his career, leaving only long enough to obtain an M.S. in chemistry from Chicago's Northwestern University in 1952.

Quarterman's research primarily involved the chemistry of fluorine. Fluorine is the most reactive chemical element, and because of this it is difficult to isolate it from the compounds in which it naturally occurs. It is impossible to do so by chemical means, and only by techniques such as the electrolysis of hydrogen fluoride can it be isolated at all. One of Quarterman's duties with the Manhattan Project had been to purify large quantities of hydro-gen fluoride, which was used to isolate the uranium-235 isotope that provided the fuel for one of the first atomic bombs, and he had designed and built a special distillation system for the purpose.

The exceptional purity of the hydrogen fluoride Quarterman produced in this manner made it possible for him to make chemical compounds from fluorine that no one else had ever made, or even thought were possible to make. His most noteworthy achievement in this area was the making of compounds from fluorine and xenon, one of the so-called inert gases. Prior to Quarterman's work, it was generally believed that it was impossible to make compounds from the inert gases because their outer rings of electrons were full, thus they could not share electrons with other elements. Quarterman proved this theory wrong when he combined xenon and fluorine to make xenon difluoride, xenon tetrafluoride, and xenon hexafluoride. Xenon difluoride, a white crystalline solid, was later demonstrated to be an excellent source for introducing fluorine into organic reactions because it is not nearly as corrosive as hydrogen fluoride, previously the source of choice for fluorine. Today xenon difluoride is widely used in the fabrication of semiconductors.

Quarterman also developed a method for using hydrogen fluoride as a means of studying the nature of other chemical compounds. In 1967 he built a special corrosion-resistant chamber with a tiny window made from two diamonds. In the chamber he dissolved in hydrogen fluoride whatever compound he wanted to study. Then he examined the X-ray and ultraviolet light bands emitted by the vibrations of the dissolved compound's molecules by shining an electromagnetic beam through the diamond window and checking out the result with a spectroscope.

Quarterman was a member of the American Association for the Advancement of Science. He died in August 1982 in Chicago.

Further Reading

McMurray, Emily J., ed. *Notable Twentieth Century Scientists*. Detroit: Gale Research, 1995, pp. 1,628–1,629.

Spangenburg, Ray, and Kit Moser. *African Americans in Science, Math, and Invention*. New York: Facts On File, 2003, pp. 198–199.

Quimby, Edith H.
(Edith Hinkley, Edith Hinkley Quimby)
(1891–1982) *physicist*

Edith Quimby was one of the first experts in the field of radiology. Her experiments with X-rays and radioactive isotopes provided the medical community with a tremendous amount of much-needed information about these important therapeutic and diagnostic tools.

Quimby was born Edith Hinkley on July 10, 1891, in Rockford, Illinois. Her father, Arthur, was an architect and farmer, and her mother, Harriet, was a homemaker. She moved with her family to Alabama and then to Boise, Idaho, where she attended high school. In 1908 she enrolled in Whitman College in Washington State and received a B.S. in mathematics and physics four years later. After teaching high school science in Nyssa, Oregon, for two years, she was accepted as a graduate student at the University of California at Berkeley, and in 1916 she received an M.A. in physics. After graduation she taught high school science in Antioch, California, for three years. In 1915 she married Shirley L. Quimby with whom she had no children.

In 1919 Quimby moved with her husband to New York City. While he taught physics at Columbia University, she conducted medical research for the New York City Memorial Hospital for Cancer and Allied Diseases. Quimby's specific assignment was to study X-rays and radiation. Although X-rays had been used to treat tumors for almost 20 years, physicians knew little about how much radiation constituted an effective treatment or about the side effects of radiation therapy on patients and therapists. For 20 years Quimby conducted experiments that provided the answers to these and a host of related questions. One result of her experiments was the development of a method for measuring how much radiation a patient's skin and body had absorbed during treatment. Once this was done, physicians could begin prescribing with confidence dosages of radiation treatment that were both safe and effective. In this, they were greatly aided by one of Quimby's many scholarly articles, "The Specification of Dosage in Radium Therapy," which appeared in the *American Journal of Roentgenology* in 1941.

In 1941 Quimby left New York Memorial to teach radiology at Cornell University Medical College. During her two-year stay at Cornell, she coauthored *Physical Foundations of Radiology* (1944), a guidebook for radiologists. In 1943 she took a similar position at Columbia University's College of Physicians and Surgeons, where she cofounded Columbia's Radiological Research Laboratory. Once at Columbia, she concentrated her research efforts on investigating the medical usefulness of radioactive isotopes as well as developing procedures for their safe handling. Her experiments ranged from determining the value of radioactive isotopes as tracers for studying the circulatory system to developing methods for using radioactive isotopes to treat cancer and thyroid disorders. Much of her work with radioactive isotopes was summed up in two books, *Radioactive Isotopes in Clinical Practices* (1958) and *Safe Handling of Radioactive Isotopes in Medical Practice* (1960). In 1960 she retired from Columbia, but she continued to experiment and write about radiology for another 20 years.

Quimby received a number of awards and honors for her work, including the American Radium Society's Janeway Medal in 1940. During World War II she was a consultant on the Manhattan Project, the U.S. effort to build the first atomic bomb, and after the war she consulted for the Atomic Energy Commission. In 1954 she was elected president of the American Radium Society. She died on October 11, 1982, in New York City.

Further Reading
Bailey, Martha J. *American Women in Science: A Biographical Dictionary.* Santa Barbara, Calif.: ABC-CLIO, 1994, p. 313.

McMurray, Emily J., ed. *Notable Twentieth-Century Scientists.* Detroit: Gale, 1995, pp. 1,629–1,631.

Yount, Lisa. *A to Z of Women in Science and Math.* New York: Facts On File, 1999, pp. 177–178.

Rabi, I. I.
(Israel Isaac Rabi, Isidor Isaac Rabi)
(1898–1988) *physicist*

I. I. Rabi won a Nobel Prize for developing the molecular beam magnetic resonance method of observing atomic spectra. This technique was later modified by other researchers for a wide range of applications from lasers to magnetic resonance imaging (MRI).

Rabi was born Israel Isaac Rabi on July 29, 1898, in Rymanov, Galicia, in the Austro-Hungarian Empire, to David and Sheindel Rabi. As an infant, he moved with his family to the United States, settling in New York City. Once in the United States, his first name was changed from Israel to Isidor. As a boy he became fascinated with radio transmission and built several pieces of radio equipment from scratch. Upon enrolling in Cornell University in 1916, he intended to study electrical engineering, but he became disillusioned with the course of study and received his B.S. in chemistry in 1919. After graduation he worked at several nondescript jobs before enrolling in Cornell's graduate physics program in 1921. Two years later he transferred to Columbia University, receiving a Ph.D. in physics in 1927. He spent the next two years touring Europe on a fellowship, and he met and studied with many of Europe's leading physicists. In 1929 he returned to the United States to teach theoretical physics at Columbia, where he remained for the rest of his career. In 1926 he married Helen Newmark with whom he had two children.

Rabi's research focused on measuring the magnetic properties of atoms, atomic nuclei, and molecules. While in Europe, he met OTTO STERN, director of the Institute of Physical Chemistry at the University of Hamburg. Stern and Walter Gerlach had made use of the molecular beam technique to determine whether or not atoms possess magnetic properties. While Stern's guest, Rabi modified the magnetic field through which Stern and Gerlach had passed their molecular beam to demonstrate that different atoms have different magnetic moments, that is, their individual magnetic fields are oriented in different directions. At Columbia he established a molecular beam laboratory to conduct experiments that demonstrated the different angular momentums, or spins, that nuclei and atoms possess because of their magnetic properties. He also developed a method for measuring the relatively weak magnetic moments of protons in a nucleus despite the presence of the stronger magnetic moments of their surrounding electrons.

In the mid-1930s, Rabi returned to his childhood fascination with radio technology, and in 1937 he used it to develop a new experimental tool known as molecular beam magnetic resonance. Rabi beamed molecules through a series of magnetic fields, the strengths of which he modified via radio frequency. Adjusting the frequencies of the fields reoriented the spins of the protons in the nuclei, which allowed him to measure the magnetic interaction between a nucleus and its surrounding electrons. Further experimentation with this technique on deuterons, nuclei consisting of one proton and one neutron, demonstrated the quadrupole moment of the deuteron, that is, the degree to which it deviates from being spherical.

The precise measurements made possible by molecular beam magnetic resonance, also known as the magnetic resonance method, enabled physicists to study the internal workings of atoms in ways not possible before. Meanwhile, CHARLES H. TOWNES and ARTHUR L. SCHAWLOW used Rabi's work as a springboard from which to develop masers, devices that produce and amplify microwaves, and lasers, devices that produce a single-color beam of light so intense it can vaporize heat-resistant materials. Perhaps most important, his work also led to the development of MRI as an incredibly powerful medical diagnostic tool. Even before these later developments, Rabi's work was recognized as being of such importance that in 1944 he was awarded the Nobel Prize in physics.

During World War II, Rabi played an important role in developing microwave radar for military applications. After the war, his attention turned increasingly away from experimentation toward administration. In 1945 he was named chair of Columbia's physics department, and under his direction the department became one of the finest in the country. He was instrumental in establishing the Brookhaven National Laboratory for Atomic Research on Long Island as a research facility for nine major eastern universities, and the Hudson Laboratory in Dobbs Ferry, New York, as a research facility for developing a way to communicate with submarines via low frequency radio. He served as science adviser to President Dwight D. Eisenhower, as a member of the Science Advisory Committee of every president from Eisenhower to Nixon, as a delegate to the NATO Science Committee, and as chair of the U.S. Atomic Energy Commission (AEC). He proposed the establishment of the Conseil Européen pour la Recherche Nucléaire (CERN), in essence the European counterpart to the AEC, as a means of stimulating and coordinating nuclear research in Europe.

Rabi retired from Columbia in 1967. He served as president of the American Physical Society and was elected to the National Academy of Sciences, the American Academy of Arts and Sciences, and the American Association for the Advancement of Science. He died on January 11, 1988, in New York City.

Further Reading

Nobelprize.org. "The Nobel Prize in Physics 1944." Available online. URL: http://nobelprize.org/physics/laureates/1944. Downloaded on February 13, 2004.

Rabi, I. I. *My Life and Times as a Physicist.* Claremont, Calif.: Claremont College, 1960.

Ramsey, Norman F. "I. I. Rabi," National Academy of Sciences, *Biographical Memoirs* 62 (1993): pp. 311–327.

Rigden, John S. *Rabi, Scientist and Citizen.* New York: Basic Books, 1987.

Wasson, Tyler, ed. *Nobel Prize Winners.* New York: H. W. Wilson, 1987, pp. 847–849.

Rainwater, L. James
(Leo James Rainwater)
(1917–1986) *physicist*

James Rainwater received a Nobel Prize for his contributions to a better understanding of atomic nuclei. His ideas, known today as the unified theory, explain the connection between the collective and individual movement of subatomic particles in a nucleus and describe the structure of the nucleus based on this connection.

Rainwater was born on December 9, 1917, in Council, Idaho. His father, Leo, was a civil engineer, and his mother, Edna, managed a general store. His father died when Rainwater was an infant, after which he moved with his mother and siblings to Hanford, California, where he grew up. He won a high school chemistry competition sponsored by the California Institute of Technology (Caltech), and after finishing high school in 1935 he enrolled in Caltech to study chemistry. About halfway through he changed his course of study, and in 1939 he received a B.S. in physics. Two years later he received an M.A. in physics from Columbia University. In 1942 he married Emma Smith with whom he had four children.

During World War II Rainwater worked on the Manhattan Project, the U.S. effort to build the first atomic bomb. This bomb worked on the principle of nuclear fission, specifically the splitting apart of the uranium atom by bombarding it with fast-moving neutrons. Little was known about fission at the time, so Rainwater experimented with neutrons in Columbia's particle accelerator, a device for studying the behavior of fast-moving subatomic particles. These experiments formed the basis of his doctoral dissertation, and in 1946 he received a Ph.D. in physics from Columbia. He remained at Columbia to teach physics and to continue his experiments with subatomic particles at Columbia's Nevis Cyclotron Laboratory.

In 1949 Rainwater shared office space with Aage Niels Bohr, a visiting Danish physicist whose father (Niels Bohr) had won a Nobel Prize in physics. Over the course of the next year, Rainwater and Bohr discussed their mutual interest in the atomic nucleus, specifically from the point of view of developing a model that explained the behavior of protons and neutrons, known collectively as nucleons. In fact, two such models had already been advanced. In 1935 GEORGE GAMOW had suggested that a nucleus was like a drop of water, and that nucleons reacted flexibly and collectively to vibration by constantly changing the nucleus's shape. In 1949 MARIA GOEPPERT MAYER had suggested that a nucleus was more like an onion in that it contained several independent layers of nucleons that orbit inside the nucleus in much the same way that electrons orbit around the nucleus. Rainwater and Bohr were dissatisfied with both models because neither model could explain why nucleons sometimes acted collectively and at other times acted independently.

After Bohr returned to Denmark in 1950, Rainwater developed his own model of the nucleus. Known as the deformed-shell or unified theory, it incorporated features of Gamow's and Mayer's models to develop a more nuanced picture of the nucleus. According to Rainwater, the interplay between the greater proportion of the nucleons, which form an inner nucleus, and the outer nucleons can influence the shape of the inner nucleus. Meanwhile, the shape of the inner nucleus determines the field in which the outer nucleons move. Usually, the inner nucleons maintain a shell around which the outer nucleons move, but on occasion the outer nucleons are able to encroach on the space occupied by the inner nucleons, thus causing the nucleus to be deformed, sometimes permanently.

Rainwater's theory was tested via an experiment devised by Bohr and his Danish colleague, Ben Roy Mottelson. The experiment confirmed that the theory offered a better model than either Gamow's liquid-drop theory or Mayer's spherical-shell theory. In 1975 Rainwater, Bohr, and Mottelson were awarded the Nobel Prize for physics for the roles they played in devising and confirming the unified theory. Although more recent experimentation has suggested that the unified theory does not explain the behavior of nucleons quite as well as had been supposed in 1975, by the end of the 20th century it still offered the best explanation for such behavior to date.

In 1950 the Nevis Laboratory put into operation a synchrocyclotron, a particle accelerator that can accelerate subatomic particles almost to the speed of light. For most of the rest of his career, Rainwater used this machine to experiment with various subatomic particles. He was particularly interested in pions, or pi mesons, highly unstable particles that help bind protons and neutrons to one another, and muons, massive particles that decay rapidly into electrons and other particles. In 1953 he and VAL L. FITCH, while conducting an experiment with muons, concluded that the radius of the nucleus of an atom of lead is much smaller than had been previously supposed.

Rainwater retired from Columbia in 1986. He died on May 31 that same year in Yonkers, New York.

Further Reading

Nobelprize.org. "The Nobel Prize in Physics 1975." Available online. URL: http://nobelprize.org/physics/laureates/1975. Downloaded on July 7, 2003.

McMurray, Emily J., ed. *Notable Twentieth-Century Scientists*. Detroit: Gale, 1995, pp. 1,635–1,636.

Wasson, Tyler, ed. *Nobel Prize Winners*. New York: H. W. Wilson, 1987, pp. 849–851.

Ramsey, Norman F.
(Norman Foster Ramsey, Jr.)
(1915–) *physicist*

Norman F. Ramsey invented the separated oscillating magnetic fields technique. Although this technique was originally designed as a tool for studying atoms and molecules by examining the light spectra they emit, it was later employed as a key feature in atomic clocks, the most accurate timekeeping devices yet devised. For this contribution, he was awarded a share of the 1989 Nobel Prize in physics.

Ramsey was born on August 27, 1915, in Washington, D.C. His father, Norman Sr., was an army officer, and his mother, Minna, was a homemaker. Because of his father's profession, he moved frequently, finally graduating from high school at age 15 in Fort Leavenworth, Kansas. His parents then moved to New York City where he entered Columbia College (today Columbia University), receiving a B.S. in mathematics in 1935. He then entered Cambridge University in England on a fellowship from Columbia. After receiving a B.S. in physics in 1938, he returned to Columbia and received a Ph.D. in physics in 1940. That same year he married Elinor Jameson with whom he had four children; she died in 1983, after which he married Ellie Welch.

Ramsey's research focused on measuring the magnetic properties of atoms and molecules. As an undergraduate student at Columbia, he used the molecular beam technique, whereby a stream of gaseous molecules is passed through a series of magnetic fields. As a graduate student, he assisted I. I. RABI, developer of the magnetic resonance method, whereby the strengths of the magnetic fields are adjusted by means of radio waves so as to obtain more precise measurements of the molecules' magnetic properties. In one of their most memorable experiments, Ramsey and Rabi demonstrated the quadrupole moment of the deuteron; a deuteron is an atom with one proton and one neutron, and its quadrupole moment is the degree to which it deviates from being spherical.

After short stints as a fellow at the Carnegie Institution of Washington and a physics professor at the University of Illinois, in 1940 Ramsey joined the staff at the Massachusetts Institute of Technology's Radiation Laboratory and helped develop microwave technology for use in radar. In 1943 he went to Los Alamos, New Mexico, to work on the Manhattan Project, the U.S. effort to build an atomic bomb during World War II, and in 1945 he returned to Columbia to teach physics. He left after a year to chair the physics department at the Brookhaven National Laboratory on New York's Long Island, and in 1947 he was named a professor of physics at Harvard University.

At Harvard, Ramsey established a laboratory for molecular beam magnetic resonance research similar to the one he had worked in at Columbia. By 1950 he had modified the magnetic resonance method to incorporate two separate oscillating fields. The interaction between these fields produces a very sharp interference pattern, which permitted him to make even more accurate measurements of a number of molecular and nuclear magnetic properties. Most of his work in this regard focused on the diatomic molecules of the hydrogen isotopes, in which the single proton in the hydrogen atom's nucleus is joined by one or two neutrons.

Meanwhile, other researchers had adapted the separated oscillating magnetic fields technique for use in atomic clocks. Time is measured by counting a certain number of periods, for example, the swinging back and forth of a pendulum or the rotation of the Earth around the Sun. An atomic clock counts the number of periods, or complete cycles of a wave, an atom makes while it resonates by measuring the atom's microwave frequency. The results are extremely accurate measurements of time; for example, the cesium clock counts more than 9.1 billion periods of a cesium atom before it registers the passage of one second of time. Ramsey's separated oscillating magnetic fields technique makes it possible to count atomic periods with extreme accuracy, and therefore plays a crucial role in the operation of an atomic clock. In 1967 he and Daniel Kleppner contributed further to the development of atomic clocks by inventing the atomic hydrogen maser, a device that amplifies the microwave frequency of hydrogen atoms so that they are easier to measure.

Ramsey retired from Harvard in 1986. Nevertheless, he continued to conduct research there and at the Institut Laue-Langevin in Grenoble, France. His publications include *Experimental Nuclear Physics* (1953), *Nuclear Moments* (1953), *Molecular Beams* (1956 and 1985), and *Quick Calculus* (1965 and 1985). He served as president of the United Chapters of Phi Beta Kappa, the Universities Research Association, and the American Physical Society. His many honors include the National Medal of Science and election to the National Academy of Sciences.

Further Reading

Broad, William J. "5 Win the Nobel Prizes in Chemistry and Physics," *New York Times*, October 13, 1989, p. I10.

IEEE History Center. Legacies. "Norman F. Ramsey." Available online. URL: http://www.ieee.org/organizations/history_center/legacies/ramsey.html. Downloaded on March 25, 2005.

Nobelprize.org. "The Nobel Prize in Physics 1989." Available online. URL: http://nobelprize.org/physics/laureates/1989. Downloaded on September 11, 2004.

Reed, Walter

(1851–1902) *bacteriologist*

Walter Reed was one of the leading medical investigators of his day. He made significant contributions to the discoveries of how to cure diphtheria and how typhoid fever and yellow fever are transmitted.

Reed was born on September 13, 1851, in Belroi, Virginia. His father, Lemuel, was a minister, and his mother, Pharaba, was a homemaker. In 1867 he enrolled in the University of Virginia; after a year of undergraduate work, he was accepted into that school's medical college, and in 1869, at age 18, he received an M.D. After graduation he moved to Brooklyn, New York, and over the next six years he served on the staffs of Kings County Hospital, Brooklyn City Hospital, and the city board of health. In 1872 he received a second M.D., this time from Bellevue Hospital Medical College in New York City.

In 1875, the year before he married Emilie Lawrence with whom he had two children, Reed was commissioned a first lieutenant in the U.S. Army and assigned to the army's medical department. He spent the next 12 years at various posts in the United States before being assigned in 1887 to the Mount Vernon Barracks in Alabama. There he came to the attention of Surgeon General Jedediah H. Baxter, who recognized Reed's medical capabilities. In 1890 Baxter transferred Reed to Fort McHenry in Balti-

more, Maryland, and arranged for Reed to study pathology and bacteriology at Johns Hopkins University under WILLIAM H. WELCH, one of the foremost medical minds of the day. Following a tour of duty in the West, in 1893 Reed was posted to Washington, D.C., where he served as curator of the Army Medical Museum, director of the museum's pathology laboratory, and professor of bacteriology and clinical microscopy at the Army Medical School. Three years later he took on the additional duties of teaching pathology and bacteriology at Columbian University (modern George Washington University) Medical School in Washington.

In 1890 Reed had taken up the study of diphtheria, a contagious disease that results from a bacterial infection of the throat. By 1898 he was able to demonstrate that diphtheria could be cured, and even prevented, by injecting patients with diphtheria antitoxins. His work in this regard led to him being put in charge of the army's Typhoid Board that same year. The army was readying troops for service in the Spanish-American War, but its training camps were rife with disease, especially typhoid fever. The board, consisting of Reed and two subordinates, set out to discover how typhoid fever spread through the camps in the hope that such knowledge could lead to a significant reduction in typhoid cases among new recruits. The board examined in minute detail every aspect of camp sanitation, housing, and hospital conditions, and it established laboratories staffed with trained bacteriologists at the camps. In 1899 the board finished its work; its final report, which was not released until 1904, found that typhoid fever was not caused by contaminated drinking water, as had been supposed, but was transmitted by flies and unsanitary practices on the part of typhoid patients and those who came in contact with them.

In 1899 Reed was assigned to investigate the causes of yellow fever. Cuba had been liberated by U.S. troops during the Spanish-American War, and the occupying force that had been left behind to stabilize the new regime was being depleted by yellow fever. Specifically, Reed was asked to determine whether or not yellow fever was caused by *Bacillus icteroides*, which in 1896 had been discovered in the blood of yellow fever patients by Italian bacteriologist Guiseppe Sanarelli. By early 1900,

Reed and Aristides Agramonte were able to determine that *Bacillus icteroides* caused hog cholera instead of yellow fever, and that it entered the bloodstreams of yellow fever patients as a secondary invader.

Meanwhile, a yellow fever epidemic had broken out in the U.S. garrison in Havana, Cuba, and in 1900 Reed was assigned to head up the army's Yellow Fever Board, also known as the Yellow Fever Commission. Reed and his fellow board members—Agramonte, James Carroll, and Jesse Lazear—traveled to Havana and set up a laboratory to study yellow fever. Unfortunately, the microscopes of the day were not powerful enough to detect the virus that causes yellow fever. Shortly after the board's arrival, yellow fever broke out in an army jail, but only one of the nine prisoners became sick. This suggested to Reed that fomites, items such as bedding and clothing that have been contaminated by patients, were not the cause of the disease, as many had supposed. Instead, Reed surmised that the patient had been infected by an insect bite.

Based on Reed's intuition, the board began investigating the theory, developed in 1881 by Cuban epidemiologist Carlos Juan Finlay, that yellow fever was transmitted by insects. Reed felt confident that the mosquito species known as *Aedes aegypti*, which is commonly found throughout Cuba, was the vector by which yellow fever was spread. To further investigate this possibility, the board established a small hutted camp where experiments were performed on volunteers who were fully briefed on the dangers involved. The first volunteer to be bitten by an infected mosquito was Carroll, who developed a severe case of yellow fever but lived. Lazear, on the other hand, was bitten and died. Other volunteers allowed themselves to be bitten by mosquitoes, to be injected with the blood of volunteers who had yellow fever, or to come in close contact with fomites.

By 1901 the Yellow Fever Board had proven conclusively that whatever caused yellow fever was injected into the bloodstream via mosquito bite. The board further demonstrated that no other method, save being injected with blood from an infected patient, was capable of spreading yellow fever; fomites were specifically ruled out as a cause. Armed with this information, army engineers under the direction of Major William Gorgas began ridding Havana of mosquitoes, and within 90 days they had eradicated yellow fever in Havana.

Following the completion of his duties in Havana, Reed returned to Washington to teach medicine. When Surgeon General George M. Sternberg retired in 1902, Reed's name was mentioned prominently as his replacement. Instead, Reed was appointed chief librarian of the Surgeon General's Library. He was also named to chair the department of pathology at Columbian. Later that year, Reed developed acute appendicitis; he was operated on at the Washington Barracks medical facility and died of complications related to the surgery on November 23, 1902. In 1906 the army acknowledged his contribution to medicine by opening a hospital in Washington and naming it Walter Reed Hospital (today Walter Reed Army Medical Center) in his honor.

Further Reading

Bean, William B. *Walter Reed: A Biography.* Charlottesville: University Press of Virginia, 1982.
Groh, Lynn. *Walter Reed, Pioneer in Medicine.* Champaign, Ill.: Garrard Pub. Co., 1971.

Reines, Frederick
(1918–1998) *physicist*

Frederick Reines codetected the neutrino, a subatomic particle with no electrical charge and virtually no mass. For this achievement he was awarded a half share of the 1995 Nobel Prize in physics.

Reines was born on March 16, 1918, in Paterson, New Jersey. His father, Israel, owned a silk mill, and his mother, Gussie, was a homemaker. As a young boy he moved with his family to Hillburn, New York, where his father opened a general store, returning with them to Paterson in time to enter high school. He went to college at the Stevens Institute of Technology in nearby Hoboken, receiving a B.S. in engineering in 1939 and an M.S. in mathematical physics in 1941, and New York University (NYU), where he received a Ph.D. in theoretical physics in 1944. In 1940 he married Sylvia Samuels with whom he had two children.

Reines's studies at NYU had focused on developing a model for the atom as it undergoes nuclear fission. Consequently, after graduation he was recruited to join the Manhattan Project, the U.S. effort to build an atomic bomb during World War II, and was assigned to the Los Alamos Scientific Laboratory in New Mexico. He remained at Los Alamos after the war, focusing his research on understanding the effects of nuclear blasts, particularly the air blast wave that a hydrogen bomb generates.

In 1951 Reines began devoting part of his research efforts to detecting the neutrino. The existence of neutrinos had been hypothesized in 1931 by Austrian physicist Wolfgang Pauli, but 20 years later they had yet to be discovered, so Reines set out to prove or disprove their existence. Pauli had theorized that neutrinos are produced in prodigious numbers via certain types of radioactive decay, and it has been estimated that one square centimeter of radioactive material from a nuclear reactor emits more than 10 billion neutrinos per second. The problem with detecting them, however, is that they rarely interact with other particles because they have no charge and virtually no mass, and so they are almost impossible to capture. It is now believed that for every trillion neutrinos that enter the atmosphere from outer space, all but one penetrate far below the Earth's surface.

Reines and Clyde L. Cowan, Jr., a Los Alamos colleague, began their search for neutrinos by examining radioactive material from a nuclear bomb test at Los Alamos. Almost immediately, however, they reasoned that neutrinos would be much easier to find in the radioactive matter produced by a nuclear reactor, and so they began examining reactor material from government-operated reactors in Hanford, Washington, and Barnwell, South Carolina. In 1953 they theorized that if a neutrino combines with a proton, the yield would be a neutron and a positron, an electron with a positive charge. That same year they began exposing protons to particle beams produced from reactor material and observing the increase in the number of positrons, which are extremely short-lived but measurable nonetheless, as well as neutrons. In short order they obtained data that indicated the production of a few neutrinos every hour. Over the next three years they intensified the strength of the particle beam while increasing the "heaviness" of the

proton target, a combination of water and cadmium chloride, and in 1956 they actually captured a few neutrinos. The collaboration ended that same year when Cowan left Los Alamos, and for the next three years Reines conducted experiments of his own on the properties of the neutrino at the Barnwell reactor.

By proving that neutrinos exist, Reines proved that the fundamental laws of conservation of energy and momentum apply to the radioactive decay of an atomic nucleus, especially after he showed that neutrinos have mass, even if only one ten-thousandth as much as an electron. He also opened the door for the use of neutrinos as a tool for probing more deeply into the inner workings of quarks, the basic building blocks of protons and neutrons. For his contribution to these developments, Reines was awarded a half share of the 1995 Nobel Prize in physics.

In 1959 Reines left Los Alamos to become head of the physics department at the Case Institute of Technology (today Case Western Reserve University) in Cleveland, Ohio. Seven years later he was named the founding dean of the School of Physical Sciences at the University of California at Irvine (UCI). At Case and UCI he put together a research group devoted to reactor neutrino physics. This group's many activities included the study of the neutrino-Mössbauer effect, whereby a neutrino functions like a photon (a packet of light energy), and participation in the 1987 discovery of neutrinos in cosmic rays emitted by a supernova, a discovery that shed much light on the role played by neutrinos in the collapse of a star.

Reines stepped down as dean in 1974 and retired from teaching in 1988, although he remained at UCI as a researcher. His honors include the National Medal of Science and election to the National Academy of Sciences and the American Academy of Arts and Sciences. He died on August 26, 1998, in Irvine.

Further Reading

Nobelprize.org. "The Nobel Prize in Physics 1995." Available online. URL: http://nobelprize.org/physics/laureates/1995. Downloaded on September 7, 2004.

University of California Irvine Department of Physics and Astronomy. "1995 Nobel Laureate Frederick Reines." Available online. URL: http://www.ps.uci.edu/physics/reines.html. Downloaded on March 25, 2005.

Wilford, John N. "2 Americans Win Nobel for Finding Tiny Particles," *New York Times*, October 12, 1995, p. B6.

Richards, Dickinson W.
(Dickinson Woodruff Richards, Jr.)
(1895–1973) *physician*

Dickinson W. Richards was one of the first medical researchers to use the catheter as a tool for studying the functions of the human heart. His work in this regard won him a Nobel Prize in physiology or medicine.

Richards was born on October 30, 1895, in Orange, New Jersey. His father, Dickinson Sr., was a lawyer, and his mother, Sally, was a homemaker. In 1917 he received an A.B. from Yale University and joined the U.S. Army, serving in France as an artillery officer during World War I. In 1919 he entered Columbia University's College of Physicians and Surgeons, and he received an M.A. in physiology in 1922 and an M.D. in 1923. He then joined the staff of New York City's Presbyterian Hospital, and in 1928 he began teaching at the College of Physicians and Surgeons. In 1945 he left Presbyterian for Bellevue Hospital, where he spent the rest of his career. In 1931 he married Constance Riley with whom he had four children.

Richards's work at Presbyterian primarily involved researching the nature and function of the heart and circulatory system. Meanwhile, Bellevue's ANDRÉ F. COURNAND, a tuberculosis researcher, was studying the lungs, and he realized that he needed to know more about the heart and the circulatory system in order to continue. In 1931 Richards joined Cournand in a joint study of the cardiopulmonary system as a means of advancing both their research efforts. At the time, most of what physiologists knew about the heart was what they had learned from dissecting and experimenting with the hearts of laboratory animals. It was assumed that the human heart operated in much the same way as animal hearts, but no one knew for sure because no one had discovered a way to study a living human heart.

By 1936 Richards and Cournand had become interested in the work of German physician Werner Forssmann. In 1929 Forssmann had inserted a catheter, a narrow flexible tube, into his own heart via a vein at his right elbow. He had hoped that this technique might serve as a useful way to inject drugs directly into the circulatory system, thus making them more effective. Richards and Cournand, however, believed that Forssmann's technique could be used as a diagnostic tool for learning more about the heart and lungs. In 1936 Cournand went to Paris to learn more about cardiac catheterization, and upon his return he and Richards began catheterizing the hearts of laboratory animals. In time they were able to insert a catheter all the way through the heart and into the lungs. When no harmful side effects showed themselves, they began catheterizing human hearts as well.

During the 1940s Richards and Cournand discovered how to use the catheter to measure blood pressure and volume in the human heart, something that had not been possible before. They also discovered how organs such as the kidneys are harmed when the volume of circulating blood is reduced due to malfunctions of the heart, especially those stemming from congenital heart disease. They also learned much about how to treat these conditions by increasing circulating blood volume via surgery and other therapeutic methods. In time their work led to the use of cardiac catheterization as a means of diagnosing and treating virtually every kind of heart disease and condition. For their contributions to the development of this important diagnostic technique, Richards, Cournand, and Forssmann were awarded equal shares of the 1956 Nobel Prize in physiology or medicine.

Richards retired from Columbia and Bellevue in 1961, but he continued to collaborate with Cournand for another 12 years. He died on February 23, 1973, in Lakeville, Connecticut.

Further Reading
The Nobel Prize Internet Archive. "Dickinson W. Richards." Available online. URL: http://almaz. com/nobel/medicine/1956c.html. Downloaded on March 25, 2005.

Nobelprize.org. "The Nobel Prize in Physiology or Medicine 1956." Available online. URL: http://nobelprize. org/medicine/laureates/1956. Downloaded on January 10, 2004.

Wasson, Tyler, ed. *Nobel Prize Winners*. New York: H. W. Wilson, 1987, pp. 862–864.

Richards, Theodore W.
(Theodore William Richards)
(1868–1928) *chemist*

Theodore W. Richards is best remembered for developing methods and an apparatus for determining the atomic weights of the elements. He and his students arrived at exact values for 55 elements, or more than half the periodic table. This accomplishment earned for him the 1914 Nobel Prize in chemistry.

Richards was born on January 31, 1868, in Germantown, Pennsylvania. His father, William, was a painter, and his mother, Anna, was a poet. He was homeschooled until age 15, when he entered Haverford College, receiving a B.A. in science in 1885. He then entered Harvard University as a senior and received a second B.A. the following year. He remained at Harvard to study chemistry, receiving an M.A. and a Ph.D. in 1888. After a year of study at the University of Göttingen in Germany, he returned to Harvard to teach chemistry. He spent his entire career at Harvard, eventually becoming chair of the chemistry department. In 1896 he married Miriam Thayer with whom he had three children.

Richards devoted practically his entire career to the accurate measurement of the weights of atoms and molecules. As a graduate student he became interested in atomic weight, the average weight of one atom of a given element in relation to a standard. The concept of atomic weight is fundamental to chemistry, because most chemical reactions take place in accordance with simple numerical relationships among atoms. Since it is almost always impossible to actually count the atoms involved, chemists measure reactants and products by weighing them and then reach their conclusions through calculations involving atomic weights. In the late 19th century, the standard for calculating atomic weight was hydrogen, the lightest element, which was assigned an atomic weight of 1 (today the standard is one-twelfth the weight of carbon-12). All other elements were then assigned weights based on the ratio between their actual weight and that of hydrogen; for example, oxygen was assigned an atomic weight of 16. Much of this work was carried out in the mid-19th century by Belgian chemist Jean S. Stas, whose accuracy was widely acknowledged by the scientific community.

By 1885, however, a growing number of chemists were beginning to question some of Stas's results. For example, actual experiments indicated that oxygen's weight was a bit less than exactly 16, the value Stas had assigned. Richards's first project was to arrive at an exact weight for oxygen; in conjunction with his mentor, Josiah P. Cooke, in 1886 he measured it to be within 0.02 percent of its current accepted value, 15.9994.

Richards then set out to determine the exact atomic weights of a number of other elements. He developed methods for expelling every trace of moisture from a substance, and he perfected the use of specific gravity, the ratio of the density of a solid or liquid to the density of water. He also reconfigured the nephelometer, an instrument designed to count bacteria, so that it could determine the density of particles suspended in a liquid by measuring the way they scatter light. By 1903 he and his assistants had determined more exact atomic weights for copper, barium, strontium, zinc, magnesium, nickel, cobalt, iron, uranium, calcium, and cesium than had previously been obtained.

In the course of his work with strontium, Richards came to the realization that much of Stas's work was flawed by tiny errors resulting from the primitive methods that had been available to him. Using his more rigorous methods and equipment, Richards recalculated the atomic weights for oxygen, silver, chlorine, bromine, iodine, potassium, sodium, nitrogen, and sulfur. These atomic weights were considered to be fundamental because these elements are the ones most commonly used to determine the atomic weights of all the other elements. By 1907 Richards had arrived at values that coincide within 0.0003 percent of the ones currently accepted for all these elements. For example, Richards revised Stas's value of 107.938 as the atomic weight of silver to 107.876, while the most current accepted value is 107.868. By providing more accurate values for the various atomic weights, Richards made it possible for chemists to measure more accurately the results of their experiments. For this immeasurably important contribution, he was awarded the 1914 Nobel Prize in chemistry.

Richards was elected to the National Academy of Sciences, and he served as president of the American Chemical Society, the American Association for the Advancement of Science, and the American Academy of Arts and Sciences. He continued to experiment with atomic weights until his death on April 2, 1928, in Cambridge, Massachusetts.

Further Reading

Conant, James B. "Theodore William Richards," National Academy of Sciences, *Biographical Memoirs* 44 (1974): pp. 251–270.

Nobelprize.org. "The Nobel Prize in Chemistry 1914." Available online. URL: http://nobelprize.org/chemistry/laureates/1914. Downloaded on January 30, 2004.

Wasson, Tyler, ed. *Nobel Prize Winners.* New York: H. W. Wilson, 1987, pp. 864–868.

Richardson, Robert C.
(Robert Coleman Richardson)
(1937–) *physicist*

Robert C. Richardson codiscovered superfluidity in an isotope of helium known as helium-3. For this discovery, he was awarded a share of the 1996 Nobel Prize in physics.

Richardson was born on June 26, 1937, in Washington, D.C., but he grew up in nearby Arlington, Virginia. His father, Robert, was a telephone lineman, and his mother, Lois, was a homemaker. He received a B.S. and an M.S. in physics from Virginia Polytechnic Institute in 1958 and 1960, respectively, and a Ph.D. from Duke University in 1966. In 1962 he married Betty McCarthy with whom he had two children.

In graduate school, Richardson became interested in low temperature physics, the study of what happens to the thermal, electrical, and magnetic properties of matter at temperatures approaching 0 K, or absolute zero. He also became interested in helium-3 and used nuclear magnetic resonance testing to study the various properties of the isotope in its solid form. Helium-3 was of particular interest at that time because of its resistance to superfluidity, the unusual properties exhibited by liquid helium when it is cooled to 2.18 K. These properties include frictionless flow, including the ability to overflow its containment vessel in defiance of the laws of viscosity, and very high heat conductivity. The standard explanation for this phenomenon involved the difference between bosons and fermions. Helium-4, the more common isotope of helium, is a boson because it contains an even number of nucleons (protons and neutrons), while helium-3 is a fermion because it contains an uneven number of nucleons. The difference between having an even or odd number of nucleons is significant because it determines angular momentum, or spin; bosons and fermions behave differently from each other because they have different spins. Consequently, it was believed that helium-4 becomes a superfluid because it is a boson while helium-3 cannot become a superfluid because it is a fermion.

In 1966 Richardson went to Cornell University in Ithaca, New York, to work as a research associate in the Laboratory of Atomic and Solid State Physics (LASSP). LASSP was under the direction of DAVID M. LEE, who focused its research on low-temperature physics, especially superfluidity. In 1967 Richardson and Lee were joined by DOUGLAS D. OSHEROFF, and the three began collaborating on a study of the magnetic properties of solid helium-3. By 1972 they had managed to cool helium-3 to 0.002 K, at which point they discovered that it, too, becomes a superfluid. Moreover, helium-3 in the superfluid phase possesses certain magnetic properties that helium-4 in the superfluid phase does not. Not only did this discovery nullify the conventional wisdom regarding the conditions required for superfluidity but also it permitted physicists to conduct some very interesting research concerning the differences in behavior between bosons and fermions, as now a boson (helium-4) and a fermion (helium-3) could be studied in a superfluid phase. For their discovery, Lee, Richardson, and Osheroff were each awarded a one-third share of the 1996 Nobel Prize in physics.

In 1968 Richardson became a professor of physics at Cornell, and in 1990 he took Lee's place as director of LASSP. His many honors include election to the National Academy of Sciences and the American Academy of Arts and Sciences. His publications include *Experimental Techniques in Condensed Matter Physics at Low Temperatures* (1988).

Further Reading

Cornell University Laboratory of Atomic and Solid State Physics. "Robert C. Richardson." Available online. URL: http://www.lassp.cornell.edu/lassp_data/rcr. html. Downloaded on March 25, 2005.

Krapp, Kristine M., ed. *Notable Twentieth-Century Scientists Supplement.* Detroit: Gale Research, 1998, pp. 390–391.

Nobelprize.org. "The Nobel Prize in Physics 1996." Available online. URL: http://nobelprize.org/physics/ laureates/1996. Downloaded on August 23, 2004.

Richter, Burton

(1931–) *physicist*

Burton Richter codiscovered the J/psi particle as well as the charmed quark and its antiquark. For these discoveries he was awarded a share of the 1976 Nobel Prize in physics.

Richter was born on March 22, 1931, in New York City. His father, Abraham, was a textile worker, and his mother, Fanny, was a homemaker. At age 17 he enrolled in the Massachusetts Institute of Technology (MIT) where he majored in physics and received a B.S. in 1952. He stayed on as a graduate student and began investigating electron-positron interactions, a positron being a subatomic particle with the same mass as an electron but with a positive charge. The positron is the electron's antiparticle, and when the two collide they disintegrate. His experiments with electrons and positrons involved the use of a particle accelerator, a device that propels subatomic particles into extremely high energy levels so that their properties can be better studied. He became so fascinated with the particle accelerator that, upon receiving a Ph.D. in physics in 1956, he solicited a position as a research assistant at Stanford (Calif.) University's High-Energy Physics Laboratory because it had one of the finest particle accelerator programs in the nation. He eventually became a professor of physics at Stanford, and in 1960 he married Laurose Becker with whom he had two children.

At Stanford, Richter continued his work with electrons and positrons. His earliest work showed that the basic tenets of quantum electrodynamics (QED), the body of theory concerning the interactions of charged particles with each other and with electromagnetic radiation, apply to electron-positron pairs. In 1957 he and several colleagues shifted the focus of the QED research to study electron-electron scattering, whereby a beam of high-energy electrons is fired into a cloud of stationary electrons. In the process, they realized that the basic design of the linear accelerator they were using caused it to lose a great deal of energy that might otherwise be transferred to the electron beam, and so they set out to build a more energy-efficient machine. By 1963 they had completed the first colliding beam storage ring, whereby two beams of particles are accelerated in concentric rings and then directed to collide head-on with one another, and over the next two years they used it to complete their study.

Meanwhile, in 1964, the year after he was named a professor of physics at the Stanford Linear Accelerator Center, Richter decided to build a colliding beam storage ring dedicated to the study of electron-positron interactions. Nine years later he completed construction of the Stanford Positron-Electron Accelerating Ring (SPEAR), which was capable of energizing particles to higher levels than any other machine then in existence. Richter and his colleagues began using SPEAR to see if they could convert extremely large amounts of energy—which they generated by firing high-energy electrons and positrons at each other—into previously unknown subatomic particles.

In 1974 Richter and his team succeeded in producing a new particle that they named the psi particle. The psi particle is a meson, meaning that it consists of two quarks, the basic building blocks of certain types of matter; by contrast, a proton and a neutron each consist of three quarks. Further investigation showed that the psi particle is composed of two previously unknown quarks. While protons and neutrons consist of different combinations of "up" and "down" quarks, the psi particle consists of a "charmed" quark and its antiquark. The charmed antiquark is the charmed quark's antiparticle, and when the two collide, they disintegrate, thus explaining the extremely short life of the psi particle. Meanwhile, SAMUEL C.C. TING discovered the psi particle at about the same time but by using a different method. Ting called his discovery the J-particle, and today it is known as the J/psi particle.

The discovery of the J/psi particle and two new quarks forced physicists to reevaluate what they thought they knew about elementary particles and the quarks that comprise them. The most surprising thing about the J/psi particle is that it has twice the mass of a proton, even though it consists of one less quark. This fact alone caused physicists to ponder the existence of other quarks with properties radically different from the ones already known, and thus it stimulated a major search for new quarks. By 1990 researchers had discovered the "beauty" quark and strongly suspected the existence of the "truth" quark. For the role he played in these developments, Richter was awarded a half share of the 1976 Nobel Prize in physics; his corecipient was Ting.

Richter continued to experiment with particle accelerators for the rest of his career. In the late 1970s he worked to gain international support for the construction of the world's most high-powered colliding beam storage ring, but the costs were prohibitively high. Undaunted, he began looking for new designs that would attain extremely high energy levels at a fraction of the cost, and in the 1980s he codeveloped the concept of the linear collider, whereby electron and positron beams from separate linear accelerators are fired at each other to produce high-energy interactions. Known as the SLAC linear collider, this machine became operational in 1990 and is more than two miles long.

In 1984 Richter was named the director of SLAC, a position he held until his retirement in 1999. His many honors include election to the National Academy of Sciences and the American Academy of Arts and Sciences and terms as president of the American Physical Society and the International Union of Pure and Applied Physics.

Further Reading

Nobelprize.org. "The Nobel Prize in Physics 1976." Available online. URL: http://nobelprize.org/physics/laureates/1976. Downloaded on September 18, 2004.

Stanford Linear Accelerator Center. "Director Emeritus Burton Richter." Available online. URL: http://www.slac.stanford.edu/grp/do/people/richter.html. Downloaded on March 25, 2005.

Wasson, Tyler, ed. *Nobel Prize Winners*. New York: H. W. Wilson, 1987, pp. 869–871.

Richter, Charles F.
(Charles Francis Richter)
(1900–1985) *seismologist*

Charles F. Richter was the coinventor of the Richter scale, a method for measuring the magnitude of an earthquake. First published in 1935, it remained the standard scale for measuring earthquakes well into the 21st century.

Richter was born on April 26, 1900, on a farm near Hamilton, Ohio. His parents divorced when he was very young, and at age nine he moved with his mother and her father to Los Angeles, California. He attended the University of Southern California for one year and then transferred to Stanford University where he received an A.B. in physics in 1920. In 1928 he married Lillian Brand, received a Ph.D. in theoretical physics from the California Institute of Technology (Caltech), and went to work at the Carnegie Institution of Washington's Seismological Laboratory in Pasadena.

The director of the Seismological Laboratory was Beno Gutenberg, a professor of geophysics at Caltech, and in 1928 Richter and Gutenberg began developing a scale for cataloging earthquakes in Southern California according to their intensity. The only scale then in existence, the Mercalli scale, classified earthquakes according to eyewitness accounts and damage reports. The problems with the Mercalli scale were that it was too subjective and that it tended to underestimate the severity of earthquakes that struck remote areas. Richter and Gutenberg began developing a scale that utilized a seismograph, a device that records the actual motion of the earth during an earthquake. They based their scale on the tremors recorded at the earthquake's epicenter, the point of ground directly above the earthquake's origin, and they made the scale logarithmic; for example, an earthquake rated 7 is ten times more severe than one rated 6. The scale was jointly published by Richter and Gutenberg in 1935 and quickly became the international standard for judging an earthquake's intensity. For some reason, however, Gutenberg's name never became attached to the scale, which is known simply as the Richter scale.

In 1937 Richter returned to Caltech as a professor of physics and seismology. He continued to collaborate with Gutenberg on establishing seismic monitoring stations around the world, and they coauthored *Seismicity of the Earth and Associated Phenomena* (1949, 1954). By 1960, when Gutenberg died, they had refined their scale to take into account the various types of seismograph then in use, as the original scale had been designed for use with a specific seismograph. On his own, Richter wrote *Elementary Seismology* (1958); this work contains everything from descriptions of major historical earthquakes to a discussion of how buildings can best be built to withstand an earthquake. He also played a major role in establishing the Southern California Seismic Array, a network of seismographs for monitoring earthquake activity in the general vicinity of California's San Andreas Fault, and in publishing the Caltech catalog of California earthquakes.

Richter retired from Caltech in 1970. He spent his remaining years working for Lindvall, Richter, and Associates, a Los Angeles–based earthquake consulting firm for government agencies and private businesses. His honors include election to the American Academy of Arts and Sciences and a term as president of the Seismological Society of America. He died on September 30, 1985, in Pasadena.

Further Reading

BookRags.com. "Biography of Charles F. Richter." Available online. URL: http://www.bookrags.com/biography/charles-f-richter. Downloaded on September 18, 2004.

McMurray, Emily J., ed. *Notable Twentieth-Century Scientists.* Detroit: Gale Research, 1995, pp. 1,677–1,680.

Robbins, Frederick C.
(Frederick Chapman Robbins)
(1916–2003) *virologist*

Along with JOHN F. ENDERS and THOMAS H. WELLER, Frederick C. Robbins discovered how to cultivate the polio virus in a laboratory. This discovery was a major step toward the development of a polio vaccine; for his role in making it, Robbins won a share of a Nobel Prize.

Robbins was born on August 25, 1916, in Auburn, Alabama. His father, William, was a college professor, and his mother, Christine, was a homemaker. As a boy he moved with his family to Columbia, Missouri, where he grew up. After receiving a B.S. from the University of Missouri in 1938, he entered Harvard Medical College and received an M.D. in 1940. Like his colleague, Weller, he then joined the staff of Children's Hospital in Boston, Massachusetts, but took a leave of absence to serve in the U.S. Army Medical Corps during World War II. While in the army, he conducted research related to infectious hepatitis, typhus fever, Q fever, and mumps. Discharged in 1946, he returned to Children's Hospital and began teaching bacteriology at Harvard Medical College. In 1948 he married Alice Northrop with whom he had two children.

While in medical school, Robbins had studied under Enders, and he had participated in some of Enders's studies of viruses. In 1948 he joined Enders's research team, of which Weller was already a part, which was conducting its work at the Research Division of Infectious Diseases at Children's Hospital. The team was primarily interested in poliomyelitis; also known as polio and infantile paralysis, it was one of the most frightening diseases that preyed on children. The team's major challenge was how to produce enough polio virus so that it could be studied thoroughly. At the time, the only way to produce polio virus was to grow it in the nerve tissue of live monkeys, but this process was expensive and tedious because the monkeys were difficult to handle and they always died from the virus. Consequently, Robbins, Enders, and Weller set out to devise a way to grow cultures of polio virus.

Building on Enders and Weller's previous work with viral cultures beginning in 1939, Robbins and his collaborators devised a way to use kidney tissue from monkeys as well as tissue from human embryos as a medium for growing polio virus. Basically, the tissue was placed in a test tube along with a chemical solution and a bit of the polio virus. By 1949 the team had perfected this process, and shortly thereafter other medical researchers began producing enough polio virus for them to conduct in-depth studies of the pathology of the disease. Consequently, an injectable polio vaccine was developed by JONAS E. SALK in 1954, and an oral polio vaccine was developed by ALBERT B. SABIN in 1960. Even before these vaccines had been developed, the work of Robbins, Enders, and Weller was recognized as being of such importance that the three were awarded equal shares of the 1954 Nobel Prize in physiology or medicine.

Robbins continued to collaborate with Enders and Weller until 1952, when he left Boston for Cleveland, Ohio. From 1952 to 1966 he served as director of the Cleveland Metropolitan General Hospital's department of pediatrics and contagious diseases, and from 1952 to 1980 he taught pediatrics at the Case Western Reserve University School of Medicine. He served as president of the Society for Pediatric Research, and he was elected to membership in the American Academy of Arts and Sciences. He died on August 4, 2003, in Cleveland.

Further Reading

Hargittai, Istvan, and Magdolna Hargittai. *Candid Science II: Conversations with Famous Biomedical Scientists.* London: Imperial College Press, 2002, pp. 498–518.

Nobelprize.org. "The Nobel Prize in Physiology or Medicine 1954." Available online. URL: http://nobelprize.org/medicine/laureates/1954. Downloaded on January 12, 2004.

Wasson, Tyler, ed. *Nobel Prize Winners.* New York: H. W. Wilson, 1987, pp. 871–873.

Rodbell, Martin
(1925–1998) *biochemist*

Martin Rodbell made important discoveries concerning cellular signal transduction, the way in which a message from a hormone is transmitted chemically into a cell so that one of the cell's enzymes is induced to take action. For these contributions, he was awarded a share of the 1994 Nobel Prize in physiology or medicine.

Rodbell was born on December 1, 1925, in Baltimore, Maryland. His father, Milton, owned a grocery store, and his mother, Shirley, was a homemaker. He entered Johns Hopkins University in 1943 to study literature but he left shortly thereafter when he was drafted into the U.S. military. After serving with the U.S. Navy in the South Pacific during World War II, he returned to Hopkins; he changed his major to biology and received a B.A. in 1949, although he remained at Hopkins an additional year to take advanced courses in chemistry. In 1950, the same year he married Barbara Ledermann with whom he had four children, he entered the University of Washington, receiving a Ph.D. in biochemistry in 1954. After a year as a research fellow at the University of Illinois at Urbana, he became a research chemist with the National Heart Institute, part of the National Institutes of Health in Bethesda, Maryland. In 1961 he transferred to the nutrition and endocrine laboratory of the National Institute of Arthritis and Metabolic Diseases.

Rodbell's early research focused on the biochemistry of lipids, the fatty components of living cells. By 1960 he had isolated and identified the chemical composition of the five lipoproteins (biochemical compounds that are composed of a lipid and a protein) on the surface of human chylomicrons, the principal form in which fat circulates in the bloodstream. By 1967 he had developed a procedure for separating the fat cells from the vascular cells in fatty tissue and another for removing most of the fat from a fat cell while retaining many of the cell's structural and metabolic aspects. He then showed that these defatted cells, which he called fat cell ghosts, remain responsive to the effects of hormones on the cell's metabolic functions. He also discovered that phospholipases, enzymes that break down certain types of lipids, have the same ability as hormones to trigger metabolic functions within fat cells.

In the mid-1960s, Rodbell became intrigued with the research of EARL W. SUTHERLAND, which shed light on the way that hormones initiate metabolic functions within a cell. Sutherland's work suggested that each hormone has a specific location, or receptor, along the cell membrane where it must attach itself in order to be recognized by the cell. Once attached, the hormone triggers the production of cyclic adenosine monophosphate, or cyclic AMP, the so-called second messenger, which then signals for the production of the specific enzyme associated with that particular receptor. Working with fat cell ghosts, in 1967 Rodbell began investigating the biochemistry of cellular signal transduction. Over the next three years, he discovered that the process requires a third messenger as well. Once a hormone attaches itself to its proper receptor, a small intracellular molecule called guanosine triphosphate (GTP) is produced. A signal indicating the presence of the hormone at the receptor is carried through the membrane by GTP to the membrane's inner wall, where it signals for the production of cyclic AMP, which in turn initiates the enzyme called for by the hormone.

Rodbell's findings informed the work of ALFRED G. GILMAN, who picked up where Rodbell had left off. By 1980 Gilman was able to show that GTP is transmitted through the cell membrane by binding to what Gilman called G-proteins, the "G" standing for GTP. The discovery of GTP and G-proteins shed much light on how cellular functions are governed, and it gave medical researchers new insights into how to cure certain diseases involving cellular malfunctions by stimulating or retarding the activities of G-proteins. Consequently, Rodbell and Gilman were each awarded a half share of the 1994 Nobel Prize in physiology or medicine, Sutherland having been awarded the prize in 1971.

In 1985 Rodbell was named scientific director of the National Institute of Environmental Health Sciences in Triangle Research Park, North Carolina. In addition to his administrative duties, he continued to conduct research, and he demonstrated that G-proteins play many roles in normal cellular function, including cell growth. His many honors include election to the National Academy of Sciences and the American Academy of Arts and Sciences. In 1994 he retired to his home in Chapel Hill, North Carolina, where he died on December 7, 1998.

Further Reading

Krapp, Kristine M., ed. *Notable Twentieth-Century Scientists Supplement*. Detroit: Gale Research, 1998, pp. 391–393.

Nobelprize.org. "The Nobel Prize in Physiology or Medicine 1994." Available online. URL: http://nobelprize.org/medicine/laureates/1994. Downloaded on June 28, 2004.

Profiles in Science, National Library of Medicine. "The Martin Rodbell Papers." Available online. URL: http://profiles.nlm.nih.gov/GG. Downloaded on March 25, 2005.

Romer, Alfred S.
(Alfred Sherwood Romer)
(1894–1973) *paleontologist*

Alfred S. Romer helped to revolutionize the study of vertebrate paleontology—the study of the fossils of prehistoric vertebrates. Trained as a zoologist and anatomist, he brought the unique (for his day) idea that fossils were the remains of once-living creatures. Unlike many scholars, he published many of his groundbreaking studies in textbooks and other popular works so that the general educated public might benefit from his discoveries as well as the academic community. By so doing, he did much to make such creatures become "alive" for his audience.

Romer was born on December 28, 1894, in White Plains, New York. His father, Henry, was a journalist, and his mother, Evelyn, was a homemaker. His parents divorced when he was 10; after living with his father in Connecticut for five years, in 1909 he returned to White Plains to live with his father's mother. After graduating from high school, he worked for a year as a railroad clerk before enrolling in Amherst College in Massachusetts where he received an A.B. in 1917. He served two years in the U.S. Army in France during World War I, and upon returning to the United States he attended Columbia University where he received a Ph.D. in zoology in 1921. He taught anatomy for two years at Bellevue Hospital Medical College in New York City, and then accepted a position with the University of Chicago as a professor of vertebrate paleontology. In 1924 he married Ruth Hibbard with whom he had three children.

At the time, the scientific community considered the study of vertebrate paleontology to be a branch of geology, as it mostly involved the study of fossils. As a zoologist and anatomist, Romer took the approach that these fossils represented creatures that had once lived and breathed. This approach did not win him many friends among the faculty at Chicago, so in 1934 he moved to Harvard University to teach zoology and to become the new curator of its Museum of Comparative Zoology, also known as the Agassiz Museum.

As a paleontologist, Romer was particularly interested in Permian tetrapods, four-legged creatures who lived approximately 250 million years ago and from whom the dinosaurs most likely descended. He wanted to trace the evolution of vertebrates from fish-like creatures from 500 million years ago to amphibians and reptiles of the Permian period, after which their evolution was much better known. He spent a great deal of time digging in the fossil-rich sediment beds of Africa and the American Southwest, and in the process he discovered a number of excellent specimens. As curator of the Agassiz Museum, he acquired a number of fossilized Permian tetrapods for its collection, in the process transforming it from a rather unimpressive museum of modern amphibians and reptiles into an important source for the study of vertebrate paleontology.

In 1946 Romer became director of the Agassiz Museum, and he devoted himself to transforming the museum as he had its collection. He increased the museum's endowment tenfold, thus permitting him to increase the size and scope of the museum's activities. Among these activities were publication of a number of studies by Romer of extinct amphibians such as the labyrinthodont (a lizard-like creature that resembled an alligator and from which all land vertebrates most likely evolved) and the pelycosaur (a sail-backed reptile that evolved into the therapsid, a mammal-like reptile from which all mammals most likely evolved). These studies were unique in that they attempted to flesh out the skeletons of the creatures in question by visualizing what their musculature might have looked like and how their nervous systems might have worked. In addition to these studies, Romer wrote several important textbooks and works for the general educated reader about vertebrate paleontology, including *Vertebrate Paleontology* (1933), *Man and the Vertebrates* (1933), *The Vertebrate Body* (1949), *Osteology of the Reptiles* (1956), *The Vertebrate Story* (1959), and *The Procession of Life* (1968).

In 1965 Romer retired from Harvard to dig for fossils in Argentina's Chañares region, an area rich in reptilian fossils from the Triassic period, during which dinosaurs first appeared. During this dig it occurred to him that fossilized Permian tetrapods found in the New World bore many striking resemblances to Permian tetrapod fossils found in Europe and Africa. As a zoologist and anatomist, he knew that the bone structure of the fossilized creatures made it impossible that they could have flown or swum from one side of the Atlantic Ocean to the other. This led him to conclude that until approximately 200 million years ago the continents of Africa and South America had been joined together, thus permitting Permian tetrapods to roam freely from one continent to the other. This conclusion offered strong supporting evidence to geologists who had proposed their own theory of continental drift.

Romer received a number of awards, including election to the National Academy of Sciences in 1944. He founded and served as first president of the Society of Vertebrate Paleontology, and he presided over the American Society of Zoologists, the Society of Systematic Zoology, the Society for the Study of Evolution, and the American Association for the Advancement of Science. He died on November 5, 1973, in Cambridge, Massachusetts.

Further Reading

Colbert, Edwin H. "Alfred Sherwood Romer," National Academy of Sciences, *Biographical Memoirs* 53 (1982): pp. 265–294.

McMurray, Emily J. *Notable Twentieth-Century Scientists.* Detroit: Gale Research, 1995, pp. 1,704–1,706.

Rose, Irwin A.
(1926–) *biochemist*

Irwin A. Rose codiscovered ubiquitin-mediated protein degradation, the process by which a cell rids itself of unwanted or defective proteins. For this contribution, he was awarded a one-third share of the 2004 Nobel Prize in chemistry.

Rose was born on July 26, 1926, in Brooklyn, New York. As a young boy he moved with his family to Spokane, Washington, where he grew up. He studied briefly at Washington State College before enlisting in the U.S. Navy during World War II. After the war he entered the University of Chicago, receiving a B.S. in chemistry in 1949 and a Ph.D. in biochemistry in 1952. He spent two years doing postdoctoral research at Case Western Reserve University in Cleveland, Ohio, and New York University, and in 1954 he was named a professor of biochemistry at the Yale University Medical School. In 1963 he left Yale to become a senior member of the department of basic science at Fox Chase Cancer Center (FCCC) in Philadelphia, Pennsylvania. In 1955 he married Zelda Budenstein with whom he had four children.

Rose's research at FCCC involved investigating the role played by protein as a cause of several forms of cancer. In the 1970s he became interested in a curious fact about protein degradation, the breaking down of protein, in the cell. Neither the construction of proteins by enzymes nor the degradation of protein outside the cell requires any energy, but the degradation of protein inside the cell does. With the assistance of the Israeli biochemists Avram Hershko and Aaron Ciechanover, Rose began investigating the role played in protein degradation by the protein ubiquitin, so named because it is found in the cells of every living organism more complex than bacteria. Despite its ubiquity, no one knew exactly what ubiquitin did, so Rose and his colleagues decided to find out.

In the early 1980s Rose, Hershko, and Ciechanover identified what is known as ubiquitin-mediated protein degradation. Whenever a protein needs to be destroyed, either because it was built incorrectly or because it is no longer needed for a specific biochemical function, it is labeled by a succession of enzymes with a strand of ubiquitin. Proteins so labeled are then directed toward structures in the cell known as proteasomes. Proteasomes act like paper shredders in that they cut up the unwanted proteins into their constituent amino acids, which are then used in the construction of other proteins. The process by which enzymes label proteins with ubiquitin requires energy, thus explaining one of the mysteries that Rose and his colleagues set out to solve.

Rose, Hershko, and Ciechanover also discovered that ubiquitin plays a role in the regulation of cell reproduction. At the end of certain stages in the reproductive cycle, certain proteins known as cyclins must be disposed of before the cycle can proceed to the next stage. Via the process known as ubiquitin-mediated proteolysis, cyclins are labeled with ubiquitin and recycled through the proteasomes. Ubiquitin-mediated proteolysis also plays important roles in DNA repair and transcription and immune response.

The identification of the ubiquitin system and the role it plays in biochemical functions has had profound implications for the developers of pharmaceutical drugs, particularly those that treat cancer. In the early 2000s, a drug that treats multiple myeloma, a form of cancer that affects the immune system, by regulating the ubiquitin system was developed, and many similar drugs are sure to follow. For discovering the ubiquitin system and describing the role it plays in protein degradation and cell reproduction, Rose, Hershko, and Ciechanover were each awarded a one-third share of the 2004 Nobel Prize in chemistry.

Rose retired from FCCC in 1995. Two years later he was named an emeritus researcher at the University of California at Irvine. His other honors include election to the National Academy of Sciences.

Further Reading

Chang, Kenneth. "Study of Cell Breakdown Captures Nobel," New York Times, October 7, 2004, p. A20.
Nobelprize.org. "The Nobel Prize in Chemistry 2004." Available online. URL: http://nobelprize.org/chemistry/laureates/2004. Downloaded on December 28, 2004.

Rous, Peyton
(Francis Peyton Rous)
(1879–1970) *pathologist*

Peyton Rous was the first medical researcher to demonstrate that viruses can cause cancer. This accomplishment won him a share of the 1966 Nobel Prize in physiology or medicine.

Rous was born on October 5, 1879, in Baltimore, Maryland. His father, Charles, was a grain broker, and his mother, Frances, was a homemaker. He received a B.A. and an M.D. from Johns Hopkins University in Baltimore in 1900 and 1905, respectively. He spent the next four years interning at the university's hospital, doing postdoctoral research at the University of Dresden in Germany, working as a laboratory assistant at the University of Michigan, and recovering from tuberculosis. Rous's research at Dresden involved lymphocytes, white blood cells that form in the lymph tissue. The paper resulting from this research impressed SIMON FLEXNER, the director of New York City's Rockefeller Institute for Medical Research (today Rockefeller University), and in 1909 he hired Rous to direct the institute's laboratory for cancer research. In 1915 Rous married Marion de Kay with whom he had three children.

Shortly after joining Rockefeller's staff, Rous began experimenting with sarcomas, or tumors, in chickens. While investigating a lump on the breast of a Plymouth Rock hen, he determined that the lump was a spindle-cell sarcoma, and that cell-free filtrates of the tumor were capable of inducing cancer into other Plymouth Rock hens via inoculation. His conclusion, that the causative agent of the sarcoma was a virus, was published in 1911. Unfortunately, other researchers attempted to duplicate his results by inoculating mice and rats with cell-free filtrates of tumors that occur in rodents, but these experiments failed to result in cancer. Consequently, the medical community dismissed Rous's discovery as an anomaly. Undeterred, he continued to experiment with what is now known as Rous sarcoma virus. He devised a method for growing viruses on chicken embryos, and in the process discovered two other strains of avian virus capable of inducing cancer in chickens.

In 1934, Rous and Richard Shope, a colleague at Rockefeller, began collaborating on the study of the Shope papilloma, a benign lesion that occurs in the skin and mucous membranes of cottontail rabbits. They determined that the Shope papilloma, which over time can develop into a malignant tumor, is also caused by a virus. Further research with Shope papilloma revealed that cancer progresses slowly and by stages, not all of a sudden as many medical researchers of the day believed, and that cancer cells often lie dormant until some agent, like a virus or a chemical, awakens them.

The work of Rous and Shope opened the eyes of other cancer researchers to the possibility that cancer in humans might be caused by viruses. By the 1950s, when the behavior of viruses and their ability to infect healthy cells were better understood, cancer researchers began looking more closely at viruses as a potential cause of cancer. By the mid-1960s, they had discovered a number of viruses that induce cancer in humans. Perhaps more importantly, Rous and Shope contributed immensely to a better understanding of how cancer develops over time. For these contributions, Rous was awarded a share of the 1966 Nobel Prize in physiology or medicine.

In addition to his work with cancer-causing viruses, Rous also made some important contributions to the preservation of whole blood. During World War I he and Joseph R. Turner, another Rockefeller colleague, devised the Rous-Turner method, which preserves whole blood in a citrate-sugar solution. This method was one of a number of developments that eventually resulted in the development of blood banks.

Rous was elected to the National Academy of Sciences and the Royal Society of England, and in 1966 he received the National Medal of Science. He served for a number of years as editor of the prestigious *Journal of Experimental Medicine*. He retired from Rockefeller in 1945, but he continued to conduct research there for another 25 years. He died on February 16, 1970, in New York City.

Further Reading

Dulbecco, Renato. "Francis Peyton Rous," National Academy of Sciences, *Biographical Memoirs* 48 (1976): pp. 275–306.

Nobelprize.org. "The Nobel Prize in Physiology or Medicine 1966." Available online. URL:http://nobelprize.org/medicine/laureates/1966. Downloaded on February 1, 2004.

Wasson, Tyler, ed. *Nobel Prize Winners*. New York: H. W. Wilson, 1987, pp. 889–891.

Rowland, F. Sherwood
(Frank Sherwood Rowland)
(1927–) *chemist*

F. Sherwood Rowland codiscovered that chlorofluorocarbons (CFCs) delete the ozone layer of the upper atmosphere. For this discovery, he was awarded a one-third share of the 1995 Nobel Prize in chemistry.

Rowland was born on June 28, 1927, in Delaware, Ohio. His father, Sidney, was a mathematics professor at Ohio Wesleyan University and his mother, Margaret, was a homemaker. He finished high school at age 16 and then entered Ohio Wesleyan; he spent a year in the U.S. Navy during World War II and received a B.A. in chemistry in 1948. He then entered the graduate program at the University of Chicago, receiving an M.S. and a Ph.D. in chemistry in 1951 and 1952, respectively. He spent the next four years teaching chemistry at Princeton University before leaving in 1956 for the University of Kansas. In 1964 he was named chair of the chemistry department at the University of California at Irvine. In 1952 he married Joan Lundberg with whom he had two children.

Rowland's early research involved radiochemistry, the chemical study of radioactive elements and their use in the study of chemical processes. He pioneered the use of radioactive tritium, an isotope of hydrogen, as a tracer for studying chemical reactions, particularly those involving photochemistry, the chemical action of light. He also had a strong interest in atmospheric science that dated back to his high school days, when he had assisted with the operation of the local volunteer weather station. In 1972 he attended a chemistry-meteorology workshop sponsored by the U.S. Atomic Energy Commission (today part of the Department of Energy), where he learned about efforts to study air mass movement by studying the movement of chlorofluorocarbons (CFCs). These man-made molecules are key ingredients in such products as aerosol-spray propellants, refrigerants, and solvents, and they were slowly building up in the upper atmosphere where it was thought they would remain inert, thus making them excellent chemical tracers. Rowland knew from his work with photochemistry, however, that CFCs would not remain inert forever because of the effects of solar radiation. In 1973 he and MARIO J. MOLINA, an Irvine colleague, undertook a study to find out what would happen to CFCs in the atmosphere.

Rowland and Molina began their joint project by looking for atmospheric mechanisms that destroy CFCs in the lower atmosphere. When they found none, they developed what is now known as the CFC–ozone depletion theory. According to this theory, CFCs drift into the upper atmosphere where they are decomposed by solar radiation. The chlorine atoms released as a result of this decomposition then catalyze a photochemical reaction that destroys ozone molecules, thus causing a significant depletion of the ozonosphere. This region in the upper atmosphere prevents temperatures on Earth from getting too hot; it also filters out certain forms of solar radiation that, if allowed to reach the Earth's surface, would kill or injure most living things. They published their findings in 1974, but because of the perceived danger to life on Earth they presented their findings to public policymakers as well. Stirred to action by Rowland and Molina's findings, by 1980 the United States, Canada, and the Scandinavian nations banned the use of CFCs in aerosol-spray dispensers.

In 1982 Rowland and Molina ended their collaboration when Molina left Irvine for the California Institute of Technology's Jet Propulsion Laboratory. By 1987 Molina had shown that the presence of ice crystals in the stratospheric clouds over the South Pole promotes chlorine-activation reactions of the very type he and Rowland had called attention to in the CFC–ozone depletion theory. This discovery explained the discovery in 1985 by other researchers that ozone depletion was taking place in the ozone layer over Antarctica. Although this depletion was shown to occur naturally at regular intervals, it was also shown that CFCs exacerbate the depletion process. These two discoveries led more than two dozen nations in 1987 to impose strict reductions on the manufacture and use of CFCs over the next 12 years. For alerting the world to the dangers of CFCs, Rowland and Molina were each awarded a one-third share of the 1995 Nobel Prize in chemistry. Their corecipient was the Dutch chemist Paul J. Crutzen.

Rowland remained at Irvine for the rest of his career. Over the years his research drifted away from radiochemistry toward atmospheric chemistry. By 2004 his research group was dedicated to studying the composition of the atmosphere in remote locations throughout the Pacific region from Alaska to New Zealand, in highly polluted cities throughout the world, and in areas with special conditions, such as burning forests, agricultural wastes, or the marine boundary layer in oceanic locations with high biological emissions. His many honors include election to the National Academy of Sciences and the American Academy of Arts and Sciences and a term as president of the American Association for the Advancement of Science.

Further Reading

Newbold, Heather, ed. *Life Stories: World-Renowned Scientists Reflect on Their Lives and on the Future of Life on Earth.* Berkeley: University of California Press, 2000.

Nobelprize.org. "The Nobel Prize in Chemistry 1995." Available online. URL: http://nobelprize.org/chemistry/laureates/1995. Downloaded on August 19, 2004.

Rowley, Janet D.
(Janet Davison, Janet Davison Rowley)
(1925–) *cytogeneticist*

Janet D. Rowley was the first to identify abnormalities in the chromosomes as a possible cause of cancer. Her work also suggested that gene therapies might offer great promise as cures for certain forms of cancer.

Rowley was born Janet Davison on April 5, 1925, in New York City. Her father, Hurford, was a business professor, and her mother, Ethel, was a high school teacher and librarian. She finished her last two years of high school as part of a special program at the University of Chicago, where she received a B.A. in philosophy in 1944, a B.S. in anatomy in 1946, and an M.D. in 1948. Also in 1948, she married Donald Rowley with whom she had four children, and for the next 21 years she focused on taking care of her family. Nevertheless, she also made time to complete her internship at Cook County Hospital and her residency at the U.S. Public Health Service (USPHS) Marine Hospital in Chicago, conduct research on mental retardation at Cook County Hospital, and teach neurology at the University of Illinois School of Medicine.

In 1961 Rowley's husband, an immunologist, decided to spend his sabbatical year in England,

and she applied for and received a USPHS research fellowship at the radiobiology laboratory of Oxford University's Churchill Hospital. By this time she had become intrigued by Down syndrome, a congenital disease that is marked by moderate to severe mental retardation. Two years earlier it had been discovered that patients with Down syndrome have 47 chromosomes rather than the normal number of 46, the extra one arising from a doubling of one of the chromosomes. As a trained cytogeneticist, Rowley was particularly interested in the connection between cells and heredity, so she spent her time at Oxford further investigating the connection between chromosomal abnormality and mental retardation. Upon returning to the United States in 1962, she became a part-time researcher at the Argonne Cancer Research Hospital (today the Franklin McLean Memorial Research Institute). In 1969 she was named to a full-time professorship at the University of Chicago Medical School and to a full-time research position at Argonne, positions she held for the rest of her career.

Having been inspired by Down syndrome, at Argonne Rowley shifted the focus of her research to cancer, specifically the various forms of blood cancer known as leukemia, because her mentor, Leon Jacobson, was a blood specialist and her research space was in his laboratory. For 10 years she studied the chromosomes of Jacobson's patients, hoping to find something unusual in their arrangement. During this period she became an expert at staining chromosomes and in using the fluorescence microscope, and in 1972 she made her first important discovery. She noted a chromosomal abnormality in patients with acute myeloblastic leukemia; specifically, a small piece of chromosome 8 had changed places, or translocated, with a small piece of chromosome 21. Two years later she discovered that, in patients with chronic myelogenous leukemia (CML), translocation had occurred between small pieces of chromosomes 9 and 22. Further studies showed that more than 90 percent of all patients diagnosed with CML display this particular translocation. She later discovered translocations between chromosomes 14 and 18 in patients with follicular lymphoma, and between chromosomes 15 and 17 in patients with acute promyelocytic leukemia. As to how such translocations take place, by 2000 she had hypothesized a connection between translocation and the consumption of heavy doses of bioflavonoids, brightly colored chemicals that occur naturally in certain fruits and vegetables. Specifically, she showed that 10 different bioflavonoids cause breaks in a gene associated with several forms of leukemia in children and adults.

As to why translocation might cause cancer, other researchers have shown that the function of a certain gene is modified and regulated by the genes adjacent to it on a chromosome, so that moving a gene's physical location can also change the way it functions. In leukemia patients, for example, it seems that the translocation of genes results in a growth-regulating gene being switched permanently "on," so that it continuously calls for the production of a particular type of cell, which results in cancer.

Rowley has been honored by the American Cancer Society and the National Cancer Institute. She served as cofounder and coeditor of *Genes, Chromosomes and Cancer,* a medical journal devoted to the genetic causes of cancer. She also edited several books concerning the genetic causes of cancer, including *Chromosomes and Cancer: From Molecules to Man* (1983), *Finding Order in Chaos* (1988), and *Advances in Understanding Genetic Changes in Cancer* (1992).

Further Reading

McMurray, Emily J., ed. *Notable Twentieth-Century Scientists.* Detroit: Gale Research, 1995, pp. 1,722–1,723.

Wasserman, Elga. *The Door in the Dream: Conversations with Eminent Women in Science.* Washington, D.C.: Joseph Henry Press, 2000, pp. 51–90.

Rubin, Vera C.
(Vera Cooper, Vera Cooper Rubin)
(1928–   ) *astronomer*

Vera C. Rubin played a major role in verifying the existence of dark matter, invisible material that may constitute most of the matter in the universe. She also demonstrated the existence of large-scale streaming and shed light on how galaxies are formed.

Rubin was born Vera Cooper on July 23, 1928, in Philadelphia, Pennsylvania. Her father, Philip, was an electrical engineer, and her mother, Rose, was a homemaker. She received three degrees in astronomy: a B.A. from Vassar College in 1948, an M.A. from Cornell University in 1951, and a Ph.D. from Georgetown University in 1954. After teaching astronomy at Georgetown for 11 years, in 1965 she joined the staff of the Carnegie Institution of Washington's Department of Terrestrial Magnetism (DTM), where she spent the rest of her career. In 1948 she married Robert Rubin with whom she had four children.

Rubin's research focused on the motion of galaxies. Shortly after arriving at DTM, she and W. Kent Ford, a DTM physicist, began measuring how fast stars in the Andromeda galaxy rotate around its center by studying changes in stellar light spectra, the patterns of electromagnetic radiation emitted by stars. This technique had been used by astronomers for years, but Rubin and Ford made use of a new technology, known as image tube intensification, that allowed them to measure minute changes in stellar light spectra more precisely. By 1970 they had discovered that stars on the edge of the galaxy are moving just as fast and in some cases faster than the stars near the center of the galaxy. This finding contradicts the prediction of the Newtonian laws of gravity, which holds that stars should move faster the closer they are to the center, in much the same way that planets nearer the Sun orbit faster than the ones farther away. In fact, a similar discovery had been made in the 1920s by Dutch astronomer Jan Oort, who had determined that stars on the periphery of the Milky Way move at the same rate as stars closer to the galaxy's center. Oort believed that this finding was an anomaly that would be cleared up once scientists developed better methods for observing matter. Ironically, by using those better methods, Rubin and Ford had proved that Oort's finding was no anomaly.

Rubin and Ford also found that a significant portion of the Andromeda galaxy's gravitational mass is neither emitting nor absorbing light, and that the percentage of nonemitting, nonabsorbing matter increases as the distance from the galaxy's center increases. By 1985 they had used image tube intensification to study the stellar light spectra of 60 spiral galaxies and had obtained the same results for each. The most plausible explanation for this phenomenon is that every galaxy contains a great deal of matter that is invisible because it emits no light spectra, and that this so-called dark matter exerts a gravitational pull on the stars on the periphery of a galaxy that increases their speed. In 1933 Swiss astronomer Fritz Zwicky suggested that dark matter might exist based on the velocities of galaxies in galaxy clusters, and in 1973 James Peebles and Jeremiah Ostriker provided a theoretical argument for the presence of dark matter in galaxies. However, Rubin and Ford's work offered the first observational evidence for the existence of dark matter as a common astrophysical phenomenon. Today astrophysicists believe that as much as 90 percent of the matter in the universe is dark matter, but exactly what dark matter is no one can say.

In 1975 Rubin and Ford demonstrated that the Milky Way and the galaxy cluster it belongs to are moving at a different speed than many of the more distant galaxies. At first this finding was labeled the Rubin-Ford effect because most astrophysicists did not accept it. However, further research demonstrated the veracity of the effect, and today it is known as "large-scale streaming." She also obtained evidence that some galaxies both rotate and counter-rotate, an indication that galaxies are formed by the merger of a dwarf galaxy with either another dwarf galaxy or a massive gas cloud possessing different physical dynamics.

Rubin published her work in *Large Scale Motions in the Universe* (1988) and *Bright Galaxies, Dark Matters* (1996). She was elected to the National Academy of Sciences. Her many awards include the National Medal of Science and the International Cosmology Prize.

Further Reading

Lightman, Alan, and Roberta Brawer. *Origins: The Lives and Worlds of Modern Cosmologists.* Cambridge, Mass.: Harvard University Press, 1990, pp. 285–305.

Yount, Lisa. "Rubin, Vera Cooper," *A to Z of Women in Science and Math.* New York: Facts On File, 1999, pp. 183–185.

Rush, Benjamin
(1746–1813) *physician*

Benjamin Rush was one of the foremost American medical theoreticians of his day. Largely as a result of his influence, a majority of American physicians employed "heroic medicine" as the standard method for treating illnesses until the late 19th century.

Rush was born on January 4, 1746, in Byberry Township, Pennsylvania. His parents, John and Susanna, were farmers. His father died when he was young, and at age eight he went to live with his uncle, Samuel Finley, in Nottingham, Maryland. After finishing at the academy that Finley ran, at age 13 Rush entered the College of New Jersey (today Princeton University) and received an A.B. one year later. In 1761 he moved to Philadelphia, Pennsylvania, where he studied medicine by serving as an apprentice to John Redman, a noted physician.

In 1766 Rush was encouraged by Redman to go to Scotland to study medicine at the University of Edinburgh, which he did. Upon receiving his M.D. in 1768, Rush received additional training at St. Thomas's Hospital in London, England. He returned to Philadelphia in 1769 and opened a medical practice. Later that same year he was appointed professor of chemistry at the College of Philadelphia, and in 1770 he wrote and published the first American textbook on chemistry, *A Syllabus of a Course of Lectures on Chemistry.* By the end of his medical career, he had published more than 60 pieces on medicine, and the reputation he received from them contributed to the long-term success of his medical practice.

In 1776 Rush married Julia Stockton with whom he had 13 children. That same year he was elected to the Continental Congress and appointed to its medical care committee. The following year he left Congress and was appointed surgeon general of the Continental Army's Middle Department. In this position, he bickered constantly with his superiors concerning what he considered to be incompetence and corruption in the army hospital system. He resigned his commission in early 1778 to return to the private practice of medicine.

In 1780 Rush was named a lecturer at the University of the State of Pennsylvania, and in 1784 he began performing surgery at the Pennsylvania Hospital. Two years later he helped set up the Philadelphia Dispensary, one of the first free clinics for the poor in the United States. In 1787 he helped found the College of Physicians of Philadelphia and assumed responsibility for the care and treatment of the Pennsylvania Hospital's insane patients. In 1791, when the College of Philadelphia and the University of the State of Pennsylvania merged to form the University of Pennsylvania, Rush was named to the chair of the institutes of medicine and clinical practice, and later to the chair of theory and practice of medicine.

Rush's medical theories often stood in sharp contrast to those of less learned practitioners. Most physicians believed that disease was caused by an imbalance in one of the four bodily "humors" or body fluids (blood, phlegm, black bile, and yellow bile), an idea that had been passed down by the ancient Greeks. Rush, on the other hand, believed that all disease was caused by morbid excitement of the nervous system, which he believed was caused by an imbalance in the circulatory system. This imbalance could be cured, he believed, only by employing a rather barbaric treatment known as bloodletting. This practice involved opening one or more of the patient's blood vessels and draining out a significant amount of blood, sometimes as much as three pints a day. In addition, Rush often prescribed the use of purgatives, whereby the patient was induced to eliminate additional harmful matter via vomiting and/or bowel movements. Taken as a whole, this therapy became known as "heroic medicine," because it required a heroic, or extreme, effort on the part of the physician.

What is perhaps more shocking than a description of heroic medicine is the fact that such methods actually seemed to work; in the hands of a skilled practitioner like Rush, they worked rather well. His theories were put to a serious test in 1793, when a yellow fever epidemic broke out in Philadelphia. During the course of the epidemic, more than 4,000 people, almost 10 percent of the city's population, died, yet more than 90 percent of Rush's patients survived. He himself fell sick twice during the epidemic, but he treated himself heroically and recovered quickly both times.

As a result of the superior results he achieved during the epidemic, Rush became a local hero, and his reputation as a medical genius spread far and wide. Many of his fellow physicians, however, condemned what they called Rush's indiscriminate use of heroic medicine. Their chief complaint was that when heroic medicine was practiced on extremely weak patients, they often died from the treatment rather than from the disease. At one point he grew so weary of their attacks that he resigned from the College of Physicians and almost relocated his practice to New York City. But despite the condemnations, Rush's methods were adopted by a great many of the approximately 3,000 students he taught during his career, and eventually heroic medicine was used by a majority of physicians in the United States.

When dealing with the insane, Rush advocated the use of much more enlightened methods.

Benjamin Rush, who signed the Declaration of Independence, was one of the most influential medical authorities of his day. *(Library of Congress, Prints and Photographs Division [LC-USZ62-97104])*

He held that mental illness results from natural causes, not from possession by demons as was believed by many. He was convinced that many cases of mental illness could be cured, as they stemmed from physical illness, and he advocated humane treatment for the mentally ill, a major departure from the conventional wisdom that held that the insane should be incarcerated in prison-like conditions, sometimes in chains. In 1812 he published *Medical Inquiries and Observations upon the Diseases of the Mind,* the first American treatise on mental illness and psychiatry.

In addition to his medical career, Rush enjoyed a noteworthy public career as well. He served in the Pennsylvania state legislature and the Continental Congress, and while in the latter body he signed the Declaration of Independence. From 1797 to 1813 he served as treasurer of the U.S. Mint, which was located in Philadelphia. He died on April 19, 1813, in Philadelphia.

Further Reading

Binger, Carl A. *Revolutionary Doctor: Benjamin Rush, 1746–1813.* New York: Norton, 1966.

Corner, George W., ed. *The Autobiography of Benjamin Rush.* Princeton, N.J.: Princeton University Press, 1948.

Goodman, Nathan G. *Benjamin Rush, Physician and Citizen, 1746–1813.* Philadelphia: University of Pennsylvania Press, 1934.

King, Lester S. *Transformations in American Medicine: From Benjamin Rush to William Osler.* Baltimore, Md.: Johns Hopkins University Press, 1991.

Russell, Henry N.
(Henry Norris Russell)
(1877–1957) *astrophysicist*

Henry Norris Russell was one of the leading astronomers of his day. He was also one of the first astrophysicists, astronomers who use physics as a tool for understanding the heavenly bodies.

Russell was born on October 25, 1877, in Oyster Bay, New York. His father, Alexander, was a minister, and his mother, Eliza, was a homemaker. After receiving a private school education, he entered Princeton University at age 16 and received a B.A.

in mathematics in 1897 and a Ph.D. in astronomy in 1900. He spent the next five years doing postdoctoral research at Cambridge University in England, and then in 1905 he returned to teach at Princeton. In 1908 he married Lucy Cole with whom he had four children; four years later he was named director of Princeton's observatory, a position he held for the rest of his career.

As an undergraduate, Russell became interested in binary stars, two stars that revolve around a common center of gravity. By the time he began teaching at Princeton he had devised two ways to determine the orbits of binary stars around each other. He later devised a method for calculating the masses of binary stars from their orbital behavior and for using information about their orbits and masses to calculate their distance from each other. Even at this early stage of his development, Russell was an unusual astronomer for his day in that he was not interested only in observing and cataloging what he observed. His was a more modern approach to astronomy in that he preferred to develop theories regarding the history and evolution of stars and then attempt to prove or disprove them via his observations. This approach led him to develop two important theories concerning stellar evolution, both of which bear his name.

By 1909 Russell had discovered that a definite correlation exists between a star's intrinsic brightness and its spectral classification type. This discovery led him to realize that there are two main classes of stars—dwarves (about the size of the Sun) and giants (which are not as common or as bright as dwarves). Whereas giants all possess the same intrinsic brightness, the brightness of dwarves varies according to their color. During the mid-1910s, both Russell and Danish astronomer Ejnar Hertzsprung, who worked independently of one another, developed a chart, known today as the Hertzsprung-Russell (HR) Diagram, that demonstrates the relationship between a star's brightness and its type or color.

Unlike Hertzsprung, who seemed content merely to state the relationship in diagram form, Russell moved beyond the discovery into the realm of theory. He concluded that a star's color indicates at what point in the "evolutionary" process it is. Russell theorized that the giants are actually young stars, and as such they are relatively cool. As giants age, their masses compress due to gravitational contraction and they become dwarves, but this process also makes them hotter. Eventually a star begins to burn itself out and cool down. Russell theorized from studying spectrograms—photographs of a star's spectral lines—that as giants heat up, they turn from red to yellow to white to blue, and they repeat this sequence as they age until they complete their evolutionary cycle by turning into small, cool red stars. Russell's theory was published in *Encyclopaedia Britannica* in 1929, and it greatly influenced the thinking of astronomers for years to come about the nature and process of stellar evolution. In recent years, much data has been collected to demonstrate that Russell's theory is incorrect; nevertheless, his thoughts on the matter inspired many of his colleagues to think more theoretically about their own work.

After World War I, Russell became interested in the physical composition of stars. He was led to this line of investigation by the work of Indian astronomer Megnad Saha, who showed that much could be learned about stars by examining their physical properties. Beginning in 1921, Russell began collaborating closely with GEORGE ELLERY HALE, whose research demonstrated that the elements making up the stars can be identified by comparing their spectral lines to the spectral lines of the basic elements. By 1931 Russell had published a number of articles concerning astrophysics, or the physics of outer space, in the *Astronomical Journal* and the *Astrophysical Journal*. The most important of these articles was a quantitative analysis of the elements making up the Sun's atmos-phere. He later expanded on this analysis by developing the Russell mixture, a composition of the elements that make up the atmospheres of most of the stars closest to Earth. Although it was greeted with much criticism at the time, today astrophysicists recognize the validity of the Russell mixture for most of the stars that are close to Earth.

Russell operated on the cutting edge of astrophysics in its early days. In addition to publishing his work for the benefit of his colleagues, he also strove to make his work understandable to the general educated public. With Raymond S. Dugan and John Q. Stewart, he authored the popular two-volume textbook, *Astronomy* (1926–27, revised in 1938 and 1945). Other popular works include *The Solar System and Its Origin* (1935) and a monthly column in the popular journal *Scientific American* from 1900 to 1943.

Russell presided over the American Astronomical Society, the American Association for the Advancement of Science, and the American Philosophical Society. He was awarded nine medals, including the gold medal of the Royal Astronomical Society of England and Mexico's Order of the Aztec Eagle. In 1947 he retired from Princeton, although he continued to conduct research until his death on February 18, 1957, in Princeton, New Jersey.

Further Reading

DeVorkin, David H. *Henry Norris Russell: Dean of American Astronomers.* Princeton, N.J.: Princeton University Press, 2000.

Shapley, Harlow. "Henry Norris Russell," National Academy of Sciences, *Biographical Memoirs* 32 (1958): pp. 353–378.

S

Sabin, Albert B.
(Albert Bruce Sabin)
(1906–1993) *immunologist*

Albert B. Sabin developed an oral vaccine for poliomyelitis, commonly known as polio. Before the vaccine, polio had been one of the major childhood diseases, killing or paralyzing hundreds of thousands of children around the world every year. After the vaccine, polio virtually disappeared as a threat to the health of children in the developed world.

Sabin was born on August 26, 1906, in Bialystok, Russia (today part of Poland). His parents, Jacob and Tillie, were silk weavers. At age 13 he emigrated with his family from Russia to the United States; they lived for awhile in Paterson, New Jersey, before settling in New York City. After completing his undergraduate work at New York University in 1927, he entered its college of medicine and received an M.D. in 1931. He spent the next two years on the medical staff at Bellevue Hospital, followed by two years of research as a National Research Council fellow at the Lister Institute of Preventive Medicine in London, England. In 1935 he returned to New York City to join the research staff of the Rockefeller Institute for Medical Research (today Rockefeller University). That same year he married Sylvia Tregillus with whom he had two children. She died in 1966, and in 1970 he married Jane Warner. They divorced the following year, and in 1972 he married Heloisa de Branchis. In 1930 he became a naturalized U.S. citizen.

Sabin began studying polio in the early 1930s, following the outbreak of a major polio epidemic in New York City. In 1936 he and Peter Olitsky, a Rockefeller colleague, cultivated poliovirus in a sample of human nervous tissue in the laboratory; this development made it much easier to study the way the virus grows and spreads. In 1939 he became chief of the division of infectious diseases at the Children's Hospital Research Foundation of the University of Cincinnati, where he also taught pediatrics. These appointments allowed him to greatly expand his research efforts concerning polio because he could develop a group of patients whom he could watch closely while also conducting research in the laboratory. In 1941 he demonstrated that poliovirus does not enter the body through the nose, as had been believed. Instead, he showed that it enters through the throat and infects the digestive tract, from where it spreads to the central nervous system.

Sabin's polio research was interrupted by World War II, during which he conducted research concerning a number of infectious diseases to which U.S. troops were being exposed. While attached to the preventive medicine division of the Office of the U.S. Surgeon General, he developed a vaccine for Japanese encephalitis. He also began the work that eventually led to the development of vaccines for sandfly fever and dengue fever.

Upon returning to Cincinnati after the war, Sabin began trying to make a vaccine for polio. He cloned the three strains of poliovirus but in such a way that they were greatly weakened, and then he demonstrated that the weakened strains would grow in the digestive tracts of chimpanzees without causing paralysis. By 1954 he had developed a vaccine from the three weakened strains that could be put on a sugar cube and taken orally. Over the next five years, the vaccine was tested thoroughly and extensively in the United States and five other countries, including a trial involving six million people in the Soviet Union. The trial's success led Soviet authorities to give the vaccine to another 77 million people under the age of 21 in 1960.

By 1961 Sabin's oral vaccine had been approved for general use in the United States, and the American Medical Association had recommended that the vaccine be given to as many people as possible as quickly as possible. Between 1962 and 1964 more than 100 million Americans, the majority of them young people, received the vaccine. It was administered on Sundays by health-care personnel at high schools and National Guard armories around the country, with people waiting patiently in line for hours to receive the cherry-flavored vaccine on a sugar cube. It has been estimated that Sabin's vaccine, along with a killed-virus vaccine developed in the early 1950s by JONAS E. SALK, save a combined total of 600,000 lives each year. In recognition of his contribution to the health of the world's children, Sabin was presented with more than 100 major awards from around the world, including the National Medal of Science, the Presidential Medal of Freedom, and the U.S. Medal of Liberty. He was elected to the National Academy of Sciences and the American Academy of Arts and Sciences.

Sabin continued to experiment with infectious diseases until he retired from Cincinnati in 1970. Over the next 18 years he served as president of the Weizmann Institute of Science in Israel, worked as a consultant to the National Cancer Institute and the National Institutes of Health, and taught biomedicine at the University of South Carolina College of Medicine. He retired permanently in 1988, and he died on March 3, 1993, in Washington, D.C.

Further Reading
Paul, John R. *A History of Poliomyelitis.* New Haven, Conn.: Yale University Press, 1971.

Sabin Vaccine Institute. "The Legacy of Albert B. Sabin." Available online. URL: http://www.sabin.org/who_legacy.htm. Downloaded on April 15, 2004.

Sabin, Florence
(Florence Rena Sabin)
(1871–1953) *anatomist*

Florence Sabin was the foremost female medical researcher of her day. Her long list of firsts includes being the first woman elected to the National Academy of Sciences.

Sabin was born on November 9, 1871, in Central City, Colorado. Her father, George, was a mining engineer, and her mother, Serena, was a homemaker. At age four she moved with her family to Denver. Three years later Sabin's mother died, and she and her sister were sent to live with an uncle in Chicago, Illinois. After 1882 Sabin lived with relatives in Vermont and boarded at the Vermont Academy, a preparatory school for girls. In 1889 she entered Smith College in Massachusetts and received a B.S. in mathematics and zoology four years later. After graduation she taught school for three years, and by 1896 she had saved enough money to attend Johns Hopkins University's medical school.

While a student, Sabin demonstrated her gifts for research and teaching by developing a model of an infant's middle and lower brain. The model was later included in *An Atlas of the Medulla and Midbrain* (1901), which became a standard text on the subject. After receiving an M.D. in 1900, she spent a year as an intern at Johns Hopkins's hospital followed by a year as a research assistant to Franklin Mall, who chaired Johns Hopkins's department of anatomy. In 1902 she was hired by Johns Hopkins to teach anatomy, thus becoming the school's first woman professor.

Sabin spent the next 23 years teaching anatomy and conducting research in embryology and histology, the study of tissues. Her specialty was the lymphatic system, which maintains the balance of fluids in tissues while removing harmful bacteria. At the time, most anatomists thought that lymph vessels developed in the embryo from spaces in the tissues, but Sabin proved that instead they bud

Florence Sabin was a world-renowned anatomist, but her research also helped eliminate tuberculosis as a killer disease. *(Library of Congress, Prints and Photographs Division [LC-USZ62-10273])*

from veins. She published her findings in *The Method and Growth of the Lymphatic System* (1913). Her discovery created a considerable amount of controversy at first, but before long it was recognized as being a major contribution to modern medicine's understanding of the lymphatic system.

While studying the embryonic development of the lymphatic system, Sabin had used a method called supravital staining. Popular in Germany, where she had learned about it while on a visit, supravital staining was relatively unknown in the United States. Her work with the lymphatic system helped demonstrate its usefulness as a medical research technique.

In 1917 Mall died, and many observers expected that Sabin would be appointed to take his place as department chair. She was not, probably because of her gender. Instead, she was made a full professor, the first woman to be so recognized by

Johns Hopkins. Unlike most of her friends and supporters, she seemed unperturbed at being passed over, and she continued to teach and conduct research at Johns Hopkins for another seven years.

In 1924 Sabin was elected to a two-year term as president of the American Association of Anatomists, the first woman to be so honored. The following year she received two more honors: election to the National Academy of Sciences, and an invitation to become a full member of the Rockefeller Institute of Medical Research (later Rockefeller University) in New York City. The institute was one of the most important medical research centers in the world, and Sabin accepted its offer to set up a section on cellular immunology. For the next 13 years she conducted research at the institute concerning the immune system, particularly the way it responds to the production and development of tuberculosis. Her research contributed to the steady decline of tuberculosis as a killer disease in the latter half of the 20th century.

In 1938 Sabin retired from the Rockefeller Institute and returned to Denver to be near her sister. Six years later, at age 73, she was appointed to chair the subcommittee on health of Colorado's Post-War Planning Committee. For the next seven years she strove mightily to address the mountain of problems that prevented Colorado from providing sufficient public health care for its residents. She lobbied state legislators for increased funding for public health facilities, staff, and training, and she helped author a collection of statutes related to public health known as the Sabin Program, most of which was passed into law in 1947. From 1947 to 1951 she also chaired Denver's board of health and hospitals.

Sabin retired from public service in 1951 to take care of her sister, who was in poor health. Florence Sabin died, having never married, on October 3, 1953, in Denver.

Further Reading

Bailey, Martha J. *American Women in Science: A Biographical Dictionary.* Santa Barbara, Calif.: ABC-CLIO, 1994, pp. 343–344.

Bleumel, Elinor. *Florence Sabin: Colorado Woman of the Century.* Boulder: University of Colorado Press, 1959.

Yount, Lisa. *A to Z of Women in Science and Math.* New York: Facts On File, 1999, pp. 186–188.

Salk, Jonas
(Jonas Edward Salk)
(1914–1995) *immunologist*

Jonas Salk developed the first vaccine for poliomyelitis, commonly known as polio. Although the Salk vaccine was eventually replaced in terms of popularity by ALBERT B. SABIN's vaccine, Salk is still remembered for the seminal role he played in ridding the world of polio, at one time a major childhood disease that killed or paralyzed hundreds of thousands of children every year.

Salk was born on October 28, 1914, in New York City. His father, Daniel, was a clothing designer, and his mother, Dora, was a homemaker. At age 15 he entered the City College of New York and received a B.S. degree in 1933. He then enrolled in the New York University (NYU) School of Medicine and received an M.D. in 1939. That same year he married Donna Lindsay with whom he had three children. They later divorced, and in 1967 he married Françoise Gilot.

After finishing an internship at New York's Mount Sinai Hospital, in 1942 Salk went to the University of Michigan School of Public Health on a National Research Council fellowship. At Michigan he renewed his acquaintance with Thomas Francis, a former professor at NYU who now headed Michigan's department of epidemiology. Francis was developing a vaccine against influenza for the U.S. military, which had just entered World War II, and Salk became one of his assistants. They soon discovered that influenza virus that had been killed in a solution of formaldehyde no longer had the power to infect, but it did stimulate the production of antibodies. By 1943 they had produced a killed-virus influenza vaccine that was effective against both the A and B strains of influenza.

In 1946 Salk was named a professor of epidemiology at Michigan, but he left a year later to become a professor of bacteriology at the University of Pittsburgh School of Medicine's Virus Research Laboratory. Over the next three years he built up the laboratory into one of the foremost centers for viral research in the United States. By 1950 he had also become interested primarily in developing a vaccine for polio, largely as a result of two unre-

lated factors. First, in 1949 JOHN F. ENDERS, THOMAS H. WELLER, and FREDERICK C. ROBBINS had developed a method for growing poliovirus in the laboratory, an accomplishment that made it much easier for immunologists to study polio. Second, Salk had gained the confidence of Daniel B. O'Connor, director of the National Foundation for Infantile Paralysis (today the March of Dimes), who placed his organization's financial support behind Salk.

In 1951 Salk's research showed that there are three strains of poliovirus—I, II, and III, also known as Brunhilde, Lansing, and Leon—meaning that an effective polio vaccine would have to immunize against all three strains. Using techniques similar to those he had used at Michigan to develop the influenza vaccine, by 1952 he had developed a polio vaccine from the killed viruses of all three strains. Field testing proved to be highly

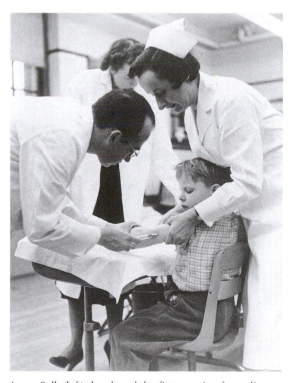

Jonas Salk (left) developed the first vaccine for polio. *(Library of Congress, Prints and Photographs Division [LC-USZ62-92227])*

successful, and he published his findings in 1953. A mass field trial of the vaccine was conducted in 1954, with similar success, and in 1955 the Salk vaccine was approved for use in the United States. By 1961 more than 200 million doses of the Salk vaccine had been administered in the United States, and it was estimated that the vaccine reduced the incidence of polio in this country by 96 percent.

Although the Salk vaccine was highly effective, it was difficult to administer, as it had to be injected via three shots, one for each poliovirus strain, plus a follow-up booster shot. In 1961 the Salk vaccine was largely replaced by the Sabin vaccine, an oral live-virus polio vaccine that had to be taken only once, and the Sabin vaccine remains the polio vaccine of choice today. Nevertheless, Salk's name is still synonymous with the polio vaccine, and for developing it he received a number of honors, including the Presidential Medal of Freedom.

In 1958 Salk began working on a vaccine to immunize against all the viruses that affect the central nervous system. This project led him to conduct some research concerning viruses as a possible cause of multiple sclerosis and cancer. In 1960 he left Pittsburgh for La Jolla, California, where he founded the Salk Institute for Biological Studies. Funded largely by the March of Dimes, the Institute became an innovative center for medical and scientific research, particularly concerning molecular biology and genetics, the neurosciences, and plant biology. Meanwhile, Salk continued his work with vaccines, and the latter part of his career was devoted to finding a vaccine for the human immunodeficiency virus (HIV), which causes AIDS. He died on June 23, 1995, in La Jolla.

Further Reading

Carter, Richard. *Breakthrough: The Saga of Jonas Salk.* New York: Trident Press, 1966.

Salk Institute for Biological Studies. "Jonas Salk." Available online. URL: http://www.salk.edu/jonassalk. Downloaded on May 7, 2004.

Sherrow, Victoria. *Jonas Salk.* New York: Facts On File, 1993.

Schally, Andrew V.
(Andrew Victor Schally)
(1926–) *neuroendocrinologist*

Andrew V. Schally was a cofounder of the field of neuroendocrinology, the study of how the central nervous system controls the endocrine system, which comprises all the glands that secrete hormones. For this achievement he was awarded a share of the 1977 Nobel Prize in physiology or medicine.

Schally was born on November 30, 1926, in Wilno, Poland, to Casimir and Maria Schally. In 1939 he moved with his family to Romania following the outbreak of World War II, relocating in 1945 to Scotland where he completed his secondary education the following year. He then enrolled in the University of London in England to study chemistry, receiving an undergraduate degree in 1950. After graduation he obtained a junior research position with the National Institute for Medical Research in London, leaving in 1952 to study endocrinology at McGill University in Montreal, Canada, where he received a Ph.D. in 1957. That same year he became a professor of physiology at the Baylor University College of Medicine in Houston, Texas. Schally was married twice: to Margaret White, with whom he had two children, and to Ana Maria de Medeiros-Comaru. In 1962 he became a naturalized U.S. citizen.

Schally's early research in endocrinology involved adrenocorticotropic hormone (ACTH), a hormone produced by the pituitary gland that regulates the activities of the adrenal cortex. This study led him to study the relationship between the hypothalamus, an integral part of the brain located at the base of the brain just above the pituitary, and the endocrine system. At the time it was known that the hormones secreted by the pituitary gland induced the other endocrine glands to secrete their various hormones, but no one knew what mechanism triggered the pituitary to produce its hormones. In the 1930s English anatomist Geoffrey W. Harris had suggested that the hypothalamus controls the pituitary by secreting hormones of its own, but he had not been able to identify a specific hypothalamic hormone.

In 1955 Schally demonstrated the presence of corticotrophin-releasing hormone (CRH) in the tissues of the hypothalamus and the pituitary, a strong indication that CRH was the hypothalamic hormone that Harris had predicted. Shortly after arriving at Baylor, Schally began collaborating with ROGER GUILLEMIN, a fellow Baylor physiology professor, in an effort to prove that the hypothalamus regulates the pituitary via the secretion of CRH. Unfortunately, their work proceeded very slowly, mostly because CRH is secreted in infinitesimally small amounts. In fact, they isolated such a small amount of CRH that Schally's 1955 findings were called into question. They parted ways in 1960 when Guillemin began conducting research at the Collège de France in Paris as well as at Baylor. Two years later Schally left Baylor to become director of the Endocrine and Polypeptide Laboratories at the Veterans Administration (VA) Medical Center in New Orleans, Louisiana, and to teach at the Tulane University School of Medicine.

Despite ending their partnership, Schally and Guillemin continued to search for the hypothalamic hormone, and they each assembled their own research team for that purpose. Their quest was made much easier after 1959, when ROSALYN YALOW announced the development of a technique known as radioimmunoassay (RIA), which she had developed as a way to measure tiny amounts of biochemical products in blood and other bodily fluids. Using RIA to study the contents of several tons of sheep hypothalamuses, in 1966 Schally isolated thyrotropin-releasing hormone (TRH), the hypothalamic hormone that induces the pituitary to stimulate the thyroid. Two years later Guillemin determined the chemical structure of TRH. In 1971 Schally and Guillemin both discovered a second hypothalamic hormone, known both as luteinizing hormone-releasing hormone (LHRH) and gonadotropin-releasing hormone (GnRH), which induces the pituitary to secrete two hormones that stimulate the production of male and female sex hormones by the gonads. That same year Schally's team determined the chemical composition of LHRH/GnRH, while Guillemin's team isolated a third hypothalamic hormone, somatostatin, which inhibits the release of growth hormone by the pituitary.

Schally and Guillemin's work cofounded the field of neuroendocrinology by showing that the brain, specifically the hypothalamus, is directly responsible for regulating the secretions of the endocrine glands. Today it is known that the hypothalamus translates electrical neural impulses, particularly those related to emotion and stress, into hormones that ultimately control the secretion of all hormones produced by the endocrine system. In addition, as a result of Schally and Guillemin's work medical researchers were better able to understand diseases and conditions related to dysfunctions of the endocrine system such as thyroid diseases, problems of infertility, diabetes, and several types of tumors. The two were recognized for their contributions to neuroendocrinology when they each received a quarter share of the 1977 Nobel Prize in physiology or medicine; the winner of the other half share was Yalow.

After receiving the Nobel Prize, Schally continued to conduct research relative to neuroendocrinology at the VA Medical Center. His other honors include election to the National Academy of Sciences and the American Association for the Advancement of Science.

Further Reading

Nobelprize.org. "The Nobel Prize in Physiology or Medicine 1977." Available online. URL: http://nobelprize.org/medicine/laureates/1977. Downloaded on June 26, 2004.

Wade, Nicholas. *The Nobel Duel: Two Scientists' 21-Year Race to Win the World's Most Coveted Research Prize.* Garden City, N.Y.: Anchor Press/Doubleday, 1981.

Wasson, Tyler, ed. *Nobel Prize Winners.* New York: H. W. Wilson, 1987, pp. 928–930.

Schawlow, Arthur L.
(Arthur Leonard Schawlow)
(1921–1999) *physicist*

Arthur L. Schawlow coinvented the laser and then developed techniques for using it to study the inner workings of atoms and molecules. For this development he was awarded a share of the 1981 Nobel Prize in physics.

Schawlow was born on May 5, 1921, in Mount Vernon, New York. His father, Arthur, was an insurance salesman, and his mother, Helen, was a homemaker. At age three he moved with his family to

Toronto, Canada, where he grew up. At age 16 he entered the University of Toronto where he received a B.S., an M.S., and a Ph.D. in physics in 1941, 1944, and 1949, respectively. He spent the next two years conducting postdoctoral research at Columbia University in New York City, and in 1951 he went to work as a research physicist for Bell Telephone Laboratories (BTL) in Murray Hill, New Jersey. That same year he married Aurelia Townes (sister of CHARLES H. TOWNES) with whom he had three children.

Schawlow's primary research interest was spectroscopy, the study of atoms and molecules by observing the light spectra they emit. At Columbia he collaborated with Charles H. Townes on the use of microwave spectroscopy to determine an atom's magnetic moment, a function of its magnetic strength. His work at BTL focused on superconductivity, the complete disappearance of electrical resistance in various solids when they are cooled to temperatures approaching absolute zero, but on the weekends he continued to collaborate with Townes. One result of this collaboration was *Microwave Spectroscopy* (1955), which they coauthored; another was the modification of the maser, which Townes had developed in 1953. "Maser" is an acronym for Microwave Amplification by Stimulated Emission of Radiation, and a maser produces and amplifies electronic radiation in the microwave region of the light spectrum.

Schawlow's idea was to extend the principles of the maser to the much shorter wavelengths of visible light. He wanted to produce a spectroscopic device that used visible light to produce coherent light—light in which the photons, or packets of light energy, have the same wavelength and oscillate in phase with each other. Working from a theory advanced by ALBERT EINSTEIN in 1917, Schawlow reasoned that such a device could develop coherent light so intense that, when beamed into an atom or molecule, the target would be stimulated to emit light of the same wavelength that could then be used to study the target's properties with extreme accuracy. By 1958 he and Townes had worked out the theoretical underpinnings of optical maser operation. At that point, Schawlow and his colleagues at BTL set out to build an optical maser, and in 1960 Theodore H. Maiman succeeded in building one.

Maiman's laser consisted of a helical flash lamp, a device used by photographers to produce brief, intense emissions of light, wrapped around a rod made from a ruby crystal. Shortly thereafter, the optical maser became known as the laser, which stands for Light Amplification by Stimulated Emission of Radiation.

In 1961 Schawlow became a professor of physics at Stanford University. Over the next 27 years he developed a series of new and improved lasers by replacing the ruby crystal with ions of inert gas and by using certain organic dyes that exhibit laser action that can be tuned to a wide range of frequencies. He also oversaw a research group that developed a number of advanced methods for using the laser as a spectroscopic device. Their work led to the development of new theoretical models for understanding the behavior of atoms and molecules in a much more sophisticated way. Designed as a spectroscopic tool, the laser quickly found a host of other uses as well. In 1975 Schawlow and Theodor Hänsch, a Stanford colleague, laid the theoretical groundwork for using a laser to cool atoms in a vapor to within fractions of a degree above absolute zero. More recently, lasers have been used to repair detached retinas, and they are employed extensively in long-distance optical fiber communications, to name but two of the countless number of applications to which they have been put to use. For coinventing the laser and for his groundbreaking contributions to laser spectroscopy, Schawlow was awarded a quarter share of the 1981 Nobel Prize in physics.

Schawlow retired from Stanford in 1991. His many honors include the National Medal of Science and election to the National Academy of Sciences and the American Academy of Arts and Sciences. He was also elected to terms as president of the Optical Society of America and the American Physical Society. He died on April 28, 1999, at his home in Stanford.

Further Reading

Chu, Steven, and Charles H. Townes. "Arthur Schawlow," National Academy of Sciences, *Biographical Memoirs* 83 (2003): pp. 196–215.

Nobelprize.org. "The Nobel Prize in Physics 1981." Available online. URL: http://nobelprize.org/physics/laureates/1981. Downloaded on August 29, 2004.

Wasson, Tyler, ed. *Nobel Prize Winners*. New York: H. W. Wilson, 1987, pp. 930–933.

Schrieffer, J. Robert
(John Robert Schrieffer)
(1931–   ) *physicist*

J. Robert Schrieffer won a share of the 1972 Nobel Prize for his contributions to the BCS theory. This theory explains superconductivity, the ability of certain metals to lose all resistance to electron flow in extreme low-temperature conditions.

Schrieffer was born on May 31, 1931, in Oak Park, Illinois, to John and Louise Schrieffer. At age nine he moved with his family to Manhasset, New York, and at age 16 to Eustis, Florida, where his parents bought a citrus grove. As an undergraduate at the Massachusetts Institute of Technology, he became interested in solid-state physics, or the science of semiconductors, elements that are neither good conductors of electricity nor good insulators. At the time, transistors, which are made from semiconductors, were replacing vacuum tubes as the primary devices for controlling and amplifying electric current in electronic applications. After receiving a B.S. in physics in 1953, he chose to attend graduate school at the University of Illinois at Urbana because JOHN BARDEEN, one of the founders of solid-state physics, was teaching electrical engineering and physics there.

During his first two years at Illinois, Schrieffer conducted research regarding the conduction of electricity on semiconductor surfaces, for which he received an M.S. in 1954. Meanwhile, Bardeen had become interested in superconductivity. Superconductivity was discovered in the 1910s, but 40 years later it remained somewhat of a mystery. By 1955 Bardeen had concluded that superconductivity results from some sort of unusual interaction that takes place between the electrons in the metal atoms and the electrons flowing through the metal, or superconductor. For the most part, however, the scientific community rejected this theory on the grounds that electrons repel each other just like the negative poles of two bar magnets repel each other.

In 1955 Schrieffer joined Bardeen and LEON N. COOPER in a project to verify Bardeen's theory.

Within a year, Cooper discovered what is now called Cooper pairs. In a Cooper pair, one electron in the superconductor forms a bond with an electron flowing through the superconductor. As the number of Cooper pairs increases, they interact with each other in such a way that completely eliminates the superconductor's resistance to the flow of electricity. Schrieffer's contribution to the collaboration was a mathematical model that explains why Cooper pairs behave as they do. In 1957 Bardeen, Cooper, and Schrieffer published their findings, which today are known as the BCS theory. Almost 50 years later, the BCS theory remained the most convincing explanation for superconductivity, and as such it informed all research involving superconductors. Since superconductivity promises to revolutionize the way electricity is transmitted and applied in a number of electronic applications, its elucidation is of tremendous importance for practical as well as theoretical reasons, and in 1972 Schrieffer, Bardeen, and Cooper were each awarded a one-third share of the Nobel Prize in physics.

In 1957 Schrieffer received a Ph.D. in physics from Illinois. His scientific career from that point on was devoted to studying superconductivity, especially in conditions of high temperature and strong magnetism, but he carried out his studies in a variety of places. After spending a year as a National Science Foundation fellow at the University of Birmingham in England and the Niels Bohr Institute in Copenhagen, Denmark, in 1958 he became a professor of physics at the University of Chicago. He left the following year to return to Illinois as a faculty member, but left after three years to accept a similar position at the University of Pennsylvania. In 1980 he went to the University of California at Santa Barbara (UCSB), where from 1984 to 1989 he served as director of the Institute for Theoretical Physics. He left UCSB in 1992 to become chief scientist at the National High Magnetic Field Laboratory at Florida State University, where he remained for the rest of his career.

In 1960 Schrieffer married Anne Thomsen with whom he had three children. His publications include *Theory of Superconductivity* (1964). His honors include the National Medal of Science, election to the National Academy of Sciences and the

American Academy of Arts and Sciences, and a term as president of the American Physical Society.

Further Reading

The Nobel Prize Internet Archive. "J. Robert Schrieffer." Available online. URL: http://almaz.com/nobel/physics/1972c.html. Downloaded on March 25, 2005.

Nobelprize.org. "The Nobel Prize in Physics 1972." Available online. URL: http://nobelprize.org/physics/laureates/1972. Downloaded on September 21, 2004.

Wasson, Tyler, ed. *Nobel Prize Winners*. New York: H. W. Wilson, 1987, pp. 215–216.

Schwartz, Melvin
(1932–) *physicist*

Melvin Schwartz initiated the development of the neutrino beam method for studying the weak nuclear interactions, the forces by which certain subatomic particles decay radioactively. He also used that method to discover the muon neutrino. For these contributions he was awarded a share of the 1988 Nobel Prize in physics.

Schwartz was born on November 2, 1932, in New York City, to Harry and Hannah Schwartz. Having decided to become a physicist while attending the Bronx High School for Science, he majored in physics at New York's Columbia University, receiving a B.S. in 1953 and a Ph.D. in 1958. He remained at Columbia for the next seven years as a member of the faculty. In 1953 he married Marilyn Fenster with whom he had two children.

In 1956 FREDERICK REINES and Clyde L. Cowan, Jr., had discovered the neutrino, a subatomic particle with no electrical charge and virtually no mass. Because of its charge and mass, a neutrino rarely interacts with matter, but when it does the result is either an electron or a muon, a particle that carries the same electrical charge (negative) as an electron but that has about 200 times the mass. Physicists wondered if this meant that there are two different types of neutrinos, so Schwartz convinced LEON M. LEDERMAN and JACK STEINBERGER, two of his Columbia colleagues, to attempt to find out. In short order they devised an experiment that required the services of the alternating gradient synchrotron (AGS), a particle accelerator that

energizes subatomic particles to extremely high energy levels, at the nearby Brookhaven National Laboratory. AGS generated a beam of high-energy protons that were fired into a block of the metal beryllium, thus blasting the beryllium atoms into billions of subatomic particles, including approximately one hundred thousand billion neutrinos. The blast drove the particles through a 40-foot-thick barrier of steel plates, which removed all of the particles except the neutrinos. Upon emerging from the steel barrier, the neutrinos entered a detector consisting of 90 one-inch aluminum sheets with a layer of neon gas separating each sheet. Of the billions of neutrinos that passed through the detector, a grand total of only 51 were captured, but this was enough for the three experimenters to study their properties. By 1962 Schwartz and his collaborators had verified the existence of two distinct types of neutrinos: electron neutrinos, which generate electrons, and muon neutrinos, which generate muons.

The "two-neutrino experiment," as it became known, demonstrated the existence of the previously unknown muon neutrino. Perhaps more important, it provided physicists with the neutrino beam, a powerful new tool for investigating nuclear forces. Previously, particle accelerators had generated beams of particles that operate according to the strong interactions, so it was difficult for them to investigate the weak interactions, the forces that govern certain types of radioactive decay. Since neutrinos are affected only by weak interactions and not by the strong interactions, the neutrino beam became the perfect tool for investigating the weak interactions, about which little was known. For the role he played in devising and carrying out the two-neutrino experiment, Schwartz was awarded a one-third share of the 1988 Nobel Prize in physics; his corecipients were Lederman and Steinberger.

In 1966 Schwartz left Columbia for California's Stanford University, which had just acquired a state-of-the-art particle accelerator. Over the next 17 years he conducted research concerning pi mesons (the subatomic particles that govern the strong interactions) and K mesons (whose patterns of radioactive decay defy several of the laws of conservation). In 1979 he cofounded and became the chief executive officer of Digital Pathways, Inc., a software development company dedicated to the secure management of data communications, and in 1983 he left Stanford to devote himself full-time to his duties at Digital. In 1991 he returned to New York to be the associate director of high energy and nuclear physics at Brookhaven. His publications include *Principles of Electrodynamics* (1972), and his honors include election to the National Academy of Sciences.

Further Reading

McMurray, Emily J., ed. *Notable Twentieth-Century Scientists.* Detroit: Gale Research, 1995, pp. 1,799–1,801.

Nobelprize.org. "The Nobel Prize in Physics 1988." Available online. URL: http://nobelprize.org/physics/laureates/1988. Downloaded on October 6, 2004.

Stanford Linear Accelerator Center. "Nobel Prize in Physics 1988." Available online. URL: http://www.slac.stanford.edu/library/nobel/nobel1988.html. Downloaded on March 25, 2005.

Schwinger, Julian S.
(Julian Seymour Schwinger)
(1918–1994) *physicist*

Julian S. Schwinger played a major role in overhauling the theories associated with quantum electrodynamics (QED), the body of theory concerning the interactions of charged particles with each other and with electromagnetic radiation. For this achievement, he was awarded a share of the 1965 Nobel Prize in physics.

Schwinger was born on February 12, 1918, in New York City. His father, Benjamin, was a dress manufacturer, and his mother, Belle, was a homemaker. A child prodigy, he taught himself the basic principles of quantum mechanics, the study of subatomic particles, while still in high school. At age 16 he entered the City College of New York, and at age 17 he published two papers in the *Physical Review,* thus becoming perhaps the youngest person to be published in that prestigious journal. This latter feat brought him to the attention of Columbia University's I. I. RABI, who convinced Schwinger to transfer to Columbia where he completed his college education. At age 18 he received an A.B. in physics and in 1939, at age 21, he received a Ph.D.

He spent the next four years as a research associate and physics instructor at the University of California at Berkeley and Purdue University, and the two years after that conducting research related to the development of the atomic bomb and radar during World War II. In 1945 he joined the faculty at Harvard University, and in 1947 he married Clarice Carrol with whom he had no children. In 1972 he retired from Harvard and joined the faculty at the University of California at Los Angeles (UCLA), where he taught until his death.

Schwinger developed an interest in QED while still in high school. QED is concerned primarily with the creation of certain subatomic particles (such as electrons and their positively charged counterparts, positrons) from electromagnetic radiation (such as light), as well as the reverse process by which a particle and its antiparticle of opposite charge (for example, an electron and a positron) negate each other and are converted into electromagnetic radiation. QED also studies the process by which charged particles inside the nucleus interact by emitting and absorbing photons, tiny packets of light that transmit electromagnetic energy. QED originated in 1928 with French physicist Paul Dirac, who described the motion of electrons in terms of quantum theory and ALBERT EINSTEIN's theory of special relativity. He was joined in this endeavor by German physicists Werner Heisenberg and Wolfgang Pauli, both of whom were among the founders of quantum mechanics. These eminent physicists were able to develop equations for calculating certain magnetic properties of the electron and the positron, but they were unable to develop equations from calculating such relatively simple things as the mass and charge of the positron and other particles found in the nucleus, thus calling into question QED's usefulness.

Schwinger's work with radar during World War II had led him to experiment extensively with microwaves, a form of electromagnetic radiation whose use is central to the operation of radar. This line of research led him to address problems related to electromagnetic radiation in terms of the principles of electrical engineering, and once he was settled at Harvard he used this insight to tackle the problems QED had not yet solved. Another key insight was his realization that the reaction of an electron's electromagnetic field alters certain of its properties such as its mass, which led him to reformulate QED's basic equations. By 1954 he had shown that two interacting particles can interact in a number of complex patterns because they change their speed and direction as they release or absorb the energy of a photon. He also developed highly intricate mathematical equations for explaining and predicting these patterns. Much of this work was published in summary form in *Selected Papers on Quantum Electrodynamics* (1958).

Meanwhile, Schwinger's efforts were being duplicated independently by RICHARD P. FEYNMAN and Japanese physicist Shinichiro Tomonaga. Feynman and Tomonaga took a less abstract approach to QED than did Schwinger, whose mathematical equations defied understanding in some cases, but all three arrived at the same basic conclusions and solutions. In this manner, they transformed QED from a theory of questionable value into one of the best working models available to physicists who study quantum mechanics. For his contribution to resuscitating QED, Schwinger was awarded a one-third share of the 1965 Nobel Prize in physics; his cowinners were Feynman and Tomonaga.

After 1954 Schwinger's research took him in a number of directions, but he focused primarily on subatomic particles and the forces that work on them. In 1957 he successfully predicted the existence of two different neutrinos, particles with no electrical charge and virtually no mass, one associated with the electron and one associated with the muon, a negatively charged particle about 200 times larger than an electron. He also developed theories about the forces that hold together nucleons (protons and neutrons), and the forces that hold together quarks, the particles that form nucleons. Much of this work was published in a three-volume work, *Particles, Sources, and Fields* (1970, 1973, 1983).

Schwinger was awarded the National Medal of Science and elected to the National Academy of Sciences. He died on July 16, 1994, in Los Angeles.

Further Reading

Mehra, Jagdish, and Kimball A. Milton. *Climbing the Mountain: The Scientific Biography of Julian Schwinger.* New York: Oxford University Press, 2000.

Nobelprize.org. "The Nobel Prize in Physics 1965." Available online. URL: http://nobelprize.org/physics/laureates/1965. Downloaded on March 29, 2004.

Schweber, Silvan S. *QED and the Men Who Made It: Dyson, Feynman, Schwinger and Tomonaga.* Princeton, N.J.: Princeton University Press, 1994.

Wasson, Tyler, ed. *Nobel Prize Winners.* New York: H. W. Wilson, 1987, pp. 943–945.

Seaborg, Glenn T.
(Glenn Theodore Seaborg)
(1912–1999) *chemist*

Glenn T. Seaborg is best remembered for the role he played in discovering 10 transuranium elements, man-made elements that do not exist in nature. More importantly, however, he explained the relationship of the transuranium elements to the natural elements and placed the transuranium elements in their proper place in the periodic table. For these achievements, he received a share of the 1951 Nobel Prize in chemistry.

Seaborg was born on April 19, 1912, in Ishpeming, Michigan, to Herman and Selma Seaborg. At age 10 he moved with his family to Southgate, California, and they eventually settled in the Los Angeles neighborhood of Watts. After receiving an A.B. in chemistry from the University of California at Los Angeles in 1934, he entered the graduate program at Cal-Berkeley and received a Ph.D. in chemistry in 1937. He spent the next two years as the personal laboratory assistant to Berkeley's GILBERT N. LEWIS, and in 1939 he accepted a position on Berkeley's faculty. In 1942 he married Helen Griggs with whom he had six children.

As a graduate student, Seaborg became interested in the transuranium elements. With an atomic number of 92, uranium is the largest element that occurs in nature. By the late 1930s physicists had learned enough about subatomic particles to reason that if a uranium nucleus could be made to accept one or more neutrons, its atomic number would be increased and the result would be a new element. This possibility was strongly suggested in a 1934 experiment at the University of Rome by ENRICO FERMI and EMILIO SEGRÈ, and in 1938 by German physicists Otto Hahn, Fritz Strassmann, and Lise

Meitner, although the results of both experiments were inconclusive in terms of nuclear fusion. Researchers at Berkeley were especially hopeful that they would succeed in this endeavor, particularly because Berkeley had a state-of-the-art nuclear research facility, the Berkeley Radiation Laboratory, that was equipped with a cyclotron, also known as an "atom smasher." The cyclotron generates an electromagnetic field to accelerate subatomic particles to extremely high velocities and then propels them into atomic nuclei in an effort to create an atomic reaction. In 1940 EDWIN M. MCMILLAN and his colleagues (including, on occasion, Seaborg) used the Berkeley cyclotron to synthesize neptunium, with an atomic number of 93.

In 1940 Seaborg and McMillan became full collaborators. That same year they and their associates bombarded uranium with deuterons, particles consisting of one proton and one neutron, in the process producing an element with an atomic number of 94. Christened plutonium, this new element was similar to neptunium in that both were silvery metals. Unlike neptunium, which has a half-life of 23 minutes, plutonium has a half-life of 24,000 years, thus making it stable enough to be used as an atomic fuel. Later experiments by other researchers showed that plutonium is an even better fuel for a nuclear bomb than uranium, from which the first atomic bomb was made. Because of his work with uranium and plutonium, Seaborg was recruited to work on the Manhattan Project, the federal government's program for building the first atomic bombs. He spent World War II at the University of Chicago's Metallurgical Laboratory, where he oversaw the first industrial production of plutonium.

In 1944 Seaborg advanced the actinide concept, by which he explained the relationship of the transuranium elements to the natural elements. In the periodic table, the natural elements with atomic weights between 1 and 57 (helium and lanthanum, respectively) and between 72 and 89 (hafnium and actinium, respectively) fit logically according to period (the number of rings of electrons) and group (the number of electrons in the outer ring). This pattern is broken by the so-called rare-earth elements, those with atomic weights between 58 and 71 (cerium and lutetium, respec-

tively). The elements behave as if they were quasi isotopes, or variations, of lanthanum. Accordingly, the rare-earth elements are given their own special "row" in the periodic table to signify their peculiar properties; they are also known as the lanthanides. In the 1920s Danish Nobel laureate Niels Bohr theorized that if elements heavier than uranium were ever discovered, they would be as similar to uranium as the rare-earth elements, or lanthanides, are to lanthanum.

Seaborg's actinide concept suggested that Bohr was half right. Seaborg agreed that the transuranium elements were similar, in terms of their chemical behavior, to a lighter element. He suggested, however, that the lighter element was not uranium but actinium, of atomic weight 89. Accordingly, the three heaviest natural elements—thorium, protactinium, and uranium—and all of the transuranium elements are quasi isotopes of actinium. Thus, he labeled these elements the actinides and suggested that they occupy a special row in the periodic table, just as the rare-earth elements do.

After returning to Berkeley in 1946, Seaborg was named director of nuclear chemical research. In this capacity, he continued to experiment with transuranium elements. By 1951 he had played a leading role in the discovery of four more transuranium elements: americium, curium, berkelium, and californium. By experimenting with these new elements, he demonstrated conclusively that they behave almost exactly the way his actinide concept predicted they would. He also demonstrated that a certain chemical agreement can be found, member for member, between the lanthanides and the actinides, based on their placement in their respective rows in the periodic table. For these achievements, Seaborg was awarded a share of the 1951 Nobel Prize in chemistry; his corecipient was his collaborator, Edwin McMillan.

Between 1951 and 1958, Seaborg codiscovered four more transuranium elements: einsteinium, fermium, mendelevium, and nobelium. He left research in 1958 to take over as Berkeley's chancellor, a position he gave up after three years to become chairman of the U.S. Atomic Energy Commission. In 1971 he returned to Berkeley and resumed his research, although he played an active role as a government adviser on policies related to nuclear energy for a number of years thereafter.

In addition to the Nobel Prize, Seaborg received a number of honors during his lifetime. He was elected to the National Academy of Sciences, the American Association for the Advancement of Science, and the American Academy of Arts and Sciences. His many medals include the highest scientific honor in the United States, the National Medal of Science. In 1997 the last of the 10 transuranium elements he codiscovered was named seaborgium in his honor. He died on February 25, 1999, at his home in Lafayette, California.

Further Reading

Nobelprize.org. "The Nobel Prize in Chemistry 1951." Available online. URL: http://nobelprize.org/chemistry/laureates/1951. Downloaded on July 5, 2003.

Seaborg, Glenn T., with Eric Seaborg. *Adventures in the Atomic Age: From Watts to Washington.* New York: Farrar, Straus and Giroux, 2001.

Wasson, Tyler, ed. *Nobel Prize Winners.* New York: H. W. Wilson, 1987, pp. 945–948.

Segrè, Emilio
(Emilio Gino Segrè)
(1905–1989) *physicist*

Emilio Segrè played a major role in the discovery of technetium, astatine, and plutonium, the first three man-made elements. He also codiscovered the antiproton, a proton with a net negative charge, for which he was awarded a share of the 1959 Nobel Prize in physics.

Segrè was born on January 30, 1905 (some sources give February 1), in Tivoli, Italy. His father, Giuseppe, was a factory owner, and his mother, Amelia, was a homemaker. At age 12 he moved with his family to Rome. After studying engineering for a few years at the University of Rome, he changed to physics and received a Ph.D. in 1928; his dissertation was directed by ENRICO FERMI. He spent the next two years in the Italian army, and the two years after that conducting postdoctoral research at the universities of Rome, Hamburg, and Amsterdam. In 1932 he returned to Rome to teach

physics and to serve as Fermi's chief collaborator. In 1936 he married Elfriede Spiro with whom he had three children; she died in 1970, and two years later he married Rosa Mines.

Prior to 1934, all of Segrè's research involved atomic spectroscopy, the study of the structure of atoms by examining the spectra, or waves of light, that they emit. In 1934, however, he and Fermi turned their attention to the study of neutrons. Together they discovered slow neutrons, neutrons that travel at such a speed that, rather than split an atomic nucleus, the process of nuclear fission, they are captured by the nucleus, the process by which the man-made and radioactive elements are produced. Over the next two years Segrè and Fermi used slow neutron bombardment to produce a number of radioactive isotopes (uncommon versions of an element that contain the same number of protons but a different number of neutrons but that behave exactly like the common version) that do not exist in nature. Many of these isotopes were later put to use by researchers as tracers for studying the behavior of certain elements and biochemical compounds.

In 1936 Segrè was named director of the physics laboratory at the University of Palermo. The following year he and a Palermo colleague, Carlo Perrier, discovered element 43, or technetium, as the by-product of molybdenum, which had been bombarded with a hydrogen isotope. Although technetium occupies a place in the middle of the periodic table, it was the first man-made element not found in nature because all of its isotopes are radioactively unstable. Two years later Segrè left Italy for the United States to become a research associate at the University of California at Berkeley's Radiation Laboratory. He continued his work with man-made elements and isotopes, and in 1940 he and two Berkeley colleagues, Dale Corson and K. R. MacKenzie, discovered element 85, or astatine, the second of the human-made elements. The following year he participated with GLENN T. SEABORG and other Berkeley colleagues in the study of plutonium, the first of the transuranium elements because its nucleus has more protons than a nucleus of uranium (the largest element found in nature).

Segrè spent World War II working on the Manhattan Project, the U.S. effort to build an atomic bomb. Upon becoming a naturalized U.S. citizen in 1944, he was named leader of the group at the Los Alamos, New Mexico, research facility that was studying the spontaneous fission rate of plutonium. Their work contributed in a major way to the design of Fat Man, a 21-kiloton plutonium bomb that was dropped on Nagasaki, Japan.

In 1946 Segrè returned to Berkeley, where he was joined two years later by OWEN CHAMBERLAIN, one of the members of his Los Alamos group. Over the next several years Segrè, Chamberlain, and others conducted experiments designed to find and identify antimatter, subatomic particles that are analogous to common particles such as the electron but with opposite charges. In 1928 French physicist Paul Dirac had postulated the existence of a so-called positive electron, a subatomic particle with the same mass as an electron but with a positive rather than a negative charge. Four years later, CARL D. ANDERSON proved Dirac's theory correct by detecting a positively charged particle with a mass about the same as an electron, which he named the positron. Anderson's discovery raised the question as to whether or not the positron was the only form of antimatter, and in 1948 Segrè and Chamberlain set out to answer this question.

Since the neutron has no net charge, it was believed that an antineutron could not exist, so Segrè and Chamberlain set out to find an antiproton, the antiparticle of the proton, which has a net positive charge. They began their work on Berkeley's 184-inch synchrocyclotron, a sophisticated device that generates an electromagnetic field to accelerate subatomic particles to extremely high velocities and then propels them into other particles in an effort to create an atomic reaction. As sophisticated as this device was, however, it was incapable of proving or disproving the question at hand. In 1955 Berkeley brought online an even more sophisticated device known as the bevatron, an extremely powerful synchrocyclotron. That same year Segrè and Chamberlain, assisted by Clyde Wiegand and Thomas Ypsilantis, conducted a number of proton-proton bombardment experiments, and the results clearly showed that antiprotons, protons with a net negative charge, do indeed exist, although they are short-lived. Meanwhile, other subatomic particles such as muons, pions, and K-mesons had been dis-

covered, and researchers eventually discovered that they had antiparticles as well. In 1956 Segrè and Chamberlain discovered the antineutron, which has the same charge as a neutron but a different magnetic moment, a function of its magnetic properties. For discovering the antiproton, Segrè and Chamberlain each received a half share of the 1959 Nobel Prize in physics.

Segrè continued to study antiparticles until his retirement in 1972. He served as editor of *Annual Review of Nuclear Science* for 20 years, and his publications include *Experimental Nuclear Physics* (1953); *Nuclei and Particles: An Introduction to Nuclear and Subnuclear Physics* (1964, 1965, 1977); *Enrico Fermi, Physicist* (1970); *From X-rays to Quarks: Modern Physicists and Their Discoveries* (1980); and *From Falling Bodies to Radio Waves: Classical Physicists and Their Discoveries* (1984). His many honors include election to the National Academy of Sciences. He died on April 22, 1989, in Lawrence, California.

Further Reading

Jackson, J. David. "Emilio Gino Segrè," National Academy of Sciences, *Biographical Memoirs* 81 (2001): pp. 317–338.

Nobelprize.org. "The Nobel Prize in Physics 1959." Available online. URL: http://nobelprize.org/physics/laureates/1959. Downloaded on August 24, 2004.

Segrè, Claudio. *Atoms, Bombs, and Eskimo Kisses: A Memoir of Father and Son.* New York: Viking, 1995.

Segrè, Emilio. *A Mind Always in Motion: The Autobiography of Emilio Segrè.* Berkeley: University of California Press, 1993.

Wasson, Tyler, ed. *Nobel Prize Winners.* New York: H. W. Wilson, 1987, pp. 950–952.

Sharp, Phillip A.
(Phillip Allen Sharp)
(1944–   ) *biologist*

Phillip A. Sharp discovered that genes in higher organisms are "split" in that their DNA contains sequences that translate into valuable genetic coding as well as sequences that translate into nonsense. For this discovery, he was awarded a share of the 1993 Nobel Prize in physiology or medicine.

Sharp was born on June 6, 1944, in Falmouth, Kentucky. He grew up in nearby McKinneysburg where his parents, Joseph and Katherin, owned a farm. After receiving a B.A. in chemistry and mathematics from Union (Ky.) College in 1966, he entered the graduate program at the University of Illinois at Urbana, receiving a Ph.D. in physical chemistry in 1969. In 1964 he married Ann Holcombe with whom he had three children.

After graduating from Illinois, Sharp spent five years doing postdoctoral research in molecular biology at the California Institute of Technology and the Cold Spring Harbor (N.Y.) Laboratory. Sharp's early research during this period focused on the behavior of genes in phages, viruses that infect bacteria, but he soon abandoned phages in favor of animal viruses. He worked briefly with SV40, a virus that causes cancer in simians, before taking up the study of human adenovirus. In humans, adenovirus causes the common cold and other upper respiratory ailments, but when injected into newborn rodents it can cause cancer. By 1974 he had mapped a number of human adenovirus genes, and he had demonstrated which of these genes are responsible for transforming healthy rodent cells into tumors.

In 1974 Sharp became a professor of biology at the Massachusetts Institute of Technology (MIT) and a researcher at its Center for Cancer Research. He continued to study the genetics of human adenovirus, but now from the point of view of how it transcribes its genome, a single set of chromosomes, into the nucleus of the host cell it infects. By using an electron microscope, he was able to observe how a viral gene produces a molecule of messenger RNA (mRNA), the complex molecule that signals the production of a certain protein. In 1977 he discovered that the gene's DNA was not duplicated exactly, but rather that large sections of a DNA string were left out of the corresponding string of mRNA. Previously it was believed that each sequence of proteins in the typical string of DNA carries a portion of its gene's coding, a belief that came from studying the DNA of simple organisms like phages and the bacteria they infect. Human adenovirus, however, has a genetic structure that more closely resembles that of humans, and so its DNA is much more complicated.

Sharp discovered that adenovirus DNA consists of two types of sequences. Some sequences, which he named exons, do indeed carry genetic coding, and these sequences signal messenger RNA (mRNA) to begin the production of specific proteins. Other sequences, which he named introns, are essentially nonsense sequences in that they do not signal mRNA to do anything. A typical adenovirus gene is composed of 15 to 20 exons, many of which are separated by an intron. At first, Sharp believed that during protein synthesis mRNA reads the exons but ignores the introns. Further experimentation showed the existence of a "precursor" mRNA molecule, which encodes introns as well as exons from viral DNA; however, enzymes then splice out the precursor mRNA's introns, leaving only the exons in a mature molecule of mRNA. Lastly he showed that introns are not always spliced out in the same exact way, but rather that the splicing enzymes act as a sort of editor in that they seem to pick and choose which sequences are to be copied and which are to be discarded.

Sharp's work shed some interesting light on the process of evolution in higher organisms. Previously it was thought that genes, and therefore species, evolve slowly because small changes in the genetic material gradually accumulate over a period of years, and this is probably how lower organisms evolve. Today it is thought that higher-order evolution might take place faster, as the process of splicing and editing mRNA makes possible wholesale yet rapid genetic changes. His discoveries further suggested that hereditary diseases or congenital defects might be caused, at least in part, by errors in the splicing/editing process. For these contributions, Sharp was awarded a half share of the 1993 Nobel Prize in physiology or medicine.

Sharp remained at MIT for the rest of his career. He served as director of the Center for Cancer Research from 1985 to 1991, and he chaired the biology department from 1991 to 1999. In 2000 he was named founding director of MIT's McGovern Institute for Brain Research. His many honors include election to the National Academy of Sciences, the American Academy of Arts and Sciences, and the American Association for the Advancement of Science. He served on the President's Advisory Council on Science and Technology, and he cofounded and chaired the scientific board of Biogen, a biotechnology firm headquartered in Geneva, Switzerland.

Further Reading

McMurray, Emily J., ed. *Notable Twentieth-Century Scientists*. Detroit: Gale Research, 1995, pp. 1,820–1,821.

MIT Department of Biology. "Phillip A. Sharp." Available online. URL: http://web.mit.edu/biology/www/facultyareas/facresearch/sharp.shtml. Downloaded on March 25, 2005.

Nobelprize.org. "The Nobel Prize in Physiology or Medicine 1993." Available online. URL: http://nobelprize.org/medicine/laureates/1993. Downloaded on July 23, 2004.

Sharpless, K. Barry
(1941–   ) *chemist*

K. Barry Sharpless developed asymmetric epoxidation, asymmetric dihydroxylation, and asymmetric aminohydroxylation, catalytic techniques that revolutionized the way a number of chemical compounds are produced. For these contributions he was awarded a half share of the 2001 Nobel Prize in chemistry.

Sharpless was born on April 28, 1941, in Philadelphia, Pennsylvania. His father was a physician and his mother was a homemaker. After receiving a B.A. in chemistry from Dartmouth College in 1963, he entered the graduate program at Stanford University, receiving a Ph.D. in organic chemistry in 1968. He spent the next two years conducting postdoctoral research at Stanford and Harvard University, and in 1970 he became a professor of chemistry at the Massachusetts Institute of Technology (MIT). In 1977 he returned to Stanford for three years before going back to MIT, which he left a second time in 1990 for the Scripps Research Institute in La Jolla, California. In 1965 he married Jan Dueser with whom he had three children.

When Sharpless finished graduate school in 1968, chemists were beginning to understand how a molecule's structure, or the three-dimensional arrangement of its atoms, affects its reactivity.

Pharmaceutical chemists had known for years that many of the drugs they produce involve molecules that come in two versions, a "right hand" and a "left hand" version, and that production processes yield roughly equal amounts of both versions. Although the two versions are composed of the exact same atoms, their structures mirror each other as the right hand mirrors the left hand. Moreover, they do not have the same effect as each other; for example, the "right hand" versions of thalidomide eases nausea in pregnant women while the "left hand" version causes serious birth defects. Consequently, the "left hand" versions of many pharmaceuticals had to be separated from the "right hand" versions and discarded, an expensive and time-consuming process. WILLIAM S. KNOWLES, a pharmaceutical chemist, sought a way to avoid producing both "right hand" and "left hand" versions of the same molecule, and in 1968 he developed a catalytic process known as asymmetrical hydrogenation. This process uses a modified catalyst that causes all of the molecules produced during the reaction to be of the "right hand" version, thus preventing the "left hand" version from even being produced.

Like many chemists, Sharpless was greatly impressed by Knowles's feat, and in the early 1970s he set out to see if other asymmetrical catalysts could be developed for reactions involving oxidation, the insertion of oxygen atoms into a molecule. He was particularly interested in converting olefins, hydrocarbon by-products of the refining of crude oil such as ethylene and propylene, into epoxides, oxygen-bearing compounds from which a number of useful products can be derived. Early on he came up with the idea of building the catalyst from tartrate, which is used extensively in baking powders and confections, and a metal. Over the next seven or eight years he experimented with more than two dozen different metals, but in every case, rather than catalyze the reaction so that only "right hand" molecules were produced, the metal prevented the reaction from occurring at all. Finally in 1980 he combined tartrate with titanium, and the result was a catalyst that produced only "right hand" molecules. He spent the next seven years perfecting the catalyst and developing the methods for using it properly before publishing his findings in 1987.

This catalytic process is known today as asymmetric epoxidation.

While he was working out the kinks concerning asymmetric epoxidation, Sharpless was also developing another asymmetric catalytic process for the oxidation of olefins, asymmetric dihydroxylation, which employs a catalyst made from osmium and quinine. Because this catalyst is a ligand (a metal atom attached to a group of nonmetal atoms), the process is also known as ligand-accelerated catalysis. In 1995 he developed a third asymmetrical catalytic process, asymmetric aminohydroxylation.

Like Knowles's asymmetric hydrogenation, Sharpless's three asymmetric catalytic processes provided chemists with powerful new tools for producing pharmaceutical drugs, as well as other products of commercial importance that are derived from olefins. For developing these new catalytic techniques, Sharpless was awarded a half share of the 2001 Nobel Prize in chemistry; one of his corecipients was Knowles and the other was the Japanese chemist Ryoji Noyori.

After 1995 Sharpless and his collaborators continued to develop new methods for selectively controlling chemical reactions. The most interesting one was "click chemistry," the use of high-energy chemical building blocks to catalyze a spontaneous and irreversible linkage reaction with complementary sites in other blocks. They also experimented with the use of chemical and biological receptor structures as templates to guide the formation of click chemistry products, so that the target of the product being produced actually plays a role in the product's development. Sharpless's many honors include election to the National Academy of Sciences and the American Academy of Arts and Sciences.

Further Reading

Chang, Kenneth. "3 Win Nobel for Better Chemical Reactions," *New York Times*, October 11, 2001, p. A20.
Nobelprize.org. "The Nobel Prize in Chemistry 2001." Available online. URL: http://nobelprize.org/chemistry/laureates/2001. Downloaded on August 18, 2004.
The Scripps Research Institute, The Sharpless Lab. "K. Barry Sharpless, Ph.D." Available online. URL: http://www.scripps.edu/chem/sharpless/cv.html. Downloaded on March 25, 2005.

Shockley, William B.
(William Bradford Shockley)
(1910–1989) *physicist*

William B. Shockley was one of the pioneers of solid-state physics, the use of semiconductors rather than vacuum tubes to control and amplify electric current in electronic applications. He and his research partners, WALTER H. BRATTAIN and JOHN BARDEEN, invented the transistor, an electronic device that revolutionized the electronics industry by making it possible to build radios, televisions, computers, and other electronic apparatuses that were smaller, less expensive, more reliable, and more energy-efficient. The technology Shockley and his partners developed and the scientific principles they discovered served as the springboard for the development of the integrated circuit, or computer chip, and the advent of microchip technology. In recognition of his work with solid-state physics, he was awarded a share of the 1956 Nobel Prize in physics.

Shockley was born on February 13, 1910, in London, England. His father, William, was a mining engineer, and his mother, Mary, was a mineral surveyor; both were American citizens. At age three he moved with his family to Palo Alto, California, where he grew up. After spending a year at the University of California at Los Angeles, he transferred to the California Institute of Technology and received a B.S. in physics in 1932. Four years later he received a Ph.D. from the Massachusetts Institute of Technology and went to work at Bell Telephone Laboratories (BTL) in Murray Hill, New Jersey. In 1933 he married Jean Bailey with whom he had three children. They divorced in 1955, after which he married Emily Lanning.

One of Shockley's first colleagues at BTL was Walter H. Brattain. Together they worked to improve an electronic device known as the thermionic valve, also called the vacuum tube because its electrodes are encased in an evacuated glass housing. BTL's parent company, American Telephone & Telegraph (AT&T), had been using vacuum tubes since the mid-1910s to amplify long-distance telephone signals. The vacuum tube performed credibly well at this task, but it was too bulky to fit everywhere it was needed and it had a relatively short life, mostly because the electrodes burned out rather quickly due to the intense heat the tube generated.

Shortly after arriving at BTL, Shockley began thinking about scrapping the vacuum tube altogether and replacing it with something entirely different. He believed a much better electronic amplifier could be built from a semiconductor, a substance that conducts a flow of electrons better than an insulator, such as glass, but not as well as a good conductor, such as copper. Radio manufacturers were already using semiconductors in radio receivers as rectifiers, devices that change alternating current to direct current, and Shockley believed that they could be used as amplifiers as well. Meanwhile, Brattain had been thinking along similar lines, and the two proposed to their superiors that they shift the focus of their research from vacuum tubes to semiconductors. At first BTL managers showed little interest, mostly because they were in the process of developing radar, a major project that demanded a great deal of BTL's resources. When vacuum tubes proved to be inadequate for handling the high-frequency microwave signals that radar requires, Shockley and Brattain were given the go-ahead to proceed with their project.

Shockley and Brattain began studying semiconductors before World War II, but their research was interrupted by the war, during which Shockley served as director of research for the U.S. Navy's Antisubmarine Warfare Operations Research Group. In 1945 he was named director of BTL's solid-state physics program, and he and Brattain were joined by John Bardeen. Shortly thereafter, it occurred to Shockley that the electrons in a semiconductor could be used to amplify an electrical signal flowing into the semiconductor in much the same way that the electrons emitted by the electrodes in a vacuum tube amplify a signal passing through the tube. The group's first attempt to do this, however, failed, thus necessitating a full-blown study of the properties of semiconductors. Led by Brattain, this study revealed that a major factor in a semiconductor's ability to conduct electrons is the percentage of impurities it contains. Further research by Shockley concerning the energy bands of semiconductor crystals showed that impurities in the semiconductor leave "holes" in its crystalline

structure that enhance the flow of electrons through the crystal. His work in this regard was later published in *Electrons and Holes in Semiconductors* (1950) and *Imperfections of Nearly Perfect Crystals* (1952).

Upon completion of these studies, in 1948 Brattain and Bardeen used the semiconductor germanium to construct the first transistor (later, transistors would be made mostly from silicon, a more abundant semiconductor). They passed an incoming electrical current through a wire to one side of a germanium crystal containing a small amount of impurities, and a signal from an electrode to the other side of the crystal. The signal from the electrode was greatly amplified by its passage through the semiconductor, even though the incoming current was much weaker than that required to create the same level of amplification in a vacuum tube. Later, Shockley improved on the efficiency of this device, known as a point-contact transistor, by using a rectifier to connect the wire carrying the amplifying current to the crystal and the wire carrying the amplified signal from the crystal. Shockley's design, known as a junction transistor, became the standard version of the transistor, and in short order the junction transistor and modified versions of it replaced the vacuum tube almost completely. For discovering the so-called transistor effect, the underlying physical principles governing the ability of a semiconductor to amplify electronic signals, Shockley was awarded a one-third share of the 1956 Nobel Prize in physics; he shared the prize with his collaborators, Brattain and Bardeen.

In 1955 Shockley resigned from BTL and established the Shockley Semiconductor Laboratory in Mountain View, California, to design and build transistors for commercial applications. Unfortunately, he was a poor business manager, and within only two years most of his top engineers had left the company to form competing firms of their own. Despite being restructured as Shockley Transistor Corporation, the company never recovered from the defections or Shockley's lack of business sense, and in 1968 it went out of business, its founder having left the company six years earlier. Nevertheless, by establishing his company in Mountain View, Shockley planted the seed that grew into the thriving semiconductor and computer chip industry known today as Silicon Valley.

Meanwhile in 1958 Shockley had begun teaching physics at Stanford University. Four years later he was named professor of engineering and applied sciences, a position he held until his retirement in 1976. His many honors included election to the National Academy of Sciences. He died on August 12, 1989, in Palo Alto.

Further Reading

Moll, John L. "William Bradford Shockley," National Academy of Sciences, *Biographical Memoirs* 68 (1996): pp. 305–324.

Nobelprize.org. "The Nobel Prize in Physics 1956." Available online. URL: http://nobelprize.org/physics/laureates/1956. Downloaded on February 21, 2004.

Wasson, Tyler, ed. *Nobel Prize Winners.* New York: H. W. Wilson, 1987, pp. 962–964.

Shull, Clifford G.
(Clifford Glenwood Shull)
(1915–2001) *physicist*

Clifford G. Shull codeveloped the neutron diffraction technique, a method for studying the atomic structure of liquid and solid matter. For this contribution he was awarded a share of the 1994 Nobel Prize in physics.

Shull was born on September 23, 1915, in Pittsburgh, Pennsylvania. His father, David, owned a hardware store and a home repair business, and his mother, Daisy, was a homemaker. He received a B.A. in physics from Pittsburgh's Carnegie Institute of Technology (today Carnegie-Mellon University) in 1937 and a Ph.D. in physics from New York University in 1941. That same year he married Martha-Nuel Summer, with whom he had three children, and went to work as a research chemist for the Texas Company (today Texaco) in Beacon, New Jersey. In 1946 he joined the staff at the Clinton Laboratory (today the Oak Ridge National Laboratory, or ORNL) in Oak Ridge, Tennessee, a top secret government facility for nuclear energy research.

As a graduate student and a Texaco researcher, Shull learned and used the traditional methods for determining the structure of condensed matter (i.e., liquids and solids) such as crystallography, gas adsorption, X-ray diffraction, and electron diffraction as tools for characterizing the physical structure of petroleum fuels and lubricants. He also experimented with neutron diffraction, specifically the paramagnetic scattering effect certain materials have on a beam of neutrons, and he focused on using this method once he was settled in at ORNL. Ernest Wollan, an ORNL colleague, had been working with neutron diffraction as well, and in 1946 they began experimenting with neutron diffraction as a tool to supplement results obtained via X-ray and electron diffraction.

By 1955 Shull and Wollan were able to show that neutrons, like X-rays and electrons, also diffract, or scatter, in predictable patterns after being beamed into a crystal or other material, and that the angle of diffraction indicates the arrangement of the atoms in the material being tested. However, they also showed that the neutron diffraction technique, unlike other methods, is able to locate the positions of hydrogen atoms in condensed matter, thus making it particularly useful to organic chemists and biochemists. Shull and Wollan also showed that the neutron diffraction technique can be used to demonstrate the magnetic properties of metals and alloys, something that X-ray diffraction cannot do.

Over the next 40 years the neutron diffraction technique proved to have a number of applications. Researchers used it to study ceramic superconductors, the structure of viruses, and the surfaces of relevance to catalytic exhaust cleaning, among other things. By the 1990s it had become the single most important technique for determining the structure and dynamics of condensed matter. For playing a major role in the development of the neutron diffraction technique, Shull was awarded a half share of the 1994 Nobel Prize in physics; had Wollan lived, he most likely would have shared the award with Shull. Shull's corecipient was the Canadian physicist Bertram N. Brockhouse.

In 1955 Shull was named a professor of physics at the Massachusetts Institute of Technology (MIT). At MIT he continued to contribute to neutron diffraction technology while also using neutron radiation to study a wide range of topics, including internal magnetization in crystals, dynamical scattering in perfect crystals, and the fundamental properties of the neutron. His honors include election to the National Academy of Sciences and the American Academy of Arts and Sciences. He retired in 1986, and he died on March 31, 2001, in Medford, Massachusetts.

Further Reading

Krapp, Kristine M., ed. *Notable Twentieth-Century Scientists Supplement.* Detroit: Gale Research, 1998, pp. 418–420.

Massachusetts Institute of Technology News Office. "Clifford G. Shull, co-winner of 1994 Nobel Prize in physics, is dead at 85." Available online. URL: http://web.mit.edu/newsoffice/2001/shull.html. Downloaded on March 25, 2005.

Nobelprize.org. "The Nobel Prize in Physics 1994." Available online. URL: http://nobelprize.org/physics/laureates/1994. Downloaded on August 21, 2004.

Simpson, George G.
(George Gaylord Simpson)
(1902–1984) *paleontologist*

As a paleontologist, George G. Simpson contributed a great deal to the body of knowledge concerning the fossil remains of early mammals. But his most important work involved contributing to the development of the scientific underpinnings for British naturalist Charles Darwin's work concerning natural selection and evolution.

Simpson was born on June 16, 1902, in Chicago, Illinois. His father, Joseph, was a lawyer, and his mother, Helen, was a homemaker. As a young boy he moved with his family to Cheyenne, Wyoming, and from there to Denver, Colorado, where he grew up. At age 16 he enrolled in the University of Colorado at Boulder where he became interested in geology. He transferred after his junior year to Yale University, receiving a Ph.B. and a Ph.D. in paleontology in 1923 and 1926, respectively. In 1923 he married Lydia Pedroja with whom he had four children; they divorced in 1938, and that same year he married Anne Roe.

While at Yale, Simpson became interested in mammals from the Mesozoic Age, particularly those found in the Americas, as this period marks the beginning of mammalian evolution. He continued to study them after graduation during a year of postdoctoral studies in England and as a staff member of the American Museum of Natural History in New York City, where he went to work in 1927. Once at the museum, however, he became more focused on the mammals of the Cenozoic Age, when mammals began to differentiate and assume their "modern" form. He spent much of his time in Argentina's Patagonia region, largely because researchers in that area had discovered a number of mammalian fossils dating back to when South America was an island continent. What made these fossils particularly interesting is the fact that they do not closely resemble fossils found in any other part of the world dating to that same time period. His work in this area, much of which was published in the mid-1930s, contributed greatly to a heightened appreciation for the diversity of early mammalian life in the Americas.

Simpson's work in Patagonia also led him to focus more and more on the mechanics of evolution. Genetics was becoming a field of major endeavor in the 1930s, and many scientists wondered if there was enough genetic variation in natural populations to account for the emergence of new species. Meanwhile, other scientists were wondering how to explain the fact that some species seemed to evolve rapidly while others evolved very slowly. Simpson provided answers for both groups by being the first to apply mathematical methods to paleontology. In so doing, he demonstrated that the key to evolution is random variation. For each species, he argued, evolution takes place at its own time and pace. He rejected the notion that evolution occurred in a straightline progression from ancient forms to modern ones. Instead, he argued that evolution resulted in many dead ends (i.e., the extinction of many species) and that the success or failure of any species's evolution is mostly dependent on random variables peculiar to the time and place in which that species dwells.

To better explain the mechanics of evolution, Simpson helped develop the synthetic theory of evolution, so named because it was derived from recent developments in anatomy, biology, botany, ecology, and genetics. He argued that evolution can take place in one of three ways. Speciation, the first way, takes place when a group of members of a species leave the main population, as occurred in South America, and develop on their own. Phyletic evolution, the second way, takes place when an entire species evolves into a new species. Quantum evolution, the third way, takes place when one or two members of a species mutate into a new species. He published much of his work regarding the synthetic theory of evolution in *Tempo and Mode in Evolution* (1944), one of the first works to espouse the synthetic theory. He followed up this book with *The Meaning of Evolution* (1949), *Evolution and Geography* (1953), *The Major Features of Evolution* (1953), *The Principles of Animal Taxonomy* (1961), and *This View of Life* (1964). These works were intended primarily for a general audience, and they did much to deepen the general public's understanding of the complexities of evolution.

In 1942 Simpson was named curator of the American Museum of Natural History, but he left that same year to serve in World War II. He returned to the museum in 1945, when he was also appointed professor of vertebrate paleontology at Columbia University. In 1959 he left the museum and Columbia to teach at Harvard University's Museum of Comparative Zoology, one of the foremost institutions of its kind in the world. In 1967 he retired to Tucson, Arizona, although he continued to write about a number of topics; his works from this period include *Why and How: Some Problems and Methods in Historical Biology* (1980) and *Fossils and the History of Life* (1983). He served as president of the Society of Vertebrate Paleontology, the Society for the Study of Evolution, the American Society of Mammalogists, the Society for Systematic Zoology, and the American Society of Zoologists. He was elected to membership in the National Academy of Sciences, and in 1966 he was awarded the National Medal of Science. He died on October 6, 1984, in Tucson.

Further Reading

Laporte, Leo F. *George Gaylord Simpson: Paleontologist and Evolutionist*. New York: Columbia University Press, 2000.

Simpson, George G. *Concession to the Improbable: An Unconventional Autobiography*. New Haven, Conn.: Yale University Press, 1978.

Smalley, Richard E.
(Richard Erret Smalley)
(1943–   ) *chemist*

Richard E. Smalley codiscovered the fullerenes, spherical arrangements of carbon atoms that possess amazing properties of strength, flexibility, and electrical conductivity. For this discovery he was awarded a share of the 1996 Nobel Prize in chemistry.

Smalley was born on June 6, 1943, in Akron, Ohio. His father, Frank, was a businessman, and his mother, Esther, was a homemaker. At age three he moved with his family to Kansas City, Missouri, where he grew up. He spent two years at Hope (Mich.) College before transferring to the University of Michigan where he received a B.S. in chemistry in 1965. After working for four years as a research chemist at a polypropylene manufacturing plant owned by the Shell Chemical Company in Woodbury, New Jersey, he entered the graduate program at Princeton University, receiving an M.A. and a Ph.D. in chemistry in 1971 and 1973, respectively. He then conducted postdoctoral research at the University of Chicago before accepting, in 1976, a position as a chemistry professor at Rice University. He was married and divorced three times and he had two children.

As a graduate student, Smalley became interested in molecular spectroscopy, the study of molecules by examining the spectrum of light they emit. At the time, one of the great problems faced by molecular spectroscopists was determining the structure of nitrogen dioxide, a relatively simple three-atom molecule. The molecule was able to resist the best efforts of spectroscopists to penetrate its secrets because of the complex nature of its rotation and vibration. Smalley's postdoctoral research involved using a supersonic free jet to cool down the molecule to about 3 K, a temperature low enough to reduce its rotation and vibration to the point that its structure could be studied in detail with a tunable laser. This experiment led to the development of supersonic beam laser spectroscopy, which made it possible to study the spectra of rotating polyatomic molecules.

At Rice, Smalley collaborated with ROBERT F. CURL, another spectroscopist, in the design and construction of increasingly sophisticated supersonic beam machines. Their efforts culminated with the laser-vaporization supersonic cluster beam machine, which froze its target molecules and then vaporized them with a laser so that their structures could be studied via a spectroscope. By 1982 Smalley and Curl had developed a supersonic beam machine capable of studying particles so small they are measured in nanometers, a nanometer being one-millionth of a millimeter long.

In 1985 Smalley and Curl froze and vaporized carbon in their latest version of the supersonic beam machine. When they went to examine the results, they discovered that the carbon gas had condensed into molecules of C_{60}, which is composed of 60 atoms of carbon linked together in the shape of a soccer ball. They named their discovery buckminsterfullerene in honor of R. Buckminster Fuller, an American architect, because buckminsterfullerene bears an uncanny resemblance to the geodesic dome that Fuller designed. Today, buckminsterfullerene is more commonly known as a buckyball. Further experimentation revealed the existence of other fullerenes, or spherical arrangements of carbon atoms, such as C_{70} and C_{240}. By experimenting with buckyballs, Smalley and Curl also discovered that by adding a few atoms of nickel or cobalt, buckyballs can be elongated into buckytubes, tubes no longer than one nanometer that possess the strength and flexibility of polymers as well as the ability to conduct electricity.

The discovery of fullerenes revolutionized the world of organic chemistry, the study of carbon and its compounds, because it demonstrated that carbon can exist in previously unknown forms. This discovery also promised to lead to new technologies such as electrical wiring or structural materials made from buckytubes. For the role he played in their discovery, Smalley received a one-third share of the 1996 Nobel Prize in chemistry; one of his corecipients was Curl.

Smalley remained at Rice for the rest of his career. He served as cofounder and first chair of the Rice Quantum Institute, founding director of the Rice Center for Nanoscale Science and Technology, and director of the Carbon Nanotechnology Laboratory. He also cofounded and served as chair of Carbon Nanotechnologies, Inc., a for-profit firm specializing in developing large-scale production and applications of buckytubes. His many honors include election to the National Academy of Sciences and the American Academy of Arts and Sciences.

Further Reading
Browne, Malcolm W. "Discoveries of Superfluid Helium, and 'Buckyballs,' Earn Nobels for 6 Scientists," *New York Times,* October 10, 1996, p. D21.
Nobelprize.org. "The Nobel Prize in Chemistry 1996." Available online. URL: http://nobelprize.org/chemistry/laureates/1996. Downloaded on August 10, 2004.
The Smalley Group, Rice University. "Richard E. Smalley." Available online. URL: http://smalley.rice.edu/smalley.cfm?doc_id=4855. Downloaded on March 25, 2005.

Smith, Hamilton O.
(Hamilton Othanel Smith)
(1931–) *molecular biologist*

Hamilton O. Smith discovered an enzyme that makes it possible to recombine sections of DNA chains, a development that helped bring about the rise of biotechnology. For this contribution, he was awarded a share of the 1978 Nobel Prize in physiology or medicine.

Smith was born on August 23, 1931, in New York City. His father, Tommie, was a college professor, and his mother, Bunnie, was a high school teacher. Smith's family divided its time between New York City and Gainesville, Florida, until he turned six, when his family moved to Urbana, Illinois, where he grew up. In 1948 he entered the University of Illinois at Urbana but transferred after two years to the University of California at Berkeley, receiving a B.S. in biology in 1952. He then entered Johns Hopkins University Medical School, receiving an M.D. in 1956. After a one-year internship at Barnes Hospital in St. Louis, Missouri, a two-year hitch in the U.S. Navy, and a three-year internship at the Henry Ford Hospital in Detroit, Michigan, in 1962 he became affiliated with the University of Michigan's department of human genetics. In 1967 he returned to Johns Hopkins to teach microbiology, where he remained for the next 30 years. In 1956 he married Elizabeth Bolton with whom he had five children.

During his intern/military years, Smith became interested in molecular biology, a field that applies biochemistry and biophysics to the study of genetics, and in his spare time he began studying this subject on his own. His first research interest in molecular biology involved bacteriophages, also known as phages, which are viruses that infect bacteria. Once settled at Michigan, he took up the study of P22, a phage that infects several strains of bacteria including *Salmonella*. He was particularly interested in P22's ability to replicate itself by inserting its genome, the collection of genes in the deoxyribonucleic acid (DNA) of its core, into a bacterium's core so that the virus's genome becomes one of the bacterium's genes, a process known as lysogeny. Thus when a colony of *Salmonella* that has been infected with P22 replicates, the replicated bacteria already contain P22 virons. Rather than kill the infected *Salmonella* immediately, these virons live somewhat as parasites in the bacteria, being released only when the bacteria are exposed to a specific phenomenon such as a chemical or ultraviolet light. By 1965 he had discovered the specific viral gene that permits P22 lysogeny to take place.

Smith next became interested in restriction/modification phenomena, the ability of certain enzymes to either cut DNA chains or protect them from being cut. This work was initiated in the late 1950s by Swiss microbiologist Werner Arber, who eventually discovered that certain bacteria protect themselves against lysogeny by producing enzymes that coat their DNA chains so that phages cannot splice their genomes into them. In addition to discovering these so-called modification enzymes, Arber also discovered restriction enzymes, enzymes that can cut up chains of a phage's DNA before the phage has time to infect the bacterium. All of Arber's restriction enzymes belong to the category now known as Type I, meaning they recognize specific DNA sequences but they cut those sequences

at random points. Nevertheless, Arber hypothesized the existence of Type II restriction enzymes, enzymes that would always cut a DNA chain at the same exact point in the sequence.

In 1966 Smith visited Arber at the University of Geneva in Switzerland to learn more about his findings. Upon returning to the United States, Smith set out to determine whether or not Arber's hypothesis was correct. Working with *Hemophilus influenzae*, another bacterium susceptible to P22 infection, in 1969 Smith discovered the first Type II restriction enzyme. Today it is known that about 100 different Type II restriction enzymes exist, each of which cuts DNA chains at different, defined regions.

Smith's discovery was a major factor in the growth of the field of biotechnology in the 1970s. Biotechnologists genetically engineer new organisms, such as strains of bacteria that biodegrade oil spills and toxic wastes or organisms that produce insulin for human consumption, by recombining DNA from two or more organisms, and the principal tool by which they cut and splice DNA is Type II restriction enzymes. Recombinant DNA techniques are also widely used by medical researchers looking to cure cancer or a variety of hereditary diseases. For his contribution to these areas, Smith was awarded a one-third share of the 1978 Nobel Prize in physiology or medicine; one of his corecipients was Arber.

Until his retirement from Johns Hopkins in 1998, Smith continued to study the restriction enzymes produced by *H. influenzae*. In addition to discovering more than a dozen DNA transformation genes in the bacterium, he also cloned the first genes that direct the production of restriction enzymes. In 1993 he was named scientific director of the Institute for Biological Energy Alternatives (IBEA), a biotech research firm in Rockville, Maryland. As a member of the scientific advisory council of IBEA's Institute for Genomic Research, he helped decode the genome of a bacterium, a major step toward identifying the sequence of the human genome.

Further Reading

The Nobel Prize Internet Archive. "Hamilton O. Smith." Available online. URL: http://almaz.com/nobel/medicine/1978c.html. Downloaded on March 25, 2005.

Nobelprize.org. "The Nobel Prize in Physiology or Medicine 1978." Available online. URL: http://nobelprize.org/medicine/laureates/1978. Downloaded on July 4, 2004.

Wasson, Tyler, ed. *Nobel Prize Winners.* New York: H. W. Wilson, 1987, pp. 983–985.

Snell, George D.
(George Davis Snell)
(1903–1996) *immunogeneticist*

George D. Snell discovered the H-2 gene and the major histocompatibility complex (MHC), both of which work together to regulate the body's immune responses to everything from viruses to transplanted tissue. These discoveries helped establish a new scientific field, immunogenetics, the study of the connection between immunology and genetics. They also earned him a share of the 1980 Nobel Prize in physiology or medicine.

Snell was born on December 19, 1903, in Bradford, Massachusetts. His father, Cullen, was a YMCA secretary, and his mother, Kathleen, was a homemaker. At age four he moved with his family to Brookline where he grew up. He received a B.S. in biology from Dartmouth College in 1926 and a D.Sc. from Harvard University in 1930. After teaching zoology for a year at Brown University, in 1931 he went to the University of Texas at Austin on a National Research Council fellowship where he conducted research under HERMANN J. MULLER. In 1933 he joined the faculty at the Washington University of St. Louis, Missouri, and in 1935 he became affiliated with the Jackson Laboratory, the world center for studies in mammalian genetics, in Bar Harbor, Maine, where he spent the rest of his career. In 1937 he married Rhoda Carson with whom he had three children.

Snell's research focused on the genetics of the laboratory mouse. As a graduate student, he identified more than two dozen visible mutations, and he established important linkages between certain genes. From Muller he learned how to alter the genetics of fruit flies by bombarding them with X-rays, thus creating any number of strange mutations, a technique he adapted for use on mice. At the Jackson Laboratory he investigated the role played by genetics in the development of cancer by transplanting tumor cells in highly inbred strains of mice. He discovered that these cells grew progressively in mice of the same strain as the donor, but that the cells were rejected by a recipient mouse of a different strain than the donor mouse. Further experimentation suggested that inbred mice share a certain dominant gene, thus suppressing the production of tumor-killing cells known as killer lymphocytes. He expanded on this line of research by investigating the rejection mechanism involving nontumorous cells. By grafting healthy skin from one mouse to another, he discovered that the grafts most likely to "take" involved mice who shared a common visible characteristic. This result allowed him to isolate the gene that seemed most responsible for rejecting transplants.

Meanwhile, Snell had been collaborating with British biologist Peter Gorer, who had distinguished the presence in mice of two antigens, proteins that attack foreign objects in the bloodstream. Although one antigen was identical in all mice, the other (Antigen II) differed depending on the strain of the mouse. In 1948 Snell and Gorer determined that Antigen II was responsible for rejecting transplanted tissue, healthy or otherwise; transplants involving mice of the same strain were successful because the mice shared the same type of Antigen II. They then labeled the gene that regulates the production of Antigen II as H-2, the "H" standing for histocompatibility, the compatibility of tissue.

For the next 25 years, Snell focused on developing a more sophisticated understanding of histocompatibility, in the process laying the groundwork for the development of immunogenetics. By 1973 he and his colleagues had determined the existence of the major histocompatibility complex (MHC)—a linked group of genes that regulates the body's immune response—and mapped the locations of many of its individual genes. Although H-2 is the most important of these genes, its effect is regulated by scores of other minor genes, at least 60 in the mouse. The identification of the MHC in the mouse led to the discovery of MHCs in virtually every vertebrate, but most important in humans. By studying the human MHC, other researchers were able to develop methods for predicting how compatible a donor organ might be in a proposed recipient. Such methods greatly increased the success rate of organ transplants and in fact made them possible on a widespread basis. For his contributions in this regard, Snell was awarded a one-third share of the 1980 Nobel Prize in physiology or medicine; one of his corecipients was BARUJ BENACERRAF and the other was the French physiologist Jean Dausset.

Snell was elected to the National Academy of Sciences and the American Academy of Arts and Sciences. His major publications include *The Biology of the Laboratory Mouse* (1941, 1966), *Cell Surface Antigens: Studies in Mammals Other Than Man* (1973), *Genetic and Biological Aspects of Histocompatibility* (1973), and *Histocompatibility* (1976). He retired from the Jackson Laboratory in 1973, and in his later years he explored the connection between human evolution and ethical behavior; the result was *Search for a Rational Ethic* (1987). He died on June 6, 1996, in Bar Harbor.

Further Reading

Mitchison, N. Avrion. "George Davis Snell," National Academy of Sciences, *Biographical Memoirs* 83 (2003): pp. 252–269.

Nobelprize.org. "The Nobel Prize in Physiology or Medicine 1980." Available online. URL: http://nobelprize.org/medicine/laureates/1980. Downloaded on June 2, 2004.

Wasson, Tyler, ed. *Nobel Prize Winners*. New York: H. W. Wilson, 1987, pp. 985–987.

Sperry, Roger W.
(Roger Wolcott Sperry)
(1913–1994) *psychobiologist*

Roger W. Sperry described the specialties of the brain's right and left hemispheres and showed how they work separately from one another, but he also demonstrated how and when they work together. For these contributions, he was awarded a share of the 1981 Nobel Prize in physiology or medicine.

Sperry was born on August 20, 1913, in Hartford, Connecticut. His father, Francis, was a banker, and his mother, Florence, was a secretary. He attended Oberlin (Ohio) College, receiving an A.B. in English in 1935 and an M.A. in psychology in 1937. He then entered the graduate program at the University of Chicago, receiving a Ph.D. in zoology in 1941. After spending the next five years as a biology research fellow at Harvard University and the Yerkes Laboratory of Primate Biology in Orange Park, Florida, in 1946 he returned to Chicago to teach anatomy. In 1954 he was named a professor of psychobiology at the California Institute of Technology (Caltech) where he remained for the next 30 years. In 1949 he married Norma Deupree with whom he had two children.

Sperry's early research focused on developmental neurobiology. In the late 1930s, conventional wisdom held that nerves were like electrical wires in that they could be interchanged with one another without interfering with an organism's ability to function. Sperry conducted a number of experiments with rats and frogs that demonstrated that nerves, unlike arteries, come "programmed"; in other words, a nerve that controls the left leg will always try to control the left leg, no matter where it is transplanted to. He also found that no amount of training, at least in the lower life-forms, can overcome a nerve's preprogrammed settings. This discovery led Sperry to advance his chemo-affinity theory, which states that the specific function carried out by a specific nerve is guided by specific chemical compounds that are produced and controlled by a specific gene. The discovery also forced a major shift in the way patients with damaged nerves are treated; previously, they had often undergone transplant surgery, whereby nerves from a different muscle group were substituted for the damaged ones, followed by intense rehabilitative training. Sperry's findings explained why such methods rarely worked, and then only after tremendous difficulty.

Sperry's next major project was to consider the role played by the corpus callosum (also known as the great cerebral commissure), the bundle of nerves that connects and separates the right and left hemispheres of the brain. In the mid-1940s, when he began this project, conventional wisdom held that the corpus callosum existed mostly just to separate the two hemispheres; however, no one really understood its function. Neurosurgeons had gone so far as to cut through it entirely as a means of reducing the frequency and severity of epileptic seizures, and they had done so without affecting the patient's personality, intelligence, or coordination. Sperry showed that the corpus callosum plays an important role in hand-eye coordination. He also showed that it is the means by which the two hemispheres communicate with each other. Even though the two halves operate within their own spheres, they must share their knowledge and memories so that each half has access to what the other one knows, and the conduit through which this sharing takes place is the corpus callosum.

Sperry's work with the corpus callosum led him to undertake a study of the so-called split-brain effect. In the 1950s, when he began this project, conventional wisdom held that the left hemisphere was more developed than the right hemisphere, mostly because the left houses the abilities associated with speech, abilities that could not be transferred to the right after the left had been injured. Sperry began experimenting on cats and humans whose hemispheres had been surgically separated. By 1965 he had demonstrated that the right hemisphere is as developed as the left and perhaps even more so. He located in the right hemisphere the abilities related to nonverbal thought such as sorting sizes and shapes, interpreting sights and sounds, appreciating music, and creating works of art. At the same time, he demonstrated that the left hemisphere is home to the abilities related to communications, motor skills, mathematical calculations, and logical thought. Sperry's brilliant description of the roles played by the right and left hemispheres won him a half share of the 1981 Nobel Prize in physiology or medicine. His corecipients were the American neurobiologist DAVID H. HUBEL and the Swedish physiologist Torsten N. Wiesel.

Meanwhile, Sperry had shifted his research focus once again, this time in an effort to understand the concept of "mind" or consciousness. Toward the end of his career, he had come to see the mind as an independent entity that emerges from the activities of the brain. In turn, the mind feeds back into the workings of the brain, which further contributes to a heightened awareness or consciousness in a never-ending cycle. He further understood that an individual's consciousness contributes to a global human consciousness, an important result of which is the development of

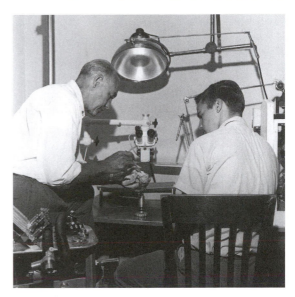

Roger Sperry (left), shown here instructing an unidentified student, demonstrated that the brain is split into two hemispheres. *(Courtesy of the California Institute of Technology)*

human values. Thus he suggested that ethics and ethical behavior are rooted, at least in part, in the physiology of the brain.

Sperry retired from Caltech in 1984. His many honors include election to the National Academy of Sciences and the American Academy of Arts and Sciences and receipt of the National Medal of Science. He died on April 17, 1994, in Pasadena, California.

Further Reading

Nobelprize.org. "The Nobel Prize in Physiology or Medicine 1981." Available online. URL: http://nobelprize.org/medicine/laureates/1981. Downloaded on June 6, 2004.

Trevarthen, Colwyn, ed. *Brain Circuits and Functions of the Mind: Essays in Honor of Roger W. Sperry.* New York: Cambridge University Press, 1990.

Voneida, Theodore J. "Roger Wolcott Sperry," National Academy of Sciences, *Biographical Memoirs* 71 (1997): pp. 315–332.

Wasson, Tyler, ed. *Nobel Prize Winners.* New York: H. W. Wilson, 1987, pp. 997–1,000.

Stakman, Elvin C.
(Elvin Charles Stakman)
(1885–1979) *botanist*

Elvin Stakman was one of the world's foremost plant pathologists. His efforts to develop disease-resistant strains of wheat and to eradicate the plant pathogens that prey on cereal grains played an integral role in bringing about the "green revolution" of the mid-20th century that vastly improved agriculture around the world.

Stakman was born on May 17, 1885, in Algoma, Wisconsin. His parents, Frederick and Emelie, were farmers. As a young boy, he moved with his family to Brownton, Minnesota, where he grew up. At age 17 he enrolled in the University of Minnesota and received a B.A. in botany in 1906. He taught in the Minnesota public schools for three years before returning to the university as an instructor of plant pathology. At the same time, he entered Minnesota's graduate program and received an M.A. and Ph.D. in plant pathology in 1910 and 1913, respectively. He was promoted to professor in 1913, and he remained at the university for the rest of his career. In 1917 he married Louise Jensen with whom he had no children.

Throughout his career, Stakman focused his research work almost entirely on controlling the fungal diseases that are deadly to wheat, the mainstay of the economy of the northern Great Plains. At the time he was in graduate school, it was believed that if a particular fungus could infect one type of cereal grain (for example, winter wheat), it could eventually develop the ability to infect other types of that grain (for example, summer wheat), even if those other types were presently immune. Known as the bridging hypothesis, this notion prevented botanists from trying to develop disease-resistant strains of cereal grain, as they believed their efforts would simply be undone once they introduced their strains into cultivation. Stakman's Ph.D. dissertation, however, proved that the bridging hypothesis is false, thus encouraging botanists to engineer strains of cereal grains that were genetically resistant to particular plant pathogens.

During the early 1900s, several epidemics of a fungal disease known as stem rust ravaged the wheat crops of the northern Great Plains. To combat future epidemics, Stakman proposed the establishment of a research center at the University of Minnesota dedicated to the study of rusts, fungal diseases that are particularly deadly to wheat. In 1915 the U.S. Department of Agriculture (USDA), with the financial assistance of several milling companies based in Minneapolis, established what later became known as the Cereal Rust Laboratory (today the Cereal Disease Laboratory) at the university. In 1916 Stakman played a major role in the laboratory's discovery of the first physiological race, or genetic subdivision, of *Puccinia graminis tritici*, a wheat stem rust that preys on *Triticum aestivum*, better known as common wheat. In time, more than 200 races of *P. graminis tritici* would be discovered, as well as a number of physiological races of the stem rusts that affect other cereal grains.

Stakman's discoveries presented botanists with a quandary. On the one hand, it was now worthwhile to develop cereal grains with genetic immunity to a particular plant pathogen. On the other hand, the growing multitude of rust races suggested that rusts were genetically reengineering themselves, thus creating new and deadly races faster than botanists could develop immune strains of cereal grains. This quandary led Stakman to his third project: the elimination of wheat rusts altogether. To this end, he determined to eradicate the barberry, a thorny shrub that serves as an alternate host for wheat stem rusts in their spore stage. During this stage, stem rusts can reproduce sexually, and on occasion this process results in a new and virulent race. In 1917 he convinced the USDA to implement a barberry eradication program, which he designed, in the northern Great Plains. Eventually, hundreds of millions of barberry plants were destroyed across the western United States, and to this day it is forbidden to plant certain barberry species in this region.

Meanwhile, Stakman worked with the Cereal Rust Laboratory (CRL) to develop a breeding program for wheat that would genetically alter wheat plants so that they were immune to rusts. To this end, he helped develop "rust nurseries" wherein researchers could identify new, virulent races of rusts. Between the two programs, the ability of rusts to wreak havoc on the region's wheat crops was greatly reduced, and the northern Great Plains began to produce bushels of wheat in record numbers. In time, Stakman's methods for safeguarding wheat would be extended to include virtually every cereal grain. Most of this activity would take place at the CRL, working in close conjunction with the university's department of plant pathology; during Stakman's tenure as both director and department chair from 1940 to 1953, the laboratory developed into an international center for rust control.

In 1941 Stakman was recruited by the Rockefeller Foundation to head up a team to investigate the agricultural needs of Mexico. Two years later, the team had identified several worthwhile projects, including the development of corn and wheat strains that were better suited to the Mexican environment. In essence, these projects were so successful toward helping Mexico feed its growing population that they sparked the so-called green revolution. This revolution involved developing new strains of fast-growing, disease-resistant crops, and included the establishment of research centers for rice in the Philippines, sorghum in India, and the common bean in Colombia, among others. At each of these three centers, researchers from the University of Minnesota, all of them trained by Stakman, played integral roles. One of his students, Norman Borlaug, won the 1970 Nobel Peace Prize for developing the Mexican wheat strains that revolutionized agriculture globally.

In 1953 Stakman retired from the University and the CRL, but he continued to serve as a consultant to the Rockefeller Foundation until his death. His publications include coauthorship of two major books, *Principles of Plant Pathology* (1957) and *Campaign against Hunger* (1967). His honors include a term as president of the American Association for the Advancement of Science, election to the National Academy of Sciences, and service on the Atomic Energy Commission and the National Science Board. He died on January 22, 1979, in St. Paul, Minnesota.

Further Reading

Christensen, Clyde M. *E. C. Stakman, Statesman of Science.* St. Paul, Minn.: American Phytopathological Society, 1984.

———. "Elvin Charles Stakman," National Academy of Sciences, *Biographical Memoirs* 61 (1992): pp. 330–349.

Stanley, Wendell M.
(Wendell Meredith Stanley)
(1904–1971) *chemist*

Wendell M. Stanley was the first biochemist to crystallize a living organism, in this case the tobacco mosaic virus (TMV). For this achievement, he was awarded a share of the 1946 Nobel Prize in chemistry.

Stanley was born on August 16, 1904, in Ridgeville, Indiana. His parents, James and Claire, were newspaper publishers. After receiving a B.S. in chemistry from Earlham (Ind.) College in 1926, he entered the graduate program at the University of Illinois at Urbana, receiving an M.S. in 1927 and a Ph.D. in chemistry in 1929. Also in 1929 he married Marian Jay with whom he had four children. After spending the next two years conducting postdoctoral research at Illinois and in Germany, in 1931 he joined the staff of the Rockefeller Institute for Medical Research (today Rockefeller University) in New York City, transferring the following year to the institute's division of plant pathology in Princeton, New Jersey.

In 1932 Stanley was assigned to a research group investigating TMV, a viral infection whose presence in a tobacco plant can be identified by a distinctive pattern of discoloration in the leaves. Stanley's assignment was to obtain the purest possible form of the virus so that other researchers could study it more easily. Using crystallization techniques developed by JAMES B. SUMNER and perfected by JOHN H. NORTHROP, a Rockefeller colleague, by 1935 Stanley had developed a method for crystallizing TMV. He then demonstrated that TMV was a large protein molecule, and that crystallized TMV could be dissolved and recrystallized repeatedly without the virus losing any of its ability to infect tobacco plants. Within a year, other investigators had demonstrated that TMV consists of rod-like particles that, in addition to protein, contain large amounts of ribonucleic acid (RNA).

Stanley's discovery that viruses can be crystallized allowed biochemists and virologists to study the molecular structures of a wide range of viruses. One result of such studies was the development of vaccines against a number of viral infections. Another result was that researchers were now able to learn more about replication, the process by which a living organism generates identical offspring, by studying viruses, the simplest form of life. For demonstrating that viruses can be prepared in pure form via crystallization, Stanley won a quarter share of the 1946 Nobel Prize in chemistry; his corecipients were Sumner and Northrop.

The U.S. entry into World War II saw Stanley shift the focus of his research from viruses that affect plants to those that affect humans. By the end of the war he had crystallized the virus that causes influenza, commonly known as flu, and developed a vaccine for it. In 1948 Rockefeller closed its Princeton facility, and Stanley left for the University of California at Berkeley where he remained for the rest of his career. As chair of the department of biochemistry, he founded the Virus Laboratory and developed it into the West Coast's foremost institute for virus research. In the mid-1950s staff members at the Virus Laboratory crystallized the virus that causes poliomyelitis, commonly known as polio.

Toward the end of his career, Stanley became one of a growing number of researchers who believe that viruses cause cancer, and his later research involved tumor viruses. He served on the board of scientific counselors of the National Cancer Institute, chaired the Tenth International Cancer Congress in 1970, and served on the board of directors of the American Cancer Society. He died on June 15, 1971, while attending a scientific conference in Salamanca, Spain.

Further Reading

Creager, Angela N. H. *The Life of a Virus: Tobacco Mosaic Virus as an Experimental Model, 1930–1965.* Chicago: University of Chicago Press, 2002.

Nobelprize.org. "The Nobel Prize in Chemistry 1946." Available online. URL: http://nobelprize.org/chemistry/laureates/1946. Downloaded on April 29, 2004.

Wasson, Tyler, ed. *Nobel Prize Winners.* New York: H. W. Wilson, 1987, pp. 1,001–1,003.

Stein, William H.
(William Howard Stein)
(1911–1980) *chemist*

Along with STANFORD MOORE, William H. Stein discovered the molecular structure of ribonuclease and showed how its structure relates to its biochemical function. This work marked the first time the complete sequence of an enzyme had been described completely, and it won Stein a share of the 1972 Nobel Prize in chemistry.

Stein was born on June 25, 1911, in New York City. His father, Fred, was a businessman, and his mother, Beatrice, was a homemaker. After receiving a B.S. in chemistry from Harvard University in 1933, he entered Harvard's graduate program but transferred a year later to Columbia University. In 1937 he received a Ph.D. in biochemistry from Columbia's College of Physicians and Surgeons and went to work as a researcher at the Rockefeller Institute of Medical Research (today Rockefeller University). In 1936 he married Phoebe Hockstader with whom he had three children.

Stein's graduate work had focused on gaining a better understanding of elastin, the amino acid that constitutes the basic substance of elastic tissue. This work qualified him to join the staff of Max Bergmann, a senior Rockefeller researcher who was trying to determine the amino acid composition of protein. After two years of assisting Bergmann, Stein was joined by Stanford Moore, and for the next three years Stein and Moore worked closely together. Their joint effort involved breaking down the proteins albumin and fibroin into their constituent amino acids and then identifying those acids. In order to do this, they had to dissolve the proteins in various solutions and then separate what had been dissolved into the various amino acids. Chromatography, the separation of mixtures into their constituents by using a solid adsorption medium, was still a rather unsophisticated field, and so they had to filter the solutions through a narrow column packed with potato starch, a slow and painstaking process. Nevertheless, by 1942 Stein and Moore had identified four of the amino acids that albumin and fibroin have in common: serine, alanine, phenylalanine, and leucine.

Stein's research was temporarily refocused by World War II, during which he remained at Rockefeller to conduct medical-related research for the U.S. Office of Scientific Research and Development. In 1945 he and Moore resumed their experiments with albumin and fibroin, but this time they were able to make use of more advanced techniques and equipment, much of which was of their own design. They discovered that resonated polystyrene resins act as a more discriminating filtering medium than potato starch, and once they started using resins in their filtering columns they were able to collect a greater amount of a particular fraction in a much shorter period of time. Later, they adapted the techniques of ion-exchange chromatography, whereby a charged filtering medium filters out the desired fraction by exchanging ions with it, for use with liquids by charging the resonated polystyrene resins, thus making this method even more effective. They also designed two important pieces of equipment, the automatic amino acid analyzer and the automatic fraction collector. This latter device uses a photoelectric cell to count the drops of amino acid being filtered out of a solution, and it has been adapted for use in so many other applications that it is now an important tool in biochemical research. As a result of all these advances, by 1953 they had identified four more constituent amino acids of albumin and fibroin: isoleucine, methionine, tyrosine, and valine.

In 1953 Stein and Moore turned their attention from protein to enzymes, specifically ribonuclease, which plays an important role in the synthesis of cellular protein. Using the filtering techniques they had developed over the years, by 1963 they had completely identified the sequence of amino acids in ribonuclease. Moreover, they were able to describe how the amino acids that make up ribonuclease's structure also control the way it functions. This achievement marked the first time that the amino-acid sequence of an enzyme had been described, and it won for Stein and Moore a quarter share each of the 1972 Nobel Prize in chemistry. The other half was awarded to CHRISTIAN B. ANFINSEN, whose work concerning the relationship between ribonuclease's structure and function concurred with Stein and Moore's results.

Stein was elected to membership in the National Academy of Sciences, the American Association for the Advancement of Science, and the American Academy of Arts and Sciences. He also served on the editorial staff of the *Journal of Biological Chemistry* for a number of years. He remained at Rockefeller until his death on February 2, 1980, in New York City.

Further Reading

Moore, Stanford. "William H. Stein," National Academy of Sciences, *Biographical Memoirs* 56 (1987): pp. 414–441.

Nobelprize.org. "The Nobel Prize in Chemistry 1972." Available online. URL: http://nobelprize.org/chemistry/laureates/1972. Downloaded on July 5, 2003.

Wasson, Tyler, ed. *Nobel Prize Winners*. New York: H. W. Wilson, 1987, pp. 1,008–1,009.

Steinberger, Jack
(1921–) *physicist*

Jack Steinberger helped design and carry out the "two-neutrino experiment." This experiment discovered the muon neutrino, and it developed the neutrino beam method for studying the weak nuclear interactions. For these contributions he was awarded a share of the 1988 Nobel Prize in physics.

Steinberger was born on May 25, 1921, in Bad Kissingen, Germany, to Ludwig and Berta Steinberger. At age 13 he left Germany with his older brother and settled in Chicago, Illinois, where he was eventually joined by the rest of his family. He studied chemistry at the Armour (later Illinois) Institute of Technology and the University of Chicago, receiving a B.S. from the latter in 1942. He then joined the U.S. Army and spent World War II at the Massachusetts Institute of Technology's Radiation Laboratory, making antennas for radar bomb sights and taking several basic physics courses. After the war he returned to Chicago and received a Ph.D. in physics in 1948. He spent the next two years at the Institute for Advanced Studies in Princeton, New Jersey, and the University of California at Berkeley, and in 1950 he joined the faculty of Columbia University in New York City.

Steinberger's research was devoted to the study of subatomic particles. As a graduate student he showed that a muon, a particle that has the same negative charge as an electron but approximately 200 times more mass, decays radioactively into an electron and two neutrinos, particles that have no electrical charge and virtually no mass. At Berkeley he experimented with mesons, particles that have more mass than an electron but not as much as a proton. He focused on pi mesons, or pions, the elementary particles that are chiefly responsible for the strong interactions, the forces that bind together protons and neutrons in an atomic nucleus. In addition to showing that pions can be formed from photons, tiny packets of electromagnetic radiation, he measured their lifetimes and showed that some pions carry no electrical charge. At Columbia he measured the spin, or the momentum of axial rotation, and parity, the distribution of matter during radioactive decay, of pions.

In 1959 Steinberger was approached by MELVIN SCHWARTZ, one of his Columbia colleagues, concerning Schwartz's idea about confirming the number of neutrinos in existence. Neutrinos had been detected three years earlier by FREDERICK REINES and Clyde L. Cowan, Jr. Because of its charge and mass, a neutrino rarely interacts with matter, but when it does it initiates the production of either an electron or a muon. Physicists wondered if this meant that there are two different types of neutrinos, so Steinberger and Schwartz recruited LEON M. LEDERMAN, a third Columbia colleague, to help them determine the answer to this question.

Using the particle accelerator, a device that energizes subatomic particles to extremely high energy levels, at the Brookhaven National Laboratory on Long Island, Steinberger, Schwartz, and Lederman devised an experiment whereby a beam of high-energy protons was generated in the accelerator and then fired into a block of the metal beryllium. The beam struck the block with so much force that the beryllium atoms were demolished into billions of subatomic particles, among which were approximately one hundred thousand billion neutrinos. The debris was blasted into a 40-foot-thick barrier of steel plates, which collected all of the particles except the neutrinos, which were propelled in a beam through the plates into a detector consisting of 90 one-inch aluminum sheets with a layer of neon gas separating each sheet. This detector collected a grand total of 51 neutrinos, whose properties were then examined by the three experimenters. By 1962 they had demonstrated the existence of two different types of neutrinos: electron neutrinos (which generate electrons) and muon neutrinos (which generate muons).

The "two-neutrino experiment," as it became known, had two important results. In addition to demonstrating the existence of the previously unknown muon neutrino, it provided physicists with the neutrino beam, a powerful new tool for investigating nuclear forces. Previously, particle accelerators had generated beams of particles that operate according to the strong interactions, so it was difficult for them to investigate the weak interactions, certain processes of radioactive decay. Since neutrinos are affected only by the weak interactions but not by the strong interactions, the neutrino beam allowed particle physicists to investigate the weak interactions, about which little was known. For his role in devising and carrying out the two-neutrino experiment, Steinberger was awarded a one-third share of the 1988 Nobel Prize in physics; his corecipients were Schwartz and Lederman.

Following completion of the two-neutrino experiment, Steinberger became interested in the K meson, one of the so-called strange particles because its radioactive decay violates some of the basic laws of conservation. In 1968 he left Columbia for the European Organization for Nuclear Research (CERN) in Geneva, Switzerland, to focus on K-meson research. He retired from CERN in 1986 to teach part-time at the Scuola Normale Superiore in Pisa, Italy, although he continued to conduct research at CERN.

Steinberger was married twice—in 1943 to Joan Beauregard with whom he had two children and in 1961 to Cynthia Alff with whom he had two children. His honors include the National Medal of Science and election to the National Academy of Sciences and the American Academy of Arts and Sciences.

Further Reading

Kleinknecht, Konrad, and Tsung-Dao Lee, eds. *Particles and Detectors: Festschrift for Jack Steinberger.* New York: Springer-Verlag, 1986.

McMurray, Emily J., ed. *Notable Twentieth-Century Scientists.* Detroit: Gale Research, 1995, pp. 1,913–1,914.

Nobelprize.org. "The Nobel Prize in Physics 1988." Available online. URL: http://nobelprize.org/physics/laureates/1988. Downloaded on October 6, 2004.

Stern, Otto
(1888–1969) *physicist*

Otto Stern was one of the first physicists to subscribe to the theories of quantum mechanics, the study of the behavior of atoms and subatomic particles. Although his experiments mostly involved confirming or denying the validity of other physicists' theories, he did much to verify the soundness of quantum mechanics as a better tool than classical mechanics for understanding atomic behavior. In 1943 he was awarded the Nobel Prize in physics.

Stern was born on February 17, 1888, in Sohrau, Germany. His father, Oskar, was a miller and grain merchant, and his mother, Eugenie, was a homemaker. At age four he moved with his family to Breslau where he grew up. As an undergraduate he studied science at several German universities, and in 1912 he received a Ph.D. in physical chemistry from the University of Breslau. He then took up postdoctoral studies at the University of Prague (in the Austro-Hungarian Empire) under noted physicist ALBERT EINSTEIN, and he moved with Einstein in 1913 to the University of Zurich in Switzerland. As Einstein's student and collaborator (they coauthored a paper in 1913 that theorized about the vibrational energy level of a diatomic hydrogen molecule), Stern joined a group of physicists who were studying theoretical physics, later known as quantum mechanics. In 1914 he became a lecturer at the University of Frankfurt, Germany, but he was drafted later that year into the German army. When World War I ended, he returned to Frankfurt as the assistant director of the Institute for Theoretical Physics. In 1921 he joined the faculty at the University of Rostock, but he left two years later to become director of the Institute of Physical Chemistry at the University of Hamburg.

In 1919 Stern began testing the theories of other physicists by using a technique known as the molecular beam. Invented in 1911 by French physicist Louis Dunoyer, this technique involved injecting molecules in a gaseous state into a large vacuum through a tiny orifice so that they entered the vacuum in a thin beam. This technique made it possible to study the molecules in a free, or noncolliding state. Within a year he was able to verify the theoretical calculations made by Scottish physicist James Clerk Maxwell concerning the velocity of gas molecules. He next used the molecular beam to settle a theoretical dispute concerning an atom's magnetic

Otto Stern developed a number of the experiments that either proved or disproved some of the early theories related to quantum mechanics, the study of the behavior of subatomic particles. *(Library of Congress, Prints and Photographs Division [LC-USZ62-121038])*

moment, the strength and direction of its magnetic field. Whereas classical physicists had postulated that the magnetic moment could take any direction, theoretical physicists had argued that it could take only two directions, either the same as or the opposite of the magnetic field. By 1922 Stern and a colleague, Walter Gerlach, had demonstrated that the latter theory was correct.

Stern then began testing the theory of French physicist Louis de Broglie that atomic particles had wavelengths. By 1931 he had proven Broglie's theory to be correct by determining the wavelength of helium atoms. Other Stern experiments determined the rotational magnetic moment of the diatomic hydrogen molecule and estimated the magnetic moment of the deuteron, a positively charged particle consisting of one proton and one neutron.

Stern's most important work with the molecular beam involved the theories of English physicist Paul Dirac concerning the magnetic moment of the proton. Dirac had theorized that the ratio of the magnetic moments of the proton and the electron was equal to the inverse ratio of their masses. In 1933 Stern published his findings that the magnetic moment of the proton was more than twice as strong as Dirac's theory had predicted. For this achievement and for his other groundbreaking work with the molecular beam, Stern was awarded the 1943 Nobel Prize in physics.

When the Nazis came to power in Germany in 1933, they began dismissing Jewish professors from the universities. Stern resigned his position at Hamburg in protest, and that same year he left Germany for the United States, having accepted a position at the Carnegie Institute of Technology in Pittsburgh, Pennsylvania. While at Carnegie Tech he continued to experiment with molecular beams until his retirement in 1946.

Stern became a naturalized citizen of the United States in 1939. He received a number of honors in his lifetime, including induction into the National Academy of Sciences in 1945. He spent his retirement in Berkeley, California, where two of his sisters lived and where he was given access to the laboratory facilities at the University of California at Berkeley. He died, having never married, on August 17, 1969, in Berkeley.

Further Reading
Nobelprize.org. "The Nobel Prize in Physics 1943." Available online. URL: http://nobelprize.org/physics/laureates/1943. Downloaded on July 14, 2003.
Segrè, Emilio. "Otto Stern," National Academy of Sciences, *Biographical Memoirs* 43 (1973): pp. 215–236.
Wasson, Tyler, ed. *Nobel Prize Winners*. New York: H. W. Wilson, 1987, pp. 1,012–1,014.

Sumner, James B.
(James Batcheller Sumner)
(1887–1955) *chemist*

James B. Sumner was the first to obtain an enzyme in pure form, and he also discovered that enzymes are complex proteins. For these contributions, he was awarded a share of the 1946 Nobel Prize in chemistry.

Sumner was born on November 19, 1887, in Canton, Massachusetts. His father, Charles, was a textile manufacturer, and his mother, Elizabeth, was a homemaker. After receiving a B.A. in chemistry from Harvard University in 1910, he worked in his uncle's textile factory and taught college chemistry before entering the graduate program at Harvard, receiving an M.A. and Ph.D. in chemistry in 1912 and 1913, respectively. In 1914 he accepted an offer to teach biochemistry at the Cornell University Medical College in Ithaca, New York. In 1915 he married Bertha Ricketts with whom he had five children. They divorced in 1930, and the following year he married Agnes Lundkvist. They divorced in 1943, and that same year he married Mary Beyer with whom he had two children.

In 1917 Sumner decided to focus his research efforts on finding out what an enzyme is. At the time, biochemists knew that enzymes catalyze, or begin, every chemical reaction that takes place in the body, and yet they understood very little about what enzymes are or exactly how they work. Part of their problem was that no one had been able to isolate a pure enzyme, and so they could not experiment directly with an enzyme. Sumner set out to rectify this problem by extracting a pure form of urease, the enzyme that catalyzes the conversion of urea, a by-product of protein metabolism, into ammonia and carbon dioxide. Working with jack beans, which are rich in urease, he spent the next nine years trying every technique he could think of to obtain a pure form of the enzyme, but to no avail. In 1921 he visited Jean Effront, at the time one of the world's foremost experts on enzymes, at Effront's laboratory at the University of Brussels in Belgium. Rather than learn anything of value from Effront, Sumner was told to abandon his project because it was too difficult to accomplish.

Undaunted, Sumner continued his experiments at Cornell. In 1926 he mixed a batch of the purest urease he had been able to obtain with acetone solvent and then refrigerated it. To his surprise, the chilled solution yielded crystals of pure urease. Having obtained a pure enzyme, he was now able to study its composition, and shortly after purifying it he discovered that urease is a protein. He published his findings that same year in the *Journal of Biological Chemistry*.

At first, Sumner's discovery was greeted with skepticism. His greatest opponents were a group of German biochemists who had also been trying to isolate a pure enzyme. They refused to believe that an American could succeed where they had failed, and they campaigned long and loud against Sumner's claims. The dispute raged for more than 10 years and was not settled until 1937 when JOHN H. NORTHROP, using better techniques than either Sumner or the Germans, isolated five enzymes and proved that they were proteins. Meanwhile, Sumner, working with Swedish biochemists Hans von Euler-Chelpin and Theodor Svedberg, had isolated other pure enzymes. In 1946 he was awarded a half share of the Nobel Prize in chemistry for contributing to a better understanding of enzymes. His corecipients were Northrop (one-quarter share) and the American chemist WENDELL M. STANLEY.

In 1947 Sumner was named director of Cornell's laboratory of enzyme chemistry, a position he held until his retirement in 1955. The following year he was elected to the National Academy of Sciences. He published his findings in *The Chemistry and Methods of Enzymes* (1943) and *The Enzymes: Chemistry and Mechanism of Action* (1950–52). He also wrote the popular textbook *Laboratory Experiments in Biological Chemistry* (1944). He died on August 12, 1955, in Buffalo, New York.

Further Reading

Maynard, Leonard A. "James Batcheller Sumner," National Academy of Sciences, *Biographical Memoirs* 31 (1958): pp. 376–396.

Nobelprize.org. "The Nobel Prize in Chemistry 1946." Available online. URL: http://nobelprize.org/chemistry/laureates/1946. Downloaded on February 9, 2004.

Wasson, Tyler, ed. *Nobel Prize Winners*. New York: H. W. Wilson, 1987, pp. 1,024–1,026.

Sutherland, Earl W.
(Earl Wilbur Sutherland, Jr.)
(1915–1974) *biochemist*

Earl W. Sutherland discovered cyclic adenosine monophosphate, or cyclic AMP, a biochemical compound that plays an important role in the metabolic production of a wide range of enzymes. For this discovery, and for demonstrating how cyclic AMP works, he was awarded the 1971 Nobel Prize in physiology or medicine.

Sutherland was born on November 19, 1915, in Burlingame, Kansas. His father, Earl, was a merchant, and his mother, Edith, was a homemaker. After receiving an A.B. from Washburn (Kans.) College in 1937, he entered the Washington University School of Medicine in St. Louis, Missouri, and received an M.D. in 1942. While in medical school, he assisted CARL F. CORI and GERTY T. CORI in their research concerning how the body metabolizes glucose, a simple sugar that circulates freely in the bloodstream and is the source of energy for cell functions. In 1937 he married Mildred Rice; they divorced in 1962, and the following year he married Claudia Sebeste with whom he had four children.

Following an internship at St. Louis's Barnes Hospital and service during World War II as a battalion surgeon in the U.S. Army, Sutherland in 1945 returned to Washington University to teach biochemistry and pharmacology. Like the Coris, his research focused on glucose, in his case the step-by-step process by which glycogen, the form in which glucose is stored in the muscles and liver, is broken down into glucose. The Coris had discovered that this conversion process is regulated in some way by epinephrine, a hormone that is secreted by the adrenal gland, and Sutherland set out to describe epinephrine's role in detail. By 1953 he was able to show that when the body feels stress, it readies itself to perform muscular activity by secreting epinephrine. In turn, epinephrine activates the enzyme phosphorylase, which exists in the liver in an inactive form. Phosphorylase then breaks down glycogen in the liver so that it can be released as glucose into the bloodstream. Phosphorylase also converts glycogen into glucose in the muscles, which use it to fuel their activities.

In 1953 Sutherland left Washington University to become director of the pharmacology department at the Case Western Reserve University School of Medicine in Cleveland, Ohio. He continued to study the glucose-glycogen conversion cycle, and by 1960 he discovered two new biochemical compounds, an enzyme known as adenal cyclase and a nucleotide known as cyclic AMP. These discoveries allowed him to describe the breakdown of glycogen into glucose in detail. By attaching itself to a receptor on the cell wall, epinephrine initiates the production of adenal cyclase, which also operates from a location on the surface of the cell. Adenal cyclase stimulates the cell to produce cyclic AMP within the cell, which then activates the cell's inactive phosphorylase so that it can break down glycogen into glucose.

The most intriguing feature of Sutherland's research was that it shed light on the way other hormones initiate metabolic functions. Sutherland hypothesized that cyclic AMP was the biochemical agent that set in motion the production of a number of enzymes inside cells. He further concluded that its production was initiated by a host of hormones and their related enzymes operating from different receptors along the cell wall. The determining factor as to which enzyme is produced by cyclic AMP is determined by the receptor positions of both the hormone and the enzyme. At first Sutherland's hypothesis was rejected by the scientific community as being too simple; many biochemists could not believe that one substance, cyclic AMP, could activate a wide range of seemingly unrelated metabolic processes. By the late 1960s, however, a number of independent researchers had demonstrated the validity of the hypothesis. For discovering cyclic AMP and demonstrating its role in cell metabolism, Sutherland was awarded the 1971 Nobel Prize in physiology or medicine.

Meanwhile, in 1963 Sutherland had been named a professor of physiology at Vanderbilt University in Nashville, Tennessee. He continued his research with cyclic AMP, and in 1965 he discovered that it is produced even in such simple organisms as bacteria. Other researchers have since determined that cyclic AMP helps microscopic organisms adapt to their environments, and they have raised the question of whether or not cyclic AMP is actually a primitive type of hormone.

In 1973 Sutherland became a research professor of biochemistry at the University of Miami (Fla.), a position he held until his death. In addition to winning the Nobel Prize, he was elected to the National Academy of Sciences and the American Association of Arts and Sciences. He died on March 9, 1974, in Miami.

Further Reading

Cori, Carl "Earl W. Sutherland," National Academy of Sciences, *Biographical Memoirs* 49 (1978): pp. 319–350.

Nobelprize.org. "The Nobel Prize in Physiology or Medicine 1971." Available online. URL: http://nobelprize.org/medicine/laureates/1971. Downloaded on April 23, 2004.

Wasson, Tyler, ed. *Nobel Prize Winners*. New York: H. W. Wilson, 1987, pp. 1,026–1,028.

T

Tarter, Jill C.
(Jill Cornell, Jill Cornell Tarter)
(1944–) *astronomer*

Jill Tarter is one of the foremost investigators in the search for intelligent life in outer space. In 1984 she cofounded the Search for Extraterrestrial Intelligence (SETI) Institute.

Tarter was born Jill Cornell on January 16, 1944, in Eastchester, New York, to Richard and Betty Cornell. After receiving a B.S. in engineering physics in 1965 from Cornell University (Ezra Cornell, for whom the school was named, was one of her ancestors), she entered the graduate program at the University of California at Berkeley, receiving an M.S. and a Ph.D. in astronomy in 1971 and 1975, respectively. She spent the next two years doing postdoctoral research on "brown dwarfs," a term she coined for small stars whose cores never get hot enough to permit nuclear fusion, at the National Aeronautics and Space Administration's (NASA) Ames Research Center in Moffett Field, California. In 1964 she married Bruce Tarter with whom she had one child; they later divorced, after which she married William Welch.

As a graduate student, Tarter became involved in SERENDIP (Search for Extraterrestrial Radio Emissions from Nearby Developed Intelligent Populations), a project sponsored by the University of California at Berkeley's Hat Creek Observatory to detect possible radio signals from alien civilizations. The project was prompted by the Green Bank equation, which was devised at a 1961 conference on extraterrestrial intelligence at the National Radio Astronomy Observatory at Green Bank, West Virginia. The brainchild of astrophysicist Frank Drake, the equation suggests, depending on how one tweaks the variables, that there may be as many as one million advanced civilizations within a few hundred light-years of Earth. It further assumes that such a civilization might try to contact other intelligent life via the transmission of radio signals, which can be beamed across interstellar distances at a relatively inexpensive cost. In 1977 Tarter became a project scientist with NASA's High Resolution Microwave Survey (HRMS), a much larger and better-funded version of SERENDIP. Over the next seven years she used radio telescopes, such as the one at the Arecibo Observatory in Puerto Rico, to monitor incoming microwave signals from 200 stars in the Milky Way Galaxy that are similar to the Sun, all the while trying to decipher potential signs of intelligent life.

In 1984 Tarter and Drake converted HRMS into the nonprofit Search for Extraterrestrial Intelligence (SETI) Institute in Mountain View, California, with Tarter assuming the position of director of the institute's Center for SETI Research. NASA provided most of the institute's funding until 1993, when Congress voted to cut NASA's $12 million appropriation for SETI research. The institute overcame this setback by establishing Project Phoenix, a private organization devoted to raising money for SETI that eventually attracted significant contributions from William R. Hewlett and David Packard, cofounders of Hewlett-Packard;

Paul Allen, cofounder of Microsoft; and Gordon Moore, chair of Intel, among others.

As director of SETI research, Tarter helped establish a global network of "listening posts" and a state-of-the-art microwave telescope array at Hat Creek Observatory. She played an integral role in the development of techniques to monitor a relatively narrow band (1,000–10,000 megahertz) of microwave frequencies, and to use pulse-sensitive filters to drown out the static emanating from Earth as a result of the increased use of cell phones, garage-door openers, and airport radars, all of which broadcast microwaves. Her many honors include election to the American Association for the Advancement of Science.

Further Reading

Jackson, Ellen. *Looking for Life in the Universe.* New York: Houghton Mifflin, 2002.

SETI Institute. "Jill Tarter." Available online. URL: http://www.seti.org/about_us/leadership/staff/jill_t.html. Downloaded on May 20, 2004.

Tatum, Edward L.
(Edward Lawrie Tatum)
(1909–1975) *geneticist*

Edward L. Tatum cofounded the branch of genetic research known as biochemical genetics, the study of the role genes play in controlling the biochemical functions of living organisms. For codeveloping the "one gene–one enzyme" concept with GEORGE W. BEADLE, and for facilitating the research of JOSHUA LEDERBERG on bacterial genetics, Tatum was awarded a share of the 1958 Nobel Prize in physiology or medicine.

Tatum was born on December 14, 1909, in Boulder, Colorado. His father, Arthur, was a chemistry professor, and his mother, Mabel, was a homemaker. As a youngster he moved with his family to Wisconsin, Illinois, Pennsylvania, and South Dakota before settling with them in 1918 in Chicago, Illinois. In 1925 the family moved to Madison, Wisconsin; two years later, Tatum entered the University of Wisconsin, receiving an A.B. in chemistry in 1932, an M.S. in microbiology in 1933, and a Ph.D. in biochemistry in 1935. In

1934 he married June Alton with whom he had two children. They divorced in 1956, and that same year he married Viola Kantor. She died in 1974, and that same year he married Elsie Bergland.

Tatum remained at Wisconsin for a year to conduct postdoctoral research. In 1936 he received a General Education Board fellowship to study at the University of Utrecht in the Netherlands, where he experimented with the nutritional requirements of various fungi. In 1937 he accepted a position as a research associate at Stanford University, where he began collaborating with Beadle on the latter's studies of genetic behavior in fruit flies. Beadle felt certain that the biochemical functions of any organism are controlled by its genes, and during the 1930s he had induced mutations in the larvae of fruit flies in an effort to prove his theory. In 1937 Tatum and Beadle began working to develop the sophisticated experimental methods required to understand the complex biochemical operations of mutated fruit flies, but by 1941 they were forced to admit that the fruit fly, simple organism though it may be, was too complex an organism on which to test their theories.

That same year, Tatum and Beadle refocused their research by shifting their attention from the fruit fly to *Neurospora crassa,* a red bread mold. Because of his earlier work with the nutritional requirements of fungi, Tatum knew that *Neurospora*'s environment could be manipulated in such a way that tracking genetic changes would be relatively easy. Tatum and Beadle used X-rays to introduce mutations into colonies of *Neurospora,* and then they varied the nutritional medium upon which the mutants grew. By noting which biochemical functions the mutants were unable to perform, and then identifying which gene had been mutated, they were able to match up a number of specific biochemical functions with the particular gene that was associated with each function. By the end of 1941, they had concluded that genes control the structure and function of enzymes, complex proteins that initiate biochemical reactions. They further concluded that each enzyme is controlled by one particular gene, a hypothesis that became known as the "one gene–one enzyme" concept. Further experimentation showed that a mutation in a gene affects only the biochemical function initiated by the enzyme that the gene controls.

Over the next several years, other geneticists provided additional evidence to validate Tatum and Beadle's one gene–one enzyme concept. In time, biochemists learned how to develop methods based on the concept that were highly useful in a variety of applications such as studying cell metabolism and developing pharmaceutical drugs from living organisms. For their achievements in the field of biochemical genetics, which they cofounded, Tatum and Beadle were each awarded a quarter share of the 1958 Nobel Prize in physiology or medicine.

Meanwhile, in 1945 Tatum had left Stanford to become a professor of botany and microbiology at Yale University. At Yale he and Lederberg, one of his graduate students, adapted the techniques Tatum and Beadle had used to study *Neurospora* for use with bacteria, specifically the K-12 strain of *Escherichia coli* (*E. coli*). In 1946 they discovered that individual *E. coli* exchange genetic material, an ability that was thought to be restricted to lifeforms that reproduce sexually. They also demonstrated that bacteria, being such a primitive life-form, are an even better research subject than *Neurospora* for understanding the way genes regulate biochemical functions. Their brief collaboration formed the basis of Lederberg's later research concerning bacterial genetics, for which he received the other half share of Tatum and Beadle's Nobel Prize.

In 1948 Tatum returned to Stanford to teach biology and biochemistry and to conduct research related to genetic processes that take place outside the nucleus of the cell. In 1957 he left Stanford for the second time, this time to join the research staff at the Rockefeller Institute for Medical Research (today Rockefeller University) in New York City, where he remained for the rest of his career. His many honors include election to the National Academy of Sciences. He died on November 5, 1975, in New York City.

Further Reading

Lederberg, Joshua. "Edward Lawrie Tatum," National Academy of Sciences, *Biographical Memoirs* 59 (1990): pp. 356–387.

Nobelprize.org. "The Nobel Prize in Physiology or Medicine 1958." Available online. URL: http://nobelprize.org/medicine/laureates/1958. Downloaded on April 21, 2004.

Wasson, Tyler, ed. *Nobel Prize Winners.* New York: H. W. Wilson, 1987, pp. 1,041–1,043.

Taube, Henry
(1915–   ) *chemist*

Henry Taube's research presented scientists with a better understanding of how electrons are transferred during a chemical reaction. For this contribution, he was awarded the 1983 Nobel Prize in chemistry.

Taube was born on November 30, 1915, in Neudorf, Saskatchewan, Canada. His parents, Samuel and Albertina, were farmers. After completing his secondary education at a boarding school, he entered the University of Saskatchewan, receiving a B.S. in chemistry in 1935 and an M.S. in photochemistry in 1937. He then came to the United States and received a Ph.D. in inorganic chemistry from the University of California at Berkeley in 1940. He remained at Berkeley for a year as a chemistry instructor before joining the faculty at Cornell University in Ithaca, New York, in 1941. Five years later he was named a professor of chemistry at the University of Chicago, and in 1962 he accepted a similar position at Stanford University in California. In 1942 he became a naturalized U.S. citizen, and in 1952 he married Mary Alice Wesche with whom he had four children.

Taube's research focused on electron transfer during chemical reactions. He was particularly interested in reactions that yield coordination compounds, substances whose chemical structures feature a central metal atom surrounded by groups of nonmetallic atoms known as ligands. Coordination compounds, such as vitamin B_{12} and chlorophyll, are distinguished by the unique three-dimensional arrangements of their atoms. Taube's early work employed metallic ions, atoms or groups of atoms whose electron configurations give them a net charge that is either positive or negative. By 1950 he had shown that when metallic ions are immersed in a water solution, the ions bond with some of the water molecules to form coordination compounds, and that the stability of the chemical bond and the arrangement of the atoms are determined by the properties of the ions. Further research along this line enabled him to explain the properties of coordination compounds in terms of their electron configurations.

Taube then set out to explain why metallic ions can exchange electrons in water solutions. Conventional wisdom suggested that such an exchange should be impossible because the water molecules insulate the ions from one another, and yet it happens, and often quite rapidly, in many reactions that yield coordination compounds. Eventually he was able to demonstrate that rather than hinder electron exchange, water molecules actually facilitate it. In essence, the chemical bond that combines a metallic ion and the water molecules into a coordination compound turns the nonmetallic ligand into a bridge that allows an electron to cross the gap between two metallic ions. Once the electron crosses the bridge, the bond is broken, thus completing the transfer.

Taube's findings explained why chemical reactions proceed at different rates of speed from one another. Previously, chemists had believed that atoms and molecules simply exchange electrons in more or less the same way, but Taube showed that the rate of reaction depends in large part on the ability of a ligand to serve as a bridge. His work also had many practical applications. For example, his demonstration of the bridge effect enabled other chemists to develop coordination compounds for use as catalysts in the production of commercial polymers such as polyethylene and polypropylene. In recognition of his accomplishments, Taube was awarded the 1983 Nobel Prize in chemistry.

Taube retired from Stanford in 1986; although he continued to tutor and conduct research there, he spent more of his time in retirement as a consultant to various chemical manufacturers. His many honors include the National Medal of Science and election to the National Academy of Sciences and the American Academy of Arts and Sciences. His publications include *Electron Transfer Reactions of Complex Ions in Solution* (1970).

Further Reading

Isied, Stephan S., ed. *Electron Transfer Reactions: Inorganic, Organometallic, and Biological Applications* [lectures in honor of Henry Taube's 80th birthday]. Washington, D.C.: American Chemical Society, 1997.

Nobelprize.org. "The Nobel Prize in Chemistry 1983." Available online. URL: http://nobelprize.org/chemistry/laureates/1983. Downloaded on August 11, 2004.

Wasson, Tyler, ed. *Nobel Prize Winners*. New York: H. W. Wilson, 1987, pp. 1,043–1,045.

Taussig, Helen B.
(Helen Brooke Taussig)
(1898–1986) *physiologist*

Helen Taussig helped develop a surgical procedure that saved the lives of thousands of children born with heart defects. For this and other contributions, she was described toward the end of her life as being "probably the best-known woman physician in the world."

Taussig was born on May 24, 1898, in Cambridge, Massachusetts. Her father, Frank, was a professor at Harvard University, and her mother, Edith, was a homemaker. As a child she was greatly influenced by her grandfather, a physician whose practice dealt mostly with children. She received a private education, and in 1917 she entered Radcliffe College, her mother's alma mater. Two years later she transferred to the University of California at Berkeley, where she received an A.B. in 1921.

After studying medicine for two years at Harvard, which did not grant degrees to women, Taussig began taking courses at Boston University Medical School. Boston did not grant degrees to women, either, but the medical school's dean, Alexander Begg, took an interest in her and encouraged her to learn more about the heart. He also encouraged her to apply to Johns Hopkins University Medical School, perhaps the finest medical school in the country that graduated women. She was admitted in 1924 and received an M.D. three years later. She spent the next three years at Johns Hopkins Hospital as a fellow in cardiology and an intern in pediatrics. In 1930 she was named director of the hospital's new Children's Heart Clinic, a position she held for 33 years.

One of Taussig's first accomplishments as director was to develop a new method for identifying heart defects. Previously, physicians applied a stethoscope to the patient's chest and listened for unusual sounds, but Taussig suffered from a partial loss of hearing. Taking advantage of advances in X-ray technology, she used a fluoroscope to produce X-ray images of the heart and chest from a variety of angles. Over time, she also became adept at diagnosing certain heart defects by observing the movement of a patient's chest while the patient breathed.

Of all the heart defects, Taussig was most interested in the ones that caused anoxemia, also known as "blue baby syndrome." Children with this condition did not get enough oxygen into their hearts; their skin was a light shade of blue, and they rarely lived to adulthood. After studying both blue babies and healthy babies for almost 10 years, she discovered that blue babies shared two problems. The first was a leaking septum, the wall that separates the chambers of the heart, and the second was that the pulmonary artery, which connects the heart to the lungs, was too narrow. As Taussig realized, these two problems are sufficient to keep most of the body's blood from ever reaching the lungs.

At this point Taussig set out to find a way to repair both problems surgically. In this quest she was aided by the work of Robert Gross, who was also a pediatric cardiologist. In 1939 Gross had devised a surgical procedure for closing an open ductus arteriosus, the artery connecting the aorta to the pulmonary artery; the ductus arteriosus remains open in the womb but normally closes at birth. One curious thing about the procedure was that although it helped otherwise normal babies, it seemed to worsen the condition of blue babies. Taussig reasoned that somehow the open ductus arteriosus was allowing more blood to reach the lungs, and she wondered if blue baby syndrome could be cured by creating an artificial opening in an artery.

Taussig first approached Gross with her idea; when he showed insufficient interest, she shared her thoughts with ALFRED BLALOCK, Johns Hopkins Hospital's chief of surgery. Blalock was much more interested, and he began working on a procedure with

Helen B. Taussig codeveloped a surgical procedure for correcting "blue baby syndrome," a heart defect in newborns. *(©Bettmann/Corbis)*

Taussig. In 1943 Blalock was able to join the subclavian artery, which in a human carries blood from the heart to the arms, to the pulmonary artery of a dog. By 1944 he was ready to try a similar procedure on a human, and that same year he effected a complete cure in a six-year-old "blue baby" via surgery. Taussig and Blalock published a joint account of the procedure the following year, and in time the procedure became known as the Blalock-Taussig operation.

In addition to curing blue baby syndrome, the Blalock-Taussig operation is noteworthy for two other reasons. First, it demonstrated to surgeons that very sick children could be operated on successfully, which opened up to those children a wide range of surgical procedures previously denied them, albeit with good intentions. Second, it suggested to surgeons that more complicated operations could be performed on adults, which eventually led to the development of open-heart surgery.

In 1962 Taussig made another contribution to children's health. She had heard from a German colleague that the drug thalidomide, which German doctors had prescribed for pregnant women as a way to control morning sickness, was causing ghastly birth defects. Taussig immediately traveled to Germany to conduct her own personal investigation. She discovered that the babies of women who had taken thalidomide were often born without arms or legs; in other words, their hands were attached directly to their shoulders while their feet were connected directly to their hips. Taussig immediately notified Frances Kelsey, a medical officer with the U.S. Food and Drug Administration. Kelsey had already denied a request from the William S. Merrell Company, the drug's manufacturer, to sell thalidomide in the United States, but the company had distributed a large quantity of the drug to physicians as samples. Armed with Taussig's report, Kelsey was able to officially notify physicians about the dangers of thalidomide, thus safeguarding the health of an untold number of American children.

Taussig retired from Johns Hopkins in 1963. She continued to conduct research on heart defects, however, and in 1965 she was elected president of the American Heart Association. Her other honors include the U.S. Medal of Freedom in 1964 and election to the National Academy of Sciences in 1973. She died on May 20, 1986, in an automobile accident in Kennett Square, Pennsylvania.

Further Reading

Bailey, Martha J. *American Women in Science: A Biographical Dictionary.* Santa Barbara, Calif.: ABC-CLIO, 1994, p. 387.

Nuland, Sherwin B. "A Triumph of Twentieth-Century Medicine: Helen Taussig and the Blue-Baby Operation," in *Doctors: The Biography of Medicine.* New York: Random House, 1989, pp. 430–455.

Yount, Lisa. *A to Z of Women in Science and Math.* New York: Facts On File, 1999, pp. 199–201.

Taylor, Joseph H.
(Joseph Hooton Taylor, Jr.)
(1941–) *astrophysicist*

Joseph H. Taylor codiscovered the first binary pulsar and provided some of the earliest evidence to support ALBERT EINSTEIN's theory of general relativ-

ity. These contributions won Taylor a share of the 1993 Nobel Prize in physics.

Taylor was born on March 29, 1941, in Philadelphia, Pennsylvania, to Joseph and Sylvia Taylor. At age seven he moved with his family to a farm in Cinnaminson, New Jersey, where he grew up. After receiving a B.A. in physics from Haverford (Pa.) College in 1963, he entered the graduate astronomy program at Harvard University.

As a boy, Taylor had been fascinated with radio, and he built a number of amateur radio sets and antennas while still in high school. He pursued this interest in graduate school by focusing on radio astronomy, the study of distant stars by examining the radio frequencies they emit. He was particularly interested in pulsars, rapidly rotating stars that emit extremely regular pulses of radio waves. Discovered in 1967 by English astronomers Jocelyn Bell and Antony Hewish, pulsars are created when the core of a supernova, a violently exploding star, collapses inward and becomes highly compressed. The result of this compression is a gravitational field so strong that radio waves, which are generated by the pulsar's extremely rapid rotation, can escape it only at the magnetic poles, where the gravitational pull is the weakest. These waves are projected in intense, sweeping beams that resemble the beams of light from a lighthouse. Most pulsars do not emit visible light, and so they can be studied only via radio astronomy. Consequently, in 1968, when Taylor received his Ph.D., there was still much to be learned about pulsars.

Taylor taught astronomy at Harvard for a year before joining the faculty at the University of Massachusetts in 1969. Four years later, he and RUSSELL A. HULSE, one of his graduate students, began searching for pulsars by using the giant radio telescope in Arecibo, Puerto Rico. Of the 40 new pulsars they discovered, by far the most interesting one was the first binary pulsar, known today as PSR1913+16. A binary pulsar consists of two pulsars that orbit each other at a distance roughly equal to that separating the Earth and the Moon, and because of their intertwined orbits their radio pulses are irregular. Of particular interest to Taylor and Hulse was the fact that PSR1913+16 rotates approximately 10 times faster than the speed at which the Earth orbits the Sun, thus making it an excellent candidate for testing some of Einstein's theories about general relativity. Einstein had theorized that celestial bodies moving at rapid rates of speed would generate gravitational radiation, or a series of waves that ripple in the curvature of spacetime. Although Taylor and Hulse were unable to provide direct evidence for the existence of gravitational radiation, they showed that PSR1913+16's orbiting period gradually diminishes with time, and in exactly the way that Einstein predicted, as a result of the emission of gravitational waves that are produced when the two stars are closest to each other. This result has been interpreted by physicists as indicating that gravitational radiation does exist. For discovering PSR1913+16 and for providing evidence to support Einstein's theory of general relativity, Taylor and Hulse were each awarded a half share of the 1993 Nobel Prize in physics.

In 1976 Taylor married Marietta Bisson with whom he had three children. Four years later he left Massachusetts to teach physics at Princeton University, where Hulse had gone to teach in 1977. He remained at Princeton for the rest of his career, and he continued to search for and study pulsars. His publications include *Pulsars* (1977), which he coauthored with Richard Manchester. His honors include election to the National Academy of Sciences and the American Academy of Arts and Sciences.

Further Reading

Bailes, Matthew, et al., eds. *Radio Pulsars: In Celebration of the Contributions of Andrew Lyne, Dick Manchester and Joe Taylor—A Festschrift Honoring Their 60th Birthdays.* San Francisco, Calif.: Astronomical Society of the Pacific, 2003.

McMurray, Emily J., ed. *Notable Twentieth-Century Scientists.* Detroit: Gale Research, 1995, pp. 1,980–1,981.

Nobelprize.org. "The Nobel Prize in Physics 1993." Available online. URL: http://nobelprize.org/physics/laureates/1993. Downloaded on October 12, 2004.

Teller, Edward
(Ede Teller)
(1908–2003) *physicist*

Edward Teller, the "father of the hydrogen bomb," is the person most responsible for the development of thermonuclear weapons. He played a central role in the conception, design, construction, testing, and inclusion in the American arsenal of the hydrogen bombs, the most destructive weapons ever developed.

Teller was born Ede Teller on January 15, 1908, in Budapest, Hungary. His father, Max, was a lawyer, and his mother, Ilona, was a homemaker. After finishing high school in 1925, he studied chemical engineering at the Karlsruhe Technische Hochschule in Karlsruhe, Germany, receiving a B.S. in 1928. He spent the next two years at the universities of Munich and Leipzig, receiving a Ph.D. in theoretical physics from the latter in 1930. After several years as a research consultant at the University of Göttingen, in 1934 he obtained a Rockefeller Foundation fellowship to study at the University of Copenhagen's Institute for Theoretical Physics. Here he met GEORGE GAMOW, who offered him a position as a physics professor at George Washington University (GWU) in Washington, D.C. In 1934 he married Augusta Harkanyi with whom he had two children.

Teller's early research interest involved quantum mechanics, the study of subatomic particles. At GWU he and Gamow theorized about the various ways in which a subatomic particle could escape an atomic nucleus via radioactive decay, and they eventually explained this phenomenon via what is now known as the Gamow-Teller selection rules for beta decay. They also worked together to use what was known about nuclear physics to explain astrophysical phenomena such as the production of heat and energy by the stars.

Teller's involvement with nuclear weapons began in 1939 when he was one of three scientists who convinced ALBERT EINSTEIN to convince President Franklin D. Roosevelt to authorize the Manhattan Project, the U.S. effort to build an atomic bomb during World War II. In 1941 Teller became a naturalized U.S. citizen, joined the Manhattan Project, and was assigned to the University of Chicago where he helped ENRICO FERMI achieve the first controlled chain reaction involving nuclear fission, in this case as a result of splitting apart uranium atoms. In 1943 Teller joined J. ROBERT OPPENHEIMER at the Los Alamos Laboratory in New Mexico where he took part in the design of the uranium bomb that was dropped on Hiroshima, Japan, in 1945.

After the war, Teller taught physics at the Institute for Nuclear Studies at the University of Chicago for three years before returning to Los Alamos in 1949. He was motivated to do so by his desire to create a superbomb, one that used nuclear fission to initiate a chain reaction involving nuclear fusion, in this case the combination of hydrogen atoms to form helium, the process by which the Sun produces heat and energy. Teller and Fermi had come up with the idea while working together in Chicago, and while at Los Alamos Teller had urged Oppenheimer to devote more attention to the development of a fusion bomb. Many of his fellow scientists, having seen what devastation atomic weapons wrought in Japan, were reluctant to work on a superbomb, but Teller believed that such a weapon was necessary to check what he perceived to be the Soviet Union's intention to dominate the world. He played a major role in convincing President Harry S Truman to authorize work on the hydrogen or thermonuclear bomb, and he oversaw its design, construction, and successful testing in the South Pacific Ocean in 1952.

That same year Teller returned to his former position at Chicago, from where he lobbied government officials to establish a Los Alamos–like facility dedicated to thermonuclear research. That year the federal government established such a facility, the Lawrence Livermore Radiation Laboratory, at the University of California at Berkeley. Teller joined its staff when it opened; he was named its associate director in 1954 and served as its director from 1958 to 1960. In these positions he played a major role in the design of increasingly sophisticated and destructive thermonuclear weapons. Meanwhile, the general public was becoming increasingly concerned about the possibility of a thermonuclear war, and to assuage their fears he wrote several books: *Our Nuclear Future* (1958), *The Legacy of Hiroshima* (1962), and *The Reluctant Revolutionary* (1964).

Teller retired from Lawrence Livermore in 1975, although he continued to work there as a consultant for a number of years thereafter. He never abandoned his interest in thermonuclear weapons, and he was a strong proponent of President Ronald Reagan's Strategic Defense Initiative, better known as Star Wars. Nevertheless, in the 1970s Teller expanded his work to include finding peaceful applications for nuclear energy. To this end he spent his remaining years as a senior research fellow at Stanford University's Hoover Institution on War, Revolution, and Peace, and he wrote several more books—*Energy: A Plan for Action* (1975), *Nuclear Energy in the Developing World* (1977), and *Energy from Heaven and Earth* (1979).

Teller's honors include the National Medal of Science, the Presidential Medal of Freedom, and election to the National Academy of Sciences and the American Academy of Arts and Sciences. He died on September 9, 2003, at his home in Palo Alto, California.

Further Reading

Blumberg, Stanley A., and Gwinn Owens. *Energy and Conflict: The Life and Times of Edward Teller.* New York: Putnam's, 1976.

Teller, Edward, with Judith L. Shoolery. *Memoirs: A Twentieth-Century Journey in Science and Politics.* Cambridge, Mass.: Perseus, 2001.

Temin, Howard M.
(Howard Martin Temin)
(1934–1994) *virologist*

Howard M. Temin discovered retroviruses, cancer-causing viruses that replicate themselves by reversing the normal transmission of genetic coding. For this discovery, he was awarded a share of the 1975 Nobel Prize in physiology or medicine.

Temin was born on December 10, 1934, in Philadelphia, Pennsylvania. His father, Henry, was an attorney, and his mother, Annette, was a homemaker. After receiving a B.S. in biology from Swarthmore College in 1955, he entered the California Institute of Technology (Caltech), receiving a Ph.D. in virology in 1959. He remained at Caltech for a year to do postdoctoral research with his mentor, RENATO DULBECCO. In 1960 Temin became associated with the McArdle Laboratory for Cancer Research at the University of Wisconsin Medical School in Madison where he remained for the rest of his career. In 1962 he married Rayla Greenberg with whom he had two children.

Temin's career was devoted to cancer research. As a graduate student at Caltech, he began studying the Rous sarcoma virus (RSV); discovered by PEYTON ROUS, RSV causes cancer in chickens. Temin was interested in how RSV replicates itself, and by 1959 he had hypothesized that this occurs after RSV integrates itself into a host cell. Further experimentation allowed him to demonstrate in 1964 that RSV, unlike many viruses, does not kill off the host cell after infecting it. Rather, it attaches its genome, or a single set of chromosomes, to the genes of the host cell; in effect, the viral genome becomes a new gene, thus transforming the host cell. Consequently, when the transformed host cell reproduces itself, the daughter cells already contain the genetic coding for RSV. These infected cells are not attacked by the chicken's immune system because the genetic coding indicates that the RSV-infected cells "belong" in the chicken. These findings coincided with those of Dulbecco, who in 1962 had demonstrated that polyoma virus, which causes cancer in mice, operates in the same way.

Temin also discovered that RSV-infected cells do not necessarily reproduce RSV. Instead, the viral genome, which Temin named a provirus, often lies dormant for a number of generations, perhaps even for millions of years, and it causes the transformed cell to release RSV only after the cell comes in contact with a certain chemical. This discovery was supported by the work of French biologist André-Michael Lwoff, who won the 1965 Nobel Prize in physiology or medicine for demonstrating the existence of prophages, viruses that infect the cells of bacteria in much the same way that RSV infects the cells of chickens. Temin's demonstration of the existence of proviruses in animal cells led other researchers to look for additional examples, and by the time of his death they had discovered more than 100 proviruses in various mammals.

The major problem with Temin's findings was the fact that RSV consists mostly of RNA, not DNA. This means that RSV transmits genetic coding from RNA to DNA, which is the exact opposite of how genetic coding is normally transmitted. At the time, it was understood that genetic coding is transmitted by messenger RNA from the DNA in a replicating cell to a daughter cell. Conventional wisdom held, therefore, that genetic coding could be transmitted from DNA to RNA but not vice versa, so the scientific community refused to accept that RSV behaved as Temin claimed. Undaunted, he continued to study RSV, and in 1970 he discovered a viral enzyme, which he named reverse transcriptase, that reverses the way genetic coding is transmitted. Simply stated, reverse transcriptase synthesizes DNA by copying the genetic coding in RNA, in this case the RNA of RSV. Temin's discovery of reverse transcriptase and his description of its abilities were duplicated independently that same year by DAVID BALTIMORE, thus demonstrating conclusively that an RNA tumor virus can integrate its genome into a host cell in the same way that certain DNA tumor viruses, like polyoma, do. Tumor viruses that make use of reverse transcriptase to copy DNA from RNA are now known as retroviruses. For helping to discover them, Temin was awarded a one-third share of the 1975 Nobel Prize in physiology or medicine; his corecipients were Dulbecco and Baltimore.

The discovery of retroviruses had major implications for medical researchers, particularly those who began studying acquired immunodeficiency syndrome (AIDS) and the virus that causes it, human immunodeficiency virus (HIV), in the 1980s. Once it was discovered that HIV is a retrovirus, researchers were better able to develop methods for combating its spread. Temin contributed to the attack on AIDS by helping to demonstrate that HIV causes AIDS; he served on the National Institutes of Health committee that named HIV, and he chaired the Global Commission on AIDS and the World Health Organization Advisory Council on HIV and AIDS. One of the tools used to fight AIDS is a method he developed for measuring how fast a host cell is transformed by a retrovirus; armed with such information, researchers can develop vaccines that target HIV based on its speed of replication.

Temin's many honors included election to the National Academy of Sciences and the American Academy of Arts and Sciences and receipt of the National Medal of Science. He died on February 9, 1994, in Madison.

Further Reading

Nobelprize.org. "The Nobel Prize in Physiology or Medicine 1975." Available online. URL: http://nobelprize.org/medicine/laureates/1975. Downloaded on June 8, 2004.

Sugden, Bill. "Howard M. Temin," National Academy of Sciences, *Biographical Memoirs* 79 (2001): pp. 336–375.

Wasson, Tyler, ed. *Nobel Prize Winners.* New York: H. W. Wilson, 1987, pp. 1,045–1,047.

Thomas, E. Donnall
(Edward Donnall Thomas)
(1920–   ) *physician*

E. Donnall Thomas was the world's foremost authority on bone marrow transplants. His contributions to medical science in this regard won him a share of the 1990 Nobel Prize in physiology or medicine.

Thomas was born on March 15, 1920, in Mart, Texas. His father, Edward, was a physician, and his mother, Angie, was a schoolteacher. He studied chemistry and chemical engineering at the University of Texas at Austin, receiving a B.A. in 1941 and an M.A. in 1943. He then entered the University of Texas Medical Branch in Galveston but transferred after a year to Harvard Medical School, receiving an M.D. in 1946. He spent the next two years as an intern and resident at the Peter Bent Brigham Hospital (today Brigham and Women's Hospital) in Boston, Massachusetts, followed by two years as a medical officer in the U.S. Army and a year of postdoctoral research at the Massachusetts Institute of Technology. In 1951 he returned to Brigham as chief medical resident, leaving in 1955 to become physician-in-chief at the Mary Imogene Bassett Hospital in Cooperstown, New York, and a professor of medicine at Columbia University's College of Physicians and Surgeons. In 1963 he joined the faculty at the University of Washington (UW) School of Medicine and the medical staff at the Seattle Public Health Hospital. In 1975 he left Seattle Hospital to become affiliated with UW's Fred Hutchinson Cancer Research Center, where he remained for the rest of his career. In 1943 he married Dorothy Martin with whom he had three children.

E. Donnall Thomas is a leading expert on bone marrow transplants. *(Courtesy of Fred Hutchinson Cancer Research Center)*

As a resident at Brigham, Thomas became interested in leukemia and other cancers of the blood. Leukemia causes the body's bone marrow to produce an abnormally large number of white blood cells, the body's frontline defense against infection, so Thomas began experimenting with bone marrow transplants as a possible cure for leukemia. Extensive research showed that a healthy individual could donate as much as one liter of bone marrow without suffering unduly. It also showed that donated bone marrow injected into a patient via a blood vessel automatically found its way to the right places in the bones, where it began producing the proper proportion of healthy red and white blood cells. After experimenting extensively with dogs, in 1956 he performed the first successful bone marrow transplant in humans. However, the donor and the recipient were identical twins, a situation that was necessitated by the fact that the body's immune system naturally rejects bone marrow from another body because it has different genetic characteristics. This situation is particularly complicated for patients with leukemia, because if the immune system does not reject the donor marrow, then the donor marrow might produce white blood cells that will attack the recipient's cells and tissues because they lack the "proper" genetic coding. He found that exposing the patient's bone marrow to irradiation by X-rays suppresses the immune system somewhat, but not enough to ensure the success of a bone marrow transplant. The future for such procedures seemed dim unless Thomas could find a way to overcome both problems.

Fortunately, developments by other researchers gave Thomas the tools he needed to ensure the success of bone marrow transplants. In 1957 GERTRUDE B. ELION developed azathioprine, a pharmaceutical drug that proved useful in suppressing the body's immune system during transplant operations. Five years later JOSEPH E. MURRAY used azathioprine during the world's first successful kidney transplant involving two nonrelated humans. Meanwhile, GEORGE D. SNELL and others were developing procedures for determining the compatibility of tissues that made it possible to match donors and recipients with greater confidence that a transplant between them would be successful. Armed with these and other tools, in 1969 Thomas's research team was able to perform the first successful bone marrow transplant between a leukemia patient and a nonidentical twin donor. By 1977 the team had developed a sophisticated procedure that combined radiation therapy and drug therapy (methotrexate instead of azathioprine) as a means of suppressing the immunological response of both the recipient's immune system and the white blood cells produced by the donated bone marrow. That same year they performed the first successful bone marrow transplant involving two unrelated humans. This procedure raised the success rate of a bone marrow transplant to almost 50 percent and made this operation a viable option for patients with certain inherited blood disorders or dysfunctional bone marrow as well as those with leukemia and other blood cancers.

Bone marrow transplants have saved the lives of tens of thousands of patients with blood disorders or conditions for which no other treatments exist. By 1990 Thomas's team alone had conducted more than 4,000 successful bone marrow transplants. Accordingly, Thomas was awarded a half share of the 1990 Nobel Prize in physiology or medicine; his corecipient was Murray. Thomas's other honors include the National Medal of Science.

Further Reading

Applebaum, Frederick R. "Dedication." *Biology of Blood and Marrow Transplantation* 6 (2000): pp. 75–76.
Nobelprize.org. "The Nobel Prize in Physiology or Medicine 1990." Available online. URL: http://nobelprize. org/medicine/laureates/1990. Downloaded on June 16, 2004.

Ting, Samuel C. C.
(Samuel Chao Chung Ting)
(1936–   ) *physicist*

Samuel C. C. Ting codiscovered the J/psi particle as well as the charmed quark and its antiquark. For these discoveries he was awarded a share of the 1976 Nobel Prize in physics.

Ting was born on January 27, 1936, in Ann Arbor, Michigan. His parents, Kuan Hai and Tsun-Ying, were students at the University of Michigan; eventually his father became a professor of engineering and his mother became a professor of psychology. As a baby he returned with his family to China, where he grew up, but he returned to the United States at age 20 to study engineering at Michigan. He soon changed his major to mathematics and physics, and he received a B.S.E. in both subjects in 1959. He remained at Michigan to attend graduate school, and in 1962 he received a Ph.D. in physics. He spent the next five years conducting research at the European Organization for Nuclear Research (CERN) in Geneva, Switzerland, and the Deutsches Elektronen Synchrotron in Hamburg, Germany, and teaching physics at Columbia University in New York City. In 1967 he joined the faculty at the Massachusetts Institute of Technology (MIT), and two years later he was named a professor of physics. In 1985 he married

Susan Marks with whom he had one child; he also had two children by a previous marriage.

In 1966, while at Columbia, Ting became interested in electron-positron pairs. A positron is a subatomic particle with the same mass as an electron but with a positive charge. It is the electron's antiparticle, meaning that when the two collide at high speed they disintegrate. He was particularly intrigued by an experiment that had been conducted at England's Cambridge University, whereby photons, or tiny packets of light energy, were used to produce electron-positron pairs. The manner of their production suggested that the underlying theories of quantum electrodynamics (QED), the body of theory concerning the interactions of charged particles with each other and with electromagnetic radiation, did not hold true for electron-positron pairs. Ting set out to corroborate these findings, and from that moment on his research focused on electrons and muons, negatively charged particles whose mass is approximately 200 times that of an electron.

In 1971 Ting began performing experiments concerning electron-positron pairs with the Alternating Gradient Synchrotron (AGS) at the Brookhaven National Laboratory on New York's Long Island. The AGS generates beams of high-intensity protons and propels them into stationary targets as a means of producing previously unknown subatomic particles. In 1974 Ting produced a totally unpredicted particle he named the J-particle. The J-particle is a meson because it consists of two quarks. A quark is one of the basic building blocks of matter; protons and neutrons, for example, consist of three quarks. Whereas protons and neutrons are composed of different combinations of "up" and "down" quarks, the J-particle consists of two previously unknown quarks, the "charmed" quark and its antiquark. The charmed antiquark is the charmed quark's antiparticle, and when the two collide, they disintegrate, thus explaining the extremely short life of the J particle. At about the same time that Ting discovered the J-particle, BURTON RICHTER discovered what he called the psi particle. Further investigation demonstrated that the J-particle and the psi particle are one and the same, and today Ting and Richter's discovery is known as the J/psi particle.

The existence of the J/psi particle had been totally unknown, although SHELDON L. GLASHOW had predicted the existence of the charmed quark 10 years before its discovery. The most surprising thing about the J/psi particle is that it has twice the mass of a proton, even though it consists of one less quark. Since the charmed quark and its antiquark clearly possess properties that are significantly different from the up and down quarks, physicists began to search for other unknown quarks. By 1990 researchers had discovered the "beauty" quark and strongly suspected the existence of a "truth" quark. For the role he played in these developments, Ting was awarded a half share of the 1976 Nobel Prize in physics; his corecipient was Richter.

Ting remained at MIT for the rest of his career. His publications include *The Search for Charm, Beauty, and Truth at High Energies* (1984). His honors include election to the National Academy of Sciences and the American Academy of Arts and Sciences.

Further Reading

Massachusetts Institute of Technology. "Samuel C. C. Ting." Available online. URL: http://www-lns.mit.edu/~eluc/AMS/ting-bio.html. Downloaded on March 25, 2005.

Nobelprize.org. "The Nobel Prize in Physics 1976." Available online. URL: http://nobelprize.org/physics/laureates/1976. Downloaded on September 20, 2004.

Wasson, Tyler, ed. *Nobel Prize Winners.* New York: H. W. Wilson, 1987, pp. 1,061–1,063.

Torrey, John
(1796–1873) *botanist*

John Torrey was the first professional botanist in the United States, as well as the last professional botanist to be self-taught. His publications and personal herbarium set the first standards for the classification and collection of plants in the United States.

Torrey was born on August 15, 1796, in New York City. His father, William, was a merchant and prison superintendent, and his mother, Margaret, was a homemaker. After receiving an M.D. from New York City's College of Physicians and Surgeons in 1818, he practiced medicine until 1824, when he was named to teach chemistry, mineralogy, and geology at the U.S. Military Academy. Three years later he returned to New York City to teach chemistry part-time at his alma mater, the College of Pharmacy at New York University, and Columbia and Princeton Universities. In 1853 he gave up teaching to become an assayer with the U.S. Mint, a position he held for the rest of his career.

As a boy, Torrey had developed an intense interest in botany from assisting Amos Eaton, a professor of natural history who was an inmate in Torrey's father's prison. Torrey collected plant specimens for the incarcerated Eaton, who in turn taught Torrey everything he knew about botany. While in college, he cofounded the Lyceum of Natural History (later known as the New York Academy of Sciences) and prepared a catalog of plants that were native to New York City and the surrounding environs that became known as "Torrey's catalog." While practicing as a medical doctor, he devoted as much of his spare time as he could to studying the plants of the northeastern United States. In 1824 he published *Flora of the Northern and Middle Sections of the United States*, a compendium of his botanical work to date. With the publication of this work, Torrey established his reputation as the foremost botanist in the country.

In 1831 Torrey published an American edition of John Lindley's *Introduction to the Natural System of Botany*. This volume introduced to American botanists the new ideas about plant classification that the leading botanists in Europe had been developing over the years. Lindley's work inspired Torrey to conduct a survey of all the plants in North America, and he was assisted ably in this task by ASA GRAY, who became his protégé in 1834. Their work on this mammoth project was slowed considerably when Torrey was named New York State botanist in 1836; nevertheless, he and Gray were able to publish two volumes of *Flora of North America*; the first volume, which consisted of seven parts, was published in 1838, while a portion of the second volume came out in 1843. Despite its incompleteness, this work served as the basis for the study of North American plants for a number of years thereafter. In 1843 Torrey also published the two-volume *Flora of the State of New York*.

Flora of North America established Torrey's reputation as a first-class botanist. Over the next three decades, government expeditions to the West sent specimens of unidentified plants for him to classify, thus giving him access to the very plants he had hoped to include in later volumes of *Flora of North America*. Although he published no more books after 1843, he did publish a number of reports on the plants he had received from across the nation. He used these plants to create a herbarium that by 1856 included 40,000 specimens. That same year he donated his herbarium and extensive collection of botanical books to Columbia University, although he continued to maintain and augment them with new specimens he received from around the country. In time, Torrey's herbarium would form the core of the New York Botanical Garden.

Torrey received two unique honors during his lifetime. In 1870 the Botanical Club of New York, which Torrey had founded 12 years earlier, was renamed the Torrey Botanical Club. The year before he died, he climbed Torreys Peak in Colorado, which a former student had named in his honor, where he collected plants that he had classified 40 years earlier. *Torreya*, a genus of approximately six species of ornamental trees and shrubs in the yew family, was also named in his honor. He died on March 10, 1873, in New York City.

Further Reading

Princeton University Educational Technologies Center. "Torrey, John." Available online. URL: http://etc.princeton.edu/CampusWWW/Companion/torrey_john.html. Downloaded on February 14, 2004.

Robins, Christine C. "John Torrey (1796–1873): His Life and Times," *Bulletin of the Torrey Botanical Club* 95 (1968): pp. 515–645.

Rodgers, Andrew D. *John Torrey: A Story of North American Botany.* Princeton, N.J.: Princeton University Press, 1942.

Townes, Charles H.
(Charles Hard Townes)
(1915–　) *physicist*

Charles H. Townes won a share of the 1964 Nobel Prize in physics for inventing the maser, a device that produces and amplifies microwaves. He also played a major role in the development of the laser, a device that is a direct offshoot of the maser.

Townes was born on July 28, 1915, in Greenville, South Carolina. His father, Henry, was an attorney, and his mother, Ellen, was a homemaker. At age 19 he received a B.A. in modern languages and a B.S. in physics from Greenville's Furman University, and a year later he received an M.A. in physics from Duke University. He then entered the graduate physics program at the California Institute of Technology, receiving a Ph.D. in 1939. That same year he joined the technical staff of the Bell Telephone Laboratories (BTL) in New York City. In 1941 he married Frances Brown with whom he had four children.

Townes's research at BTL focused on microwaves, electromagnetic radiation having higher frequencies and longer wavelengths than visible light. His time at BTL coincided with World War II, and so most of his research involved the wartime applications of microwave technology, such as the development of radar bombing systems. After the war he focused more on the use of microwaves as a tool of spectroscopy, the study of the structure of atoms and molecules by examining the light spectra they emit.

In 1948 Townes left BTL to become a professor of physics at Columbia University. His research continued to focus on microwave spectroscopy, and in 1951 he came up with the idea for a totally new spectroscopic device. His idea was based on ALBERT EINSTEIN's 1917 theory that when an atom or molecule absorbs electromagnetic radiation, that radiation must stimulate the atom or molecule to emit the same kind of radiation in such a way that might amplify the radiation. Consequently, if one bombarded an atom with microwaves, then that atom might emit microwaves strong enough that a spectroscopist could study them as a way of understanding the inner workings of that atom. After working on his idea for two years, in 1953 Townes succeeded in developing a device that proved the correctness of Einstein's theory. This device employed a beam of ammonia ions that passed along the axis of a cylindrical cage of metal rods, the charges of the rods alternating between positive and negative. The nonuniform electrical field pro-

duced by the rods excited the ammonia ions, which were then projected through a tiny hole into a resonator, a metal box that resonates at the same frequency as that emitted by the ammonia ions. The frequency of the wavelength is amplified as the ions enter the resonator. He called this device a maser, an acronym for Microwave Amplification by Stimulated Emission of Radiation.

Meanwhile, Townes had been collaborating with ARTHUR L. SCHAWLOW on several projects involving microwave technology, including the coauthorship of *Microwave Spectroscopy* (1955). During the course of their collaboration Schawlow, who worked at BTL, had the idea of developing an optical maser by substituting visible light for microwaves. In 1958 Townes and Schawlow had worked out the theoretical underpinnings of optical maser operation. Over the next two years, Schawlow and his colleagues experimented with optical masers, and in 1960 BTL's Theodore H. Maiman succeeded in building one from a helical flash lamp, a device used by photographers to produce brief, intense emissions of light, wrapped around a rod made from a ruby crystal. Shortly thereafter, the optical maser became known as the laser, which stands for Light Amplification by Stimulated Emission of Radiation.

At first, masers and lasers were used primarily as spectroscopic devices, and in this role they led to a number of important discoveries concerning the structure of atoms and molecules. Very quickly, however, they also proved to have a number of other applications in medicine and industry, and today they are used in a number of ways that Townes could hardly have imagined. For his role in the development of masers and lasers, he was awarded a half share of the 1964 Nobel Prize in physics. His corecipients were the Soviet physicists Nicolay G. Basov and Alexandr M. Prokhorov.

In 1959 Townes left Columbia to serve as vice president and director of research of the Institute for Defense Analyses in Washington, D.C. Two years later he was named provost of the Massachusetts Institute of Technology (MIT) as well as a professor of physics. In 1967 he joined the faculty at the University of California at Berkeley and shifted his interest to astrophysics. Over the next 19 years he implemented a multicampus program that employed electromagnetic radiation, particularly radio and infrared waves, thus making it easier for radio astronomers to study the chemical makeup of outer space. His many honors include election to the National Academy of Sciences. He retired from teaching in 1986 to focus on astrophysical research, but he returned to the classroom in 1994. His many honors include the National Medal of Science and election to the National Academy of Sciences and the American Academy of Arts and Sciences.

Further Reading

Backer, Donald C., ed. *The Galactic Center: Proceedings from the Symposium Honoring C.H. Townes, Berkeley, CA, 1986.* New York: American Institute of Physics, 1987.

Nobelprize.org. "The Nobel Prize in Physics 1964." Available online. URL: http://nobelprize.org/physics/laureates/1964. Downloaded on August 30, 2004.

Townes, Charles H. *How the Laser Happened: Adventures of a Scientist.* New York: Oxford University Press, 1999.

Wasson, Tyler, ed. *Nobel Prize Winners.* New York: H. W. Wilson, 1987, pp. 1,071–1,073.

Tsui, Daniel C.
(Daniel Chee Tsui)
(1939–) *physicist*

Daniel C. Tsui codiscovered the fractional quantum Hall effect, whereby electrons behave as if they possess a fraction of their electrical charge. As a result, he was awarded a share of the 1998 Nobel Prize in physics.

Tsui was born on February 28, 1939, in a remote village in Henan Province, China. At age 13 his parents sent him to boarding school in Hong Kong, where he grew up. In 1958 he came to the United States to attend Augustana (Ill.) College, receiving a B.A. in physics three years later. He then entered the graduate physics program at the University of Chicago and received an M.S. and a Ph.D. in 1967. In 1964 he married Linda Varland with whom he had two children.

After remaining at Chicago for an additional year to conduct postdoctoral research, in 1968 Tsui went to work for the Bell Telephone Laboratories

(BTL) in Murray Hill, New Jersey. His early work at BTL involved solid-state physics, the study of how electrons flow through semiconductors, substances that conduct electricity better than nonconductors such as glass but not as well as good conductors such as copper. In the 1970s he helped develop a transistor, an electronic control device, which routes electrons between the interfaces of two semiconductors in a gaseous flow so narrow that it is essentially two-dimensional.

In 1980 Tsui became interested in the work of German physicist Klaus von Klitzing concerning magnetism's effect on electron flow. One hundred years earlier, American physicist Edwin H. Hall had discovered that when an electric current flows through a solid material in the presence of a strong magnetic field, the electrons are drawn to one side of the material, thus creating a transverse electric field at right angles to the direction of the current. The result, known today as the Hall effect, is that one side of the material becomes positively charged while the other side becomes negatively charged. Hall also showed that the voltage generated by the Hall effect varies with changes in the field's strength in a smooth and continuous pattern, but by chilling the electrons to temperatures approaching absolute zero and then subjecting them to a very strong magnetic field, Klitzing showed that Hall-effect voltage varies in discrete steps, as if in accordance with the laws of quantum mechanics.

In 1981 Tsui and Horst L. Störmer, a BTL colleague, undertook a detailed study of the quantum Hall effect as demonstrated by Klitzing. Using lower temperatures and stronger magnets than Klitzing had used, they showed that Klitzing's quantized steps were actually a collection of peaks and valleys that bore only a passing resemblance to discrete steps, and that these peaks and valleys corresponded to fractional, not integral, values. They concluded that these peaks and valleys result from the presence of electrons that have only a fractional negative charge. This conclusion, however, flew in the face of everything that was known about electrons, since it was understood that an electron carries an integral charge of 1 and it had been demonstrated repeatedly that an electron cannot be fragmented into smaller, constituent particles.

An explanation for Tsui and Störmer's discovery was offered in 1983 by ROBERT B. LAUGHLIN. Laughlin theorized that low temperature and high magnetism combine to create a kind of quantum fluid, and that the magnetic field further acts upon the fluid in the same way that a storm acts upon the sea. The magnetic field, or "wind," creates excitations, or "eddies," in the quantum fluid, thus forcing the electrons to share their electrical charges with the eddies. In turn, the eddies take on the characteristics of quasiparticles in that each carries a small fraction of an electron's charge.

In the 15 years following Tsui and Störmer's discovery of a new quantum fluid with fractionally charged excitations, physicists remained somewhat baffled by the discovery. Nevertheless, the discovery, known today as the fractional quantum Hall effect, promises to open the door to new and exciting technologies in the future. For this reason, Tsui and Störmer were each awarded a one-third share of the 1998 Nobel Prize in physics; their corecipient was Laughlin.

In 1982 Tsui left BTL to teach physics and electrical engineering at Princeton University, although the primary focus of his research remained the fractional quantum Hall effect. His honors include election to the National Academy of Sciences.

Further Reading

McMurray, Emily J., ed. *Notable Twentieth-Century Scientists*. Detroit: Gale Research, 1995, pp. 2,051–2,052.
Nobelprize.org. "The Nobel Prize in Physics 1998." Available online. URL: http://nobelprize.org/physics/laureates/1998. Downloaded on October 13, 2004.
Princeton University, Department of Electrical Engineering. "Daniel C. Tsui." Available online. URL: http://www.ee.princeton.edu/people/Tsui.php. Downloaded on March 25, 2005.

Turner, Charles H.
(Charles Henry Turner)
(1867–1923) *entomologist*

Charles H. Turner was one of the first entomologists to describe a complete cycle of behavior for a certain species of insect. In the course of his career, he demonstrated that the sensory capabilities of insects, especially ants and bees, are actually quite diverse and are sensitive to a variety of external stimuli.

Turner was born on February 3, 1867, in Cincinnati, Ohio. His father, Thomas, was a custodian, and his mother, Adeline, was a nurse. After graduating from high school, he enrolled in the University of Cincinnati and received a B.S. in 1891 and an M.S. in 1892. After graduation, he worked for a year as an assistant in the university's biology laboratory, a position he had held previously for a year. In 1893 he accepted the position of professor of biology and head of the department of science and agriculture at Clark University (today Clark-Atlanta University) in Atlanta, Georgia. He stayed at Clark until 1905, after which he taught biology at high schools in Tennessee and Georgia while working on a Ph.D. in zoology at the University of Chicago, which he received in 1907. The following year he moved to St. Louis, Missouri, to teach biology at Sumner High School, where he remained for the rest of his career. In 1888 he married Leontine Troy with whom he had two children; she died in 1904, and he later married Lillian Porter.

By the time Turner earned his Ph.D., he had already published a number of research articles, mostly in the *Journal of Comparative Neurology*. His work from this period focused on the morphology of the forms and structures of various animal species. While at Chicago, however, he became interested in the neurological and psychological aspects of animal behavior in general, but specifically the learning abilities of insects, particularly ants and bees. His most important contribution in this regard was his description of how certain ant species behave while returning to their nests in the wild. This pattern became known as "Turner's circling" because it described the complete cycle of steps ants always go through as they return to their colony after a food-hunting expedition.

Turner made a number of other interesting observations about insects. He discovered that ants are capable of differentiating between various landscape features, and that they respond to these features as well as to light and scent as part of their circling pattern. He discovered that ant lions lie motionless for long periods of time because they suffer from "terror paralysis" in response to external stimuli, not as some sort of survival strategy. He showed that honey bees can identify certain colors, patterns, and smells, that they have a sense of time, and that wasps and burrowing bees can identify landmarks close to their nests. He discovered that cockroaches can learn from trial and error and possess a certain amount of short-term memory. He also proved that some insects can hear well enough to be able to tell the difference between certain pitches.

Surprisingly, given the sophisticated nature of the experiments he conducted, Turner conducted all of his research in his spare time and at his own expense. In addition, he developed his own methods and experiments for identifying the learning abilities of his subjects, as very little work of this type had been done by zoologists. Despite the difficulties he faced in the course of developing and conducting his experiments, he had little trouble getting his work published. In all, he published more than 70 scholarly articles, most of them in prestigious journals such as *Journal of Animal Behavior, Science, American Naturalist,* and *Biological Bulletin.*

In 1922 Turner retired from teaching and moved back to Chicago, where one of his children lived. He died in Chicago on February 14, 1923.

Further Reading

Abramson, Charles I., et al., eds. *Selected Papers and Biography of Charles Henry Turner (1867–1923), Pioneer of Comparative Animal Behavior Studies.* Lewiston, N.Y.: Edward Mellen Press, 2003.

Hayden, Robert C. *Seven African-American Scientists.* Brookfield, Conn.: Twenty-First Century Books, 1992, pp. 34–57.

Spangenburg, Ray, and Kit Moser. *African Americans in Science, Math, and Invention.* New York: Facts On File, 2003, pp. 212–213.

U

Urey, Harold C.
(Harold Clayton Urey)
(1893–1981) *chemist*

Harold C. Urey won a Nobel Prize for discovering "heavy water," so named because it contains atoms of a hydrogen isotope that has a higher atomic weight than the normal form of hydrogen. Urey also contributed to the development of modern medical diagnostic techniques and to a better understanding of the origins of life on Earth.

Urey was born on April 29, 1893, in Walkerton, Indiana. His father, Samuel, was a minister, and his mother, Cora, was a homemaker. He finished high school in 1911, and then he taught in several rural schools before entering Montana State College (today the University of Montana) in 1914. After receiving a B.S. in zoology with a minor in chemistry in 1917, he went to work as a research chemist for the Bartlett Chemical Company in Philadelphia, Pennsylvania. In 1919 he returned to his alma mater to teach chemistry. Two years later he entered the graduate chemistry program at the University of California at Berkeley where he studied under GILBERT N. LEWIS, the dean of physical chemists in the United States. Upon receiving a Ph.D. in chemistry in 1923, he spent a year studying with renowned physicist Niels Bohr in Copenhagen, Denmark, before accepting a position as a chemistry professor at Johns Hopkins University in Baltimore, Maryland. In 1926 he married Frieda Daum with whom he had four children.

As a student of both Lewis and Bohr, Urey developed a strong interest in physical chemistry, which concerns itself with how quantum mechanics, the behavior of subatomic particles, applies to chemistry. While at Johns Hopkins, he developed the concept of electron spin, or angular momentum, as a way to explain the fine lines in the light spectra of atoms. In 1930 he coauthored the first American textbook of physical chemistry, *Atoms, Molecules, and Quanta*.

In 1929 Urey left Johns Hopkins for a similar position at Columbia University in New York City. Shortly after arriving at Columbia, Urey became interested in isotopes, forms of a chemical element having the same number of protons but a different number of neutrons. An isotope behaves almost exactly like the common form of its element, but the difference in the number of neutrons makes it a little bit lighter or heavier than the common form. In 1931 he charted all the known isotopes, an exercise that led him to hypothesize the existence of two isotopes of hydrogen, hydrogen-2 and hydrogen-3, which had yet to be discovered in nature. He then devised a method for distilling liquid hydrogen that would evaporate the common hydrogen atoms, or hydrogen-1, faster than the two heavier isotopes. Upon examining the spectral lines of the residue, he discovered the existence of hydrogen-2, which he named deuterium because it has one proton and one neutron (common hydrogen has one proton and no neutrons). In 1932 he and Edward Washburn, a Columbia colleague, developed an electrolytic method for isolating deuterium, and in the process they discovered "heavy water," a water molecule that consists of one atom of oxygen and two atoms of deuterium. In 1934 other researchers used Urey's methods to discover hydrogen-3, also known as tritium because it has one proton and two neutrons. These discoveries demonstrated clearly what physical chemistry had to offer to the study of chemistry in general, and in 1934 Urey was awarded the Nobel Prize in chemistry.

Urey continued to experiment with isotope separation, and by 1940 he had isolated isotopes of carbon, oxygen, nitrogen, and sulfur. Other researchers at Columbia adapted these isotopes for use as medical tracers. By observing the unique spectral lines of isotopes, researchers can trace the progress of a harmless solution as it travels through the human body, thus making diagnostic medicine much easier to practice. His work with isotopes led him to be recruited to work on the Manhattan Project, the U.S. project to build an atomic bomb during World War II. He oversaw a research group at Columbia working to isolate the isotope uranium-235, which is more fissionable than uranium-238, the normal form. Eventually, the group was able to produce enough uranium-235 to build the atomic bomb that was dropped on Hiroshima, Japan. Despite his wartime involvement, or perhaps because of it, Urey later became such a strong opponent of nuclear weaponry that he was investigated by the House Un-American Activities Committee.

In 1945 Urey left Columbia for the University of Chicago's Institute for Nuclear Studies. At Chicago he shifted his research focus to geochemistry and planetary science. In 1947 he developed a method for calculating the temperature of the oceans as far back as 180 million years ago via measuring the percentage of oxygen-18 in fossilized sea creatures. This work led one of his students, Gerald J. Wasserburg, to develop a method for dating minerals by using potassium-40 and argon-40. In *The Planets* (1952), Urey theorized that Earth's mantle, core, and silicate layers had been formed from a cloud of dust. He also theorized that its earliest atmosphere had consisted of methane, ammonia, and water vapor, and that life evolved via the

reactions among these chemicals caused by ultraviolet radiation from the sun. Later research by one of his students, Sidney Miller, showed that passing an electrical charge through such an atmosphere results in the production of two amino acids and several nucleic acids, the building blocks of life. This result led to the theory that the first form of life on Earth might have been sparked into existence by a bolt of lightning. In the mid-1950s he and Harmon Craig, another student, developed the modern method for classifying meteorites.

In 1958 Urey left Chicago for the University of California at San Diego (UCSD). Shortly after arriving, he began urging the National Aeronautics and Space Administration (NASA) to explore the Moon. Urey had theorized that the Moon was older than Earth, and that it had always been a cold body. He served as a consultant to NASA's Ranger program in the early 1960s and the Apollo 11 mission in 1969, which brought back 47 pounds of moon rocks. Urey was one of six scientists invited to examine the rocks, but to his dismay they proved to be of volcanic origin. Nevertheless, they did substantiate his claim that the Moon was formed independently of Earth, and that it is very old.

Urey retired in 1970, although he continued to do some work at UCSD until 1981. He served as the first editor of the *Journal of Chemical Physics*, he was elected to the National Academy of Sciences, and he was awarded the National Medal of Science. He died on January 5, 1981, at his home in La Jolla, California.

Further Reading

Arnold, James R. "Harold Clayton Urey," National Academy of Sciences, *Biographical Memoirs* 68 (1995): pp. 363–411.

Craig, Harmon, et al. *Isotopic and Cosmic Chemistry.* Amsterdam: North-Holland Pub. Co., 1964.

Nobelprize.org. "The Nobel Prize in Chemistry 1934." Available online. URL: http://nobelprize.org/chemistry/laureates/1934. Downloaded on February 12, 2004.

Wasson, Tyler, ed. *Nobel Prize Winners.* New York: H. W. Wilson, 1987, pp. 1,080–1,082.

Van Allen, James A.
(James Alfred Van Allen)
(1914–   ) *astrophysicist*

James A. Van Allen discovered the Van Allen belts, two zones of high-energy charged particles that are trapped at high altitudes by the Earth's magnetic field. He also played an important role in the U.S. space program by designing some of the earliest rockets, satellites, and test equipment and by leading the call for the creation of the National Aeronautics and Space Administration (NASA).

Van Allen was born on September 7, 1914, in Mount Pleasant, Iowa. His father, Alfred, was an attorney, and his mother, Alma, was a homemaker. He studied physics and chemistry at Iowa Wesleyan College, receiving a B.S. in 1935, and nuclear physics at the University of Iowa, receiving an M.S. in 1936 and a Ph.D. in 1939. He spent the next three years conducting research on terrestrial magnetism at the Carnegie Institution of Washington (D.C.), after which he served as a naval officer during World War II. In 1945 he married Abigail Halsey with whom he had five children.

In 1946 Van Allen was appointed to head the high-altitude research program at the Applied Physics Laboratory of Johns Hopkins University in Baltimore, Maryland. In this capacity he oversaw the modification of a captured German V-2 rocket into the Aerobee, the first rocket designed specifically for scientific purposes. By 1950 several Aerobees containing cameras and magnetometers,

devices that measure the intensity of the Earth's magnetic field, had been launched into the upper atmosphere.

In 1951 Van Allen was named a professor of physics at the University of Iowa. While at Iowa he continued to conduct research on subjects concerning the upper atmosphere. Between 1952 and 1955 he supervised expeditions to the North Pole whose purpose was to study the intensity of cosmic rays. These rays originate in outer space and contain particles, not photons, and only at the poles are they not deflected, thus making it possible there to measure their original intensity accurately. In 1956 and 1957 he oversaw cosmic ray experiments in the continental United States and in the upper atmosphere over the Equator. In 1957 he developed a new technique for exploring the upper atmosphere known as the rockoon. This technique involved launching a rocket from a balloon from about 15 miles above the Earth's surface, thus making it possible to attain altitudes never before reached by a scientific rocket. With the help of others, he designed the Explorer-class satellites, the first scientific satellites to be put into Earth's orbit, and all of the scientific equipment that they carried.

In 1958, using data obtained by the Explorer I satellite, Van Allen hypothesized the existence of what is known today as the Van Allen belts. These two zones of radioactive material in the upper atmosphere move along the lines of force of the Earth's magnetic field. The inner zone is centered approximately 1,800 miles above the Earth's surface. It consists mostly of high-energy protons, which are believed to be the product of cosmic rays colliding with the atoms and molecules of the upper atmosphere. The outer zone, centered about 10,000 miles from the Earth's surface, is a mix of low-energy protons and high-energy electrons from unknown sources in outer space and charged helium atoms from the Sun. Further experiments by Van Allen and other researchers confirmed his findings and showed that the Van Allen belts play a role in such terrestrial phenomena as the Aurora Borealis, or Northern Lights, and magnetic storms, temporary disturbances of the Earth's magnetic field that are induced by radiation and streams of charged particles from the Sun.

Van Allen also played an important role in the development of two major scientific institutions. In 1950 he and British geophysicist Sydney Chapman conceived of an idea that led to the establishment of the first International Geophysical Year (IGY) in 1957–58; IGYs have been held ever since, and they have brought together international support for a variety of scientific projects designed to increase our understanding of the Earth. In 1957 Van Allen led a group of scientists who called for the establishment of a national agency whose purpose would be to explore outer space; the result of this call was the creation of NASA the following year.

Van Allen retired from Iowa in 1985. His publications include *Scientific Uses of Earth Satellites* (1956), *Pioneer: First to Jupiter, Saturn, and Beyond* (1980), *Origins of Magnetospheric Physics* (1983), and *924 Elementary Problems and Answers in Solar System Astronomy* (1993). His honors include election to the National Academy of Sciences and a term as president of the American Geophysical Union.

Further Reading

McMurray, Emily J., ed. *Notable Twentieth-Century Scientists*. Detroit: Gale Research, 1995, pp. 2,070–2,072.
Sputnik Biographies. "James A. Van Allen (1914–)." Available online. URL: http://www.hq.nasa.gov/office/pao/History/sputnik/vanallen.html. Downloaded on March 25, 2005.
"Van Allen, James A(lfred)," *Current Biography* 20 (1959): pp. 461–463.

Van de Graaff, Robert J.
(Robert Jemison Van de Graaff)
(1901–1967) *physicist*

Robert J. Van de Graaff invented the Van de Graaff generator, a device for producing very high electric voltages. This device served as the energy source for the first particle accelerators, and as such played an important role in the development of quantum mechanics, the study of subatomic particles.

Van de Graaff was born on December 20, 1901, in Tuscaloosa, Alabama. His father, Adrian, was a judge, and his mother, Minnie, was a homemaker. He studied mechanical engineering at the University of Alabama where he received a B.S. in 1922 and an M.S. in 1923. After a year as a research assistant at the Alabama Power Company, he went to Europe to study physics, first at the Sorbonne in Paris, France, and then at Oxford University, where he received a B.S. in 1926 and a Ph.D. in 1928.

Van de Graaff began studying subatomic particles while at the Sorbonne. Shortly after leaving there for Oxford, he recognized the need for a device that could propel beams of subatomic particles into higher energy levels so that their behavior could be studied in greater detail. Following a year of postdoctoral research at Oxford, in 1929 he became a National Research Council fellow at Princeton University and began building what is now known as the Van de Graaff generator. This device deposits an electrical charge on a moving belt of insulating fabric. The belt then carries the charge into a smooth, round, insulated metal shell of approximately 15 feet in diameter where the charge is passed to the shell. The movement of the belt increases the voltage of the charge on the outside of the shell until either an electrical breakdown occurs or the charge is discharged intentionally. In this manner, a charge of more than 10 million volts can be generated, which was sufficient for powering the first particle accelerators. These devices propelled subatomic particles, such as protons, into atoms and molecules at incredibly high velocities so as to cause collisions, the results of which were then studied for insights into the nature of both the particles and their targets.

In 1931 Van de Graaff became a research associate at the Massachusetts Institute of Technology (MIT); three years later MIT named him a professor of physics. By 1933 the first Van de Graaff generator was completely operational. Not until 1938, however, when it was housed in a pressurized chamber, did it work to its full potential as an energy source for a particle accelerator. Meanwhile, in 1937 Van de Graaff had built a smaller version of his generator to power a medical X-ray machine at the Harvard Medical School's hospital. During World War II, he headed MIT's High Voltage Radiographic Project, which developed X-ray machines for testing naval artillery shells. In 1946 he cofounded and became chief scientist of the High Voltage Engineering Corporation (HVEC); headquartered in Boston, Massachusetts, HVEC designed and manufactured Van de Graaff generators for use in hospitals and research laboratories. In 1960 he resigned from MIT to focus full-time on his duties at HVEC.

Because of the Van de Graaff generator, physicists around the world were able to obtain much valuable information about the properties of subatomic particles. For this contribution, Van de Graaff was awarded the American Physical Society's 1967 Tom W. Bonner Prize. In 1936 he married Catherine Boyden with whom he had two children. He died on January 16, 1967, in Boston.

Further Reading

Garraty, John A., and Mark C. Carnes, eds. *Dictionary of American Biography*, Supplement 8. New York: Charles Scribner's Sons, 1988, pp. 665–666.

McMurray, Emily J., ed. *Notable Twentieth-Century Scientists*. Detroit: Gale Research, 1995, pp. 2,072–2,075.

Resonance Research Corp. "Historical Notes—Robert J. Van de Graaff and Van de Graaff High Voltage Electrostatics Generators Development." Available online. URL: http://www.resonanceresearch.com/ Robert-J-Van-de-Graaff-high-voltage-electrostatic-generators.htm. Downloaded on March 25, 2005.

Van Hise, Charles R.
(Charles Richard Van Hise)
(1857–1918) *geologist*

Charles R. Van Hise is best remembered for his contributions to higher education as president of the University of Wisconsin. However, he was also one of the foremost geologists of his day, and his work shed light on the physical and chemical processes via which rock is formed and deformed.

Van Hise was born on May 29, 1857, near Fulton, Wisconsin. His parents, William and Mary, were farmers. At age 13 he moved with his family to a farm near Evansville, Wisconsin, where he completed his secondary education. In 1874 he enrolled in the University of Wisconsin and received a B.S. in metallurgical engineering five years later. Upon graduating he was offered a position as an instructor of metallurgy on Wisconsin's faculty, which he accepted. Over the next 24 years he also taught geology, mineralogy, and petrology at Wisconsin, and he taught briefly at the University of Chicago as a nonresident professor of structural geology and metamorphic geology. In 1881 he married Alice Ring with whom he had three children.

Upon joining the Wisconsin faculty in 1879, Van Hise began collaborating with his former geology professor, Roland Irving, on a study of the Precambrian rock of northern Wisconsin. Van Hise's work in this regard was accepted as his master's thesis, and in 1882 he received an M.S. from Wisconsin. That same year he and Irving began a geological study of the Lake Superior region under the auspices of the U.S. Geological Survey (USGS), which Van Hise was forced to continue on his own after Irving died in 1888. The project was completed four years later, and the reports from the study, issued in seven volumes by the USGS, served as Van Hise's doctoral dissertation. In 1892 he received the first Ph.D. ever awarded by the University of Wisconsin.

Van Hise specialized in geologic formations dating back to the Precambrian Age, a period in Earth's history prior to about 600 million years ago. His training in metallurgy proved to be particularly helpful in studying the iron ranges of the Lake Superior region, and his reports on the Mesabi and other ranges contributed immeasurably to their commercial exploitation.

At the time Van Hise entered the field of geology, it was considered to be little more than the collection and classification of rocks, and it was just barely considered to be a scientific discipline of its own. Van Hise did much to change this situation, as he strove to understand the scientific principles that governed the development of rock. His treatise on the deformation of rock strata as the result of geologic change, *Principles of North American Pre-Cambrian Geology* (1896), contributed to the development of structural geology, the study of rock deformation on a large and small scale. Similarly, his classic study of the physical and chemical principles that underlie geologic change, *A Treatise on Metamorphism* (1904), contributed to the development of metamorphic geology, the study of how rock changes as a result of processes different from the ones by which it was formed. Together, the two books helped stake geology's claim to being a legitimate scientific discipline.

In 1903 Van Hise gave up his teaching and research responsibilities to become president of the University of Wisconsin, a position he held until his death. In this capacity he did much to make Wisconsin one of the best public universities in the nation. He also served terms as president of the Geological Society of America, the National Association of State Universities, the National Academy of Sciences, the American Association for the Advancement of Science, and the International Geological Congress in Stockholm, Sweden. He died on November 19, 1918, in Milwaukee from complications arising from minor surgery.

Further Reading

Chamberlin, Thomas C. "Charles Richard Van Hise," National Academy of Sciences, *Biographical Memoirs* 17 (1924): pp. 143–151.

Vance, Maurice M. *Charles Richard Van Hise, Scientist Progressive*. Madison: State Historical Society of Wisconsin, 1960.

Wisconsin Electronic Reader. "President Van Hise." Available online. URL: http://www.library.wisc.edu/etext/WIReader/WER0746.html. Downloaded on August 3, 2003.

Van Vleck, John H.
(John Hasbrouck Van Vleck)
(1899–1980) *physicist*

John H. Van Vleck is known as the "father of modern magnetism" because he was the first to explain magnetism in terms of quantum mechanics, the behavior of subatomic particles. His major scientific contribution was to offer a better understanding of the relationship between electrons and magnetism, and for this contribution he was awarded a share of the 1977 Nobel Prize in physics. He also made a major contribution to the field of physical chemistry by advancing the ligand field theory, which explains the nature of certain molecular bonds in terms of electron behavior.

Van Vleck was born on March 13, 1899, in Middletown, Connecticut. His father, Edward, was a mathematics professor, and his mother, Hester, was a homemaker. At age seven he moved with his family to Madison, Wisconsin, where his father had accepted a teaching position at the University of Wisconsin. After receiving an A.B. in physics from Wisconsin in 1920, he entered the graduate program at Harvard University and received a Ph.D. in physics in 1922. He taught physics for a year at Harvard and then for five years at the University of Minnesota before returning in 1928 to Wisconsin, this time to teach. In 1934 he returned to Harvard, where he remained for the rest of his career. In 1927 he married Abigail Pearson with whom he had no children.

Van Vleck's primary research interest throughout his career was magnetism. While teaching at Minnesota and Wisconsin, he began studying diamagnetism and paramagnetism; diamagnetic materials are not susceptible to induced magnetism while paramagnetic materials are slightly susceptible. These magnetic phenomena had been named and studied in 1845 by English physicist Michael Faraday, but they remained poorly understood 80 years later. By applying the principles of quantum mechanics, which itself was not widely understood at the time, Van Vleck was able to offer the first satisfactory theory for the electric and magnetic behavior of diamagnetic and paramagnetic gases. His theory explained the nature of diamagnetism and paramagnetism in terms of electron behavior, and showed why diamagnetism is not affected by changes in temperature while paramagnetism usually is. He also demonstrated the existence of a form of paramagnetism that is not susceptible to temperature changes, known today as Van Vleck paramagnetism. His work regarding these magnetic phenomena was published in 1932 in *The Theory of Electric and Magnetic Susceptibilities*.

In the early 1930s, Van Vleck departed briefly from his work with magnetism to study the nature of molecular bonds involving ligands. A ligand is one of a group of atoms or molecules that are bound to a central atom, usually of a metallic element, and that are capable of donating electrons to form a molecular bond. At the time, HANS A. BETHE had theorized that metal-ligand linkages are strictly ionic; that is, they are formed between a positively charged central atom and negatively charged ligands. This theory, however, failed to explain some features of metal-ligand linkages, so Van Vleck applied the principles of quantum mechanics to the problem, as he had done previously with magnetism. By 1935 he was able to demonstrate that the orbits of the electrons in the central atom and the ligands overlap to a small degree, something which Bethe's theory assumed did not happen at all. He further discovered that some electrons involved in a metal-ligand linkage become delocalized so that they orbit the nuclei of the central atom and the ligands. Further experimentation by other researchers indicated that Van Vleck's theory, now known as the ligand field theory, offers a more complete explanation of metal-ligand linkages.

After 1935 Van Vleck refocused his primary research on magnetism. He became particularly interested in the discovery by Dutch physicist Cornelis J. Gorter that paramagnetic ions can lose their equilibrium (by either gaining or losing energy) when subjected to an oscillating magnetic field. By 1941 Van Vleck had developed a precise set of calculations for determining relaxation, the process by which these ions regain their equilibrium once they are no longer in the presence of the magnetic field. That same year he also hypothesized that an oscillating magnetic field's ability to affect a paramagnetic ion's equilibrium would be restricted in extremely low temperatures. In the 1960s other researchers demonstrated the existence of this effect, known today as the phonon bottleneck. In 1952 he offered an explanation for ferromagnetism, the natural magnetism of certain elements, by combining two competing theories. The Heisenberg model suggested that the electrons in a ferromagnetic substance are localized on certain ions, while the itinerant model suggested that they are completely delocalized and "wander" about through the substance's structure. Van Vleck's minimum polarity model offered a more comprehensive explanation of ferromagnetism by suggesting that the electrons are

indeed localized, but that they shift constantly from one ion to another. To date, no satisfactory model for explaining ferromagnetism exists, but the minimum polarity model remains the better of the three. For this achievement, Van Vleck was awarded a one-third share of the 1977 Nobel Prize in physics; his corecipients were the American physicist PHILIP W. ANDERSON and the British physicist Nevill F. Mott.

Van Vleck received the National Medal of Science and was elected to membership in the National Academy of Sciences and the American Association of Arts and Sciences; he also served a term as president of the American Physical Society. In 1969 he retired to his home in Cambridge, Massachusetts, where he died on October 27, 1980.

Further Reading

Anderson, Philip W. "John Hasbrouck Van Vleck," National Academy of Sciences, *Biographical Memoirs* 56 (1987): pp. 501–540.

Nobelprize.org. "The Nobel Prize in Physics 1977." Available online. URL: http://nobelprize.org/ physics/laureates/1977. Downloaded on March 9, 2004.

Wasson, Tyler, ed. *Nobel Prize Winners.* New York: H. W. Wilson, 1987, pp. 1,086–1,088.

Varmus, Harold E.
(Harold Eliot Varmus)
(1939–) *virologist*

Harold E. Varmus played a major role in discovering that potentially cancerous cells are found in virtually every living organism; otherwise normal, these cells contain within them a gene that can initiate the production of cancerous cells once it is mutated by the proper agent. For this contribution he was awarded a share of the 1989 Nobel Prize in physiology or medicine.

Varmus was born on December 18, 1939, in Freeport, New York. His father, Frank, was a physician, and his mother, Beatrice, was a social worker. After receiving a B.A. from Amherst (Mass.) College in 1961 and an M.A. from Harvard University in 1962 (both degrees were in English literature), he entered Columbia University's College of Physicians and Surgeons and received an M.D. in 1966.

He spent the next four years completing his internship and residency at New York's Columbia-Presbyterian Hospital and conducting postdoctoral research at the National Institutes of Health (NIH) in Bethesda, Maryland. In 1970 he became a professor of microbiology at the University of California at San Francisco (UCSF). In 1969 he married Constance Casey with whom he had two children.

Varmus's primary research interest was retroviruses, cancer-causing viruses that replicate themselves by using RNA to synthesize DNA, a reversal of the normal transmission of genetic coding. In 1970 HOWARD M. TEMIN and DAVID BALTIMORE discovered reverse transcriptase, the enzyme by which RNA encodes DNA. That same year, Varmus and J. MICHAEL BISHOP, a UCSF colleague, began studying reverse transcriptase, and eventually they were able to demonstrate exactly how reverse transcriptase works. Next, Varmus and Bishop undertook a study of viral RNA and viral DNA in both normal and infected cells, and then they began to study viruses as a cause of cancer.

Varmus and Bishop focused on Rous sarcoma virus (RSV), a virus that PEYTON ROUS had shown to cause cancer in chickens. Rous also showed that cancer does not develop all of a sudden, as many researchers had believed, but rather slowly and by stages. He further demonstrated that cancer cells sometimes lie dormant until a particular biochemical factor, like a virus or a chemical, awakens them. Other researchers had suggested that the outbreak of cancer in a host cell was controlled by a viral gene known as *src*. When a virus infects a host cell, it often implants its genome, a set of chromosomes, into the host's DNA where it functions as if were one of the cell's original genes. Varmus and Bishop, assisted by their junior colleagues Dominique Stehelin and Deborah Spector, provided conclusive evidence that *src* is responsible for initiating the spread of RSV. However, they also discovered that *src* is not a viral gene but is a normal growth-controlling gene of the host cell that has become part of the viral genome via recombination, the process whereby a virus and its host cell exchange genetic material. The *src* gene then lies dormant until some agent causes it to mutate into a cancer gene.

Varmus and Bishop then began searching for *src*-like genes in other species. By 1976 they were able to show that proto-oncogenes, as they labeled them, were present in virtually every species they investigated. Even more surprisingly, they discovered that proto-oncogenes, despite being infected by the viral genome, continue to play a role in regulating cellular functions, just as if they had never been infected. Proto-oncogenes trigger the production of cancer cells only after they are mutated by a particular agent, usually another retrovirus or a chemical carcinogen, but until then they function as normal, healthy genes of the organism to which they originally belonged.

Varmus and Bishop's discoveries advanced cancer research significantly, even though they showed that cancer is a much tougher opponent to defeat than was previously believed. By showing that some cancers are genetically coded, however, they presented medical researchers with some additional tools to use in the fight against cancer. Varmus and Bishop also showed why most human cancers occur late in life, as it takes many decades for proto-oncogenes to mutate into cancer-producing genes. For their contributions to cancer research, Varmus and Bishop were each awarded a half share of the 1989 Nobel Prize in physiology or medicine.

Varmus remained at UCSF until 1993, when he returned to NIH as its director. He left after six years to become president and chief executive officer of Memorial Sloan-Kettering Cancer Center in New York City. In 2000 he cofounded the Public Library of Science, an electronic publishing site that provides complete access to the most important journals of the life sciences. His many honors include election to the National Academy of Sciences and the American Academy of Arts and Sciences.

Further Reading

McMurray, Emily J. *Notable Twentieth-Century Scientists.* Detroit: Gale Research, 1995, pp. 2,083–2,084.

Memorial Sloan-Kettering Cancer Center. "President's Pages." Available online. URL: http://www.mskcc. org/mskcc/html/515.cfm. Downloaded on March 25, 2005.

Nobelprize.org. "The Nobel Prize in Physiology or Medicine 1989." Available online. URL: http://nobelprize. org/medicine/laureates/1989. Downloaded on July 9, 2004.

Waksman, Selman A.
(Selman Abraham Waksman)
(1888–1973) *microbiologist*

Selman A. Waksman developed the first antibiotic drugs, one of which proved to be a very effective treatment for tuberculosis. This major contribution to world health won him the 1952 Nobel Prize in physiology or medicine.

Waksman was born on July 22, 1888, in Novaia-Priluka, Russia. His father, Jacob, was a weaver, and his mother, Fradia, was a merchant. After completing the European equivalent of a high school education in 1910, he emigrated to the United States and went to live with some cousins in Metuchen, New Jersey. In 1911 he entered Rutgers College, receiving a B.Sc. and an M.Sc. in agriculture in 1915 and 1916, respectively. After receiving a Ph.D. in biochemistry from the University of California at Berkeley in 1918, he became a microbiologist at the New Jersey Agricultural Experimental Station in New Brunswick and a professor of soil microbiology at Rutgers. In 1916 he became a naturalized U.S. citizen and married Bertha Mitnik with whom he had one child.

As a student at Rutgers, Waksman became interested in soil microbes, microscopic organisms that live in earth. He undertook a study of the physiological and biochemical properties of the soil microbes known as actinomycetes, some of which are capable of killing plants and other microbes. At the time, so little was known about these bacteria that they were thought to be fungi; Waksman's study contributed significantly to a better understanding of them. Upon joining the staff at the Experimental Station, he began studying the way microbes affect soil fertility. In 1921 he described how soil microbes decompose material in a compost pile, and by the end of the decade he could describe how they decompose peat, humus, and human and animal waste as well. His work in these areas was published in *Enzymes* (1926), *Principles of Soil Microbiology* (1927), and *The Soil and the Microbe* (1931).

Waksman shifted his research back to the study of actinomycetes in 1932 following a discovery by RENÉ DUBOS, a former student and colleague. Dubos had isolated an enzyme produced by soil microbes that could decompose the protective shell surrounding the bacteria that cause pneumonia. Thus inspired, Waksman began looking for "killer" actinomycetes that could be used to combat tuberculosis. At the time, tuberculosis was a deadly killer and one of the leading causes of death in young people around the world. A deadly bacterial infection that is impervious to penicillin, tuberculosis was known to last only a short time in soil; Waksman believed the reason might be that certain actinomycetes were lethal to the tubercle bacillus, the microbe that causes tuberculosis.

In 1940 Waksman developed the first antibiotic (a term coined by Waksman) from an enzyme produced by a certain type of actinomycetes known as streptomycetes. Named actinomycin, this antibiotic proved to be deadly to the tubercle bacillus.

Unfortunately, it was so toxic that it was too harmful to administer to humans, although later researchers were able to develop it into a chemotherapy treatment for Hodgkin's disease, cancer of the lymph system. Two years later Waksman and his associates developed two more antibiotics, clavacin and streptothricin; milder than actinomycin, they were still too toxic for humans. Then, in 1943, Waksman and a student assistant, Albert Schatz, developed streptomycin. This antibiotic kills the tubercle bacillus without also killing humans, consequently making it a highly effective treatment for tuberculosis. In time, it was discovered that streptomycin is also an effective treatment for tularemia, bacterial meningitis, endocarditis, and infections of the pulmonary and urinary tracts. The patent for streptomycin, which Waksman assigned to Rutgers, was considered to be one of the most valuable patents in the world, and in 1952 Waksman was voted one of the 100 most outstanding people in the world. That same year he was awarded the 1952 Nobel Prize in physiology or medicine.

In 1949 Waksman became director of the Rutgers Institute of Microbiology ("Rutgers" was later changed to "Waksman" in his honor). In addition to the antibiotics named above, he developed neomycin, grisein, candicidin, candidin, and fradicin; the first of these is widely used to treat skin and eye infections, while the last was named in honor of his mother. He served as president of the American Society for Microbiology and founded the Foundation for Microbiology as a means of supporting microbiological research around the world. He retired from Rutgers in 1958 but continued to experiment and to work as a consultant to industry for a number of years. He died on August 16, 1973, in Hyannis, Massachusetts.

Further Reading

Nobelprize.org. "The Nobel Prize in Physiology or Medicine 1952." Available online. URL: http://nobelprize.org/medicine/laureates/1952. Downloaded on February 11, 2004.

Waksman, Selman A. *My Life with the Microbes*. New York: Simon and Schuster, 1954.

Wasson, Tyler, ed. *Nobel Prize Winners*. New York: H. W. Wilson, 1987, pp. 1,094–1,095.

Wald, George
(1906–1997) *physiologist*

George Wald was a pioneer in the discovery of the physiological processes of vision. For his contributions in this area, he received a share of the 1967 Nobel Prize in physiology or medicine.

Wald was born on November 18, 1906, in New York City. His father, Isaac, was a tailor, and his mother, Ernestine, was a homemaker. In 1927 he received a B.S. in biology from New York University's Washington Square College and entered the graduate zoology program at Columbia University, receiving an M.S. in 1928 and a Ph.D. in 1932. He spent the next two years as a National Research Council fellow studying biochemistry at the University of Heidelberg in Germany, the University of Zurich in Switzerland, and the University of Chicago. In 1934 he joined the faculty at Harvard University where he remained for the rest of his career. In 1931 he married Frances Kingsley with whom he had two children. They divorced in 1958, and later that year he married Ruth Hubbard, his research assistant, with whom he had two children.

As a graduate student, Wald had studied the visual performance of the fruit fly, and he discovered that this performance closely resembles that of more complex living things. Moreover, his mentor at Columbia, Selig Hecht, had done some groundbreaking work with the photosensory systems of simple organisms, and he had demonstrated that these systems operate in conformance with the known principles of photochemistry. Hecht had hypothesized that the photosensory systems of simple organisms are based on the decomposition or rearrangement of the molecular structure of some unknown photosensitive substance, a hypothesis that Wald would later prove to be largely correct for sophisticated organisms as well. Thus inspired, Wald's lifelong research interest involved the biochemistry of vision. One of his first discoveries was that the retina's yellow pigments, which are found in the eye's natural lens, filter out ultraviolet light and allow the eye to focus on the light in the visible spectrum. His most important work concerned the role played by vitamin A in the proper functioning of the vision system.

While at Heidelberg, Wald had discovered that the retina contains significant amounts of vitamin A. In the 1940s he began studying rods, or rod-shaped photoreceptor cells in the retina that distinguish different shades of gray, and he showed that they contain a significant amount of a pigment known as rhodopsin or visual purple. Moreover, he demonstrated that rhodopsin is composed of a protein called opsin and a derivative of vitamin A known as vitamin A aldehyde or retinal, and in 1950 he synthesized rhodopsin in the laboratory. In the 1950s he began studying cones, or cone-shaped photoreceptor cells in the retina that distinguish the different colors, and he showed that they contain pigments that are sensitive to red, yellow, and green. Again, he demonstrated that these pigments are also composed of opsin and various forms of retinal. In the 1960s he discovered that the blue-sensitive pigment, like all the other pigments in the retina, is a compound of opsin and a particular form of retinal. Shortly thereafter he discovered that color blindness results from the lack of one of the visual pigments, which itself results from the lack of vitamin A in the body. These discoveries alerted the medical community to the fact that the body needs significant amounts of vitamin A in order to maintain its visual system in good working order.

Wald's discoveries also demonstrate that the process of sending light-sensory information from the eye to the brain begins with a biochemical reaction in the retina. As light strikes that part of the pigment containing the vitamin A, the pigment changes its molecular form in such a way that leads eventually to the excitation of the photoreceptor cells. Once excited, they generate discrete electric signals, which are transmitted to the brain via the optic nerve. For the role he played in explaining the physiology of vision, he was awarded a one-third share of the 1967 Nobel Prize in physiology or medicine. One of his corecipients was H. KEFFER HARTLINE, whose work contributed to a better understanding of the biophysical aspects of vision, and the other was the Swedish physiologist Ragnar Granit.

Wald was elected to membership in the National Academy of Sciences and the American Academy of Arts and Sciences. He retired from Harvard in 1977, and he spent the rest of his life working for political causes, particularly those that opposed war and the proliferation of nuclear weapons. From 1980 until his death he served as vice president of the Permanent People's Tribunal, an organization based in Rome, Italy, that is concerned with international human rights. He died on April 12, 1997, in Cambridge, Massachusetts.

Further Reading

Dowling, John E. "George Wald," National Academy of Sciences, *Biographical Memoirs* 78 (2000): pp. 299–317.

Nobelprize.org. "The Nobel Prize in Physiology or Medicine 1967." Available online. URL: http://nobelprize.org/medicine/laureates/1967. Downloaded on April 14, 2004.

Wasson, Tyler, ed. *Nobel Prize Winners.* New York: H. W. Wilson, 1987, pp. 1,095–1,097.

Watson, James D.
(James Dewey Watson, Jr.)
(1928–   ) *molecular biologist*

James D. Watson played a central role in one of the most important developments in biology in the 20th century, the discovery of the structure of deoxyribonucleic acid (DNA), the carrier of genetic information at the molecular level. Watson's discovery redirected the study of genetics and heredity and had vast implications for the future of medical research. For this accomplishment, he was awarded a share of the 1962 Nobel Prize in physiology or medicine.

Watson was born on April 6, 1928, in Chicago, Illinois. His father, James, was a businessman, and his mother, Jean, was a homemaker. At age 15 he entered the University of Chicago, receiving both a Ph.B. and a B.S. in zoology in 1947. He then enrolled in the graduate program at the University of Indiana where he studied under SALVADOR E. LURIA. Luria was a pioneer in the field of molecular biology and one of the leading members of the so-called phage school, an informal group of researchers who worked collaboratively but independently on the study of phages, viruses that infect bacteria. At the time it was believed that phages transmit genetic coding from one organism to another via their viral protein, and the phage school was actively engaged in determining whether or not this was so. Watson became a junior member of the phage school while at Indiana, where he studied the effects of X-rays on phage multiplication.

After receiving a Ph.D. in zoology in 1950, Watson spent the next year conducting postdoctoral research at the University of Copenhagen in Denmark and the Naples Zoological Station in Italy. In Naples he met Maurice H. F. Wilkins, a British biophysicist who was studying the way X-rays are diffracted by crystallized molecules of DNA, a form of nucleic acid that is frequently found in phages. Wilkins's research greatly interested Watson; like several other phage researchers, he had begun to suspect that a phage's nucleic acid, and not its viral protein, was the actual carrier of genetic coding. Inspired by Wilkins, Watson decided to learn more about DNA, and in 1951 he received a grant from the National Foundation for Infantile Paralysis to study biochemistry in England at Cambridge University's Cavendish Laboratories. Here he became associated with Francis H. C. Crick, at the time a graduate student studying the structure of protein.

Over the next two years, Watson and Crick developed a model of the DNA molecule. They drew upon a variety of sources for data and ideas: the X-ray diffraction studies of Wilkins and others; LINUS C. PAULING's demonstration of the helical structure of polypeptides, the molecules from which proteins are constructed; Austrian-American biochemist Erwin Chargaff's research concerning the symmetrical relationship among adenine, cytosine, guanine, and thymine—the nitrogen-bearing bases from which DNA is constructed; and Watson's work, completed in 1952, showing that the protein structure of the tobacco mosaic virus is helical. By 1953 Watson and Crick had concluded that the DNA molecule looks like two long ladders. Each step in a ladder consists of a pair of bases, either adenine and thymine or cytosine and guanine, that are connected end-to-end at the middle of the step. Each link between the steps is composed of a phosphate compound and a sugar known as deoxyribose, arranged so that only the deoxyribose connects with the steps. The steps can be arranged in infinite varieties of adenine-thymine pairs and cytosine-guanine pairs. Because of the internal stresses caused by the chemical arrangement, the two ladders intertwine with each other in a double-helix arrangement like two spiral staircases.

In 1953 Watson and Crick described their model of the DNA molecule in a short paper in the scientific journal *Nature*. Almost immediately thereafter, their findings were corroborated by Wilkins and other researchers. Later that year, Watson and Crick published another paper in *Nature* in which they described the genetic implications of the structure of the DNA molecule. They hypothesized that genetic coding is carried along the middle of the molecule's steps. When the molecule replicates itself, each of the two ladders simply splits in half along the middle of the steps where the two bases connect. Because of the precise arrangement of the compounds composing the steps and links, the ladder halves reconstruct themselves into complete ladders that are identical to the original ladders, only now there are two sets of ladders instead of one. This hypothesis was corroborated in 1959 by ARTHUR KORNBERG.

By explaining in detail how the DNA molecule is constructed and how it replicates, Watson and Crick made it possible for geneticists to develop amazing new insights into the mysteries of life and reproduction. They also opened the door to the possibility of finding cures for a number of hereditary diseases and conditions that previously were believed to be untreatable. For this remarkable achievement, Watson, Crick, and Wilkins were each awarded a one-third share of the 1962 Nobel Prize in physiology or medicine.

Meanwhile, in 1953 Watson's grant had expired, and he spent the next two years at the California Institute of Technology (Caltech). As a research fellow in biology, he investigated the role played by ribonucleic acid (RNA) as the messenger that transmits genetic code during the replication of a DNA molecule. He then returned to the Cavendish Laboratories for a year, where he and Crick teamed up once again, this time to propose a model for the structure of viruses. In 1956 he was named professor of biology at Harvard University, where he continued to investigate the role played by RNA in protein synthesis. In 1968 he became the part-time director of the Laboratory of Quantitative Biology at Cold Spring Harbor, New York, a world center for research in molecular biology that had served as the unofficial headquarters of the phage school. In 1976 he left Harvard to direct the laboratory full-time; in this capacity he facilitates the work of other biological researchers, with an emphasis on cancer research. From 1989 to 1991 he also served as director of the Human Genome Project of the National Institutes of Health, an ambitious research program designed to identify the composition and role played by each of the human body's 100,000 or so genes.

Watson authored *The Molecular Biology of the Gene* (1965) and coauthored *The Molecular Biology of the Cell* (1983), both of which became widely used as college textbooks. He was elected to the National Academy of Sciences and the American Academy of Arts and Sciences, and he was awarded the Presidential Medal of Freedom. In 1968 he married Elizabeth Lewis with whom he has two children.

Further Reading

McElheny, Victor K. *Watson and DNA: Making a Scientific Revolution.* Cambridge, Mass.: Perseus Publishing, 2003.

Nobelprize.org. "The Nobel Prize in Physiology or Medicine 1962." Available online. URL: http://nobelprize. org/medicine/laureates/1962. Downloaded on April 19, 2004.

Wasson, Tyler, ed. *Nobel Prize Winners.* New York: H. W. Wilson, 1987, pp. 1,105–1,107.

Watson, James D. *The Double Helix, a Personal Account of the Discovery of the Structure of DNA.* New York: Atheneum, 1968.

Weinberg, Steven
(1933–   ) *physicist*

Steven Weinberg codeveloped the electroweak unification theory, which links together the seemingly unrelated physical forces of electromagnetism and the weak interactions. For this contribution, he was awarded a share of the 1979 Nobel Prize in physics.

Weinberg was born on May 3, 1933, in New York City. His father, Frederick, was a court stenog-rapher, and his mother, Eva, was a homemaker. As a boy he attended the Bronx High School of Science, and while in high school he decided to become a theoretical physicist. In 1954 he married Louise Goldwasser with whom he had one child and received a B.S. in physics from Cornell University in Ithaca, New York. He spent the following year at the Institute for Theoretical Physics (today the Niels Bohr Institute) in Copenhagen, Denmark, after which he entered the graduate physics program at Princeton University, receiving a Ph.D. in 1957. He then joined the faculty at the University of California at Berkeley.

Weinberg's work as a theoretical physicist focused on developing a grand unified theory for linking together the four elementary forces of physics, namely, electromagnetism, gravity, and the strong and weak interactions. Much progress in this direction had already been made by British physicist James Clerk Maxwell, who had shown that electricity and magnetism are both manifestations of electromagnetism. Later, RICHARD P. FEYNMAN, JULIAN S. SCHWINGER, and others developed quantum electrodynamics, which explains the strong interactions, the forces that hold together protons and neutrons in an atomic nucleus, in terms of electromagnetism.

In the early 1960s Weinberg became interested in the work of SHELDON L. GLASHOW, a fellow classmate from his high school and undergraduate days. Glashow was attempting to explain the weak interactions, which are responsible for certain forms of radioactive decay, in terms of electromagnetism and the strong interactions. The key to developing such a connection involved the existence of gauge bosons, messenger particles that actually carry the weak interactions in much the same way that electrons and photons, tiny packets of light energy, carry electromagnetism. Glashow's theory required four gauge bosons; one of these could be the photon, but the existence of the other three was problematic because they would have to have no mass, thus making them virtually impossible to detect.

By 1968 Weinberg had overcome the problems with Glashow's theory by proposing that the three missing gauge bosons did not have to be massless. Because the range of any given force tends to be inversely proportional to the mass of the particle transmitting it, Weinberg concluded that the gauge bosons carrying the weak interactions could be relatively large since the weak interactions operate over extremely short distances on the order of 10^{-16} centimeters. He postulated the existence of three gauge bosons, which he labeled W^+, W^-, and Z^0, and he speculated that in addition to carrying the weak interactions these particles also carry electrical charges of positive, negative, and neutral, respectively. This theory was codeveloped independently by Pakistani physicist Abdus Salam, and so it became known as the Weinberg-Salam theory. Weinberg also proposed that the W and Z particles are produced when a proton and an antiproton collide head-on at extremely high energy levels. This theory was confirmed in 1973 by researchers at the European Organization for Nuclear Research (CERN) in Geneva, Switzerland, thus offering the first experimental evidence to support the Weinberg-Salam theory.

The combined effort of Weinberg, Glashow, and Salam concerning unified theory is known today as the electroweak unification theory. Thirty-five years after its promulgation, it remains a valid attempt to unify the forces of electromagnetism and the weak interactions. The value of the theory was recognized in 1979 when Weinberg, Salam, and Glashow were each awarded a one-third share of the Nobel Prize in physics.

In 1969 Weinberg left Berkeley for the Massachusetts Institute of Technology. Four years later he moved to nearby Harvard University while also becoming a senior scientist at the Smithsonian Astrophysical Observatory in Cambridge, Massachusetts, where he pursued a growing interest in the physical origins of the universe. In 1982 he was named a professor of physics and astronomy at the University of Texas at Austin. His publications include *Gravitation and Cosmology: Principles and Applications of the General Theory of Relativity* (1972), *The Discovery of Subatomic Particles* (1983), *Dreams of a Final Theory* (1992), *The First Three Minutes: A Modern View of the Origin of the Universe* (1993), *The Quantum Theory of Fields* (1998), *Facing Up: Science and Its Cultural Adversaries* (2001), and *Glory and Terror: The Growing Nuclear Danger* (2004). His honors include the National Medal of Science and election to the National Academy of Sciences and the American Academy of Arts and Sciences.

Further Reading

Department of Physics, University of Texas at Austin Theory Group. "Professor Steven Weinberg." Available online. URL: http://www.ph.utexas.edu/~weintech/weinberg.html. Downloaded on March 25, 2005.

Nobelprize.org. "The Nobel Prize in Physics 1979." Available online. URL: http://nobelprize.org/physics/laureates/1979. Downloaded on October 2, 2004.

Wasson, Tyler, ed. *Nobel Prize Winners.* New York: H. W. Wilson, 1987, pp. 1,107–1,109.

Welch, William H.
(William Henry Welch)
(1850–1934) *pathologist*

William H. Welch made several contributions to the field of bacteriology. He is best remembered, however, for building Johns Hopkins University Medical School into one of the finest in the nation, in the process transforming the way medicine is taught in the United States.

Welch was born on April 8, 1850, in Norfolk, Connecticut. His father, William, was a physician and his mother, Emeline, was a homemaker. After graduating from Yale University in 1870, he spent two years as an apprentice to his father and as a chemistry student at Yale's Sheffield Scientific School. In 1872 he enrolled in the College of Surgeons and Physicians in New York City, receiving an M.D. three years later. He then became an intern at New York's Bellevue Hospital, but left after a year to study medicine in Germany at the universities of Strasburg, Breslau, and Leipzig. In 1878 he returned to New York City where he established the country's first teaching laboratory in pathology, the study of the origins, nature, and courses of diseases. Six years later he was hired to teach pathology at Johns Hopkins University in Baltimore, Maryland. Before he assumed his duties in 1885, however, he spent a year in Germany becoming acquainted with the latest developments in bacteriology.

Unlike other U.S. medical schools of the day, Johns Hopkins was intended to focus on research as well as patient care. To this end, Welch devoted much of his early years at Hopkins to medical research. The Johns Hopkins Hospital opened in 1889, thus giving Welch the opportunity to conduct various experiments on its patients. In 1891 he made two important discoveries. The first was that gas gangrene, a gangrenous infection that develops primarily in deep wounds because of air bubbles in the blood, is caused by bacteria. Further experimentation resulted in the identification of the bacillus in question as *Clostridium welchii,* also known as Welch's bacillus. The second was the existence of *Staphylococcus epidermidis albus,* a type of bacteria that lives in the deep layers of the skin and is not killed when the outer layer of the skin is disinfected, thus causing infections in deep surgical wounds. This discovery led to the development of subcutaneous stitching and disinfection as a means of preventing infections below the skin as a result of surgery. In 1892 he and one of his first students at Hopkins, SIMON FLEXNER, demonstrated the pathological effects of the toxin produced by the bacillus that causes diphtheria.

In 1893 the Johns Hopkins Medical School was officially opened, and Welch was named its first dean. This position forced him to abandon any serious research efforts of his own, and the rest of his medical career focused on administrative duties rather than research. Nevertheless, he continued to maintain an interest in the experimental work of his students, whose numbers included GEORGE H. WHIPPLE, PEYTON ROUS, and WALTER REED, while turning Hopkins into perhaps the finest medical school in the country. Two of his major innovations were to require medical students at Hopkins to be college graduates and to admit women as the equals of men, innovations that would spread quickly to medical schools across the country.

Welch stepped down as dean of the medical school in 1898, but he continued to wield a considerable amount of influence over the operation of the medical school and the hospital. In addition to recruiting some of the finest medical practitioners in the United States to come to Hopkins to teach,

in 1913, as the university's acting president, he oversaw the professionalization of the medical school's teaching staff. Previously, medical professors had worked part-time for their schools while maintaining private practices. Welch's innovation, to put all teaching staff on full-time pay, improved the quality of teaching by recruiting highly skilled medical practitioners who were primarily interested in teaching and research. Over the next 30 years, this innovation became the norm at all American medical schools.

Welch played an important role in the administration of a number of other medical-related institutions. As president of the Rockefeller Institute for Medical Research's first advisory board, he hired Flexner to be the institute's first director of laboratories. As president of its board of scientific directors from 1901 to 1933, he oversaw the institute's development of a school of hygiene and public health at Hopkins, with Welch as its first dean. Meanwhile, he also served as president of the American Association for the Advancement of Science, the American Medical Association, and the National Academy of Sciences, and he chaired the executive committee of the Carnegie Institution of Washington. He helped form the National Research Council and transform the Peking Union Medical College into the first modern medical school in China.

Welch retired from Hopkins in 1931. He died, having never married, on April 30, 1934, in Baltimore.

Further Reading
Fleming, Donald. *William H. Welch and the Rise of Modern Medicine.* Baltimore, Md.: Johns Hopkins University Press, 1987.

Flexner, Simon, and James T. Flexner. *William Henry Welch and the Heroic Age of American Medicine.* New York: Dover Publications, 1966.

Weller, Thomas H.
(Thomas Huckle Weller)
(1915–   ) *virologist*

Thomas H. Weller was a key member of the research team that discovered how to grow the polio virus under laboratory conditions. This discovery, which led shortly thereafter to the development of a polio vaccine, won for Weller a share of a Nobel Prize.

Weller was born on June 15, 1915, in Ann Arbor, Michigan. His father, Carl, was a college professor, and his mother, Elsie, was a homemaker. He attended the University of Michigan and received an A.B. and an M.S. in medical zoology in 1936 and 1937, respectively. He then entered Harvard Medical School where he studied comparative medicine and tropical medicine en route to receiving an M.D. in 1940. He then joined the staff of Boston's Children's Hospital, taking a leave of absence in 1942 to serve in the U.S. Army Medical Corps during World War II. In 1945 he married Kathleen Fahey with whom he had four children.

While in medical school, Weller had been a student of JOHN F. ENDERS, and he had collaborated with Enders in the study of viruses. The Enders research team, which Weller joined in 1939, specialized in coming up with new techniques for cultivating viruses in the laboratory. When Enders established a laboratory for investigating infectious diseases at the Boston Children's Hospital in 1946, Weller became his chief assistant, and in 1949 he assumed the position of assistant director of the laboratory, which was officially known as the Research Division of Infectious Diseases. Meanwhile, he taught comparative pathology and tropical medicine at Harvard Medical College's School of Public Health.

Working in collaboration with Enders and FREDERICK C. ROBBINS, Weller began studying poliomyelitis, a crippling childhood disease that is also known as polio and infantile paralysis. Prior to 1946, poliomyelitis was difficult to study because researchers could grow the polio virus only in the nerve tissue of live monkeys. This problem limited the amount of the virus available to study and prevented researchers from learning how polio develops in human tissue; but in 1949 Weller, Enders, and Robbins adapted the culture-growing techniques Enders and Weller had devised to work with polio virus cultures, and from that point on they were able to produce enough polio virus to permit researchers to begin studying polio in a serious manner. The procedure basically involved mixing cultures of kidney tissue from monkeys with cultures of human embryos in test tubes, and then introducing the polio virus.

As a result of Weller, Enders, and Robbins's achievement, medical researchers were able to observe the polio virus as it grew and developed in living human cells under laboratory conditions. Thus the stage was set for the development of an injectable polio vaccine by JONAS SALK in 1954 and an oral polio vaccine by ALBERT B. SABIN in 1960. For their work regarding the in vitro growth of the polio virus, Weller, Enders, and Robbins were awarded equal shares of the 1954 Nobel Prize in physiology or medicine.

Weller, Enders, and Robbins continued to work together until 1952, when Robbins left Children's Hospital. Working without him, Weller and Enders developed methods for growing lab cultures of the Coxsackie, chicken pox, cytomegalovirus, and German measles viruses, and in the late 1950s they produced a measles vaccine that went into widespread distribution in 1963. Meanwhile, Weller began branching out on his own. He isolated the virus that causes chicken pox and showed that this virus also causes shingles; his work in this regard led to the development of a chicken pox vaccine by Japanese virologist Michiaki Takahashi in 1974. Weller also showed that cytomegalovirus causes cytomegalic inclusion disease in infants and that a fetal infection with this disease often results in mental retardation and cerebral palsy. Lastly, he demonstrated that Coxsackie virus causes epidemic pleurodynia, which is characterized by sudden chest pain and a mild fever.

Weller retired from Harvard and Children's Hospital in 1985, although he continued to write and review articles about virology.

Further Reading

The Nobel Prize Internet Archive. "Thomas Huckle Weller." Available online. URL://almaz.com/nobel/medicine/1954b.html. Downloaded on March 25, 2005.

Nobelprize.org. "The Nobel Prize in Physiology or Medicine 1954." Available online. URL: http://nobelprize.org/medicine/laureates/1954. Downloaded on January 12, 2004.

Wasson, Tyler, ed. *Nobel Prize Winners*. New York: H. W. Wilson, 1987, pp. 1,109–1,110.

Whipple, George H.
(George Hoyt Whipple)
(1878–1976) *pathologist*

George H. Whipple played a major role in the development of liver therapy as a treatment for pernicious anemia. For this contribution, he was awarded a share of the 1934 Nobel Prize in physiology or medicine.

Whipple was born on August 28, 1878, in Ashland, New Hampshire. His father, Ashley, was a physician, and his mother, Anna, was a homemaker. After receiving an A.B. from Yale University in 1900, he taught school in Ossining, New York, for a year before enrolling in Johns Hopkins Medical School. He received an M.D. in 1905 and then remained at Hopkins for another nine years, first as an assistant to WILLIAM H. WELCH but later as a professor of pathology. During this period he also served for a year as pathologist at Panama's Ancon Hospital and studied in Europe at the universities of Heidelberg and Vienna. In 1914, the same year he married Katharine Waring with whom he had two children, he accepted a professorship in pathology at the University of California at San Francisco (UCSF) Medical School, eventually becoming the school's dean. He left in 1921 to become dean of the new school of medicine and dentistry at the University of Rochester in New York, a position he held for the rest of his career.

At first, Whipple's research interest involved the liver and its relationship to various diseases and medical conditions. At Johns Hopkins he studied the ability of liver cells to regenerate themselves in patients suffering from the adverse effects of anesthesia via chloroform. This course of study led him to investigate jaundice, a condition closely associated with chloroform poisoning and liver injury. In the course of this latter investigation, however, he realized that he needed to know more about hemoglobin, the protein coloring matter of the red blood corpuscles that carries oxygen to the tissues. Thus in 1920 he began a full-blown study of anemia, a deficiency of hemoglobin in the blood that leads to a reduction in the number of red blood cells and causes weakness and breathlessness.

In Panama, Whipple had studied anemia caused by parasitic infections. At UCSF he undertook a study of secondary anemia, which is caused by the loss of blood. He and his assistant, Freida Robscheit-Robbins, bled dogs until they became anemic and then put them on a variety of diets to see which one was best capable of restoring the dogs' red blood count. He soon found out that diets rich in raw liver contributed to the quick creation of new red blood cells that were filled with hemoglobin. He continued to experiment with secondary anemia at Rochester, but here he induced long-term anemia in dogs by withdrawing blood on an ongoing basis. The results of this experiment were that the consumption of large amounts of raw liver, with or without other meats or vegetables, led in short order to the production of plenty of healthy red blood cells.

Whipple's work inspired GEORGE R. MINOT and WILLIAM P. MURPHY, two Boston physicians who were looking for a cure for pernicious anemia, at the time a fatal blood disease. Using Whipple's discoveries concerning liver-rich diets as a springboard, Minot and Murphy were able to develop a highly effective treatment known as liver therapy. Liver therapy not only saved patients' lives but also prevented the symptoms of pernicious anemia from recurring. For their work in this regard, Whipple, Minot, and Murphy were awarded equal shares of the 1934 Nobel Prize in physiology or medicine.

Whipple's research was greatly curtailed by his duties as dean of Rochester's medical school. Nevertheless, later in his career he took up the study of how the body stores and releases proteins, the subject of his only book, *The Dynamic Equilibrium of Body Proteins* (1956). He retired from all academic duties in 1955. He died on February 1, 1976, in Rochester.

Further Reading
Corner, George W. *George Hoyt Whipple and His Friends: The Life-Story of a Nobel Prize Pathologist*. Philadelphia: Lippincott, 1963.

Nobelprize.org. "The Nobel Prize in Physiology or Medicine 1934." Available online. URL: http://nobelprize.org/medicine/laureates/1934. Downloaded on January 22, 2004.

Wasson, Tyler, ed. *Nobel Prize Winners*. New York: H. W. Wilson, 1987, pp. 1,112–1,114.

Wieman, Carl E.
(Carl Edwin Wieman)
(1951–   ) *physicist*

Carl E. Wieman participated in the development of Bose-Einstein condensates, a bizarre state of matter in which atoms behave like photons, packets of light energy. For this development, he was awarded a share of the 2001 Nobel Prize in physics.

Wieman was born on March 26, 1951, in Corvallis, Oregon, but he grew up in a remote logging community in the Oregon backwoods. His father, Orr, worked in a sawmill, and his mother, Alison, was a homemaker. When it came time for him to enter the seventh grade, he moved with his family to Corvallis. As an undergraduate at the Massachusetts Institute of Technology (MIT), he became interested in laser spectroscopy, the use of lasers to study the inner workings of atoms and molecules. After receiving a B.S. in physics in 1973, he went to Stanford University where ARTHUR L. SCHAWLOW and others were doing groundbreaking work with laser spectroscopy. At Stanford he developed techniques for studying the spectra of polarized light and then used these techniques to obtain a more accurate measurement of the Lamb shift, the energy difference between two positions in the orbital pattern of electrons that in theory should be exactly the same.

After receiving a Ph.D. in physics in 1977, Wieman became a research scientist at the University of Michigan. For the next seven years he studied atomic parity violation, or how the weak interaction of radioactive decay disrupts the symmetry of the wave function of subatomic particles. His initial efforts involved the use of microwave spectroscopy to study hydrogen, but later he switched to the study of cesium via laser spectroscopy. In 1984, the same year he married Sarah Gilbert, he joined the research staff at the Joint Institute for Laboratory Astrophysics (today known officially as JILA), a joint institute of the University of Colorado at Boulder and the National Institute of Standards and Technology.

Carl Wieman (above) and Eric Cornell demonstrated the existence of Bose-Einstein condensates, a state of matter wherein atoms behave like light waves rather than particles. *(Courtesy of Colorado University–Boulder Office of Public Relations; photo by Ken Abbott)*

At JILA he continued his work with cesium, and in 1986 he obtained the best measurement for parity violation to that date.

Wieman continued to study parity violation for a number of years thereafter. Nevertheless, his work in this regard employed state-of-the-art laser technology, and as this technology improved he became increasingly interested in laser cooling and trapping. He was particularly interested in the work of STEVEN CHU and WILLIAM D. PHILLIPS, who had designed and built the first atom trap and the first magneto-optic atom trap, respectively. After developing an improved yet scaled down version of the magneto-optic trap from a simple diode laser and a vapor cell,

Wieman embarked on an ambitious program to use laser cooling and trapping to develop Bose-Einstein condensates (BEC), a state of matter that exists only at temperatures near absolute zero and in which atoms merge into a single wavelike entity. The existence of BEC had been postulated in the 1920s by world-renowned physicists ALBERT EINSTEIN and Satyendra Nath Bose. All attempts to develop them, however, had failed because no means existed to chill molecules to a sufficiently low temperature.

In 1990 Wieman was joined at JILA by ERIC A. CORNELL, and over the next five years they worked to develop the necessary apparatus and techniques for reaching temperatures of less than one-millionth of a degree above absolute zero. One such technique is evaporative cooling, whereby the overall temperature of the atoms is reduced by removing the fastest-moving, or the "hottest," atoms from the sample. Another involves the use of a rotating magnetic field to prevent the coldest atoms from leaving the trap. Finally, in 1995, they succeeded in supercooling about 2,000 atoms in a dilute gas of rubidium, after which the atoms began behaving as if they were one gigantic atom. Further experiments by other researchers showed that BEC actually behaves more like a beam of light, which suggests that at extremely low temperatures matter and energy become interchangeable.

The development of BEC shed new light on the ability of matter to behave as if it were light. This development also promised to have many practical applications, especially for so-called quantum computers, futuristic computers that would operate with unimaginable speed. For developing BEC, Wieman and Cornell were each awarded a one-third share of the 2001 Nobel Prize in physics. Their corecipient was the German physicist Wolfgang Ketterle. Weiman's other honors include election to the National Academy of Sciences and the American Academy of Arts and Sciences.

Further Reading

Glanz, James. "3 Researchers Based in U.S. Win Nobel Prize in Physics," *New York Times*, October 10, 2001, p. A14.

Nobelprize.org. "The Nobel Prize in Physics 2001." Available online. URL: http://nobelprize.org/physics/laureates/2001. Downloaded on September 4, 2004.

University of Colorado at Boulder. "Carl E. Wieman." Available online. URL: http://www.colorado.edu/NewsServices/nobel/wieman.html. Downloaded on March 25, 2005.

Wieschaus, Eric F.
(1947–) *embryologist*

Eric F. Wieschaus helped discover how genes regulate the early development of an embryo. For his role in this discovery, he was awarded a share of the 1995 Nobel Prize in physiology or medicine.

Wieschaus was born on June 7, 1947, in South Bend, Indiana. At age six he moved with his family to Birmingham, Alabama, where he grew up. After receiving a B.S. in biology from the University of Notre Dame in 1969, he entered the graduate program at Yale University and received a Ph.D. in experimental embryology in 1974. As a student, his research focused on the embryology of *Drosophila melanogaster*, the common fruit fly, which had long been a favorite subject of geneticists. He was particularly interested in how the various cells that eventually form the fruit fly's 14 distinct segments become arranged together into segments in the embryo.

Wieschaus left Yale for the University of Zurich in Switzerland, where he spent four years as a postdoctoral fellow doing research on the development of the *Drosophila* embryo. During this time he met Christiane Nüsslein-Volhard, a fellow postdoctoral researcher who shared his interests in *Drosophila* segmentation. Following the completion of his fellowship in 1978, he went to the European Molecular Biology Laboratory in Heidelberg, Germany, where he was named a group leader of the project to identify the genes in the fruit fly genome. He was joined shortly thereafter by Nüsslein-Volhard, and over the next three years they spent their spare time conducting their own experiments on the origins of fruit fly segmentation in oogenesis, the process by which a primary egg cell becomes a mature egg. In 1981 Wieschaus and Nüsslein-Volhard went their separate ways; he returned to the United States to teach genetics and developmental biology at Princeton University while she joined the faculty at the Max Planck Institute in Tübingen, Germany. Nevertheless, they continued to coordinate their experiments with one another's and to compare notes on a regular basis.

Eventually Wieschaus and Nüsslein-Volhard were able to identify three sets of genes, 15 genes total, that govern fruit fly segmentation. One set arranges all of the cells in the proper order from head to tail, another set separates the cells into the various segments, and the last set orients each segment head to tail. Moreover, they were able to demonstrate that these genes begin their work during oogenesis and not during later stages of embryological growth as had been suspected by other researchers. By looking for the origins of segmentation at the earliest stages of embryonic development, they helped demonstrate how the genes regulate the growth of a single cell into a complex, multicellular organism. For this contribution, they were each awarded a one-third share of the 1995 Nobel Prize in physiology or medicine. Their corecipient was EDWARD B. LEWIS.

Wieschaus remained at Princeton for the rest of his career. His later work involved the way that genes control changes in cell shape in the fruit fly embryo and how they regulate the development of the embryo's cytoskeleton, the system of filaments that organizes the cell's contents and maintains the cell's shape. In 1983 he married Trudi Schüpbach with whom he had three children.

Further Reading

Altman, Lawrence K. "Work on Body of Fruit Fly Wins Nobel," *New York Times,* October 10, 1995, p. C1.

Nobelprize.org. "The Nobel Prize in Physiology or Medicine 1995." Available online. URL: http://nobelprize.org/medicine/laureates/1995. Downloaded on July 23, 2004.

Princeton University, Department of Molecular Biology. "Wieschous Lab." Available online. URL: http://www.molbio.princeton.edu/labs/wieschous. Downloaded on March 25, 2005.

Wigner, Eugene P.
(Eugene Paul Wigner)
(1902–1995) *physicist*

Eugene P. Wigner contributed in a number of important ways to a better understanding of quantum mechanics, the study of subatomic particles. He authored more than 500 scholarly papers that shed light on virtually every area of nuclear physics, but his most important contribution was to demonstrate the symmetry of the forces that act upon subatomic particles. This latter contribution was acknowledged in 1963 when he was awarded the Nobel Prize in physics.

Wigner was born on November 17, 1902, in Budapest, Hungary. His father, Antal, managed a leather tanning factory, and his mother, Erzsébet, was a homemaker. He studied at the Technical University in Budapest for a year before transferring to the Technische Hochschule in Berlin, Germany, where he received a diploma and a Ph.D. in chemical engineering in 1924 and 1925, respectively. He worked for his father for a year, and then from 1926 to 1930 he conducted research and taught physics at the Technische Hochschule and the University of Göttingen.

Despite his academic training in chemical engineering, Wigner was actually more interested in mathematical, or theoretical, physics. He was particularly interested in quantum mechanics, which had its origins in the 1920s in the German universities. While at the Technische Hochschule and Göttingen, he set for himself the ambitious goal of establishing quantum mechanics as the foundation for all ventures into theoretical physics. His earliest success in this regard came in 1927 when he introduced the use of group theory, the mathematics of symmetry, as a tool for better understanding the behavior of electrons as they rotate around a nucleus. Four years later he published his most important work, a treatise on group theory for physicists; it was published in German, at the time the language in which most cutting-edge works about physics were written. It was the first book about group theory that was written with physicists, not mathematicians, in mind, and it quickly came to be one of the influential works in quantum mechanics. One of the many ideas presented in this book was the Wigner-Eckart theorem; this theorem offers a formal expression of the conservation laws of angular momentum, the relationship between an electron's inertia and its angular velocity. In 1959 this book was translated into English as *Group Theory and Its Application to the Quantum Mechanics of Atomic Spectra.*

Between 1930 and 1933, Wigner shuttled back and forth between the two German schools and Princeton University before settling permanently in the United States in 1933, and for the next three years he taught exclusively at Princeton. In 1933 he and Frederick Seitz, a Princeton graduate student, advanced the Wigner-Seitz cellular method as a way of better understanding the lattice structure of single-element crystals. Over the next two years he described the way a particle beam scatters neutrons, and he defined metals in terms of their electron structure. In 1935 he and JOHN BARDEEN developed the Wigner-Bardeen work function, a useful tool for solving a Schrödinger wave equation, the fundamental equation for describing the wave motion of subatomic particles.

In 1936 Wigner was named to a professorship at the University of Wisconsin, where he became a collaborator of Gregory Breit. In 1936 Wigner and Breit determined that some force other than electromagnetism governs the interaction of nucleons (protons and neutrons) in a nucleus. Seventy years later, this force is not much better understood; scientists now consider that nucleons are held together by the weak nuclear force while quarks, the building blocks of nucleons, are held together by the strong nuclear force. Wigner and Breit also postulated the Breit-Wigner theory, which explains in terms of the resonance, or energy level, of the neutron why some nuclei absorb stray neutrons while others do not. This theory contributed significantly to the discovery of nuclear fission in 1938. Wigner also developed the supermultiplet theory, which emphasizes the symmetry of the forces acting on subatomic particles even when their electrical charges, as is usually the case with nucleons, are different. This theory would later have profound implications for researchers studying the various properties of quarks.

In 1938, the same year he returned to Princeton, Wigner turned his attention to the Lorentz transformations, a set of mathematical equations that relate the space and time coordinates of two systems moving at a constant velocity relative to each other. He used these equations to provide a complete classification of nucleons and electrons in terms of the effect that time and space have on their physical dimensions. In an unpublished paper written in 1940 but circulated widely among his friends and colleagues, he reworked the mathematics of angular momentum and introduced the famous three-*j* symbols known as Clebsch-Gordan or Wigner coefficients and the six-*j* symbols known as Racah coefficients.

Wigner was a major player in the development of nuclear weapons in the United States. In 1939 he helped convince ALBERT EINSTEIN to write his famous letter to President Franklin D. Roosevelt that is credited with initiating the Manhattan Project, the production of the first atomic bombs. As one of the chiefs of the Manhattan Project's Metallurgical Laboratory, Wigner oversaw the design and construction of the nuclear reactors that produced the plutonium for one of the atomic bombs dropped on Japan during World War II. After the war, he served for two years as director of research and development for the nuclear reactors at the Oak Ridge National Laboratory in Tennessee.

In 1947 Wigner returned to teaching at Princeton, where he remained for the next 24 years. His major contribution during this period was to initiate the use of random matrices to explain the scattering of particles during a nuclear reaction. His collaborator in this effort was Leonard Eidenbud, a former graduate student; their work, which became known as the R-matrix theory, served as a cornerstone for the development of the quantum theory of chaos. In 1958 Wigner and Eisenbud coauthored *Nuclear Structure;* that same year he and another former graduate student, Alvin M. Weinberg, coauthored *The Physical Theory of Neutron Chain Reactions.*

In 1963 Wigner won a half share of the Nobel Prize in physics for his contributions to quantum mechanics but particularly for his work regarding the symmetry of nuclear forces. He shared the award with people who conducted different types of experiments from his: American physicist MARIA GOEPPERT MAYER and German physicist J. Hans D. Jensen. His many other honors include the National Medal of Science and the U.S. Medal for Merit. He served a term as president of the American Physical Society and was elected to the National Academy of Sciences, the American

Association for the Advancement of Science, and the American Academy of Arts and Sciences.

Wigner retired from Princeton in 1971, but for the next 14 years he taught on an occasional basis at Louisiana State University. In 1936 he married Amelia Frank, who died the following year; in 1941 he married Mary Wheeler with whom he had two children. She died in 1977, and two years later he married Eileen Hamilton. In 1937 he became a naturalized U.S. citizen. He died on New Year's Day, 1995, in Princeton, New Jersey.

Further Reading

Nobelprize.org. "The Nobel Prize in Physics 1963." Available online. URL: http://nobelprize.org/physics/laureates/1963. Downloaded on March 11, 2004.

Seitz, Frederick, Erich Vogt, and Alvin M. Weinberg. "Eugene Paul Wigner," National Academy of Sciences, *Biographical Memoirs* 74 (1998): pp. 364–388.

Wasson, Tyler, ed. *Nobel Prize Winners*. New York: H. W. Wilson, 1987, pp. 1,125–1,127.

Wigner, Eugene P. *The Recollections of Eugene P. Wigner as Told to Andrew Szanton*. New York: Plenum Press, 1992.

Wilczek, Frank
(Frank Anthony Wilczek)
(1951–) *physicist*

Frank Wilczek was one of three physicists who developed a theory to explain why quarks, the basic building blocks of nucleons (protons and neutrons), cannot be separated from one another even though they sometimes behave as if they are separated. For this contribution, he was awarded a share of the 2004 Nobel Prize in physics.

Wilczek was born on May 15, 1951, in Mineola, New York, to Frank J. and Mary Rose Wilczek. After receiving a B.S. in mathematics from the University of Chicago in 1970, he entered the graduate program at Princeton University and received an M.A. in mathematics in 1971. He then entered Princeton's graduate physics program and became the first graduate student to be supervised by DAVID J. GROSS. Wilczek and Gross began looking for an answer to one of particle physics' most perplexing questions: What is the nature of the force that

binds together quarks? In 1964 MURRAY GELL-MANN had theorized that nucleons are not basic particles but are themselves composed of particles that he named quarks. By 1970 Gell-Mann's theory had been verified by a number of experiments. However, the results of these experiments suggested that the strong nuclear force, the force that binds together quarks, gets stronger as the distance between quarks increases and weaker as the distance between them decreases. Thus, it is impossible to remove a quark from a nucleon, and a single quark has never been found outside a nucleon; yet quarks seem to move about within nucleons as if they are not bound together with anything. This property, known as asymptotic freedom, is unknown in the other known forces of nature, for instance, electromagnetism, gravity, and the weak nuclear force, which governs certain forms of radioactive decay. For these three forces, an increase in the distance over which the force must operate results in a decrease in the force's power, thus making the strong nuclear force unique among the basic forces of nature. Not surprisingly, theoretical physicists were unable to reconcile this anomaly, and therefore they were unable to understand how quarks behave in a nucleon.

After only two years of collaborating, Wilczek and Gross were able to provide an elegant solution to this problem. They developed an ingenious mathematical formula for describing the asymptotic freedom of quarks. Simply stated, they demonstrated that the beta function, which is always positive in formulas involving the other three forces, can be negative for the strong nuclear force. This development made it possible for physicists to understand—mathematically—the behavior of quarks. Wilczek and Gross published their formula in a 1973 issue of the prestigious physics journal *Physical Review Letters*; that same issue also contained a paper by H. DAVID POLITZER, who had duplicated Wilczek and Gross's work independently. The formula was verified experimentally shortly thereafter, and it helped lay the groundwork for the development of quantum chromodynamics, the body of theory that explains in detail how quarks interact within a nucleon. For developing a mathematical explanation for asymptotic freedom, Wilczek, Gross, and Politzer were each awarded a one-third share of the 2004 Nobel Prize in physics.

Wilczek received a Ph.D. in 1973, but he remained at Princeton for an additional year to teach physics. In 1974 he joined the faculty at the Institute for Theoretical Physics (today the Kavli Institute for Theoretical Physics) at the University of California at Santa Barbara. In 1989 he returned to Princeton to teach and conduct research at the Institute for Advanced Study, and in 2000 he joined the faculty at the Massachusetts Institute of Technology. His publications include *Longing for the Harmonies* (1988), *Geometric Phases in Physics* (1989), and *Fractional Statistics and Anyon Super-conductivity* (1990). His other honors include election to the National Academy of Sciences and the American Academy of Arts and Sciences.

In 1973 he married Elizabeth Devire with whom he had two children.

Further Reading

Nobelprize.org. "The Nobel Prize in Physics 2004." Available online. URL: http://nobelprize.org/physics/laureates/2004. Downloaded on December 30, 2004.

Overbye, Dennis. "Three Americans Win Nobel for Particle Physics Work," *New York Times*, October 6, 2004, p. A18.

Physics@MIT. "Frank Wilczek, 2004 Nobel Laureate." Available online. URL: http://web.mit.edu/physics/facultyandstaff/faculty/frank_wilczek.html. Downloaded on March 25, 2005.

Wilson, Kenneth G.
(Kenneth Geddes Wilson)
(1936–) *physicist*

Kenneth G. Wilson developed a powerful technique for understanding what happens during phase transitions, when bulk matter changes from one phase to another. This contribution won him the 1982 Nobel Prize in physics.

Wilson was born on June 8, 1936, in Waltham, Massachusetts. His father, Edgar, taught chemistry at Harvard University, and his mother, Emily, was a homemaker. At age 16 he entered Harvard, receiving a B.A. in mathematics and physics in 1956. He

spent the next six years studying theoretical physics at the California Institute of Technology (Caltech) and Harvard, receiving a Ph.D. from Caltech in 1961. In 1962 he went to Geneva, Switzerland, to conduct research at the European Organization for Nuclear Research (CERN), and the following year he joined the faculty at Cornell University in Ithaca, New York.

While in graduate school, Wilson had become interested in quantum electrodynamics (QED), the study of the interactions between subatomic particles in the electromagnetic field within an atomic nucleus. His dissertation involved the study of the K-meson, one of the so-called strange particles because of the way it decays via radioactivity. Part of this project involved using a highly arcane mathematical tool known as renormalization group theory to better understand the K-meson's unique properties. At Cornell the focus of his work shifted from QED to a subject more suited to a classical physicist, phase transitions. A phase transition is the process by which a substance changes from one phase to another; the most common examples of phase transitions are water turning into ice and vice versa. Phase transitions had been studied for more than a century and yet they were not entirely understood. Wilson began developing a method for using renormalization group theory to understand exactly what happens at a phase transition's critical point, the moment at which the substance has the same density, pressure, and temperature in both phases, by breaking down each transition into a series of smaller steps. By 1971, when he first published his work in this regard, he had developed renormalization group theory into a powerful tool for understanding the critical phenomena associated with phase transitions. In Wilson's hands, renormalization group theory was made to give a complete theoretical description of the behavior close to the critical point while also providing methods for making the crucial calculations associated with phase transitions. Renormalization group theory proved to be so important a predictive tool for physicists and chemists alike that Wilson was awarded a Nobel Prize for developing it.

In the early 1970s Wilson modified renormalization group theory so that it applied to the strong interactions, the forces that bind together protons and neutrons in the nucleus. Meanwhile, he became interested in large-scale scientific computing and the organizational problems associated with it. In the 1980s he and his wife, the former Alison Brown whom he had married in 1982, began developing a computer support program for scientific research, and in 1985 he was named director of Cornell's Center for Theory and Simulation in Science and Engineering, one of five national supercomputer centers created by the National Science Foundation. In 1988 he left Cornell to be a distinguished professor of physics at Ohio State University, and in this position he pushed for educational reform in Ohio and the nation. He published his theories regarding educational reform in *Redesigning Education* (1994). His honors include election to the National Academy of Sciences and the American Academy of Arts and Sciences.

Further Reading

Book Rags.com. "Biography of Kenneth Geddes Wilson." Available online. URL: http://www.bookrags.com/biography/kenneth-geddes-wilson. Downloaded on March 25, 2005.

Nobelprize.org. "The Nobel Prize in Physics 1982." Available online. URL: http://nobelprize.org/physics/laureates/1982. Downloaded on October 2, 2004.

Wasson, Tyler, ed. *Nobel Prize Winners*. New York: H. W. Wilson, 1987, pp. 1,136–1,138.

Wilson, Robert W.
(Robert Woodrow Wilson)
(1936–) *astrophysicist*

Robert W. Wilson helped validate the big bang theory of creation by discovering that a low level of cosmic microwave radiation permeates the universe. This discovery won him a share of the 1978 Nobel Prize in physics.

Wilson was born on January 10, 1936, in Houston, Texas. His father, Ralph, worked for an oil well service company, and his mother, Fannie, was a homemaker. In 1957 he received a B.A. in physics from Rice University and entered the graduate physics program at the California Institute of Technology (Caltech). At Caltech he became interested in radio astronomy—the use of the various wave-bands of electromagnetic radiation to explore outer space—and he participated in a project by the Owens Valley Radio Observatory to develop a radio map of the Milky Way. He remained at Caltech as a postdoctoral fellow for a year after receiving his Ph.D. in 1962 to complete this and other projects. In 1958 he married Elizabeth Sawin with whom he had three children.

In 1963 Wilson went to work in the radio research laboratory at Bell Telephone Laboratories (BTL) in Holmdel, New Jersey. Almost immediately, he began collaborating with ARNO A. PENZIAS in a project to use radio astronomy to detect various molecules and chemical compounds in deep space. Over the next 10 years they identified and mapped the distribution of carbon monoxide, hydrocyanic acid, and ethyl alcohol, as well as an isotope of hydrogen known as deuterium.

In 1964 Wilson and Penzias began using a new, highly sensitive horn reflector antenna. While they were tuning it to seven centimeters, a bandwidth they hoped would minimize background noise from cosmic interference, they accidentally discovered a faint yet persistent low-level noise signal at about three degrees above absolute zero. They began searching for the origin of this signal, and eventually they were forced to conclude that there is no single source, but rather that the signal represents a low level of cosmic microwave radiation that exists in every corner of the universe.

This discovery was very important because of the light it shed on the origins of the universe itself. In 1948 GEORGE GAMOW had developed the big bang theory based on evidence supplied by EDWIN HUBBLE that showed that the universe is expanding. Gamow theorized that about 15 billion years ago a ball of matter, in essence the universe in highly condensed form, exploded and began expanding rapidly. Gamow further theorized that part of the residue of the big bang was a low level of radiation that permeated the universe in the same way that a flash of light permeates the vicinity of a giant firecracker immediately after it explodes. Gamow's theory was greeted with much skepticism at first, but once Wilson and Penzias demonstrated that the "flash of light" from the explosion still lingers throughout the universe, the theory gained acceptance. Forty years later it was acknowledged by the scientific community as the best explanation for the origins of the universe. For the role they played in confirming the big bang theory, Wilson and Penzias were each awarded a quarter share of the 1978 Nobel Prize in physics. Their corecipient was the Soviet physicist Pyotr L. Kapitsa.

Wilson remained at BTL until 1994, when he was named a senior scientist at the Harvard-Smithsonian Center for Astrophysics in Cambridge, Massachusetts. His honors include election to the American Academy of Arts and Sciences.

Further Reading

The Nobel Prize Internet Archive. "Robert W. Wilson." Available online. URL: http://almaz.com/noble/physics/1978c.html. Dowloaded on March 25, 2005.

Nobelprize.org. "The Nobel Prize in Physics 1978." Available online. URL: http://nobelprize.org/physics/laureates/1978. Downloaded on September 29, 2004.

Wasson, Tyler, ed. *Nobel Prize Winners.* New York: H. W. Wilson, 1987, pp. 1,138–1,140.

Wong-Staal, Flossie
(Flossie Wong, Yee-ching Wong)
(1946–) *virologist*

Flossie Wong-Staal codiscovered HIV, the virus that causes AIDS. Her subsequent work with HIV/AIDS involved the search for a cure for AIDS and a vaccine for HIV.

Wong-Staal was born Yee-ching Wong on August 27, 1946, in Canton, China. Her father, Sueh-fung, was a textile importer-exporter, and her mother was a homemaker. At age six she moved with her family to Hong Kong where she grew up. When the teachers at her English-language school asked her father to give her an English first name, he named her Flossie after a recent typhoon. After finishing high school, she arrived in the United States to attend the University of California at Los Angeles, receiving a B.A. and a Ph.D. in molecular biology in 1968 and 1972, respectively. She spent a year conducting postdoctoral research at the University of California at San Diego (UCSD), and then in 1973 she became a research investigator at the National Cancer Institute (NCI) in Bethesda, Maryland, eventually rising to the position of sec-

tion chief in the laboratory of tumor cell biology. In 1971 she married Steven Staal with whom she had two children; they later divorced.

Wong-Staal's research at NCI involved cancer-causing viruses. At the time, several viruses, such as Rous sarcoma virus, were known to cause cancer in mammals, but none had been discovered that caused cancer in humans. Working closely with NCI colleague Robert Gallo, Wong-Staal focused on retroviruses, viruses that replicate themselves by transmitting genetic coding from RNA to DNA, the exact opposite of how genetic coding is normally transmitted. In 1981 she and Gallo discovered human T-cell leukemia virus (HTLV); a retrovirus, HTLV was the first virus known to cause cancer in humans. Within two years she and Gallo had discovered two more retroviruses, HTLV-2 and HTLV-3, which were similar to HTLV. Meanwhile, the world was being hit with the first wave of acquired immunodeficiency syndrome (AIDS), a deadly disease that kills its victims by crippling their autoimmune systems. Shortly after discovering HTLV-3 in 1983, she and Gallo also demonstrated that HTLV-3 causes AIDS, and today HTLV-3 is known as human immunodeficiency virus (HIV). Their findings concerning HTLV-3/HIV were confirmed contemporaneously but independently by researchers at the Pasteur Institute in Paris, France.

Having codiscovered HIV, Wong-Staal turned her attention to studying its biochemical properties. In 1984 she cloned HIV and mapped it genetically, in the process identifying the chemical composition of each of its genes. Further study showed that many of the HIV genes control the virus's growth so that its initial development is much slower than most viruses, even though once it develops into AIDS it spreads very rapidly. This discovery explained why HIV lies dormant in its victims for so long before causing AIDS.

In 1990 Wong-Staal returned to UCSD, this time as a professor of biology/medicine and director of the Center for AIDS Research. In this position she guided the center's efforts to develop a vaccine for HIV as well as to develop treatments for patients with HIV. Because HIV contains a number of genes that work to repress its initial growth, her efforts concerning the treatment of HIV focused on identifying the gene that controls the other growth-inhibiting genes and developing drug treatments to stimulate this gene to work nonstop. Much of her work concerning HIV appears in *Retrovirus Biology and Human Disease* (1990), which she coauthored with Gallo; *Genetic Structure and Regulation of HIV* (1991); and *AIDS Vaccine Research* (2002).

Further Reading

Women's Lives. "Flossie Wong-Staal." Available online. URL: http://www.edwardsly.com/wongsta.htm. Downloaded on March 25, 2005.

"Wong-Staal, Flossie," *Current Biography Yearbook* 62 (2001): pp. 595–596.

Yount, Lisa. *A to Z of Women in Science and Math.* New York: Facts On File, 1999, pp. 211–212.

Woodward, R. B.
(Robert Burns Woodward)
(1917–1979) *chemist*

R. B. Woodward was considered by many to be the 20th century's leading practitioner of organic synthesis, the production of organic compounds by combining their chemical constituents in a laboratory rather than from naturally occurring substances. During his career, he synthesized more than a dozen organic compounds, most of which had pharmaceutical applications, in the process making them easier and cheaper to produce. For this achievement, he was awarded the 1965 Nobel Prize in chemistry.

Woodward was born on April 10, 1917, in Boston, Massachusetts, to Arthur and Margaret Woodward. His father died when he was two years old, and shortly thereafter he moved with his mother and his stepfather to Quincy, where he grew up. At age 16 he entered the Massachusetts Institute of Technology (MIT), receiving a B.S. in chemistry in 1936 and a Ph.D. in organic chemistry in 1937. After teaching for a semester at the University of Illinois, he joined the faculty at Harvard University where he remained for the rest of his career. In 1938 he married Irja Pullman with whom he had two children; they later divorced, and in 1946 he married Eudoxia Muller, with whom he had two children before their divorce in 1966.

In 1941 Woodward was placed in charge of Harvard's advanced organic chemistry laboratory. This position made it easy for him to recruit assistants from the chemistry department's graduate students, and it is estimated that he employed as many as 400 different assistants during his career. That same year he began working to synthesize quinine, a derivative of cinchona bark that was in great demand during World War II because of its value as an antimalarial drug. Quinine is also one of the key constituents in iodoquinine sulfate, which at the time was used in sunglasses and camera lens filters to polarize light, and so he was able to gain financial support for his quest from Edwin F. Land of the Polaroid Corporation. By 1944 Woodward had synthesized quinine, but only via a process that required the production of 20 intermediate compounds. It was a stunning achievement, particularly given the fact that chemists had been trying without success to synthesize quinine since the 1850s, and it established Woodward's reputation early on.

Woodward's ability to succeed where others had failed was the result of two factors. First, earlier chemists had tried to synthesize compounds by trial and error, a tedious and generally unsuccessful process that requires lots of time and patience. Woodward, on the other hand, had the uncanny ability to see in his mind the chemical structure of the compound he intended to synthesize, and he planned out every step involved in its synthesis before he set foot in the laboratory. Second, earlier chemists had available to them methods and equipment that were crude compared to what Woodward had at his disposal. As early as 1940, he had grasped the importance to organic synthesis of spectroscopy, the study of the patterns of light that every substance emits. Over the next two years he published four papers demonstrating how the structures of certain molecules could be better understood by studying their spectral lines of ultraviolet light. Consequently, he pioneered the use of spectroscopic equipment in chemistry at a time when such equipment was being used mostly by physicists. He also made extensive use of crystallography, the study of chemical compounds in the form of crystals, and chromatography, the separation of a chemical compound into its constituent parts via filtration.

After synthesizing quinine, Woodward turned his full attention to the synthesis of penicillin, an antibiotic agent derived from the green mold *Penicillium notatum*. By 1945 he had succeeded, and over the next 20 years he synthesized other compounds with therapeutic applications. The most important ones include cortisone, a steroid produced by the human adrenal cortex used to treat arthritis; oxytetracycline, a derivative of the bacterium *Streptomyces rimosus* that is used to treat streptococcal and staphylococcal infections; cevine, a derivative of sabadilla seeds that is used as a delousing agent; gliotoxin, an antiviral agent produced by the fungus *Trichoderma viride;* colchicine, a derivative of the autumn crocus that is used to treat gout; and reserpine, a derivative of the plant *Rauwolfia serpentina* that is used to treat high blood pressure and certain nervous disorders. In several cases Woodward's synthetic compounds were more therapeutic, less toxic, or less likely to cause harmful side effects than the natural version. In 1963 Woodward formed a working relationship with Ciba Ltd. (today Ciba-Geigy), a Swiss pharmaceutical firm. That same year it opened the Woodward Research Institute in Basel, Switzerland; directed by Woodward, the institute engaged in basic pharmacological research while also collaborating with his operations at Harvard.

Woodward synthesized nonpharmaceutical organic compounds as well. In the 1940s he synthesized toxic substances and hallucinogens such as patulin, strychnine, and lysergic acid, as well as the steroid cholesterol, and he defined the structure of the antibiotics Terramycin and aureomycin as well as of tetrodotoxin, the deadly poison of the puffer fish. In 1955 he began synthesizing chlorophyll, the green coloring matter of leaves and plants; his success five years later was hailed as a major accomplishment for synthetic chemistry. It also shed much light on the workings of the biological molecules in chlorophyll, and by extension the process of photosynthesis. His most spectacular achievement, however, was the synthesis in 1972 of vitamin B_{12}. This accomplishment required the production of more than 100 intermediate products and was achieved through the cooperation of dozens of researchers in the United States and Switzerland. The success of this project led Woodward and ROALD HOFFMANN, one of his Harvard collaborators, to develop the Woodward-Hoffmann rules, which define certain chemical reactions in terms not only of the energy level of the shared electrons but also in terms of the symmetry of the shared electrons. The Woodward-Hoffmann rules are explained in great detail in their book, *The Conservation of Orbital Symmetry* (1970).

Woodward's ability to synthesize organic compounds that no one else had been able to synthesize won him the 1965 Nobel Prize in chemistry. His many other honors and awards include the National Medal of Science and membership in the National Academy of Sciences and the American Academy of Arts and Sciences. He died from a heart attack on July 8, 1979, in Cambridge, Massachusetts.

Further Reading

Barton, Derek, ed. *R. B. Woodward Remembered: A Collection of Papers in Honour of Robert Burns Woodward, 1917–1979*. New York: Pergamon Press, 1982.

Blout, Elkan. "Robert Burns Woodward," National Academy of Sciences, *Biographical Memoirs* 80 (2002): pp. 366–387.

Nobelprize.org. "The Nobel Prize in Chemistry 1965." Available online. URL: http://nobelprize.org/chemistry/laureates/1965. Downloaded on May 5, 2004.

Wasson, Tyler, ed. *Nobel Prize Winners*. New York: H. W. Wilson, 1987, pp. 1,147–1,148.

Wright, Jane C.
(Jane Cooke Wright)
(1919–) *medical researcher*

Jane C. Wright was a pioneer in the field of cancer chemotherapy. Although her research yielded little in the way of positive results, she paved the way for the success of future researchers by shedding much light on the nature of tumors as well as on a wide range of potential chemotherapy drugs.

Wright was born on November 30, 1919, in New York City. Her father was LOUIS T. WRIGHT and her mother, Corinne, was a homemaker. In 1942 she received a B.A. from Smith (Mass.) College and entered New York Medical College, receiving an M.D. three years later. She spent the next three years completing her internship and residency at New York City's Bellevue and Harlem hospitals, and in 1947 she married David Jones with whom she had two children.

In 1948 Wright went to work as a physician for the New York City public schools. That same year, her father established the Harlem Hospital Cancer Research Foundation as a center for conducting some of the first clinical tests of cancer chemotherapy drugs, and she became a clinician with the foundation the following year. When her father died in 1952, she took over his duties as head of the foundation and moved it to more modern facilities at the New York University Medical School.

When Wright joined the foundation, cancer chemotherapy was in its infancy. The only drug known to be an effective treatment for cancer was mechlorethamine, whose effectiveness against certain lymphomas, tumors arising in the human lymphatic system, had been demonstrated by other researchers in the mid-1940s. Consequently, Wright and her colleagues had to discover virtually everything about how to treat tumors with drugs. They established trial-and-error testing involving animals and tissue cultures for a number of potential chemotherapy drugs, including triethylene melamine, triethylene phosphoramide, puromycin, ACTH, folic acid antagonists, actinomycin D, streptonigrin, mithramycin, and fluorouracil. They discovered that tumors are unique in that they do not always grow or react to treatment the same way; some tumors spread rapidly in one patient but slowly in another, some treatments that are effective against tumors in animals or tissue cultures are not effective when administered to humans, and some drugs are effective against one type of tumor but not another. Not surprisingly, her research generated much more failure than success.

Nevertheless, Wright and her colleagues did make progress, as certain drugs were proven to be effective under certain conditions. For example, they showed that triethylene thiophosphoramide is an effective treatment for advanced malignant melanoma, or skin cancer, while Dihydro E. 73 possesses certain anticancer properties that make it a useful treatment for a number of different tumors. She developed the techniques known as isolation perfusion, whereby a solid tumor is saturated with a

chemotherapeutic drug, and regional perfusion, whereby the general area, usually in the head or neck, is saturated. Perhaps the most significant result of Wright's work, however, is the knowledge that chemotherapy can be an effective way to treat most forms of cancer, and that researchers need to be patient but hopeful as they continue their search for effective chemotherapeutic agents.

In 1964 Wright cofounded the American Society of Clinical Oncology and served as its first secretary-treasurer. She also served on the President's Commission on Heart Disease, Cancer, and Stroke and the National Advisory Cancer Council. In 1967 she was named a dean and a professor of surgery at her alma mater, New York Medical College, as well as head of its cancer research laboratory. Although she stepped down as dean in 1975, she continued to teach and conduct research until her retirement in 1987.

Further Reading

McMurray, Emily J., ed. *Notable Twentieth Century Scientists.* Detroit: Gale Research, 1995, pp. 2,257–2,258.

Spangenburg, Ray, and Kit Moser. *African Americans in Science, Math, and Invention.* New York: Facts On File, 2003, pp. 228–230.

Yount, Lisa. *A to Z of Women in Science and Math.* New York: Facts On File, 1999, pp. 212–213.

Wright, Louis T.
(Louis Tompkins Wright)
(1891–1952) *medical researcher*

Louis Wright devised and supervised the testing of some of the first cancer chemotherapy drugs. He also supervised some of the first clinical tests of antibiotic drugs and invented two devices for handling fractured bones.

Wright was born on July 22, 1891, in La Grange, Georgia. His father, Ceah, was a physician and minister, and his mother, Lula, was a homemaker. When he was three, his father died, and he moved shortly thereafter with his mother to Atlanta. When he was eight, his mother married William F. Penn, a physician who encouraged Louis to follow in his footsteps by taking him on his rounds. In 1911 he graduated from Atlanta's Clark

University and enrolled in Harvard Medical School, receiving an M.D. four years later. After completing a two-year internship at Freedmen's Hospital in Washington, D.C., in 1917 he returned to Atlanta to join his stepfather's practice. When the United States entered World War I later that same year, he volunteered for the U.S. Army and served with distinction in France as a medical officer. In 1918 he married Corinne Cooke with whom he had two children.

After the war, Wright settled in New York City, his wife's hometown, and opened a private practice. In 1920 he was hired as a clinical assistant by Harlem Hospital, where he spent the rest of his medical career. In 1938 he was named director of surgery, and 10 years later he was elected president of the hospital's medical board.

Rather than concentrate in any one field, Wright devoted his research efforts to several unrelated but important areas. The first was the detection of diphtheria in African Americans. At the turn of the century, diphtheria was a deadly disease because it interfered with the ability of people, especially children, to breathe. In the early 1900s, pediatrician Bela Schick developed the Schick test to identify persons who had no immunity to diphtheria. The test involved injecting a small amount of diphtheria toxin under the skin; those without immunity would experience inflammation of the skin in the immediate vicinity of the test. The Schick test proved to be a valuable tool for fighting diphtheria, but a number of physicians refused to perform the test on blacks, saying that the pigments in the skin of African Americans would make inflammation impossible to detect. Wright scoffed at this notion, and while he was an intern at Freedmen's Hospital he proved that the Schick test worked just as well on African Americans as it did on light-skinned people.

Wright's duties as a surgeon at Harlem Hospital brought him into regular contact with broken bones of all sorts, and he eventually became an expert on treating fractures. He developed two devices that improved the handling of fractured bones—a neck brace for handling upper vertebrae that had been fractured or dislocated, and a special metal plate for treating certain fractures of the femur (thigh bone). In 1937 he was invited to write the chapter on head injuries for Charles Scudder's

The Treatment of Fractures (1938), at the time of its publication the most comprehensive medical textbook on the subject.

Lastly, Wright helped set up and then supervised the testing of a number of important drugs. In 1948 he organized a team of doctors at Harlem Hospital to conduct the first clinical tests on humans of Aureomycin, one of the first antibiotic drugs. Later that same year, he established the Harlem Hospital Cancer Research Foundation; under his direction, the foundation conducted some of the first clinical tests of chemotherapy drugs. As a result of his work with the foundation, Wright became one of the first experts in the use of chemotherapy, and he shared his expertise with other physicians via dozens of articles in leading scientific and medical journals.

Wright was also active in the civil rights movement. He was involved in the affairs of the National Association for the Advancement of Colored People (NAACP) all his adult life, and from 1935 to 1952 he chaired its board of directors. Largely as a result of his influence and agitation, Harlem Hospital became one of the first hospitals in the United States to integrate its medical staff. Drawing on his experiences in this regard, in 1937 he helped establish an NAACP program to eliminate discrimination in health care. He was particularly opposed to segregated hospitals because he believed that separate was not equal, especially when it came to health care. He died of a heart attack on October 8, 1952, in New York City.

Further Reading

Cobb, William M. "Louis Tompkins Wright, 1891–1952," *Journal of the National Medical Association* 45 (March 1953): pp. 130–148.

Spangenburg, Ray, and Kit Moser. *African Americans in Science, Math, and Invention.* New York: Facts On File, 2003, pp. 230–231.

Wright, Sewall
(Sewall Green Wright)
(1889–1988) *biologist*

Sewall Wright was a major contributor to the neo-Darwinian theory of evolution. He also helped to make animal husbandry more of an exact science.

Wright was born on December 21, 1889, in Melrose, Massachusetts. His father, Philip, was a college professor, and his mother, Elizabeth, was a homemaker. At age three he moved with his family to Galesburg, Illinois, where his father had accepted a position on the faculty of Lombard College. He finished high school at age 15 and then enrolled at Lombard, receiving a B.A. in mathematics in 1911.

Wright became interested in evolution while in high school, when he read Charles Darwin's *Origin of Species* in its entirety. It was not until his senior year at Lombard, however, that he became interested in biology. He spent the summer after graduation at the Carnegie Institution of Washington's experimental evolution station at Cold Spring Harbor in New York, and then he entered the graduate program at the University of Illinois, receiving an M.A. in biology in 1912. His twin interests in evolution and biology then led him to Harvard University, where he studied genetics while earning a Ph.D. in zoology, which he received in 1915.

Wright continued to experiment with genetics after leaving Harvard and going to work for the U.S. Department of Agriculture in Washington, D.C. As a senior worker in animal husbandry, his duties were to conduct research that might help improve livestock breeding. To this end he studied the effects of inbreeding and crossbreeding on livestock and guinea pigs. A gifted mathematician, he developed a statistical method known as path analysis to gain a better understanding of the genetic factors that determine various body characteristics such as coat and eye color. He also pioneered the use of detailed observations and exact record-keeping of various pedigrees of animals over several generations as a means of better understanding the effects of inbreeding and crossbreeding, and his methods contributed to making animal breeding a more exact science. At the time, however, much of his research fell outside the parameters of the department's work, and in 1926 he joined the faculty at the University of Chicago. Meanwhile, in 1921 he had married Louise Williams with whom he had three children.

At Chicago, Wright continued his experiments with inbreeding and crossbreeding but from a more theoretical perspective. By 1931 he had reached the conclusion that evolution does not always take place as the result of natural selection. His work with small herds of animals led him to conclude that sometimes, by chance, a gene that is carried by only a few members in a small, isolated population might not be passed along but instead might disappear altogether from that population. One result, he reasoned, might be the evolution of a new species via a process that has nothing to do with natural selection. This theory, known alternately as genetic drift and the Sewall Wright effect, aroused much controversy among evolutionists. In time, Wright became involved in a rather bitter feud with British geneticist Robert A. Fisher, the informal leader of the faction that rejected genetic drift on the grounds that this sort of variance could be analyzed only in large populations.

Despite Wright's difficulties with Fisher, these two men, along with British geneticist J. B. S. Haldane, laid the groundwork for what became known as the neo-Darwinian synthesis of evolution. Wright, Fisher, and Haldane developed sophisticated mathematical models for studying the parameters of evolutionary change. These models demonstrated that evolution takes place only partly in accordance with Darwinian selection theory; of equal importance is the role played by the laws of genetics, as expressed in the work of Gregor Mendel, Hugo de Vries, and

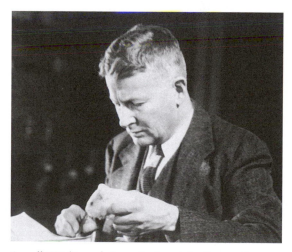

Sewall Wright made important contributions to the theory of evolution. *(Courtesy of the University of Chicago)*

others. Wright's work, in particular, informed Theodosius Dobzhansky's *Genetics and the Origin of Species* (1937); by combining Wright's mathematical models with Dobzhansky's experimental evidence, this work led directly to the development of modern evolution theory.

In 1955 Wright retired from Chicago, only to take a faculty position at the University of Wisconsin in Madison. He retired a second time five years later, although he remained active at Wisconsin until his death. In 1968 he published the first volume of the four-volume *Evolution and the Genetics of Populations*; the remaining volumes came out in 1969, 1977, and 1978. This work summarized his own ideas about genetics and evolution while restating the major developments that had taken place in mathematical evolutionary theory during the previous 50 years. Late in his life, Wright became interested in philosophy, and he developed what became known as panpsychic dualism, the idea that all matter, even the most elementary particles, is infused with some sort of consciousness.

Wright served as president of the American Society of Zoologists, the Genetics Society of America, the American Society of Naturalists, and the Society for the Study of Evolution. His many honors include election to the National Academy of Sciences and receipt of the National Medal of Science. He died on March 3, 1988, in Madison.

Further Reading

Crow, James F. "Sewall Wright," National Academy of Sciences, *Biographical Memoirs* 64 (1994): pp. 439–469.

Provine, William B. *Sewall Wright and Evolutionary Biology.* Chicago: University of Chicago Press, 1986.

Wrinch, Dorothy Maud
(1894–1976) *biochemist, biochemical theorist*

Dorothy Wrinch was a controversial figure in the scientific community in the 1930s. Hailed by many as the "woman Einstein" for her cyclol theory of protein structure, she was also dismissed by many as a lightweight because of her lack of professional training. Although her theory never became accepted, it helped to encourage many scientists to look at problems in their discipline from a multidisciplinary point of view.

Wrinch was born on September 12, 1894, in Rosario, Argentina. Her father, Hugh, was an engineer, and her mother, Ada, was a homemaker. As a child she moved with her parents to London, England. In 1913 she enrolled in Cambridge College's Girton College where she studied mathematics and philosophy and received a B.A. four years later. After spending a fifth year at Girton as a research scholar, in 1918 she entered London's University College where she taught mathematics while earning her M.Sc. (1920) and D.Sc. (1921) in mathematics. She spent another two years (1921–23) at Girton as a research fellow before becoming a part-time mathematics instructor in the five women's colleges of Oxford University. While at Oxford she received another set of graduate degrees in mathematics. In 1922 she married John Nicholson but did not take his name; they had one child before separating in 1930 and divorcing in 1938.

Trained as an applied mathematician, Wrinch was actually more interested in the philosophy of science, particularly the way in which scientists thought while investigating a particular problem. In this sense she was inspired by the British philosophers Bertrand Russell and Alfred North Whitehead, who combined mathematics and logic in their groundbreaking work, *Principia Mathematica*, and by ALBERT EINSTEIN, whose theory of general relativity combined physics, geometry, and logic. In 1931 she left Oxford to pursue a career as a theoretical scientist. Over the next three years she used several fellowships to study physics, chemistry, and biology at four major European universities. In 1934 she began studying the mechanics of chromosomes, but she did so from the perspective of the potential theory, which previously had been limited to determine the distribution of electric charge over a given mass. By 1936 she had published five articles on the nature and behavior of chromosomes.

Meanwhile, Wrinch had become active in the proceedings of the Biotheoretical Gathering. Cofounded by her in 1932, this group was particularly impressed by the many roles proteins play in the structure and function of living organisms, and its members sought to explain the mystery of life by learning more about proteins and the handful of different amino acids from which they are composed. In 1936 she published a paper concerning her cyclol theory of protein structure. Most biologists believed that the connections between amino acids in proteins were linear, but Wrinch argued otherwise. She posited that the linkages were hollow, hexagonal structures that she called cyclols, and that cyclols more closely resembled a piece of fabric than a piece of chain.

Wrinch's cyclol theory attracted a surprising number of detractors in the late 1930s. Largely because of her lack of advanced training and experience in biology or chemistry, she was denigrated and ridiculed by most experts in both fields. One detractor dismissed the cyclol theory as being incompatible with the laws of thermodynamics. Others pointed out that cyclols do not exist in nature and could not be synthesized in the laboratory; however, these detractors were proven wrong in the 1950s when cyclols were discovered in nature as well as reproduced under laboratory conditions. More damning was an accusation by one of her colleagues in the Biotheoretical Gathering that she had plagiarized the work of other members. Prevented by her lack of biochemical training from conducting her own experiments to prove or disprove the cyclol theory, she was forced to wait patiently for other researchers to do this work for her. None did, and by the end of the decade she had become the laughingstock of English academia.

In 1939 Wrinch left England and came to the United States to accept a position as a lecturer in chemistry at Johns Hopkins University. Two years later she married Otto Glaser, vice president of Amherst College in Massachusetts, with whom she had no children, and moved to Massachusetts to be a visiting professor at Amherst and two women's colleges. In 1943 she became a naturalized citizen of the United States and accepted a full-time position as a professor of physics at Smith College. She retired from Smith in 1971 to Woods Hole, Massachusetts. She died on February 11, 1976, in Falmouth, Massachusetts.

Further Reading

Abir-Am, Pnina G. "Synergy or Clash: Disciplinary and Marital Strategies in the Career of Mathematical Biologist Dorothy Wrinch." In Pnina G. Abir-Am and Dorinda Outram, eds., *Uneasy Careers and Intimate Lives: Women in Science 1789–1979.* New Brunswick, N.J.: Rutgers University Press, 1987, pp. 239–280.

Julian, Maureen M. "Women in Crystallography." In G. Kass-Simon and Patricia Farnes, eds., *Women of Science: Righting the Record.* Bloomington: University of Indiana Press, 1990, pp. 364–368.

Yount, Lisa. *A to Z of Women in Science and Math.* New York: Facts On File, 1999, pp. 213–214.

Y, Z

Yalow, Rosalyn
(Rosalyn Sussman, Rosalyn Sussman Yalow)
(1921–) *medical physicist*

Rosalyn Yalow codeveloped a method for measuring minute concentrations of peptide hormones in blood and other bodily fluid samples. For this development, she won a share of a Nobel Prize, thus becoming the first U.S.-born female scientist to win a Nobel.

Yalow was born Rosalyn Sussman on July 19, 1921, in New York City. Her father, Simon, was a small businessman, and her mother, Clara, was a homemaker. By age eight she had decided to pursue a career as a scientist, and when she enrolled in New York's Hunter College in 1936 she decided to study nuclear physics. Upon receiving an A.B. in physics in 1941, she went to the University of Illinois at Champaign-Urbana where she received an M.S. in 1942 and a Ph.D. in physics in 1945. In 1943 she married Aaron Yalow with whom she had two children. After graduation she returned to New York City to work as an engineer at the Federal Telecommunications Laboratory. When her research group was relocated out of town in 1946, she returned to Hunter College, this time as a physics professor.

Yalow's interest in nuclear physics had led her to study and conduct research with radioisotopes, radioactive isotopes of elements that are not normally radioactive. This interest led her to become interested in medical physics, and in 1947 she was introduced to EDITH H. QUIMBY, cofounder of Columbia University's Radiological Research Laboratory. Quimby's research involved investigating the medical usefulness of radioisotopes as well as developing procedures for their safe handling. Through Quimby, Yalow was able to obtain a research position at the Veterans Administration (VA) Hospital in New York City. Her primary duties were to organize one of the first radioisotope laboratories in the country, under the auspices of the VA Medical Research Program, and then conduct research as to how radioisotopes could be used to treat cancer. Part of her job involved designing and building the equipment she needed, as it did not exist commercially. After working part-time at the VA Hospital for three years, in 1950 she left Hunter to concentrate full-time on her research with radioisotopes.

In 1950 Yalow began a research partnership with Solomon Berson, who had just joined the VA Hospital's staff. Their first joint project involved using radioisotopes to determine blood volume. Later they developed ways to use radioisotopes to diagnose thyroid diseases, to study the metabolism of iodine, and to study the distribution of globin, the protein component of red blood corpuscles. In essence, their research involved finding ways to attach radioisotopes to various biochemical components, which could then be used as tracers.

In 1956 Yalow and Berson discovered that the immune system of diabetics produced antibodies to the insulin they injected, because injected insulin comes from animals and not humans. Yalow and Berson adapted this discovery to develop the incredibly powerful diagnostic tool known as radioimmunoassay (RIA). In essence, they injected a sample of the bodily substance they

Rosalyn S. Yalow codeveloped radioimmunoassay, a method for determining the amount of certain biomolecules in a given sample of blood or other bodily fluid. *(Library of Congress, Prints and Photographs Division [LC-USZ62-122235])*

wanted to test for into an animal, which then produced antibodies to the substance. Then they mixed radioisotopes with the antibodies and another sample of the bodily substance. The antibodies attach themselves to the substance, thus preventing the radioisotopes from attaching. By measuring the amount of unattached radioisotopes, they were able to tell how much of the substance the sample contained.

In 1959 Yalow and Berson published their findings concerning RIA. Almost immediately, other researchers began developing uses for RIA, as it proved to be a very sensitive and simple means for measuring peptide hormones, such as insulin and cortisone, which occur in very small amounts in the blood and other bodily fluids. The development of RIA permitted medical research concerning the

peptide hormones to move forward. In time RIA was adapted for use in hundreds of other applications, such as detecting the presence of viruses or illegal drugs in the bloodstream and determining the optimum dosages for prescription drugs. In recognition of the importance of their discovery, Yalow was awarded a half share of the 1977 Nobel Prize for physiology or medicine. Berson would surely have shared in the prize had he not died in 1972. Instead, her corecipients were the American physiologists ROGER GUILLEMIN and ANDREW V. SCHALLY.

After Berson's death, Yalow continued to conduct research regarding peptide hormones. She and her colleagues described the physiology of insulin, cortisone, and growth hormone and shed much light on how the abnormal secretion of these hormones results in a variety of diseases. She also returned to teaching, joining the faculty of the Mount Sinai School of Medicine, the Montefiore Hospital and Medical Center, and the Albert Einstein College of Medicine, all in New York City. She was elected to the National Academy of Sciences in 1975.

Yalow retired from the VA Hospital in 1991, but she continued to conduct research there for several years thereafter. After 1991 she began lecturing on the need for more nuclear power and the importance of scientific training for people in general and women in particular.

Further Reading

Hargittai, Istvan, and Magdolna Hargittai. *Candid Science II: Conversations with Famous Biomedical Scientists.* London: Imperial College Press, 2002, pp. 518–524.

Nobelprize.org. "The Nobel Prize in Physiology or Medicine 1977." Available online. URL: http://nobelprize. org/medicine/laureates/1977. Downloaded on September 4, 2003.

Wasson, Tyler, ed. *Nobel Prize Winners.* New York: H. W. Wilson, 1987, pp. 1,148–1,150.

Yang, Chen Ning
(Franklin Yang, Frank Yang)
(1922–) *physicist*

Chen Ning Yang hypothesized that the laws of parity conservation do not necessarily apply to interactions involving subatomic particles. Known today as parity violation, his hypothesis was proven correct in 1957, and that same year Yang was awarded a share of the Nobel Prize in physics. The speed with which the Nobel committee acted to recognize Yang's achievement was unprecedented, and it testifies to the importance of parity violation as a means of understanding the behavior of the elementary particles.

Yang was born on September 22, 1922, in Hofei, Anwhei, China, but his early life was spent in Beijing. His father, Ke Chuan, was a mathematics professor at Tsinghua University in Beijing, and his mother, Meng, was a homemaker. As a boy he adopted the name Franklin in honor of one of his boyhood heroes, BENJAMIN FRANKLIN; in the United States he is known as Franklin or Frank, but elsewhere he is known as Chen Ning. Following the invasion of China by Japan in the late 1930s, he moved with his family to Kunming in Yunnan Province. He received a B.S. in physics from the National Southwest Associated University in Kunming in 1942 and an M.S. in physics from Tsinghua, which had relocated temporarily to Kunming, in 1944. After teaching high school mathematics for two years, in 1946 he came to the United States to attend the University of Chicago, receiving a Ph.D. in theoretical physics in 1948. He remained at Chicago for an additional year as an assistant to ENRICO FERMI, and in 1949 he joined the staffs of the Institute for Advanced Study in Princeton, New Jersey, and the Brookhaven National Laboratory in Upton, New York. In 1950 he married Chih Li Tu with whom he had three children, and in 1964 he became a naturalized U.S. citizen.

While at Chicago, Yang developed a working relationship with TSUNG-DAO LEE, at the time a fellow graduate student. They resumed their collaboration in 1951 when Lee joined Yang at the Institute for Advanced Study, and they continued it after Lee obtained a position at Columbia University in New York City, just down the road from Yang's office at Brookhaven. Their primary interest involved the theory of the weak interactions, one of which causes subatomic particles to decay via radioactivity, a process known as beta decay. In the early 1950s it was generally believed that

the weak interactions, like all the other physical forces, obey the laws of parity conservation. These laws state that every physical reaction occurs symmetrically, without regard to up, down, left, right, clockwise, or counterclockwise. For example, when an ice cube melts, the water does not flow mostly to the left but in all directions evenly. In 1953, however, Yang and Lee discovered that when the K-meson, one of the so-called strange particles because it takes trillions of times longer to decay than it does to form, undergoes beta decay, it does not always yield the same products. Sometimes a K-meson decays into three pi mesons, but sometimes it decays into only two, thus suggesting that the laws of parity conservation are being violated.

Yang and Lee set out to discover what experimental evidence, if any, supports the notion that parity conservation holds for the weak interactions. They were somewhat surprised to discover that there was none, as every experiment that they could find involving the weak interactions had been conducted on the assumption that parity conservation is a given. At this point they were forced to conclude that parity violation might explain the behavior of K-mesons during beta decay. Being theoreticians and not experimenters, in 1956 they suggested a set of experiments that could be performed to determine whether or not parity conservation holds for beta decay. The following year Chinese-American physicist Chienshiung Wu conducted their experiments with a radioactive isotope of cobalt, cobalt-60. Wu was able to demonstrate that as cobalt-60 undergoes beta decay, the particles it emits have a remarkable preference for moving in the "up" direction, a clear violation of parity conservation.

Yang and Lee's experiments, as conducted by Wu, offered the first clear-cut evidence that parity violation occurs during beta decay. Other experiments conducted over the next several years offered further support for parity violation during other weak interactions, of which there are approximately 20. Consequently, physicists were forced to reevaluate their ideas about the laws of conservation as they apply to particles. Eventually, they discovered that the laws of conservation regarding charge conjugation and time are also violated during certain weak interactions. For proposing the experiments that forced this reevaluation, Yang and Lee were each awarded a half share of the 1957 Nobel Prize in physics.

Parity violation was not Yang's only important contribution to particle physics. In 1954 he and a Brookhaven colleague, Robert L. Mills, developed the Yang-Mills theory. This theory attempts to explain the fundamental interactions of elementary particles in fields of electricity, magnetism, and gravity. In time, the Yang-Mills theory provided much of the underpinnings for efforts by other researchers to develop a so-called grand unified theory, whereby the four known physical forces—electromagnetism, gravity, and the strong and weak interactions—could be demonstrated to be manifestations of one "superforce." Yang was also one of the first to apply the mathematical theories of braid groups and knot theory to statistical mechanics, the study of the behavior of large systems of elementary particles.

In 1966 Yang was named a professor of physics at the State University of New York in Stony Brook, a position he held for more than 30 years. In 1998 he returned to Beijing to teach at Tsinghua University, where he spent the remainder of his career. His honors include the National Medal of Science and election to the National Academy of Sciences. He also served terms as president of the Association of Asia Pacific Physical Sciences and the Asia Pacific Center of Theoretical Physics. His publications include *Elementary Particles and Weak Interactions* (1957), which he coauthored with Lee; *Elementary Particles* (1961); *Theory of Charged Vector Mesons Interacting with the Electromagnetic Field* (1963); and *Braid Group, Knot Theory, and Statistical Mechanics* (1989).

Further Reading

Liu, Chao Shiuan, and Shing-Tung Yau, eds. *Chen Ning Yang: A Great Physicist of the Twentieth Century.* Cambridge, Mass.: International Press, 1995.

Nobelprize.org. "The Nobel Prize in Physics 1957." Available online. URL: http://nobelprize.org/physics/laureates/1957. Downloaded on September 24, 2004.

Wasson, Tyler, ed. *Nobel Prize Winners.* New York: H. W. Wilson, 1987, pp. 1,150–1,152.

Zewail, Ahmed H.
(Ahmed Hassan Zewail)
(1946–) *chemist*

Ahmed H. Zewail developed femtochemistry, the use of fast laser techniques to record the actual events that take place during the transition state in a chemical reaction. For this achievement, he was awarded the 1999 Nobel Prize in chemistry.

Zewail was born on February 26, 1946, in Damanhur, Egypt, but he grew up in nearby Disuq. His father, Hassan, was a government official and businessman, and his mother, Rawhia, was a homemaker. After finishing high school, he entered Alexandria University, receiving a B.S. and an M.S. in chemistry in 1967 and 1969, respectively. He then came to the United States to study at the University of Pennsylvania, receiving a Ph.D. in 1974. After two years as a postdoctoral fellow at the University of California at Berkeley, in 1976 he joined

Ahmed Zewail developed a method for using lasers to take pictures of a chemical reaction during the transition state. *(Courtesy of Ahmed H. Zewail)*

the faculty at the California Institute of Technology (Caltech). In 1989 he married Dema Zewail with whom he had two children; he also had two children by a previous marriage.

Zewail's research involved the use of spectroscopy, the study of the spectral lines of atoms and molecules, to study the structures of various chemical compounds. His graduate research focused on dimers, molecules composed of two identical, simpler molecules, and his postdoctoral research included the use of a picosecond laser, a laser whose burst of light is measured in millionths of a millionth of a second, to study the process of dimerization. At Caltech he took up the challenge of finding out what actually happens to a reacting dimer as it passes through its transition state, that intermediate stage when its two constituent molecules either bond together or break apart. This was a daunting task because the transition state lasts no longer than a dozen or so femtoseconds, or millionths of a billionth of a second, and most chemists doubted that photographing the transition state would ever be possible.

Despite such skepticism, Zewail spent his first 11 years at Caltech working toward this goal, and by 1987 he had succeeded. His "camera" was a fast laser technique whereby the flashes of intense light lasted for only a few tens of femtoseconds. The first flash initiated the reaction, and the subsequent flashes followed the events. The first experiments demonstrated in slow motion how chemical bonds are stretched and broken in rather simple reactions, but as his methods and equipment became more sophisticated he was able to study more complex reactions. Over the next 12 years he demonstrated that many of the theories about what happens during the transition state were wrong, thus forcing chemists to rethink much of what they thought they knew about chemical reactions.

Femtochemistry revolutionized the study of all branches of chemistry, but particularly of biochemistry, as it gave medical researchers a better understanding of what happens during biochemical functions. For developing femtochemistry, Zewail was awarded the 1999 Nobel Prize in chemistry.

In 1996 Zewail was named director of the National Science Foundation Laboratory for Molecular Sciences at Caltech. He also served as editor of *Laser Chemistry* and *Journal of Physical Chemistry*. His other honors include election to the National Academy of Sciences and the American Academy of Arts and Sciences.

Further Reading

California Institute of Technology. "Ahmed Zewail." Available online. URL: http://www.its.caltech.edu/~femto. Downloaded on March 25, 2005.

Nobelprize.org. "The Nobel Prize in Chemistry 1999." Available online. URL: http://nobelprize.org/chemistry/laureates/1999. Downloaded on August 20, 2004.

Zewail, Ahmed H. *Voyage through Time: Walks of Life to the Nobel Prize.* Cairo: American University in Cairo Press, 2002.

BIBLIOGRAPHY AND RECOMMENDED SOURCES

Bailey, Martha J. *American Women in Science: 1950 to the Present.* Santa Barbara, Calif.: ABC-CLIO, 1998.

Carey, Charles W., Jr. *American Inventors, Entrepreneurs, and Business Visionaries.* New York: Facts On File, 2002.

Contemporary Black Biography, Profiles from the International Black Community. Detroit: Gale Research, 1992.

Dictionary of American Biography. New York: Charles Scribner's Sons, 1996.

Elliot, Clark A., ed. *Biographical Index to American Science: The Seventeenth Century to 1920.* New York: Greenwood Press, 1990.

Garraty, John A., and Mark C. Carnes, eds. *American National Biography.* New York: Oxford University Press, 1999.

Gillispie, Charles C., ed. *Dictionary of Scientific Biography.* New York: Scribner, 1980.

Hargittai, Istvan, and Magdolna Hargittai. *Candid Science II: Conversations with Famous Biomedical Scientists.* London: Imperial College Press, 2002.

Harris, Jonathan. *Scientists in the Shaping of America.* Menlo Park, Calif.: Addison-Wesley, 1971.

Kalte, Pamela, and Katherine H. Nemeh. *American Men & Women of Science: A Biographical Dictionary of Today's Leaders in Physical, Biological and Related Sciences.* Detroit: Gale Research, 2003.

Krapp, Kristine M., ed. *Notable Twentieth-Century Scientists Supplement.* Detroit: Gale Research, 1998.

McGraw-Hill Modern Scientists and Engineers. New York: McGraw-Hill, 1980.

McMurray, Emily J., ed. *Notable Twentieth-Century Scientists.* Detroit: Gale Research, 1995.

National Academy of Sciences. *Biographical Memoirs.* Washington, D.C.: National Academy of Sciences, 1877–.

Nobelprize.org. "The Nobel Prize." Available online. URL: http://nobelprize.org. Downloaded on October 18, 2004.

Serafini, Anthony. *Legends in Their Own Time: A Century of American Physical Scientists.* New York: Plenum Books, 1993.

Spangenburg, Ray, and Kit Moser. *African Americans in Science, Math, and Invention.* New York: Facts On File, 2003.

Wasson, Tyler, ed. *Nobel Prize Winners.* New York: H. W. Wilson, 1987.

Yount, Lisa. *A to Z of Women in Science and Math.* New York: Facts On File, 1999.

Zuckerman, Harriet. *Scientific Elite: Nobel Laureates in the United States.* New York: Free Press, 1977.

ENTRIES BY DISCIPLINE

ANATOMIST
Sabin, Florence

ASTRONOMER
Banneker, Benjamin
Cannon, Annie J.
Faber, Sandra M.
Fleming, Williamina
Hubble, Edwin
Kuiper, Gerard P.
Leavitt, Henrietta
Maury, Antonia
Mitchell, Maria
Newcomb, Simon
Rubin, Vera C.
Tarter, Jill C.

ASTROPHYSICIST
Chandrasekhar, Subrahmanyan
Fowler, William A.
Gamow, George
Geller, Margaret J.
Hale, George Ellery
Hulse, Russell A.
Penzias, Arno A.
Russell, Henry N.
Taylor, Joseph H.
Van Allen, James A.
Wilson, Robert W.

BACTERIOLOGIST
Reed, Walter

BIOCHEMIST
Altman, Sidney
Anfinsen, Christian B.
Berg, Paul
Bloch, Konrad
Boyer, Paul D.
Cohen, Stanley
Cori, Carl F.
Cori, Gerty T.
Doisy, Edward A.
Du Vigneaud, Vincent
Edelman, Gerald M.
Fischer, Edmond H.
Furchgott, Robert F.
Gilman, Alfred G.
Holley, Robert W.
Ignarro, Louis J.
Kendall, Edward C.
Khorana, H. Gobind
Kornberg, Arthur
Krebs, Edwin G.
Landsteiner, Karl
Lipmann, Fritz A.
Merrifield, R. Bruce
Moore, Stanford
Murad, Ferid
Nirenberg, Marshall W.
Ochoa, Severo
Rodbell, Martin
Rose, Irwin A.
Sutherland, Earl W.
Wrinch, Dorothy Maud

BIOGENETICIST
Horvitz, H. Robert

BIOLOGIST
Carson, Rachel
Claude, Albert
Just, Ernest E.
Sharp, Phillip A.
Wright, Sewall

BIOPHYSICIST
Hartline, H. Keffer
Hauptman, Herbert A.

BLOOD PLASMA SCIENTIST
Drew, Charles R.

BOTANIST
Carver, George Washington
Dodge, Bernard O.
Gray, Asa
Hoagland, Dennis R.
Stakman, Elvin C.
Torrey, John

CELL BIOLOGIST
Blobel, Günter
Palade, George E.

CHEMIST
Brown, Herbert C.
Calvin, Melvin

Cech, Thomas R.
Corey, Elias J.
Cram, Donald J.
Curl, Robert F.
Fenn, John B.
Flory, Paul J.
Giauque, William F.
Hall, Lloyd A.
Heeger, Alan J.
Hill, Henry A.
Hoffmann, Roald
Julian, Percy L.
Knowles, William S.
Langmuir, Irving
Lee, Yuan T.
Lewis, Gilbert N.
Libby, Willard F.
MacDiarmid, Alan G.
Molina, Mario J.
Mulliken, Robert S.
Mullis, Kary B.
Northrop, John H.
Olah, George A.
Onsager, Lars
Pauling, Linus C.
Pedersen, Charles J.
Quarterman, Lloyd A.
Richards, Theodore W.
Rowland, F. Sherwood
Seaborg, Glenn T.
Sharpless, K. Barry
Smalley, Richard E.
Stanley, Wendell M.
Stein, William H.
Sumner, James B.
Taube, Henry
Urey, Harold C.
Woodward, R. B.
Zewail, Ahmed H.

COMPUTER SCIENTIST
Emeagwali, Philip
Hopper, Grace

CYTOGENETICIST
Rowley, Janet D.

ELECTRICAL ENGINEER
Kilby, Jack S.

EMBRYOLOGIST
Wieschaus, Eric F.

ENTOMOLOGIST
Turner, Charles H.

GENETICIST
Beadle, George W.
Hartwell, Leland H.
Lederberg, Joshua
Lewis, Edward B.
McClintock, Barbara
Morgan, Thomas Hunt
Muller, Hermann J.
Tatum, Edward L.

GEOLOGIST
Agassiz, Louis
Dana, James D.
Powell, John Wesley
Van Hise, Charles R.

GEOPHYSICIST
Press, Frank

IMMUNOGENETICIST
Benacerraf, Baruj
Snell, George D.

IMMUNOLOGIST
Sabin, Albert B.
Salk, Jonas

MEDICAL PHYSICIST
Yalow, Rosalyn

MEDICAL RESEARCHER
Kountz, Samuel L. Jr.
Wright, Jane C.
Wright, Louis T.

METEOROLOGIST
Anderson, Charles E.

MICROBIOLOGIST
Colwell, Rita C.
Dubos, René
Hazen, Elizabeth L.
Waksman, Selman A.

MOLECULAR BIOLOGIST
Bishop, J. Michael
Delbrück, Max
Gilbert, Walter
Hershey, Alfred D.
Luria, Salvador E.
Nathans, Daniel
Smith, Hamilton O.
Watson, James D.

MOLECULAR GENETICIST
Brown, Michael S.
Goldstein, Joseph L.

NEUROBIOLOGIST
Greengard, Paul
Hubel, David H.
Kandel, Eric R.
Prusiner, Stanley B.

NEUROEMBRYOLOGIST
Levi-Montalcini, Rita

NEUROENDOCRINOLOGIST
Guillemin, Roger
Schally, Andrew V.

NEUROPHARMACOLOGIST
Axelrod, Julius

NEUROPHYSIOLOGIST
Gasser, Herbert S.

OCEANOGRAPHER
Maury, Matthew F.

PALEONTOLOGIST
Romer, Alfred S.
Simpson, George G.

PATHOLOGIST
Flexner, Simon
Hinton, William A.
Minot, George R.
Murphy, William P.
Rous, Peyton
Welch, William H.
Whipple, George H.

PERINATOLOGIST
Apgar, Virginia

PHARMACOLOGIST
Elion, Gertrude B.
Hitchings, George H.

PHYSICAL ANTHROPOLOGIST
Cobb, W. Montague

PHYSICAL CHEMIST
Herschbach, Dudley R.
Karle, Jerome
Lipscomb, William N.
Marcus, Rudolph A.

PHYSICIAN
Blumberg, Baruch S.
Cournand, André F.
Richards, Dickinson W.
Rush, Benjamin
Thomas, E. Donnall

PHYSICIST
Alvarez, Luis W.
Anderson, Carl D.
Anderson, Philip W.
Bardeen, John
Bethe, Hans A.
Bloch, Felix
Blodgett, Katharine B.
Bloembergen, Nicolaas
Brattain, Walter H.
Bridgman, P. W.
Chamberlain, Owen
Chu, Steven
Compton, Arthur H.

Cooper, Leon N.
Cormack, Allan M.
Cornell, Eric A.
Cronin, James W.
Davis, Raymond, Jr.
Davisson, Clinton J.
Dehmelt, Hans G.
Einstein, Albert
Fermi, Enrico
Feynman, Richard P.
Fitch, Val L.
Franklin, Benjamin
Friedman, Jerome I.
Gell-Mann, Murray
Giacconi, Riccardo
Giaever, Ivar
Gibbs, J. Willard
Glaser, Donald A.
Glashow, Sheldon L.
Gourdine, Meredith C.
Gross, David J.
Henry, Joseph
Hofstadter, Robert
Imes, Elmer S.
Kendall, Henry W.
Kohn, Walter
Kusch, Polykarp
Lamb, Willis E. Jr.
Laughlin, Robert B.
Lawrence, Ernest O.
Lederman, Leon M.
Lee, David M.
Lee, Tsung-Dao
Mayer, Maria Goeppert
McMillan, Edwin M.
Michelson, Albert A.
Millikan, Robert A.
Oppenheimer, Julius R.
Osheroff, Douglas D.
Perl, Martin L.
Phillips, William D.
Politzer, H. David
Purcell, Edward M.
Quimby, Edith H.
Rabi, I. I.
Rainwater, L. James

Ramsey, Norman F.
Reines, Frederick
Richardson, Robert C.
Richter, Burton
Schawlow, Arthur L.
Schrieffer, J. Robert
Schwartz, Melvin
Schwinger, Julian S.
Segrè, Emilio
Shockley, William B.
Shull, Clifford G.
Steinberger, Jack
Stern, Otto
Teller, Edward
Ting, Samuel C. C.
Townes, Charles H.
Tsui, Daniel C.
Van de Graaff, Robert J.
Van Vleck, John H.
Weinberg, Steven
Wieman, Carl E.
Wigner, Eugene P.
Wilczek, Frank
Wilson, Kenneth G.
Yang, Chen Ning

PHYSIOLOGIST
Axel, Richard
Békésy, Georg von
Blalock, Alfred
Buck, Linda B.
Erlanger, Joseph
Hench, Philip S.
Taussig, Helen B.
Wald, George

PSYCHOBIOLOGIST
Sperry, Roger W.

PSYCHOPHYSIOLOGIST
Cowings, Patricia S.

ROCKET SCIENTIST
von Braun, Wernher
Goddard, Robert H.

SCIENCE ADMINISTRATOR
Bache, Alexander D.

SEISMOLOGIST
Richter, Charles F.

SURGEON
De Bakey, Michael E.
Huggins, Charles B.

Murray, Joseph E.

TERATOLOGIST
Apgar, Virginia

VIROLOGIST
Baltimore, David
Dulbecco, Renato
Enders, John F.

Gajdusek, D. Carleton
Robbins, Frederick C.
Temin, Howard M.
Varmus, Harold E.
Weller, Thomas H.
Wong-Staal, Flossie

ZOOLOGIST
Fossey, Dian

Entries by Year of Birth

1700–1799
Banneker, Benjamin
Franklin, Benjamin
Henry, Joseph
Rush, Benjamin
Torrey, John

1800–1849
Agassiz, Louis
Bache, Alexander D.
Dana, James D.
Gibbs, J. Willard
Gray, Asa
Maury, Matthew F.
Mitchell, Maria
Newcomb, Simon
Powell, John Wesley

1850–1859
Fleming, Williamina
Michelson, Albert A.
Reed, Walter
Van Hise, Charles R.
Welch, William H.

1860–1869
Cannon, Annie J.
Carver, George Washington
Flexner, Simon
Hale, George Ellery
Landsteiner, Karl
Leavitt, Henrietta
Maury, Antonia

Millikan, Robert A.
Morgan, Thomas Hunt
Richards, Theodore W.
Turner, Charles H.

1870–1879
Dodge, Bernard O.
Einstein, Albert
Erlanger, Joseph
Lewis, Gilbert N.
Rous, Peyton
Russell, Henry N.
Sabin, Florence
Whipple, George H.

1880–1884
Bridgman, P. W.
Davisson, Clinton J.
Goddard, Robert H.
Hinton, William A.
Hoagland, Dennis R.
Imes, Elmer S.
Just, Ernest E.
Langmuir, Irving

1885–1889
Gasser, Herbert S.
Hazen, Elizabeth L.
Hubble, Edwin
Kendall, Edward C.
Minot, George R.
Stakman, Elvin C.
Stern, Otto

Sumner, James B.
Waksman, Selman A.
Wright, Sewall

1890–1894
Compton, Arthur H.
Doisy, Edward A.
Hall, Lloyd A.
Muller, Hermann J.
Murphy, William P.
Northrop, John H.
Quimby, Edith H.
Romer, Alfred S.
Urey, Harold C.
Wright, Louis T.
Wrinch, Dorothy Maud

1895–1899
Békésy, Georg von
Blalock, Alfred
Blodgett, Katharine B.
Claude, Albert
Cori, Carl F.
Cori, Gerty T.
Cournand, André F.
Enders, John F.
Giauque, William F.
Hench, Philip S.
Julian, Percy L.
Lipmann, Fritz A.
Mulliken, Robert S.
Rabi, I. I.
Richards, Dickinson W.

Taussig, Helen B.
Van Vleck, John H.

1900–1904
Beadle, George W.
Brattain, Walter H.
Cobb, W. Montague
Drew, Charles R.
Dubos, René
Du Vigneaud, Vincent
Fermi, Enrico
Gamow, George
Hartline, H. Keffer
Huggins, Charles B.
Lawrence, Ernest O.
McClintock, Barbara
Onsager, Lars
Oppenheimer, Julius R.
Pauling, Linus C.
Pedersen, Charles J.
Richter, Charles F.
Simpson, George G.
Snell, George D.
Stanley, Wendell M.
Van de Graaff, Robert J.
Wigner, Eugene P.

1905–1909
Anderson, Carl D.
Apgar, Virginia
Bardeen, John
Bethe, Hans A.
Bloch, Felix
Carson, Rachel
De Bakey, Michael E.
Delbrück, Max
Hershey, Alfred D.
Hitchings, George H.
Hopper, Grace
Kuiper, Gerard P.
Levi-Montalcini, Rita
Libby, Willard F.
Mayer, Maria Goeppert
McMillan, Edwin M.
Ochoa, Severo
Sabin, Albert B.
Segrè, Emilio

Tatum, Edward L.
Teller, Edward
Wald, George

1910–1914
Alvarez, Luis W.
Axelrod, Julius
Bloch, Konrad
von Braun, Wernher
Brown, Herbert C.
Calvin, Melvin
Chandrasekhar, Subrahmanyan
Davis, Raymond, Jr.
Dulbecco, Renato
Flory, Paul J.
Fowler, William A.
Kusch, Polykarp
Lamb, Willis E. Jr.
Luria, Salvador E.
Moore, Stanford
Palade, George E.
Purcell, Edward M.
Salk, Jonas
Seaborg, Glenn T.
Shockley, William B.
Sperry, Roger W.
Stein, William H.
Van Allen, James A.

1915–1919
Anderson, Charles E.
Anfinsen, Christian B.
Boyer, Paul D.
Cram, Donald J.
Elion, Gertrude B.
Fenn, John B.
Feynman, Richard P.
Furchgott, Robert F.
Hauptman, Herbert A.
Hill, Henry A.
Hofstadter, Robert
Karle, Jerome
Knowles, William S.
Kornberg, Arthur
Krebs, Edwin G.
Lewis, Edward B.
Lipscomb, William N.

Murray, Joseph E.
Quarterman, Lloyd A.
Rainwater, L. James
Ramsey, Norman F.
Reines, Frederick
Robbins, Frederick C.
Schwinger, Julian S.
Shull, Clifford G.
Sutherland, Earl W.
Taube, Henry
Townes, Charles H.
Weller, Thomas H.
Woodward, R. B.
Wright, Jane C.

1920–1924
Anderson, Philip W.
Benacerraf, Baruj
Bloembergen, Nicolaas
Chamberlain, Owen
Cohen, Stanley
Cormack, Allan M.
Dehmelt, Hans G.
Fischer, Edmond H.
Fitch, Val L.
Gajdusek, D. Carleton
Guillemin, Roger
Holley, Robert W.
Khorana, H. Gobind
Kilby, Jack S.
Kohn, Walter
Lederman, Leon M.
Marcus, Rudolph A.
Merrifield, R. Bruce
Press, Frank
Schawlow, Arthur L.
Steinberger, Jack
Thomas, E. Donnall
Yalow, Rosalyn
Yang, Chen Ning

1925–1929
Berg, Paul
Blumberg, Baruch S.
Corey, Elias J.
Edelman, Gerald M.
Gell-Mann, Murray

Giaever, Ivar
Glaser, Donald A.
Gourdine, Meredith C.
Greengard, Paul
Hubel, David H.
Kandel, Eric R.
Kendall, Henry W.
Lederberg, Joshua
Lee, Tsung-Dao
MacDiarmid, Alan G.
Nathans, Daniel
Nirenberg, Marshall W.
Olah, George A.
Perl, Martin L.
Rodbell, Martin
Rose, Irwin A.
Rowland, F. Sherwood
Rowley, Janet D.
Rubin, Vera C.
Schally, Andrew V.
Watson, James D.

1930–1934
Colwell, Rita C.
Cooper, Leon N.
Cronin, James W.
Curl, Robert F.
Fossey, Dian
Friedman, Jerome I.
Giacconi, Riccardo
Gilbert, Walter
Glashow, Sheldon L.
Herschbach, Dudley R.

Kountz, Samuel L. Jr.
Lee, David M.
Penzias, Arno A.
Richter, Burton
Schrieffer, J. Robert
Schwartz, Melvin
Smith, Hamilton O.
Temin, Howard M.
Weinberg, Steven

1935–1939
Altman, Sidney
Baltimore, David
Bishop, J. Michael
Blobel, Günter
Hartwell, Leland H.
Heeger, Alan J.
Hoffmann, Roald
Lee, Yuan T.
Murad, Ferid
Richardson, Robert C.
Ting, Samuel C. C.
Tsui, Daniel C.
Varmus, Harold E.
Wilson, Kenneth G.
Wilson, Robert W.

1940–1944
Brown, Michael S.
Faber, Sandra M.
Gilman, Alfred G.
Goldstein, Joseph L.
Gross, David J.

Ignarro, Louis J.
Molina, Mario J.
Mullis, Kary B.
Prusiner, Stanley B.
Sharp, Phillip A.
Sharpless, K. Barry
Smalley, Richard E.
Tarter, Jill C.
Taylor, Joseph H.

1945–1949
Axel, Richard
Buck, Linda B.
Cech, Thomas R.
Chu, Steven
Cowings, Patricia S.
Geller, Margaret J.
Horvitz, H. Robert
Osheroff, Douglas D.
Phillips, William D.
Politzer, H. David
Wieschaus, Eric F.
Wong-Staal, Flossie
Zewail, Ahmed H.

1950–
Cornell, Eric A.
Emeagwali, Philip
Hulse, Russell A.
Laughlin, Robert B.
Wieman, Carl E.
Wilczek, Frank

Locators in **boldface** indicate main entries. Locators in *italic* indicate photographs.